MW01005384

THE LOEB CLASSICAL LIBRARY

FOUNDED BY JAMES LOEB

EDITED BY

G. P. GOOLD

SOPHOCLES

II

LCL 21

SOPHOCLES

ANTIGONE · THE WOMEN OF TRACHIS · PHILOCTETES OEDIPUS AT COLONUS

EDITED AND TRANSLATED BY

HUGH LLOYD-JONES

HARVARD UNIVERSITY PRESS
CAMBRIDGE, MASSACHUSETTS
LONDON, ENGLAND
1994

Library of Congress Cataloging-in-Publication Data

Sophocles.
[Works. English & Greek.]
Sophocles / edited and translated by Hugh Lloyd-Jones.
p.   cm. — (Loeb classical library; 20–21)
Includes bibliographical references.
ISBN 0–674–99557–0 (v. 1).   ISBN 0–674–99558–9 (v. 2)
1. Sophocles—Translations into English.
2. Greek drama (Tragedy)—Translations into English.
3. Mythology, Greek—Drama.
I. Lloyd-Jones, Hugh.   II. Title.   III. Series.
PA4414.A1L56   1992   92–19295
882′.01—dc20   CIP

Typeset by Chiron, Inc, Cambridge, Massachusetts.
Printed in Great Britain by St Edmundsbury Press Ltd,
Bury St Edmunds, Suffolk, on acid-free paper.
Bound by Hunter & Foulis Ltd, Edinburgh, Scotland.

CONTENTS

SIGLA

Π 13   P.Oxy. 1805 + 3787, saec. ii–iii
Π 14   P.Oxy. 3688, saec. v–vi
Π 15   P.Amst. inv. 68, saec. iii

PHILOCTETES
l   LΛK
r   the common source of G (Laur. CS 152), Q
        (Paris. supp. gr. 109), and R
a   AUY
S   (lines 1–1297)
V
z   ZgZo
t   TTa

Π 16   P.Berol. inv. 17058, saec. iv–v

OEDIPUS AT COLONUS
l   LΛK
r   QR
a   AUY
V   (lines 1338–779)
z   the common source of Zn (Paris. gr. 2787), Zo
t   TTa

Π 17   P.Mich. 3.1400, saec. ii–iii

Σ   scholium
lm.   lemma
γρ   γράφεται
ac   ante correctionem
pc   post correctionem
s.l.   supra lineam
cett.   ceteri

ANTIGONE

ΤΑ ΤΟΥ ΔΡΑΜΑΤΟΣ ΠΡΟΣΩΠΑ

Ἀντιγόνη
Ἰσμήνη
Χορὸς Θηβαίων γερόντων
Κρέων
Φύλαξ
Αἵμων
Τειρεσίας
Ἄγγελος
Εὐρυδίκη

Antigone
Ismene
Chorus of Theban Elders
Creon
Guard
Haemon
Tiresias
Messenger
Eurydice

Scene: In front of the palace at Thebes.
Time: Just after the battle in which the Thebans have repulsed the Argive attack, and the brothers Eteocles and Polynices have killed each other.

ΑΝΤΙΓΟΝΗ

ΑΝΤΙΓΟΝΗ

Ὦ κοινὸν αὐτάδελφον Ἰσμήνης κάρα,
ἆρ' οἶσθ' ὅτι Ζεὺς τῶν ἀπ' Οἰδίπου κακῶν —
ἆ, ποῖον οὐχὶ νῶν ἔτι ζώσαιν τελεῖ;
οὐδὲν γὰρ οὔτ' ἀλγεινὸν οὔτ' ἄτης γέμον
5 οὔτ' αἰσχρὸν οὔτ' ἄτιμόν ἐσθ', ὁποῖον οὐ
τῶν σῶν τε κἀμῶν οὐκ ὄπωπ' ἐγὼ κακῶν.
καὶ νῦν τί τοῦτ' αὖ φασι πανδήμῳ πόλει
κήρυγμα θεῖναι τὸν στρατηγὸν ἀρτίως;
ἔχεις τι κεἰσήκουσας; ἤ σε λανθάνει
10 πρὸς τοὺς φίλους στείχοντα τῶν ἐχθρῶν κακά;

ΙΣΜΗΝΗ

ἐμοὶ μὲν οὐδεὶς μῦθος, Ἀντιγόνη, φίλων
οὔθ' ἡδὺς οὔτ' ἀλγεινὸς ἵκετ' ἐξ ὅτου
δυοῖν ἀδελφοῖν ἐστερήθημεν δύο,
μιᾷ θανόντοιν ἡμέρᾳ διπλῇ χερί·
15 ἐπεὶ δὲ φροῦδός ἐστιν Ἀργείων στρατὸς
ἐν νυκτὶ τῇ νῦν, οὐδὲν οἶδ' ὑπέρτερον,
οὔτ' εὐτυχοῦσα μᾶλλον οὔτ' ἀτωμένη.

ΑΝΤΙΓΟΝΗ

ἤδη καλῶς, καί σ' ἐκτὸς αὐλείων πυλῶν

2 ὅτι Hermann: ὅ τι codd.

4

ANTIGONE

The stage building represents the royal palace at Thebes.
ANTIGONE *and* ISMENE *enter from the central door.*

ANTIGONE

My own sister Ismene, linked to myself, are you aware that
Zeus ... ah, which of the evils that come from Oedipus is
he not accomplishing while we still live? No, there is noth-
ing painful or laden with destruction or shameful or dis-
honouring among your sorrows and mine that I have not
witnessed. And now what is this proclamation that they say
the general has lately made to the whole city? Have you
any knowledge? Have you heard anything? Or have you
failed to notice the evils from our enemies as they come
against our friends?

ISMENE

To me, Antigone, no word about our friends has come,
either agreeable or painful, since we two were robbed of
two brothers, who perished on one day each at the other's
hand. Since the Argive army left during this night, I know
nothing further, nothing that improves my fortune or
brings me nearer to disaster.

ANTIGONE

I knew it well, and I summoned you out of the gates of the

---

[3] ἆ, ποῖον Ll.-J.: ὁποῖον codd.
[4] ἄτης γέμον Hermann: ἄτης ἄτερ codd.

τοῦδ' οὕνεκ' ἐξέπεμπον, ὡς μόνη κλύοις.

ΙΣΜΗΝΗ

20   τί δ' ἔστι; δηλοῖς γάρ τι καλχαίνουσ' ἔπος.

ΑΝΤΙΓΟΝΗ

οὐ γὰρ τάφου νῷν τὼ κασιγνήτω Κρέων
τὸν μὲν προτίσας, τὸν δ' ἀτιμάσας ἔχει;
Ἐτεοκλέα μέν, ὡς λέγουσι, σὺν δίκης
χρήσει δικαίᾳ καὶ νόμῳ, κατὰ χθονὸς
25   ἔκρυψε τοῖς ἔνερθεν ἔντιμον νεκροῖς·
τὸν δ' ἀθλίως θανόντα Πολυνείκους νέκυν
ἀστοῖσί φασιν ἐκκεκηρῦχθαι τὸ μὴ
τάφῳ καλύψαι μηδὲ κωκῦσαί τινα,
ἐᾶν δ' ἄκλαυτον, ἄταφον, οἰωνοῖς γλυκὺν
30   θησαυρὸν εἰσορῶσι πρὸς χάριν βορᾶς.
τοιαῦτά φασι τὸν ἀγαθὸν Κρέοντα σοὶ
κἀμοί, λέγω γὰρ κἀμέ, κηρύξαντ' ἔχειν,
καὶ δεῦρο νεῖσθαι ταῦτα τοῖσι μὴ εἰδόσιν
σαφῆ προκηρύξοντα, καὶ τὸ πρᾶγμ' ἄγειν
35   οὐχ ὡς παρ' οὐδέν, ἀλλ' ὃς ἂν τούτων τι δρᾷ,
φόνον προκεῖσθαι δημόλευστον ἐν πόλει.
οὕτως ἔχει σοι ταῦτα, καὶ δείξεις τάχα
εἴτ' εὐγενὴς πέφυκας εἴτ' ἐσθλῶν κακή.

ΙΣΜΗΝΗ

τί δ', ὦ ταλαῖφρον, εἰ τάδ' ἐν τούτοις, ἐγὼ
40   λύουσ' ἂν εἴθ' ἅπτουσα προσθείμην πλέον;

23–24 σὺν δίκης χρήσει G. H. Müller: σὺν δίκῃ χρησθεὶς codd.
40 εἴθ' ἅπτουσα Porson: ἢ θάπτουσα codd.

6

courtyard because I wished you to hear this alone.

ISMENE

But what is it? It is clear that you are brooding over something you are going to say.

ANTIGONE

Why, has not Creon honoured one of our brothers and dishonoured the other in the matter of their burial? Eteocles, they say, in accordance with justice and with custom he has hidden beneath the earth, honoured among the dead below. But as for the unhappy corpse of Polynices, they say it has been proclaimed to the citizens that none shall conceal it in a grave or lament for it, but that they should leave it unwept for, unburied, a rich treasure house for birds as they look out for food. This is the proclamation which they say the good Creon has made to you and to me—yes, I count myself also—and he is coming this way to make the proclamation clear to those who do not know of it. He is not treating the matter as unimportant, but for anyone who does any of these things death in the city is ordained, by stoning at the people's hand. There you have the way things stand, and you will soon show whether your nature is noble or you are the cowardly descendant of valiant ancestors.

ISMENE

But, my poor dear, if this is how things stand, what could I contribute by trying to untie or to tie the knot?

ΑΝΤΙΓΟΝΗ

εἰ ξυμπονήσεις καὶ ξυνεργάσῃ σκόπει.

ΙΣΜΗΝΗ

ποῖόν τι κινδύνευμα; ποῦ γνώμης ποτ᾽ εἶ;

ΑΝΤΙΓΟΝΗ

εἰ τὸν νεκρὸν ξὺν τῇδε κουφιεῖς χερί.

ΙΣΜΗΝΗ

ἦ γὰρ νοεῖς θάπτειν σφ᾽, ἀπόρρητον πόλει;

ΑΝΤΙΓΟΝΗ

45 τὸν γοῦν ἐμόν, καὶ τὸν σόν, ἢν σὺ μὴ θέλῃς,
ἀδελφόν· οὐ γὰρ δὴ προδοῦσ᾽ ἁλώσομαι.

ΙΣΜΗΝΗ

ὦ σχετλία, Κρέοντος ἀντειρηκότος;

ΑΝΤΙΓΟΝΗ

ἀλλ᾽ οὐδὲν αὐτῷ τῶν ἐμῶν <μ᾽> εἴργειν μέτα.

ΙΣΜΗΝΗ

οἴμοι· φρόνησον, ὦ κασιγνήτη, πατὴρ
50 ὡς νῷν ἀπεχθὴς δυσκλεής τ᾽ ἀπώλετο
πρὸς αὐτοφώρων ἀμπλακημάτων, διπλᾶς
ὄψεις ἀράξας αὐτὸς αὐτουργῷ χερί·
ἔπειτα μήτηρ καὶ γυνή, διπλοῦν ἔπος,
πλεκταῖσιν ἀρτάναισι λωβᾶται βίον·
55 τρίτον δ᾽ ἀδελφὼ δύο μίαν καθ᾽ ἡμέραν
αὐτοκτονοῦντε τὼ ταλαιπώρω μόρον
κοινὸν κατειργάσαντ᾽ ἐπαλλήλοιν χεροῖν.
νῦν δ᾽ αὖ μόνα δὴ νὼ λελειμμένα σκόπει

8

ANTIGONE

ANTIGONE
Consider whether you will share the pain and the labour!

ISMENE
What dangerous thing is to be done? What have you in mind?

ANTIGONE
Will you bury the dead man, together with this hand of mine?

ISMENE
Are you thinking of burying him, when it has been forbidden to the city?

ANTIGONE
Well, I will bury my brother, and yours, if you will not; I will not be caught betraying him.

ISMENE
Reckless one, when Creon has forbidden it?

ANTIGONE
But he has no right to keep me from my own!

ISMENE
Woe! Think, sister, of how our father perished hated and ill-famed, through the crimes he had himself detected, after striking both his eyes himself, with his own hand! And then his mother and his wife, two names in one, did violence to her life with twisted noose; and, thirdly, our two brothers, on one day killing each other, did themselves both to death at one another's hands. And now consider how much the worse will be the fate of us two, who are left

---

⁴⁶ spurium apud antiquos habitum esse testatur Didymus
⁴⁸ suppl. Brunck

ὅσῳ κάκιστ᾽ ὀλούμεθ᾽, εἰ νόμου βίᾳ
60 ψῆφον τυράννων ἢ κράτη παρέξιμεν.
ἀλλ᾽ ἐννοεῖν χρὴ τοῦτο μὲν γυναῖχ᾽ ὅτι
ἔφυμεν, ὡς πρὸς ἄνδρας οὐ μαχουμένα·
ἔπειτα δ᾽ οὕνεκ᾽ ἀρχόμεσθ᾽ ἐκ κρεισσόνων
καὶ ταῦτ᾽ ἀκούειν κἄτι τῶνδ᾽ ἀλγίονα.
65 ἐγὼ μὲν οὖν αἰτοῦσα τοὺς ὑπὸ χθονὸς
ξύγγνοιαν ἴσχειν, ὡς βιάζομαι τάδε,
τοῖς ἐν τέλει βεβῶσι πείσομαι. τὸ γὰρ
περισσὰ πράσσειν οὐκ ἔχει νοῦν οὐδένα.

ΑΝΤΙΓΟΝΗ

οὔτ᾽ ἂν κελεύσαιμ᾽ οὔτ᾽ ἄν, εἰ θέλοις ἔτι
70 πράσσειν, ἐμοῦ γ᾽ ἂν ἡδέως δρῴης μέτα.
ἀλλ᾽ ἴσθ᾽ ὁποία σοι δοκεῖ, κεῖνον δ᾽ ἐγὼ
θάψω. καλόν μοι τοῦτο ποιούσῃ θανεῖν.
φίλη μετ᾽ αὐτοῦ κείσομαι, φίλου μέτα,
ὅσια πανουργήσασ᾽· ἐπεὶ πλείων χρόνος
75 ὃν δεῖ μ᾽ ἀρέσκειν τοῖς κάτω τῶν ἐνθάδε.
ἐκεῖ γὰρ αἰεὶ κείσομαι· σὺ δ᾽ εἰ δοκεῖ
τὰ τῶν θεῶν ἔντιμ᾽ ἀτιμάσασ᾽ ἔχε.

ΙΣΜΗΝΗ

ἐγὼ μὲν οὐκ ἄτιμα ποιοῦμαι, τὸ δὲ
βίᾳ πολιτῶν δρᾶν ἔφυν ἀμήχανος.

ΑΝΤΙΓΟΝΗ

80 σὺ μὲν τάδ᾽ ἂν προὔχοι· ἐγὼ δὲ δὴ τάφον
χώσουσ᾽ ἀδελφῷ φιλτάτῳ πορεύσομαι.

alone, if in despite of the law we flout the decision of the ruler or his power. Why, we must remember that we are women, who cannot fight against men, and then that we are ruled by those whose power is greater, so that we must consent to this and to other things even more painful! So I shall beg those beneath the earth to be understanding, since I act under constraint, but I shall obey those in authority; for there is no sense in actions that exceed our powers.

ANTIGONE

I would not tell you to do it, and even if you were willing to act after all I would not be content for you to act with me! Do you be the kind of person you have decided to be, but I shall bury him! It is honourable for me to do this and die. I am his own and I shall lie with him who is my own, having committed a crime that is holy, for there will be a longer span of time for me to please those below than there will be to please those here. As for you, if it is your pleasure, dishonour what the gods honour!

ISMENE

I am not dishonouring them, but I do not have it in me to act against the will of the people of the city.

ANTIGONE

You may offer that excuse; but I shall go to heap up a tomb for my dearest brother!

ΙΣΜΗΝΗ

οἴμοι, ταλαίνης ὡς ὑπερδέδοικά σου.

ΑΝΤΙΓΟΝΗ

μὴ 'μοῦ προτάρβει· τὸν σὸν ἐξόρθου πότμον.

ΙΣΜΗΝΗ

ἀλλ' οὖν προμηνύσῃς γε τοῦτο μηδενὶ
85   τοὔργον, κρυφῇ δὲ κεῦθε, σὺν δ' αὕτως ἐγώ.

ΑΝΤΙΓΟΝΗ

οἴμοι, καταύδα· πολλὸν ἐχθίων ἔσῃ
σιγῶσ', ἐὰν μὴ πᾶσι κηρύξῃς τάδε.

ΙΣΜΗΝΗ

θερμὴν ἐπὶ ψυχροῖσι καρδίαν ἔχεις.

ΑΝΤΙΓΟΝΗ

ἀλλ' οἶδ' ἀρέσκουσ' οἷς μάλισθ' ἁδεῖν με χρή.

ΙΣΜΗΝΗ

90   εἰ καὶ δυνήσῃ γ'· ἀλλ' ἀμηχάνων ἐρᾷς.

ΑΝΤΙΓΟΝΗ

οὐκοῦν, ὅταν δὴ μὴ σθένω, πεπαύσομαι.

ΙΣΜΗΝΗ

ἀρχὴν δὲ θηρᾶν οὐ πρέπει τἀμήχανα.

ΑΝΤΙΓΟΝΗ

εἰ ταῦτα λέξεις, ἐχθαρῇ μὲν ἐξ ἐμοῦ,
ἐχθρὰ δὲ τῷ θανόντι προσκείσῃ δίκῃ.
95   ἀλλ' ἔα με καὶ τὴν ἐξ ἐμοῦ δυσβουλίαν
παθεῖν τὸ δεινὸν τοῦτο· πείσομαι γὰρ οὖν
τοσοῦτον οὐδὲν ὥστε μὴ οὐ καλῶς θανεῖν.

ANTIGONE

ISMENE

Alas, how I fear for you, poor creature!

ANTIGONE

Have no fears for me! Make your own course go straight!

ISMENE

Well, tell no one of this act beforehand, but keep it secret, and so shall I.

ANTIGONE

Ah, tell them all! I shall hate you far more if you remain silent, and do not proclaim this to all.

ISMENE

Your heart is fiery in a matter that is chilling.

ANTIGONE

Why, I know that I am giving pleasure to those I must please most!

ISMENE

If you have the strength! But you are in love with the impossible.

ANTIGONE

Then when my strength fails I shall be at rest.

ISMENE

But to begin with it is wrong to hunt for what is impossible.

ANTIGONE

If you say that, you will be hated by me, and you will justly incur the hatred of the dead man. Let me and my rashness suffer this awful thing! I shall suffer nothing so dire that my death will not be one of honour.

SOPHOCLES

ΙΣΜΗΝΗ

ἀλλ' εἰ δοκεῖ σοι, στεῖχε· τοῦτο δ' ἴσθ', ὅτι
ἄνους μὲν ἔρχῃ, τοῖς φίλοις δ' ὀρθῶς φίλη.

ΧΟΡΟΣ

100   ἀκτὶς ἀελίου, τὸ κάλ-   στρ. α'
      λιστον ἑπταπύλῳ φανὲν
      Θήβᾳ τῶν προτέρων φάος,
      ἐφάνθης ποτ' ὦ χρυσέας
      ἀμέρας βλέφαρον, Διρκαί-
105   ων ὑπὲρ ῥεέθρων μολοῦσα,
      τὸν †λεύκασπιν Ἀργόθεν
      φῶτα βάντα πανσαγίᾳ†
      φυγάδα πρόδρομον ὀξυτόρῳ
      κινήσασα χαλινῷ·
110   ὃς ἐφ' ἡμετέρᾳ γῇ Πολυνείκους
      ἀρθεὶς νεικέων ἐξ ἀμφιλόγων
      ὀξέα κλάζων
      αἰετὸς ἐς γῆν ὣς ὑπερέπτα,
      λευκῆς χιόνος πτέρυγι στεγανὸς
115   πολλῶν μεθ' ὅπλων
      ξύν θ' ἱπποκόμοις κορύθεσσιν.
      στὰς δ' ὑπὲρ μελάθρων φονώ-   ἀντ. α'
      σαισιν ἀμφιχανὼν κύκλῳ
      λόγχαις ἑπτάπυλον στόμα
120   ἔβα, πρίν ποθ' ἁμετέρων
      αἱμάτων γένυσιν πλησθῆ-
      ναί <τε> καὶ στεφάνωμα πύργων
      πευκάενθ' Ἥφαιστον ἑλεῖν.

14

ISMENE

Well, if you wish to, go! But know this much, that in your going you are foolish, but truly dear to those who are your own.

Exeunt ANTIGONE *and* ISMENE. *The* CHORUS *of elderly men, leading citizens of Thebes, enters the orchestra.*

CHORUS

Beam of the sun, fairer than all that have shone before for seven-gated Thebes, finally you shone forth, eye of golden day, coming over the streams of Dirce, you who moved off in headlong flight the man with white shield that came from Argos in his panoply, with a bridle of constraint that pierced him sharply, him that was raised up against our land by the contentious quarrels of Polynices,[a] and flew to our country, loudly screaming like an eagle sheathed in snow-white pinion, with many weapons and with helmets with horsehair plumes; he paused above our houses, ringing round the seven gates with spears that longed for blood; but he went, before his jaws had been glutted with our gore and the fire-god's pine-fed flame had taken the walls that crown our city. Such was the din of battle

---

[a] Polynices had persuaded Adrastus, king of Argos, to lead an army against Thebes, where his brother Eteocles had excluded him from power. Each of the seven gates of Thebes had been attacked by one of seven famous warriors; the seventh gate had been attacked by Polynices and defended by his brother.

---

[110] ὃς ... Πολυνείκους Scaliger: ὃν ... Πολυνείκης codd. et Π 11

[117] φονώσαισιν e schol. Bothe: φοναῖσιν K: φο(ι)νίαισιν cett.

SOPHOCLES

τοῖος ἀμφὶ νῶτ' ἐτάθη
125 πάταγος Ἄρεος, ἀντιπάλῳ
δυσχείρωμα δράκοντος.
Ζεὺς γὰρ μεγάλης γλώσσης κόμπους
ὑπερεχθαίρει, καί σφας ἐσιδὼν
πολλῷ ῥεύματι προσνισομένους,
130 χρυσοῦ καναχῆς ὑπεροπτείαις,
παλτῷ ῥιπτεῖ πυρὶ βαλβίδων
ἐπ' ἄκρων ἤδη
νίκην ὁρμῶντ' ἀλαλάξαι·
ἀντιτύπᾳ δ' ἐπὶ γᾷ πέσε τανταλωθεὶς   στρ. β'
135 πυρφόρος ὃς τότε μαινομένᾳ ξὺν ὁρμᾷ
βακχεύων ἐπέπνει
ῥιπαῖς ἐχθίστων ἀνέμων.
εἶχε δ' ἄλλα τάδ'· <ἀλλ'>
ἄλλ' ἐπ' ἄλλοις ἐπενώ-
μα στυφελίζων μέγας Ἄ-
140 ρης δεξιόσειρος.
ἑπτὰ λοχαγοὶ γὰρ ἐφ' ἑπτὰ πύλαις
ταχθέντες ἴσοι πρὸς ἴσους ἔλιπον
Ζηνὶ τροπαίῳ πάγχαλκα τέλη,
πλὴν τοῖν στυγεροῖν, ὣ πατρὸς ἑνὸς
145 μητρός τε μιᾶς φύντε καθ' αὑτοῖν
δικρατεῖς λόγχας στήσαντ' ἔχετον
κοινοῦ θανάτου μέρος ἄμφω.
ἀλλὰ γὰρ ἁ μεγαλώνυμος ἦλθε Νίκα   ἀντ. β'
τᾷ πολυαρμάτῳ ἀντιχαρεῖσα Θήβᾳ,
150 ἐκ μὲν δὴ πολέμων

16

stretched about his back, hard for the dragon's adversary to vanquish.

For Zeus detests the boasts of a proud tongue, and when he saw them advancing in full flood, with the arrogance of flashing gold, with the fire he hurls he flung down him who was already hastening to shout forth his victory on the topmost ramparts.[a]

And he fell upon the hard ground, shaken down, the torchbearer who in the fury of his mad rush breathed upon us with the blast of hateful winds. This indeed went otherwise; and different fates were dispensed to different persons by the mighty war-god who shattered them, a horse that carried our chariot to victory.

For seven captains posted against seven gates, man against man, left behind their brazen weapons for Zeus the god of trophies, except for the unhappy two, who, sprung of one father and one mother, set their strong spears against each other and both shared a common death.

But since Victory whose name is glorious has come, her joy responding to the joy of Thebes with many chariots,

---

[a] Capaneus, one of the Seven Against Thebes.

---

125 ἀντιπάλῳ] -ου L s.l., a s.l.
126 δράκοντος V et s.l. in a: δράκοντι cett.
130 ὑπεροπτείαις Musgrave: -είας K: -ίας cett.
138 <ἀλλ'> ἄλλ' ἐπ' Ll.-J.: ἄλλα δ' ἐπ' t: ἄλλα τάδ' ἐπ' cett.

17

τῶν νῦν θέσθε λησμοσύναν,
θεῶν δὲ ναοὺς χοροῖς
παννύχοις πάντας ἐπέλ-
θωμεν, ὁ Θήβας δ' ἐλελί-
χθων Βάκχιος ἄρχοι.

155 ἀλλ' ὅδε γὰρ δὴ βασιλεὺς χώρας,
†Κρέων ὁ Μενοικέως,† . . . νεοχμὸς
νεαραῖσι θεῶν ἐπὶ συντυχίαις
χωρεῖ τίνα δὴ μῆτιν ἐρέσσων,
ὅτι σύγκλητον τήνδε γερόντων
160 προὔθετο λέσχην,
κοινῷ κηρύγματι πέμψας;

KΡΕΩΝ

ἄνδρες, τὰ μὲν δὴ πόλεος ἀσφαλῶς θεοὶ
πολλῷ σάλῳ σείσαντες ὤρθωσαν πάλιν·
ὑμᾶς δ' ἐγὼ πομποῖσιν ἐκ πάντων δίχα
165 ἔστειλ' ἱκέσθαι, τοῦτο μὲν τὰ Λαΐου
σέβοντας εἰδὼς εὖ θρόνων ἀεὶ κράτη,
τοῦτ' αὖθις, ἡνίκ' Οἰδίπους ὤρθου πόλιν,

        ❋   ❋   ❋   ❋   ❋

κἀπεὶ διώλετ', ἀμφὶ τοὺς κείνων ἔτι
παῖδας μένοντας ἐμπέδοις φρονήμασιν.
170 ὅτ' οὖν ἐκεῖνοι πρὸς διπλῆς μοίρας μίαν
καθ' ἡμέραν ὤλοντο παίσαντές τε καὶ
πληγέντες αὐτόχειρι σὺν μιάσματι,
ἐγὼ κράτη δὴ πάντα καὶ θρόνους ἔχω
γένους κατ' ἀγχιστεῖα τῶν ὀλωλότων.

after the recent wars be forgetful, and let us visit all the temples of the gods with all-night dances, and may the Bacchic god who shakes the land of Thebes be ruler!

But here comes the new king of the land, ... Creon, under the new conditions given by the gods; what plan is he turning over, that he has proposed this assembly of elders for discussion, summoning them by general proclamation?

Enter CREON.

CREON

Sirs, the gods have shaken the city's fortunes with a heavy shaking, but now they have set them right in safety. And I have summoned you out of all the people by emissaries, knowing well first that you have always reverenced the power of the throne of Laius, and second that when Oedipus guided the city <with my sister as his wife, you always served them faithfully,> and when he perished, you persisted in loyalty towards their children. So now that they have perished by twofold ruin on a single day, striking and being struck by the polluting violence of one another, I hold the power and the throne by reason of my kinship with the dead.

---

151 θέσθε laz: θέσθαι RSVt
167 post hunc versum lacunam statuit Dindorf

175   ἀμήχανον δὲ παντὸς ἀνδρὸς ἐκμαθεῖν
ψυχήν τε καὶ φρόνημα καὶ γνώμην, πρὶν ἂν
ἀρχαῖς τε καὶ νόμοισιν ἐντριβὴς φανῇ.
ἐμοὶ γὰρ ὅστις πᾶσαν εὐθύνων πόλιν
μὴ τῶν ἀρίστων ἅπτεται βουλευμάτων,
180   ἀλλ' ἐκ φόβου του γλῶσσαν ἐγκλῄσας ἔχει,
κάκιστος εἶναι νῦν τε καὶ πάλαι δοκεῖ·
καὶ μεῖζον' ὅστις ἀντὶ τῆς αὑτοῦ πάτρας
φίλον νομίζει, τοῦτον οὐδαμοῦ λέγω.
ἐγὼ γάρ, ἴστω Ζεὺς ὁ πάνθ' ὁρῶν ἀεί,
185   οὔτ' ἂν σιωπήσαιμι τὴν ἄτην ὁρῶν
στείχουσαν ἀστοῖς ἀντὶ τῆς σωτηρίας,
οὔτ' ἂν φίλον ποτ' ἄνδρα δυσμενῆ χθονὸς
θείμην ἐμαυτῷ, τοῦτο γιγνώσκων ὅτι
ἥδ' ἐστὶν ἡ σῴζουσα καὶ ταύτης ἔπι
190   πλέοντες ὀρθῆς τοὺς φίλους ποιούμεθα.
τοιοῖσδ' ἐγὼ νόμοισι τήνδ' αὔξω πόλιν.
καὶ νῦν ἀδελφὰ τῶνδε κηρύξας ἔχω
ἀστοῖσι παίδων τῶν ἀπ' Οἰδίπου πέρι·
Ἐτεοκλέα μέν, ὃς πόλεως ὑπερμαχῶν
195   ὄλωλε τῆσδε, πάντ' ἀριστεύσας δορί,
τάφῳ τε κρύψαι καὶ τὰ πάντ' ἐφαγνίσαι
ἃ τοῖς ἀρίστοις ἔρχεται κάτω νεκροῖς·
τὸν δ' αὖ ξύναιμον τοῦδε, Πολυνείκη λέγω,
ὃς γῆν πατρῴαν καὶ θεοὺς τοὺς ἐγγενεῖς
200   φυγὰς κατελθὼν ἠθέλησε μὲν πυρὶ
πρῆσαι κατ' ἄκρας, ἠθέλησε δ' αἵματος
κοινοῦ πάσασθαι, τοὺς δὲ δουλώσας ἄγειν,

There is no way of getting to know a man's spirit and thought and judgment, until he has been seen to be versed in government and in the laws. Yes, to me anyone who while guiding the whole city fails to set his hand to the best counsels, but keeps his mouth shut by reason of some fear seems now and has always seemed the worst of men; and him who rates a dear one higher than his native land, him I put nowhere. I would never be silent, may Zeus who sees all things for ever know it, when I saw ruin coming upon the citizens instead of safety, nor would I make a friend of the enemy of my country, knowing that this is the ship that preserves us, and that this is the ship on which we sail and only while she prospers can we make our friends.

These are the rules by which I make our city great; and now in consonance with them I have made to the citizens this proclamation touching the sons of Oedipus. Eteocles, who died fighting for this city, having excelled in battle, we shall hide in the tomb and we shall render to him all the rites that come to the noblest of the dead below. But his brother, I mean Polynices, who came back from exile meaning to burn to the ground his native city and the gods of his race, and meaning to drink the people's blood and to enslave its people, as for him it is proclaimed to this

SOPHOCLES

τοῦτον πόλει τῇδ' ἐκκεκήρυκται τάφῳ
μήτε κτερίζειν μήτε κωκῦσαί τινα,
205 ἐᾶν δ' ἄθαπτον καὶ πρὸς οἰωνῶν δέμας
καὶ πρὸς κυνῶν ἐδεστὸν αἰκισθέν τ' ἰδεῖν.
τοιόνδ' ἐμὸν φρόνημα, κοὔποτ' ἔκ γ' ἐμοῦ
τιμῇ προέξουσ' οἱ κακοὶ τῶν ἐνδίκων.
ἀλλ' ὅστις εὔνους τῇδε τῇ πόλει, θανὼν
210 καὶ ζῶν ὁμοίως ἔκ γ' ἐμοῦ τιμήσεται.

ΧΟΡΟΣ
σοὶ ταῦτ' ἀρέσκει, παῖ Μενοικέως, ποεῖν
τὸν τῇδε δύσνουν καὶ τὸν εὐμενῆ πόλει·
νόμῳ δὲ χρῆσθαι παντί, τοῦτ' ἔνεστί σοι
καὶ τῶν θανόντων χὠπόσοι ζῶμεν πέρι.

ΚΡΕΩΝ
215 ὡς ἂν σκοποὶ νῦν ἦτε τῶν εἰρημένων —

ΧΟΡΟΣ
νεωτέρῳ τῳ τοῦτο βαστάζειν πρόθες.

ΚΡΕΩΝ
ἀλλ' εἴσ' ἕτοιμοι τοῦ νεκροῦ γ' ἐπίσκοποι.

ΧΟΡΟΣ
τί δῆτ' ἂν ἄλλ' ἐκ τοῦδ' ἐπεντέλλοις ἔτι;

ΚΡΕΩΝ
τὸ μὴ 'πιχωρεῖν τοῖς ἀπιστοῦσιν τάδε.

ΧΟΡΟΣ
220 οὐκ ἔστιν οὕτω μῶρος ὃς θανεῖν ἐρᾷ.

city that none shall bury or lament, but they shall leave his
body unburied for birds and dogs to devour and savage.
That is my way of thinking, and never by my will shall bad
men exceed good men in honour. No, whoever is loyal to
the city in death and life alike shall from me have honour.

CHORUS

It is your pleasure, son of Menoeceus, to do this to the man
who is hostile and to the man who is loyal to the city; and
you have power to observe every rule with regard to the
dead and to us who are alive.

CREON

So that you may see that my orders are observed . . .

CHORUS

Give this burden to some younger man to bear!

CREON

But men are ready who will guard the corpse!

CHORUS

Then what other command have you to give?

CREON

You must not give way to those who disobey in this.

CHORUS

There is no one foolish enough to desire death.

---

²⁰³ ἐκκεκήρυκται τάφῳ Musgrave: -ύχθαι τάφῳ codd.: -ύχθαι
λέγω Nauck
²⁰⁸ τιμῇ Linwood: -ὴν codd.
²¹¹ ποιεῖν (sic) K in marg. (coni. Martin): Κρέον vel Κρέων codd.
²¹³ τοῦτ' Platt: πού τ' codd.
²¹⁸ ἀλλ' ἐκ τοῦδ' Pallis: ἄλλῳ (ἄλλο L s.l.) τοῦτ' codd.

ΚΡΕΩΝ

καὶ μὴν ὁ μισθός γ' οὗτος. ἀλλ' ὑπ' ἐλπίδων
ἄνδρας τὸ κέρδος πολλάκις διώλεσεν.

ΦΥΛΑΞ

ἄναξ, ἐρῶ μὲν οὐχ ὅπως τάχους ὕπο
δύσπνους ἱκάνω κοῦφον ἐξάρας πόδα.
225 πολλὰς γὰρ ἔσχον φροντίδων ἐπιστάσεις,
ὁδοῖς κυκλῶν ἐμαυτὸν εἰς ἀναστροφήν·
ψυχὴ γὰρ ηὔδα πολλά μοι μυθουμένη,
"τάλας, τί χωρεῖς οἷ μολὼν δώσεις δίκην;
τλήμων, μένεις αὖ; κεἰ τάδ' εἴσεται Κρέων
230 ἄλλου παρ' ἀνδρός, πῶς σὺ δῆτ' οὐκ ἀλγυνῇ;"
τοιαῦθ' ἑλίσσων ἤνυτον σχολῇ βραδύς,
χοὔτως ὁδὸς βραχεῖα γίγνεται μακρά.
τέλος γε μέντοι δεῦρ' ἐνίκησεν μολεῖν
σοί· κεἰ τὸ μηδὲν ἐξερῶ, φράσω δ' ὅμως.
235 τῆς ἐλπίδος γὰρ ἔρχομαι δεδραγμένος,
τὸ μὴ παθεῖν ἂν ἄλλο πλὴν τὸ μόρσιμον.

ΚΡΕΩΝ

τί δ' ἐστὶν ἀνθ' οὗ τήνδ' ἔχεις ἀθυμίαν;

ΦΥΛΑΞ

φράσαι θέλω σοι πρῶτα τἀμαυτοῦ· τὸ γὰρ
πρᾶγμ' οὔτ' ἔδρασ' οὔτ' εἶδον ὅστις ἦν ὁ δρῶν,
240 οὐδ' ἂν δικαίως ἐς κακὸν πέσοιμί τι.

ΚΡΕΩΝ

εὖ γε στοχάζῃ κἀποφάργνυσαι κύκλῳ
τὸ πρᾶγμα. δηλοῖς δ' ὥς τι σημανῶν νέον.

ANTIGONE

CREON

Well, that is the reward; but hope has often caused the love
of gain to ruin men.

Enter GUARD.

GUARD

King, I will not say that I come breathless with running,
having plied a nimble foot! I had many worries that held
me up, turning this way and that in my journey as I thought
of going back. Yes, my mind spoke many words to me:
"Wretch, why are you going to a place where you will pay
the penalty? Poor fellow, are you staying behind, then?
And if Creon learns this from another man, how shall you
escape affliction?" As I pondered on such thoughts I made
my way slowly, with delays, and so a short journey became
a long one. But in the end the thought that prevailed was
that of coming here to you; and even if what I say amounts
to nothing, still I will tell you; for I come clutching at the
hope that I cannot suffer anything but what is fated.

CREON

But what is it that so troubles you?

GUARD

First I want to tell you about myself; I did not do the deed,
nor did I see who did, and I could not with justice come to
any harm.

CREON

You are skilfully setting fences and palisades around the
matter, and it is clear that you have some news to tell us.

---

229 μένεις Kᵃᶜ: μενεῖς cett.

ΦΥΛΑΞ

τὰ δεινὰ γάρ τοι προστίθησ' ὄκνον πολύν.

ΚΡΕΩΝ

οὔκουν ἐρεῖς ποτ', εἶτ' ἀπαλλαχθεὶς ἄπει;

ΦΥΛΑΞ

245 καὶ δὴ λέγω σοι. τὸν νεκρόν τις ἀρτίως
θάψας βέβηκε κἀπὶ χρωτὶ διψίαν
κόνιν παλύνας κἀφαγιστεύσας ἃ χρή.

ΚΡΕΩΝ

τί φής; τίς ἀνδρῶν ἦν ὁ τολμήσας τάδε;

ΦΥΛΑΞ

οὐκ οἶδ'· ἐκεῖ γὰρ οὔτε του γενῆδος ἦν
250 πλῆγμ', οὐ δικέλλης ἐκβολή· στύφλος δὲ γῆ
καὶ χέρσος, ἀρρὼξ οὐδ' ἐπημαξευμένη
τροχοῖσιν, ἀλλ' ἄσημος οὑργάτης τις ἦν.
ὅπως δ' ὁ πρῶτος ἡμὶν ἡμεροσκόπος
δείκνυσι, πᾶσι θαῦμα δυσχερὲς παρῆν.
255 ὁ μὲν γὰρ ἠφάνιστο, τυμβήρης μὲν οὔ,
λεπτὴ δ' ἄγος φεύγοντος ὣς ἐπῆν κόνις.
σημεῖα δ' οὔτε θηρὸς οὔτε του κυνῶν
ἐλθόντος, οὐ σπάσαντος ἐξεφαίνετο.
λόγοι δ' ἐν ἀλλήλοισιν ἐρρόθουν κακοί,
260 φύλαξ ἐλέγχων φύλακα, κἂν ἐγίγνετο
πληγὴ τελευτῶσ', οὐδ' ὁ κωλύσων παρῆν.
εἷς γάρ τις ἦν ἕκαστος οὑξειργασμένος,
κοὐδεὶς ἐναργής, ἀλλ' ἔφευγε μὴ εἰδέναι.

ANTIGONE

GUARD

Yes, serious matters make one very nervous.

CREON

Will you not out with it, and then take yourself away?

GUARD

Well, I will tell you! Someone has just gone off after bury-
ing the body, sprinkling its flesh with thirsty dust and per-
forming the necessary rites.

CREON

What are you saying? What man has dared to do this?

GUARD

I do not know; there was no mark of an axe, no earth
turned up by a mattock; the earth was hard and dry, unbro-
ken and with no tracks of wheels; the doer left no mark.
And when the first daytime watcher showed us, it was a
disagreeable surprise for all. He had vanished, not buried
in a tomb, but covered with a light dust, as though put
there by someone to avoid pollution; and there were no
signs of any animal or dog that had come and torn the
body. Hard words were bandied between us, one guard
questioning another, and it might have ended with a blow,
and no one was there to stop it; for each of us was the doer,
but no one manifestly so, but he escaped detection.

---

259 post hunc versum aliquid forsitan interciderit

27

ἦμεν δ' ἕτοῖμοι καὶ μύδρους αἴρειν χεροῖν,
265 καὶ πῦρ διέρπειν, καὶ θεοὺς ὁρκωμοτεῖν
τὸ μήτε δρᾶσαι μήτε τῳ ξυνειδέναι
τὸ πρᾶγμα βουλεύσαντι μήτ' εἰργασμένῳ.
τέλος δ' ὅτ' οὐδὲν ἦν ἐρευνῶσιν πλέον,
λέγει τις εἷς ὃ πάντας ἐς πέδον κάρα
270 νεῦσαι φόβῳ προὔτρεψεν· οὐ γὰρ εἴχομεν
οὔτ' ἀντιφωνεῖν οὔθ' ὅπως δρῶντες καλῶς
πράξαιμεν. ἦν δ' ὁ μῦθος ὡς ἀνοιστέον
σοὶ τοὔργον εἴη τοῦτο κοὐχὶ κρυπτέον.
καὶ ταῦτ' ἐνίκα, κἀμὲ τὸν δυσδαίμονα
275 πάλος καθαιρεῖ τοῦτο τἀγαθὸν λαβεῖν.
πάρειμι δ' ἄκων οὐχ ἑκοῦσιν, οἶδ' ὅτι·
στέργει γὰρ οὐδεὶς ἄγγελον κακῶν ἐπῶν.

ΧΟΡΟΣ
ἄναξ, ἐμοί τοι μή τι καὶ θεήλατον
τοὔργον τόδ' ἡ ξύννοια βουλεύει πάλαι.

ΚΡΕΩΝ
280 παῦσαι, πρὶν ὀργῆς καί με μεστῶσαι λέγων,
μὴ 'φευρεθῇς ἄνους τε καὶ γέρων ἅμα.
λέγεις γὰρ οὐκ ἀνεκτὰ δαίμονας λέγων
πρόνοιαν ἴσχειν τοῦδε τοῦ νεκροῦ πέρι.
πότερον ὑπερτιμῶντες ὡς εὐεργέτην
285 ἔκρυπτον αὐτόν, ὅστις ἀμφικίονας
ναοὺς πυρώσων ἦλθε κἀναθήματα
καὶ γῆν ἐκείνων καὶ νόμους διασκεδῶν;
ἢ τοὺς κακοὺς τιμῶντας εἰσορᾷς θεούς;

And we were ready to lift lumps of molten lead and to go through fire and to swear by the gods that we had not done the deed and did not know who had planned it or who had done it. And finally, when our search had done us no good, one of us said a thing that made us all bow our heads to the ground in terror; for we could not answer him nor see what action would help us to escape disaster. What he said was that we had to report the matter to you and not conceal it. This view prevailed, and the lot constrained me, poor fellow, to accept this privilege. So here I am, no less unwelcome than unwilling, I know; for no one loves the messenger who brings bad news.

CHORUS

King, my anxious thought has long been advising me that this action may have been prompted by the gods.

CREON

Cease, before your words fill me with rage, so that you may not be found to be not only an old man but a fool! What you say is intolerable, that the gods are concerned for this corpse! Did they conceal it so as to do him great honour as a benefactor, him who came to burn their colonnaded temples and their offerings and to destroy their country and its laws? Do you see the gods honouring evil men? It is not

---

[269] ὁ Nauck: ὅς codd.

οὐκ ἔστιν. ἀλλὰ ταῦτα καὶ πάλαι πόλεως
290 ἄνδρες μόλις φέροντες ἐρρόθουν ἐμοὶ
κρυφῇ, κάρα σείοντες, οὐδ' ὑπὸ ζυγῷ
λόφον δικαίως εἶχον, ὡς στέργειν ἐμέ.
ἐκ τῶνδε τούτους ἐξεπίσταμαι καλῶς
παρηγμένους μισθοῖσιν εἰργάσθαι τάδε.
295 οὐδὲν γὰρ ἀνθρώποισιν οἷον ἄργυρος
κακὸν νόμισμ' ἔβλαστε. τοῦτο καὶ πόλεις
πορθεῖ, τόδ' ἄνδρας ἐξανίστησιν δόμων·
τόδ' ἐκδιδάσκει καὶ παραλλάσσει φρένας
χρηστὰς πρὸς αἰσχρὰ πράγμαθ' ἵστασθαι βροτῶν·
300 πανουργίας δ' ἔδειξεν ἀνθρώποις ἔχειν
καὶ παντὸς ἔργου δυσσέβειαν εἰδέναι.
ὅσοι δὲ μισθαρνοῦντες ἤνυσαν τάδε,
χρόνῳ ποτ' ἐξέπραξαν ὡς δοῦναι δίκην.
ἀλλ' εἴπερ ἴσχει Ζεὺς ἔτ' ἐξ ἐμοῦ σέβας,
305 εὖ τοῦτ' ἐπίστασ', ὅρκιος δέ σοι λέγω,
εἰ μὴ τὸν αὐτόχειρα τοῦδε τοῦ τάφου
εὑρόντες ἐκφανεῖτ' ἐς ὀφθαλμοὺς ἐμούς,
οὐχ ὑμὶν Ἅιδης μοῦνος ἀρκέσει, πρὶν ἂν
ζῶντες κρεμαστοὶ τήνδε δηλώσηθ' ὕβριν,
310 ἵν' εἰδότες τὸ κέρδος ἔνθεν οἰστέον
τὸ λοιπὸν ἁρπάζητε, καὶ μάθηθ' ὅτι
οὐκ ἐξ ἅπαντος δεῖ τὸ κερδαίνειν φιλεῖν.
ἐκ τῶν γὰρ αἰσχρῶν λημμάτων τοὺς πλείονας
ἀτωμένους ἴδοις ἂν ἢ σεσωμένους.

so! But long since men in the city who find it hard to bear me have been murmuring against me, unwilling to keep their necks beneath the yoke, as justice demands, so as to put up with me. I know well that these people have been bribed by those men to do this thing. There is no institution so ruinous for men as money; money sacks cities, money drives men from their homes! Money by its teaching perverts men's good minds so that they take to evil actions! Money has shown men how to practise villainy, and taught them impiousness in every action! But those who to earn their fee have contrived to do this thing have ensured that in time they will pay the penalty. Well, if Zeus is still revered through my authority, know this for certain, and I speak to you on oath! If you do not find the author of this burial and reveal him to my eyes, a single Hades shall not suffice for you, before all have been strung up alive to expose this insolence, so that for the future you may know where you can get your profit when you plunder, and learn that you must not grow used to making money out of everything. One sees more people ruined than one has seen preserved by shameful gains.

ΦΥΛΑΞ

315 εἰπεῖν τι δώσεις, ἢ στραφεὶς οὕτως ἴω;

ΚΡΕΩΝ

οὐκ οἶσθα καὶ νῦν ὡς ἀνιαρῶς λέγεις;

ΦΥΛΑΞ

ἐν τοῖσιν ὠσὶν ἢ 'πὶ τῇ ψυχῇ δάκνῃ;

ΚΡΕΩΝ

τί δὲ ῥυθμίζεις τὴν ἐμὴν λύπην ὅπου;

ΦΥΛΑΞ

ὁ δρῶν σ' ἀνιᾷ τὰς φρένας, τὰ δ' ὦτ' ἐγώ.

ΚΡΕΩΝ

320 οἴμ' ὡς λάλημα, δῆλον, ἐκπεφυκὸς εἶ.

ΦΥΛΑΞ

οὔκουν τό γ' ἔργον τοῦτο ποιήσας ποτέ.

ΚΡΕΩΝ

καὶ ταῦτ' ἐπ' ἀργύρῳ γε τὴν ψυχὴν προδούς.

ΦΥΛΑΞ

φεῦ·
ἦ δεινόν, ᾧ δοκεῖ γε, καὶ ψευδῆ δοκεῖν.

ΚΡΕΩΝ

κόμψευέ νυν τὴν δόξαν· εἰ δὲ ταῦτα μὴ
325 φανεῖτέ μοι τοὺς δρῶντας, ἐξερεῖθ' ὅτι
τὰ δειλὰ κέρδη πημονὰς ἐργάζεται.

ΦΥΛΑΞ

ἀλλ' εὑρεθείη μὲν μάλιστ'· ἐὰν δέ τοι
ληφθῇ τε καὶ μή, τοῦτο γὰρ τύχη κρινεῖ,

32

GUARD

Will you let me say something, or must I turn my back and leave like this?

CREON

Do you not know even now how your words pain me?

GUARD

Is it your ears or your mind that feels the pain?

CREON

Why do you try to locate the pain I feel?

GUARD

The doer pains your mind, but I your ears.

CREON

Ah, you are a chatterer by nature, it is clear!

GUARD

But never one who did this thing!

CREON

You did, because you gave away your life for money!

GUARD

Oh! It is dangerous for the believer to believe what is not true.

CREON

Well, you split hairs about belief! But if you do not reveal the doers to me, you shall testify that low desire for profit is the cause of pain!

Exit CREON.

GUARD

Why, let him be found by all means! But whether he is found or not, for that is something that fortune will decide,

33

οὐκ ἔσθ' ὅπως ὄψῃ σὺ δεῦρ' ἐλθόντα με.
330 καὶ νῦν γὰρ ἐκτὸς ἐλπίδος γνώμης τ' ἐμῆς
σωθεὶς ὀφείλω τοῖς θεοῖς πολλὴν χάριν.

ΧΟΡΟΣ

πολλὰ τὰ δεινὰ κοὐδὲν ἀν-   στρ. α΄
θρώπου δεινότερον πέλει·
τοῦτο καὶ πολιοῦ πέραν
335 πόντου χειμερίῳ νότῳ
χωρεῖ, περιβρυχίοισιν
περῶν ὑπ' οἴδμασιν, θεῶν
τε τὰν ὑπερτάταν, Γᾶν
ἄφθιτον, ἀκαμάταν ἀποτρύεται,
340 ἰλλομένων ἀρότρων ἔτος εἰς ἔτος,
ἱππείῳ γένει πολεύων.
κουφονόων τε φῦλον ὀρ-   ἀντ. α΄
νίθων ἀμφιβαλὼν ἄγει
καὶ θηρῶν ἀγρίων ἔθνη
345 πόντου τ' εἰναλίαν φύσιν
σπείραισι δικτυοκλώστοις,
περιφραδὴς ἀνήρ· κρατεῖ
δὲ μηχαναῖς ἀγραύλου
350 θηρὸς ὀρεσσιβάτα, λασιαύχενά θ'
ἵππον ὀχμάζεται ἀμφὶ λόφον ζυγῷ
οὔρειόν τ' ἀκμῆτα ταῦρον.
καὶ φθέγμα καὶ ἀνεμόεν   στρ. β΄
355 φρόνημα καὶ ἀστυνόμους
ὀργὰς ἐδιδάξατο καὶ δυσαύλων

you will never see me coming here again! Indeed, this time I have got off safely beyond my own hopes and my own judgment, and I am deeply grateful to the gods!

Exit GUARD.

CHORUS

Many things are formidable, and none more formidable than man! He crosses the gray sea beneath the winter wind, passing beneath the surges that surround him; and he wears away the highest of the gods, Earth, immortal and unwearying, as his ploughs go back and forth from year to year, turning the soil with the aid of the breed of horses.

And he captures the tribe of thoughtless birds and the races of wild beasts and the watery brood of the sea, catching them in the woven coils of nets, man the skilful. And he contrives to overcome the beast that roams the mountain, and tames the shaggy-maned horse and the untiring mountain bull, putting a yoke about their necks.

And he has learned speech and wind-swift thought and the temper that rules cities, and how to escape the expo-

---

³⁵¹ ὀχμάζεται Schöne: ἔξεται l: ἄξεται codd. plerique ἀμφὶ λόφον ζυγῷ Schöne et Franz: ἀμφίλοφον ζυγὸν codd.

πάγων ὑπαίθρεια καὶ
δύσομβρα φεύγειν βέλη
360 παντοπόρος· ἄπορος ἐπ' οὐδὲν ἔρχεται
τὸ μέλλον· Ἅιδα μόνον
φεῦξιν οὐκ ἐπάξεται·
νόσων δ' ἀμηχάνων φυγὰς
ξυμπέφρασται.

365 σοφόν τι τὸ μηχανόεν   ἀντ. β'
τέχνας ὑπὲρ ἐλπίδ' ἔχων
τοτὲ μὲν κακόν, ἄλλοτ' ἐπ' ἐσθλὸν ἕρπει.
νόμους παρείρων χθονὸς
θεῶν τ' ἔνορκον δίκαν
370 ὑψίπολις· ἄπολις ὅτῳ τὸ μὴ καλὸν
ξύνεστι τόλμας χάριν.
μήτ' ἐμοὶ παρέστιος
γένοιτο μήτ' ἴσον φρονῶν
375 ὃς τάδ' ἔρδοι.
εἰ δαιμόνιον τέρας ἀμφινοῶ
τόδε· πῶς <δ'> εἰδὼς ἀντιλογήσω
τήνδ' οὐκ εἶναι παῖδ' Ἀντιγόνην;
ὦ δύστηνος καὶ δυστήνου
380 πατρὸς Οἰδιπόδα,
τί ποτ'; οὐ δή που σέ γ' ἀπιστοῦσαν
τοῖς βασιλείοις ἀπάγουσι νόμοις
καὶ ἐν ἀφροσύνῃ καθελόντες;

ΦΥΛΑΞ
ἥδ' ἔστ' ἐκείνη τοὔργον ἡ 'ξειργασμένη·

sure of the inhospitable hills and the sharp arrows of the rain, all-resourceful; he meets nothing in the future without resource; only from Hades shall he apply no means of flight; and he has contrived escape from desperate maladies.

Skilful beyond hope is the contrivance of his art, and he advances sometimes to evil, at other times to good. When he applies the laws of the earth and the justice the gods have sworn to uphold he is high in the city; outcast from the city is he with whom the ignoble consorts for the sake of gain. May he who does such things never sit by my hearth or share my thoughts!

The GUARD *leads in* ANTIGONE.

I am at a loss; is this a godsent portent? But how shall I deny, since I know it, that this is the young Antigone? Unhappy one and child of an unhappy father, Oedipus, what is this? Surely they do not lead you captive for disobedience to the king's laws, having detected you in folly?

GUARD

This is the one that did the deed! We caught her burying

---

357 ὑπαίθρεια Boeckh: αἴθρια codd.
368 παρείρων] γεραίρων Reiske
376 εἰ Reiske: ἐς codd.

385 τήνδ᾽ εἵλομεν θάπτουσαν. ἀλλὰ ποῦ Κρέων;

ΧΟΡΟΣ

ὅδ᾽ ἐκ δόμων ἄψορρος ἐς δέον περᾷ.

ΚΡΕΩΝ

τί δ᾽ ἔστι; ποίᾳ ξύμμετρος προὔβην τύχῃ;

ΦΥΛΑΞ

ἄναξ, βροτοῖσιν οὐδέν ἐστ᾽ ἀπώμοτον.
ψεύδει γὰρ ἡ ᾽πίνοια τὴν γνώμην· ἐπεὶ
390 σχολῇ ποθ᾽ ἥξειν δεῦρ᾽ ἂν ἐξηύχουν ἐγὼ
ταῖς σαῖς ἀπειλαῖς, αἷς ἐχειμάσθην τότε.
ἀλλ᾽ ἡ γὰρ εὐκτὸς καὶ παρ᾽ ἐλπίδας χαρὰ
ἔοικεν ἄλλῃ μῆκος οὐδὲν ἡδονῇ,
ἥκω, δι᾽ ὅρκων καίπερ ὢν ἀπώμοτος,
395 κόρην ἄγων τήνδ᾽, ἣ καθῃρέθη τάφον
κοσμοῦσα. κλῆρος ἐνθάδ᾽ οὐκ ἐπάλλετο,
ἀλλ᾽ ἔστ᾽ ἐμὸν θοὔρμαιον, οὐκ ἄλλου, τόδε.
καὶ νῦν, ἄναξ, τήνδ᾽ αὐτός, ὡς θέλεις, λαβὼν
καὶ κρῖνε κἀξέλεγχ᾽· ἐγὼ δ᾽ ἐλεύθερος
400 δίκαιός εἰμι τῶνδ᾽ ἀπηλλάχθαι κακῶν.

ΚΡΕΩΝ

ἄγεις δὲ τήνδε τῷ τρόπῳ πόθεν λαβών;

ΦΥΛΑΞ

αὐτὴ τὸν ἄνδρ᾽ ἔθαπτε· πάντ᾽ ἐπίστασαι.

ΚΡΕΩΝ

ἦ καὶ ξυνίης καὶ λέγεις ὀρθῶς ἃ φής;

---

392 εὐκτὸς Bothe: ἐκτὸς codd.   402 αὐτὴ Wilson: αὕτη codd.

the body! But where is Creon?

CHORUS

He is here, returning from the house just when he is needed.

Enter CREON.

CREON

What is the matter? What is the event that makes my coming opportune?

GUARD

King, there is nothing that mortals can swear is impossible! For second thoughts show one's judgment to be wrong; why, I scarcely would have thought I would come here again because of your threats, which at that time battered me. But since the delight that one has prayed for beyond hope is unlike any other pleasure by a long way, I have come, though I had sworn never to do so, bringing this girl, who was caught adorning the grave. No lots were cast in this case, but the gift of fortune belongs to me and to no other. And now, king, take her yourself and judge her and convict her; but I am free, and have the right to be released from these troubles!

CREON

How did you take her, and from where have you brought her?

GUARD

She herself was burying the man! You know it all!

CREON

Do you understand, and are you saying correctly what you are telling me?

ΦΥΛΑΞ

ταύτην γ' ἰδὼν θάπτουσαν ὃν σὺ τὸν νεκρὸν
405 ἀπεῖπας. ἆρ' ἔνδηλα καὶ σαφῆ λέγω;

ΚΡΕΩΝ

καὶ πῶς ὁρᾶται κἀπίληπτος ᾑρέθη;

ΦΥΛΑΞ

τοιοῦτον ἦν τὸ πρᾶγμ'. ὅπως γὰρ ἥκομεν,
πρὸς σοῦ τὰ δείν' ἐκεῖν' ἐπηπειλημένοι,
πᾶσαν κόνιν σήραντες ἣ κατεῖχε τὸν
410 νέκυν, μυδῶν τε σῶμα γυμνώσαντες εὖ,
καθήμεθ' ἄκρων ἐκ πάγων ὑπήνεμοι,
ὀσμὴν ἀπ' αὐτοῦ μὴ βάλῃ πεφευγότες,
ἐγερτὶ κινῶν ἄνδρ' ἀνὴρ ἐπιρρόθοις
κακοῖσιν, εἴ τις τοῦδ' ἀφειδήσοι πόνου.
415 χρόνον τάδ' ἦν τοσοῦτον, ἔστ' ἐν αἰθέρι
μέσῳ κατέστη λαμπρὸς ἡλίου κύκλος
καὶ καῦμ' ἔθαλπε· καὶ τότ' ἐξαίφνης χθονὸς
τυφὼς ἀγείρας σκηπτόν, οὐράνιον ἄχος,
πίμπλησι πεδίον, πᾶσαν αἰκίζων φόβην
420 ὕλης πεδιάδος, ἐν δ' ἐμεστώθη μέγας
αἰθήρ· μύσαντες δ' εἴχομεν θείαν νόσον.
καὶ τοῦδ' ἀπαλλαγέντος ἐν χρόνῳ μακρῷ,
ἡ παῖς ὁρᾶται κἀνακωκύει πικρῶς
ὄρνιθος ὀξὺν φθόγγον, ὡς ὅταν κενῆς
425 εὐνῆς νεοσσῶν ὀρφανὸν βλέψῃ λέχος·
οὕτω δὲ χαὕτη, ψιλὸν ὡς ὁρᾷ νέκυν,
γόοισιν ἐξώμωξεν, ἐκ δ' ἀρὰς κακὰς
ἠρᾶτο τοῖσι τοὔργον ἐξειργασμένοις.

GUARD

Yes, I saw her burying the corpse whose burial you for-
bade! Is what I say clear and exact?

CREON

And how was she sighted and taken in the act?

GUARD

It was like this! When we went back, after those terrible
threats of yours, we swept away all the dust that covered
the corpse, carefully stripped the mouldering body, and
then sat shielded by the hilltops from the wind, avoiding
the smell that might have come to us from it, each man
watchfully arousing his neighbour with volleys of abuse, if
anyone seemed likely to neglect this task. This lasted until
the bright circle of the sun took its place in the sky and the
midday heat began to roast us; and then suddenly a
whirlwind on the ground raised up a storm, a trouble in the
air, and filled the plain, tormenting all the foliage of the
woods that covered the ground there; and the vast sky was
filled with it, and we shut our eyes and endured the god-
sent affliction.

And when after a long time this went away, we saw the
girl; she cried out bitterly, with a sound like the piercing
note of a bird when she sees her empty nest robbed of her
young; just so did she cry out, weeping, and called down
curses on those who had done the deed. At once she

---

[412] post hunc versum lacunam statuit Meineke
[418] ἀγείρας Radermacher: ἀείρας codd.
[423] πικρῶς Bothe: πικρᾶς codd.

καὶ χερσὶν εὐθὺς διψίαν φέρει κόνιν,
430 ἔκ τ᾽ εὐκροτήτου χαλκέας ἄρδην πρόχου
χοαῖσι τρισπόνδοισι τὸν νέκυν στέφει.
χἠμεῖς ἰδόντες ἱέμεσθα, σὺν δέ νιν
θηρώμεθ᾽ εὐθὺς οὐδὲν ἐκπεπληγμένην,
καὶ τάς τε πρόσθεν τάς τε νῦν ἠλέγχομεν
435 πράξεις· ἄπαρνος δ᾽ οὐδενὸς καθίστατο,
ἅμ᾽ ἡδέως ἔμοιγε κἀλγεινῶς ἅμα.
τὸ μὲν γὰρ αὐτὸν ἐκ κακῶν πεφευγέναι
ἥδιστον, ἐς κακὸν δὲ τοὺς φίλους ἄγειν
ἀλγεινόν. ἀλλὰ πάντα ταῦθ᾽ ἥσσω λαβεῖν
440 ἐμοὶ πέφυκε τῆς ἐμῆς σωτηρίας.

ΚΡΕΩΝ

σὲ δή, σὲ τὴν νεύουσαν ἐς πέδον κάρα,
φής, ἢ καταρνῇ μὴ δεδρακέναι τάδε;

ΑΝΤΙΓΟΝΗ

καὶ φημὶ δρᾶσαι κοὐκ ἀπαρνοῦμαι τὸ μή.

ΚΡΕΩΝ

σὺ μὲν κομίζοις ἂν σεαυτὸν ᾗ θέλεις
445 ἔξω βαρείας αἰτίας ἐλεύθερον·
σὺ δ᾽ εἰπέ μοι μὴ μῆκος, ἀλλὰ συντόμως,
ᾔδησθα κηρυχθέντα μὴ πράσσειν τάδε;

ΑΝΤΙΓΟΝΗ

ᾔδη· τί δ᾽ οὐκ ἔμελλον; ἐμφανῆ γὰρ ἦν.

ΚΡΕΩΝ

καὶ δῆτ᾽ ἐτόλμας τούσδ᾽ ὑπερβαίνειν νόμους;

brought in her hands thirsty dust, and from the well-wrought brazen urn that she was carrying she poured over the corpse a threefold libation. When we saw it we made haste and at once seized her, she being in no way surprised, and charged her with her earlier action and with this. She denied none of it, which gave me pleasure and pain at once. For to have escaped oneself from trouble is most pleasant, but to bring friends into danger is painful. But all this matters less to me than my own safety!

CREON

You there, you that are bowing down your head towards the ground, do you admit, or do you deny, that you have done this?

ANTIGONE

I say that I did it and I do not deny it.

CREON

(to GUARD) You may take yourself to wherever you please, free from the heavy charge.

Exit GUARD.

(to ANTIGONE) But do you tell me, not at length, but briefly: did you know of the proclamation forbidding this?

ANTIGONE

I knew it; of course I knew it. It was known to all.

CREON

And yet you dared to transgress these laws?

SOPHOCLES

ΑΝΤΙΓΟΝΗ

450 οὐ γάρ τί μοι Ζεὺς ἦν ὁ κηρύξας τάδε,
οὐδ' ἡ ξύνοικος τῶν κάτω θεῶν Δίκη
τοιούσδ' ἐν ἀνθρώποισιν ὥρισεν νόμους,
οὐδὲ σθένειν τοσοῦτον ᾠόμην τὰ σὰ
κηρύγμαθ' ὥστ' ἄγραπτα κἀσφαλῆ θεῶν
455 νόμιμα δύνασθαι θνητά γ' ὄνθ' ὑπερδραμεῖν.
οὐ γάρ τι νῦν γε κἀχθές, ἀλλ' ἀεί ποτε
ζῇ ταῦτα, κοὐδεὶς οἶδεν ἐξ ὅτου 'φάνη.
τούτων ἐγὼ οὐκ ἔμελλον, ἀνδρὸς οὐδενὸς
φρόνημα δείσασ', ἐν θεοῖσι τὴν δίκην
460 δώσειν· θανουμένη γὰρ ἐξῄδη, τί δ' οὔ;
κεἰ μὴ σὺ προυκήρυξας. εἰ δὲ τοῦ χρόνου
πρόσθεν θανοῦμαι, κέρδος αὔτ' ἐγὼ λέγω.
ὅστις γὰρ ἐν πολλοῖσιν ὡς ἐγὼ κακοῖς
ζῇ, πῶς ὅδ' οὐχὶ κατθανὼν κέρδος φέρει;
465 οὕτως ἔμοιγε τοῦδε τοῦ μόρου τυχεῖν
παρ' οὐδὲν ἄλγος· ἀλλ' ἄν, εἰ τὸν ἐξ ἐμῆς
μητρὸς θανόντ' ἄθαπτον <ὄντ'> ἠνεσχόμην,
κείνοις ἂν ἤλγουν· τοῖσδε δ' οὐκ ἀλγύνομαι.
σοὶ δ' εἰ δοκῶ νῦν μῶρα δρῶσα τυγχάνειν,
470 σχεδόν τι μώρῳ μωρίαν ὀφλισκάνω.

ΧΟΡΟΣ

δῆλον· τὸ γέννημ' ὠμὸν ἐξ ὠμοῦ πατρὸς
τῆς παιδός· εἴκειν δ' οὐκ ἐπίσταται κακοῖς.

ΚΡΕΩΝ

ἀλλ' ἴσθι τοι τὰ σκλήρ' ἄγαν φρονήματα

44

ANTIGONE

ANTIGONE

Yes, for it was not Zeus who made this proclamation, nor
was it Justice who lives with the gods below that estab-
lished such laws among men, nor did I think your procla-
mations strong enough to have power to overrule, mortal
as they were, the unwritten and unfailing ordinances of the
gods. For these have life, not simply today and yesterday,
but for ever, and no one knows how long ago they were
revealed. For this I did not intend to pay the penalty
among the gods for fear of any man's pride. I knew that I
would die, of course I knew, even if you had made no proc-
lamation. But if I die before my time, I account that gain.
For does not whoever lives among many troubles, as I do,
gain by death? So it is in no way painful for me to meet
with this death; if I had endured that the son of my own
mother should die and remain unburied, that would have
given me pain, but this gives me none. And if you think my
actions foolish, that amounts to a charge of folly by a fool!

CHORUS

It is clear! The nature of the girl is savage, like her father's,
and she does not know how to bend before her troubles.

CREON

Why, know that over-stubborn wills are the most apt to fall,

---

455 θνητά γ᾽ ὄνθ᾽ Bruhn: θνητὸν ὄνθ᾽ codd.
467 <ὄντ᾽> ἠνεσχόμην Blaydes: ἠ(ν)σχόμην νέκυν codd.
plerique: ἠνεσχόμην νέκυν Zo
471 δῆλον Nauck: δηλοῖ codd.

SOPHOCLES

πίπτειν μάλιστα, καὶ τὸν ἐγκρατέστατον
475 σίδηρον ὀπτὸν ἐκ πυρὸς περισκελῆ
θραυσθέντα καὶ ῥαγέντα πλεῖστ᾽ ἂν εἰσίδοις.
σμικρῷ χαλινῷ δ᾽ οἶδα τοὺς θυμουμένους
ἵππους καταρτυθέντας· οὐ γὰρ ἐκπέλει
φρονεῖν μέγ᾽ ὅστις δοῦλός ἐστι τῶν πέλας.
480 αὕτη δ᾽ ὑβρίζειν μὲν τότ᾽ ἐξηπίστατο,
νόμους ὑπερβαίνουσα τοὺς προκειμένους·
ὕβρις δ᾽, ἐπεὶ δέδρακεν, ἥδε δευτέρα,
τούτοις ἐπαυχεῖν καὶ δεδρακυῖαν γελᾶν.
ἦ νῦν ἐγὼ μὲν οὐκ ἀνήρ, αὕτη δ᾽ ἀνήρ,
485 εἰ ταῦτ᾽ ἀνατεὶ τῇδε κείσεται κράτη.
ἀλλ᾽ εἴτ᾽ ἀδελφῆς εἴθ᾽ ὁμαιμονεστέρα
τοῦ παντὸς ἡμῖν Ζηνὸς ἑρκείου κυρεῖ,
αὐτή τε χἠ ξύναιμος οὐκ ἀλύξετον
μόρου κακίστου· καὶ γὰρ οὖν κείνην ἴσον
490 ἐπαιτιῶμαι τοῦδε βουλεῦσαι τάφου.
καί νιν καλεῖτ᾽· ἔσω γὰρ εἶδον ἀρτίως
λυσσῶσαν αὐτὴν οὐδ᾽ ἐπήβολον φρενῶν.
φιλεῖ δ᾽ ὁ θυμὸς πρόσθεν ᾑρῆσθαι κλοπεὺς
τῶν μηδὲν ὀρθῶς ἐν σκότῳ τεχνωμένων.
495 μισῶ γε μέντοι χὤταν ἐν κακοῖσί τις
ἁλοὺς ἔπειτα τοῦτο καλλύνειν θέλῃ.

ΑΝΤΙΓΟΝΗ
θέλεις τι μεῖζον ἢ κατακτεῖναί μ᾽ ἑλών;

ΚΡΕΩΝ
ἐγὼ μὲν οὐδέν· τοῦτ᾽ ἔχων ἅπαντ᾽ ἔχω.

46

and the toughest iron, baked in the fire till it is hard, is most often, you will see, cracked and shattered! I know that spirited horses are controlled by a small bridle; for pride is impossible for anyone who is another's slave. This girl knew well how to be insolent then, transgressing the established laws; and after her action, this was a second insolence, to exult in this and to laugh at the thought of having done it. Indeed, now I am no man, but she is a man, if she is to enjoy such power as this with impunity. But whether she is my sister's child or closer in affinity than our whole family linked by Zeus of the hearth, she and her sister shall not escape a dreadful death! Yes, I hold her equally guilty of having planned this burial! Call her! I saw her lately in the house raving, having lost control of her wits. The mind is often detected in deceit beforehand, when people are planning nefarious deeds in darkness; but I hate also those who are caught out in evil deeds and then try to gloss them over.

ANTIGONE
Do you wish for anything more than to take me and kill me?

CREON
Not I! When I have that, I have everything.

ΑΝΤΙΓΟΝΗ

τί δῆτα μέλλεις; ὡς ἐμοὶ τῶν σῶν λόγων
500 ἀρεστὸν οὐδέν, μηδ' ἀρεσθείη ποτέ,
οὕτω δὲ καὶ σοὶ τἄμ' ἀφανδάνοντ' ἔφυ.
καίτοι πόθεν κλέος γ' ἂν εὐκλεέστερον
κατέσχον ἢ τὸν αὐτάδελφον ἐν τάφῳ
τιθεῖσα; τούτοις τοῦτο πᾶσιν ἁνδάνειν
505 λέγοιμ' ἄν, εἰ μὴ γλῶσσαν ἐγκλῄοι φόβος.
ἀλλ' ἡ τυραννὶς πολλά τ' ἄλλ' εὐδαιμονεῖ
κἄξεστιν αὐτῇ δρᾶν λέγειν θ' ἃ βούλεται.

ΚΡΕΩΝ

σὺ τοῦτο μούνη τῶνδε Καδμείων ὁρᾷς.

ΑΝΤΙΓΟΝΗ

ὁρῶσι χοὖτοι· σοὶ δ' ὑπίλλουσι στόμα.

ΚΡΕΩΝ

510 σὺ δ' οὐκ ἐπαιδῇ, τῶνδε χωρὶς εἰ φρονεῖς;

ΑΝΤΙΓΟΝΗ

οὐδὲν γὰρ αἰσχρὸν τοὺς ὁμοσπλάγχνους σέβειν.

ΚΡΕΩΝ

οὔκουν ὅμαιμος χὠ καταντίον θανών;

ΑΝΤΙΓΟΝΗ

ὅμαιμος ἐκ μιᾶς τε καὶ ταὐτοῦ πατρός.

ΚΡΕΩΝ

πῶς δῆτ' ἐκείνῳ δυσσεβῆ τιμᾷς χάριν;

505 λέγοιμ' Ll.-J.: λέγοιτ' codd.

48

ANTIGONE

Then why do you delay? There is nothing to please me in your words, and may there never be, and just so my attitude displeases you. Yet how could I have gained greater glory than by placing my own brother in his grave? I would say that all these men would approve this, if it were not that fear shuts their mouths. But kingship is fortunate in many ways, and in particular it has power to do and say what it wishes.

CREON

You alone among these Cadmeans see this.

ANTIGONE

These men too see it; but they curb their tongues to please you.

CREON

Are you not ashamed at thinking differently from them?

ANTIGONE

There is no shame in showing regard for those of one's own stock.

CREON

Was not he who died on the other side also your brother?

ANTIGONE

My brother with the same mother and the same father.

CREON

Then how can you render the other a grace which is impious towards him?

ΑΝΤΙΓΟΝΗ

515 οὐ μαρτυρήσει ταῦθ' ὁ κατθανὼν νέκυς.

ΚΡΕΩΝ

εἴ τοί σφε τιμᾷς ἐξ ἴσου τῷ δυσσεβεῖ.

ΑΝΤΙΓΟΝΗ

οὐ γάρ τι δοῦλος, ἀλλ' ἀδελφὸς ὤλετο.

ΚΡΕΩΝ

πορθῶν δὲ τήνδε γῆν· ὁ δ' ἀντιστὰς ὕπερ.

ΑΝΤΙΓΟΝΗ

ὅμως ὅ γ' Ἅιδης τοὺς νόμους τούτους ποθεῖ.

ΚΡΕΩΝ

520 ἀλλ' οὐχ ὁ χρηστὸς τῷ κακῷ λαχεῖν ἴσος.

ΑΝΤΙΓΟΝΗ

τίς οἶδεν εἰ κάτω 'στὶν εὐαγῆ τάδε;

ΚΡΕΩΝ

οὔτοι ποθ' οὑχθρός, οὐδ' ὅταν θάνῃ, φίλος.

ΑΝΤΙΓΟΝΗ

οὔτοι συνέχθειν, ἀλλὰ συμφιλεῖν ἔφυν.

ΚΡΕΩΝ

κάτω νυν ἐλθοῦσ', εἰ φιλητέον, φίλει
525 κείνους· ἐμοῦ δὲ ζῶντος οὐκ ἄρξει γυνή.

ΧΟΡΟΣ

καὶ μὴν πρὸ πυλῶν ἥδ' Ἰσμήνη,
φιλάδελφα κάτω δάκρυ' εἰβομένη·
νεφέλη δ' ὀφρύων ὕπερ αἱματόεν

ANTIGONE

The dead body will not bear witness to that.

CREON

Yes, if you honour him equally with the impious one.

ANTIGONE

It was not a slave, but my brother who had died.

CREON

But he was trying to destroy this country, and the other stood against him to protect it.

ANTIGONE

None the less, Hades demands these laws.

CREON

But the noble man has not equal claim to honour with the evil.

ANTIGONE

Who knows if this action is free from blame in the world below?

CREON

An enemy is never a friend, even when he is dead.

ANTIGONE

I have no enemies by birth, but I have friends by birth.

CREON

Then go below and love those friends, if you must love them! But while I live a woman shall not rule!

CHORUS

See, here before the gates is Ismene, dropping tears of love for her sister; and a cloud over her eyes marks her flushed

ῥέθος αἰσχύνει,
530 τέγγουσ᾽ εὐῶπα παρειάν.

ΚΡΕΩΝ

σὺ δ᾽, ἢ κατ᾽ οἴκους ὡς ἔχιδν᾽ ὑφειμένη
λήθουσά μ᾽ ἐξέπινες, οὐδ᾽ ἐμάνθανον
τρέφων δύ᾽ ἄτα κἀπαναστάσεις θρόνων,
φέρ᾽, εἰπὲ δή μοι, καὶ σὺ τοῦδε τοῦ τάφου
535 φήσεις μετασχεῖν, ἢ ᾽ξομῇ τὸ μὴ εἰδέναι;

ΙΣΜΗΝΗ

δέδρακα τοὔργον, εἴπερ ἥδ᾽ ὁμορροθεῖ,
καὶ ξυμμετίσχω καὶ φέρω τῆς αἰτίας.

ΑΝΤΙΓΟΝΗ

ἀλλ᾽ οὐκ ἐάσει τοῦτό γ᾽ ἡ δίκη σ᾽, ἐπεὶ
οὔτ᾽ ἠθέλησας οὔτ᾽ ἐγὼ ᾽κοινωσάμην.

ΙΣΜΗΝΗ

540 ἀλλ᾽ ἐν κακοῖς τοῖς σοῖσιν οὐκ αἰσχύνομαι
ξύμπλουν ἐμαυτὴν τοῦ πάθους ποιουμένη.

ΑΝΤΙΓΟΝΗ

ὧν τοὔργον Ἅιδης χοἱ κάτω ξυνίστορες·
λόγοις δ᾽ ἐγὼ φιλοῦσαν οὐ στέργω φίλην.

ΙΣΜΗΝΗ

μήτοι, κασιγνήτη, μ᾽ ἀτιμάσῃς τὸ μὴ οὐ
545 θανεῖν τε σὺν σοὶ τὸν θανόντα θ᾽ ἁγνίσαι.

ΑΝΤΙΓΟΝΗ

μὴ ᾽μοὶ θάνῃς σὺ κοινά, μηδ᾽ ἃ μὴ ᾽θιγες
ποιοῦ σεαυτῆς. ἀρκέσω θνῄσκουσ᾽ ἐγώ.

face, wetting her fair cheeks!

Enter ISMENE.

CREON

You, whom I never noticed as like a viper hiding in the house you sucked my blood—nor did I know that I was rearing up two plagues and two subverters of the throne—come, tell me, do you admit being a party to this burial, or will you swear that you know nothing?

ISMENE

I did the deed, if she agrees, and I take and bear my share of the blame.

ANTIGONE

Why, justice will not allow you this, since you refused and I was not your associate!

ISMENE

But in your time of trouble I am not ashamed to make myself a fellow voyager in your suffering.

ANTIGONE

Hades and those below know to whom the deed belongs! And I do not tolerate a loved one who shows her love only in words.

ISMENE

Sister, do not so dishonour me as not to let me die with you and grant the dead man the proper rites!

ANTIGONE

Do not try to share my death, and do not claim as your own something you never put a hand to! My death will be enough!

---

536 ὁμορροθεῖ] -θῶ Nauck

ΙΣΜΗΝΗ

καὶ τίς βίου μοι σοῦ λελειμμένη πόθος;

ΑΝΤΙΓΟΝΗ

Κρέοντ' ἐρώτα· τοῦδε γὰρ σὺ κηδεμών.

ΙΣΜΗΝΗ

550   τί ταῦτ' ἀνιᾷς μ' οὐδὲν ὠφελουμένη;

ΑΝΤΙΓΟΝΗ

ἀλγοῦσα μὲν δῆτ', εἰ γελῶ γ', ἐν σοὶ γελῶ.

ΙΣΜΗΝΗ

τί δῆτ' ἂν ἀλλὰ νῦν σ' ἔτ' ὠφελοῖμ' ἐγώ;

ΑΝΤΙΓΟΝΗ

σῶσον σεαυτήν. οὐ φθονῶ σ' ὑπεκφυγεῖν.

ΙΣΜΗΝΗ

οἴμοι τάλαινα, κἀμπλάκω τοῦ σοῦ μόρου;

ΑΝΤΙΓΟΝΗ

555   σὺ μὲν γὰρ εἵλου ζῆν, ἐγὼ δὲ κατθανεῖν.

ΙΣΜΗΝΗ

ἀλλ' οὐκ ἐπ' ἀρρήτοις γε τοῖς ἐμοῖς λόγοις.

ΑΝΤΙΓΟΝΗ

καλῶς σὺ μὲν τοῖς, τοῖς δ' ἐγὼ 'δόκουν φρονεῖν.

ΙΣΜΗΝΗ

καὶ μὴν ἴση νῷν ἐστιν ἡ 'ξαμαρτία.

ΑΝΤΙΓΟΝΗ

θάρσει. σὺ μὲν ζῇς, ἡ δ' ἐμὴ ψυχὴ πάλαι
560   τέθνηκεν, ὥστε τοῖς θανοῦσιν ὠφελεῖν.

54

ANTIGONE

ISMENE
And what desire for life will be mine if you leave me?

ANTIGONE
Ask Creon! You are his champion!

ISMENE
Why do you give me such pain, when it does you no good?

ANTIGONE
It grieves me to mock you, if I do mock you.

ISMENE
What help can I still give you, now that things have come to this?

ANTIGONE
Save yourself! I do not grudge you your escape.

ISMENE
Ah me, am I to miss sharing your death?

ANTIGONE
Yes, you chose life, and I chose death!

ISMENE
But I did not fail to speak out!

ANTIGONE
Some thought you were right, and some thought I was.

ISMENE
Why, our offence is equal!

ANTIGONE
Be comforted! You are alive, but my life has long been dead, so as to help the dead.

---

560 ὠφελεῖν] -εῖς Dobree

ΚΡΕΩΝ

τὼ παῖδέ φημι τώδε τὴν μὲν ἀρτίως
ἄνουν πεφάνθαι, τὴν δ᾽ ἀφ᾽ οὗ τὰ πρῶτ᾽ ἔφυ.

ΙΣΜΗΝΗ

οὐ γάρ ποτ᾽, ὦναξ, οὐδ᾽ ὃς ἂν βλάστῃ μένει
νοῦς τοῖς κακῶς πράσσουσιν, ἀλλ᾽ ἐξίσταται.

ΚΡΕΩΝ

565 σοὶ γοῦν, ὅθ᾽ εἵλου σὺν κακοῖς πράσσειν κακά.

ΙΣΜΗΝΗ

τί γὰρ μόνη μοι τῆσδ᾽ ἄτερ βιώσιμον;

ΚΡΕΩΝ

ἀλλ᾽ ἥδε μέντοι — μὴ λέγ᾽· οὐ γὰρ ἔστ᾽ ἔτι.

ΙΣΜΗΝΗ

ἀλλὰ κτενεῖς νυμφεῖα τοῦ σαυτοῦ τέκνου;

ΚΡΕΩΝ

ἀρώσιμοι γὰρ χἀτέρων εἰσὶν γύαι.

ΙΣΜΗΝΗ

570 οὐχ ὥς γ᾽ ἐκείνῳ τῇδε τ᾽ ἦν ἡρμοσμένα.

ΚΡΕΩΝ

κακὰς ἐγὼ γυναῖκας υἱέσι στυγῶ.

ΙΣΜΗΝΗ

ὦ φίλταθ᾽ Αἷμον, ὥς σ᾽ ἀτιμάζει πατήρ.

ΚΡΕΩΝ

ἄγαν γε λυπεῖς καὶ σὺ καὶ τὸ σὸν λέχος.

CREON

I say that one of these girls has only now been revealed as
mad, but the other has been so from birth.

ISMENE

Yes, king, those who are miserable lose even such sense as
they have; it leaves them.

CREON

It left you, when you chose to do evil with evildoers.

ISMENE

How can I live alone without her?

CREON

Why, she—Do not say it, for she no longer exists!

ISMENE

But will you kill her who is to be your son's bride?

CREON

Yes, for the furrows of others can be ploughed!

ISMENE

It would not be as fitting as for him and for her.

CREON

I hate evil wives for my son!

ISMENE

Dearest Haemon, how your father dishonours you!

CREON

You cause me excessive pain, you and the marriage you talk
of!

---

572 Antigonae tribuit ed. Aldina

ΙΣΜΗΝΗ

ἦ γὰρ στερήσεις τῆσδε τὸν σαυτοῦ γόνον;

ΚΡΕΩΝ

575 Ἅιδης ὁ παύσων τούσδε τοὺς γάμους ἐμοί.

ΙΣΜΗΝΗ

δεδογμέν', ὡς ἔοικε, τήνδε κατθανεῖν.

ΚΡΕΩΝ

καὶ σοί γε κἀμοί. μὴ τριβὰς ἔτ', ἀλλά νιν
κομίζετ' εἴσω, δμῶες· ἐκ δὲ τοῦδε χρὴ
γυναῖκας εἶναι τάσδε μηδ' ἀνειμένας.
580 φεύγουσι γάρ τοι χοὶ θρασεῖς, ὅταν πέλας
ἤδη τὸν Ἅιδην εἰσορῶσι τοῦ βίου.

ΧΟΡΟΣ

εὐδαίμονες οἷσι κακῶν ἄγευστος αἰών.   στρ. α'
οἷς γὰρ ἂν σεισθῇ θεόθεν δόμος, ἄτας
585 οὐδὲν ἐλλείπει γενεᾶς ἐπὶ πλῆθος ἕρπον·
ὥστε ποντίας ἁλὸς
οἶδμα δυσπνόοις ὅταν
Θρήσσησιν ἔρεβος ὕφαλον ἐπιδράμῃ πνοαῖς,
590 κυλίνδει βυσσόθεν
κελαινὰν θῖνα καὶ δυσάνεμοι
στόνῳ βρέμουσιν ἀντιπλῆγες ἀκταί.
ἀρχαῖα τὰ Λαβδακιδᾶν οἴκων ὁρῶμαι   ἀντ. α'
595 πήματα φθιτῶν ἐπὶ πήμασι πίπτοντ',
οὐδ' ἀπαλλάσσει γενεὰν γένος, ἀλλ' ἐρείπει
θεῶν τις, οὐδ' ἔχει λύσιν.

574 choro tribuit Boeckh

58

ANTIGONE

ISMENE
Will you indeed rob your son of her?

CREON
It is Hades who will prevent this marriage for me.

ISMENE
It is decided, it seems, that she shall die.

CREON
By you and by me! Let there be no delay, but take her in, henchmen! From now on these two must be women, and must not be on the loose. Yes, even those who are bold try to escape, when they see Hades already near to their lives.

ANTIGONE and ISMENE are taken inside.

CHORUS
Fortunate are they whose lifetime never tastes of evil! For those whose house is shaken by the gods, no part of ruin is wanting, as it marches against the whole of the family; like the swell of the deep sea, when darkness runs beneath the water, brought by the dire blast of winds from Thrace, it rolls up from the bottom the black sand and the wind-vexed shores resound before its impact.

From ancient times I see the troubles of the dead of the Labdacid house falling hard upon one another, nor does one generation release another, but some one of the gods shatters them, and they have no means of deliverance. For

---

[576] Ismenae tribuunt Kat, choro cett., Antigonae Boeckh

[586] ante ὥστε add. ὁμοῖον codd., del. Seidler

[591] δυσάνεμοι Hartung: -ον codd.: -ῳ Jacobs

[592] βρέμουσιν Zo (coni. Jacobs): βρέμουσι δ' cett.

[595] φθιτῶν Hermann: φθιμένων codd.

νῦν γὰρ ἐσχάτας ὑπὲρ
600 ῥίζας ἐτέτατο φάος ἐν Οἰδίπου δόμοις·
κατ᾽ αὖ νιν φοινία
θεῶν τῶν νερτέρων ἀμᾷ κοπίς,
λόγου τ᾽ ἄνοια καὶ φρενῶν Ἐρινύς.

τεάν, Ζεῦ, δύνασιν τίς ἀν-   στρ. β′
605 δρῶν ὑπερβασία κατάσχοι;
τὰν οὔθ᾽ ὕπνος αἱρεῖ ποθ᾽ ὁ †παντογήρως†
οὔτ᾽ ἀκάματοι θεῶν
μῆνες, ἀγήρως δὲ χρόνῳ δυνάστας
κατέχεις Ὀλύμπου
610 μαρμαρόεσσαν αἴγλαν.
τό τ᾽ ἔπειτα καὶ τὸ μέλλον
καὶ τὸ πρὶν ἐπαρκέσει
νόμος ὅδ᾽· οὐδέν᾽ ἕρπει
θνατῶν βίοτος πάμπολυς ἐκτὸς ἄτας.

615 ἁ γὰρ δὴ πολύπλαγκτος ἐλ-   ἀντ. β′
πὶς πολλοῖς μὲν ὄνησις ἀνδρῶν,
πολλοῖς δ᾽ ἀπάτα κουφονόων ἐρώτων·
εἰδότι δ᾽ οὐδὲν ἕρπει,
πρὶν πυρὶ θερμῷ πόδα τις προσαύσῃ.
620 σοφίᾳ γὰρ ἔκ του
κλεινὸν ἔπος πέφανται,
τὸ κακὸν δοκεῖν ποτ᾽ ἐσθλὸν
τῷδ᾽ ἔμμεν ὅτῳ φρένας
θεὸς ἄγει πρὸς ἄταν·
625 πράσσει δ᾽ ὀλίγος τὸν χρόνον ἐκτὸς ἄτας.
ὅδε μὴν Αἵμων, παίδων τῶν σῶν
νέατον γέννημ᾽· ἆρ᾽ ἀχνύμενος

lately the light spread out above the last root in the house
of Oedipus; it too is mown down by the bloody chopper of
the infernal gods, folly in speech and the Erinys in the
mind.

Zeus, what arrogance of men could restrict your power?
Neither sleep the all-conquering nor the unwearying
months of the gods defeats it, but as a ruler time cannot
age, you occupy the dazzling glare of Olympus. For
present, future and past this law shall suffice: to none
among mortals shall great wealth come without disaster.

For widely wandering hope brings profit to many men,
but to many the deception of thoughtless longings; and a
man knows nothing when it comes upon him, until he
scalds his foot in blazing fire. For in wisdom someone has
revealed the famous saying, that evil seems good to him
whose mind the god is driving towards disaster; but the
small man fares throughout his time without disaster.

Here is Haemon, the latest born among your sons! Is

---

599 ὑπέρ] ὅπερ K s.l., coni. Hermann
600 ἐτέτατο Brunck: τέτατο codd.: <ὁ> τέτατο Hermann
602 κοπίς Jortin: κόνις codd.
606 παντογήρως] πάντ' ἀγρεύων Jebb: alii alia
607 ἀκάματοι θεῶν] θεῶν ἄκματοι Hermann
613–14 οὐδέν' . . . πάμπολυς Ll.-J. (οὐδέν' iam Aldina, πάμπολυς
Musgrave): οὐδὲν ἕρπει θνατῶν βιότῳ πάμπολις codd.
ἕρπει] ἕρπειν Heath, qui etiam πάμπολύ γ' coniecit
618 εἰδότι δ'] εὖ εἰδόσιν Wilamowitz, del. ἕρπει
625 ὀλίγος τὸν Ll.-J.: ὀλιγοστὸν codd.: ὀλίγιστον Bergk

SOPHOCLES

[τῆς μελλογάμου νύμφης]
τάλιδος ἥκει μόρον Ἀντιγόνης,
630   ἀπάτης λεχέων ὑπεραλγῶν;

ΚΡΕΩΝ

τάχ᾽ εἰσόμεσθα μάντεων ὑπέρτερον.
ὦ παῖ, τελείαν ψῆφον ἆρα μὴ κλυὼν
τῆς μελλονύμφου πατρὶ λυσσαίνων πάρει;
ἢ σοὶ μὲν ἡμεῖς πανταχῇ δρῶντες φίλοι;

ΑΙΜΩΝ

635   πάτερ, σός εἰμι· καὶ σύ με γνώμας ἔχων
χρηστὰς ἀπορθοῖς, αἷς ἔγωγ᾽ ἐφέψομαι.
ἐμοὶ γὰρ οὐδεὶς ἀξιώσεται γάμος
μείζων φέρεσθαι σοῦ καλῶς ἡγουμένου.

ΚΡΕΩΝ

οὕτω γάρ, ὦ παῖ, χρὴ διὰ στέρνων ἔχειν,
640   γνώμης πατρῴας πάντ᾽ ὄπισθεν ἑστάναι.
τούτου γὰρ οὕνεκ᾽ ἄνδρες εὔχονται γονὰς
κατηκόους φύσαντες ἐν δόμοις ἔχειν,
ὡς καὶ τὸν ἐχθρὸν ἀνταμύνωνται κακοῖς,
καὶ τὸν φίλον τιμῶσιν ἐξ ἴσου πατρί.
645   ὅστις δ᾽ ἀνωφέλητα φιτύει τέκνα,
τί τόνδ᾽ ἂν εἴποις ἄλλο πλὴν αὑτῷ πόνους
φῦσαι, πολὺν δὲ τοῖσιν ἐχθροῖσιν γέλων;
μή νύν ποτ᾽, ὦ παῖ, τὰς φρένας γ᾽ ὑφ᾽ ἡδονῆς
γυναικὸς οὕνεκ᾽ ἐκβάλῃς, εἰδὼς ὅτι
650   ψυχρὸν παραγκάλισμα τοῦτο γίγνεται,
γυνὴ κακὴ ξύνευνος ἐν δόμοις. τί γὰρ
γένοιτ᾽ ἂν ἕλκος μεῖζον ἢ φίλος κακός;

62

he angry at the fate of his affianced one, Antigone, grieving
at the baffled hope of marriage?

Enter HAEMON.

CREON

We shall soon have better knowledge than prophets could
have given us. My son, now that you have heard the valid
decision against your destined bride, are you here in rage
against your father, or are we dear to you, no matter what
we do?

HAEMON

Father, I belong to you, and you keep me straight with
your good judgments, which I shall follow. Yes, in my eyes
no marriage shall be more highly valued than your right
guidance.

CREON

Yes, my son, that is how your mind should be, thinking that
all things rank second to your father's judgment. This is
why men pray that they may beget and keep in their houses
obedient offspring, so that they may requite the enemy
with evil and honour the friend as they honour their father.
But as for the man who fathers children who give him no
help, what can you say that he begets but trouble for him-
self, and much delight for his enemies? Never let go your
good sense, my son, for sake of the pleasure that a woman
gives, knowing that this thing is an armful that grows cold,
an evil woman sharing your bed in your house. For what
wound could be deeper than a dear one who is evil? So

---

[628] om. Zot   [635] με Blaydes: μοι Sazt: μου LRV

[637] ἀξιώσεται Musgrave: ἄξιος vel ἀξίως (ἔσται) codd.

[640] ἑστάναι] ἱστάναι Musgrave

[645] φιτεύει Livineius: φυτεύει codd.

ἀποπτύσας οὖν ὥστε δυσμενῆ μέθες
τὴν παῖδ' ἐν Ἅιδου τήνδε νυμφεύειν τινί.
655 ἐπεὶ γὰρ αὐτὴν εἷλον ἐμφανῶς ἐγὼ
πόλεως ἀπιστήσασαν ἐκ πάσης μόνην,
ψευδῆ γ' ἐμαυτὸν οὐ καταστήσω πόλει,
ἀλλὰ κτενῶ. πρὸς ταῦτ' ἐφυμνείτω Δία
ξύναιμον· εἰ γὰρ δὴ τά γ' ἐγγενῆ φύσει
660 ἄκοσμα θρέψω, κάρτα τοὺς ἔξω γένους.
ἐν τοῖς γὰρ οἰκείοισιν ὅστις ἔστ' ἀνὴρ
χρηστός, φανεῖται κἀν πόλει δίκαιος ὤν.
ὅστις δ' ὑπερβὰς ἢ νόμους βιάζεται,
ἢ τοὐπιτάσσειν τοῖς κρατύνουσιν νοεῖ,
665 οὐκ ἔστ' ἐπαίνου τοῦτον ἐξ ἐμοῦ τυχεῖν.
ἀλλ' ὃν πόλις στήσειε, τοῦδε χρὴ κλύειν
καὶ σμικρὰ καὶ δίκαια καὶ τἀναντία.
καὶ τοῦτον ἂν τὸν ἄνδρα θαρσοίην ἐγὼ
καλῶς μὲν ἄρχειν, εὖ δ' ἂν ἄρχεσθαι θέλειν,
670 δορός τ' ἂν ἐν χειμῶνι προστεταγμένον
μένειν δίκαιον κἀγαθὸν παραστάτην.
ἀναρχίας δὲ μεῖζον οὐκ ἔστιν κακόν.
αὕτη πόλεις ὄλλυσιν, ἥδ' ἀναστάτους
οἴκους τίθησιν, ἥδε συμμάχου δορὸς
675 τροπὰς καταρρήγνυσι· τῶν δ' ὀρθουμένων
σώζει τὰ πολλὰ σώμαθ' ἡ πειθαρχία.
οὕτως ἀμυντέ' ἐστὶ τοῖς κοσμουμένοις,
κοὔτοι γυναικὸς οὐδαμῶς ἡσσητέα.
κρεῖσσον γάρ, εἴπερ δεῖ, πρὸς ἀνδρὸς ἐκπεσεῖν,
680 κοὐκ ἂν γυναικῶν ἥσσονες καλοίμεθ' ἄν.

respue this girl as an enemy and allow her to marry some-
one in Hades! For since I caught her openly disobeying,
alone out of all the city, I shall not show myself false to the
city, but I shall kill her! In the face of that let her keep
invoking the Zeus of kindred! If those of my own family
whom I keep are to show no discipline, how much more
will those outside my family! The man who acts rightly in
family matters will be seen to be righteous in the city also.
But whoever transgresses or does violence to the laws, or is
minded to dictate to those in power, that man shall never
receive praise from me. One must obey the man whom the
city sets up in power in small things and in justice and in its
opposite. This is the man whom I would trust to be a good
ruler and a good subject, and when assigned his post in the
storm of battle to prove a true and noble comrade in the
fight. But there is no worse evil than insubordination! This
it is that ruins cities, this it is that destroys houses, this it is
that shatters and puts to flight the warriors on its own side!
But what saves the lives of most of those that go straight is
obedience! In this way we have to protect discipline, and
we must never allow a woman to vanquish us. If we must
perish, it is better to do so by the hand of a man, and then
we cannot be called inferior to women.

653 ἀποπτύσας Blaydes: ἀλλ᾽ ἀποπτύσας KRZc: ἀλλὰ πτύσας
cett.   οὖν ὥστε Blaydes: ὡσεί τε codd.
659 τά γ᾽ Erfurdt: τάδ᾽ a: τά τ᾽ cett.
663–67 post 671 traiecit Seidler: del. Blaydes
666–67 del. Dawe
667 σμικρὰ] πικρὰ van Eldik
674 συμμάχου Reiske: συμμάχῃ lR: σὺν μάχῃ cett.

ΧΟΡΟΣ

ἡμῖν μέν, εἰ μὴ τῷ χρόνῳ κεκλέμμεθα,
λέγειν φρονούντως ὧν λέγεις δοκεῖς πέρι.

ΑΙΜΩΝ

πάτερ, θεοὶ φύουσιν ἀνθρώποις φρένας,
πάντων ὅσ' ἐστὶ κτημάτων ὑπέρτατον,
685 ἐγὼ δ' ὅπως σὺ μὴ λέγεις ὀρθῶς τάδε,
οὔτ' ἂν δυναίμην μήτ' ἐπισταίμην λέγειν·
[γένοιτο μέντἂν χἀτέρᾳ καλῶς ἔχον.]
σὺ δ' οὐ πέφυκας πάντα προσκοπεῖν ὅσα
λέγει τις ἢ πράσσει τις ἢ ψέγειν ἔχει.
690 τὸ γὰρ σὸν ὄμμα δεινὸν ἀνδρὶ δημότῃ
λόγοις τοιούτοις οἷς σὺ μὴ τέρψῃ κλύων·
ἐμοὶ δ' ἀκούειν ἔσθ' ὑπὸ σκότου τάδε,
τὴν παῖδα ταύτην οἷ' ὀδύρεται πόλις,
πασῶν γυναικῶν ὡς ἀναξιωτάτη
695 κάκιστ' ἀπ' ἔργων εὐκλεεστάτων φθίνει·
ἥτις τὸν αὑτῆς αὐτάδελφον ἐν φοναῖς
πεπτῶτ' ἄθαπτον μήθ' ὑπ' ὠμηστῶν κυνῶν
εἴασ' ὀλέσθαι μήθ' ὑπ' οἰωνῶν τινος·
οὐχ ἥδε χρυσῆς ἀξία τιμῆς λαχεῖν;
700 τοιάδ' ἐρεμνὴ σῖγ' ὑπέρχεται φάτις.
ἐμοὶ δὲ σοῦ πράσσοντος εὐτυχῶς, πάτερ,
οὐκ ἔστιν οὐδὲν κτῆμα τιμιώτερον.
τί γὰρ πατρὸς θάλλοντος εὐκλείᾳ τέκνοις
ἄγαλμα μεῖζον, ἢ τί πρὸς παίδων πατρί;
705 μή νυν ἓν ἦθος μοῦνον ἐν σαυτῷ φόρει,

ANTIGONE

CHORUS

To us, if we are not led astray by our old age, you seem to
speak sensibly about the things you speak of.

HAEMON

Father, it is the gods who give men intelligence, the most
precious of all possessions, and I could never say, and may
I never know how to say, that what you say is wrong. [But a
different view might be correct.] But it is not in your
nature to foresee people's words or actions or the objects
of their censure; for your countenance is alarming to a sub-
ject when he speaks words that give you no pleasure. But
for me it is possible to hear under cover this, how the city is
lamenting for this girl, saying that no woman ever deserved
it less, but that she is to perish miserably for actions that
are glorious, she who did not allow her own brother who
had fallen in the slaughter to remain unburied or to be des-
troyed by savage dogs or birds. Does not she deserve, they
ask, to be honoured with a golden prize? Such is the dark
saying that is silently advancing. For me, father, nothing is
more precious than your good fortune; for what distinction
can be greater for children than a father who flourishes in
high repute, or greater for a father than sons who do so?
Do not wear the garment of one mood only, thinking that

---

687 del. Heimreich   χἀτέρᾳ K in linea, coni. Musgrave:
χἀτέρως R: χἀτέρῳ cett.

688 σὺ LγρY: σοῦ La: σοὶ L s.l., Ra   οὐ πέφυκας Lγρ: οὖν
πέφυκα codd.

690 lacunam post hunc versum statuit Dindorf

700 ὑπέρχεται Herwerden: ἐπέρχεται codd.

703 εὐκλείᾳ Johnson: -ας codd.

ὡς φὴς σύ, κοὐδὲν ἄλλο, τοῦτ' ὀρθῶς ἔχειν.
ὅστις γὰρ αὐτὸς ἢ φρονεῖν μόνος δοκεῖ,
ἢ γλῶσσαν, ἣν οὐκ ἄλλος, ἢ ψυχὴν ἔχειν,
οὗτοι διαπτυχθέντες ὤφθησαν κενοί.

710 ἀλλ' ἄνδρα, κεἴ τις ᾖ σοφός, τὸ μανθάνειν
πόλλ' αἰσχρὸν οὐδὲν καὶ τὸ μὴ τείνειν ἄγαν.
ὁρᾷς παρὰ ῥείθροισι χειμάρροις ὅσα
δένδρων ὑπείκει, κλῶνας ὡς ἐκσῴζεται,
τὰ δ' ἀντιτείνοντ' αὐτόπρεμν' ἀπόλλυται.

715 αὕτως δὲ ναὸς ὅστις ἐν κράτει πόδα
τείνας ὑπείκει μηδέν, ὑπτίοις κάτω
στρέψας τὸ λοιπὸν σέλμασιν ναυτίλλεται.
ἀλλ' εἶκε θυμοῦ καὶ μετάστασιν δίδου.
γνώμη γὰρ εἴ τις κἀπ' ἐμοῦ νεωτέρου

720 πρόσεστι, φήμ' ἔγωγε πρεσβεύειν πολὺ
φῦναι τὸν ἄνδρα πάντ' ἐπιστήμης πλέων·
εἰ δ' οὖν, φιλεῖ γὰρ τοῦτο μὴ ταύτῃ ῥέπειν,
καὶ τῶν λεγόντων εὖ καλὸν τὸ μανθάνειν.

ΧΟΡΟΣ

ἄναξ, σέ τ' εἰκός, εἴ τι καίριον λέγει,
725 μαθεῖν, σέ τ' αὖ τοῦδ'· εὖ γὰρ εἴρηται διπλῇ.

ΚΡΕΩΝ

οἱ τηλικοίδε καὶ διδαξόμεσθα δὴ
φρονεῖν πρὸς ἀνδρὸς τηλικοῦδε τὴν φύσιν;

ΑΙΜΩΝ

μηδέν γ' ὃ μὴ δίκαιον· εἰ δ' ἐγὼ νέος,
οὐ τὸν χρόνον χρὴ μᾶλλον ἢ τἄργα σκοπεῖν.

your opinion and no other must be right! For whoever think that they themselves alone have sense, or have a power of speech or an intelligence that no other has, these people when they are laid open are found to be empty. It is not shameful for a man, even if he is wise, often to learn things and not to resist too much. You see how when rivers are swollen in winter those trees that yield to the flood retain their branches, but those that offer resistance perish, trunk and all. Just so whoever in command of a ship keeps the sheet taut, and never slackens it, is overturned and thereafter sails with his oarsmen's benches upside down. No, retreat from your anger and allow yourself to change; for if I too, young as I am, have some judgment, I say that it is best by far if a man is altogether full of knowledge; but that, since things are not accustomed to go that way, it is also good to learn from those who give good counsel.

CHORUS

King, it is proper, if he says anything that is to the point, that you should learn from him, and you, Haemon, from Creon; for true things have been said on both sides.

CREON

So men of my age are to be taught sense by a man of your age?

HAEMON

Nothing but what is right! If I am young, one must not consider my age rather than my merits.

---

715 ἐν κράτει Ll.-J.: ἐγκρατεῖ L in linea, R: -ῇ vel -ῆς cett.
728 γ' ὃ Tournier: τὸ codd.

SOPHOCLES

ΚΡΕΩΝ

730 ἔργον γάρ ἐστι τοὺς ἀκοσμοῦντας σέβειν;

ΑΙΜΩΝ

οὐδ' ἂν κελεύσαιμ' εὐσεβεῖν ἐς τοὺς κακούς.

ΚΡΕΩΝ

οὐχ ἥδε γὰρ τοιᾷδ' ἐπείληπται νόσῳ;

ΑΙΜΩΝ

οὔ φησι Θήβης τῆσδ' ὁμόπτολις λεώς.

ΚΡΕΩΝ

πόλις γὰρ ἡμῖν ἁμὲ χρὴ τάσσειν ἐρεῖ;

ΑΙΜΩΝ

735 ὁρᾷς τόδ' ὡς εἴρηκας ὡς ἄγαν νέος;

ΚΡΕΩΝ

ἄλλῳ γὰρ ἢ 'μοὶ χρή με τῆσδ' ἄρχειν χθονός;

ΑΙΜΩΝ

πόλις γὰρ οὐκ ἔσθ' ἥτις ἀνδρός ἐσθ' ἑνός.

ΚΡΕΩΝ

οὐ τοῦ κρατοῦντος ἡ πόλις νομίζεται;

ΑΙΜΩΝ

καλῶς ἐρήμης γ' ἂν σὺ γῆς ἄρχοις μόνος.

ΚΡΕΩΝ

740 ὅδ', ὡς ἔοικε, τῇ γυναικὶ συμμαχεῖ.

ΑΙΜΩΝ

εἴπερ γυνὴ σύ· σοῦ γὰρ οὖν προκήδομαι.

---

736 με Dobree: om. K: γε cett.

ANTIGONE

CREON
Is it a merit to show regard for those who cause disorder?

HAEMON
It is not that I would ask you to show regard for evildoers.

CREON
Is not she afflicted with this malady?

HAEMON
This people of Thebes that shares our city does not say so.

CREON
Is the city to tell me what orders I shall give?

HAEMON
Do you notice that what you have said is spoken like a very young man?

CREON
Must I rule this land for another and not for myself?

HAEMON
Yes, there is no city that belongs to a single man!

CREON
Is not the city thought to belong to its ruler?

HAEMON
You would be a fine ruler over a deserted city!

CREON
This man, it seems, is fighting on the woman's side.

HAEMON
If you are a woman; because it is you for whom I feel concern.

ΚΡΕΩΝ

ὦ παγκάκιστε, διὰ δίκης ἰὼν πατρί;

ΑΙΜΩΝ

οὐ γὰρ δίκαιά σ' ἐξαμαρτάνονθ' ὁρῶ.

ΚΡΕΩΝ

ἁμαρτάνω γὰρ τὰς ἐμὰς ἀρχὰς σέβων;

ΑΙΜΩΝ

745   οὐ γὰρ σέβεις, τιμάς γε τὰς θεῶν πατῶν.

ΚΡΕΩΝ

ὦ μιαρὸν ἦθος καὶ γυναικὸς ὕστερον.

ΑΙΜΩΝ

οὔ τἂν ἕλοις ἥσσω γε τῶν αἰσχρῶν ἐμέ.

ΚΡΕΩΝ

ὁ γοῦν λόγος σοι πᾶς ὑπὲρ κείνης ὅδε.

ΑΙΜΩΝ

καὶ σοῦ γε κἀμοῦ, καὶ θεῶν τῶν νερτέρων.

ΚΡΕΩΝ

750   ταύτην ποτ' οὐκ ἔσθ' ὡς ἔτι ζῶσαν γαμεῖς.

ΑΙΜΩΝ

ἥδ' οὖν θανεῖται καὶ θανοῦσ' ὀλεῖ τινα.

ΚΡΕΩΝ

ἦ κἀπαπειλῶν ὧδ' ἐπεξέρχῃ θρασύς;

747 οὔ τἂν Erfurdt: οὐκ ἄν γ' at: οὐκ ἄν cett.

ANTIGONE

CREON

You villain, by disputing against your father?

HAEMON

Because I see that you are offending against justice!

CREON

Am I offending when I show regard for my own office?

HAEMON

You show no regard when you trample on the honours due to the gods!

CREON

Contemptible character, inferior to a woman!

HAEMON

You will not find me vanquished by what is shameful.

CREON

Well, everything you say is on behalf of her.

HAEMON

And of you and of me, and of the infernal gods!

CREON

You shall never marry this woman while she is alive!

HAEMON

Then she will die and by her death she will destroy another.

CREON

Have you the insolence to come out against me with threats?

SOPHOCLES

ΑΙΜΩΝ

τίς δ' ἔστ' ἀπειλὴ πρός σ' ἐμὰς γνώμας λέγειν;

ΚΡΕΩΝ

κλαίων φρενώσεις, ὢν φρενῶν αὐτὸς κενός.

ΑΙΜΩΝ

755 εἰ μὴ πατὴρ ἦσθ', εἶπον ἄν σ' οὐκ εὖ φρονεῖν.

ΚΡΕΩΝ

γυναικὸς ὢν δούλευμα, μὴ κώτιλλέ με.

ΑΙΜΩΝ

βούλῃ λέγειν τι καὶ λέγων μηδὲν κλύειν;

ΚΡΕΩΝ

ἄληθες; ἀλλ' οὐ, τόνδ' Ὄλυμπον, ἴσθ' ὅτι,
χαίρων ἔτι ψόγοισι δεννάσεις ἐμέ.
760 ἄγετε τὸ μῖσος, ὡς κατ' ὄμματ' αὐτίκα
παρόντι θνῄσκῃ πλησία τῷ νυμφίῳ.

ΑΙΜΩΝ

οὐ δῆτ' ἔμοιγε, τοῦτο μὴ δόξῃς ποτέ,
οὔθ' ἥδ' ὀλεῖται πλησία, σύ τ' οὐδαμὰ
τοὐμὸν προσόψῃ κρᾶτ' ἐν ὀφθαλμοῖς ὁρῶν,
765 ὡς τοῖς θέλουσι τῶν φίλων μαίνῃ συνών.

ΧΟΡΟΣ

ἁνήρ, ἄναξ, βέβηκεν ἐξ ὀργῆς ταχύς·
νοῦς δ' ἐστὶ τηλικοῦτος ἀλγήσας βαρύς.

753 πρός σ' ἐμὰς Ll.-J.: πρὸς κενὰς codd.
759 ἔτι Dobree: ἐπὶ codd.

74

ANTIGONE

HAEMON
What kind of threat is it for me to tell you my decisions?

CREON
You will regret your lecturing of me, when you yourself understand nothing!

HAEMON
If you were not my father, I would say you had no sense.

CREON
Slave of a woman that you are, do not try to cajole me!

HAEMON
Do you wish to speak but not to listen to him you speak to?

CREON
Do you say that? Why, by that Olympus which we see, be sure of it, you shall not continue to abuse me with your reproaches with impunity! Bring the hateful creature, so that she may die at once close at hand, in the sight of her bridegroom!

HAEMON
She shall not die close to me, never imagine it, and you shall never more set eyes upon my face, so that you can rave on in the company of those friends who will endure it!

Exit HAEMON.

CHORUS
King, the man is gone, swiftly, in his rage; and the temper of one of his age is formidable under pain.

SOPHOCLES

ΚΡΕΩΝ

δράτω, φρονείτω μεῖζον ἢ κατ' ἄνδρ' ἰών·
τὰ δ' οὖν κόρα τάδ' οὐκ ἀπαλλάξει μόρου.

ΧΟΡΟΣ

770 ἄμφω γὰρ αὐτὰ καὶ κατακτεῖναι νοεῖς;

ΚΡΕΩΝ

οὐ τήν γε μὴ θιγοῦσαν· εὖ γὰρ οὖν λέγεις.

ΧΟΡΟΣ

μόρῳ δὲ ποίῳ καί σφε βουλεύῃ κτανεῖν;

ΚΡΕΩΝ

ἄγων ἐρῆμος ἔνθ' ἂν ᾖ βροτῶν στίβος
κρύψω πετρώδει ζῶσαν ἐν κατώρυχι,
775 φορβῆς τοσοῦτον ὅσον ἄγος φεύγειν προθείς,
ὅπως μίασμα πᾶσ' ὑπεκφύγῃ πόλις.
κἀκεῖ τὸν Ἅιδην, ὃν μόνον σέβει θεῶν,
αἰτουμένη που τεύξεται τὸ μὴ θανεῖν,
ἢ γνώσεται γοῦν ἀλλὰ τηνικαῦθ' ὅτι
780 πόνος περισσός ἐστι τὰν Ἅιδου σέβειν.

ΧΟΡΟΣ

Ἔρως ἀνίκατε μάχαν,   στρ. α'
Ἔρως, ὃς ἐν κτήμασι πίπτεις,
ὃς ἐν μαλακαῖς παρειαῖς
νεάνιδος ἐννυχεύεις,
785 φοιτᾷς δ' ὑπερπόντιος ἔν τ'
ἀγρονόμοις αὐλαῖς·
καί σ' οὔτ' ἀθανάτων φύξιμος οὐδεὶς
οὔθ' ἀμερίων σέ γ' ἀν-

76

CREON

Let him act so, let him go and show more than a man's pride! But he shall not save those two girls from death!

CHORUS

Then have you a mind to kill both of them?

CREON

Not the one that did not touch the corpse; you are right!

CHORUS

And by what death do you plan to kill her?

CREON

I shall take her to where there is a path which no man treads, and hide her, still living, in a rocky cavern, putting out enough food to escape pollution,[a] so that the whole city may avoid contagion. And there she can pray to Hades, the only one among the gods whom she respects, and perhaps be spared from death; or else she will learn, at that late stage, that it is wasted effort to show regard for things in Hades.

Exit CREON.

CHORUS

Love invincible in battle, Love who falls upon men's property, you who spend the night upon the soft cheeks of a girl, and travel over the sea and through the huts of dwellers in the wild! None among the immortals can escape

---

[a] Creon believes that if he supplies Antigone with a token quantity of food he will escape the pollution caused by his killing a member of his own family.

---

775 ὅσον Blaydes: ὡς codd.   φεύγειν Hartung: μόνον codd.
789 σέ γ' Blaydes: ἐπ' codd.

790 θρώπων, ὁ δ' ἔχων μέμηνεν.
σὺ καὶ δικαίων ἀδίκους   ἀντ. α′
φρένας παρασπᾷς ἐπὶ λώβᾳ·
σὺ καὶ τόδε νεῖκος ἀνδρῶν
ξύναιμον ἔχεις ταράξας·
795 νικᾷ δ' ἐναργὴς βλεφάρων
ἵμερος εὐλέκτρου
νύμφας, τῶν μεγάλων πάρεδρος ἐν ἀρχαῖς
θεσμῶν· ἄμαχος γὰρ ἐμ-
800 παίζει θεὸς Ἀφροδίτα.
νῦν δ' ἤδη 'γὼ καὐτὸς θεσμῶν
ἔξω φέρομαι τάδ' ὁρῶν, ἴσχειν δ'
οὐκέτι πηγὰς δύναμαι δακρύων,
τὸν παγκοίτην ὅθ' ὁρῶ θάλαμον
805 τήνδ' Ἀντιγόνην ἀνύτουσαν.

ΑΝΤΙΓΟΝΗ

ὁρᾶτέ μ', ὦ γᾶς πατρίας πολῖται   στρ. β′
τὰν νεάταν ὁδὸν
στείχουσαν, νέατον δὲ φέγ-
γος λεύσσουσαν ἀελίου,
810 κοὔποτ' αὖθις· ἀλλά μ' ὁ παγ-
κοίτας Ἅιδας ζῶσαν ἄγει
τὰν Ἀχέροντος
ἀκτάν, οὔθ' ὑμεναίων
ἔγκληρον, οὔτ' ἐπὶ νυμ-
815 φείοις πώ μέ τις ὕμνος ὕ-
μνησεν, ἀλλ' Ἀχέροντι νυμφεύσω.

78

you, nor any among mortal men, and he who has you is mad.

You wrench just men's minds aside from justice, doing them violence; it is you who have stirred up this quarrel between men of the same blood. Victory goes to the visible desire that comes from the eyes of the beautiful bride,[a] desire that has its throne beside those of the mighty laws; for irresistible in her sporting is the goddess Aphrodite.

ANTIGONE is brought in from the palace under guard.

But now I myself am carried beyond the laws at this sight, and I can no longer restrain the stream of tears, when I see Antigone here passing to the bridal chamber where all come to rest.

ANTIGONE

Behold me, citizens of my native land, as I make my last journey, and look on the light of the sun for the last time, and never more; Hades who lulls all to sleep is taking me, still living, to the shore of Acheron, without the bridal that was my due, nor has any song been sung for me at my marriage, but I shall be the bride of Acheron.

---

[a] The early Greeks believed that desire was darted from the eyes of the person who inspired it into those of the person who felt it.

---

[797] πάρεδρος ἐν] σύνθρονος Arndt
[814] ἐπὶ νυμφείοις Bergk: ἐπὶ νυμφίδιος fere codd.

ΧΟΡΟΣ

οὔκουν κλεινὴ καὶ ἔπαινον ἔχουσ᾽
ἐς τόδ᾽ ἀπέρχῃ κεῦθος νεκύων;
οὔτε φθινάσιν πληγεῖσα νόσοις
820 οὔτε ξιφέων ἐπίχειρα λαχοῦσ᾽,
ἀλλ᾽ αὐτόνομος ζῶσα μόνη δὴ
θνητῶν Ἅιδην καταβήσῃ.

ΑΝΤΙΓΟΝΗ

ἤκουσα δὴ λυγροτάταν ὀλέσθαι   ἀντ. β´
τὰν Φρυγίαν ξέναν
825 Ταντάλου Σιπύλῳ πρὸς ἄ-
κρῳ, τὰν κισσὸς ὡς ἀτενὴς
πετραία βλάστα δάμασεν,
καί νιν ὄμβροι τακομέναν,
ὡς φάτις ἀνδρῶν,
830 χιών τ᾽ οὐδαμὰ λείπει,
τέγγει δ᾽ ὑπ᾽ ὀφρύσι παγ-
κλαύτοις δειράδας· ᾇ με δαί-
μων ὁμοιοτάταν κατευνάζει.

ΧΟΡΟΣ

ἀλλὰ θεός τοι καὶ θεογεννής,
835 ἡμεῖς δὲ βροτοὶ καὶ θνητογενεῖς.
καίτοι φθιμένῃ μέγα κἀκοῦσαι
τοῖς ἰσοθέοις ἔγκληρα λαχεῖν
ζῶσαν καὶ ἔπειτα θανοῦσαν.

---

828 ὄμβροι Musgrave: -ος Zc s.l., coni. Gleditsch: -ῳ cett.
836 μέγα κἀκοῦσαι Seyffert: μέγ᾽ ἀκοῦσαι codd.

CHORUS

Is it not with glory and with praise that you depart to this cavern of the dead? Not smitten by wasting maladies nor paid the wages of the sword, of your own will you alone of mortals while yet alive descend to Hades.

ANTIGONE

I have heard that the Phrygian stranger, Tantalus' daughter,[a] died the saddest death, near lofty Sipylus; her did the growth of the rock, like clinging ivy, subdue, and as she melts away rain, as men say, and snow never leave her, and with her ever-weeping eyes she soaks the mountain ridges; very like her am I, as the god sends me to sleep.

CHORUS

But she was a goddess and the child of gods,[b] and we are mortal and the children of mortals; yet it is a great thing for the departed to have the credit of a fate like that of those equal to gods, both in life and later in death.

[a] Niobe, who was the subject of plays by both Aeschylus and Sophocles.

[b] Niobe's father Tantalus is commonly called a son of Zeus.

ΑΝΤΙΓΟΝΗ

οἴμοι γελῶμαι.   στρ. γ'
τί με, πρὸς θεῶν πατρῴων,
840   οὐκ οἰχομέναν ὑβρίζεις,
ἀλλ' ἐπίφαντον;
ὦ πόλις, ὦ πόλεως
πολυκτήμονες ἄνδρες·
ἰὼ Διρκαῖαι κρῆναι Θή-
845   βας τ' εὐαρμάτου ἄλσος, ἔμ-
πας ξυμμάρτυρας ὔμμ' ἐπικτῶμαι,
οἷα φίλων ἄκλαυτος, οἵοις νόμοις
πρὸς ἕρμα τυμβόχωστον ἔρ-
χομαι τάφου ποταινίου·
850   ἰὼ δύστανος, βροτοῖς
οὔτε <νεκρὸς> νεκροῖσιν
μέτοικος, οὐ ζῶσιν, οὐ θανοῦσιν.

ΧΟΡΟΣ

προβᾶσ' ἐπ' ἔσχατον θράσους
ὑψηλὸν ἐς Δίκας βάθρον
855   προσέπεσες, ὦ τέκνον, ποδί.
πατρῷον δ' ἐκτίνεις τιν' ἆθλον.

ΑΝΤΙΓΟΝΗ

ἔψαυσας ἀλγει-   ἀντ. γ'
νοτάτας ἐμοὶ μερίμνας,
πατρὸς τριπολίστου οἴτου
860   τοῦ τε πρόπαντος
ἁμετέρου πότμου
κλεινοῖς Λαβδακίδαισιν.

82

ANTIGONE

Ah, I am being mocked! Why, in the name of the gods of my fathers, do you insult me not when I am gone, but while I am still visible? O city, O rich men of the city! Ah, fountains of Dirce and grove of Thebes of the fine chariots, you at least I can call to witness how unwept by friends, under what laws I come to the heaped-up mound of my strange tomb. Ah, unhappy one, living neither among mortals nor as a shade among the shades, neither with the living nor with the dead!

CHORUS

Advancing to the extreme of daring, you stumbled against the lofty altar of Justice, my child! And you are paying for some crime of your fathers.

ANTIGONE

You have touched on a thought most painful for me, the fate of my father, thrice renewed, and the whole of our destiny, that of the famous Labdacids. Ah, the disaster of

---

840 οἰχομέναν Martin: ὀλ(λ)ομέναν vel ὀλλυμέναν codd.

848 ἕρμα S, sch. L, coni. Hermann: ἔργμα fere codd.

851 οὔτε <νεκρὸς> Gleditsch: οὔτ' ἐν fere codd.

855 ποδί Bruhn: πολύν LSV: πολύ fere cett.

859 τριπολίστου Ll.-J.: -ιστον codd.   οἴτου Ll.-J.: οἶτον KPc, coni. Brunck: οἶκτον fere codd.

ἰὼ ματρῷαι λέκτρων ἆ-
ται κοιμήματά τ' αὐτογέν-
865 νητ' ἐμῷ πατρὶ δυσμόρου ματρός·
οἵων ἐγώ ποθ' ἁ ταλαίφρων ἔφυν·
πρὸς οὓς ἀραῖος ἄγαμος ἅδ'
ἐγὼ μέτοικος ἔρχομαι.
ἰὼ δυσπότμων κασί-
870 γνητε γάμων κυρήσας,
θανὼν ἔτ' οὖσαν κατήναρές με.

ΧΟΡΟΣ

σέβειν μὲν εὐσέβειά τις,
κράτος δ', ὅτῳ κράτος μέλει,
παραβατὸν οὐδαμᾷ πέλει,
875 σὲ δ' αὐτόγνωτος ὤλεσ' ὀργά.

ΑΝΤΙΓΟΝΗ

ἄκλαυτος, ἄφιλος, ἀνυμέναι-   ἐπ.
ος <ἁ> ταλαίφρων ἄγομαι
τὰν ἑτοίμαν ὁδόν.
οὐκέτι μοι τόδε λαμπάδος ἱερὸν
880 ὄμμα θέμις ὁρᾶν ταλαίνᾳ·
τὸν δ' ἐμὸν πότμον ἀδάκρυτον
οὐδεὶς φίλων στενάζει.

ΚΡΕΩΝ

ἆρ' ἴστ' ἀοιδὰς καὶ γόους πρὸ τοῦ θανεῖν
ὡς οὐδ' ἂν εἷς παύσαιτ' ἄν, εἰ χρείη, χέων;
885 οὐκ ἄξεθ' ὡς τάχιστα, καὶ κατηρεφεῖ
τύμβῳ περιπτύξαντες, ὡς εἴρηκ' ἐγώ,

ANTIGONE

marriage with his mother, and my father's incestuous
couplings with his ill-fated mother! From what parents
was I born, miserable one! To them I go, to live with them,
accursed, unmarried! Ah, brother who made a disastrous
marriage,[a] in your death you have destroyed my life!

CHORUS

The respect you showed is a noble kind of respect; but
power, in the hands of him to whom it belongs, is in no way
to be flouted, and you were destroyed by your self-willed
passion.

ANTIGONE

Unwept, friendless, unwedded, I am conducted, unhappy
one, along the way that lies before me! No longer may I,
poor creature, look upon the sacred eye of the shining sun;
and my fate, unwept for, is lamented by no friend.

Enter CREON.

CREON

Do you not know that no one would cease to pour forth
songs and lamentations before death, if need be? Will you
not lead her off as soon as possible, and when you have
enclosed her in the encompassing tomb, as I have ordered,

---

[a] Adrastus' support for Polynices was the consequence of the
latter's marriage with his daughter Argeia.

---

878 ἑτοίμαν] πυμάταν Reiske
884 χέων Blaydes: λέγειν codd.: λέγων Vauvilliers

ἄφετε μόνην ἐρῆμον, εἴτε χρῇ θανεῖν
εἴτ' ἐν τοιαύτῃ ζῶσα τυμβεύειν στέγῃ·
ἡμεῖς γὰρ ἁγνοὶ τοὐπὶ τήνδε τὴν κόρην·
890   μετοικίας δ' οὖν τῆς ἄνω στερήσεται.

ΑΝΤΙΓΟΝΗ

ὦ τύμβος, ὦ νυμφεῖον, ὦ κατασκαφὴς
οἴκησις ἀείφρουρος, οἷ πορεύομαι
πρὸς τοὺς ἐμαυτῆς, ὧν ἀριθμὸν ἐν νεκροῖς
πλεῖστον δέδεκται Φερσέφασσ' ὀλωλότων·
895   ὧν λοισθία 'γὼ καὶ κάκιστα δὴ μακρῷ
κάτειμι, πρίν μοι μοῖραν ἐξήκειν βίου.
ἐλθοῦσα μέντοι κάρτ' ἐν ἐλπίσιν τρέφω
φίλη μὲν ἥξειν πατρί, προσφιλὴς δὲ σοί,
μῆτερ, φίλη δὲ σοί, κασίγνητον κάρα·
900   ἐπεὶ θανόντας αὐτόχειρ ὑμᾶς ἐγὼ
ἔλουσα κἀκόσμησα κἀπιτυμβίους
χοὰς ἔδωκα· νῦν δέ, Πολύνεικες, τὸ σὸν
δέμας περιστέλλουσα τοιάδ' ἄρνυμαι.
καίτοι σ' ἐγὼ 'τίμησα τοῖς φρονοῦσιν εὖ.
905   οὐ γάρ ποτ' οὔτ' ἂν εἰ τέκν' ὧν μήτηρ ἔφυν
οὔτ' εἰ πόσις μοι κατθανὼν ἐτήκετο,
βίᾳ πολιτῶν τόνδ' ἂν ᾐρόμην πόνον.
τίνος νόμου δὴ ταῦτα πρὸς χάριν λέγω;
πόσις μὲν ἄν μοι κατθανόντος ἄλλος ἦν,
910   καὶ παῖς ἀπ' ἄλλου φωτός, εἰ τοῦδ' ἤμπλακον,
μητρὸς δ' ἐν Ἅιδου καὶ πατρὸς κεκευθότοιν
οὐκ ἔστ' ἀδελφὸς ὅστις ἂν βλάστοι ποτέ.
τοιῷδε μέντοι σ' ἐκπροτιμήσασ' ἐγὼ

leave her alone, isolated, whether she wishes to die or to be
entombed living in such a dwelling. For we are guiltless
where this girl is concerned; but she shall be deprived of
residence with us here above the ground.

ANTIGONE

O tomb, O bridal chamber, O deep-dug home, to be
guarded for ever, where I go to join those who are my own,
of whom Persephassa[a] has already received a great
number, dead, among the shades! Of these I am the last
and my descent will be the saddest of all, before the term
of my life has come. But when I come there, I am
confident that I shall come dear to my father, dear to you,
my mother, and dear to you, my own brother; since when
you died it was I that with my own hands washed you and
adorned you and poured libations on your graves; and now,
Polynices, for burying your body I get this reward! Yet in
the eyes of the wise I did well to honour you; for never, had
children of whom I was the mother or had my husband
perished and been mouldering there, would I have taken
on myself this task, in defiance of the citizens. In virtue of
what law do I say this? If my husband had died, I could
have had another, and a child by another man, if I had lost
the first, but with my mother and my father in Hades
below, I could never have another brother. Such was the
law for whose sake I did you special honour, but to

---

[a] Persephone.

904–20 del. Lehrs (905–13 iam A. Jacob): 911–12 citat Aristo-
teles, *Rhet.* 1417 a 32–33
905 τέκν᾽ ὦν C. Winckelmann: τέκνων codd.

87

νόμῳ, Κρέοντι ταῦτ' ἔδοξ' ἁμαρτάνειν
915 καὶ δεινὰ τολμᾶν, ὦ κασίγνητον κάρα.
καὶ νῦν ἄγει με διὰ χερῶν οὕτω λαβὼν
ἄλεκτρον, ἀνυμέναιον, οὔτε του γάμου
μέρος λαχοῦσαν οὔτε παιδείου τροφῆς,
ἀλλ' ὧδ' ἔρημος πρὸς φίλων ἡ δύσμορος
920 ζῶσ' ἐς θανόντων ἔρχομαι κατασκαφάς·
ποίαν παρεξελθοῦσα δαιμόνων δίκην;
τί χρή με τὴν δύστηνον ἐς θεοὺς ἔτι
βλέπειν; τίν' αὐδᾶν ξυμμάχων; ἐπεί γε δὴ
τὴν δυσσέβειαν εὐσεβοῦσ' ἐκτησάμην.
925 ἀλλ' εἰ μὲν οὖν τάδ' ἐστὶν ἐν θεοῖς καλά,
παθόντες ἂν ξυγγνοῖμεν ἡμαρτηκότες·
εἰ δ' οἵδ' ἁμαρτάνουσι, μὴ πλείω κακὰ
πάθοιεν ἢ καὶ δρῶσιν ἐκδίκως ἐμέ.

ΧΟΡΟΣ

ἔτι τῶν αὐτῶν ἀνέμων αὐταὶ
930 ψυχῆς ῥιπαὶ τήνδε γ' ἔχουσιν.

ΚΡΕΩΝ

τοιγὰρ τούτων τοῖσιν ἄγουσιν
κλαύμαθ' ὑπάρξει βραδυτῆτος ὕπερ.

ΑΝΤΙΓΟΝΗ

οἴμοι, θανάτου τοῦτ' ἐγγυτάτω
τοὔπος ἀφῖκται.

ΚΡΕΩΝ

935 θαρσεῖν οὐδὲν παραμυθοῦμαι
μὴ οὐ τάδε ταύτῃ κατακυροῦσθαι.

88

ANTIGONE

Creon I seemed to do wrong and to show shocking reck-
lessness, O my own brother. And now he leads me thus by
the hands, without marriage, without bridal, having no
share in wedlock or in the rearing of children, but thus
deserted by my friends I come living, poor creature, to the
caverns of the dead. What justice of the gods have I
transgressed? Why must I still look to the gods, unhappy
one? Whom can I call on to protect me? For by acting
piously I have been convicted of impiety. Well, if this is
approved among the gods, I should forgive them for what I
have suffered, since I have done wrong; but if they are the
wrongdoers, may they not suffer worse evils than those
they are unjustly inflicting upon me!

CHORUS

The same blasts of the same winds of the spirit still possess
her.

CREON

Therefore there shall be trouble for those conducting her
on account of their slowness!

ANTIGONE

Ah me, this saying has come close to death!

CREON

I can give you no hope that the sentence will not be accom-
plished thus.

---

⁹²⁷ πλείω] μείω Vauvilliers

89

ΑΝΤΙΓΟΝΗ

ὦ γῆς Θήβης ἄστυ πατρῷον
καὶ θεοὶ προγενεῖς,
ἄγομαι δὴ 'γὼ κοὐκέτι μέλλω.
940 λεύσσετε, Θήβης οἱ κοιρανίδαι,
τὴν βασιλειδῶν μούνην λοιπήν,
οἷα πρὸς οἵων ἀνδρῶν πάσχω,
τὴν εὐσεβίαν σεβίσασα.

ΧΟΡΟΣ

ἔτλα καὶ Δανάας οὐράνιον φῶς   στρ. α'
945 ἀλλάξαι δέμας ἐν χαλκοδέτοις αὐλαῖς ·
κρυπτομένα δ' ἐν τυμβή-
ρει θαλάμῳ κατεζεύχθη ·
καίτοι <καὶ> γενεᾷ τίμιος, ὦ παῖ παῖ,
950 καὶ Ζηνὸς ταμιεύεσκε γονὰς χρυσορύτους.
ἀλλ' ἁ μοιριδία τις δύνασις δεινά ·
οὔτ' ἄν νιν ὄλβος οὔτ' Ἄρης,
οὐ πύργος, οὐχ ἁλίκτυποι
κελαιναὶ νᾶες ἐκφύγοιεν.
955 ζεύχθη δ' ὀξύχολος παῖς ὁ Δρύαντος,   ἀντ. α'
Ἠδωνῶν βασιλεύς, κερτομίοις ὀργαῖς
ἐκ Διονύσου πετρώ-
δει κατάφαρκτος ἐν δεσμῷ.
οὕτω τᾶς μανίας δεινὸν ἀποστάζει
960 ἀνθηρόν τε μένος. κεῖνος ἐπέγνω μανίαις
ψαύων τὸν θεὸν ἐν κερτομίοις γλώσσαις.
παύεσκε μὲν γὰρ ἐνθέους
γυναῖκας εὔιόν τε πῦρ,
965 φιλαύλους τ' ἠρέθιζε μούσας.

ANTIGONE

ANTIGONE

Ancestral city of the land of Thebes and gods of my forebears, I am led away and there is delay no longer! Look, rulers of Thebes, upon the last of the royal house, what things I am suffering from what men, for having shown reverence for reverence!

ANTIGONE is led away.

CHORUS

Danae too endured an exchange of heaven's light for the brass-fastened dwelling, and immured in the tomblike chamber she was held prisoner. Yet she came of an honoured house, my daughter, and had the keeping of the seed of Zeus that flowed in gold.[a] But the power of fate is strange; neither wealth nor martial valour, nor a wall, nor black ships crashing through the sea can escape it.

Held prisoner, too, was the quickly angered son of Dryas, the king of the Edonians,[b] for his mocking fury pent by Dionysus in a rocky prison. Thus the fierce, exuberant force of his madness drained away. He learned too late that he was mad in laying hands on the god, with mocking tongue; for he tried to check the inspired women and the Bacchic fire, and provoked the music of their pipes.

[a] Danae, the daughter of Acrisius, king of Argos, was mother of Perseus by Zeus.

[b] Lycurgus; see *Iliad* 6, 130 f and the fragments of Aeschylus' tetralogy about him.

---

941 βασιλειδῶν G. Wolff: βασιλείαν t: βασιλίδα cett.
948 suppl. Hermann
952 ὄλβος Scaliger: ὄμβρος codd.
965 μούσας Ll.-J.: Μούσας vulgo

παρὰ δὲ κυανέων πελαγέων διδύμας ἁλὸς   στρ. βʹ
ἀκτᾷ Βοσπορίᾳ <τόπος ἦν> ὁ Θρηΐκων
970   Σαλμυδησσός, ἵν' ἀγχίπτολις Ἄ-
ρης δισσοῖσι Φινεΐδαις
εἶδεν ἀρατὸν ἕλκος
τυφλωθὲν ἐξ ἀγρίας δάμαρτος
ἀλαὸν ἀλαστόροισιν ὀμμάτων κύκλοις
975   ἀραχθέντων ὑφ' αἱματηραῖς
χείρεσσι καὶ κερκίδων ἀκμαῖσιν.

κατὰ δὲ τακόμενοι μέλεοι μελέαν πάθαν   ἀντ. βʹ
980   κλαῖον, ματρὸς ἔχοντες ἀνυμφεύτου γονάν·
ἁ δὲ σπέρμα μὲν ἀρχαιογόνων
<ἦν> ἄνασσ' Ἐρεχθεϊδᾶν,
τηλεπόροις δ' ἐν ἄντροις
τράφη θυέλλησιν ἐν πατρῴαις
985   Βορεὰς ἄμιππος ὀρθόποδος ὑπὲρ πάγου
θεῶν παῖς· ἀλλὰ κἀπ' ἐκείνᾳ
Μοῖραι μακραίωνες ἔσχον, ὦ παῖ.

ΤΕΙΡΕΣΙΑΣ

Θήβης ἄνακτες, ἥκομεν κοινὴν ὁδὸν
δύ' ἐξ ἑνὸς βλέποντε· τοῖς τυφλοῖσι γὰρ
990   αὕτη κέλευθος ἐκ προηγητοῦ πέλει.

ΚΡΕΩΝ

τί δ' ἔστιν, ὦ γεραιὲ Τειρεσία, νέον;

966 post πελαγέων habent codd. πετρῶν, quod del. Brunck
969 ἀκτᾷ Βοσπορίᾳ Ll.-J.: -αὶ -όριαι codd.   <τόπος ἦν> Ll.-
J.   Θρηΐκων Herkenrath: Θρηκῶν codd.

And by the shore of the Bosphorus of the dark waters of the double sea was the Thracian place Salmydessus, where Ares whose city is nearby saw the accursed blinding wound inflicted on the two sons of Phineus[a] by his cruel wife, robbing of sight the circles of their eyes that cried for vengeance, torn out by her bloody hands and the sharp points of her distaff.

And as they pined away they sadly wept for their sad affliction, the children of a mother unhappy in her marriage. She by birth was a princess of the ancient house of the sons of Erechtheus; but she was reared in distant caves, among her father's storm winds, a daughter of Boreas riding with the others beyond the steep mountain, a child of the gods. But even upon her the long-lived Fates bore hard, my child.

Enter the blind prophet TIRESIAS, *led by a boy.*

TIRESIAS

Lords of Thebes, we have come, journeying together, two with one pair of eyes; the blind have this way of travelling with a guide.

CREON

What is the matter, aged Tiresias?

---

[a] The Thracian king Phineus was first married to Cleopatra, a daughter of Boreas, the North Wind, by Oreithyia, a daughter of the Athenian king Erechtheus. Phineus' children by Cleopatra were blinded by his second wife, Eidothea.

---

975 ἀραχθέντων Seidler: ἀραχθὲν ἐγχέων fere codd.
980 ἀνυμφεύτου Meineke: -ευτον fere codd.
982 <ἦν> ἄνασσ' anon. ap. Wilamowitz: ἄντασ' codd.

SOPHOCLES

ΤΕΙΡΕΣΙΑΣ

ἐγὼ διδάξω, καὶ σὺ τῷ μάντει πιθοῦ.

ΚΡΕΩΝ

οὔκουν πάρος γε σῆς ἀπεστάτουν φρενός.

ΤΕΙΡΕΣΙΑΣ

τοιγὰρ δι᾽ ὀρθῆς τήνδ᾽ ἐναυκλήρεις πόλιν.

ΚΡΕΩΝ

995 ἔχω πεπονθὼς μαρτυρεῖν ὀνήσιμα.

ΤΕΙΡΕΣΙΑΣ

φρόνει βεβὼς αὖ νῦν ἐπὶ ξυροῦ τύχης.

ΚΡΕΩΝ

τί δ᾽ ἔστιν; ὡς ἐγὼ τὸ σὸν φρίσσω στόμα.

ΤΕΙΡΕΣΙΑΣ

γνώσῃ, τέχνης σημεῖα τῆς ἐμῆς κλυών.
ἐς γὰρ παλαιὸν θᾶκον ὀρνιθοσκόπον
1000 ἵζων, ἵν᾽ ἦν μοι παντὸς οἰωνοῦ λιμήν,
ἀγνῶτ᾽ ἀκούω φθόγγον ὀρνίθων, κακῷ
κλάζοντας οἴστρῳ καὶ βεβαρβαρωμένῳ·
καὶ σπῶντας ἐν χηλαῖσιν ἀλλήλους φοναῖς
ἔγνων· πτερῶν γὰρ ῥοῖβδος οὐκ ἄσημος ἦν.
1005 εὐθὺς δὲ δείσας ἐμπύρων ἐγευόμην
βωμοῖσιν παμφλέκτοισιν· ἐκ δὲ θυμάτων
Ἥφαιστος οὐκ ἔλαμπεν, ἀλλ᾽ ἐπὶ σποδῷ
μυδῶσα κηκὶς μηρίων ἐτήκετο
κἄτυφε κἀνέπτυε, καὶ μετάρσιοι
1010 χολαὶ διεσπείροντο, καὶ καταρρυεῖς

94

TIRESIAS

I will explain, and do you obey the prophet!

CREON

In the past I have not been used to depart from your counsel.

TIRESIAS

That is why you steered the ship of this city straight.

CREON

I can testify from experience that it was profitable.

TIRESIAS

Think, for you are again upon a razor's edge!

CREON

What is the matter! Your way of speaking frightens me!

TIRESIAS

You shall learn, when you hear the indications of my art! As I took my place on my ancient seat for observing birds, where I can mark every bird of omen, I heard a strange sound among them, since they were screeching with dire, incoherent frenzy; and I knew that they were tearing each other with bloody claws, for there was a whirring of wings that made it clear. At once I was alarmed, and attempted burnt sacrifice at the altar where I kindled fire; but the fire god raised no flame from my offerings. Over the ashes a dank slime oozed from the thigh bones, smoked and sputtered; the gall was sprayed high into the air, and the thighs,

μηροὶ καλυπτῆς ἐξέκειντο πιμελῆς.
τοιαῦτα παιδὸς τοῦδ᾽ ἐμάνθανον πάρα
φθίνοντ᾽ ἀσήμων ὀργίων μαντεύματα.
ἐμοὶ γὰρ οὗτος ἡγεμών, ἄλλοις δ᾽ ἐγώ.
1015 καὶ ταῦτα τῆς σῆς ἐκ φρενὸς νοσεῖ πόλις.
βωμοὶ γὰρ ἡμῖν ἐσχάραι τε παντελεῖς
πλήρεις ὑπ᾽ οἰωνῶν τε καὶ κυνῶν βορᾶς
τοῦ δυσμόρου πεπτῶτος Οἰδίπου γόνου.
κᾆτ᾽ οὐ δέχονται θυστάδας λιτὰς ἔτι
1020 θεοὶ παρ᾽ ἡμῶν οὐδὲ μηρίων φλόγα,
οὐδ᾽ ὄρνις εὐσήμους ἀπορροιβδεῖ βοάς,
ἀνδροφθόρου βεβρῶτες αἵματος λίπος.
    ταῦτ᾽ οὖν, τέκνον, φρόνησον. ἀνθρώποισι γὰρ
τοῖς πᾶσι κοινόν ἐστι τοὐξαμαρτάνειν·
1025 ἐπεὶ δ᾽ ἁμάρτῃ, κεῖνος οὐκέτ᾽ ἔστ᾽ ἀνὴρ
ἄβουλος οὐδ᾽ ἄνολβος, ὅστις ἐς κακὸν
πεσὼν ἀκεῖται μηδ᾽ ἀκίνητος πέλει.
αὐθαδία τοι σκαιότητ᾽ ὀφλισκάνει.
ἀλλ᾽ εἶκε τῷ θανόντι, μηδ᾽ ὀλωλότα
1030 κέντει. τίς ἀλκὴ τὸν θανόντ᾽ ἐπικτανεῖν;
εὖ σοι φρονήσας εὖ λέγω· τὸ μανθάνειν δ᾽
ἥδιστον εὖ λέγοντος, εἰ κέρδος λέγοι.

KΡΕΩΝ

ὦ πρέσβυ, πάντες ὥστε τοξόται σκοποῦ
τοξεύετ᾽ ἀνδρὸς τοῦδε, κοὐδὲ †μαντικῆς
1035 ἄτρωτος ὑμῖν εἰμι· τῶν δ᾽ ὑπαὶ γένους†
ἐξημπόλημαι κἀκπεφόρτισμαι πάλαι.

streaming with liquid, lay bare of the fat that had concealed
them. Such was the ruin of the prophetic rites by which I
vainly sought a sign, as I learned from this boy; for he
guides me, as I guide others. And it is your will that has put
this plague upon the city; for our altars and our braziers,
one and all, are filled with carrion brought by birds and
dogs from the unhappy son of Oedipus who fell. And the
gods are no longer accepting the prayers that accompany
sacrifice or the flame that consumes the thigh bones, and
the cries screamed out by the birds no longer give me signs
. . . for they have eaten fat compounded with a dead man's
blood.

Think upon this, my son! All men are liable to make
mistakes; and when a man does this, he who after getting
into trouble tries to repair the damage and does not remain
immovable is not foolish or miserable. Obstinacy lays you
open to the charge of blundering. Give way to the dead
man, and do not continue to stab him as he lies dead! I am
well disposed to you, and my advice is good; and it is a
pleasure to learn from a good adviser, if his advice brings
profit.

CREON

Aged man, all of you shoot at me like archers aiming at a
target, and I am not unscathed by your prophetic art; long
since I have been sold and exported by your tribe! Make

[1021] del. Reeve, 1021–22 Paley; fortasse lacuna post 1021 sta-
tuenda est

[1034] κοὐδ' ἐκ μαντικῆς Wecklein

[1035] ἄτρωτος Pallis: ἄπρακτος codd.

κερδαίνετ᾽, ἐμπολᾶτε τἀπὸ Σάρδεων
ἤλεκτρον, εἰ βούλεσθε, καὶ τὸν Ἰνδικὸν
χρυσόν· τάφῳ δ᾽ ἐκεῖνον οὐχὶ κρύψετε,
1040 οὐδ᾽ εἰ θέλουσ᾽ οἱ Ζηνὸς αἰετοὶ βορὰν
φέρειν νιν ἁρπάζοντες ἐς Διὸς θρόνους·
οὐδ᾽ ὣς μίασμα τοῦτο μὴ τρέσας ἐγὼ
θάπτειν παρήσω κεῖνον· εὖ γὰρ οἶδ᾽ ὅτι
θεοὺς μιαίνειν οὔτις ἀνθρώπων σθένει.
1045 πίπτουσι δ᾽, ὦ γεραιὲ Τειρεσία, βροτῶν
χοἰ πολλὰ δεινοὶ πτώματ᾽ αἴσχρ᾽, ὅταν λόγους
αἰσχροὺς καλῶς λέγωσι τοῦ κέρδους χάριν.

ΤΕΙΡΕΣΙΑΣ

φεῦ·
ἆρ᾽ οἶδεν ἀνθρώπων τις, ἆρα φράζεται —

ΚΡΕΩΝ

τί χρῆμα; ποῖον τοῦτο πάγκοινον λέγεις;

ΤΕΙΡΕΣΙΑΣ

1050 ὅσῳ κράτιστον κτημάτων εὐβουλία;

ΚΡΕΩΝ

ὅσῳπερ, οἶμαι, μὴ φρονεῖν πλείστη βλάβη.

ΤΕΙΡΕΣΙΑΣ

ταύτης σὺ μέντοι τῆς νόσου πλήρης ἔφυς.

ΚΡΕΩΝ

οὐ βούλομαι τὸν μάντιν ἀντειπεῖν κακῶς.

ΤΕΙΡΕΣΙΑΣ

καὶ μὴν λέγεις, ψευδῆ με θεσπίζειν λέγων.

your profits, import electrum from Sardis if you wish, and
gold from India! But you shall not hide him in the grave,
even if Zeus' eagles should snatch the body and bear the
carrion up to their master's throne! Not even then shall I
take fright at this pollution and allow him to be buried; for
I well know that no mortals have power to pollute the gods.
And even men who are clever at many things fall shame-
fully, when they skilfully speak shameful words in the pur-
suit of gain!

TIRESIAS
Alack! Does any man know, does any man understand—

CREON
What thing? What is this general statement you are mak-
ing?

TIRESIAS
How much the best of all possessions is good counsel!

CREON
Just as much, I think, as foolishness is the greatest plague.

TIRESIAS
But that is the malady from which you suffer!

CREON
I do not wish to reply rudely to the prophet.

TIRESIAS
Yet you speak rudely, saying that my prophecies are false.

[1037] τἀπὸ Blaydes: τὰ πρὸ L in linea: τὸν πρὸ L s.l., Λa Zo

ΚΡΕΩΝ

1055 τὸ μαντικὸν γὰρ πᾶν φιλάργυρον γένος.

ΤΕΙΡΕΣΙΑΣ

τὸ δ' αὖ τυράννων αἰσχροκέρδειαν φιλεῖ.

ΚΡΕΩΝ

ἆρ' οἶσθα ταγοὺς ὄντας οὓς ψέγεις λέγων;

ΤΕΙΡΕΣΙΑΣ

οἶδ'· ἐξ ἐμοῦ γὰρ τήνδ' ἔχεις σώσας πόλιν.

ΚΡΕΩΝ

σοφὸς σὺ μάντις, ἀλλὰ τἀδικεῖν φιλῶν.

ΤΕΙΡΕΣΙΑΣ

1060 ὄρσεις με τἀκίνητα διὰ φρενῶν φράσαι.

ΚΡΕΩΝ

κίνει, μόνον δὲ μὴ 'πὶ κέρδεσιν λέγων.

ΤΕΙΡΕΣΙΑΣ

οὕτω γὰρ ἤδη καὶ δοκῶ τὸ σὸν μέρος;

ΚΡΕΩΝ

ὡς μὴ 'μπολήσων ἴσθι τὴν ἐμὴν φρένα.

ΤΕΙΡΕΣΙΑΣ

ἀλλ' εὖ γέ τοι κάτισθι μὴ πολλοὺς ἔτι
1065 τρόχους ἁμιλλητῆρας ἡλίου τελῶν,
ἐν οἷσι τῶν σῶν αὐτὸς ἐκ σπλάγχνων ἕνα
νέκυν νεκρῶν ἀμοιβὸν ἀντιδοὺς ἔσῃ,
ἀνθ' ὧν ἔχεις μὲν τῶν ἄνω βαλὼν κάτω,

CREON

Yes, all you prophets are an avaricious race.

TIRESIAS

Rulers, also, are prone to be corrupt.

CREON

Do you know that those whom you rebuke have power?

TIRESIAS

Yes; for it is through me that you saved this city.

CREON

You are a skilful prophet, but given to dishonesty.

TIRESIAS

You will provoke me into telling you things that should not be dug up!

CREON

Do so, only do not speak for the sake of profit!

TIRESIAS

That is what you already think I do.

CREON

Know that you will never be able to trade on my judgment!

TIRESIAS

Then know well that you shall not accomplish many racing courses of the sun, and in that lapse of time you shall give in exchange for corpses the corpse of one from your own loins, in return for having hurled below one of those above,

---

¹⁰⁵⁶ δ' αὖ Hartung: δ' ἐκ codd.

¹⁰⁵⁷ οὓς Kapsomenos: ἃ SVR: ἃν cett.   ψέγεις Wecklein: λέγεις codd.

¹⁰⁶⁵ ἡλίου τελῶν] ἥλιον τελεῖν C. Winckelmann

ψυχήν γ᾽ ἀτίμως ἐν τάφῳ κατοικίσας,
1070 ἔχεις δὲ τῶν κάτωθεν ἐνθάδ᾽ αὖ θεῶν
ἄμοιρον, ἀκτέριστον, ἀνόσιον νέκυν.
ὧν οὔτε σοὶ μέτεστιν οὔτε τοῖς ἄνω
θεοῖσιν, ἀλλ᾽ ἐκ σοῦ βιάζονται τάδε.
τούτων σε λωβητῆρες ὑστεροφθόροι
1075 λοχῶσιν Ἅιδου καὶ θεῶν Ἐρινύες,
ἐν τοῖσιν αὐτοῖς τοῖσδε ληφθῆναι κακοῖς.
καὶ ταῦτ᾽ ἄθρησον εἰ κατηργυρωμένος
λέγω· φανεῖ γὰρ οὐ μακροῦ χρόνου τριβὴ
ἀνδρῶν γυναικῶν σοῖς δόμοις κωκύματα.
1080 ἔχθρᾳ δὲ πᾶσαι συνταράσσονται πόλεις

❀   ❀   ❀   ❀

ὅσων σπαράγματ᾽ ἢ κύνες καθήγνισαν
ἢ θῆρες, ἤ τις πτηνὸς οἰωνός, φέρων
ἀνόσιον ὀσμὴν ἑστιοῦχον ἐς πόλιν.
τοιαῦτά σοι, λυπεῖς γάρ, ὥστε τοξότης
1085 ἀφῆκα θυμῷ καρδίας τοξεύματα
βέβαια, τῶν σὺ θάλπος οὐχ ὑπεκδράμῃ.
    ὦ παῖ, σὺ δ᾽ ἡμᾶς ἄπαγε πρὸς δόμους, ἵνα
τὸν θυμὸν οὗτος ἐς νεωτέρους ἀφῇ,
καὶ γνῷ τρέφειν τὴν γλῶσσαν ἡσυχαιτέραν
1090 τὸν νοῦν τ᾽ ἀμείνω τῶν φρενῶν ὧν νῦν φέρει.

ΧΟΡΟΣ
ἀνήρ, ἄναξ, βέβηκε δεινὰ θεσπίσας.
ἐπιστάμεσθα δ᾽, ἐξ ὅτου λευκὴν ἐγὼ
τήνδ᾽ ἐκ μελαίνης ἀμφιβάλλομαι τρίχα,
μή πώ ποτ᾽ αὐτὸν ψεῦδος ἐς πόλιν λακεῖν.

102

blasphemously lodging a living person in a tomb, and you have kept here something belonging to the gods below, a corpse deprived, unburied, unholy. Neither you nor the gods above have any part in this, but you have inflicted it upon them! On account of this there lie in wait for you the doers of outrage who in the end destroy, the Erinyes of Hades and the gods, so that you will be caught up in these same evils. Consider whether I tell you this because I have been bribed! For after no long lapse of time there shall be lamentations of men and women in your house; and all the cities are stirred up by enmity ... (corpses) of which fragments have been consecrated by dogs or beasts, or some winged bird, carrying the unholy scent to the city with its hearths. These are the arrows which like an archer, since you provoke me, I have shot in anger at your heart, sure arrows, whose sting you will not escape.

Boy, lead me home, so that this man may discharge his anger against younger persons, and may learn to keep his tongue quieter and his mind more sensible than the intelligence he has at present!

Exit TIRESIAS.

CHORUS
The man is gone, king, after uttering a fearful prophecy; and I know that since this hair, once black, now white, has clothed my head, he has never spoken a falsehood to the city.

1069 γ' Dawe: τ' codd.   1080 ἔχθρᾳ Reiske: ἐχθραὶ
codd.   post hunc versum lacunam statuit Ll.-J.: 1080–83 del.
A. Jacob   1083 πόλιν] πόλον Nauck   1084 σοι ZfZc: σου
cett.   1090 ὧν Brunck: ἣ codd.

SOPHOCLES

ΚΡΕΩΝ

1095 ἔγνωκα καὐτὸς καὶ ταράσσομαι φρένας·
τό τ᾽ εἰκαθεῖν γὰρ δεινόν, ἀντιστάντα δὲ
Ἄτης πατάξαι θυμὸν ἐν λίνῳ πάρα.

ΧΟΡΟΣ

εὐβουλίας δεῖ, παῖ Μενοικέως, †λαβεῖν†.

ΚΡΕΩΝ

τί δῆτα χρὴ δρᾶν; φράζε· πείσομαι δ᾽ ἐγώ.

ΧΟΡΟΣ

1100 ἐλθὼν κόρην μὲν ἐκ κατώρυχος στέγης
ἄνες, κτίσον δὲ τῷ προκειμένῳ τάφον.

ΚΡΕΩΝ

καὶ ταῦτ᾽ ἐπαινεῖς καὶ δοκεῖ παρεικαθεῖν;

ΧΟΡΟΣ

ὅσον γ᾽, ἄναξ, τάχιστα· συντέμνουσι γὰρ
θεῶν ποδώκεις τοὺς κακόφρονας Βλάβαι.

ΚΡΕΩΝ

1105 οἴμοι· μόλις μέν, καρδίας δ᾽ ἐξίσταμαι
τὸ δρᾶν· ἀνάγκῃ δ᾽ οὐχὶ δυσμαχητέον.

ΧΟΡΟΣ

δρᾶ νυν τάδ᾽ ἐλθὼν μηδ᾽ ἐπ᾽ ἄλλοισιν τρέπε.

ΚΡΕΩΝ

ὧδ᾽ ὡς ἔχω στείχοιμ᾽ ἄν· ἴτ᾽ ἴτ᾽ ὀπάονες,
οἵ τ᾽ ὄντες οἵ τ᾽ ἀπόντες, ἀξίνας χεροῖν
1110 ὁρμᾶσθ᾽ ἑλόντες εἰς ἐπόψιον τόπον.

CREON

I know it myself, and my mind is disturbed! For to yield
would be terrible, but if I resist, my will may run into the
fowler's net of disaster.

CHORUS

You have need of good counsel, son of Menoeceus!

CREON

What must I do? Tell me, and I will obey!

CHORUS

Go and release the girl from the subterranean dwelling,
and make a tomb for him who lies there!

CREON

Is that what you approve, and do you think I should give
way?

CHORUS

As soon as possible, king! Swift avengers from the gods cut
off those who think mistakenly.

CREON

Alack! It comes hard, but I renounce my heart's purpose,
and shall act! One cannot fight against superior force.

CHORUS

Go, then, and do it, and do not leave it to others!

CREON

I will go, just as I am! Come, come, my servants, present
and absent, take picks in your hands and rush to the

[1097] Ἄτης ... λίνῳ Ll.-J.: Ἄτη ... δεινῷ codd.
[1098] λαβεῖν lV: λαχεῖν Zf: Κρέον SaZot, K in marg.: τὰ νῦν
Rauchenstein   [1102] δοκεῖ Rauchenstein: δοκεῖς codd.

ἐγὼ δ᾿, ἐπειδὴ δόξα τῇδ᾿ ἐπεστράφη,
αὐτός τ᾿ ἔδησα καὶ παρὼν ἐκλύσομαι.
δέδοικα γὰρ μὴ τοὺς καθεστῶτας νόμους
ἄριστον ᾖ σῴζοντα τὸν βίον τελεῖν.

ΧΟΡΟΣ

1115 πολυώνυμε, Καδμείας   στρ. α´
νύμφας ἄγαλμα
καὶ Διὸς βαρυβρεμέτα
γένος, κλυτὰν ὃς ἀμφέπεις
Ἰταλίαν, μέδεις δὲ
1120 παγκοίνοις Ἐλευσινίας
Δηοῦς ἐν κόλποις, ὦ Βακχεῦ,
Βακχᾶν ματρόπολιν Θήβαν
ναιετῶν παρ᾿ ὑγρὸν
Ἰσμηνοῦ ῥέεθρον, ἀγρίου τ᾿
1125 ἐπὶ σπορᾷ δράκοντος.
σὲ δ᾿ ὑπὲρ διλόφου πέτρας   ἀντ. α´
στέροψ ὄπωπε
λιγνύς, ἔνθα Κωρύκιαι
στείχουσι Νύμφαι Βακχίδες
1130 Κασταλίας τε νᾶμα.
καί σε Νυσαίων ὀρέων
κισσήρεις ὄχθαι χλωρά τ᾿ ἀ-
κτὰ πολυστάφυλος πέμπει
ἀμβρότων ἐπέων
1135 εὐαζόντων Θηβαΐας
ἐπισκοποῦντ᾿ ἀγυιάς.

ground that you can see! Since my decision has been thus reversed, I who imprisoned her shall myself be present to release her! I am afraid that it is best to end one's life in obedience to the established laws!

Exit CREON.

You who have many names, pride of the Cadmean bride[a] and of Zeus the loud-thunderer, you who rule famous Italy, and lord it in the hollows of Demeter of Eleusis, open to all, Bacchic god, who live in the mother city of the Bacchants, Thebes, by the watery flow of Ismenus, near to the seed of the savage dragon!

Upon you looks the fiery flame of pitch beyond the rock with double peak, where walk the Corycian Bacchic nymphs, and where is the Castalian spring.[b] And the ivy-covered slopes of the hills of Nysa and the green coast with many grapes send you here, while voices divine cry "euhoe," as you visit the streets of Thebes.

[a] Semele, daughter of Cadmus, king of Thebes, was the mother of Dionysus.

[b] During the winter months, when Apollo was with the Hyperboreans, his brother Dionysus occupied his shrine at Delphi.

---

¹¹²³ ναιετῶν Dindorf: ναίων codd.
¹¹³⁴ ἐπέων] ἐπετᾶν Pallis

τὰν ἐκ πασᾶν τιμᾷς   στρ. β′
ὑπερτάταν πόλεων
ματρὶ σὺν κεραυνίᾳ·
1140 νῦν δ᾽, ὡς βιαίας ἔχεται
πάνδαμος πόλις ἐπὶ νόσου,
μολεῖν καθαρσίῳ ποδὶ Παρνασίαν
1145 ὑπὲρ κλειτὺν ἢ στονόεντα πορθμόν.
ἰὼ πῦρ πνεόντων   ἀντ. β′
χοράγ᾽ ἄστρων, νυχίων
φθεγμάτων ἐπίσκοπε,
Ζηνὸς γένεθλον, προφάνηθ᾽,
1150 ὦναξ, σαῖς ἅμα περιπόλοις
Θυίασιν, αἵ σε μαινόμεναι πάννυχοι
χορεύουσι τὸν ταμίαν Ἴακχον.

ΑΓΓΕΛΟΣ

1155 Κάδμου πάροικοι καὶ δόμων Ἀμφίονος,
οὐκ ἔσθ᾽ ὁποῖον στάντ᾽ ἂν ἀνθρώπου βίον
οὔτ᾽ αἰνέσαιμ᾽ ἂν οὔτε μεμψαίμην ποτέ.
τύχη γὰρ ὀρθοῖ καὶ τύχη καταρρέπει
τὸν εὐτυχοῦντα τόν τε δυστυχοῦντ᾽ ἀεί·
1160 καὶ μάντις οὐδεὶς τῶν καθεστώτων βροτοῖς.
Κρέων γὰρ ἦν ζηλωτός, ὡς ἐμοί, ποτέ,
σώσας μὲν ἐχθρῶν τήνδε Καδμείαν χθόνα,
λαβών τε χώρας παντελῆ μοναρχίαν
ηὔθυνε, θάλλων εὐγενεῖ τέκνων σπορᾷ·

1149 post ἐπίσκοπε add. παῖ codd., del. Schubert   Ζηνὸς
Bothe: Διὸς codd.: Δῖον Seyffert   προφάνηθ᾽ ὦναξ Bergk: προ-
φάνηθι ναξίαις codd.

ANTIGONE

Her do you honour above all cities, together with your
mother, victim of the lightning; and now, since the whole
city is gripped by the assault of plague, come with cleans-
ing movement over the slope of Parnassus, or the resound-
ing strait!

Hail, leader of the dance of the stars breathing fire,
master of the voices heard by night, son of Zeus, appear,
king, with your attendant Thyiads,[a] who in their frenzy
dance all night in honour of their lord Iacchus![b]

Enter MESSENGER.

MESSENGER

Neighbours of Cadmus and the house of Amphion,[c] there
is no state of human life that I would praise or blame as
though it had come to a stop; for fortune makes straight
and fortune brings down the fortunate or the unfortunate
man at all times, and no prophet can tell mortals what is
ordained. Why, Creon once was enviable, as it seemed to
me; he had saved this Cadmean land from enemies, had
acquired the all-powerful kingship of the land, and was
guiding it, happy with a noble brood of children.

[a] Maenads.

[b] The name of a deity invoked during the Eleusinian Mysteries,
in all probability identical with Dionysus.

[c] With his brother Zethus Amphion was the legendary builder
of the walls of Thebes.

1165   καὶ νῦν ἀφεῖται πάντα. καὶ γὰρ ἡδοναὶ
        ὅταν προδῶσιν ἀνδρός, οὐ τίθημ᾽ ἐγὼ
        ζῆν τοῦτον, ἀλλ᾽ ἔμψυχον ἡγοῦμαι νεκρόν.
        πλούτει τε γὰρ κατ᾽ οἶκον, εἰ βούλῃ, μέγα,
        καὶ ζῆ τύραννον σχῆμ᾽ ἔχων, ἐὰν δ᾽ ἀπῇ
1170   τούτων τὸ χαίρειν, τἄλλ᾽ ἐγὼ καπνοῦ σκιᾶς
        οὐκ ἂν πριαίμην ἀνδρὶ πρὸς τὴν ἡδονήν.

ΧΟΡΟΣ

τί δ᾽ αὖ τόδ᾽ ἄχθος βασιλέων ἥκεις φέρων;

ΑΓΓΕΛΟΣ

τεθνᾶσιν· οἱ δὲ ζῶντες αἴτιοι θανεῖν.

ΧΟΡΟΣ

καὶ τίς φονεύει; τίς δ᾽ ὁ κείμενος; λέγε.

ΑΓΓΕΛΟΣ

1175 Αἵμων ὄλωλεν· αὐτόχειρ δ᾽ αἱμάσσεται.

ΧΟΡΟΣ

πότερα πατρῴας, ἢ πρὸς οἰκείας χερός;

ΑΓΓΕΛΟΣ

αὐτὸς πρὸς αὑτοῦ, πατρὶ μηνίσας φόνου.

ΧΟΡΟΣ

ὦ μάντι, τοὔπος ὡς ἄρ᾽ ὀρθὸν ἤνυσας.

ΑΓΓΕΛΟΣ

ὡς ὧδ᾽ ἐχόντων τἄλλα βουλεύειν πάρα.

[1165] καὶ γὰρ ἡδοναὶ Seyffert: τὰς γὰρ ἡδονὰς codd.
[1166] ἀνδρός] ἄνδρας Zot: ἄνδρα Eustathius

And now all has been let go; for when a man's pleasures
have abandoned him, I do not consider him a living being,
but an animated corpse. Enjoy great wealth in your house,
if you will, and live in royal style; but if you take no delight
in these things, I would not purchase all the rest for the
shadow of smoke, compared with pleasure.

CHORUS

But what is this new burden for the princes that you come
bringing?

MESSENGER

They are dead! And those who are alive are guilty of their
deaths!

CHORUS

And who is the murderer? and who lies low? Tell me!

MESSENGER

Haemon is dead; and his own hand has shed his blood.[a]

CHORUS

Was it by his father's hand or by his own?

MESSENGER

He died at his own hand, in anger against his father for the
murder he committed.

CHORUS

Prophet, how true, then, was your word!

MESSENGER

You may take counsel in the knowledge that this is so.

---

[a] An untranslatable pun; the name Haemon resembles the
Greek word for blood.

SOPHOCLES

ΧΟΡΟΣ

1180   καὶ μὴν ὁρῶ τάλαιναν Εὐρυδίκην ὁμοῦ
       δάμαρτα τὴν Κρέοντος· ἐκ δὲ δωμάτων
       ἤτοι κλυοῦσα παιδὸς ἢ τύχῃ περᾷ.

ΕΥΡΥΔΙΚΗ

       ὦ πάντες ἀστοί, τῶν λόγων ἐπῃσθόμην
       πρὸς ἔξοδον στείχουσα, Παλλάδος θεᾶς
1185   ὅπως ἱκοίμην εὐγμάτων προσήγορος.
       καὶ τυγχάνω τε κλῇθρ' ἀνασπαστοῦ πύλης
       χαλῶσα, καί με φθόγγος οἰκείου κακοῦ
       βάλλει δι' ὤτων· ὑπτία δὲ κλίνομαι
       δείσασα πρὸς δμωαῖσι κἀποπλήσσομαι.
1190   ἀλλ' ὅστις ἦν ὁ μῦθος αὖθις εἴπατε·
       κακῶν γὰρ οὐκ ἄπειρος οὖσ' ἀκούσομαι.

ΑΓΓΕΛΟΣ

       ἐγώ, φίλη δέσποινα, καὶ παρὼν ἐρῶ,
       κοὐδὲν παρήσω τῆς ἀληθείας ἔπος.
       τί γάρ σε μαλθάσσοιμ' ἂν ὧν ἐς ὕστερον
1195   ψεῦσται φανούμεθ'· ὀρθὸν ἀλήθει' ἀεί.
       ἐγὼ δὲ σῷ ποδαγὸς ἑσπόμην πόσει
       πεδίον ἐπ' ἄκρον, ἔνθ' ἔκειτο νηλεὲς
       κυνοσπάρακτον σῶμα Πολυνείκους ἔτι·
       καὶ τὸν μέν, αἰτήσαντες ἐνοδίαν θεὸν
1200   Πλούτωνά τ' ὀργὰς εὐμενεῖς κατασχεθεῖν,
       λούσαντες ἁγνὸν λουτρόν, ἐν νεοσπάσιν
       θαλλοῖς ὃ δὴ 'λέλειπτο συγκατῄθομεν,
       καὶ τύμβον ὀρθόκρανον οἰκείας χθονὸς

112

ANTIGONE

CHORUS

Now I see the unhappy Eurydice close by, Creon's wife; she is coming from the house, perhaps because she has heard about her son.

Enter EURYDICE.

EURYDICE

All you citizens, I heard the news as I was about to leave the house so as to go to address prayers to the goddess Pallas; and I chanced to be loosening the bolt of the gate to open it when the accent of disaster in the house struck my ears, and in terror I fell back into the arms of my servants, and was struck dumb. But whatever the news was, tell it again! For you will have a listener not without experience of disaster.

MESSENGER

I was there, dear mistress, and will tell you, and I shall suppress no word of the truth. For why should I try to soothe you with words which will later brand me as a liar? Truth is always best. I accompanied your husband on foot to the edge of the plain, where the unpitied corpse of Polynices still lay, torn by the dogs. Praying the goddess of the crossway[a] and Pluto to restrain their wrath in mercy, we washed it with purifying water, and among newly uprooted bushes burned what was left. And we heaped up a tall burial mound of our own earth, and after that

[a] Hecate.

[1182] περᾷ Brunck: πάρα codd.

χώσαντες αὖθις πρὸς λιθόστρωτον κόρης
1205 νυμφεῖον Ἅιδου κοῖλον εἰσεβαίνομεν.
φωνῆς δ᾽ ἄπωθεν ὀρθίων κωκυμάτων
κλύει τις ἀκτέριστον ἀμφὶ παστάδα,
καὶ δεσπότῃ Κρέοντι σημαίνει μολών·
τῷ δ᾽ ἀθλίας ἄσημα περιβαίνει βοῆς
1210 ἕρποντι μᾶλλον ἆσσον, οἰμώξας δ᾽ ἔπος
ἵησι δυσθρήνητον, "ὦ τάλας ἐγώ,
ἆρ᾽ εἰμὶ μάντις; ἆρα δυστυχεστάτην
κέλευθον ἕρπω τῶν παρελθουσῶν ὁδῶν;
παιδός με σαίνει φθόγγος. ἀλλά, πρόσπολοι,
1215 ἴτ᾽ ἆσσον ὠκεῖς, καὶ παραστάντες τάφῳ
ἀθρήσατ᾽, ἀγμὸν χώματος λιθοσπαδῆ
δύντες πρὸς αὐτὸ στόμιον, εἰ τὸν Αἵμονος
φθόγγον συνίημ᾽, ἢ θεοῖσι κλέπτομαι."
τάδ᾽ ἐξ ἀθύμου δεσπότου κελεύμασιν
1220 ἠθροῦμεν· ἐν δὲ λοισθίῳ τυμβεύματι
τὴν μὲν κρεμαστὴν αὐχένος κατείδομεν,
βρόχῳ μιτώδει σινδόνος καθημμένην,
τὸν δ᾽ ἀμφὶ μέσσῃ περιπετῆ προσκείμενον,
εὐνῆς ἀποιμώζοντα τῆς κάτω φθορὰν
1225 καὶ πατρὸς ἔργα καὶ τὸ δύστηνον λέχος.
ὁ δ᾽ ὡς ὁρᾷ σφε, στυγνὸν οἰμώξας ἔσω
χωρεῖ πρὸς αὐτὸν κἀνακωκύσας καλεῖ·
"ὦ τλῆμον, οἷον ἔργον εἴργασαι· τίνα
νοῦν ἔσχες; ἐν τῷ συμφορᾶς διεφθάρης;
1230 ἔξελθε, τέκνον, ἱκέσιός σε λίσσομαι."
τὸν δ᾽ ἀγρίοις ὄσσοισι παπτήνας ὁ παῖς,
πτύσας προσώπῳ κοὐδὲν ἀντειπών, ξίφους

114

approached the maiden's hollow bridal chamber of death
with its stony floor. And we heard some way off a voice of
loud wailing around the unconsecrated nuptial room, and
went to tell our master Creon. As he came nearer, the
indistinct sound of a pitiful cry floated about him, and with
a groan he uttered a lamenting word, "O my unhappy self,
am I a prophet? am I travelling on the saddest path of all
the ways I have come in the past? I recognise my son's
voice! Come, attendants, swiftly come near, stand by the
tomb, and look, entering the gap made by the tearing away
of the stones, to see whether I know the voice of Haemon,
or the gods deceive me!" At these orders from our master
in his desperation we looked upon the scene; and at the
bottom of the tomb we saw her hanging by the neck,
caught in the woven noose of a piece of linen, and him
lying near, his arms about her waist, lamenting for the ruin
of his bride in the world below and the actions of his father
and his miserable marriage. But when Creon saw him,
with a dreadful groan he came inside towards him, and
with wailing accents called on him: "Wretch, what a thing
you have done! What was in your mind? At what point
of disaster did you lose your reason? Come out, my son, I
beg you as a suppliant!" But his son glared at him with fu-
rious eyes, spat in his face, and returning no answer

---

¹²¹⁶ ἀγμὸν Ll.-J.: ἁρμὸν codd.
¹²¹⁹ post hunc versum lacunam statuit Hermann
¹²²⁵ versus forte delendus

115

SOPHOCLES

ἕλκει διπλοῦς κνώδοντας, ἐκ δ' ὁρμωμένου
πατρὸς φυγαῖσιν ἤμπλακ'· εἶθ' ὁ δύσμορος
1235 αὑτῷ χολωθείς, ὥσπερ εἶχ', ἐπενταθεὶς
ἤρεισε πλευραῖς μέσσον ἔγχος, ἐς δ' ὑγρὸν
ἀγκῶν' ἔτ' ἔμφρων παρθένῳ προσπτύσσεται,
καὶ φυσιῶν ὀξεῖαν ἐκβάλλει ῥοὴν
λευκῇ παρειᾷ φοινίου σταλάγματος.
1240 κεῖται δὲ νεκρὸς περὶ νεκρῷ, τὰ νυμφικὰ
τέλη λαχὼν δείλαιος ἔν γ' Ἅιδου δόμοις,
δείξας ἐν ἀνθρώποισι τὴν ἀβουλίαν
ὅσῳ μέγιστον ἀνδρὶ πρόσκειται κακόν.

ΧΟΡΟΣ

τί τοῦτ' ἂν εἰκάσειας; ἡ γυνὴ πάλιν
1245 φρούδη, πρὶν εἰπεῖν ἐσθλὸν ἢ κακὸν λόγον.

ΑΓΓΕΛΟΣ

καὐτὸς τεθάμβηκ'· ἐλπίσιν δὲ βόσκομαι
ἄχη τέκνου κλυοῦσαν ἐς πόλιν γόου
οὐκ ἀξιώσειν, ἀλλ' ὑπὸ στέγης ἔσω
δμωαῖς προθήσειν πένθος οἰκεῖον στένειν.
1250 γνώμης γὰρ οὐκ ἄπειρος, ὥσθ' ἁμαρτάνειν.

ΧΟΡΟΣ

οὐκ οἶδ'· ἐμοὶ δ' οὖν ἥ τ' ἄγαν σιγὴ βαρὺ
δοκεῖ προσεῖναι χἠ μάτην πολλὴ βοή.

ΑΓΓΕΛΟΣ

ἀλλ' εἰσόμεσθα, μή τι καὶ κατάσχετον
κρυφῇ καλύπτει καρδίᾳ θυμουμένῃ,
1255 δόμους παραστείχοντες· εὖ γὰρ οὖν λέγεις.

116

drew his two-edged sword. As his father darted back to
escape him, he missed him; then the unhappy man, furious
with himself, just as he was, pressed himself against the
sword and drove it, half its length, into his side. Still living,
he clasped the maiden in the bend of his feeble arm, and
pouring forth a sharp jet of blood, he stained her white
cheek. He lay, a corpse holding a corpse, having achieved
his marriage rites, poor fellow, in the house of Hades, hav-
ing shown by how much the worst evil among mortals is
bad counsel.

Exit EURYDICE.

CHORUS
What do you make of this? The lady has departed, before
uttering a good or a bad word.

MESSENGER
I too am afraid; but I am sustained by hope that after hear-
ing of the sorrows of her son she will not demand a lamen-
tation in the city, but will order her servants to mourn a
private sorrow in the house, indoors; for she is free from
the inexperience in judgment that might lead to error.

CHORUS
I do not know; but to me both excessive silence and loud
crying to no end seem grievous.

MESSENGER
Well, we shall know, whether indeed she is not hiding
some secret purpose in her impassioned heart, by entering

1241 ἔν γ᾽ Heath: εἰν Kat: ἐν cett.
1247 γόου Pearson: γόους codd.

καὶ τῆς ἄγαν γάρ ἐστί που σιγῆς βάρος.

ΧΟΡΟΣ

καὶ μὴν ὅδ᾽ ἄναξ αὐτὸς ἐφήκει
μνῆμ᾽ ἐπίσημον διὰ χειρὸς ἔχων,
εἰ θέμις εἰπεῖν, οὐκ ἀλλοτρίαν
1260 ἄτην, ἀλλ᾽ αὐτὸς ἁμαρτών.

ΚΡΕΩΝ

ἰὼ   στρ. α´
φρενῶν δυσφρόνων ἁμαρτήματα
στερεὰ θανατόεντ᾽,
ὦ κτανόντας τε καὶ
θανόντας βλέποντες ἐμφυλίους.
1265 ὤμοι ἐμῶν ἄνολβα βουλευμάτων.
ἰὼ παῖ, νέος νέῳ ξὺν μόρῳ,
αἰαῖ αἰαῖ,
ἔθανες, ἀπελύθης,
ἐμαῖς οὐδὲ σαῖσι δυσβουλίαις.

ΧΟΡΟΣ

1270 οἴμ᾽ ὡς ἔοικας ὀψὲ τὴν δίκην ἰδεῖν.

ΚΡΕΩΝ

οἴμοι,
ἔχω μαθὼν δείλαιος· ἐν δ᾽ ἐμῷ κάρᾳ
θεὸς τότ᾽ ἄρα τότε με μέγα βάρος ἔχων
ἔπαισεν, ἐν δ᾽ ἔσεισεν ἀγρίαις ὁδοῖς,
1275 οἴμοι λακπάτητον ἀντρέπων χαράν.
φεῦ φεῦ, ἰὼ πόνοι βροτῶν δύσπονοι.

the house. Yes, you are right; excessive silence also has its dangers.

Exit MESSENGER, and from the side enter CREON, carrying the body of HAEMON.

CHORUS

Here comes the king himself, bearing in his arms an all too clear reminder; if we may say so, his ruin came not from others, but from his own error.

CREON

Woe for the errors of my mistaken mind, obstinate and fraught with death! You look on kindred that have done and suffered murder! Alas for the disaster caused by my decisions! Ah, my son, young and newly dead, alas, alas, you died, you were cut off, through my folly, not through your own!

CHORUS

Alas, you seem to have seen justice only late!

CREON

Alas, I have learned, unhappy as I am; then it was, then, that a god bearing a great weight struck my head, and hurled me into ways of cruelty, overthrowing my joy so that it was trodden under foot! Ah, ah, woe for the sad troubles of men!

1273 με huc traiecit Meineke: post βάρος praebent codd.
1275 λακπάτητον] λεωπάτητον a

119

ΑΓΓΕΛΟΣ

ὦ δέσποθ', ὡς ἔχων τε καὶ κεκτημένος,
τὰ μὲν πρὸ χειρῶν τάδε φέρεις, τὰ δ' ἐν δόμοις
1280 ἔοικας ἥκειν καὶ τάχ' ὄψεσθαι κακά.

ΚΡΕΩΝ

τί δ' ἔστιν αὖ κάκιον ἐκ κακῶν ἔτι;

ΑΓΓΕΛΟΣ

γυνὴ τέθνηκε, τοῦδε παμμήτωρ νεκροῦ,
δύστηνος, ἄρτι νεοτόμοισι πλήγμασιν.

ΚΡΕΩΝ

ἰώ,   ἀντ. α΄
ἰὼ δυσκάθαρτος Ἅιδου λιμήν,
1285 τί μ' ἄρα τί μ' ὀλέκεις;
ὦ κακάγγελτά μοι
προπέμψας ἄχη, τίνα θροεῖς λόγον;
αἰαῖ, ὀλωλότ' ἄνδρ' ἐπεξειργάσω.
τί φής, παῖ, τί δ' αὖ λέγεις μοι νέον,
1290 αἰαῖ αἰαῖ,
σφάγιον ἐπ' ὀλέθρῳ,
γυναικεῖον ἀμφικεῖσθαι μόρον;

ΧΟΡΟΣ

ὁρᾶν πάρεστιν· οὐ γὰρ ἐν μυχοῖς ἔτι.

ΚΡΕΩΝ

οἴμοι,
1295 κακὸν τόδ' ἄλλο δεύτερον βλέπω τάλας.
τίς ἄρα, τίς με πότμος ἔτι περιμένει;

ANTIGONE

Enter MESSENGER.

MESSENGER

My lord, you carry this sorrow in your arms with full rights of ownership, and it seems that soon you will enter and see other sorrows in the house.

CREON

What is there that is yet more evil, coming after evils?

MESSENGER

Your wife is dead, own mother of this dead man, unhappy one, through wounds newly inflicted!

CREON

Woe, woe, all-receiving Hades, never to be appeased, why, why do you destroy me? You who convey to me the evil news of sorrow, what story do you tell? Alas, you have killed a dead man a second time! What are you saying, boy? What new message of my wife's death, alas, alas, lies upon me, bringing destruction after death?

CHORUS

You can see it! It is no longer hidden indoors.

CREON

Alas, I see this second disaster, miserable one! What fate, what fate still awaits me? I held only now my son in my

---

¹²⁷⁸ ἐξάγγελος t: ἄγγελος Zo: οἰκέτης fere codd.

¹²⁷⁹ φέρεις Brunck: φέρων codd.

¹²⁸¹ ἐκ Canter: ἢ codd.

¹²⁸⁹ τί δ' αὖ Ll.-J.: τίνα codd.

ἔχω μὲν ἐν χείρεσσιν ἀρτίως τέκνον,
τάλας, τὰν δ' ἔναντα προσβλέπω νεκρόν.
1300 φεῦ φεῦ μᾶτερ ἀθλία, φεῦ τέκνον.

ΑΓΓΕΛΟΣ

†ἥ δ' ὀξύθηκτος ἥδε βωμία πέριξ†

    ❊   ❊   ❊   ❊   ❊

λύει κελαινὰ βλέφαρα, κωκύσασα μὲν
τοῦ πρὶν θανόντος Μεγαρέως κενὸν λέχος,
αὖθις δὲ τοῦδε, λοίσθιον δὲ σοὶ κακὰς
1305 πράξεις ἐφυμνήσασα τῷ παιδοκτόνῳ.

ΚΡΕΩΝ

αἰαῖ αἰαῖ,   στρ. β′
ἀνέπταν φόβῳ. τί μ' οὐκ ἀνταίαν
ἔπαισέν τις ἀμφιθήκτῳ ξίφει;
1310 δείλαιος ἐγώ, αἰαῖ,
δειλαίᾳ δὲ συγκέκραμαι δύᾳ.

ΑΓΓΕΛΟΣ

ὡς αἰτίαν γε τῶνδε κἀκείνων ἔχων
πρὸς τῆς θανούσης τῆσδ' ἐπεσκήπτου μόρων.

ΚΡΕΩΝ

ποίῳ δὲ κἀπελύετ' ἐν φοναῖς τρόπῳ;

ΑΓΓΕΛΟΣ

1315 παίσασ' ὑφ' ἧπαρ αὐτόχειρ αὑτήν, ὅπως
παιδὸς τόδ' ᾔσθετ' ὀξυκώκυτον πάθος.

arms, ah misery, and now I see her, a corpse, before me.
Ah, ah, unhappy mother, ah, my son!

MESSENGER

Pierced by the sharp sword . . . near the altar, she . . . closed
her darkening eyes, after she had lamented the empty mar-
riage bed of Megareus, who died earlier, and had called
down curses upon you, the killer of your son.

CREON

Alas, alas! My mind leaps up with fear! Why has no one
struck me to the heart with a two-edged sword? Miserable
am I, alas, and miserable the woe with which I am com-
pounded!

MESSENGER

You were reproached by the dead as guilty of those deaths
and these.

CREON

But in what fashion did she meet her bloody end?

MESSENGER

With her own hand she struck herself beneath the liver, so
that she experienced the suffering of her son, loudly to be
lamented.

1298 τὰν δ' Postgate: τήνδ' R: τάδ' L: τόνδ' a
1301 ὀξυθήκτῳ βωμία περὶ ξίφει Arndt   lacunam post
hunc versum statuit Brunck
1303 κενὸν Seyffert: κλεινὸν codd.   λέχος] λάχος Bothe
1310 αἰαῖ Erfurdt: φεῦ φεῦ codd.
1313 μόρων KSt: μόρῳ cett.
1314 κἀπελύετ' Pearson: κἀπελύσατ' codd.

ΚΡΕΩΝ

ὤμοι μοι, τάδ᾽ οὐκ ἐπ᾽ ἄλλον βροτῶν
ἐμᾶς ἁρμόσει ποτ᾽ ἐξ αἰτίας.
ἐγὼ γάρ σ᾽, ἐγώ σ᾽ ἔκανον, ὦ μέλεος,
1320   ἐγώ, φάμ᾽ ἔτυμον. ἰὼ πρόσπολοι,
ἄγετέ μ᾽ ὅτι τάχιστ᾽, ἄγετέ μ᾽ ἐκποδών,
1325   τὸν οὐκ ὄντα μᾶλλον ἢ μηδένα.

ΧΟΡΟΣ

κέρδη παραινεῖς, εἴ τι κέρδος ἐν κακοῖς·
βράχιστα γὰρ κράτιστα τὰν ποσὶν κακά.

ΚΡΕΩΝ

ἴτω ἴτω,   ἀντ. β΄
φανήτω μόρων ὁ κάλλιστ᾽ ἔχων
1330   ἐμοὶ τερμίαν ἄγων ἁμέραν
ὕπατος· ἴτω ἴτω,
ὅπως μηκέτ᾽ ἆμαρ ἄλλ᾽ εἰσίδω.

ΧΟΡΟΣ

μέλλοντα ταῦτα. τῶν προκειμένων τι χρὴ
1335   πράσσειν. μέλει γὰρ τῶνδ᾽ ὅτοισι χρὴ μέλειν.

ΚΡΕΩΝ

ἀλλ᾽ ὧν ἐρῶ μέν, ταῦτα συγκατηυξάμην.

ΧΟΡΟΣ

μή νυν προσεύχου μηδέν· ὡς πεπρωμένης
οὐκ ἔστι θνητοῖς συμφορᾶς ἀπαλλαγή.

1322 τάχιστ᾽ Erfurdt: τάχος codd.
1329 ἔχων Pallis: ἐμῶν codd.

124

ANTIGONE

CREON

Ah me, this can never be transferred to any other mortal, acquitting me! For it was I that killed you, unhappy one, I, I speak the truth! Ah! attendants, lead me off at once, lead me out of the way, me who am no more than nothing!

CHORUS

Your counsel is good, if there is any good among troubles; for when one is face to face with troubles, quickest is best!

CREON

Let it come, let it come! May it appear, the best of deaths for me, bringing my final day, the best fate of all! Let it come, let it come, so that I may never look upon another day!

CHORUS

That lies in the future; but we must attend to present tasks; the future is a care to those responsible.

CREON

What I desire I have already prayed for.

CHORUS

Utter no prayers now! There is no escape from calamity for mortals.

ΚΡΕΩΝ

ἄγοιτ' ἂν μάταιον ἄνδρ' ἐκποδών,
1340 ὅς, ὦ παῖ, σέ τ' οὐχ ἑκὼν κατέκανον
σέ τ' αὖ τάνδ', ὤμοι μέλεος, οὐδ' ἔχω
πρὸς πότερον ἴδω, πᾷ κλιθῶ· πάντα γὰρ
1345 λέχρια τὰν χεροῖν, τὰ δ' ἐπὶ κρατί μοι
πότμος δυσκόμιστος εἰσήλατο.

ΧΟΡΟΣ

πολλῷ τὸ φρονεῖν εὐδαιμονίας
πρῶτον ὑπάρχει· χρὴ δὲ τά γ' ἐς θεοὺς
1350 μηδὲν ἀσεπτεῖν· μεγάλοι δὲ λόγοι
μεγάλας πληγὰς τῶν ὑπεραύχων
ἀποτείσαντες
γήρᾳ τὸ φρονεῖν ἐδίδαξαν.

1340 κατέκανον W. Schneider: κατέκτανον codd.
1341 σέ Hermann: ὅς σέ codd.   αὖ τάνδ' Seidler: αὐτάν codd.
1343 πρὸς Seidler: ὅπᾳ πρὸς codd.
1344 κλιθῶ Musgrave: καὶ θῶ codd.
1345 τὰν Brunck: τάδ' ἐν codd.

CREON

Lead me out of the way, useless man that I am, who killed you, my son, not by my own will, and you here too, ah, miserable one; I do not know which to look on, which way to lean; for all that is in my hands has gone awry, and fate hard to deal with has leapt upon my head.

Exeunt CREON *and his attendants.*

CHORUS

Good sense is by far the chief part of happiness; and we must not be impious towards the gods. The great words of boasters are always punished with great blows, and as they grow old teach them wisdom.

THE WOMEN OF TRACHIS

ΤΑ ΤΟΥ ΔΡΑΜΑΤΟΣ ΠΡΟΣΩΠΑ

Δηάνειρα
Δούλη τροφός
Ὕλλος
Χορὸς γυναικῶν Τραχινίων
Ἄγγελος
Λίχας
Πρέσβυς
Ἡρακλῆς

Deianeira
Nurse
Hyllus
Chorus of Women of Trachis
Messenger
Lichas
Doctor
Heracles

Scene: In front of the house in Trachis where Heracles is living as the guest of Ceyx.

ΤΡΑΧΙΝΙΑΙ

ΔΗΙΑΝΕΙΡΑ

Λόγος μὲν ἔστ' ἀρχαῖος ἀνθρώπων φανεὶς
ὡς οὐκ ἂν αἰῶν' ἐκμάθοις βροτῶν, πρὶν ἂν
θάνῃ τις, οὔτ' εἰ χρηστὸς οὔτ' εἴ τῳ κακός·
ἐγὼ δὲ τὸν ἐμόν, καὶ πρὶν εἰς Ἅιδου μολεῖν,
5 ἔξοιδ' ἔχουσα δυστυχῆ τε καὶ βαρύν,
ἥτις πατρὸς μὲν ἐν δόμοισιν Οἰνέως
ναίουσ' ἔτ' ἐν Πλευρῶνι νυμφείων ὄτλον
ἄλγιστον ἔσχον, εἴ τις Αἰτωλὶς γυνή.
μνηστὴρ γὰρ ἦν μοι ποταμός, Ἀχελῷον λέγω,
10 ὅς μ' ἐν τρισὶν μορφαῖσιν ἐξῄτει πατρός,
φοιτῶν ἐναργὴς ταῦρος, ἄλλοτ' αἰόλος
δράκων ἑλικτός, ἄλλοτ' ἀνδρείῳ κύτει
βούπρῳρος· ἐκ δὲ δασκίου γενειάδος
κρουνοὶ διερραίνοντο κρηναίου ποτοῦ.
15 τοιόνδ' ἐγὼ μνηστῆρα προσδεδεγμένη
δύστηνος ἀεὶ κατθανεῖν ἐπηυχόμην,
πρὶν τῆσδε κοίτης ἐμπελασθῆναί ποτε.
   χρόνῳ δ' ἐν ὑστέρῳ μέν, ἀσμένῃ δέ μοι,

THE WOMEN OF TRACHIS

The stage building represents the house at Trachis where
Heracles has been living in exile. Enter DEIANEIRA, *fol-*
lowed by the NURSE.

DEIANEIRA

There is an ancient saying among men, once revealed to
them, that you cannot understand a man's life before he is
dead, so as to know whether he has a good or bad one. But
I know well, even before going to Hades, that the one I
have is unfortunate and sorrowful. While I still lived in the
house of my father Oeneus, in Pleuron, I suffered painful
affliction in the matter of my wedding, if any Aetolian
woman did. For I had as a wooer a river, I mean Achelous,
who came in three shapes to ask my father for me, at some
times manifest as a bull, at others as a darting, coiling ser-
pent, and again at others with a man's trunk and a bull's
head; and from his shaggy beard there poured streams of
water from his springs. Expecting such a suitor as that I
was always praying, poor creature, that I might die before
ever coming near his bed. But at the last moment, and to

---

[7] ἔτ᾽ ἐν Vitus Winshemius: ἐν L: ἐνὶ VRa   ὅτλον Lγρ:
ὄκνον fere cett.

[12–13] κύτει βούπρῳρος Strabo 10,458: τύπῳ βούκρανος codd.

[17] τῆσδε] τοῦδε Wunder

ὁ κλεινὸς ἦλθε Ζηνὸς ᾽Αλκμήνης τε παῖς·
20 ὃς εἰς ἀγῶνα τῷδε συμπεσὼν μάχης
ἐκλύεταί με. καὶ τρόπον μὲν ἂν πόνων
οὐκ ἂν διείποιμ᾽· οὐ γὰρ οἶδ᾽· ἀλλ᾽ ὅστις ἦν
θακῶν ἀταρβὴς τῆς θέας, ὅδ᾽ ἂν λέγοι.
ἐγὼ γὰρ ἥμην ἐκπεπληγμένη φόβῳ
25 μή μοι τὸ κάλλος ἄλγος ἐξεύροι ποτέ.
τέλος δ᾽ ἔθηκε Ζεὺς ἀγώνιος καλῶς,
εἰ δὴ καλῶς. λέχος γὰρ Ἡρακλεῖ κριτὸν
ξυστᾶσ᾽ ἀεί τιν᾽ ἐκ φόβου φόβον τρέφω,
κείνου προκηραίνουσα. νὺξ γὰρ εἰσάγει
30 καὶ νὺξ ἀπωθεῖ διαδεδεγμένη πόνον.
κἀφύσαμεν δὴ παῖδας, οὓς κεῖνός ποτε,
γῄτης ὅπως ἄρουραν ἔκτοπον λαβών,
σπείρων μόνον προσεῖδε κἀξαμῶν ἅπαξ·
τοιοῦτος αἰὼν εἰς δόμους τε κἀκ δόμων
35 ἀεὶ τὸν ἄνδρ᾽ ἔπεμπε λατρεύοντά τῳ.
    νῦν δ᾽ ἡνίκ᾽ ἄθλων τῶνδ᾽ ὑπερτελὴς ἔφυ,
ἐνταῦθα δὴ μάλιστα ταρβήσασ᾽ ἔχω.
ἐξ οὗ γὰρ ἔκτα κεῖνος Ἰφίτου βίαν,
ἡμεῖς μὲν ἐν Τραχῖνι τῇδ᾽ ἀνάστατοι
40 ξένῳ παρ᾽ ἀνδρὶ ναίομεν, κεῖνος δ᾽ ὅπου
βέβηκεν οὐδεὶς οἶδε· πλὴν ἐμοὶ πικρὰς
ὠδῖνας αὐτοῦ προσβαλὼν ἀποίχεται.
σχεδὸν δ᾽ ἐπίσταμαί τι πῆμ᾽ ἔχοντά νιν·
χρόνον γὰρ οὐχὶ βαιόν, ἀλλ᾽ ἤδη δέκα
45 μῆνας πρὸς ἄλλοις πέντ᾽ ἀκήρυκτος μένει.

my relief, there came the famous son of Zeus and
Alcmene, who contended with him in battle and released
me. I cannot tell of the manner of his struggle, for I know
nothing of it; whoever was sitting there not terrified by the
sight, he could tell you. For I was sitting there struck
numb with fear that my beauty might end by bringing me
pain. But in the end Zeus the god of contests decided well,
if it was well; for I clove to Heracles as the bride he had
won, and always nourish one fear after another, in my anx-
iety for him; night brings trouble, and the succeeding night
pushes it away. We had, indeed, children, whom he, like a
farmer who has taken over a remote piece of ploughland,
regards only when he sows and when he reaps. Such is the
life that was always sending my husband home or away
from home in servitude to a certain man.[a]

But now that he has surmounted those ordeals has
come the moment of my greatest fear. For since he killed
the mighty Iphitus we have been uprooted and have lived
here in Trachis with a foreign friend, but where *he* is no
one knows; except that when he went away he afflicted me
with sharp pains here. And I am almost sure that he is
suffering from some trouble, for we have had no news of
him for no small lapse of time, but for fifteen months now.

[a] Deianeira does not deign to mention the name of the hated
enemy Eurystheus, king of Mycenae and Heracles' cousin, under
whose orders Heracles performed his labours.

20–21 μάχης et πόνων permutavit Herwerden
42 αὐτοῦ] αὑτοῦ Hermann
43–48 del. Reeve (43 iam Dindorf, 44–48 Wunder)

κἄστιν τι δεινὸν πῆμα· τοιαύτην ἐμοὶ
δέλτον λιπὼν ἔστειχε· τὴν ἐγὼ θαμὰ
θεοῖς ἀρῶμαι πημονῆς ἄτερ λαβεῖν.

ΤΡΟΦΟΣ

δέσποινα Δηάνειρα, πολλὰ μέν σ' ἐγὼ
50   κατεῖδον ἤδη πανδάκρυτ' ὀδύρματα
τὴν Ἡράκλειον ἔξοδον γοωμένην·
νῦν δ', εἰ δίκαιον τοὺς ἐλευθέρους φρενοῦν
γνώμαισι δούλαις, κἀμὲ χρὴ φράσαι τὸ σόν·
πῶς παισὶ μὲν τοσοῖσδε πληθύεις, ἀτὰρ
55   ἀνδρὸς κατὰ ζήτησιν οὐ πέμπεις τινά,
μάλιστα δ' ὅνπερ εἰκὸς Ὕλλον, εἰ πατρὸς
νέμοι τιν' ὥραν τοῦ καλῶς πράσσειν δοκεῖν;
ἐγγὺς δ' ὅδ' αὐτὸς ἀρτίπους θρῴσκει δόμοις,
ὥστ' εἴ τί σοι πρὸς καιρὸν ἐννέπειν δοκῶ,
60   πάρεστι χρῆσθαι τἀνδρὶ τοῖς τ' ἐμοῖς λόγοις.

ΔΗΙΑΝΕΙΡΑ

ὦ τέκνον, ὦ παῖ, κἀξ ἀγεννήτων ἄρα
μῦθοι καλῶς πίπτουσιν· ἥδε γὰρ γυνὴ
δούλη μέν, εἴρηκεν δ' ἐλεύθερον λόγον.

ΥΛΛΟΣ

ποῖον; δίδαξον, μῆτερ, εἰ διδακτά μοι.

ΔΗΙΑΝΕΙΡΑ

65   σὲ πατρὸς οὕτω δαρὸν ἐξενωμένου
τὸ μὴ πυθέσθαι ποῦ 'στιν αἰσχύνην φέρειν.

---

⁵³ τὸ σόν LR: τόσον at
⁵⁵ ἀνδρὸς] τἀνδρὸς Wecklein

And it is some grave trouble; such is the tablet that he left for me when he went; often I pray to the gods that my receiving it did not mean disaster.

NURSE

Deianeira, my mistress, often in the past I have seen you bewail the absence of Heracles with tearful lamentations. But now, if it is right for slaves to instruct free persons with their opinions, I must indicate what you should do. How comes it that you have so many sons, yet you do not send any of them to search for their father, and above all Hyllus, whom it would be natural to send, if he cares at all that we should think his father prospers. And he is here near the house, speeding with nimble feet, so that if you think my speech hits the mark, you can make use of the man and of my words.

Enter HYLLUS.

DEIANEIRA

My child, my son, so even words from those of lowly birth can fall out well; this woman is a slave, but the word she has spoken is that of a free person.

HYLLUS

What word? Explain it to me, mother, if you can!

DEIANEIRA

She says that when your father has been absent for so long it is shameful that you do not inquire as to his whereabouts.

---

57 ὥραν L: ὤραν cett.   καλῶς] κακῶς Roscher
58 fort. interpungendum post αὐτὸς   δόμοις Wakefield: -ους codd.
66 φέρειν Valckenaer: -ει codd.

137

ΥΛΛΟΣ

ἀλλ' οἶδα, μύθοις γ' εἴ τι πιστεύειν χρεών.

ΔΗΙΑΝΕΙΡΑ

καὶ ποῦ κλύεις νιν, τέκνον, ἱδρῦσθαι χθονός;

ΥΛΛΟΣ

τὸν μὲν παρελθόντ' ἄροτον ἐν μήκει χρόνου
70 Λυδῇ γυναικί φασί νιν λάτριν πονεῖν.

ΔΗΙΑΝΕΙΡΑ

πᾶν τοίνυν, εἰ καὶ τοῦτ' ἔτλη, κλύοι τις ἄν.

ΥΛΛΟΣ

ἀλλ' ἐξαφεῖται τοῦδέ γ', ὡς ἐγὼ κλύω.

ΔΗΙΑΝΕΙΡΑ

ποῦ δῆτα νῦν ζῶν ἢ θανὼν ἀγγέλλεται;

ΥΛΛΟΣ

Εὔβοιδα χώραν φασίν, Εὐρύτου πόλιν,
75 ἐπιστρατεύειν αὐτόν, ἢ μέλλειν ἔτι.

ΔΗΙΑΝΕΙΡΑ

ἆρ' οἶσθα δῆτ', ὦ τέκνον, ὡς ἔλειπέ μοι
μαντεῖα πιστὰ τῆσδε τῆς χρείας πέρι;

ΥΛΛΟΣ

τὰ ποῖα, μῆτερ; τὸν λόγον γὰρ ἀγνοῶ.

ΔΗΙΑΝΕΙΡΑ

ὡς ἢ τελευτὴν τοῦ βίου μέλλει τελεῖν,
80 ἢ τοῦτον ἄρας ἆθλον εἰς τό γ' ὕστερον
τὸν λοιπὸν ἤδη βίοτον εὐαίων' ἔχειν.
ἐν οὖν ῥοπῇ τοιᾷδε κειμένῳ, τέκνον,

HYLLUS
Why, I know, if we can believe what people say!

DEIANEIRA
And where in the world do they say he is situated, my son?

HYLLUS
As for the past year, they say that he was long a slave to a
Lydian woman.

DEIANEIRA
Then one might hear anything, if he put up even with that!

HYLLUS
But he is released from that condition, as I hear.

DEIANEIRA
Then where is he reported to be, alive or dead?

HYLLUS
They say he is marching against a place in Euboea, the city
of Eurytus, or is about to do so.

DEIANEIRA
Do you know, my son, that he left me prophecies we can
trust regarding this hour of need?

HYLLUS
What prophecies, mother? I do not know the story.

DEIANEIRA
That either he is about to come to the end of his life, or he
will accomplish this ordeal and for the future live from now
on happily. So since he stands at such a crisis, my son, will

---

^{77} χρείας Hense: χώρας codd.
^{80} τό γ᾽ Reiske: τὸν codd.
^{81} τὸν] τὸ Rz

οὐκ εἶ ξυνέρξων, ἡνίκ᾽ ἢ σεσώμεθα
[ἢ πίπτομεν σοῦ πατρὸς ἐξολωλότος]
85 κείνου βίον σώσαντος, ἢ οἰχόμεσθ᾽ ἅμα;

ΥΛΛΟΣ

ἀλλ᾽ εἶμι, μῆτερ· εἰ δὲ θεσφάτων ἐγὼ
βάξιν κατῄδη τῶνδε, κἂν πάλαι παρῆ.
ἀλλ᾽ ὁ ξυνήθης πότμος οὐκ εἴα πατρὸς
ἡμᾶς προταρβεῖν οὐδὲ δειμαίνειν ἄγαν.
90 νῦν δ᾽ ὡς ξυνίημ᾽, οὐδὲν ἐλλείψω τὸ μὴ
πᾶσαν πυθέσθαι τῶνδ᾽ ἀλήθειαν πέρι.

ΔΗΙΑΝΕΙΡΑ

χώρει νυν, ὦ παῖ· καὶ γὰρ ὑστέρῳ, τό γ᾽ εὖ
πράσσειν ἐπεὶ πύθοιτο, κέρδος ἐμπολᾷ.

ΧΟΡΟΣ

ὃν αἰόλα νὺξ ἐναριζομένα   στρ. α'
95 τίκτει κατευνάζει τε φλογιζόμενον,
"Αλιον "Αλιον αἰτῶ
τοῦτο, καρῦξαι τὸν Ἀλκμή-
νας· πόθι μοι πόθι μοι
ναίει ποτ᾽, ὦ λαμπρᾷ στεροπᾷ φλεγέθων;
100 ἢ Ποντίας αὐλῶνας, ἢ
δισσαῖσιν ἀπείροις κλιθείς;
εἴπ᾽, ὦ κρατιστεύων κατ᾽ ὄμμα.

---

84 del. Bentley
85 del. Vauvilliers
88–89 del. Hermann, post 91 traiecit Brunck
88 ἀλλ᾽ Brunck: νῦν δ᾽ codd.: πρὶν δ᾽ Wakefield   εἴα Vauvilliers: ἐᾷ codd.

you not go and help him, since either we are saved if he has
saved his life or we are gone with him?

Why, I will go, mother! If I had known the import of these
prophecies, I would have been there long since. But his
accustomed fate did not allow us to fear for my father or to
be too much alarmed. But now that I understand, I will
leave nothing undone to learn the whole truth about these
matters.

Then go, my son! Even if one is late, one is better off for
learning of a success.

Exeunt HYLLUS *and* NURSE. *Enter the* CHORUS *of
women of Trachis.*

You whom spangled Night brings forth as she is
slaughtered and whom she lulls to sleep as you blaze with
fire, Sun, Sun, I beg this of you, that you proclaim a search
for the son of Alcmene! Where, where does he abide, you
who glow with brilliant light? In the channels of the Black
Sea? Or leaning against the two continents?[a] Tell me, you
who are supreme in the kingdom of the eye!

---

  [a] "The channels of the Black Sea" means the Bosporus, the Pro-
pontis, and the Hellespont. The Greeks called the Straits of
Gibraltar the Pillars of Heracles, so that Sophocles could imagine
Heracles as leaning on two pillars, one in Europe and one in Africa.

  90–91 del. Dindorf
  98 post alterum μοι codd. habent παῖς, del. Wunder
  100 Ποντίας Ll.-J.: ποντίας L: -ίους vel -ίας cett.

ποθουμένᾳ γὰρ φρενὶ πυνθάνομαι   ἀντ. α'
τὰν ἀμφινεικῆ Δηιάνειραν ἀεί,
105 οἷά τιν' ἄθλιον ὄρνιν,
οὔποτ' εὐνάζειν ἀδάκρυ-
τον βλεφάρων πόθον, ἀλλ'
εὔμναστον ἀνδρὸς δεῖμα τρέφουσαν ὁδοῦ
ἐνθυμίοις εὐναῖς ἀναν-
110 δρώτοισι τρύχεσθαι, κακὰν
δύστανον ἐλπίζουσαν αἶσαν.
πολλὰ γὰρ ὥστ' ἀκάμαντος   στρ. β'
ἢ νότου ἢ βορέα τις
κύματ' <ἂν> εὑρέι πόντῳ
115 βάντ' ἐπιόντα τ' ἴδοι,
οὕτω δὲ τὸν Καδμογενῆ
τρέφει, τὸ δ' αὔξει βιότου
πολύπονον ὥσπερ πέλαγος
Κρήσιον· ἀλλά τις θεῶν
120 αἰὲν ἀναμπλάκητον Ἄι-
δα σφε δόμων ἐρύκει.
ὧν ἐπιμεμφομένας ἁ-   ἀντ. β'
δεῖα μέν, ἀντία δ' οἴσω.
φαμὶ γὰρ οὐκ ἀποτρύειν
125 ἐλπίδα τὰν ἀγαθὰν
χρῆναί σ'· ἀνάλγητα γὰρ οὐδ'
ὁ πάντα κραίνων βασιλεὺς
ἐπέβαλε θνατοῖς Κρονίδας·
ἀλλ' ἐπὶ πῆμα καὶ χαρὰν

142

For I learn that with an ever yearning heart Deianeira, she who was fought over, like some sorrowful bird can never lull to sleep without tears the longing of her eyes, but, nourishing a fear that keeps in mind the absence of her husband, she is worn away on her anxious couch bereft of him, fearing, poor woman, a miserable fate.

For just as one may see many waves coming, stirred up by the unwearying south wind or the north wind, and many following in the broad sea, so does a Cretan sea of life that is full of troubles sustain the man born in Thebes and make him great; but some one of the gods always keeps him free of error and far from the halls of Hades.

When you complain of this fortune, I feel with you, but I shall oppose you; for I say that you should not wear away all hopefulness. Not even the son of Cronos, who ordains all things, has given mortals a fate free from pain; but as it

---

106 ἀδάκρυτον Dawe: ἀδακρύτων codd.

108 τρέφουσαν Casaubon: φέρουσαν codd.

114 <ἂν> Wakefield: <ἐν> Erfurdt

117 τρέφει] στρέφει Reiske

129 χαρὰν K: χαρὰ vel χαρᾷ cett.

130　πᾶσι κυκλοῦσιν οἷον ἄρ-
　　κτου στροφάδες κέλευθοι.
　　μένει γὰρ οὔτ' αἰόλα　　　　　　　ἐπ.
　　νὺξ βροτοῖσιν οὔτε κῆ-
　　ρες οὔτε πλοῦτος, ἀλλ' ἄφαρ
　　βέβακε, τῷ δ' ἐπέρχεται
135　χαίρειν τε καὶ στέρεσθαι.
　　ἃ καὶ σὲ τὰν ἄνασσαν ἐλπίσιν λέγω
　　τάδ' αἰὲν ἴσχειν· ἐπεὶ τίς ὧδε
140　τέκνοισι Ζῆν' ἄβουλον εἶδεν;

ΔΗΙΑΝΕΙΡΑ

　　πεπυσμένη μέν, ὡς ἀπεικάσαι, πάρει
　　πάθημα τοὐμόν· ὡς δ' ἐγὼ θυμοφθορῶ
　　μήτ' ἐκμάθοις παθοῦσα, νῦν δ' ἄπειρος εἶ.
　　τὸ γὰρ νεάζον ἐν τοιοῖσδε βόσκεται
145　χώροισιν αὑτοῦ, καί νιν οὐ θάλπος θεοῦ,
　　οὐδ' ὄμβρος, οὐδὲ πνευμάτων οὐδὲν κλονεῖ,
　　ἀλλ' ἡδοναῖς ἄμοχθον ἐξαίρει βίον
　　ἐς τοῦθ', ἕως τις ἀντὶ παρθένου γυνὴ
　　κληθῇ, λάβῃ τ' ἐν νυκτὶ φροντίδων μέρος,
150　ἤτοι πρὸς ἀνδρὸς ἢ τέκνων φοβουμένη.
　　τότ' ἄν τις εἰσίδοιτο, τὴν αὑτοῦ σκοπῶν
　　πρᾶξιν, κακοῖσιν οἷς ἐγὼ βαρύνομαι.
　　　πάθη μὲν οὖν δὴ πόλλ' ἔγωγ' ἐκλαυσάμην·
　　ἓν δ', οἷον οὔπω πρόσθεν, αὐτίκ' ἐξερῶ.
155　ὁδὸν γὰρ ἦμος τὴν τελευταίαν ἄναξ
　　ὡρμᾶτ' ἀπ' οἴκων Ἡρακλῆς, τότ' ἐν δόμοις
　　λείπει παλαιὰν δέλτον ἐγγεγραμμένην

144

were the revolving paths of the Bear[a] bring to all suffering and joy in turn.

For neither spangled Night nor spirits of death nor riches abide for mortals, but joy or loss at once is gone, and then comes back. Wherefore I tell you, the queen, always to hold to this in hope; for who has seen Zeus so lacking in counsel for his children?

DEIANEIRA

You are here, it seems, in the knowledge that I suffer; but may you never learn to know through suffering such agony of heart as mine, of which you now have no experience. For such are the places of its own where youth is nourished, and it is afflicted neither by the sun god's heat, nor by rain, nor any winds, but uplifts its life in pleasures, untroubled, till the time when one is called a woman rather than a maiden, and gets during the night one's share of worries, fearing for one's husband or one's children. Then one could see, looking at his own condition, what evils I am burdened with.

So the sufferings I have wept over are many; but there is one which I have never known before of which I shall now tell you. When lord Heracles was starting from home on his last expedition, he left in the house an ancient tablet

[a] Cf. *Iliad* 18, 487 f: "The Great Bear ... wheels round in the same place."

ξυνθήμαθ᾽, ἁμοὶ πρόσθεν οὐκ ἔτλη ποτέ,
πολλοὺς ἀγῶνας ἐξιών, οὕτω φράσαι,
160 ἀλλ᾽ ὥς τι δράσων εἷρπε κοὐ θανούμενος.
νῦν δ᾽ ὡς ἔτ᾽ οὐκ ὢν εἶπε μὲν λέχους ὅ τι
χρείη μ᾽ ἑλέσθαι κτῆσιν, εἶπε δ᾽ ἣν τέκνοις
μοῖραν πατρῴας γῆς διαίρετον νέμοι,
χρόνον προτάξας ὡς τρίμηνος ἡνίκ᾽ ἂν
165 χώρας ἀπείη κἀνιαύσιος βεβώς,
τότ᾽ ἢ θανεῖν χρείη σφε τῷδε τῷ χρόνῳ,
ἢ τοῦθ᾽ ὑπεκδραμόντα τοῦ χρόνου τέλος
τὸ λοιπὸν ἤδη ζῆν ἀλυπήτῳ βίῳ.
τοιαῦτ᾽ ἔφραζε πρὸς θεῶν εἱμαρμένα
170 τῶν Ἡρακλείων ἐκτελευτᾶσθαι πόνων,
ὡς τὴν παλαιὰν φηγὸν αὐδῆσαί ποτε
Δωδῶνι δισσῶν ἐκ πελειάδων ἔφη.
καὶ τῶνδε ναμέρτεια συμβαίνει χρόνου
τοῦ νῦν παρόντος ὡς τελεσθῆναι χρεών·
175 ὥσθ᾽ ἡδέως εὕδουσαν ἐκπηδᾶν ἐμὲ
φόβῳ, φίλαι, ταρβοῦσαν, εἴ με χρὴ μένειν
πάντων ἀρίστου φωτὸς ἐστερημένην.

ΧΟΡΟΣ

εὐφημίαν νῦν ἴσχ᾽· ἐπεὶ καταστεφῆ
στείχονθ᾽ ὁρῶ τιν᾽ ἄνδρα πρὸς χάριν λόγων.

---

159 οὕτω Tournier: οὔπω LRU: οὔπω cett.
164 τρίμηνος Wakefield: -ον codd.
165 κἀνιαύσιος] -ιον Brunck

146

with writing. Never in the past, though he went out to
many ordeals, had he brought himself to give me such
instructions, but he would go as though about to do some
deed and not to die. But now, as though he was no more,
he told me what I was to take as my dowry, and what share
of his ancestral land he was allotting to his children. He
fixed a time: when he had been absent for a year and three
months he was fated either to die at that moment or to sur-
vive that moment of crisis and for the future to live a life
free from pain. Such a fate appointed by the gods was to
be the end, he said, of the troubles of Heracles, as he had
heard the ancient oak at Dodona[a] say through the two
doves. And the exact moment when this should be fulfilled
falls at the time now present; so that while sleeping sweetly
I suddenly start with fear, afraid it is my fate to live on
robbed of the noblest of all men.

CHORUS

Be silent now, for I see a man wearing a garland coming to
bring us news!

Enter MESSENGER.

[a] In Epirus, the seat of an ancient oracle of Zeus, whose
priestesses were called doves.

169–70 del. Bergk
170 del. Wunder
174 ὡς] ᾧ Hense
179 χάριν KR: χαρὰν cett.

ΑΓΓΕΛΟΣ

180 δέσποινα Δηάνειρα, πρῶτος ἀγγέλων
ὄκνου σε λύσω· τὸν γὰρ Ἀλκμήνης τόκον
καὶ ζῶντ' ἐπίστω καὶ κρατοῦντα κἀκ μάχης
ἄγοντ' ἀπαρχὰς θεοῖσι τοῖς ἐγχωρίοις.

ΔΗΙΑΝΕΙΡΑ

τίν' εἶπας, ὦ γεραιέ, τόνδε μοι λόγον;

ΑΓΓΕΛΟΣ

185 τάχ' ἐς δόμους σοὺς τὸν πολύζηλον πόσιν
ἥξειν, φανέντα σὺν κράτει νικηφόρῳ.

ΔΗΙΑΝΕΙΡΑ

καὶ τοῦ τόδ' ἀστῶν ἢ ξένων μαθὼν λέγεις;

ΑΓΓΕΛΟΣ

ἐν βουθερεῖ λειμῶνι πρὸς πολλοὺς θροεῖ
Λίχας ὁ κῆρυξ ταῦτα· τοῦ δ' ἐγὼ κλυὼν
190 ἀπῇξ', ὅπως σοι πρῶτος ἀγγείλας τάδε
πρὸς σοῦ τι κερδάναιμι καὶ κτώμην χάριν.

ΔΗΙΑΝΕΙΡΑ

αὐτὸς δὲ πῶς ἄπεστιν, εἴπερ εὐτυχεῖ;

ΑΓΓΕΛΟΣ

οὐκ εὐμαρείᾳ χρώμενος πολλῇ, γύναι.
κύκλῳ γὰρ αὐτὸν Μηλιεὺς ἅπας λεὼς
195 κρίνει περιστάς, οὐδ' ἔχει βῆναι πρόσω.
†τὸ γὰρ ποθοῦν† ἕκαστος ἐκμαθεῖν θέλων

---

188 πρὸς πολλοὺς Hermann: πρόσπολος codd.
195 περιστάς Paley: παραστάς codd.

148

MESSENGER

Queen Deianeira, I before any other messenger shall set
you free from fear! Know that the son of Alcmene is alive
and victorious, and is bringing the first fruits from the bat-
tle to the gods of the land!

DEIANEIRA

What is this news that you have told me, aged man?

MESSENGER

Soon your much envied husband shall come to your home,
appearing with victorious might!

DEIANEIRA

And from which citizen or which stranger have you learned
the story that you tell me?

MESSENGER

In the meadow where the cows graze in summer the herald
Lichas is telling this story to a crowd; I heard it from him
and hurried off, so that I might be the first to report it and
so gain some reward from you and acquire your favour.

DEIANEIRA

But why is he himself not here, if indeed fortune favours
him?

MESSENGER

Things are not easy for him, lady;[a] the whole people of
Malis is standing around him and questioning him, and he
cannot take a step forward, since in his eagerness to learn

---

[a] The Messenger does not realise that Deianeira was thinking
not of Lichas but of Heracles.

<hr/>

[196] τὸ γὰρ ποθοῦν] fort. πόθῳ γὰρ εἷς

SOPHOCLES

οὐκ ἂν μεθεῖτο, πρὶν καθ' ἡδονὴν κλύειν.
οὕτως ἐκεῖνος οὐχ ἑκὼν ἑκουσίοις
ξύνεστιν· ὄψῃ δ' αὐτὸν αὐτίκ' ἐμφανῆ.

ΔΗΙΑΝΕΙΡΑ

200 ὦ Ζεῦ, τὸν Οἴτης ἄτομον ὃς λειμῶν' ἔχεις,
ἔδωκας ἡμῖν ἀλλὰ σὺν χρόνῳ χαράν.
φωνήσατ', ὦ γυναῖκες, αἵ τ' εἴσω στέγης
αἵ τ' ἐκτὸς αὐλῆς, ὡς ἄελπτον ὄμμ' ἐμοὶ
φήμης ἀνασχὸν τῆσδε νῦν καρπούμεθα.

ΧΟΡΟΣ

205 ἀνολολυξάτω δόμος
ἐφεστίοις ἀλαλαγαῖς
ὁ μελλόνυμφος· ἐν δὲ κοινὸς ἀρσένων
ἴτω κλαγγὰ τὸν εὐφαρέτραν
Ἀπόλλω προστάταν,
210 ὁμοῦ δὲ παιᾶνα παι-
ᾶν' ἀνάγετ', ὦ παρθένοι,
βοᾶτε τὰν ὁμόσπορον
Ἄρτεμιν Ὀρτυγίαν, ἐλαφαβόλον, ἀμφίπυρον,
215 γείτονάς τε Νύμφας.
αἴρομαι οὐδ' ἀπώσομαι
τὸν αὐλόν, ὦ τύραννε τᾶς ἐμᾶς φρενός.
ἰδού μ' ἀναταράσσει,
εὐοῖ,
ὁ κισσὸς ἄρτι Βακχίαν
220 ὑποστρέφων ἅμιλλαν.

150

what he desires to know each of them will not let him go till he has heard it to his satisfaction. So he is detained, according to their will but contrary to his own; but soon you shall see him face to face.

DEIANEIRA

O Zeus, to whom belongs the meadow of Oeta, never cropped by the scythe, at long last you have granted us delight! Speak out, women, both inside the house and outside the court, since now we are enjoying the dawning, beyond all hope, of this radiant news!

CHORUS

Let the house that is to receive the bridegroom utter a cry of joy, with shouts of triumph at the hearth! And let a song from the men also go up in honour of him of the fine quiver, Apollo the protector, and do you raise up the paean, the paean,[a] O maidens! Call upon his sister, Artemis of Ortygia, the shooter of deer, the bearer of torches, and her neighbouring nymphs!

I rise up, nor shall I reject the pipe, you who are the ruler of my mind! See, the ivy excites me—Euoi! —whirl-

[a] This word is both a title of Apollo and the name of a kind of song addressed to him or to his sister Artemis.

---

198 ἐκουσίοις Nauck: ἐκοῦσι δὲ codd.
205 ἀνολολυξάτω Burges: ἀνολολύξετε LRa: -ξατε KZg δόμος Burges: -οις codd.
206 ἀλαλαγαῖς z: ἀλαλαῖς LR, quo recepto ἐφεστίοισιν Blaydes
207 ὅ] ἁ Erfurdt
209 Ἀπόλλω Dindorf: -ωνα codd.
212 τάν <θ'> Musgrave
216 αἴρομαι Ll.-J.: ἀείρομ' codd.

ἰὼ ἰὼ Παιάν·
ἴδε ἴδ', ὦ φίλα γύναι·
τάδ' ἀντίπρωρα δή σοι
βλέπειν πάρεστ' ἐναργῆ.

ΔΗΙΑΝΕΙΡΑ

225 ὁρῶ, φίλαι γυναῖκες, οὐδέ μ' ὄμματος
φρουρὰν παρῆλθε, τόνδε μὴ λεύσσειν στόλον·
χαίρειν δὲ τὸν κήρυκα προὐννέπω, χρόνῳ
πολλῷ φανέντα, χαρτὸν εἴ τι καὶ φέρεις.

ΛΙΧΑΣ

ἀλλ' εὖ μὲν ἵγμεθ', εὖ δὲ προσφωνούμεθα,
230 γύναι, κατ' ἔργου κτῆσιν· ἄνδρα γὰρ καλῶς
πράσσοντ' ἀνάγκη χρηστὰ κερδαίνειν ἔπη.

ΔΗΙΑΝΕΙΡΑ

ὦ φίλτατ' ἀνδρῶν, πρῶθ' ἃ πρῶτα βούλομαι
δίδαξον, εἰ ζῶνθ' Ἡρακλῆ προσδέξομαι.

ΛΙΧΑΣ

ἔγωγέ τοί σφ' ἔλειπον ἰσχύοντά τε
235 καὶ ζῶντα καὶ θάλλοντα κοὐ νόσῳ βαρύν.

ΔΗΙΑΝΕΙΡΑ

ποῦ γῆς; πατρῴας, εἴτε βαρβάρου, λέγε.

ΛΙΧΑΣ

ἀκτή τις ἔστ' Εὐβοΐς, ἔνθ' ὁρίζεται
βωμοὺς τέλη τ' ἔγκαρπα Κηναίῳ Διί.

226 φρουρὰν Musgrave: -ὰ codd.

ing me around in the Bacchic rush! Oh, oh, Paean! See, see, dear lady! You can look on this before your eyes, in all clarity.

Enter LICHAS *with a group of female captives, including* IOLE.

DEIANEIRA

I see, dear women, nor does the sight of this procession escape my watchful eye; and I welcome you the herald, who have now at last appeared, if indeed your news is welcome.

LICHAS

I am happy in my coming and happy in your salutation, lady, which fits what the action has achieved; when a man enjoys success, he must profit by the speaking of favourable words!

DEIANEIRA

Dearest of men, tell me first what I wish for first, whether I shall receive Heracles alive!

LICHAS

I left him strong, alive, and flourishing, and not afflicted by any sickness.

DEIANEIRA

In what country? His own, or a foreign land? Tell me!

LICHAS

There is a cape in Euboea where he is marking off altars and offering due first fruits to Zeus of Mount Cenaeum.

ΔΗΙΑΝΕΙΡΑ

εὐκταῖα φαίνων, ἢ 'πὸ μαντείας τινός;

ΛΙΧΑΣ

240 εὐχαῖς, ὅθ' ᾔρει τῶνδ' ἀνάστατον δορὶ
χώραν γυναικῶν ὧν ὁρᾷς ἐν ὄμμασιν.

ΔΗΙΑΝΕΙΡΑ

αὗται δέ, πρὸς θεῶν, τοῦ ποτ' εἰσὶ καὶ τίνες;
οἰκτραὶ γάρ, εἰ μὴ ξυμφοραὶ κλέπτουσί με.

ΛΙΧΑΣ

ταύτας ἐκεῖνος Εὐρύτου πέρσας πόλιν
245 ἐξείλεθ' αὑτῷ κτῆμα καὶ θεοῖς κριτόν.

ΔΗΙΑΝΕΙΡΑ

ἦ κἀπὶ ταύτῃ τῇ πόλει τὸν ἄσκοπον
χρόνον βεβὼς ἦν ἡμερῶν ἀνήριθμον;

ΛΙΧΑΣ

οὔκ, ἀλλὰ τὸν μὲν πλεῖστον ἐν Λυδοῖς χρόνον
κατείχεθ', ὥς φησ' αὐτός, οὐκ ἐλεύθερος,
250 ἀλλ' ἐμποληθείς. τῷ λόγῳ δ' οὐ χρὴ φθόνον,
γύναι, προσεῖναι, Ζεὺς ὅτου πράκτωρ φανῇ.
κεῖνος δὲ πραθεὶς Ὀμφάλῃ τῇ βαρβάρῳ
ἐνιαυτὸν ἐξέπλησεν, ὡς αὐτὸς λέγει,
χοὔτως ἐδήχθη τοῦτο τοὔνειδος λαβὼν
255 ὥσθ' ὅρκον αὑτῷ προσβαλὼν διώμοσεν,
ἦ μὴν τὸν ἀγχιστῆρα τοῦδε τοῦ πάθους
ξὺν παιδὶ καὶ γυναικὶ δουλώσειν ἔτι.
κοὐχ ἡλίωσε τοὔπος, ἀλλ' ὅθ' ἁγνὸς ἦν,
στρατὸν λαβὼν ἐπακτὸν ἔρχεται πόλιν

154

DEIANEIRA

Revealing his fulfilment of a vow, or because of some prophet's words?

LICHAS

Because of a vow, since he had conquered and devastated the land of these women whom you see with your own eyes.

DEIANEIRA

And they, pray tell me, whom do they belong to and who are they? They deserve pity, if their calamity does not deceive me.

LICHAS

He picked them out, after he had sacked the city of Eurytus, as a choice prize for himself and for the gods.

DEIANEIRA

Was it to attack this city that he was gone for that unspeakable length of time, whose days were countless?

LICHAS

No, for most of the time he was detained among the Lydians, as he says himself; he was not free, but had been sold. No resentment should attach to the story, lady, since Zeus is known to be responsible. Heracles was sold to the barbarian Omphale and served out a year, as he himself tells me. And he was so much stung at having this shame set upon him that he put himself on oath and swore that in all truth he would yet enslave the man who had brought about this affliction together with his child and wife. And he did not fail to keep his word, but once he had been purified he raised a mercenary army and went against the city of

---

²⁵⁰ τῷ λόγῳ Margoliouth: τοῦ λόγου codd.

260 τὴν Εὐρυτείαν. τόνδε γὰρ μεταίτιον
  μόνον βροτῶν ἔφασκε τοῦδ᾽ εἶναι πάθους ·
  ὃς αὐτὸν ἐλθόντ᾽ ἐς δόμους ἐφέστιον,
  ξένον παλαιὸν ὄντα, πολλὰ μὲν λόγοις
  ἐπερρόθησε, πολλὰ δ᾽ ἀτηρᾷ φρενί,
265 λέγων χεροῖν μὲν ὡς ἄφυκτ᾽ ἔχων βέλη
  τῶν ὧν τέκνων λείποιτο πρὸς τόξου κρίσιν,
  †φώνει δέ, δοῦλος ἀνδρὸς ὡς ἐλευθέρου,
  ῥαίοιτο·† δείπνοις δ᾽ ἡνίκ᾽ ἦν ᾠνωμένος,
  ἔρριψεν ἐκτὸς αὐτόν. ὧν ἔχων χόλον,
270 ὡς ἵκετ᾽ αὖθις Ἴφιτος Τιρυνθίαν
  πρὸς κλειτύν, ἵππους νομάδας ἐξιχνοσκοπῶν,
  τότ᾽ ἄλλοσ᾽ αὐτὸν ὄμμα, θητέρᾳ δὲ νοῦν
  ἔχοντ᾽, ἀπ᾽ ἄκρας ἧκε πυργώδους πλακός.
  ἔργου δ᾽ ἕκατι τοῦδε μηνίσας ἄναξ,
275 ὁ τῶν ἁπάντων Ζεὺς πατὴρ Ὀλύμπιος,
  πρατόν νιν ἐξέπεμψεν, οὐδ᾽ ἠνέσχετο,
  ὁθούνεκ᾽ αὐτὸν μοῦνον ἀνθρώπων δόλῳ
  ἔκτεινεν. εἰ γὰρ ἐμφανῶς ἠμύνατο,
  Ζεύς τἂν συνέγνω ξὺν δίκῃ χειρουμένῳ.
280 ὕβριν γὰρ οὐ στέργουσιν οὐδὲ δαίμονες.
  κεῖνοι δ᾽ ὑπερχλίοντες ἐκ γλώσσης κακῆς
  αὐτοὶ μὲν Ἅιδου πάντες εἰσ᾽ οἰκήτορες,
  πόλις δὲ δούλη · τάσδε δ᾽ ἅσπερ εἰσορᾷς
  ἐξ ὀλβίων ἄζηλον εὑροῦσαι βίον
285 χωροῦσι πρὸς σέ · ταῦτα γὰρ πόσις τε σὸς
  ἐφεῖτ᾽, ἐγὼ δέ, πιστὸς ὢν κείνῳ, τελῶ.
  αὐτὸν δ᾽ ἐκεῖνον, εὖτ᾽ ἂν ἁγνὰ θύματα

Eurytus; for he it was whom he held responsible, alone among mortals, for what he had suffered. When Heracles had come to his house and was at his hearth, being an old friend, Eurytus had reviled him greatly with insults coming from a baneful mind, saying that, though he held in his hands arrows that could not be escaped, he was inferior to Eurytus' own sons when matched in archery, and [that he was a slave who was crushed by the mere voice of a free man.[a]] And at dinner when he was full of wine he threw him out. Angry at this, when Iphitus[b] came later to the ridge of Tiryns, on the track of wandering horses, as he had his eye in one place and his mind in another Heracles hurled him from the high platform of the fortress. It was on account of this deed that the lord, Olympian Zeus, the father of all, sent him to be sold. He did not tolerate it, because this was the only man he had killed by treachery; if he had fought him openly, Zeus would have pardoned him, since he had worsted his enemy in just fashion, for the gods also do not put up with violent crime. They in the arrogance fed by their evil speech now all inhabit Hades, and their city is enslaved; and these women whom you see come to you, having exchanged their good fortune for an unenviable life. These were your husband's orders, which I execute in loyalty to him. And as for himself, think of him

[a] The text is wholly uncertain here.
[b] Son of Eurytus.

---

267 φώνει] φωνεῖ Zo
268 ὠνωμένος Porson: οἰν- codd.
274–75 an ἄναξ et πατὴρ permutanda?

ῥέξῃ πατρῴῳ Ζηνὶ τῆς ἁλώσεως,
φρόνει νιν ὡς ἥξοντα· τοῦτο γὰρ λόγου
290 πολλοῦ καλῶς λεχθέντος ἥδιστον κλύειν.

ΧΟΡΟΣ

ἄνασσα, νῦν σοι τέρψις ἐμφανὴς κυρεῖ,
τῶν μὲν παρόντων, τὰ δὲ πεπυσμένη λόγῳ.

ΔΗΙΑΝΕΙΡΑ

πῶς δ᾽ οὐκ ἐγὼ χαίροιμ᾽ ἄν, ἀνδρὸς εὐτυχῆ
κλύουσα πρᾶξιν τήνδε, πανδίκῳ φρενί;
295 πολλή ᾽στ᾽ ἀνάγκη τῇδε τοῦτο συντρέχειν.
ὅμως δ᾽ ἔνεστι τοῖσιν εὖ σκοπουμένοις
ταρβεῖν τὸν εὖ πράσσοντα, μὴ σφαλῇ ποτε.
ἐμοὶ γὰρ οἶκτος δεινὸς εἰσέβη, φίλαι,
ταύτας ὁρώσῃ δυσπότμους ἐπὶ ξένης
300 χώρας ἀοίκους ἀπάτοράς τ᾽ ἀλωμένας,
αἳ πρὶν μὲν ἦσαν ἐξ ἐλευθέρων ἴσως
ἀνδρῶν, τανῦν δὲ δοῦλον ἴσχουσιν βίον.
 ὦ Ζεῦ τροπαῖε, μή ποτ᾽ εἰσίδοιμί σε
πρὸς τοὐμὸν οὕτω σπέρμα χωρήσαντά ποι,
305 μηδ᾽, εἴ τι δράσεις, τῆσδέ γε ζώσης ἔτι.
οὕτως ἐγὼ δέδοικα τάσδ᾽ ὁρωμένη.
 ὦ δυστάλαινα, τίς ποτ᾽ εἶ νεανίδων;
ἄνανδρος, ἢ τεκνοῦσσα; πρὸς μὲν γὰρ φύσιν
πάντων ἄπειρος τῶνδε, γενναία δέ τις.
310 Λίχα, τίνος ποτ᾽ ἐστὶν ἡ ξένη βροτῶν;
τίς ἡ τεκοῦσα, τίς δ᾽ ὁ φιτύσας πατήρ;
ἔξειπ᾽· ἐπεί νιν τῶνδε πλεῖστον ᾤκτισα

as about to come, once he has rendered holy sacrifice to
Zeus his father in return for the city's capture; in the long
story happily recounted, this is the most delightful thing to
hear.

CHORUS

Queen, now your delight is manifest; part of your pleasure
is before your eyes, and the rest you have heard described.

DEIANEIRA

And how should I not rejoice at hearing of my husband's
successful action, with every right? Without fail, my joy
must match his triumph. But none the less it is the way of
those who consider things with care to fear for the man
who is fortunate, in case he may one day come to grief.
Yes, a strange pity comes upon me, dear women, when I
see these unhappy ones homeless and fatherless, astray in a
foreign land; perhaps they were formerly the children of
free men, but now their life is one of slavery.

Zeus, god of trophies, may I never see you go against
my offspring in this fashion; if you do so, may it not be
while I still live! Such is my fear as I look upon these
women.

Unhappy one, who among all young girls are you? Have
you no husband, or are you a mother? You look as though
you know nothing of all these things, but you are some
noble person. Lichas, who among human beings is the
stranger? Who is her mother, and who is the father that
gave her life? Tell me, because I pitied her most when I

---

[292] τὰ Scaliger: τῶν codd.   λόγῳ La: -ων cett.
[308] τεκνοῦσσα Brunck: τεκνοῦσα v.l. in L et a: τεκοῦσα codd.

βλέπουσ', ὅσωπερ καὶ φρονεῖν οἶδεν μόνη.

ΛΙΧΑΣ

τί δ' οἶδ' ἐγώ; τί δ' ἄν με καὶ κρίνοις; ἴσως
315 γέννημα τῶν ἐκεῖθεν οὐκ ἐν ὑστάτοις.

ΔΗΙΑΝΕΙΡΑ

μὴ τῶν τυράννων; Εὐρύτου σπορά τις ἦν;

ΛΙΧΑΣ

οὐκ οἶδα· καὶ γὰρ οὐδ' ἀνιστόρουν μακράν.

ΔΗΙΑΝΕΙΡΑ

οὐδ' ὄνομα πρός του τῶν ξυνεμπόρων ἔχεις;

ΛΙΧΑΣ

ἥκιστα· σιγῇ τοὐμὸν ἔργον ἤνυτον.

ΔΗΙΑΝΕΙΡΑ

320 εἴπ', ὦ τάλαιν', ἀλλ' ἡμὶν ἐκ σαυτῆς· ἐπεὶ
καὶ ξυμφορά τοι μὴ εἰδέναι σέ γ' ἥτις εἶ.

ΛΙΧΑΣ

οὔ τἄρα τῷ γε πρόσθεν οὐδὲν ἐξ ἴσου
χρόνῳ διήσει γλῶσσαν, ἥτις οὐδαμὰ
προύφηνεν οὔτε μείζον' οὔτ' ἐλάσσονα,
325 ἀλλ' αἰὲν ὠδίνουσα συμφορᾶς βάρος
δακρυρροεῖ δύστηνος, ἐξ ὅτου πάτραν
διήνεμον λέλοιπεν. ἡ δέ τοι τύχη
κακὴ μὲν αὐτή γ', ἀλλὰ συγγνώμην ἔχει.

ΔΗΙΑΝΕΙΡΑ

ἡ δ' οὖν ἐάσθω, καὶ πορευέσθω στέγας
330 οὕτως ὅπως ἥδιστα, μηδὲ πρὸς κακοῖς

160

saw her, in as much as she alone can feel and understand.

LICHAS

How do I know? Why should you question me? Perhaps she is the child of people not among the lowest over there.

DEIANEIRA

Is she of the royal house? Had Eurytus any children?

LICHAS

I do not know; you see, I did not ask many questions.

DEIANEIRA

Have you not learned her name from one of her fellow travellers?

LICHAS

No, indeed! I did my work in silence.

DEIANEIRA

Tell me, poor girl, yourself! It is a pity for me not to know who you are.

LICHAS

If she gives tongue, it will not be like the past, for she has come out with nothing great or small, but has always wept, poor creature, in grievous travail, ever since she left her windswept native land; her fortune in itself is bad, but it deserves understanding.

DEIANEIRA

Well, let her be, and let her go into the house just as she wishes, and receive no new pain from me on top of the

---

323 διήσει Wakefield: διοίσει codd.
328 αὐτή KZg: αὕτη Zo: αὐτῇ cett.

τοῖς οὖσιν ἄλλην πρός γ' ἐμοῦ λύπην λάβῃ·
ἅλις γὰρ ἡ παροῦσα. πρὸς δὲ δώματα
χωρῶμεν ἤδη πάντες, ὡς σύ θ' οἷ θέλεις
σπεύδῃς, ἐγὼ δὲ τἄνδον ἐξαρκῆ τιθῶ.

ΑΓΓΕΛΟΣ

335   αὐτοῦ γε πρῶτον βαιὸν ἀμμείνασ', ὅπως
μάθῃς, ἄνευ τῶνδ', οὕστινάς γ' ἄγεις ἔσω
ὧν τ' οὐδὲν εἰσήκουσας ἐκμάθῃς ἃ δεῖ.
τούτων — ἔχω γὰρ πάντ' — ἐπιστήμων ἐγώ.

ΔΗΙΑΝΕΙΡΑ

τί δ' ἔστι; τοῦ με τήνδ' ἐφίστασαι βάσιν;

ΑΓΓΕΛΟΣ

340   σταθεῖσ' ἄκουσον· καὶ γὰρ οὐδὲ τὸν πάρος
μῦθον μάτην ἤκουσας, οὐδὲ νῦν δοκῶ.

ΔΗΙΑΝΕΙΡΑ

πότερον ἐκείνους δῆτα δεῦρ' αὖθις πάλιν
καλῶμεν, ἢ 'μοὶ ταῖσδέ τ' ἐξειπεῖν θέλεις;

ΑΓΓΕΛΟΣ

σοὶ ταῖσδέ τ' οὐδὲν εἴργεται, τούτους δ' ἔα.

ΔΗΙΑΝΕΙΡΑ

345   καὶ δὴ βεβᾶσι, χὠ λόγος σημαινέτω.

ΑΓΓΕΛΟΣ

ἀνὴρ ὅδ' οὐδὲν ὧν ἔλεξεν ἀρτίως
φωνεῖ δίκης ἐς ὀρθόν, ἀλλ' ἢ νῦν κακός,
ἢ πρόσθεν οὐ δίκαιος ἄγγελος παρῆν.

troubles that she has; the pain she has at present is enough.
And now let us all go into the house, so that you may hasten
to wherever you wish to go and I may make preparations
inside.

Exeunt LICHAS and the prisoners.

MESSENGER

Wait here first for a little, so that you may learn without
their being present who it is that you are taking in and
learn fully things of which you have heard nothing! About
these I am informed, for I know all!

DEIANEIRA

What is it? Why are you halting my departure?

MESSENGER

Stand here and listen! What I said before was worth your
hearing, and I think this will be too.

DEIANEIRA

Shall we call them back here, or do you wish to speak to me
and to these women?

MESSENGER

To you and to these I may speak freely, but let the others
be!

DEIANEIRA

Well, they are gone, so let your story be told!

MESSENGER

None of what this man has just told you is the truth, but
either he is a liar now, or he gave a false report before.

---

³³¹ ἄλλην Zo: λύπην LRa   λάβῃ Blaydes: -οι codd.
³³⁸ ἐπιστήμων Jackson, qui v. sic interpunxit: ἐπιστήμην codd.

163

ΔHIANEIPA

τί φής; σαφῶς μοι φράζε πᾶν ὅσον νοεῖς·
350 ἃ μὲν γὰρ ἐξείρηκας ἀγνοίᾳ μ' ἔχει.

ΑΓΓΕΛΟΣ

τούτου λέγοντος τἀνδρὸς εἰσήκουσ' ἐγώ,
πολλῶν παρόντων μαρτύρων, ὡς τῆς κόρης
ταύτης ἕκατι κεῖνος Εὔρυτόν θ' ἕλοι
τήν θ' ὑψίπυργον Οἰχαλίαν, Ἔρως δέ νιν
355 μόνος θεῶν θέλξειεν αἰχμάσαι τάδε,
οὐ τἀπὶ Λυδοῖς οὐδ' ὑπ' Ὀμφάλῃ πόνων
λατρεύματ', οὐδ' ὁ ῥιπτὸς Ἰφίτου μόρος·
ὃν νῦν παρώσας οὗτος ἔμπαλιν λέγει.
ἀλλ' ἡνίκ' οὐκ ἔπειθε τὸν φυτοσπόρον
360 τὴν παῖδα δοῦναι, κρύφιον ὡς ἔχοι λέχος,
ἔγκλημα μικρὸν αἰτίαν θ' ἑτοιμάσας
ἐπιστρατεύει πατρίδα [τὴν ταύτης, ἐν ᾗ
τὸν Εὔρυτον τόνδ' εἶπε δεσπόζειν θρόνων,
κτείνει τ' ἄνακτα πατέρα] τῆσδε καὶ πόλιν
365 ἔπερσε. καὶ νῦν, ὡς ὁρᾷς, ἥκει δόμους
ἐς τούσδε πέμπων οὐκ ἀφροντίστως, γύναι,
οὐδ' ὥστε δούλην· μηδὲ προσδόκα τόδε·
οὐδ' εἰκός, εἴπερ ἐντεθέρμανται πόθῳ.
ἔδοξεν οὖν μοι πρὸς σὲ δηλῶσαι τὸ πᾶν,
370 δέσποιν', ὃ τοῦδε τυγχάνω μαθὼν πάρα.
καὶ ταῦτα πολλοὶ πρὸς μέσῃ Τραχινίων
ἀγορᾷ συνεξήκουον ὡσαύτως ἐμοί,
ὥστ' ἐξελέγχειν· εἰ δὲ μὴ λέγω φίλα,

DEIANEIRA

What are you saying? Tell me truly all that is in your mind!
For as to the subject of your speech, I am all ignorance.

MESSENGER

I heard this man saying, before many witnesses, that it was
on account of this girl that Heracles brought down Eurytus
and the high towers of Oechalia, and that it was Eros alone
among the gods that bewitched him into this deed of arms,
not the doings among the Lydians or his servitude under
Omphale or Iphitus, hurled to his death. And now he
pushes this story aside and tells a different one!

No, when he failed to persuade her father to give him
his daughter, to have as his secret love, he trumped up a
petty accusation and a pretext, and marched against her
country [in which he said this Eurytus was king, killed the
king her father,] and sacked the city. And now, as you see,
he has come back, sending her not without forethought,
lady, or as a slave; do not expect that, nor is it likely, if
indeed he is inflamed with desire.

I thought, then, that I should tell you all, my lady, that I
had heard from him; and many of the men of Trachis heard
this in the centre of the market place, just as I did, so that
you can question them; and if what I say is not agreeable, I

---

^{356} ὑπ᾽ Herwerden: ἐπ᾽ vel ἀπ᾽ codd.

$^{362-64}$ τὴν ... πατέρα del. Dobree

^{366} ἐς Brunck: ὡς codd.: πρὸς Schneidewin

^{372} post hunc v. deficit R

οὐχ ἥδομαι, τὸ δ' ὀρθὸν ἐξείρηχ' ὅμως.

ΔΗΙΑΝΕΙΡΑ

375 οἴμοι τάλαινα, ποῦ ποτ' εἰμὶ πράγματος;
τίν' ἐσδέδεγμαι πημονὴν ὑπόστεγον
λαθραῖον; ὦ δύστηνος· ἆρ' ἀνώνυμος
πέφυκεν, ὥσπερ οὑπάγων διώμνυτο,
ἡ κάρτα λαμπρὰ καὶ κατ' ὄμμα καὶ φύσιν;

ΑΓΓΕΛΟΣ

380 πατρὸς μὲν οὖσα γένεσιν Εὐρύτου †ποτὲ†
Ἰόλη 'καλεῖτο, τῆς ἐκεῖνος οὐδαμὰ
βλάστας ἐφώνει δῆθεν οὐδὲν ἱστορῶν.

ΧΟΡΟΣ

ὄλοιντο μή τι πάντες οἱ κακοί, τὰ δὲ
λαθραῖ' ὃς ἀσκεῖ μὴ πρέπονθ' αὑτῷ κακά.

ΔΗΙΑΝΕΙΡΑ

385 τί χρὴ ποεῖν, γυναῖκες; ὡς ἐγὼ λόγοις
τοῖς νῦν παροῦσιν ἐκπεπληγμένη κυρῶ.

ΧΟΡΟΣ

πεύθου μολοῦσα τἀνδρός, ὡς τάχ' ἂν σαφῆ
λέξειεν, εἴ νιν πρὸς βίαν κρίνειν θέλοις.

ΔΗΙΑΝΕΙΡΑ

ἀλλ' εἶμι· καὶ γὰρ οὐκ ἀπὸ γνώμης λέγεις.

ΑΓΓΕΛΟΣ

390 ἡμεῖς δὲ προσμένωμεν; ἢ τί χρὴ ποεῖν;

---

379 hunc v. nuntio tribuit a   ἡ κάρτα Heath: ἦ καὶ τὰ codd.: ἦ
κάρτα Canter: ἦν κάρτα Wilamowitz   ὄμμα] ὄνομα Fröhlich

166

take no pleasure in it, but none the less I have told the truth.

DEIANEIRA

Ah me, what is my situation? What disaster have I taken into my house, unknowingly? Has she no name, as he who brought her swore, she who is dazzling in her looks and in her person?

MESSENGER

She is the daughter of Eurytus and was called Iole, she of whose origin he said nothing, since of course he had not asked!

CHORUS

A curse not on all evildoers, but on him who practises in secret evil that ill suits one in his place!

DEIANEIRA

What must I do, women? The story we have heard leaves me struck dumb.

CHORUS

Go and question the man, since perhaps he will tell the truth, if you are willing to force him to give answer.

DEIANEIRA

Why, I will go! Your advice is wise.

MESSENGER

And are we to wait here? Or what must we do?

---

[380] ποτέ] σπορά Blaydes   post hunc v. lacunam statuit Radermacher

[390] nuntio tribuit Hermann, Deianeirae a: choro cett.

SOPHOCLES

ΔΗΙΑΝΕΙΡΑ

μίμν', ὡς ὅδ' ἀνὴρ οὐκ ἐμῶν ὑπ' ἀγγέλων
ἀλλ' αὐτόκλητος ἐκ δόμων πορεύεται.

ΛΙΧΑΣ

τί χρή, γύναι, μολόντα μ' Ἡρακλεῖ λέγειν;
δίδαξον, ὡς ἕρποντος, εἰσορᾷς, ἐμοῦ.

ΔΗΙΑΝΕΙΡΑ

395 ὡς ἐκ ταχείας σὺν χρόνῳ βραδεῖ μολὼν
ᾄσσεις, πρὶν ἡμᾶς κἀννεώσασθαι λόγους.

ΛΙΧΑΣ

ἀλλ' εἴ τι χρῄζεις ἱστορεῖν, πάρειμ' ἐγώ.

ΔΗΙΑΝΕΙΡΑ

ἦ καὶ τὸ πιστὸν τῆς ἀληθείας νεμεῖς;

ΛΙΧΑΣ

ἴστω μέγας Ζεύς, ὧν γ' ἂν ἐξειδὼς κυρῶ.

ΔΗΙΑΝΕΙΡΑ

400 τίς ἡ γυνὴ δῆτ' ἐστὶν ἣν ἥκεις ἄγων;

ΛΙΧΑΣ

Εὐβοιίς· ὧν δ' ἔβλαστεν οὐκ ἔχω λέγειν.

ΑΓΓΕΛΟΣ

οὗτος, βλέφ' ὧδε. πρὸς τίν' ἐννέπειν δοκεῖς;

ΛΙΧΑΣ

σὺ δ' ἐς τί δή με τοῦτ' ἐρωτήσας ἔχεις;

ΑΓΓΕΛΟΣ

τόλμησον εἰπεῖν, εἰ φρονεῖς, ὅ σ' ἱστορῶ.

---

[396] κἀννεώσασθαι Hermann: καὶ νεώσασθαι codd.: ἀνανεώσ-
ασθαι Eustathius, novit sch.   [397–433] personarum vices in codd.
varie turbatas restituit Tyrwhitt

168

DEIANEIRA

Wait, since of his own volition, without my having sent any message, this man is coming out of the house!

Enter LICHAS.

LICHAS

Lady, what am I to go and say to Heracles? Tell me, since I am leaving, as you see.

DEIANEIRA

How quickly you are rushing away, you who came so slowly, before I can renew our talk!

LICHAS

Why, if you wish to ask any questions, here I am!

DEIANEIRA

Will you tell the truth, so that I can believe you?

LICHAS

Let mighty Zeus know it, I shall tell all I know!

DEIANEIRA

Who is the woman whom you brought?

LICHAS

One from Euboea; and who her parents were I cannot tell.

MESSENGER

You there, look this way! To whom do you think that you are speaking?

LICHAS

But why have you asked me that question?

MESSENGER

If you are wise you will bring yourself to answer the question that I ask!

ΛΙΧΑΣ

405 πρὸς τὴν κρατοῦσαν Δηάνειραν, Οἰνέως
κόρην, δάμαρτά θ᾽ Ἡρακλέους, εἰ μὴ κυρῶ
λεύσσων μάταια, δεσπότιν τε τὴν ἐμήν.

ΑΓΓΕΛΟΣ

τοῦτ᾽ αὖτ᾽ ἔχρῃζον, τοῦτό σου μαθεῖν. λέγεις
δέσποιναν εἶναι τήνδε σήν;

ΛΙΧΑΣ

δίκαια γάρ.

ΑΓΓΕΛΟΣ

410 τί δῆτα; ποίαν ἀξιοῖς δοῦναι δίκην,
ἢν εὑρεθῇς ἐς τήνδε μὴ δίκαιος ὤν;

ΛΙΧΑΣ

πῶς μὴ δίκαιος; τί ποτε ποικίλας ἔχεις;

ΑΓΓΕΛΟΣ

οὐδέν. σὺ μέντοι κάρτα τοῦτο δρῶν κυρεῖς.

ΛΙΧΑΣ

ἄπειμι. μῶρος δ᾽ ἦ πάλαι κλύων σέθεν.

ΑΓΓΕΛΟΣ

415 οὔ, πρίν γ᾽ ἂν εἴπῃς ἱστορούμενος βραχύ.

ΛΙΧΑΣ

λέγ᾽ εἴ τι χρῄζεις· καὶ γὰρ οὐ σιγηλὸς εἶ.

ΑΓΓΕΛΟΣ

τὴν αἰχμάλωτον, ἣν ἔπεμψας ἐς δόμους,
κάτοισθα δήπου;

LICHAS

To the lady Deianeira, the daughter of Oeneus and wife of
Heracles, if I can believe my eyes, and my mistress.

MESSENGER

That is what I wanted you to say, just that! You say that she
is your mistress?

LICHAS

Yes, she is!

MESSENGER

What then? What penalty do you think that you should pay
if you are caught being disloyal to her?

LICHAS

How do you mean, "disloyal"? What is this dark saying?

MESSENGER

There is none! But that is certainly what you are doing!

LICHAS

I shall be off; I was a fool to listen to you for so long.

MESSENGER

No, not before you have answered a brief question!

LICHAS

Speak, if you wish to! You are not a silent man!

MESSENGER

The prisoner whom you escorted to the house—you know
about her?

ΛΙΧΑΣ

φημί· πρὸς τί δ' ἱστορεῖς;

ΑΓΓΕΛΟΣ

οὔκουν σὺ ταύτην, ἣν ὑπ' ἀγνοίας ὁρᾷς,

420 Ἰόλην ἔφασκες Εὐρύτου σπορὰν ἄγειν;

ΛΙΧΑΣ

ποίοις ἐν ἀνθρώποισι; τίς πόθεν μολὼν

σοὶ μαρτυρήσει ταῦτ' ἐμοῦ κλυεῖν παρών;

ΑΓΓΕΛΟΣ

πολλοῖσιν ἀστῶν. ἐν μέσῃ Τραχινίων

ἀγορᾷ πολύς σου ταῦτά γ' εἰσήκουσ' ὄχλος.

ΛΙΧΑΣ

ναί·

425 κλυεῖν γ' ἔφασκον. ταὐτὸ δ' οὐχὶ γίγνεται

δόκησιν εἰπεῖν κἀξακριβῶσαι λόγον.

ΑΓΓΕΛΟΣ

ποίαν δόκησιν; οὐκ ἐπώμοτος λέγων

δάμαρτ' ἔφασκες Ἡρακλεῖ ταύτην ἄγειν;

ΛΙΧΑΣ

ἐγὼ δάμαρτα; πρὸς θεῶν, φράσον, φίλη

430 δέσποινα, τόνδε τίς ποτ' ἐστὶν ὁ ξένος.

ΑΓΓΕΛΟΣ

ὃς σοῦ παρὼν ἤκουσεν ὡς ταύτης πόθῳ

πόλις δαμείη πᾶσα, κοὐχ ἡ Λυδία

πέρσειεν αὐτήν, ἀλλ' ὁ τῆσδ' ἔρως φανείς.

LICHAS

Yes; why do you ask me?

MESSENGER

Did you not say that this girl that you were bringing, whom you look on as though you did not know her, was Iole, daughter of Eurytus?

LICHAS

Among what people? Who, from where, can bear you witness that he heard me say this?

MESSENGER

Among many of the citizens! In the middle of the market place of the men of Trachis a crowd heard you say this.

LICHAS

Yes . . . I said that I had heard it; but it is not the same thing to say what you think is true and to give a definite account. .

MESSENGER

What do you mean by "think"? Did you not swear on oath that you were bringing her as wife to Heracles?

LICHAS

As wife? I beg you, dear mistress, tell me who this stranger is!

MESSENGER

A man who was there to hear you say that it was because of his desire for this girl that the whole city was conquered, and that it was not the Lydian woman that was its ruin, but the manifestation of his love for her.

ΛΙΧΑΣ

ἄνθρωπος, ὦ δέσποιν᾽, ἀποστήτω· τὸ γὰρ
435 νοσοῦντι ληρεῖν ἀνδρὸς οὐχὶ σώφρονος.

ΔΗΙΑΝΕΙΡΑ

μή, πρός σε τοῦ κατ᾽ ἄκρον Οἰταῖον νάπος
Διὸς καταστράπτοντος, ἐκκλέψῃς λόγον.
οὐ γὰρ γυναικὶ τοὺς λόγους ἐρεῖς κακῇ,
οὐδ᾽ ἥτις οὐ κάτοιδε τἀνθρώπων, ὅτι
440 χαίρειν πέφυκεν οὐχὶ τοῖς αὐτοῖς ἀεί.
Ἔρωτι μέν νυν ὅστις ἀντανίσταται
πύκτης ὅπως ἐς χεῖρας, οὐ καλῶς φρονεῖ.
οὗτος γὰρ ἄρχει καὶ θεῶν ὅπως θέλει,
κἀμοῦ γε· πῶς δ᾽ οὐ χἀτέρας οἵας γ᾽ ἐμοῦ;
445 ὥστ᾽ εἴ τι τὠμῷ γ᾽ ἀνδρὶ τῇδε τῇ νόσῳ
ληφθέντι μεμπτός εἰμι, κάρτα μαίνομαι,
ἢ τῇδε τῇ γυναικί, τῇ μεταιτίᾳ
τοῦ μηδὲν αἰσχροῦ μηδ᾽ ἐμοὶ κακοῦ τινος.
οὐκ ἔστι ταῦτ᾽. ἀλλ᾽ εἰ μὲν ἐκ κείνου μαθὼν
450 ψεύδῃ, μάθησιν οὐ καλὴν ἐκμανθάνεις·
εἰ δ᾽ αὐτὸς αὑτὸν ὧδε παιδεύεις, ὅταν
θέλῃς λέγεσθαι χρηστός, ὀφθήσῃ κακός.
ἀλλ᾽ εἰπὲ πᾶν τἀληθές· ὡς ἐλευθέρῳ
ψευδεῖ καλεῖσθαι κὴρ πρόσεστιν οὐ καλή.
455 ὅπως δὲ λήσεις, οὐδὲ τοῦτο γίγνεται·
πολλοὶ γὰρ οἷς εἴρηκας, οἳ φράσουσ᾽ ἐμοί.
κεἰ μὲν δέδοικας, οὐ καλῶς ταρβεῖς, ἐπεὶ
τὸ μὴ πυθέσθαι, τοῦτό μ᾽ ἀλγύνειεν ἄν·

THE WOMEN OF TRACHIS

LICHAS

Mistress, let the fellow go away! To talk nonsense to a man
who is sick is not the behaviour of a rational person.

DEIANEIRA

By Zeus whose lightning strikes the lofty glades of Oeta, do
not conceal your story! The woman you will be telling it to
is not evil, nor is she ignorant of the ways of men, that they
do not always take pleasure in the same things. Whoever
stands up to Eros like a boxer is a fool; for he rules even the
gods just as he pleases, and he rules me; how should he not
rule another woman like me? So that if I blame my hus-
band for being taken by this sickness, I am surely mad, or if
I blame this woman, who has caused no shame or trouble
for me. It cannot be! But if it is on his instructions that you
are lying, you are learning no honourable lesson; and if you
have schooled yourself in this fashion, when you wish to be
called honest, you will be seen as criminal. Come, tell the
whole truth! For a free man, it is a discreditable affliction
to be called a liar. Nor is it possible for you to escape
detection; for there are many people to whom you spoke,
and they will tell me.

And if you are afraid, your fear does you no credit, since
not learning, that is what would distress me. But why is it

---

445 γ' ἀνδρὶ Schaefer: τἀνδρὶ codd.
452 λέγεσθαι Ll.-J.: γενέσθαι codd.

τὸ δ᾽ εἰδέναι τί δεινόν; οὐχὶ χἀτέρας
460 πλείστας ἀνὴρ εἷς Ἡρακλῆς ἔγημε δή;
κοὔπω τις αὐτῶν ἔκ γ᾽ ἐμοῦ λόγον κακὸν
ἠνέγκατ᾽ οὐδ᾽ ὄνειδος· ἥδε τ᾽ οὐδ᾽ ἂν εἰ
κάρτ᾽ ἐντακείη τῷ φιλεῖν, ἐπεί σφ᾽ ἐγὼ
ᾤκτιρα δὴ μάλιστα προσβλέψασ᾽, ὅτι
465 τὸ κάλλος αὐτῆς τὸν βίον διώλεσεν,
καὶ γῆν πατρῴαν οὐχ ἑκοῦσα δύσμορος
ἔπερσε κἀδούλωσεν. ἀλλὰ ταῦτα μὲν
ῥείτω κατ᾽ οὖρον· σοὶ δ᾽ ἐγὼ φράζω κακὸν
πρὸς ἄλλον εἶναι, πρὸς δ᾽ ἔμ᾽ ἀψευδεῖν ἀεί.

ΧΟΡΟΣ

470 πείθου λεγούσῃ χρηστά, κοὐ μέμψῃ χρόνῳ
γυναικὶ τῇδε, κἀπ᾽ ἐμοῦ κτήσῃ χάριν.

ΛΙΧΑΣ

ἀλλ᾽, ὦ φίλη δέσποιν᾽, ἐπεί σε μανθάνω
θνητὴν φρονοῦσαν θνητὰ κοὐκ ἀγνώμονα,
πᾶν σοι φράσω τἀληθὲς οὐδὲ κρύψομαι.
475 ἔστιν γὰρ οὕτως ὥσπερ οὗτος ἐννέπει.
ταύτης ὁ δεινὸς ἵμερός ποθ᾽ Ἡρακλῆ
διῆλθε, καὶ τῆσδ᾽ οὕνεχ᾽ ἡ πολύφθορος
καθῃρέθη πατρῷος Οἰχαλία δορί.
καὶ ταῦτα, δεῖ γὰρ καὶ τὸ πρὸς κείνου λέγειν,
480 οὔτ᾽ εἶπε κρύπτειν οὔτ᾽ ἀπηρνήθη ποτέ,
ἀλλ᾽ αὐτός, ὦ δέσποινα, δειμαίνων τὸ σὸν
μὴ στέρνον ἀλγύνοιμι τοῖσδε τοῖς λόγοις,
ἥμαρτον, εἴ τι τῶνδ᾽ ἁμαρτίαν νέμεις.

so terrible to know? Has not one man, Heracles, lain with
many women? And never yet has any of them incurred evil
speech or a reproach from *me*; and this one never would,
even if he should become absorbed in his passion for her,
since I pitied her most of all when my eyes lit on her,
because her beauty had destroyed her life, and by no fault
of hers, poor creature, she had brought her native land to
ruin and to slavery. But let all this stream in the wind! I
tell you to be devious to another, but to me always to tell
the truth!

CHORUS

Obey, for what she says is right, and you will never have
cause to blame this lady, and will win my gratitude!

LICHAS

Well, dear mistress, since I can see that you, being mortal,
think like a mortal and not unreasonably, I will tell you the
whole truth, and will not conceal it. Yes, it is just as this
man says; a fearsome passion for this girl one day came
over Heracles, and it was for her sake that her unfortunate
native city of Oechalia was conquered with the spear.
And—for I must give him too his due—he did not tell me
to conceal this or deny it, but I myself, mistress, afraid I
might wound your heart by telling you this story, did
wrong, if you count any of this as wrong.

---

483 τῶνδ' Dawe: τήνδ' codd.

SOPHOCLES

ἐπεί γε μὲν δὴ πάντ' ἐπίστασαι λόγον,
485 κείνου τε καὶ σὴν ἐξ ἴσου κοινὴν χάριν
καὶ στέργε τὴν γυναῖκα καὶ βούλου λόγους
οὓς εἶπας ἐς τήνδ' ἐμπέδως εἰρηκέναι.
ὡς τἄλλ' ἐκεῖνος πάντ' ἀριστεύων χεροῖν
τοῦ τῆσδ' ἔρωτος εἰς ἅπανθ' ἥσσων ἔφυ.

ΔΗΙΑΝΕΙΡΑ

490 ἀλλ' ὧδε καὶ φρονοῦμεν ὥστε ταῦτα δρᾶν,
κοὔτοι νόσον γ' ἐπακτὸν ἐξαρούμεθα,
θεοῖσι δυσμαχοῦντες. ἀλλ' εἴσω στέγης
χωρῶμεν, ὡς λόγων τ' ἐπιστολὰς φέρῃς,
ἅ τ' ἀντὶ δώρων δῶρα χρὴ προσαρμόσαι,
495 καὶ ταῦτ' ἄγῃς. κενὸν γὰρ οὐ δίκαιά σε
χωρεῖν προσελθόνθ' ὧδε σὺν πολλῷ στόλῳ.

ΧΟΡΟΣ

μέγα τι σθένος ἁ Κύπρις· ἐκφέρεται νίκας
ἀεί.   στρ.
καὶ τὰ μὲν θεῶν
500 παρέβαν, καὶ ὅπως Κρονίδαν ἀπάτασεν οὐ λέγω
οὐδὲ τὸν ἔννυχον Ἅιδαν,
ἢ Ποσειδάωνα τινάκτορα γαίας·
ἀλλ' ἐπὶ τάνδ' ἄρ' ἄκοιτιν
<τίνες> ἀμφίγυοι κατέβαν πρὸ γάμων,
505 τίνες πάμπληκτα παγκόνιτά τ' ἐξ-
ῆλθον ἄεθλ' ἀγώνων;
ὁ μὲν ἦν ποταμοῦ σθένος, ὑψίκερω
τετραόρου   ἀντ.
φάσμα ταύρου,
178

But since you know the whole story, both for his sake and your own show kindness to the woman, and wish the things you said regarding her not to have been said in vain. For he who in all other matters has excelled in might has been altogether vanquished by his passion for this girl.

DEIANEIRA

Why, I am indeed minded to do this, and I shall not take on myself a sickness that is foreign to me, in a vain struggle against the gods. But let us go into the house, so that you may take away the message that I charge you with, and may also carry gifts in exchange for gifts that I must attach. It would not be right for you to go empty-handed after having come here with so large a train.

All three enter the house.

CHORUS

A mighty power is the Cyprian![a] Always she carries off victories. The stories of the gods I pass over, nor do I relate how she tricked the son of Kronos, or Hades shrouded in darkness, or Poseidon the shaker of earth. But to win this bride what mighty antagonists entered the lists for the sake of the marriage? Who set out for the ordeal of the contest amid many blows and much dust?

One was a mighty river, appearing as a bull, long-

---

[a] Aphrodite.

---

[504] suppl. Hermann

510 Ἀχελῷος ἀπ' Οἰνιαδᾶν, ὁ δὲ Βακχίας ἄπο
ἦλθε παλίντονα Θήβας
τόξα καὶ λόγχας ῥόπαλόν τε τινάσσων,
παῖς Διός· οἳ τότ' ἀολλεῖς
ἴσαν ἐς μέσον ἱέμενοι λεχέων·

515 μόνα δ' εὔλεκτρος ἐν μέσῳ Κύπρις
ῥαβδονόμει ξυνοῦσα.
τότ' ἦν χερός, ἦν δὲ τό-   ἐπ.
ξων πάταγος,
ταυρείων τ' ἀνάμιγδα κεράτων·

520 ἦν δ' ἀμφίπλεκτοι κλίμακες, ἦν δὲ μετώ-
πων ὀλόεντα
πλήγματα καὶ στόνος ἀμφοῖν.
ἁ δ' εὐῶπις ἁβρὰ
τηλαυγεῖ παρ' ὄχθῳ

525 ἧστο τὸν ὃν προσμένουσ' ἀκοίταν.
†ἐγὼ δὲ μάτηρ μὲν οἷα φράζω·†
τὸ δ' ἀμφινείκητον ὄμμα νύμφας
ἐλεινὸν ἀμμένει <τέλος>·
κἀπὸ ματρὸς ἄφαρ βέβαχ',

530 ὥστε πόρτις ἐρήμα.

ΔΗΙΑΝΕΙΡΑ

ἦμος, φίλαι, κατ' οἶκον ὁ ξένος θροεῖ
ταῖς αἰχμαλώτοις παισὶν ὡς ἐπ' ἐξόδῳ,
τῆμος θυραῖος ἦλθον ὡς ὑμᾶς λάθρᾳ,
τὰ μὲν φράσουσα χερσὶν ἀτεχνησάμην,

horned, four-legged, Achelous from Oeniadae; and the
other came from Bacchic Thebes, brandishing his spring-
ing bow, his spears, and his club, the son of Zeus. They
then met together in the middle, longing for her bed; and
alone in the centre the beautiful Cyprian was there to
umpire in the contest.

Then there was a clatter of fists and of the quiver, and of
the bull's horns, all together; and legs were wound around
waists, and deadly blows struck foreheads, and groans
came from both. But she in her delicate beauty sat by a
distant hill, awaiting her bridegroom. [I tell the tale as
though I had been there];[a] but the face of the bride who is
the object of their strife waits there piteously. And sud-
denly she is gone from her mother, like a calf that has wan-
dered.

Enter DEIANEIRA.

DEIANEIRA

Dear women, while the stranger is speaking to the captive
girls, on the point of leaving, I have come out of doors to
you without his noticing, partly to tell you what I have been

---

[a] The text is uncertain here.

---

[526] μάτηρ] θατὴρ Zielinski
[528] suppl. Gleditsch

535 τὰ δ᾽ οἷα πάσχω συγκατοικτιουμένη.
  κόρην γάρ, οἶμαι δ᾽ οὐκέτ᾽, ἀλλ᾽ ἐζευγμένην,
  παρεσδέδεγμαι, φόρτον ὥστε ναυτίλος,
  λωβητὸν ἐμπόλημα τῆς ἐμῆς φρενός.
  καὶ νῦν δύ᾽ οὖσαι μίμνομεν μιᾶς ὑπὸ
540 χλαίνης ὑπαγκάλισμα. τοιάδ᾽ Ἡρακλῆς,
  ὁ πιστὸς ἡμῖν κἀγαθὸς καλούμενος,
  οἰκούρι᾽ ἀντέπεμψε τοῦ μακροῦ χρόνου.
  ἐγὼ δὲ θυμοῦσθαι μὲν οὐκ ἐπίσταμαι
  νοσοῦντι κείνῳ πολλὰ τῇδε τῇ νόσῳ,
545 τὸ δ᾽ αὖ ξυνοικεῖν τῇδ᾽ ὁμοῦ τίς ἂν γυνὴ
  δύναιτο, κοινωνοῦσα τῶν αὐτῶν γάμων;
  ὁρῶ γὰρ ἥβην τὴν μὲν ἕρπουσαν πρόσω,
  τὴν δὲ φθίνουσαν· ὧν <δ᾽> ἀφαρπάζειν φιλεῖ
  ὀφθαλμὸς ἄνθος, τῶνδ᾽ ὑπεκτρέπει πόδα.
550 ταῦτ᾽ οὖν φοβοῦμαι μὴ πόσις μὲν Ἡρακλῆς
  ἐμὸς καλῆται, τῆς νεωτέρας δ᾽ ἀνήρ.
  ἀλλ᾽ οὐ γάρ, ὥσπερ εἶπον, ὀργαίνειν καλὸν
  γυναῖκα νοῦν ἔχουσαν· ᾗ δ᾽ ἔχω, φίλαι,
  λυτήριον λύπημα, τῇδ᾽ ὑμῖν φράσω.
555 ἦν μοι παλαιὸν δῶρον ἀρχαίου ποτὲ
  θηρός, λέβητι χαλκέῳ κεκρυμμένον,
  ὃ παῖς ἔτ᾽ οὖσα τοῦ δασυστέρνου παρὰ
  Νέσσου φθίνοντος ἐκ φονῶν ἀνειλόμην,
  ὃς τὸν βαθύρρουν ποταμὸν Εὔηνον βροτοὺς
560 μισθοῦ ᾽πόρευε χερσίν, οὔτε πομπίμοις
  κώπαις ἐρέσσων οὔτε λαίφεσιν νεώς.
  ὃς κἀμέ, τὸν πατρῷον ἡνίκα στόλον

doing, and partly to get comfort from you for my suffering. For I have taken in the maiden—but I think she is no maiden, but taken by him—as a captain takes on a cargo, a merchandise that does outrage to my feelings. And now the two of us remain beneath one blanket for him to embrace; such is the reward that Heracles, he who is called true and noble, has sent me for having kept the house so long. I do not know how to be angry with my husband now that he is suffering severely from this malady; yet what woman could live together with this girl, sharing a marriage with the same man? For I see her youth advancing, and mine perishing; and the desiring eye turns away from those whose bloom it snatches. This is why I am afraid that Heracles may be called my husband, but the younger woman's man. But as I said it is not honourable for a woman of sense to be angry; and I shall tell you what means I have of remedying pain.

I had an ancient gift from a monster long ago, hidden in a brazen pot, a thing I received as a girl at the death of Nessus, who for a fee used to carry people across the broad flow of the river Evenus, not by plying oars to transport them nor by a ship with sails, but in his arms. While he was

---

548 suppl. Zippmann
549 τῶνδ' Zippmann: τῶν δ' codd.

ξὺν Ἡρακλεῖ τὸ πρῶτον εὖνις ἑσπόμην,
φέρων ἐπ᾽ ὤμοις, ἡνίκ᾽ ἦ 'ν μέσῳ πόρῳ,
565 ψαύει ματαίαις χερσίν· ἐκ δ᾽ ἤϋσ᾽ ἐγώ,
χὠ Ζηνὸς εὐθὺς παῖς ἐπιστρέψας χεροῖν
ἧκεν κομήτην ἰόν· ἐς δὲ πλεύμονας
στέρνων διερροίζησεν. ἐκθνῄσκων δ᾽ ὁ θὴρ
τοσοῦτον εἶπε· "παῖ γέροντος Οἰνέως,
570 τοσόνδ᾽ ὀνήσῃ τῶν ἐμῶν, ἐὰν πίθῃ,
πορθμῶν, ὁθούνεχ᾽ ὑστάτην σ᾽ ἔπεμψ᾽ ἐγώ·
ἐὰν γὰρ ἀμφίθρεπτον αἷμα τῶν ἐμῶν
σφαγῶν ἐνέγκῃ χερσίν, ᾗ μελάγχολος
ἔβαψεν ἰὸς θρέμμα Λερναίας ὕδρας,
575 ἔσται φρενός σοι τοῦτο κηλητήριον
τῆς Ἡρακλείας, ὥστε μήτιν᾽ εἰσιδὼν
στέρξει γυναῖκα κεῖνος ἀντὶ σοῦ πλέον."
τοῦτ᾽ ἐννοήσασ᾽, ὦ φίλαι, δόμοις γὰρ ἦν
κείνου θανόντος ἐγκεκλημένον καλῶς,
580 χιτῶνα τόνδ᾽ ἔβαψα, προσβαλοῦσ᾽ ὅσα
ζῶν κεῖνος εἶπε· καὶ πεπείρανται τάδε.
κακὰς δὲ τόλμας μήτ᾽ ἐπισταίμην ἐγὼ
μήτ᾽ ἐκμάθοιμι, τάς τε τολμώσας στυγῶ.
φίλτροις δ᾽ ἐάν πως τήνδ᾽ ὑπερβαλώμεθα
585 τὴν παῖδα καὶ θέλκτροισι τοῖς ἐφ᾽ Ἡρακλεῖ,
μεμηχάνηται τοὔργον, εἴ τι μὴ δοκῶ
πράσσειν μάταιον· εἰ δὲ μή, πεπαύσομαι.

ΧΟΡΟΣ
ἀλλ᾽ εἴ τις ἐστὶ πίστις ἐν τοῖς δρωμένοις,
δοκεῖς παρ᾽ ἡμῖν οὐ βεβουλεῦσθαι κακῶς.

carrying me upon his shoulders, when I was first accompanying Heracles as bride, after my father had sent me off, while I was in mid-stream he laid lustful hands upon me, and I called out. At once the son of Zeus turned and let fly a feathered arrow, and it went whizzing through his chest into his lungs. As he expired the monster said so much: "Child of aged Oeneus, you shall get this benefit from being carried by me, if you will follow my instructions, because you were the last of my passengers. If you take away in your hands the clotted blood from my wound, where the poison's black gall, the creation of the hydra of Lerna, dyed it, it shall be a charm for the mind of Heracles, so that he shall never more see and love another woman instead of you." I remembered this, my dears, for when he was dead I had carefully locked it up at home, and dyed this tunic, adding all the things he while he still lived had told me; and this has been accomplished.

Of rash crimes may I never know or learn anything, and I detest women who perform them. But in the hope that I may somehow overcome this girl with spells and charms, the deed has been contrived . . . unless you think that what I am doing is foolish! If so, I shall abandon it.

CHORUS

Why, if one can have any faith in the performance, we think you have not been ill-advised.

573–74 μελάγχολος . . . ἰὸς Dobree: -ους . . . ἰοὺς codd.

ΔΗΙΑΝΕΙΡΑ

590 οὕτως ἔχει γ᾽ ἡ πίστις, ὡς τὸ μὲν δοκεῖν
ἔνεστι, πείρᾳ δ᾽ οὐ προσωμίλησά πω.

ΧΟΡΟΣ

ἀλλ᾽ εἰδέναι χρὴ δρῶσαν· ὡς οὐδ᾽ εἰ δοκεῖς
ἔχειν, ἔχοις ἂν γνῶμα, μὴ πειρωμένη.

ΔΗΙΑΝΕΙΡΑ

ἀλλ᾽ αὐτίκ᾽ εἰσόμεσθα· τόνδε γὰρ βλέπω
595 θυραῖον ἤδη· διὰ τάχους δ᾽ ἐλεύσεται.
μόνον παρ᾽ ὑμῶν εὖ στεγοίμεθ᾽· ὡς σκότῳ
κἂν αἰσχρὰ πράσσῃς, οὔποτ᾽ αἰσχύνῃ πεσῇ.

ΛΙΧΑΣ

τί χρὴ ποεῖν; σήμαινε, τέκνον Οἰνέως·
ὡς ἐσμὲν ἤδη τῷ μακρῷ χρόνῳ βραδεῖς.

ΔΗΙΑΝΕΙΡΑ

600 ἀλλ᾽ αὐτὰ δή σοι ταῦτα καὶ πράσσω, Λίχα,
ἕως σὺ ταῖς ἔσωθεν ἠγορῶ ξέναις,
ὅπως φέρῃς μοι τόνδε ταναϋφῆ πέπλον,
δώρημ᾽ ἐκείνῳ τἀνδρὶ τῆς ἐμῆς χερός.
διδοὺς δὲ τόνδε φράζ᾽ ὅπως μηδεὶς βροτῶν
605 κείνου πάροιθεν ἀμφιδύσεται χροΐ,
μηδ᾽ ὄψεταί νιν μήτε φέγγος ἡλίου
μήθ᾽ ἕρκος ἱερὸν μήτ᾽ ἐφέστιον σέλας,
πρὶν κεῖνος αὐτὸν φανερὸς ἐμφανῶς σταθεὶς
δείξῃ θεοῖσιν ἡμέρᾳ ταυροσφάγῳ.
610 οὕτω γὰρ ηὔγμην, εἴ ποτ᾽ αὐτὸν ἐς δόμους

THE WOMEN OF TRACHIS

DEIANEIRA

My faith extends so far, that I can believe it, but I have
never put it to the test.

CHORUS

Well, you must know when you take action, since even if
you think you have one, you have no way of testing it unless
you try it.

DEIANEIRA

Well, we shall soon know, for I see this man already at the
door, and he will soon be here. Only do you cover my
tracks loyally, for in darkness even if what you do is shame-
ful you will never be put to shame.

Enter LICHAS.

LICHAS

What am I to do? Tell me, child of Oeneus, for we are
already late by a long stretch of time.

DEIANEIRA

But this is the very thing I have been seeing to, Lichas,
while you were speaking with the foreign women inside the
house, so that you may take for me this fine-woven robe, a
gift for that man from my hand. And when you give it to
him, take care that no other person puts it on but he, and
that neither the light of the sun nor the sacred precinct nor
the blaze at the altar light upon it before he, standing there
conspicuous in the sight of all, shall show it to the gods on
the day when oxen shall be slaughtered. For this was my
vow, that if ever I saw or heard of his safe return home, I

---

⁶⁰² ταναϋφῆ Wunder: γ᾽ εὐϋφῆ codd.

ἴδοιμι σωθέντ᾽ ἢ κλύοιμι, πανδίκως
στελεῖν χιτῶνι τῷδε, καὶ φανεῖν θεοῖς
θυτῆρα καινῷ καινὸν ἐν πεπλώματι.
καὶ τῶνδ᾽ ἀποίσεις σῆμ᾽, ὃ κεῖνος εὐμαθὲς
615 σφραγῖδος ἕρκει τῷδ᾽ ἐπὸν μαθήσεται.
  ἀλλ᾽ ἕρπε, καὶ φύλασσε πρῶτα μὲν νόμον,
τὸ μὴ ᾽πιθυμεῖν πομπὸς ὢν περισσὰ δρᾶν·
ἔπειθ᾽ ὅπως ἂν ἡ χάρις κείνου τέ σοι
κἀμοῦ ξυνελθοῦσ᾽ ἐξ ἁπλῆς διπλῆ φανῇ.

ΛΙΧΑΣ

620 ἀλλ᾽ εἴπερ Ἑρμοῦ τήνδε πομπεύω τέχνην
βέβαιον, οὔ τι μὴ σφαλῶ γ᾽ ἐν σοί ποτε,
τὸ μὴ οὐ τόδ᾽ ἄγγος ὡς ἔχει δεῖξαι φέρων,
λόγων τε πίστιν ὧν λέγεις ἐφαρμόσαι.

ΔΗΙΑΝΕΙΡΑ

στείχοις ἂν ἤδη. καὶ γὰρ ἐξεπίστασαι
625 τά γ᾽ ἐν δόμοισιν ὡς ἔχοντα τυγχάνει.

ΛΙΧΑΣ

ἐπίσταμαί τε καὶ φράσω σεσωμένα.

ΔΗΙΑΝΕΙΡΑ

ἀλλ᾽ οἶσθα μὲν δὴ καὶ τὰ τῆς ξένης ὁρῶν
προσδέγματ᾽ αὐτός, ὥς σφ᾽ ἐδεξάμην φίλως.

ΛΙΧΑΣ

ὥστ᾽ ἐκπλαγῆναι τοὐμὸν ἡδονῇ κέαρ.

---

611 sunt qui post πανδίκως interpungant
615 ἐπὸν μαθήσεται Billerbeck: ἐπ᾽ ὄμμα θήσεται codd.

would duly clothe him in this tunic, and reveal to the gods a new sacrificer wearing a new robe. And you shall carry with you a token, which he shall easily recognise because it is upon the circle of my seal.

But go, and first of all observe the rule that a messenger must not be distracted from his message, and also make sure that his gratitude and mine shall be combined, so that you get double thanks.

LICHAS

Why, if I exercise reliably this art that belongs to Hermes, I shall never fail when I do so for you, so that I shall bring this vessel and show it just as it is, and add the assurance given by the words that you have spoken.

DEIANEIRA

Depart at once, for you know well how things stand in the house!

LICHAS

I know, and I shall explain that all is well.

DEIANEIRA

Well, you know as an eyewitness about the welcome of the foreign girl, how kindly I received her.

LICHAS

So that my heart felt a delightful surprise!

---

623 λέγεις Wunder: ἔχεις codd.
628 αὐτός Bergk: αὐτὴν codd.

189

SOPHOCLES

ΔHIANEIPA

630 τί δῆτ' ἂν ἄλλο γ' ἐννέποις; δέδοικα γὰρ
μὴ πρῲ λέγοις ἂν τὸν πόθον τὸν ἐξ ἐμοῦ,
πρὶν εἰδέναι τἀκεῖθεν εἰ ποθούμεθα.

ΧΟΡΟΣ

ὦ ναύλοχα καὶ πετραῖα θερμὰ λουτρὰ καὶ
πάγους   στρ. α΄
635 Οἴτας παραναιετάοντες, οἵ τε μέσσαν
Μηλίδα πὰρ λίμναν
χρυσαλακάτου τ' ἀκτὰν κόρας,
ἔνθ' Ἑλλάνων ἀγοραὶ Πυλάτιδες κλέονται,
640 ὁ καλλιβόας τάχ' ὑμὶν αὐλὸς οὐκ ἀναρσίαν   ἀντ. α΄
ἀχῶν καναχὰν ἐπάνεισιν, ἀλλὰ θείας
ἀντίλυρον μούσας.
ὁ γὰρ Διὸς Ἀλκμήνας κόρος
645 σοῦται πάσας ἀρετᾶς λάφυρ' ἔχων ἐπ' οἴκους·
ὃν ἀπόπτολιν εἴχομεν πάντα   στρ. β΄
δυοκαιδεκάμηνον ἀμμένουσαι
χρόνον, πελάγιον, ἴδριες οὐ-
650 δέν· ἅ δέ οἱ φίλα δάμαρ τάλαιναν
δυστάλαινα καρδίαν
πάγκλαυτος αἰὲν ὤλλυτο·
νῦν δ' Ἄρης οἰστρηθεὶς
ἐξέλυσ' ἐπιπόνων ἁμερᾶν.
655 ἀφίκοιτ' ἀφίκοιτο· μὴ σταίη   ἀντ. β΄
πολύκωπον ὄχημα ναὸς αὐτῷ,
πρὶν τάνδε πρὸς πόλιν ἀνύσει-
ε, νασιῶτιν ἑστίαν ἀμείψας,

190

DEIANEIRA

What else could you say to him? For I am afraid you might
be premature in saying how I long for him, before knowing
if I am longed for there.

Exit LICHAS and DEIANEIRA.

CHORUS

Dwellers by the harbour and the hot springs by the rocks
and by the gulf of Malis in the centre and the coast belong-
ing to the maiden of the golden distaff,[a] where lie the
famous places of assembly of the Greeks at the Gates, soon
shall the beautiful sound of the pipe rise up for you again,
in no hateful strain of sorrows, but responding to the Muse
divine! For Alcmene's son by Zeus is hastening home,
bearing the trophies of all valour, he who was altogether
absent from our city while we waited for twelve months in
ignorance, across the sea; and his dear wife was ever per-
ishing in misery in her sad heart. But now the war god
goaded to fury has released him from days of toil.

May he come, may he come! May the many oars of the
ship that bears him make no stop before he makes his way
to this city, leaving the altar on the island where we are told

---

[a] Artemis; the place meant is Thermopylae.

---

639 κλέονται Musgrave: καλέονται codd.
642 ἀχῶν Elmsley: ἰάχων codd.
645 σοῦται Elmsley: σεῦται codd.
650 τάλαιναν Dindorf; τάλαινα codd.
654 ἐπιπόνων ἁμερᾶν Erfurdt: -ον -αν codd.

SOPHOCLES

ἔνθα κλῄζεται θυτήρ·
660 ὅθεν μόλοι †πανάμερος,
τᾶς Πειθοῦς παγχρίστῳ
συγκραθεὶς ἐπὶ προφάσει θηρός†.

ΔΗΙΑΝΕΙΡΑ

γυναῖκες, ὡς δέδοικα μὴ περαιτέρω
πεπραγμέν' ᾖ μοι πάνθ' ὅσ' ἀρτίως ἔδρων.

ΧΟΡΟΣ

665 τί δ' ἔστι, Δηάνειρα, τέκνον Οἰνέως;

ΔΗΙΑΝΕΙΡΑ

οὐκ οἶδ'· ἀθυμῶ δ' εἰ φανήσομαι τάχα
κακὸν μέγ' ἐκπράξασ' ἀπ' ἐλπίδος καλῆς.

ΧΟΡΟΣ

οὐ δή τι τῶν σῶν Ἡρακλεῖ δωρημάτων;

ΔΗΙΑΝΕΙΡΑ

μάλιστά γ'· ὥστε μήποτ' ἂν προθυμίαν
670 ἄδηλον ἔργου τῳ παραινέσαι λαβεῖν.

ΧΟΡΟΣ

δίδαξον, εἰ διδακτόν, ἐξ ὅτου φοβῇ.

ΔΗΙΑΝΕΙΡΑ

τοιοῦτον ἐκβέβηκεν, οἷον, ἢν φράσω,
γυναῖκες, ὑμῖν θαῦμ' ἀνέλπιστον βαλεῖν.
ᾧ γὰρ τὸν ἐνδυτῆρα πέπλον ἀρτίως
675 ἔχριον, ἀργῆς οἰὸς εὐείρῳ πόκῳ,
τοῦτ' ἠφάνισται διάβορον πρὸς οὐδενὸς
τῶν ἔνδον, ἀλλ' ἔδεστον ἐξ αὑτοῦ φθίνει,

that he is sacrificing! May he come from there, deeply desired, united in love through the monster's beguilement of persuasion.

Enter DEIANEIRA.

DEIANEIRA
Women, I am afraid that in all I lately did I went too far!

CHORUS
What is the matter, Deianeira, child of Oeneus?

DEIANEIRA
I do not know; but I am in despair at the thought that I may soon be shown to have done great harm in the expectation of good.

CHORUS
Surely not in the matter of your gift to Heracles?

DEIANEIRA
Indeed, so that I shall never advise anyone to show eager haste in any business that he does not understand.

CHORUS
Explain to me, if you can, the cause of your fear!

DEIANEIRA
Such a thing has happened, women, that if I tell you of it it will make you desperately wonder! The thing with which I lately rubbed the robe he was to put on, the woolly fleece of a white sheep, has vanished, eaten away by nothing in the house, but consumed by itself, and it is crumbling

---

660 πανάμερος] πανίμερος Mudge
662 συντακεὶς Paley, quo recepto θηρὸς ὕπο παρφάσει Pearson
673 βαλεῖν Ll.-J.: λαβεῖν codd.
675 ἀργῆς Bergk: ἀργῆτ' codd.

καὶ ψῇ κατ᾽ ἄκρας σπιλάδος. ὡς δ᾽ εἰδῇς ἅπαν,
ᾗ τοῦτ᾽ ἐπράχθη, μείζον᾽ ἐκτενῶ λόγον.

680   ἐγὼ γὰρ ὧν ὁ θήρ με Κένταυρος, πονῶν
πλευρὰν πικρᾷ γλωχῖνι, προυδιδάξατο
παρῆκα θεσμῶν οὐδέν, ἀλλ᾽ ἐσῳζόμην,
χαλκῆς ὅπως δύσνιπτον ἐκ δέλτου γραφήν·
[καί μοι τάδ᾽ ἦν πρόρρητα καὶ τοιαῦτ᾽ ἔδρων·]
685   τὸ φάρμακον τοῦτ᾽ ἄπυρον ἀκτῖνός τ᾽ ἀεὶ
θερμῆς ἄθικτον ἐν μυχοῖς σῴζειν ἐμέ,
ἕως ἂν ἀρτίχριστον ἁρμόσαιμί που.
κἄδρων τοιαῦτα. νῦν δ᾽, ὅτ᾽ ἦν ἐργαστέον,
ἔχρισα μὲν κατ᾽ οἶκον ἐν δόμοις κρυφῇ
690   μαλλῷ, σπάσασα κτησίου βοτοῦ λάχνην,
κἄθηκα συμπτύξασ᾽ ἀλαμπὲς ἡλίου
κοίλῳ ζυγάστρῳ δῶρον, ὥσπερ εἴδετε.
    ἔξω δ᾽ ἀποστείχουσα δέρκομαι φάτιν
ἄφραστον, ἀξύμβλητον ἀνθρώπῳ μαθεῖν.
695   τὸ γὰρ κάταγμα τυγχάνω ῥίψασά πως
[τῆς οἰός, ᾧ προὔχριον, ἐς μέσην φλόγα,]
ἀκτῖν᾽ ἐς ἡλιῶτιν· ὡς δ᾽ ἐθάλπετο,
ῥεῖ πᾶν ἄδηλον καὶ κατέψηκται χθονί,
μορφῇ μάλιστ᾽ εἰκαστὸν ὥστε πρίονος
700   ἐκβρώμαθ᾽ ἂν βλέψειας ἐν τομῇ ξύλου.
τοιόνδε κεῖται προπετές. ἐκ δὲ γῆς, ὅθεν
προὔκειτ᾽, ἀναζέουσι θρομβώδεις ἀφροί,
γλαυκῆς ὀπώρας ὥστε πίονος ποτοῦ
χυθέντος ἐς γῆν Βακχίας ἀπ᾽ ἀμπέλου.
705   ὥστ᾽ οὐκ ἔχω τάλαινα ποῖ γνώμης πέσω·

down from the top of a stone slab. But so that you can know the whole story of how this was done, I shall speak at greater length.

I neglected none of the instructions which the monster gave me, his side pained by the cruel arrow's point, but observed them, like writing hard to wash away from a bronze tablet. [These were his orders, and these I carried out.] I was to keep in a secret place the unguent, far from the fire and never warmed by the sun's ray, until I should apply it, newly rubbed, on something; and that is what I did. Now, when it was time to act, I rubbed it in secret, in a room inside the house, with a fleece of wool, a tuft pulled from a sheep belonging to our flock, folded it, and placed the gift, which the sun had never touched, in a container, as you saw.

And when I was going out I saw a thing too strange for words, beyond human understanding. I happened to have thrown the piece of sheep's wool [with which I had rubbed in the ointment right onto the hot floor] into the sun's ray; and when it grew warm, it melted away into nothing and crumbled on the ground, looking most like the sawdust you see when somebody cuts wood. So there it lay, where it had fallen; and from the ground where it was lying clotted foam boiled up, as when the rich liquid from the blue-green fruit is poured upon the ground from the vine of Bacchus.

So I do not know, in my trouble, what decision to come

---

[684] del. Wunder   [693] ἔξω Ll.-J.: εἴσω codd.

[696] del. Dobree

[700] ἐκβρώμαθ' ἂν βλέψειας Tyrrell: -ατ' ἂν βλέψειας a: -ατ' ἐκβλέψειας Lt

ὁρῶ δέ μ' ἔργον δεινὸν ἐξειργασμένην.
πόθεν γὰρ ἄν ποτ', ἀντὶ τοῦ θνῄσκων ὁ θὴρ
ἐμοὶ παρέσχ' εὔνοιαν, ἧς ἔθνῃσχ' ὕπερ;
οὐκ ἔστιν, ἀλλὰ τὸν βαλόντ' ἀποφθίσαι
710 χρῄζων ἔθελγέ μ'· ὧν ἐγὼ μεθύστερον,
ὅτ' οὐκέτ' ἀρκεῖ, τὴν μάθησιν ἄρνυμαι.
μόνη γὰρ αὐτόν, εἴ τι μὴ ψευσθήσομαι
γνώμης, ἐγὼ δύστηνος ἐξαποφθερῶ·
τὸν γὰρ βαλόντ' ἄτρακτον οἶδα καὶ θεὸν
715 Χείρωνα πημήναντα, χὦνπερ ἂν θίγῃ,
φθείρει τὰ πάντα κνώδαλ'· ἐκ δὲ τοῦδ' ὅδε
σφαγῶν διελθὼν ἰὸς αἵματος μέλας
πῶς οὐκ ὀλεῖ καὶ τόνδε; δόξῃ γοῦν ἐμῇ.
καίτοι δέδοκται, κεῖνος εἰ σφαλήσεται,
720 ταὐτῇ σὺν ὁρμῇ κἀμὲ συνθανεῖν ἅμα.
ζῆν γὰρ κακῶς κλύουσαν οὐκ ἀνασχετόν,
ἥτις προτιμᾷ μὴ κακὴ πεφυκέναι.

ΧΟΡΟΣ

ταρβεῖν μὲν ἔργα δείν' ἀναγκαίως ἔχει,
τὴν δ' ἐλπίδ' οὐ χρὴ τῆς τύχης κρίνειν πάρος.

ΔΗΙΑΝΕΙΡΑ

725 οὐκ ἔστιν ἐν τοῖς μὴ καλοῖς βουλεύμασιν
οὐδ' ἐλπίς, ἥτις καὶ θράσος τι προξενεῖ.

ΧΟΡΟΣ

ἀλλ' ἀμφὶ τοῖς σφαλεῖσι μὴ 'ξ ἑκουσίας
ὀργὴ πέπειρα, τῆς σε τυγχάνειν πρέπει.

to; and I see that I have done a terrible thing. For why, in return for what, could the monster have done a kindness to me, the cause of his death? It cannot be; but he cajoled me, wishing to destroy the man who had shot him; this I learn too late, when the knowledge cannot serve me. For if I am not to prove mistaken in my judgment, I alone, miserable one, shall be his ruin; I know that the arrow that struck him tormented even Chiron, who was immortal, and it destroys all the beasts whom it touches. How shall the black poison of the blood, coming from the fatal wound, not destroy my husband also? That is my belief. Well, I have determined, if he comes to grief, that with the same movement I too shall die with him. For a woman whose care is to be good cannot bear to live and to enjoy evil repute.

CHORUS

Dreadful actions must needs inspire fear; but one should not expect the worst before the thing has happened.

DEIANEIRA

When one has proved ill-advised, there is no hope that can furnish any confidence.

CHORUS

But when people come to grief through no fault of their own, anger is softened, and you should benefit from this.

---

715 χὦνπερ Wakefield: χὦσπερ La
717 αἵματος] αἱματοῦς Wunder

ΔHIANEIPA

τοιαῦτά τἂν λέξειεν οὐχ ὁ τοῦ κακοῦ
730 κοινωνός, ἀλλ' ᾧ μηδὲν ἔστ' οἴκοι βαρύ.

ΧΟΡΟΣ

σιγᾶν ἂν ἁρμόζοι σε τὸν πλείω λόγον,
εἰ μή τι λέξεις παιδὶ τῷ σαυτῆς· ἐπεὶ
πάρεστι, μαστὴρ πατρὸς ὃς πρὶν ᾤχετο.

ΥΛΛΟΣ

ὦ μῆτερ, ὡς ἂν ἐκ τριῶν σ' ἓν εἱλόμην,
735 ἢ μηκέτ' εἶναι ζῶσαν, ἢ σεσωμένην
ἄλλου κεκλῆσθαι μητέρ', ἢ λῴους φρένας
τῶν νῦν παρουσῶν τῶνδ' ἀμείψασθαί ποθεν.

ΔHIANEIPA

τί δ' ἔστιν, ὦ παῖ, πρός γ' ἐμοῦ στυγούμενον;

ΥΛΛΟΣ

τὸν ἄνδρα τὸν σὸν ἴσθι, τὸν δ' ἐμὸν λέγω
740 πατέρα, κατακτείνασα τῇδ' ἐν ἡμέρᾳ.

ΔHIANEIPA

οἴμοι, τίν' ἐξήνεγκας, ὦ τέκνον, λόγον;

ΥΛΛΟΣ

ὃν οὐχ οἷόν τε μὴ τελεσθῆναι· τὸ γὰρ
φανθὲν τίς ἂν δύναιτ' <ἂν> ἀγένητον ποεῖν;

---

729 τἂν Blaydes: δ' ἂν codd.
730 οἴκοι Wakefield: -οις codd.
743 suppl. anon.

DEIANEIRA

That is the kind of thing that a person who has no trouble of his own would say, but not the one to whom the evil belongs.

CHORUS

As to the rest of the story you should be silent, unless you are going to say something to your son; for he who had gone to look for his father is now present.

Enter HYLLUS.

HYLLUS

Mother, I would choose one of three things, that you should no longer be alive, or that you should survive but be called someone else's mother, or that you should somehow acquire a better heart than the one you have!

DEIANEIRA

And what is it I have done, my son, that is so hateful?

HYLLUS

Know that on this day you have killed your husband—yes, my father!

DEIANEIRA

Ah me, what words have you brought out, my son?

HYLLUS

Words that cannot fail to be accomplished; for when one has seen a thing, how can one cause it never to have happened?

SOPHOCLES

ΔHIANEIPA

πῶς εἶπας, ὦ παῖ; τοῦ παρ' ἀνθρώπων μαθὼν
745 ἄζηλον οὕτως ἔργον εἰργάσθαι με φής;

ΥΛΛΟΣ

αὐτὸς βαρεῖαν ξυμφορὰν ἐν ὄμμασιν
πατρὸς δεδορκὼς κοὐ κατὰ γλῶσσαν κλυών.

ΔHIANEIPA

ποῦ δ' ἐμπελάζεις τἀνδρὶ καὶ παρίστασαι;

ΥΛΛΟΣ

εἰ χρὴ μαθεῖν σε, πάντα δὴ φωνεῖν χρεών.
750 ὅθ' εἷρπε κλεινὴν Εὐρύτου πέρσας πόλιν,
νίκης ἄγων τροπαῖα κἀκροθίνια,
ἀκτή τις ἀμφίκλυστος Εὐβοίας ἄκρον
Κήναιόν ἐστιν, ἔνθα πατρῴῳ Διὶ
βωμοὺς ὁρίζει τεμενίαν τε φυλλάδα·
755 οὗ νιν τὰ πρῶτ' ἐσεῖδον ἄσμενος πόθῳ.
μέλλοντι δ' αὐτῷ πολυθύτους τεύχειν σφαγὰς
κῆρυξ ἀπ' οἴκων ἵκετ' οἰκεῖος Λίχας,
τὸ σὸν φέρων δώρημα, θανάσιμον πέπλον·
ὃν κεῖνος ἐνδύς, ὡς σὺ προὐξεφίεσο,
760 ταυροκτονεῖ μὲν δώδεκ' ἐντελεῖς ἔχων
λείας ἀπαρχὴν βοῦς· ἀτὰρ τὰ πάνθ' ὁμοῦ
ἑκατὸν προσῆγε συμμιγῆ βοσκήματα.
καὶ πρῶτα μὲν δείλαιος ἵλεῳ φρενὶ
κόσμῳ τε χαίρων καὶ στολῇ κατηύχετο·
765 ὅπως δὲ σεμνῶν ὀργίων ἐδαίετο
φλὸξ αἱματηρὰ κἀπὸ πιείρας δρυός,

DEIANEIRA

What have you said, my son? On whose warrant do you say
that I have done a deed so much to be deplored?

HYLLUS

I saw with my own eyes my father's dire calamity; I did not
hear tell of it.

DEIANEIRA

Where did you approach him and stand by?

HYLLUS

If you must hear the story, I must tell you all. When he
returned from sacking the city of Eurytus, bringing the tro-
phies of victory and the first fruits—there is a sea-swept
cape in Euboea, Mount Cenaeum, where he was marking
off altars and a sacred grove for Zeus his father. That is
where I first saw him, much relieved, for I had missed him.
And as he was about to slaughter the many beasts for
sacrifice, there came from home his own herald, Lichas,
bringing your gift, the robe of death. He put it on, as you
had instructed, and slew twelve bulls without a blemish, as
the first fruits of the spoils; but in all he was bringing up a
hundred cattle of all kinds. At first, poor man, he spoke the
prayer cheerfully, rejoicing in the fine attire. But when the
bloodshot flame from the sacred offerings and from the
resinous pine blazed up, the sweat came up upon his body,

---

[760] ἔχων] ἐλὼν ?

ἱδρὼς ἀνήει χρωτί, καὶ προσπτύσσεται
πλευραῖσιν ἀρτίκολλος, ὥστε τέκτονος
χιτών, ἅπαν κατ᾽ ἄρθρον· ἦλθε δ᾽ ὀστέων
770 ὀδαγμὸς ἀντίσπαστος· εἶτα φοίνιος
ἐχθρᾶς ἐχίδνης ἰὸς ὣς ἐδαίνυτο.
    ἐνταῦθα δὴ ᾽βόησε τὸν δυσδαίμονα
Λίχαν, τὸν οὐδὲν αἴτιον τοῦ σοῦ κακοῦ,
ποίαις ἐνέγκοι τόνδε μηχαναῖς πέπλον·
775 ὁ δ᾽ οὐδὲν εἰδὼς δύσμορος τὸ σὸν μόνης
δώρημ᾽ ἔλεξεν, ὥσπερ ἦν ἐσταλμένον.
κἀκεῖνος ὡς ἤκουσε καὶ διώδυνος
σπαραγμὸς αὐτοῦ πλευμόνων ἀνθήψατο,
μάρψας ποδός νιν, ἄρθρον ᾗ λυγίζεται,
780 ῥίπτει πρὸς ἀμφίκλυστον ἐκ πόντου πέτραν·
κόμης δὲ λευκὸν μυελὸν ἐκραίνει, μέσου
κρατὸς διασπαρέντος αἵματός θ᾽ ὁμοῦ.
ἅπας δ᾽ ἀνηυφήμησεν οἰμωγῇ λεώς,
τοῦ μὲν νοσοῦντος, τοῦ δὲ διαπεπραγμένου·
785 κοὐδεὶς ἐτόλμα τἀνδρὸς ἀντίον μολεῖν.
ἐσπᾶτο γὰρ πέδονδε καὶ μετάρσιος,
βοῶν, ἰύζων· ἀμφὶ δ᾽ ἐκτύπουν πέτραι,
Λοκρῶν τ᾽ ὄρειοι πρῶνες Εὐβοίας τ᾽ ἄκραι.
ἐπεὶ δ᾽ ἀπεῖπε, πολλὰ μὲν τάλας χθονὶ
790 ῥίπτων ἑαυτόν, πολλὰ δ᾽ οἰμωγῇ βοῶν,
τὸ δυσπάρευνον λέκτρον ἐνδατούμενος
σοῦ τῆς ταλαίνης καὶ τὸν Οἰνέως γάμον
οἷον κατακτήσαιτο λυμαντὴν βίου,
τότ᾽ ἐκ προσέδρου λιγνύος διάστροφον

and the thing clung closely to his sides, as a carpenter's tunic might, at every joint; and a biting pain came, tearing at his bones; then a bloody poison like that of a hateful serpent fed upon him.

Next he shouted at the unhappy Lichas, who was in no way guilty of your crime, asking him through what scheme he had brought the robe. And Lichas, who knew nothing, poor fellow, told him that was your gift alone, as he had been instructed. When Heracles heard it, and an agonising convulsion laid hold of his lungs, he seized him by the foot, where the ankle plays in the socket, and hurled him onto the seaswept rock; and the white brains poured out from his hair, as his head was shattered. And the whole people cried out with awe at the sickness of the one and the undoing of the other; but no one dared to come near the man. For the pain dragged him downwards and upwards, shouting and screaming; and the rocks around resounded, the mountain promontories of Locri and the Euboean peaks. But when he gave over, hurling himself often to the ground and uttering many loud cries, dwelling upon his disastrous marriage with you, wretched one, and on how the alliance he had made with Oeneus had ruined his life, then he lifted up his rolling eye above the smoke

---

[767] προσπτύσσεται Musgrave: -ετο codd.

[770] φοίνιος Pierson: -ίας codd.

[783] ἀνηυφήμησεν Dindorf: ἀνευ- Π 13, sch. E. *Tro.* 573: ἀνευφώνησεν fere cett.

[788] prius τ' Diog. Laert. 10, 137: om. codd.

795 ὀφθαλμὸν ἄρας εἶδέ μ' ἐν πολλῷ στρατῷ
δακρυρροοῦντα, καί με προσβλέψας καλεῖ·
"ὦ παῖ, πρόσελθε, μὴ φύγῃς τοὐμὸν κακόν,
μηδ' εἴ σε χρὴ θανόντι συνθανεῖν ἐμοί·
ἀλλ' ἆρον ἔξω, καὶ μάλιστα μέν με θὲς
800 ἐνταῦθ' ὅπου με μή τις ὄψεται βροτῶν·
εἰ δ' οἶκτον ἴσχεις, ἀλλά μ' ἔκ γε τῆσδε γῆς
πόρθμευσον ὡς τάχιστα, μηδ' αὐτοῦ θάνω."
τοσαῦτ' ἐπισκήψαντος, ἐν μέσῳ σκάφει
θέντες σφε πρὸς γῆν τήνδ' ἐκέλσαμεν μόλις
805 βρυχώμενον σπασμοῖσι. καί νιν αὐτίκα
ἢ ζῶντ' ἐσόψεσθ' ἢ τεθνηκότ' ἀρτίως.
    τοιαῦτα, μῆτερ, πατρὶ βουλεύσασ' ἐμῷ
καὶ δρῶσ' ἐλήφθης, ὧν σε ποίνιμος Δίκη
τείσαιτ' Ἐρινύς τ'. εἰ θέμις δ', ἐπεύχομαι·
810 θέμις δ', ἐπεί μοι τὴν θέμιν σὺ προὔβαλες,
πάντων ἄριστον ἄνδρα τῶν ἐπὶ χθονὶ
κτείνασ', ὁποῖον ἄλλον οὐκ ὄψῃ ποτέ.

ΧΟΡΟΣ

τί σῖγ' ἀφέρπεις; οὐ κάτοισθ' ὁθούνεκα
ξυνηγορεῖς σιγῶσα τῷ κατηγόρῳ;

ΥΛΛΟΣ

815 ἐᾶτ' ἀφέρπειν. οὖρος ὀφθαλμῶν ἐμῶν
αὐτῇ γένοιτ' ἄπωθεν ἑρπούσῃ καλός.
ὄγκον γὰρ ἄλλως ὀνόματος τί δεῖ τρέφειν
μητρῷον, ἥτις μηδὲν ὡς τεκοῦσα δρᾷ;
ἀλλ' ἑρπέτω χαίρουσα· τὴν δὲ τέρψιν ἣν
820 τὠμῷ δίδωσι πατρί, τήνδ' αὐτὴ λάβοι.

that clung about him and saw me weeping in the middle of
the throng. And when he had sighted me he called me,
saying, "Boy, come here, do not run away from my trouble,
not even if you have to share my death! Lift me and take
me out of this, and, if you can, place me where no man can
look upon me! But if you pity me, transport me at least out
of this country; let me not die here!" When he had given
this command, we put him right into a boat, and with much
trouble brought him to this land, bellowing as the spasms
seized him. In a moment you will see him, either alive or
lately dead.

These are the plot and the action, mother, of which you
are convicted, for which may avenging Justice and the Eri-
nys punish you! And if right permits it, I utter a curse on
you! And right does permit it, since you have made it right
for me, killing the noblest man upon the earth, one such as
you shall never see again!

Exit DEIANEIRA.

CHORUS

Why do you depart in silence? Do you not know that your
silence seconds the accuser?

HYLLUS

Let her depart! May a fair wind carry her far from my
sight! For why should one vainly honour the dignity of the
name of mother, when none of her actions are a mother's?
Let her go; farewell to her; and may she have for her own
the joy she gave my father!

Exit HYLLUS.

---

806 ἐσόψεσθ᾽] ἔτ᾽ ὄψεσθ᾽ Meineke

ΧΟΡΟΣ

ἴδ' οἷον, ὦ παῖδες, προσέμειξεν ἄφαρ   στρ. α´
τοὔπος τὸ θεοπρόπον ἡμῖν
τᾶς παλαιφάτου προνοίας,
ὅ τ' ἔλακεν, ὁπότε τελεόμηνος ἐκφέροι
825 δωδέκατος ἄροτος, ἀναδοχὰν τελεῖν πόνων
τῷ Διὸς αὐτόπαιδι·
καὶ τάδ' ὀρθῶς
ἔμπεδα κατουρίζει.
πῶς γὰρ ἂν ὁ μὴ λεύσσων
ἔτι ποτ' ἔτ' ἐπίπονον
830 ἔχοι θανὼν λατρείαν;
εἰ γάρ σφε Κενταύρου φονίᾳ νεφέλᾳ   ἀντ. α´
χρίει δολοποιὸς ἀνάγκα
πλευρά, προστακέντος ἰοῦ,
ὃν τέκετο θάνατος, ἔτεκε δ' αἰόλος δράκων,
835 πῶς ὅδ' ἂν ἀέλιον ἕτερον ἢ τανῦν ἴδοι,
δεινοτέρῳ μὲν ὕδρας
προστετακὼς
φάσματι; μελαγχαίτᾳ τ'
ἄμμιγά νιν αἰκίζει
ὑπόφονα δολόμυ-
840 θα κέντρ' ἐπιζέσαντα.
ὧν ἅδ' ἁ τλάμων ἄοκνος   στρ. β´
μεγάλαν προσορῶσα δόμοισι
βλάβαν νέων ἀίσσου-
σαν γάμων τὰ μὲν αὐτὰ

CHORUS

See, maidens, how swiftly there has come upon us the oracular saying of the ancient prophecy, which declared that when the twelfth ploughing should accomplish its tale of months, it should bring relief from his labours for the true son of Zeus! And now those words are wafted surely to fulfilment; for how could one who sees no longer maintain still, still in death his toilsome servitude?

For if the cunning constraint of the Centaur with its deadly snare stings his sides, as the poison soaks in whose mother was the darting snake and whose begetter was Death, how could he look upon tomorrow's sun, being glued to an apparition deadlier than the Hydra? And he suffers every torture from the deadly sting caused by the cunning words of the black-haired one as it boils up.

Of this the poor woman had no foreboding when she saw the great disaster of the new marriage speeding

---

836 δεινοτέρῳ Ll.-J.: -τάτῳ codd.

838 post αἰκίζει add. Νέσ(σ)ου θ᾽ codd., del. Erfurdt

839 ὑπόφονα Hermann: ὕπο φοίνια Laz

841 ἄοκνος Musgrave: ἄοκνον codd.

843 ἀίσσουσαν Nauck: ἀισσόντων codd.   αὐτὰ Blaydes: οὔ τι codd.

προσέβαλεν, τὰ δ' ἀπ' ἀλλόθρου
845 γνώμας μολόντ' ὀλεθρίαισι συναλλαγαῖς
ἦ που ὀλοὰ στένει,
ἦ που ἀδινῶν χλωρὰν
τέγγει δακρύων ἄχναν.
ἁ δ' ἐρχομένα μοῖρα προφαίνει δολίαν
850 καὶ μεγάλαν ἄταν.
ἔρρωγεν παγὰ δακρύων,   ἀντ. β′
κέχυται νόσος, ὦ πόποι, οἷον
ἀναρσίων <ὕπ'> οὔπω
<τοῦδε σῶμ'> ἀγακλειτὸν
855 ἐπέμολεν πάθος οἰκτίσαι.
ἰὼ κελαινὰ λόγχα προμάχου δορός,
ἃ τότε θοὰν νύμφαν
ἄγαγες ἀπ' αἰπεινᾶς
·τάνδ' Οἰχαλίας αἰχμᾷ·
860 ἁ δ' ἀμφίπολος Κύπρις ἄναυδος φανερὰ
τῶνδ' ἐφάνη πράκτωρ.

<ΤΡΟΦΟΣ

ἰώ μοι.>

ΧΟΡΟΣ

πότερον ἐγὼ μάταιος, ἢ κλύω τινὸς
οἴκτου δι' οἴκων ἀρτίως ὁρμωμένου;
865 τί φημι;
ἠχεῖ τις οὐκ ἄσημον, ἀλλὰ δυστυχῆ
κωκυτὸν εἴσω, καί τι καινίζει στέγη.

towards the house; part of the deed she herself supplied,
but part came from another's will, at a fatal meeting.
Much, I think, does she in her ruin lament it; thickly fall
the tears whose pale dew she sheds. And Fate as it
approaches foreshadows a treacherous and a great disaster.

The flood of tears has burst forth; the plague streams
over him, alas; so piteous an affliction have his enemies
never brought upon his glorious form. Alas for the black
point of the defending spear, which then brought the
swiftly running bride from lofty Oechalia by its might! And
the Cyprian, silent in attendance, is revealed as the doer of
these things.

Enter the NURSE.

\<NURSE

Ah me!\>

CHORUS

Am I deluded, or do I hear a lamentation just arising in the
house? What am I saying? Someone is uttering no muted
cry, but one of sorrow, and there is new trouble in the

---

[844] ἀλλόθρου Erfurdt: ἀλλοθρόου codd.
[854] suppl. Jebb   post ἀγάκλειτον add. Ἡρακλέους codd.,
del. Dindorf
[862] suppl. Meineke

ξύνες δὲ
τήνδ' ὡς ἀγηθὴς καὶ συνωφρυωμένη
870 χωρεῖ πρὸς ἡμᾶς γραῖα σημανοῦσά τι.

ΤΡΟΦΟΣ

ὦ παῖδες, ὡς ἄρ' ἡμὶν οὐ σμικρῶν κακῶν
ἦρξεν τὸ δῶρον Ἡρακλεῖ τὸ πόμπιμον.

ΧΟΡΟΣ

τί δ', ὦ γεραιά, καινοποιηθὲν λέγεις;

ΤΡΟΦΟΣ

βέβηκε Δηάνειρα τὴν πανυστάτην
875 ὁδῶν ἁπασῶν ἐξ ἀκινήτου ποδός.

ΧΟΡΟΣ

οὐ δή ποθ' ὡς θανοῦσα;

ΤΡΟΦΟΣ

πάντ' ἀκήκοας.

ΧΟΡΟΣ

τέθνηκεν ἡ τάλαινα;

ΤΡΟΦΟΣ

δεύτερον κλύεις.

ΧΟΡΟΣ

τάλαιν'· ὀλέθρου τίνι τρόπῳ θανεῖν σφε φής;

ΤΡΟΦΟΣ

σχετλίῳ τὰ πρός γε πρᾶξιν.

ΧΟΡΟΣ

εἰπέ, τῷ μόρῳ,
880 γύναι, ξυντρέχει;

house. Notice how sadly, and with what a cloud upon her
eyes, the old woman is approaching us to tell us something.

NURSE

Children, the gift that was sent to Heracles has proved to
be the start of no small evils!

CHORUS

What is the new event, aged woman, of which you speak?

NURSE

Without movement of her foot Deianeira has gone on the
last of all journeys!

CHORUS

Surely not in death?

NURSE

You have heard it all.

CHORUS

Is the poor lady dead?

NURSE

You are hearing it a second time.

CHORUS

Poor lady! By what manner of death do you say she per-
ished?

NURSE

A grim death, as regards the doing of it.

CHORUS

Tell us, woman, how she met her end!

---

869 ἀγηθὴς M. Schmidt: ἀήθης codd.
878 ὀλέθρου Blaydes: ὀλεθρία codd.
879 σχετλίῳ τὰ Hermann: σχετλιώτατα codd.

211

SOPHOCLES

ΤΡΟΦΟΣ

ταύτην διηίστωσεν <ἄμφηκες ξίφος>.

ΧΟΡΟΣ

τίς θυμός, ἢ τίνες νόσοι,
τάνδ᾽ αἰχμᾷ βέλεος κακοῦ
ξυνεῖλε; πῶς ἐμήσατο
885 πρὸς θανάτῳ θάνατον
ἀνύσασα μόνα στονόεντος
ἐν τομᾷ σιδάρου;
ἐπεῖδες — ὦ μάταια — τάνδε <τὰν> ὕβριν;

ΤΡΟΦΟΣ

ἐπεῖδον, ὡς δὴ πλησία παραστάτις.

ΧΟΡΟΣ

890 τίς ἦνεν; φέρ᾽ εἰπέ.

ΤΡΟΦΟΣ

αὐτὴ πρὸς αὑτῆς χειροποιεῖται τάδε.

ΧΟΡΟΣ

τί φωνεῖς;

ΤΡΟΦΟΣ

σαφηνῆ.

ΧΟΡΟΣ

ἔτεκ᾽ ἔτεκε μεγάλαν
ἀνέορτος ἅδε νύμφα
895 δόμοισι τοῖσδ᾽ Ἐρινύν.

212

NURSE

She was pierced <by a two-edged sword>.

CHORUS

What passion, or what affliction, took her off with the point
of its cruel dart? How did she contrive it, achieving alone
death after a death, by the stroke of the cruel iron? Did
you—ah, the futility!—see this violent deed?

NURSE

I saw it, as one standing nearby!

CHORUS

Who did the deed? Come, tell us!

NURSE

She struck herself with her own hand!

CHORUS

What are you saying?

NURSE

The truth!

CHORUS

The offspring, the offspring of the bride without a wedding
in the house is a mighty Erinys!

---

⁸⁸¹ ταύτην Ll.-J.: αὑτὴν codd.   suppl. Ll.-J. (ἀμφήκει
ξίφει iam Henderson)
⁸⁸³ αἰχμᾷ Hermann: -ὰ t: -ὰν cett.
^{886–87} στονόεντος . . . σιδάρου choro tribuit Maas, nutrici codd.
⁸⁸⁸ ὦ μάταια Dawe: ὦ ματαῖα L: ὦ ματαία cett.   suppl.
Blaydes
⁸⁹⁰ τίς ἦνεν; Wunder: τίς ἦν; πῶς; codd.

ΤΡΟΦΟΣ

ἄγαν γε· μᾶλλον δ' εἰ παροῦσα πλησία
ἔλευσσες οἷ' ἔδρασε, κάρτ' ἂν ᾤκτισας.

ΧΟΡΟΣ

καὶ ταῦτ' ἔτλη τις χεὶρ γυναικεία κτίσαι;

ΤΡΟΦΟΣ

δεινῶς γε· πεύσῃ δ', ὥστε μαρτυρεῖν ἐμοί.
900 ἐπεὶ παρῆλθε δωμάτων εἴσω μόνη,
καὶ παῖδ' ἐν αὐλαῖς εἶδε κοῖλα δέμνια
στορνύνθ', ὅπως ἄψορρον ἀντῴη πατρί,
κρύψασ' ἑαυτὴν ἔνθα μή τις εἰσίδοι,
βρυχᾶτο μὲν βωμοῖσι προσπίπτουσ' ὅτι
905 γένοιντ' ἐρῆμοι, κλαῖε δ' ὀργάνων ὅτου
ψαύσειεν οἷς ἐχρῆτο δειλαία πάρος·
ἄλλῃ δὲ κἄλλῃ δωμάτων στρωφωμένη,
εἴ του φίλων βλέψειεν οἰκετῶν δέμας,
ἔκλαιεν ἡ δύστηνος εἰσορωμένη,
910 αὐτὴ τὸν αὑτῆς δαίμον' ἀνακαλουμένη.
[καὶ τὰς ἄπαιδας ἐς τὸ λοιπὸν οὐσίας.]
ἐπεὶ δὲ τῶνδ' ἔληξεν, ἐξαίφνης σφ' ὁρῶ
τὸν Ἡράκλειον θάλαμον εἰσορμωμένην.
κἀγὼ λαθραῖον ὄμμ' ἐπεσκιασμένη
915 φρούρουν· ὁρῶ δὲ τὴν γυναῖκα δεμνίοις
τοῖς Ἡρακλείοις στρωτὰ βάλλουσαν φάρη.
ὅπως δ' ἐτέλεσε τοῦτ', ἐπενθοροῦσ' ἄνω
καθέζετ' ἐν μέσοισιν εὐνατηρίοις,
καὶ δακρύων ῥήξασα θερμὰ νάματα

214

NURSE

That is all too true! and if you had been close at hand to see
the nature of her action, you would indeed have pitied her.

CHORUS

And did a woman bring herself to do this with her own
hand?

NURSE

In awful fashion; and you shall learn it, so that you can bear
me witness. When she had gone into the house alone, and
had seen her son in the courtyard preparing a litter, so that
he could go back and meet his father, she hid herself
where nobody could see her; falling upon the altars, she
cried out that they would become desolate, and she wept
whenever she touched any of the things she, poor woman,
had used in the past. She moved this way and that way in
the house, and if she saw the face of any of her dear atten-
dants, she wept as she looked upon them, herself lament-
ing for her fate [and for her childless existence in the
future].

And when she had ceased from that, suddenly I saw her
burst into the marriage chamber of Heracles, and watched
her, hiding my face; and I saw the woman casting blankets
on the bed of Heracles. When she had finished that, she
leapt up and took her place in the middle of the bed. Hot
streams of tears burst from her eyes, and she said, "O my

---

905 γένοιντ᾽ ἐρῆμοι Nauck: γένοιτ᾽ ἐρήμη codd.
911 del. L. Dindorf
918 εὐνατηρίοις Dindorf: εὐναστ- codd.

920 ἔλεξεν, "ὦ λέχη τε καὶ νυμφεῖ᾽ ἐμά,
τὸ λοιπὸν ἤδη χαίρεθ᾽, ὡς ἔμ᾽ οὔποτε
δέξεσθ᾽ ἔτ᾽ ἐν κοίταισι ταῖσδ᾽ εὐνάτριαν."
τοσαῦτα φωνήσασα συντόνῳ χερὶ
λύει τὸν αὑτῆς πέπλον, οὗ χρυσήλατος
925 προὔκειτο μαστῶν περονίς, ἐκ δ᾽ ἐλώπισεν
πλευρὰν ἅπασαν ὠλένην τ᾽ εὐώνυμον.
κἀγὼ δρομαία βᾶσ᾽, ὅσονπερ ἔσθενον,
τῷ παιδὶ φράζω τῆς τεχνωμένης τάδε.
κἀν ᾧ τὸ κεῖσε δεῦρό τ᾽ ἐξορμώμεθα,
930 ὁρῶμεν αὐτὴν ἀμφιπλῆγι φασγάνῳ
πλευρὰν ὑφ᾽ ἧπαρ καὶ φρένας πεπληγμένην.
ἰδὼν δ᾽ ὁ παῖς ᾤμωξεν· ἔγνω γὰρ τάλας
τοὔργον κατ᾽ ὀργὴν ὡς ἐφάψειεν τόδε,
ὄψ᾽ ἐκδιδαχθεὶς τῶν κατ᾽ οἶκον οὕνεκα
935 ἄκουσα πρὸς τοῦ θηρὸς ἔρξειεν τάδε.
    κἀνταῦθ᾽ ὁ παῖς δύστηνος οὔτ᾽ ὀδυρμάτων
ἐλείπετ᾽ οὐδέν, ἀμφί νιν γοώμενος,
οὔτ᾽ ἀμφιπίπτων στόμασιν, ἀλλὰ πλευρόθεν
πλευρὰν παρεὶς ἔκειτο πόλλ᾽ ἀναστένων,
940 ὥς νιν ματαίως αἰτίᾳ βάλοι κακῇ,
κλαίων ὁθούνεχ᾽ εἷς δυοῖν ἔσοιθ᾽ ἅμα,
πατρός τ᾽ ἐκείνης τ᾽, ὠρφανισμένος βίον.
τοιαῦτα τἀνθάδ᾽ ἐστίν. ὥστ᾽ εἴ τις δύο
ἢ κἀπὶ πλείους ἡμέρας λογίζεται,
945 μάταιός ἐστιν· οὐ γὰρ ἔσθ᾽ ἥ γ᾽ αὔριον
πρὶν εὖ πάθῃ τις τὴν παροῦσαν ἡμέραν.

bridal bed, farewell now for ever, since you will never again receive me to lie upon this couch." Having said so much, with a sweeping hand she loosed her robe, where a gold pin lay above her breasts, and bared all her side and her left arm. And I ran with all my strength, and warned her son of what she was about. And in the time in which I was running there and back, we saw that she had struck herself with a two-edged sword in the side below the liver and the seat of life. When he saw, her son cried out; for he realised, poor man, that he had charged her with the crime in anger, having learned too late from those in the house that that monster had got her to do this act in innocence.

Then her unhappy son never ceased to lament, weeping over her, nor to cover her with kisses, but lying side by side with her he uttered many a groan, saying that he had charged her falsely with the crime, and weeping because now he would be bereft of both, his father and her also. That is how things stand here; so that if anyone reckons on two days or more, he is acting foolishly, for there is no tomorrow till one has got through today in happiness.

Exit NURSE.

---

924 οὗ Schaefer: ᾧ codd.
941 εἷς Nauck: ἐκ codd.
942 βίον Wakefield: βίου codd.
944 κἀπὶ West: καὶ codd.: κἄτι Herwerden

ΧΟΡΟΣ

πότερα πρότερον ἐπιστένω,   στρ. α΄
πότερα μέλεα περαιτέρω,
δύσκριτ' ἔμοιγε δυστάνῳ.
950 τάδε μὲν ἔχομεν ὁρᾶν δόμοις,   ἀντ. α΄
τάδε δὲ μένομεν ἐν ἐλπίσιν·
κοινὰ δ' ἔχειν τε καὶ μέλλειν.
εἴθ' ἀνεμόεσσά τις γένοιτ' ἔπουρος ἑστιῶτις
     αὔρα,   στρ. β΄
955 ἥτις μ' ἀποικίσειεν ἐκ τόπων, ὅπως
τὸν Ζηνὸς ἄλκιμον γόνον
μὴ ταρβαλέα θάνοιμι
μοῦνον εἰσιδοῦσ' ἄφαρ·
ἐπεὶ ἐν δυσαπαλλάκτοις ὀδύναις
960 χωρεῖν πρὸ δόμων λέγουσιν,
ἄσπετον θέαμα.
ἀγχοῦ δ' ἄρα κοὐ μακρὰν προὔκλαιον,
     ὀξύφωνος ὡς ἀηδών.   ἀντ. β΄
ξένων γὰρ ἐξόμιλος ἅδε τις στάσις.
965 πᾷ δ' αὖ φορεῖ νιν; ὡς φίλου
προκηδομένα βαρεῖαν
ἄψοφον φέρει βάσιν.
αἰαῖ· ὅδ' ἀναύδατος φέρεται.
τί χρή, φθίμενόν νιν, ἢ καθ'
970 ὕπνον ὄντα κρῖναι;

---

⁹⁴⁸ μέλεα Musgrave: τέλεα fere codd.
⁹⁵¹ μένομεν Erfurdt: μέλλομεν codd.   ἐν Blaydes: ἐπ' codd.

218

CHORUS

Which case shall I lament for first? Which is the sadder?
It is hard for me, poor creature, to decide.

The one we can see in the house, the other we await in
expectation; seeing and waiting to see are just the same.

I wish a breath of wind would come to the house to waft
me from this place, to save me from dying at once with fear
at the mere sight of the mighty son of Zeus; for they say
that he is approaching before the house in agony that can-
not be got rid of, a sight unspeakable.

So when I lamented like the shrill-voiced nightingale, it
was for what was near, not what was far! For here is a party
of strangers, come from far away. Where, now, are they
carrying him? As though caring for one dear to them they
are planting silently their heavy tread. Alas, he is speech-
less as he is borne along. Must I judge him to be dead, or
sleeping?

Enter men carrying HERACLES *in a litter,* HYLLUS, *and the*
DOCTOR.

---

956 Ζηνὸς t: Διὸς cett.: Δῖον Nauck
961 θέαμα C. Schenkl: τι θαῦμα codd.
964 στάσις Meineke: βάσις codd.
968 ἀναύδατος Erfurdt: ἄναυδος codd.
969 φθίμενον Hermann: θανόντα codd.

ΥΛΛΟΣ

οἴμοι ἐγὼ σοῦ, πάτερ, ὦ μέλεος,
τί πάθω; τί δὲ μήσομαι; οἴμοι.

ΠΡΕΣΒΥΣ

σίγα, τέκνον, μὴ κινήσῃς
975 ἀγρίαν ὀδύνην πατρὸς ὠμόφρονος.
ζῇ γὰρ προπετής. ἀλλ' ἴσχε δακὼν
στόμα σόν.

ΥΛΛΟΣ

πῶς φής, γέρον; ἦ ζῇ;

ΠΡΕΣΒΥΣ

οὐ μὴ 'ξεγερεῖς τὸν ὕπνῳ κάτοχον
κἀκκινήσεις κἀναστήσεις
980 φοιτάδα δεινὴν
νόσον, ὦ τέκνον.

ΥΛΛΟΣ

ἀλλ' ἐπί μοι μελέῳ
βάρος ἄπλετον· ἐμμέμονεν φρήν.

ΗΡΑΚΛΗΣ

ὦ Ζεῦ,
ποῖ γᾶς ἥκω; παρὰ τοῖσι βροτῶν
985 κεῖμαι πεπονημένος ἀλλήκτοις
ὀδύναις; οἴμοι <μοι> ἐγὼ τλάμων·
ἁ δ' αὖ μιαρὰ βρύκει. φεῦ.

978 'ξεγερεῖς Dawes: 'ξεγείρεις L: 'ξεγείρῃς L s.l., cett.
986 suppl. Brunck

HYLLUS

Alas for you, father! Unhappy am I! What will become of me? What shall I do? Alas!

DOCTOR

Quiet, my son, do not arouse the savage pain of your stern father! He lives, though he is prostrate. Bite your lips and control yourself!

HYLLUS

What do you say, aged man? Is he alive?

DOCTOR

You must not wake him from the sleep that holds him, nor stir and rouse up the awful malady that comes and goes, my son!

HYLLUS

But an awful weight of misery rests upon me! My mind is insane!

HERACLES

O Zeus, where in the world have I come? Among what mortals do I lie, racked by unceasing pains? Alas for me in my misery! Again this cursed plague consumes me! Ah!

ΠΡΕΣΒΥΣ

ἆρ' ἐξῄδη σ' ὅσον ἦν κέρδος
σιγῇ κεύθειν καὶ μὴ σκεδάσαι
990 τῷδ' ἀπὸ κρατὸς
βλεφάρων θ' ὕπνον;

ΥΛΛΟΣ
οὐ γὰρ ἔχω πῶς ἂν
στέρξαιμι κακὸν τόδε λεύσσων.

ΗΡΑΚΛΗΣ
ὦ Κηναία κρηπὶς βωμῶν,
997 ἢν μή ποτ' ἐγὼ προσιδεῖν ὁ τάλας
998a/994a ὤφελον ὅσσοις, ἱερῶν οἵαν
994b οἵων ἐπί μοι
995 μελέῳ χάριν ἤνυσω, ὦ Ζεῦ·
οἵαν μ' ἄρ' ἔθου λώβαν, οἵαν,
998b τόδ' ἀκήλητον
μανίας ἄνθος καταδερχθῆναι.
1000 τίς γὰρ ἀοιδός, τίς ὁ χειροτέχνας
ἰατορίας, ὃς τάνδ' ἄταν
χωρὶς Ζηνὸς κατακηλήσει;
θαῦμ' ἂν πόρρωθεν ἰδοίμαν.
ἐέ,   στρ.
< – – – ∪ – >
ἐᾶτέ μ' ἐᾶτέ με
1005 δύσμορον εὐνᾶσθαι,
ἐᾶτέ με δύστανον.
πᾷ <πᾷ> μου ψαύεις; ποῖ κλίνεις;
ἀπολεῖς μ', ἀπολεῖς.

222

DOCTOR

Did I not know how useful it would be to keep quiet, and
not to banish sleep from his head and eyes?

HYLLUS

Yes, but I do not know how I can bear to look upon this
agony!

HERACLES

Rock of Cenaeum where the altars stand, I wish I had
never set eyes on you, wretch that I am, such is the thanks
you have rendered me for such sacrifices, O Zeus! What
outrage have you done upon me, what outrage, so that I see
this ever-growing madness, not to be appeased! Who is the
charmer, who the surgeon that shall lull to sleep this
plague, other than Zeus? Even from far off I should
wonder at such a one.

Ah . . . Let me sleep, let me sleep, unhappy one, let me
sleep in my misery! Where are you touching me? Where
are you laying me? You will kill me, you will kill me! You

994a-96 post 998 ὅσσοις traiecit Wunder
994b οἵων J. F. Martin: ἀνθ᾽ ὧν θυμάτων codd.
1004 lacunam indicavit Coxon
1005 εὐνᾶσθαι Ellendt: εὐνάσαι vel εὐνᾶσαι codd.
1007 suppl. Seidler

ἀνατέτροφας ὅ τι καὶ μύσῃ.
1010 ἧπταί μου, τοτοτοῖ, ἅδ᾽ αὖθ᾽ ἕρπει. πόθεν ἔστ᾽, ὦ
Ἕλλανες πάντων ἀδικώτατοι ἀνέρες, οἷς δὴ
πολλὰ μὲν ἐν πόντῳ, κατά τε δρία πάντα καθαίρων,
ὠλεκόμαν ὁ τάλας, καὶ νῦν ἐπὶ τῷδε νοσοῦντι
οὐ πῦρ, οὐκ ἔγχος τις ὀνήσιμον οὔ ποτε τρέψει;
ἐέ,
1015 οὐδ᾽ ἀπαράξαι <μου> κρᾶτα βίου θέλει
<–∪∪–> μολὼν τοῦ στυγεροῦ; φεῦ φεῦ.

ΠΡΕΣΒΥΣ

ὦ παῖ τοῦδ᾽ ἀνδρός, τοὔργον τόδε μεῖζον ἀνήκει
ἢ κατ᾽ ἐμὰν ῥώμαν· σὺ δὲ σύλλαβε. †σοί τε γὰρ ὄμμα
1020 ἔμπλεον ἢ δι᾽ ἐμοῦ† σώζειν.

ΥΛΛΟΣ

                    ψαύω μὲν ἔγωγε,
λαθίπονον δ᾽ ὀδύναν οὔτ᾽ ἔνδοθεν οὔτε θύραθεν
ἔστι μοι ἐξανύσαι βιότου· τοιαῦτα νέμει Ζεύς.

ΗΡΑΚΛΗΣ

<ἒ ἔ.>   ἀντ.
ὦ παῖ, ποῦ ποτ᾽ εἶ;
τᾷδέ με τᾷδέ με
1025 πρόσλαβε κουφίσας.
ἒ ἔ, ἰὼ δαῖμον.
θρώσκει δ᾽ αὖ, θρώσκει δειλαία
διολοῦσ᾽ ἡμᾶς
1030 ἀπότιβατος ἀγρία νόσος.
ἰὼ ἰὼ Παλλάς, τόδε μ᾽ αὖ λωβᾶται. ἰὼ παῖ,

have roused up every part that had been lulled to rest!

It has hold of me, ah, ah, here it comes again! What are your origins, Greeks, most unrighteous of all men, for whom I destroyed myself, ridding you of pests, many in the sea and in all the forests, and now in my agony will no one bring fire or a weapon that can help me?

Ah, ah! Will no one come and lop off my head, ending the misery of my life? Ah, ah!

DOCTOR

Son of this man, this work is too hard for my strength! Help me, [for you have more power than I to preserve him].

HYLLUS

I am putting my hand to him; but neither from inside nor from outside can I manage to achieve a surgery that would cause him to forget his trouble! Such is the lot that Zeus assigns him.

HERACLES

Ah, ah! My son, where are you? Here, here raise me, take hold of me! Ah, ah, O god! It leaps up again, the evil thing, it leaps up to destroy me, the cruel plague, irresistible!

Ah, ah, Pallas,[a] again it does me outrage! Ah, my son,

---

[a] He calls upon Athena, who has always protected him.

1011 Ἕλλανες πάντων Koechly: πάντων Ἑλλάνων codd.
οἷς Wakefield: οὒς codd.
1014 οὔ ποτε τρέψει Ll.-J.: οὐκ ἀποτρέψει la
1015 suppl. Blaydes
1017 <παυσίπονος> vel <λυσίπονος> ex. gr. Ll.-J.
1019–20 fort. σοί γε τὸ σῶμα ἐς πλέον ἥβα ἐμοῦ (H.-C. Günther:
γε Ll.-J.: ἐς πλέον J. F. Martin)   1023 suppl. Dain

225

SOPHOCLES

τὸν φύτορ᾽ οἰκτίρας, ἀνεπίφθονον εἴρυσον ἔγχος,
1035 παῖσον ἐμᾶς ὑπὸ κληδός· ἀκοῦ δ᾽ ἄχος, ᾧ μ᾽
  ἐχόλωσεν
σὰ μάτηρ ἄθεος, τὰν ὧδ᾽ ἐπίδοιμι πεσοῦσαν
1040 αὔτως, ὧδ᾽ αὔτως, ὥς μ᾽ ὤλεσεν. ὦ γλυκὺς
  Ἅιδας,
<ἒ ἔ.>
ὦ Διὸς αὐθαίμων,
εὔνασον εὔνασόν μ᾽
ὠκυπέτᾳ μόρῳ τὸν μέλεον φθίσας.

ΧΟΡΟΣ

κλύουσ᾽ ἔφριξα τάσδε συμφοράς, φίλαι,
1045 ἄνακτος, οἵαις οἷος ὢν ἐλαύνεται.

ΗΡΑΚΛΗΣ

ὦ πολλὰ δὴ καὶ θερμά, καὶ λόγῳ κακά,
καὶ χερσὶ καὶ νώτοισι μοχθήσας ἐγὼ·
κοὔπω τοιοῦτον οὔτ᾽ ἄκοιτις ἡ Διὸς
προὔθηκεν οὔθ᾽ ὁ στυγνὸς Εὐρυσθεὺς ἐμοὶ
1050 οἷον τόδ᾽ ἡ δολῶπις Οἰνέως κόρη
καθῆψεν ὤμοις τοῖς ἐμοῖς Ἐρινύων
ὑφαντὸν ἀμφίβληστρον, ᾧ διόλλυμαι.
πλευραῖσι γὰρ προσμαχθὲν ἐκ μὲν ἐσχάτας
βέβρωκε σάρκας, πλεύμονός τ᾽ ἀρτηρίας
1055 ῥοφεῖ ξυνοικοῦν· ἐκ δὲ χλωρὸν αἷμά μου
πέπωκεν ἤδη, καὶ διέφθαρμαι δέμας
τὸ πᾶν, ἀφράστῳ τῇδε χειρωθεὶς πέδῃ.
κοὐ ταῦτα λόγχη πεδιάς, οὔθ᾽ ὁ γηγενὴς
στρατὸς Γιγάντων, οὔτε θήρειος βία,
226

take pity on your father, draw a sword that none can blame
and strike beneath my collar-bone! Heal the agony with
which your godless mother has enraged me! May I see her
fall in the same way, the very same, in which she has des-
troyed me! O delightful Hades!

Ah, ah! O brother of Zeus, put me to sleep, put me to
sleep, with a swift death killing the miserable one!

CHORUS

I shuddered as I heard of this disaster of our lord, my
dears; such is he and such the plagues that harry him!

HERACLES

Many and savage, evil even to relate, have been the labours
of my arms and my back! And never yet has the wife of
Zeus or hateful Eurystheus set such a thing upon me as the
woven covering of the Erinyes which the daughter of
Oeneus with beguiling face has put upon my shoulders, by
which I am perishing! It has clung to my sides and eaten
away my inmost flesh, and lives with me to devour the
channels of my lungs. Already it has drunk my fresh blood,
and my whole body is ruined, now that I am mastered by
this unspeakable bondage. The spearmen of the plain
never did such a thing, nor the earth-born army of the
Giants, nor the violence of the monsters, nor Greece, nor

[1034] φύτορ' Dindorf: φύσαντ' codd.

[1037] τὰν Seidler: ἂν codd.

[1040] ὦ γλυκὺς Ἅιδας huc traiecit Seidler: post 1041 αὐθαίμων
praebent codd.

[1041] suppl. Dain

[1042] μ' huc traiecit Erfurdt: post prius εὔνασον praebent Laz

[1046] "dictu gravia" Cicero, Tusc. Disp. 2,20

227

1060 οὔθ᾽ Ἑλλάς, οὔτ᾽ ἄγλωσσος, οὔθ᾽ ὅσην ἐγὼ
γαῖαν καθαίρων ἱκόμην, ἔδρασέ πω·
γυνὴ δέ, θῆλυς οὖσα κἄνανδρος φύσιν,
μόνη με δὴ καθεῖλε φασγάνου δίχα.

ὦ παῖ, γενοῦ μοι παῖς ἐτήτυμος γεγώς,
1065 καὶ μὴ τὸ μητρὸς ὄνομα πρεσβεύσῃς πλέον.
δός μοι χεροῖν σαῖν αὐτὸς ἐξ οἴκου λαβὼν
ἐς χεῖρα τὴν τεκοῦσαν, ὡς εἰδῶ σάφα
εἰ τοὐμὸν ἀλγεῖς μᾶλλον ἢ κείνης ὁρῶν
λωβητὸν εἶδος ἐν δίκῃ κακούμενον.
1070 ἴθ᾽, ὦ τέκνον, τόλμησον· οἴκτιρόν τέ με
πολλοῖσιν οἰκτρόν, ὅστις ὥστε παρθένος
βέβρυχα κλαίων, καὶ τόδ᾽ οὐδ᾽ ἂν εἷς ποτε
τόνδ᾽ ἄνδρα φαίη πρόσθ᾽ ἰδεῖν δεδρακότα,
ἀλλ᾽ ἀστένακτος αἰὲν εἰχόμην κακοῖς.
1075 νῦν δ᾽ ἐκ τοιούτου θῆλυς ηὕρημαι τάλας.
καὶ νῦν προσελθὼν στῆθι πλησίον πατρός,
σκέψαι δ᾽ ὁποίας ταῦτα συμφορᾶς ὕπο
πέπονθα· δείξω γὰρ τάδ᾽ ἐκ καλυμμάτων.
ἰδού, θεᾶσθε πάντες ἄθλιον δέμας,
1080 ὁρᾶτε τὸν δύστηνον, ὡς οἰκτρῶς ἔχω.
αἰαῖ, ὦ τάλας,
αἰαῖ.
ἔθαλψέ μ᾽ ἄτης σπασμὸς ἀρτίως ὅδ᾽ αὖ,
διῆξε πλευρῶν, οὐδ᾽ ἀγύμναστόν μ᾽ ἐᾶν
ἔοικεν ἡ τάλαινα διάβορος νόσος.
1085 ὦναξ Ἀΐδη, δέξαι μ᾽,
ὦ Διὸς ἀκτίς, παῖσον.

the barbarian lands, nor every country that I came to in my purifying work. But a woman, a female and unmanly in her nature, alone has brought me down, without a sword.

My son, become my true-born son, and do not honour the name of your mother more! Take your mother from the house with your own hands and give her into mine, so that I may know for certain whether you suffer more at seeing my body tortured than at seeing hers justly mal-treated! Come, my son, bring yourself to do it! Pity me, pitiable in many ways, I who am crying out, weeping like a girl, and no one can say he saw this man do such a thing before, but though racked with torments I never would lament! But now such a thing has shown me as a womanish creature.

And now draw near and stand close to your father, and see what a calamity has done this to me; for I will show it to you without a veil. Look, gaze, all of you, on my miser-able body, see the unhappy one, his pitiable state! Alas, unhappy one, alas! Again a spasm of torture has burned me, it has darted through my sides, and the ruthless devouring malady seems never to leave me without tor-ment. O lord Hades, receive me! O lightning of Zeus,

---

1062 κἄνανδρος Tournier: κοὐκ ἀνδρὸς codd.
1074 εἰχόμην Meineke: ἑσπόμην codd.: εἱπόμην sch. ad Aj. 318
1082 ἔθαλψέ μ' K, coni. Hermann: ἔθαλψεν cett.

ἔνσεισον, ὦναξ, ἐγκατάσκηψον βέλος,
πάτερ, κεραυνοῦ. δαίνυται γὰρ αὖ πάλιν,
ἤνθηκεν, ἐξώρμηκεν. ὦ χέρες χέρες,
1090 ὦ νῶτα καὶ στέρν᾽, ὦ φίλοι βραχίονες,
ὑμεῖς ἐκεῖνοι δὴ καθέσταθ᾽, οἵ ποτε
Νεμέας ἔνοικον, βουκόλων ἀλάστορα,
λέοντ᾽, ἄπλατον θρέμμα κἀπροσήγορον,
βίᾳ κατειργάσασθε, Λερναίαν θ᾽ ὕδραν,
1095 διφυᾶ τ᾽ ἄμεικτον ἱπποβάμονα στρατὸν
θηρῶν, ὑβριστήν, ἄνομον, ὑπέροχον βίαν,
Ἐρυμάνθιόν τε θῆρα, τόν θ᾽ ὑπὸ χθονὸς
Ἅιδου τρίκρανον σκύλακ᾽, ἀπρόσμαχον τέρας,
δεινῆς Ἐχίδνης θρέμμα, τόν τε χρυσέων
1100 δράκοντα μήλων φύλακ᾽ ἐπ᾽ ἐσχάτοις τόποις.
ἄλλων τε μόχθων μυρίων ἐγευσάμην,
κοὐδεὶς τροπαῖ᾽ ἔστησε τῶν ἐμῶν χερῶν.
νῦν δ᾽ ὧδ᾽ ἄναρθος καὶ κατερρακωμένος
τυφλῆς ὑπ᾽ ἄτης ἐκπεπόρθημαι τάλας,
1105 ὁ τῆς ἀρίστης μητρὸς ὠνομασμένος,
ὁ τοῦ κατ᾽ ἄστρα Ζηνὸς αὐδηθεὶς γόνος.
ἀλλ᾽ εὖ γέ τοι τόδ᾽ ἴστε, κἂν τὸ μηδὲν ὦ,
κἂν μηδὲν ἔρπω, τήν γε δράσασαν τάδε
χειρώσομαι κἀκ τῶνδε. προσμόλοι μόνον,
1110 ἵν᾽ ἐκδιδαχθῇ πᾶσιν ἀγγέλλειν ὅτι
καὶ ζῶν κακούς γε καὶ θανὼν ἐτεισάμην.

ΧΟΡΟΣ

ὦ τλῆμον Ἑλλάς, πένθος οἷον εἰσορῶ <σ᾽>
ἕξουσαν, ἀνδρὸς τοῦδέ γ᾽ εἰ σφαλεῖσ᾽ ἔσῃ.

strike me! Hurl down your thunderbolt, lord, cast it upon me, father! For again it is feasting on me, it has blossomed, it is launched! O hands, hands, O back and shoulders, O dear arms, are you they that once by force subdued the dweller in Nemea, the scourge of herdsmen, the lion, a creature none could approach and none confront, and the Lernaean Hydra, and the fierce army of the monsters, with two natures and with horses' feet, insolent, lawless, over-whelming in their might,[a] and the beast of Erymanthus, and the three-headed dog of Hades below the earth, a por-tent irresistible, the nursling of dread Echidna, and the serpent that guarded the golden apples in its place remote? And I sampled many thousand other labours, and none yet has raised a trophy for victory against my might! But now with joints unhinged and torn to rags I am miser-ably conquered by blind ruin, I, called the child of the nob-lest of mothers, I, saluted as the son of Zeus among the stars! But know this for certain, even if I amount to noth-ing and I cannot move, I shall chastise her who has done this, even in this condition! Let her only come near, so that she may be taught to proclaim to all that both in life and death I have punished evildoers!

CHORUS

Unhappy Greece, what mourning I see will be yours, if you are deprived of this man!

[a] The Centaurs.

1112 suppl. Ll.-J.
1113 σφαλεῖσ' ἔσῃ Meineke: σφαλήσεται codd.

ΥΛΛΟΣ

ἐπεὶ παρέσχες ἀντιφωνῆσαι, πάτερ,
1115 σιγὴν παρασχὼν κλῦθί μου νοσῶν ὅμως.
αἰτήσομαι γάρ σ' ὧν δίκαια τυγχάνειν.
δός μοι σεαυτόν, μὴ τοιοῦτον ὡς δάκνῃ
θυμῷ δύσοργος. οὐ γὰρ ἂν γνοίης ἐν οἷς
χαίρειν προθυμῇ κἀν ὅτοις ἀλγεῖς μάτην.

ΗΡΑΚΛΗΣ

1120 εἰπὼν ὃ χρῄζεις λῆξον· ὡς ἐγὼ νοσῶν
οὐδὲν ξυνίημ' ὧν σὺ ποικίλλεις πάλαι.

ΥΛΛΟΣ

τῆς μητρὸς ἥκω τῆς ἐμῆς φράσων ἐν οἷς
νῦν ἔστ' ἐν οἷς θ' ἥμαρτεν οὐχ ἑκουσία.

ΗΡΑΚΛΗΣ

ὦ παγκάκιστε, καὶ παρεμνήσω γὰρ αὖ
1125 τῆς πατροφόντου μητρός, ὡς κλύειν ἐμέ;

ΥΛΛΟΣ

ἔχει γὰρ οὕτως ὥστε μὴ σιγᾶν πρέπειν.

ΗΡΑΚΛΗΣ

οὐ δῆτα τοῖς γε πρόσθεν ἡμαρτημένοις.

ΥΛΛΟΣ

ἀλλ' οὐδὲ μὲν δὴ τοῖς γ' ἐφ' ἡμέραν ἐρεῖς.

1117 τοιοῦτον Mudge: τοσοῦτον codd.
1123 ἔστ' ἐν Harleianus 5734 (coni. Blaydes): ἔστιν cett.

HYLLUS

Since you have given me leave to answer you, father, be
silent and hear me, sick though you are, for I shall make a
request which in justice should be granted. Lend yourself
to me, not in such a mood that you are out of temper and
are stung to anger; else you could not learn how mistaken is
your desire for satisfaction and how mistaken your resent-
ment.

HERACLES

Say what you wish and then leave off! For I am sick, and
understand none of the subtleties you have long been talk-
ing.

HYLLUS

I have come to tell you about my mother, how it now
stands with her and how she did wrong by accident.

HERACLES

You utter villain, have you again made mention of the
mother who has killed your father, in my hearing?

HYLLUS

Yes, for things stand so with her that silence would be
wrong.

HERACLES

Indeed no, when you think of the wrong she did before!

HYLLUS

Not when you consider what she has done this day as well!

ΗΡΑΚΛΗΣ

λέγ᾽, εὐλαβοῦ δὲ μὴ φανῇς κακὸς γεγώς.

ΥΛΛΟΣ

1130 λέγω. τέθνηκεν ἀρτίως νεοσφαγής.

ΗΡΑΚΛΗΣ

πρὸς τοῦ; τέρας τοι διὰ κακῶν ἐθέσπισας.

ΥΛΛΟΣ

αὐτὴ πρὸς αὑτῆς, οὐδενὸς πρὸς ἐκτόπου.

ΗΡΑΚΛΗΣ

οἴμοι· πρὶν ὡς χρῆν σφ᾽ ἐξ ἐμῆς θανεῖν χερός;

ΥΛΛΟΣ

κἂν σοῦ στραφείη θυμός, εἰ τὸ πᾶν μάθοις.

ΗΡΑΚΛΗΣ

1135 δεινοῦ λόγου κατῆρξας· εἰπὲ δ᾽ ᾗ νοεῖς.

ΥΛΛΟΣ

ἅπαν τὸ χρῆμ᾽ ἥμαρτε χρηστὰ μωμένη.

ΗΡΑΚΛΗΣ

χρήστ᾽, ὦ κάκιστε, πατέρα σὸν κτείνασα δρᾷ;

ΥΛΛΟΣ

στέργημα γὰρ δοκοῦσα προσβαλεῖν σέθεν
ἀπήμπλαχ᾽, ὡς προσεῖδε τοὺς ἔνδον γάμους.

ΗΡΑΚΛΗΣ

1140 καὶ τίς τοσοῦτος φαρμακεὺς Τραχινίων;

1136 μωμένη Π 13, Κ: μνωμένη cett.

234

HERACLES

Speak, but take care that you are not revealed to be a trai-
tor!

HYLLUS

I will speak; she is dead, newly slain!

HERACLES

At whose hand? A miracle, told by a prophet who speaks
evil!

HYLLUS

By her own hand, not that of any other.

HERACLES

Ah me! Before she could die at my hand, as she should
have done?

HYLLUS

Even your mind would be altered, if you were to learn all.

HERACLES

What you have begun to say is dire; but tell me what you
have a mind to tell!

HYLLUS

She did altogether wrong, but her intent was good.

HERACLES

Was it a good action, villain, to kill your father?

HYLLUS

Why, she went wrong thinking that she was applying a phil-
tre, having seen the bride who is in the house!

HERACLES

And who among the men of Trachis is so great a sorcerer?

235

ΥΛΛΟΣ

Νέσσος πάλαι Κένταυρος ἐξέπεισέ νιν
τοιῷδε φίλτρῳ τὸν σὸν ἐκμῆναι πόθον.

ΗΡΑΚΛΗΣ

ἰοὺ ἰοὺ δύστηνος, οἴχομαι τάλας.
ὄλωλ' ὄλωλα, φέγγος οὐκέτ' ἔστι μοι.
1145 οἴμοι, φρονῶ δὴ ξυμφορᾶς ἵν' ἔσταμεν.
ἴθ', ὦ τέκνον· πατὴρ γὰρ οὐκέτ' ἔστι σοι·
κάλει τὸ πᾶν μοι σπέρμα σῶν ὁμαιμόνων,
κάλει δὲ τὴν τάλαιναν Ἀλκμήνην, Διὸς
μάτην ἄκοιτιν, ὡς τελευταίαν ἐμοῦ
1150 φήμην πύθησθε θεσφάτων ὅσ' οἶδ' ἐγώ.

ΥΛΛΟΣ

ἀλλ' οὔτε μήτηρ ἐνθάδ', ἀλλ' ἐπακτίᾳ
Τίρυνθι συμβέβηκεν ὥστ' ἔχειν ἕδραν,
παίδων τε τοὺς μὲν ξυλλαβοῦσ' αὐτὴ τρέφει,
τοὺς δ' ἂν τὸ Θήβης ἄστυ ναίοντας μάθοις·
1155 ἡμεῖς δ' ὅσοι πάρεσμεν, εἴ τι χρή, πάτερ,
πράσσειν, κλυόντες ἐξυπηρετήσομεν.

ΗΡΑΚΛΗΣ

σὺ δ' οὖν ἄκουε τοὔργον· ἐξήκεις δ' ἵνα
φανεῖς ὁποῖος ὢν ἀνὴρ ἐμὸς καλῇ.
ἐμοὶ γὰρ ἦν πρόφαντον ἐκ πατρὸς πάλαι,
1160 πρὸς τῶν πνεόντων μηδενὸς θανεῖν ποτε,
ἀλλ' ὅστις Ἅιδου φθίμενος οἰκήτωρ πέλοι.
ὅδ' οὖν ὁ θὴρ Κένταυρος, ὡς τὸ θεῖον ἦν
πρόφαντον, οὕτω ζῶντά μ' ἔκτεινεν θανών.
φανῶ δ' ἐγὼ τούτοισι συμβαίνοντ' ἴσα

HYLLUS

Nessus the Centaur long ago persuaded her to inflame your passion with such a love charm.

HERACLES

Ah, ah, misery, I am done for! I am dead, I am dead, there is no longer light for me! Ah me, I know now in what a calamity I stand! Go, my son—your father is no more—summon the whole brood of your siblings, and summon the unhappy Alcmene, in vain the bedfellow of Zeus, so that you may learn the last message of the oracles I know!

HYLLUS

But your mother is not here; she has come to terms with Tiryns by the shore so as to reside there; some of your children she has taken with her, and others you may learn are living in the town of Thebes. But we who are present, father, will obey you and will render any service that we must perform.

HERACLES

Well, hear what must be done! You have come to a point where you will show what sort of a man you are, you that are said to be my son. It was predicted to me by my father long ago that I should never die at the hand of any of the living, but at that of one who was dead and lived in Hades. So this monster the Centaur, as the divine prophecy had foretold, has killed me, I being alive and he dead. And I shall reveal new prophecies that fit with these, saying the

---

[1160] ποτε Musgrave: ὕπο codd.

SOPHOCLES

1165 μαντεῖα καινά, τοῖς πάλαι ξυνήγορα,
ἃ τῶν ὀρείων καὶ χαμαικοιτῶν ἐγὼ
Σελλῶν ἐσελθὼν ἄλσος ἐξεγραψάμην
πρὸς τῆς πατρῴας καὶ πολυγλώσσου δρυός,
ἥ μοι χρόνῳ τῷ ζῶντι καὶ παρόντι νῦν
1170 ἔφασκε μόχθων τῶν ἐφεστώτων ἐμοὶ
λύσιν τελεῖσθαι· κἀδόκουν πράξειν καλῶς.
τὸ δ᾽ ἦν ἄρ᾽ οὐδὲν ἄλλο πλὴν θανεῖν ἐμέ·
τοῖς γὰρ θανοῦσι μόχθος οὐ προσγίγνεται.
ταῦτ᾽ οὖν ἐπειδὴ λαμπρὰ συμβαίνει, τέκνον,
1175 δεῖ σ᾽ αὖ γενέσθαι τῷδε τἀνδρὶ σύμμαχον,
καὶ μὴ ᾽πιμεῖναι τοὐμὸν ὀξῦναι στόμα,
ἀλλ᾽ αὐτὸν εἰκαθόντα συμπράσσειν, νόμον
κάλλιστον ἐξευρόντα, πειθαρχεῖν πατρί.

ΥΛΛΟΣ
ἀλλ᾽, ὦ πάτερ, ταρβῶ μὲν ἐς λόγου στάσιν
1180 τοιάνδ᾽ ἐπελθών, πείσομαι δ᾽ ἅ σοι δοκεῖ.

ΗΡΑΚΛΗΣ
ἔμβαλλε χεῖρα δεξιὰν πρώτιστά μοι.

ΥΛΛΟΣ
ὡς πρὸς τί πίστιν τήνδ᾽ ἄγαν ἐπιστρέφεις;

ΗΡΑΚΛΗΣ
οὐ θᾶσσον οἴσεις μηδ᾽ ἀπιστήσεις ἐμοί;

ΥΛΛΟΣ
ἰδού, προτείνω, κοὐδὲν ἀντειρήσεται.

1167 ἐξεγραψάμην Elmsley et Dobree: εἰσ- codd.

238

same as the prophecies of old, that when I entered the grove of the Selli[a] who live in the mountains and sleep upon the ground I wrote down at the dictation of the ancestral oak with many voices. It said that at the time that is now alive and present my release from the labours that stood over me should be accomplished; and I thought I should be happy, but it meant no more than that I should die; for the dead do not have to labour. So now that this is clearly being fulfilled, my son, you must fight at my side, and not wait until my words grow sharp, but comply and work with me, finding that it is the noblest of laws that bids a man obey his father.

HYLLUS

Father, I am afraid at coming in our talk to such a point, but I will obey your decisions.

HERACLES

First place your right hand in mine!

HYLLUS

For what purpose do you demand this pledge, more strongly than you need to?

HERACLES

Will you not give me your hand at once and not disobey me?

HYLLUS

See, here it is, and your command shall not be gainsaid!

[a] They were the priests of the ancient oracle of Zeus at Dodona.

ΗΡΑΚΛΗΣ

1185 ὄμνυ Διός νυν τοῦ με φύσαντος κάρα.

ΥΛΛΟΣ

ἦ μὴν τί δράσειν; καὶ τόδ' ἐξειπεῖν σε δεῖ.

ΗΡΑΚΛΗΣ

ἦ μὴν ἐμοὶ τὸ λεχθὲν ἔργον ἐκτελεῖν.

ΥΛΛΟΣ

ὄμνυμ' ἔγωγε, Ζῆν' ἔχων ἐπώμοτον.

ΗΡΑΚΛΗΣ

εἰ δ' ἐκτὸς ἔλθοις, πημονὰς εὔχου λαβεῖν.

ΥΛΛΟΣ

1190 οὐ μὴ λάβω· δράσω γάρ· εὔχομαι δ' ὅμως.

ΗΡΑΚΛΗΣ

οἶσθ' οὖν τὸν Οἴτης Ζηνὸς ὑψίστου πάγον;

ΥΛΛΟΣ

οἶδ', ὡς θυτήρ γε πολλὰ δὴ σταθεὶς ἄνω.

ΗΡΑΚΛΗΣ

ἐνταῦθά νυν χρὴ τοὐμὸν ἐξάραντά σε
σῶμ' αὐτόχειρα καὶ ξὺν οἷς χρῄζεις φίλων,
1195 πολλὴν μὲν ὕλην τῆς βαθυρρίζου δρυὸς
κείραντα, πολλὸν δ' ἄρσεν' ἐκτεμόνθ' ὁμοῦ
ἄγριον ἔλαιον, σῶμα τοὐμὸν ἐμβαλεῖν,
καὶ πευκίνης λαβόντα λαμπάδος σέλας
πρῆσαι. γόου δὲ μηδὲν εἰσίτω δάκρυ,

1186 ἐξειπεῖν σε δεῖ Heimsoeth: ἐξειρήσεται codd.
1191 ὑψίστου Wakefield: ὕψιστον codd.

240

HERACLES

Now swear by the head of Zeus who was my father!

HYLLUS

What must I swear to do? You must tell me that also!

HERACLES

You must swear to perform the action that I speak of!

HYLLUS

I swear, calling Zeus to witness!

HERACLES

Pray, too, that you may incur penalties if you depart from this!

HYLLUS

I shall not incur them, for I shall do it; but none the less I pray for this!

HERACLES

Then do you know the mountain of Oeta, which belongs to highest Zeus?

HYLLUS

I know it, having often stood up there to sacrifice.

HERACLES

You must lift my body and carry it there with your own hands and with those of your friends you choose. When you have cut down much timber from the deeply rooted trees and many branches of the tough wild olive, throw my body onto the wood; then take a burning torch of pinewood and set fire to it. And let me see no tear of lamentation,

---

1199 εἰσίδω Jackson: εἰσίτω codd.

1200 ἀλλ᾽ ἀστένακτος κἀδάκρυτος, εἴπερ εἶ
τοῦδ᾽ ἀνδρός, ἔρξον· εἰ δὲ μή, μενῶ σ᾽ ἐγὼ
καὶ νέρθεν ὢν ἀραῖος εἰσαεὶ βαρύς.

ΥΛΛΟΣ

οἴμοι, πάτερ, τί εἶπας; οἷά μ᾽ εἴργασαι.

ΗΡΑΚΛΗΣ

ὁποῖα δραστέ᾽ ἐστίν· εἰ δὲ μή, πατρὸς
1205 ἄλλου γενοῦ του μηδ᾽ ἐμὸς κληθῇς ἔτι.

ΥΛΛΟΣ

οἴμοι μάλ᾽ αὖθις, οἷά μ᾽ ἐκκαλῇ, πάτερ,
φονέα γενέσθαι καὶ παλαμναῖον σέθεν.

ΗΡΑΚΛΗΣ

οὐ δῆτ᾽ ἔγωγ᾽, ἀλλ᾽ ὧν ἔχω παιώνιον
καὶ μοῦνον ἰατῆρα τῶν ἐμῶν κακῶν.

ΥΛΛΟΣ

1210 καὶ πῶς ὑπαίθων σῶμ᾽ ἂν ἰῴμην τὸ σόν;

ΗΡΑΚΛΗΣ

ἀλλ᾽ εἰ φοβῇ πρὸς τοῦτο, τἄλλα γ᾽ ἔργασαι.

ΥΛΛΟΣ

φορᾶς γέ τοι φθόνησις οὐ γενήσεται.

ΗΡΑΚΛΗΣ

ἦ καὶ πυρᾶς πλήρωμα τῆς εἰρημένης;

ΥΛΛΟΣ

ὅσον γ᾽ ἂν αὐτὸς μὴ ποτιψαύων χεροῖν·
1215 τὰ δ᾽ ἄλλα πράξω κοὐ καμῇ τοὐμὸν μέρος.

but do the work without mourning and without weeping, if you are this man's son! If you do not, I shall remain as a grievous curse upon you even below the earth!

HYLLUS

Alas, father, what have you said? What are you doing to me?

HERACLES

What must be done! And if not, become the son of some other father and be called mine no more!

HYLLUS

Alas once more, what a demand you are making of me, father, to have the guilt of your murder on my hands!

HERACLES

Not I, but to be the healer and the only curer of the ills from which I suffer!

HYLLUS

And how could I heal your body by setting light to it?

HERACLES

Well, if you are afraid of that, do at least the rest!

HYLLUS

I shall not grudge the act of carrying you there.

HERACLES

And also that of piling up the pyre?

HYLLUS

Except that I shall not put my own hands to it.[a] But the rest I shall do and I shall not fail you.

[a] The usual story was that the pyre was lit by Philoctetes.

ΗΡΑΚΛΗΣ

ἀλλ' ἀρκέσει καὶ ταῦτα· πρόσνειμαι δέ μοι
χάριν βραχεῖαν πρὸς μακροῖς ἄλλοις διδούς.

ΥΛΛΟΣ

εἰ καὶ μακρὰ κάρτ' ἐστίν, ἐργασθήσεται.

ΗΡΑΚΛΗΣ

τὴν Εὐρυτείαν οἶσθα δῆτα παρθένον;

ΥΛΛΟΣ

1220   Ἰόλην ἔλεξας, ὥς γ' ἐπεικάζειν ἐμέ.

ΗΡΑΚΛΗΣ

ἔγνως. τοσοῦτον δή σ' ἐπισκήπτω, τέκνον·
ταύτην, ἐμοῦ θανόντος, εἴπερ εὐσεβεῖν
βούλῃ, πατρῴων ὁρκίων μεμνημένος,
προσθοῦ δάμαρτα, μηδ' ἀπιστήσῃς πατρί·
1225   μηδ' ἄλλος ἀνδρῶν τοῖς ἐμοῖς πλευροῖς ὁμοῦ
κλιθεῖσαν αὐτὴν ἀντὶ σοῦ λάβῃ ποτέ,
ἀλλ' αὐτός, ὦ παῖ, τοῦτο κήδευσον λέχος.
πείθου· τὸ γάρ τοι μεγάλα πιστεύσαντ' ἐμοὶ
σμικροῖς ἀπιστεῖν τὴν πάρος συγχεῖ χάριν.

ΥΛΛΟΣ

1230   οἴμοι. τὸ μὲν νοσοῦντι θυμοῦσθαι κακόν,
τὸ δ' ὧδ' ὁρᾶν φρονοῦντα τίς ποτ' ἂν φέροι;

ΗΡΑΚΛΗΣ

ὡς ἐργασείων οὐδὲν ὧν λέγω θροεῖς.

1220 ὥς γ' Schaefer: ὥστ' codd.

244

HERACLES

That much will suffice; but grant me in addition a small favour, over and above great things!

HYLLUS

Even if it is a great one, it shall surely be done.

HERACLES

You know, surely, the daughter of Eurytus?

HYLLUS

You mean Iole, as I guess.

HERACLES

You are right! This is the charge I lay on you, my son: when I am dead, if you wish to show loyalty, remembering the oath you swore your father, make her your wife, and do not disobey me; and let no other man but you take her, who has lain by my side, but make this marriage yourself! Obey, for to fail me in small things when you have complied with me in great ones annihilates your earlier kindness.

HYLLUS

Alas! To be angry with a sick man is wrong; but who could bear to see you thinking as you are?

HERACLES

You speak as though you intend to do none of the things I ask.

ΥΛΛΟΣ

τίς γάρ ποθ', ἥ μοι μητρὶ μὲν θανεῖν μόνη
μεταίτιος, σοὶ δ' αὖθις ὡς ἔχεις ἔχειν,
1235 τίς ταῦτ' ἄν, ὅστις μὴ 'ξ ἀλαστόρων νοσοῖ,
ἕλοιτο; κρεῖσσον κἀμέ γ', ὦ πάτερ, θανεῖν
ἢ τοῖσιν ἐχθίστοισι συνναίειν ὁμοῦ.

ΗΡΑΚΛΗΣ

ἀνὴρ ὅδ' ὡς ἔοικεν οὐ νεμεῖν ἐμοὶ
φθίνοντι μοῖραν· ἀλλά τοι θεῶν ἀρὰ
1240 μενεῖ σ' ἀπιστήσαντα τοῖς ἐμοῖς λόγοις.

ΥΛΛΟΣ

οἴμοι, τάχ', ὡς ἔοικας, ὡς νοσεῖς φανεῖς.

ΗΡΑΚΛΗΣ

σὺ γάρ μ' ἀπ' εὐνασθέντος ἐκκινεῖς κακοῦ.

ΥΛΛΟΣ

δείλαιος, ὡς ἐς πολλὰ τἀπορεῖν ἔχω.

ΗΡΑΚΛΗΣ

οὐ γὰρ δικαιοῖς τοῦ φυτεύσαντος κλύειν.

ΥΛΛΟΣ

1245 ἀλλ' ἐκδιδαχθῶ δῆτα δυσσεβεῖν, πάτερ;

ΗΡΑΚΛΗΣ

οὐ δυσσέβεια, τοὐμὸν εἰ τέρψεις κέαρ.

ΥΛΛΟΣ

ἢ πράσσειν ἄνωγας οὖν με πανδίκως τάδε;

1241 φανεῖς Axt: φράσεις codd.

246

HYLLUS

Why, when she is the sole cause of my mother's death, and of your being in the state you are, who could make this choice, who that has not been made sick by avenging deities? It would be better, father, for me too to die than to live together with my greatest enemy.

HERACLES

It seems that this man will not accord me, who am dying, what is my due! But a curse from the gods shall await you if you disobey my orders!

HYLLUS

Alas, you will soon show, it seems, how sick you are!

HERACLES

Yes, for you have stirred me up again after my pain had been lulled to sleep.

HYLLUS

Unhappy as I am, how many perplexities confront me!

HERACLES

Yes, because you refuse to obey your father!

HYLLUS

But am I then to learn to be disloyal, father?

HERACLES

It is not disloyalty, if you rejoice my heart!

HYLLUS

Then do you order me in all solemnity to do this?

SOPHOCLES

ΗΡΑΚΛΗΣ

ἔγωγε· τούτων μάρτυρας καλῶ θεούς.

ΥΛΛΟΣ

τοιγὰρ ποήσω, κοὐκ ἀπώσομαι, τὸ σὸν
1250 θεοῖσι δεικνὺς ἔργον. οὐ γὰρ ἄν ποτε
κακὸς φανείην σοί γε πιστεύσας, πάτερ.

ΗΡΑΚΛΗΣ

καλῶς τελευτᾷς, κἀπὶ τοῖσδε τὴν χάριν
ταχεῖαν, ὦ παῖ, πρόσθες, ὡς πρὶν ἐμπεσεῖν
σπαραγμὸν ἤ τιν' οἶστρον ἐς πυράν με θῇς.
1255 ἄγ' ἐγκονεῖτ', αἴρεσθε. παυλά τοι κακῶν
αὕτη, τελευτὴ τοῦδε τἀνδρὸς ὑστάτη.

ΥΛΛΟΣ

ἀλλ' οὐδὲν εἴργει σοὶ τελειοῦσθαι τάδε,
ἐπεὶ κελεύεις κἀξαναγκάζεις, πάτερ.

ΗΡΑΚΛΗΣ

ἄγε νυν, πρὶν τήνδ' ἀνακινῆσαι
1260 νόσον, ὦ ψυχὴ σκληρά, χάλυβος
λιθοκόλλητον στόμιον παρέχουσ',
ἀνάπαυε βοήν, ὡς ἐπίχαρτον
τελεοῦσ' ἀεκούσιον ἔργον.

ΥΛΛΟΣ

αἴρετ', ὀπαδοί, μεγάλην μὲν ἐμοὶ
1265 τούτων θέμενοι συγγνωμοσύνην,
μεγάλην δὲ θεῶν ἀγνωμοσύνην
εἰδότες ἔργων τῶν πρασσομένων,

248

HERACLES

Yes! I call the gods to witness it!

HYLLUS

Then I will do it, and shall not refuse, showing the action to
the gods as yours! For I could never be shown up as a trai-
tor if I obeyed you, father.

HERACLES

You make a good end, and on top of this swiftly grant me
this favour, to place me on the pyre before another attack
comes to tear me or to sting me! Come, make haste, lift
me up! This is my rest from labour, the final end of this
man.

HYLLUS

Why, there is nothing to prevent these things from being
accomplished, since you command and you compel me,
father.

Enter HYLLUS' companions, who lift up the stretcher.

HERACLES

Come now, before you stir up again this malady, stubborn
soul, apply a bit set with stones and let no cry escape me,
accomplishing this unwelcome task as though it were a
pleasure!

HYLLUS

Lift him, companions, showing great sympathy with me in
what has happened, and knowing of the great unkindness
of the gods displayed in these events, gods who beget us

1259–78 del. Hartung
1263 τελεοῦσ' L. Dindorf: τελέως codd.

οἳ φύσαντες καὶ κληζόμενοι
πατέρες τοιαῦτ' ἐφορῶσι πάθη.
1270 τὰ μὲν οὖν μέλλοντ' οὐδεὶς ἐφορᾷ,
τὰ δὲ νῦν ἑστῶτ' οἰκτρὰ μὲν ἡμῖν,
αἰσχρὰ δ' ἐκείνοις,
χαλεπώτατα δ' οὖν ἀνδρῶν πάντων
τῷ τήνδ' ἄτην ὑπέχοντι.
1275   λείπου μηδὲ σύ, παρθέν', ἐπ' οἴκων,
μεγάλους μὲν ἰδοῦσα νέους θανάτους,
πολλὰ δὲ πήματα <καὶ> καινοπαθῆ,
κοὐδὲν τούτων ὅ τι μὴ Ζεύς.

1270–78 choro tribuit Bergk
1275–78 Hyllo continuant ZgT, choro tribuunt Π 14, KTa, partim
choro partim Hyllo cett.
1275 ἐπ' Lγρ et sch., t: ἀπ' Laz
1277 suppl. Bentley

and are called our fathers but who look on such sufferings as these! The future none can see, and the present is pitiful for us and shameful for them, and harder than on any other man upon him who is enduring this calamity.

Do not be left behind in the house, maiden;[a] you have lately seen terrible deaths, and many sufferings unprecedented, and none of these things is not Zeus.

---

[a] These words are addressed to the leader of the Chorus.

PHILOCTETES

ΤΑ ΤΟΥ ΔΡΑΜΑΤΟΣ ΠΡΟΣΩΠΑ

Ὀδυσσεύς
Νεοπτόλεμος
Χορός
Φιλοκτήτης
Ἔμπορος
Ἡρακλῆς

Odysseus
Neoptolemus
Chorus of Neoptolemus' Sailors
Philoctetes
Merchant
Heracles

Scene: The deserted island of Lemnos.
Time: A little before the end of the Trojan War.

ΦΙΛΟΚΤΗΤΗΣ

ΟΔΥΣΣΕΥΣ

Ἀκτὴ μὲν ἥδε τῆς περιρρύτου χθονὸς
Λήμνου, βροτοῖς ἄστιπτος οὐδ᾽ οἰκουμένη,
ἔνθ᾽, ὦ κρατίστου πατρὸς Ἑλλήνων τραφεὶς
Ἀχιλλέως παῖ Νεοπτόλεμε, τὸν Μηλιᾶ
5 Ποίαντος υἱὸν ἐξέθηκ᾽ ἐγώ ποτε —
ταχθεὶς τόδ᾽ ἔρδειν τῶν ἀνασσόντων ὕπο —
νόσῳ καταστάζοντα διαβόρῳ πόδα ·
ὅτ᾽ οὔτε λοιβῆς ἡμὶν οὔτε θυμάτων
παρῆν ἑκήλοις προσθιγεῖν, ἀλλ᾽ ἀγρίαις
10 κατεῖχ᾽ ἀεὶ πᾶν στρατόπεδον δυσφημίαις,
βοῶν, ἰύζων. ἀλλὰ ταῦτα μὲν τί δεῖ
λέγειν; ἀκμὴ γὰρ οὐ μακρῶν ἡμῖν λόγων,
μὴ καὶ μάθῃ μ᾽ ἥκοντα κἀκχέω τὸ πᾶν
σόφισμα τῷ νιν αὐτίχ᾽ αἱρήσειν δοκῶ.
15 ἀλλ᾽ ἔργον ἤδη σὸν τὰ λοίφ᾽ ὑπηρετεῖν,
σκοπεῖν θ᾽ ὅπου ᾽στ᾽ ἐνταῦθα δίστομος πέτρα
τοιάδ᾽, ἵν᾽ ἐν ψύχει μὲν ἡλίου διπλῆ
πάρεστιν ἐνθάκησις, ἐν θέρει δ᾽ ὕπνον
δι᾽ ἀμφιτρῆτος αὐλίου πέμπει πνοή.
20 βαιὸν δ᾽ ἔνερθεν ἐξ ἀριστερᾶς τάχ᾽ ἂν
ἴδοις ποτὸν κρηναῖον, εἴπερ ἐστὶ σῶν.

256

PHILOCTETES

Scene: the uninhabited island of Lemnos. Enter ODYSSEUS
and NEOPTOLEMUS, *with a scout.*

ODYSSEUS

This is the shore of the seagirt land of Lemnos, untrodden
by mortals, not inhabited. Here it was, you who were
reared as the son of the noblest father among the Greeks,
son of Achilles, Neoptolemus, that I once put ashore the
Malian, the son of Poeas—on the orders of those in
command—whose foot was dripping from a malady that
was eating it away; since we could not pour libations or
sacrifice in peace, but he filled the entire camp with savage
and ill-omened cries, shouting and screaming. But why
must I talk of that? It is not the moment for long conversa-
tion, for fear he should learn that I have come, and I should
spill out the whole scheme by which I plan at once to take
him. But from now on your task is to help me, and to see
where in this place there is a cave with two mouths, such
that when it is cold there is a double seat in the sun, and in
summer a breeze wafts sleep through the cavern with its
opening at both ends. A little below it, on the left, you
may see a spring with drinking water, if it is still there. Go

---

¹¹ ἰύζων r: στενάζων cett.

257

SOPHOCLES

ἅ μοι προσελθὼν σῖγα †σήμαιν'† εἶτ' ἔχει
χῶρον τὸν αὐτὸν τόνδ' ἔτ', εἶτ' ἄλλῃ κυρεῖ,
ὡς τἀπίλοιπα τῶν λόγων σὺ μὲν κλύῃς,
25 ἐγὼ δὲ φράζω, κοινὰ δ' ἐξ ἀμφοῖν ἴῃ.

ΝΕΟΠΤΟΛΕΜΟΣ

ἄναξ Ὀδυσσεῦ, τοὔργον οὐ μακρὰν λέγεις·
δοκῶ γὰρ οἷον εἶπας ἄντρον εἰσορᾶν.

ΟΔΥΣΣΕΥΣ

ἄνωθεν, ἢ κάτωθεν; οὐ γὰρ ἐννοῶ.

ΝΕΟΠΤΟΛΕΜΟΣ

τόδ' ἐξύπερθε, καὶ στίβου γ' οὐδεὶς κτύπος.

ΟΔΥΣΣΕΥΣ

30 ὅρα καθ' ὕπνον μὴ καταυλισθεὶς κυρῇ.

ΝΕΟΠΤΟΛΕΜΟΣ

ὁρῶ κενὴν οἴκησιν ἀνθρώπων δίχα.

ΟΔΥΣΣΕΥΣ

οὐδ' ἔνδον οἰκοποιός ἐστί τις τροφή;

ΝΕΟΠΤΟΛΕΜΟΣ

στιπτή γε φυλλὰς ὡς ἐναυλίζοντί τῳ.

ΟΔΥΣΣΕΥΣ

τὰ δ' ἄλλ' ἐρῆμα, κοὐδέν ἐσθ' ὑπόστεγον;

ΝΕΟΠΤΟΛΕΜΟΣ

35 αὐτόξυλόν γ' ἔκπωμα, φλαυρουργοῦ τινος

22 σήμαιν'] μάνθαν' Dawe
23 τὸν αὐτὸν Blaydes: πρὸς αὐτὸν codd.   τόνδ' ἔτ' Elmsley:
τόνδε γ' a: τόνδ' fere cett.

258

forward quietly, and tell me whether he still occupies the same place or he is somewhere else; so that for the rest of our discussion you may listen and I explain, and each may make his contribution.

NEOPTOLEMUS

Lord Odysseus, the task you speak of does not lie far off; for I think I see a cave such as you have told me of.

ODYSSEUS

Above or below? I do not understand.

NEOPTOLEMUS

This is above; and I hear no sound of a footstep.

ODYSSEUS

Take care he is not bivouacked there asleep!

NEOPTOLEMUS

I see an empty dwelling with no man there.

ODYSSEUS

And are there none of the things that make a home in there?

NEOPTOLEMUS

Yes, a bed of leaves pressed down, as though for someone who camps there.

ODYSSEUS

But is the rest bare, and is there nothing there beneath the roof?

NEOPTOLEMUS

Yes, a cup made from a single piece of wood, the work of a

τεχνήματ᾽ ἀνδρός, καὶ πυρεῖ᾽ ὁμοῦ τάδε.

ΟΔΥΣΣΕΥΣ
κείνου τὸ θησαύρισμα σημαίνεις τόδε.

ΝΕΟΠΤΟΛΕΜΟΣ
ἰοὺ ἰού· καὶ ταῦτά γ᾽ ἄλλα θάλπεται
ῥάκη, βαρείας του νοσηλείας πλέα.

ΟΔΥΣΣΕΥΣ
40 ἀνὴρ κατοικεῖ τούσδε τοὺς τόπους σαφῶς,
κἄστ᾽ οὐχ ἑκάς που. πῶς γὰρ ἂν νοσῶν ἀνὴρ
κῶλον παλαιᾷ κηρὶ προστείχοι μακράν;
ἀλλ᾽ ἢ ᾽πὶ φορβῆς μαστὺν ἐξελήλυθεν,
ἢ φύλλον εἴ τι νώδυνον κάτοιδέ που.
45 τὸν οὖν παρόντα πέμψον ἐς κατασκοπήν,
μὴ καὶ λάθῃ με προσπεσών· ὡς μᾶλλον ἂν
ἕλοιτ᾽ ἔμ᾽ ἢ τοὺς πάντας Ἀργείους λαβεῖν.

ΝΕΟΠΤΟΛΕΜΟΣ
ἀλλ᾽ ἔρχεταί τε καὶ φυλάξεται στίβος.
σὺ δ᾽ εἴ τι χρῄζεις, φράζε δευτέρῳ λόγῳ.

ΟΔΥΣΣΕΥΣ
50 Ἀχιλλέως παῖ, δεῖ σ᾽ ἐφ᾽ οἷς ἐλήλυθας
γενναῖον εἶναι, μὴ μόνον τῷ σώματι,
ἀλλ᾽ ἤν τι καινόν, ὧν πρὶν οὐκ ἀκήκοας,
κλύῃς, ὑπουργεῖν, ὡς ὑπηρέτης πάρει.

ΝΕΟΠΤΟΛΕΜΟΣ
τί δῆτ᾽ ἄνωγας;

poor craftsman, and with it stones for making fire.

ODYSSEUS

The treasures that you are describing must be his.

NEOPTOLEMUS

Ah, ah! Here is something else, rags drying in the sun, stained with matter from some grievous sore!

ODYSSEUS

Clearly this is the place where the man lives, and he must be not far off; for how could a man whose leg is stricken with an ancient affliction travel far? But either he has gone off to look for food, or perhaps he knows some healing herb. So send the man you have with you to look out, in case he should suddenly fall upon me. How much rather he would take me than all the other Argives!

NEOPTOLEMUS

The man is going, and the path shall be guarded. If there is anything you want, speak again and tell me!

ODYSSEUS

Son of Achilles, the mission you have come on demands that you show your nobility; not only with your body, but if you are told something new, such as you have not heard earlier, you must give your help, since you are here to help me.

NEOPTOLEMUS

What are your orders?

---

⁴² προστείχοι Herwerden: προσβαίη codd.
⁴³ μαστὸν Toup: νόστον codd.

ΟΔΥΣΣΕΥΣ

τὴν Φιλοκτήτου σε δεῖ
55 ψυχὴν ὅπως λόγοισιν ἐκκλέψεις λέγων,
ὅταν σ' ἐρωτᾷ τίς τε καὶ πόθεν πάρει,
λέγειν, Ἀχιλλέως παῖς· τόδ' οὐχὶ κλεπτέον·
πλεῖς δ' ὡς πρὸς οἶκον, ἐκλιπὼν τὸ ναυτικὸν
στράτευμ' Ἀχαιῶν, ἔχθος ἐχθήρας μέγα,
60 οἵ σ' ἐν λιταῖς στείλαντες ἐξ οἴκων μολεῖν,
μόνην γ' ἔχοντες τήνδ' ἅλωσιν Ἰλίου,
οὐκ ἠξίωσαν τῶν Ἀχιλλείων ὅπλων
ἐλθόντι δοῦναι κυρίως αἰτουμένῳ,
ἀλλ' αὔτ' Ὀδυσσεῖ παρέδοσαν· λέγων ὅσ' ἂν
65 θέλῃς καθ' ἡμῶν ἔσχατ' ἐσχάτων κακά.
τούτῳ γὰρ οὐδέν μ' ἀλγυνεῖς· εἰ δ' ἐργάσῃ
μὴ ταῦτα, λύπην πᾶσιν Ἀργείοις βαλεῖς.
εἰ γὰρ τὰ τοῦδε τόξα μὴ ληφθήσεται,
οὐκ ἔστι πέρσαι σοι τὸ Δαρδάνου πέδον.
70   ὡς δ' ἔστ' ἐμοὶ μὲν οὐχί, σοὶ δ' ὁμιλία
πρὸς τόνδε πιστὴ καὶ βέβαιος, ἔκμαθε.
σὺ μὲν πέπλευκας οὔτ' ἔνορκος οὐδενὶ
οὔτ' ἐξ ἀνάγκης οὔτε τοῦ πρώτου στόλου,
ἐμοὶ δὲ τούτων οὐδέν ἐστ' ἀρνήσιμον.
75 ὥστ' εἴ με τόξων ἐγκρατὴς αἰσθήσεται,
ὄλωλα καὶ σὲ προσδιαφθερῶ ξυνών.
ἀλλ' αὐτὸ τοῦτο δεῖ σοφισθῆναι, κλοπεὺς
ὅπως γενήσῃ τῶν ἀνικήτων ὅπλων.
ἔξοιδα, παῖ, φύσει σε μὴ πεφυκότα
80 τοιαῦτα φωνεῖν μηδὲ τεχνᾶσθαι κακά·

ODYSSEUS

You must beguile the mind of Philoctetes by your words.
When he asks you who you are and what is your family, say
"the son of Achilles"; that you need not conceal. And you
are sailing for home, having left the fleet of the Achaeans
after conceiving a great hatred for them, who after sending
to implore you to come from home, this being their only
hope of taking Ilium, when you had come refused to give
you the arms of Achilles, when you asked for them with full
rights, but had handed them over to Odysseus. And you
may add as many of the most extreme insults against me as
you please, for by that you will give me no pain, but if you
fail to do it, you will give grief to all the Argives. For if this
man's bow is not captured, it is impossible for you to con-
quer the land of Dardanus.

Now learn why it is possible for you, but not for me, to
talk with this man without distrust or danger! When you
sailed, you had sworn no oath to anyone, you were not
compelled, and you were not part of the first expedition;
but I can deny none of these charges. So if he catches sight
of me while he is master of his bow, I am dead, and I shall
cause the death of you, my companion, also. This is the
thing that we must scheme for, for you to steal the invinci-
ble weapon! I know, my son, that by nature you are not the
sort of man to speak such words or to plot to harm others.

---

[55] λόγοισιν] δόλοισιν Gedike

[61] γ' Seyffert: δ' Lr: om. a

[66] τούτῳ Buttmann: τούτων codd.

[79] παῖ Erfurdt: καὶ codd.

ἀλλ' ἡδὺ γάρ τι κτῆμα τῆς νίκης λαβεῖν,
τόλμα· δίκαιοι δ' αὖθις ἐκφανούμεθα.
νῦν δ' εἰς ἀναιδὲς ἡμέρας μέρος βραχὺ
δός μοι σεαυτόν, κᾆτα τὸν λοιπὸν χρόνον
85 κέκλησο πάντων εὐσεβέστατος βροτῶν.

ΝΕΟΠΤΟΛΕΜΟΣ

ἐγὼ μὲν οὓς ἂν τῶν λόγων ἀλγῶ κλύων,
Λαερτίου παῖ, τούσδε καὶ πράσσειν στυγῶ·
ἔφυν γὰρ οὐδὲν ἐκ τέχνης πράσσειν κακῆς,
οὔτ' αὐτὸς οὔθ', ὥς φασιν, οὑκφύσας ἐμέ.
90 ἀλλ' εἴμ' ἑτοῖμος πρὸς βίαν τὸν ἄνδρ' ἄγειν
καὶ μὴ δόλοισιν· οὐ γὰρ ἐξ ἑνὸς ποδὸς
ἡμᾶς τοσούσδε πρὸς βίαν χειρώσεται.
πεμφθείς γε μέντοι σοὶ ξυνεργάτης ὀκνῶ
προδότης καλεῖσθαι· βούλομαι δ', ἄναξ, καλῶς
95 δρῶν ἐξαμαρτεῖν μᾶλλον ἢ νικᾶν κακῶς.

ΟΔΥΣΣΕΥΣ

ἐσθλοῦ πατρὸς παῖ, καὐτὸς ὢν νέος ποτὲ
γλῶσσαν μὲν ἀργόν, χεῖρα δ' εἶχον ἐργάτιν·
νῦν δ' εἰς ἔλεγχον ἐξιὼν ὁρῶ βροτοῖς
τὴν γλῶσσαν, οὐχὶ τἄργα, πάνθ' ἡγουμένην.

ΝΕΟΠΤΟΛΕΜΟΣ

100 τί οὖν μ' ἄνωγας ἄλλο πλὴν ψευδῆ λέγειν;

ΟΔΥΣΣΕΥΣ

λέγω σ' ἐγὼ δόλῳ Φιλοκτήτην λαβεῖν.

---

83 ἀναιδὲς] ὄνειδος Housman

PHILOCTETES

But—it is a pleasure to acquire a possession by a victory—
bring yourself to do it, and in due course we shall be shown
to have been in the right. Now give yourself to me for a
few hours of shamelessness, and later for the rest of time
be called the most dutiful of mortals!

NEOPTOLEMUS

Son of Laertius,[a] things which it distresses me to hear spo-
ken of are things which I hate to do! It is my nature to do
nothing by treacherous plotting; that is my nature, and it
was also my father's nature. But I am ready to take the
man by force and not by cunning; with only one foot he will
not get the better of us who are so many. I was sent to help
you, but I am unwilling to be called a traitor; I had rather
come to grief, my lord, while acting honestly than triumph
by treachery.

ODYSSEUS

Son of a noble father, I too when I was young had a tongue
that was inactive but an arm that was active; but when I
come to put it to the proof I see that it is the tongue, not
actions, that rules in all things for mortals.

NEOPTOLEMUS

Then what are you telling me to say except lies?

ODYSSEUS

I am telling you to take Philoctetes by a trick.

[a] The father of Odysseus is sometimes called Laertes, some-
times Laertius, and sometimes Lartius.

ΝΕΟΠΤΟΛΕΜΟΣ

τί δ' ἐν δόλῳ δεῖ μᾶλλον ἢ πείσαντ' ἄγειν;

ΟΔΥΣΣΕΥΣ

οὐ μὴ πίθηται· πρὸς βίαν δ' οὐκ ἂν λάβοις.

ΝΕΟΠΤΟΛΕΜΟΣ

οὕτως ἔχει τι δεινὸν ἰσχύος θράσος;

ΟΔΥΣΣΕΥΣ

105   ἰούς <γ'> ἀφύκτους καὶ προπέμποντας φόνον.

ΝΕΟΠΤΟΛΕΜΟΣ

οὐκ ἆρ' ἐκείνῳ γ' οὐδὲ προσμεῖξαι θρασύ;

ΟΔΥΣΣΕΥΣ

οὔ, μὴ δόλῳ λαβόντα γ', ὡς ἐγὼ λέγω.

ΝΕΟΠΤΟΛΕΜΟΣ

οὐκ αἰσχρὸν ἡγῇ δῆτα τὸ ψευδῆ λέγειν;

ΟΔΥΣΣΕΥΣ

οὔκ, εἰ τὸ σωθῆναί γε τὸ ψεῦδος φέρει.

ΝΕΟΠΤΟΛΕΜΟΣ

110   πῶς οὖν βλέπων τις ταῦτα τολμήσει λακεῖν;

ΟΔΥΣΣΕΥΣ

ὅταν τι δρᾷς εἰς κέρδος, οὐκ ὀκνεῖν πρέπει.

ΝΕΟΠΤΟΛΕΜΟΣ

κέρδος δ' ἐμοὶ τί τοῦτον ἐς Τροίαν μολεῖν;

105 suppl. Dobree
108 δῆτα τὸ Vauvilliers: δὴ τάδε lV: δῆτα τὰ cett.
110 λακεῖν L: λαλεῖν cett.

PHILOCTETES

NEOPTOLEMUS

But why must I take him by a trick rather than by persuasion?

ODYSSEUS

He will never be persuaded, and you could not take him by force.

NEOPTOLEMUS

Has he such wondrous confidence in strength?

ODYSSEUS

Yes, inescapable arrows that convey death.

NEOPTOLEMUS

Then can one not dare even to approach him?

ODYSSEUS

No, unless you take him by a trick, as I am telling you to do.

NEOPTOLEMUS

Do you not think it disgraceful to tell lies?

ODYSSEUS

Not if the lie brings us salvation!

NEOPTOLEMUS

With what kind of a face will one be able to utter such words?

ODYSSEUS

When you are doing something to gain advantage, it is wrong to hesitate.

NEOPTOLEMUS

But what advantage is it for me if he should come to Troy?

SOPHOCLES

ΟΔΥΣΣΕΥΣ

αἱρεῖ τὰ τόξα ταῦτα τὴν Τροίαν μόνα.

ΝΕΟΠΤΟΛΕΜΟΣ

οὐκ ἆρ' ὁ πέρσων, ὡς ἐφάσκετ', εἴμ' ἐγώ;

ΟΔΥΣΣΕΥΣ

115 οὔτ' ἂν σὺ κείνων χωρὶς οὔτ' ἐκεῖνα σοῦ.

ΝΕΟΠΤΟΛΕΜΟΣ

θηρατέ' <ἂν> γίγνοιτ' ἄν, εἴπερ ὧδ' ἔχει.

ΟΔΥΣΣΕΥΣ

ὡς τοῦτό γ' ἔρξας δύο φέρῃ δωρήματα.

ΝΕΟΠΤΟΛΕΜΟΣ

ποίω; μαθὼν γὰρ οὐκ ἂν ἀρνοίμην τὸ δρᾶν.

ΟΔΥΣΣΕΥΣ

σοφός τ' ἂν αὑτὸς κἀγαθὸς κεκλῇ' ἅμα.

ΝΕΟΠΤΟΛΕΜΟΣ

120 ἴτω· ποήσω, πᾶσαν αἰσχύνην ἀφείς.

ΟΔΥΣΣΕΥΣ

ἦ μνημονεύεις οὖν ἅ σοι παρήνεσα;

ΝΕΟΠΤΟΛΕΜΟΣ

σάφ' ἴσθ', ἐπείπερ εἰσάπαξ συνήνεσα.

ΟΔΥΣΣΕΥΣ

σὺ μὲν μένων νῦν κεῖνον ἐνθάδ' ἐκδέχου,
ἐγὼ δ' ἄπειμι, μὴ κατοπτευθῶ παρών,
125 καὶ τὸν σκοπὸν πρὸς ναῦν ἀποστελῶ πάλιν.
καὶ δεῦρ', ἐάν μοι τοῦ χρόνου δοκῆτέ τι

PHILOCTETES

ODYSSEUS

This bow is the one thing that takes Troy.

NEOPTOLEMUS

Then am I not the one who is to capture it, as you said?

ODYSSEUS

You cannot capture it without the bow, nor the bow without you.

NEOPTOLEMUS

It would be worth trying to get it, if that is the case.

ODYSSEUS

Yes, since if you do that you win two prizes.

NEOPTOLEMUS

What prizes? If you tell me, I shall not refuse to act.

ODYSSEUS

You would be called clever, and at the same time valiant.

NEOPTOLEMUS

Let it be! I will do it, casting off all shame!

ODYSSEUS

Then do you remember my instruction?

NEOPTOLEMUS

Be sure I do, now that I have once consented.

ODYSSEUS

Do you stay here now and wait for him; I will be off, so as not to be seen by him, and shall send the scout back to the ship. And if you seem to me to be taking too long, I will

---

[116] suppl. Elmsley

κατασχολάζειν, αὖθις ἐκπέμψω πάλιν
τοῦτον τὸν αὐτὸν ἄνδρα, ναυκλήρου τρόποις
μορφὴν δολώσας, ὡς ἂν ἀγνοίᾳ προσῇ·
130 οὗ δῆτα, τέκνον, ποικίλως αὐδωμένου
δέχου τὰ συμφέροντα τῶν ἀεὶ λόγων.
ἐγὼ δὲ πρὸς ναῦν εἶμι, σοὶ παρεὶς τάδε·
Ἑρμῆς δ' ὁ πέμπων δόλιος ἡγήσαιτο νῷν
Νίκη τ' Ἀθάνα Πολιάς, ἢ σῴζει μ' ἀεί.

ΧΟΡΟΣ

135 τί χρὴ τί χρή με, δέσποτ', ἐν ξένᾳ ξένον   στρ. α΄
στέγειν, ἢ τί λέγειν πρὸς ἄνδρ' ὑπόπταν;
φράζε μοι.
τέχνα γὰρ τέχνας ἑτέρας
προὔχει καὶ γνώμα παρ' ὅτῳ τὸ θεῖον
140 Διὸς σκῆπτρον ἀνάσσεται.
σὲ δ', ὦ τέκνον, τόδ' ἐλήλυθεν
πᾶν κράτος ὠγύγιον· τό μοι ἔννεπε
τί σοι χρεὼν ὑπουργεῖν.

ΝΕΟΠΤΟΛΕΜΟΣ

νῦν μέν, ἴσως γὰρ τόπον ἐσχατιαῖς
145 προσιδεῖν ἐθέλεις ὅντινα κεῖται,
δέρκου θαρσῶν· ὁπόταν δὲ μόλῃ
δεινὸς ὁδίτης τῶνδ' οὐκ μελάθρων,
πρὸς ἐμὴν αἰεὶ χεῖρα προχωρῶν
πειρῶ τὸ παρὸν θεραπεύειν.

147 οὐκ Linwood: ἐκ codd.

send back that same man, disguising him as a sea captain, so that he will not be known. As he tells a cunning tale, my son, do you get what advantage you can from whatever words are spoken. I will go to the ship, leaving this to you; and may Hermes the escorter lead us with his guile, and Athena of the City, who is Victory, always my protectress.

Exit ODYSSEUS *with the scout, and enter the* CHORUS, *consisting of* NEOPTOLEMUS' *sailors.*

CHORUS
A stranger in a strange land, what am I to hide, my lord, and what am I to say to a suspicious man? Tell me; for his skill and judgment are better than another's, his in whose hands the divine sceptre of Zeus is wielded. And to you, my son, has come all this ancient power; wherefore, tell me what I must do to help you!

NEOPTOLEMUS
Now—for you may wish to see the place out in the wilds where he reposes—you can look with confidence! And when the dread traveller from this domain returns, advance as I signal to you from time to time, and try to render the aid the present time requires!

ΧΟΡΟΣ

150 μέλον πάλαι μέλημά μοι λέγεις, ἄναξ,   ἀντ. α΄
φρουρεῖν ὄμμ' ἐπὶ σῷ μάλιστα καιρῷ·
νῦν δέ μοι
λέγ' αὐλὰς ποίας ἔνεδρος
ναίει καὶ χῶρον τίν' ἔχει. τὸ γάρ μοι
155 μαθεῖν οὐκ ἀποκαίριον,
μὴ προσπεσών με λάθῃ ποθέν·
τίς τόπος, ἢ τίς ἕδρα; τίν' ἔχει στίβον,
ἔναυλον ἢ θυραῖον;

ΝΕΟΠΤΟΛΕΜΟΣ

οἶκον μὲν ὁρᾷς τόνδ' ἀμφίθυρον
160 πετρίνης κοίτης.

ΧΟΡΟΣ

ποῦ γὰρ ὁ τλήμων αὐτὸς ἄπεστιν;

ΝΕΟΠΤΟΛΕΜΟΣ

δῆλον ἔμοιγ' ὡς φορβῆς χρείᾳ
στίβον ὀγμεύει τῇδε πέλας που.
ταύτην γὰρ ἔχειν βιοτῆς αὐτὸν
165 λόγος ἐστὶ φύσιν, θηροβολοῦντα
πτηνοῖς ἰοῖς σμυγερὸν σμυγερῶς,
οὐδέ τιν' αὐτῷ
παιῶνα κακῶν ἐπινωμᾶν.

ΧΟΡΟΣ

οἰκτίρω νιν ἔγωγ', ὅπως,   στρ. β΄
170 μή του κηδομένου βροτῶν
μηδὲ σύντροφον ὄμμ' ἔχων,

CHORUS

The care that you assign me has long been in my thoughts,
my lord, that my eye should ever be vigilant for what you
most need. But now tell me what bivouacs he inhabits and
what place he has; for it is needful that I know this, for fear
he should suddenly fall upon me from somewhere. What
is his place? Where does he rest? Where is he walking, at
home or abroad?

NEOPTOLEMUS

You see here his home, with its two openings, where he
reposes on the rock.

CHORUS

Yes; where has the sufferer gone away to?

NEOPTOLEMUS

It is clear to me that it is the need for food that makes him
trail his painful step somewhere near here. For that is the
kind of life that he is said to lead, shooting beasts with his
winged arrows, painfully in his pain, and none, they say,
draws near him to heal his afflictions.

CHORUS

I pity him, in that with none among mortals to care for him
and with no companion he can look on, miserable, always

---

¹⁵⁰ ἄναξ Vt: ἄναξ τὸ σὸν Lraz: τὸ σὸν Benedict
¹⁵⁶ προσπεσών huc traiecit Hermann: post λάθῃ habent codd.
¹⁶³ τῇδε Blaydes: τήνδε r: τόνδε cett.
¹⁶⁶ σμυγερὸν σμυγερῶς Brunck: στ- στ- codd.

δύστανος, μόνος αἰεί,
νοσεῖ μὲν νόσον ἀγρίαν,
ἀλύει δ' ἐπὶ παντί τω
175 χρείας ἱσταμένῳ. πῶς ποτε πῶς δύσμορος
    ἀντέχει;
ὦ παλάμαι θεῶν,
ὦ δύστανα γένη βροτῶν,
οἷς μὴ μέτριος αἰών.
180 οὗτος πρωτογόνων ἴσως   ἀντ. β'
οἴκων οὐδενὸς ὕστερος,
πάντων ἄμμορος ἐν βίῳ
κεῖται μοῦνος ἀπ' ἄλλων
στικτῶν ἢ λασίων μετὰ
185 θηρῶν, ἔν τ' ὀδύναις ὁμοῦ
λιμῷ τ' οἰκτρὸς ἀνήκεστ' ἀμερίμνητά τ' ἔχων
    βάρη.
ἁ δ' ἀθυρόστομος
Ἀχὼ τηλεφανὴς πικραῖς
190 οἰμωγαῖς ὑπακούει.

ΝΕΟΠΤΟΛΕΜΟΣ

οὐδὲν τούτων θαυμαστὸν ἐμοί·
θεῖα γάρ, εἴπερ κἀγώ τι φρονῶ,
καὶ τὰ παθήματα κεῖνα πρὸς αὐτὸν
τῆς ὠμόφρονος Χρύσης ἐπέβη,
195 καὶ νῦν ἃ πονεῖ δίχα κηδεμόνων,
οὐκ ἔσθ' ὡς οὐ θεῶν του μελέτῃ
τοῦ μὴ πρότερον τόνδ' ἐπὶ Τροίᾳ

274

alone, he suffers from a cruel sickness and is bewildered by
each need as it arises. How, how does the unhappy man
hold out? O contrivances of the gods! O unhappy race of
mortals to whom life is unkind!

This man, inferior, perhaps, to none of the houses of
the first rank, lies without a share of anything in life, far
from all others, with beasts dappled or hairy, and pitiable
in his pain and hunger he endures afflictions incurable and
uncared for. And she whose mouth has no bar, Echo,
appearing far off responds to his bitter cries of lamenta-
tion.

NEOPTOLEMUS

None of these things is a surprise to me. For it was by the
will of the gods, if I have any understanding, that those
sufferings came upon him from cruel Chryse, and his
present troubles without companions must be the work of
the gods, so that he cannot direct against Troy his irresist-

---

¹⁷⁷ θεῶν Lachmann: θνητῶν codd.
¹⁸⁷ ἀμερίμνητά τ᾽ Page: μεριμνήματ᾽ codd.
^{187–88} βάρη. ἁ δ᾽ Hermann: βαρεῖα δ᾽ codd.
^{189–90} πικραῖς οἰμωγαῖς Ast: -ᾱς -ᾱς codd.
¹⁹⁰ ὑπακούει Auratus: ὑπόκειται codd.
¹⁹⁶ ἔσθ᾽ ὡς Porson: ἔσθ᾽ vel ἔστιν ὅπως codd.

τεῖναι τὰ θεῶν ἀμάχητα βέλη,
πρὶν ὅδ' ἐξήκοι χρόνος, ᾧ λέγεται
200 χρῆναί σφ' ὑπὸ τῶνδε δαμῆναι.

ΧΟΡΟΣ

εὔστομ' ἔχε, παῖ.

ΝΕΟΠΤΟΛΕΜΟΣ
τί τόδε;

ΧΟΡΟΣ
προὐφάνη κτύπος,   στρ. γ΄
φωτὸς σύντροφος ὡς τειρομένου <του>,
ἢ που τᾷδ' ἢ τᾷδε τόπων.
205 βάλλει βάλλει μ' ἐτύμα
φθογγά του στίβον κατ' ἀνάγ-
καν ἕρποντος, οὐδέ με λά-
θει βαρεῖα τηλόθεν αὐ-
δὰ τρυσάνωρ· διάσημα θρηνεῖ.
210 ἀλλ' ἔχε, τέκνον —

ΝΕΟΠΤΟΛΕΜΟΣ
λέγ' ὅ τι.

ΧΟΡΟΣ
φροντίδας νέας·   ἀντ. γ΄
ὡς οὐκ ἔξεδρος, ἀλλ' ἔντοπος ἀνήρ,
οὐ μολπὰν σύριγγος ἔχων,
ὡς ποιμὴν ἀγροβάτας,
215 ἀλλ' ἤ που πταίων ὑπ' ἀνάγ-
κας βοᾷ τηλωπὸν ἰω-

ible weapons until the time has arrived when it is fated to
be conquered by them.

CHORUS

Be silent, my son!

NEOPTOLEMUS

What is this?

CHORUS

A sound rang out, such as might haunt the lips of a man in
agony, this way, I think, or that. It strikes me, it strikes me,
the true voice of one who treads his path under constraint;
I do not mistake from far off the grievous cry of a man in
distress; the lament he utters rings out clearly!

But take, my son . . .

NEOPTOLEMUS

Tell me what!

CHORUS

New counsels! For the man is not far from home, but he is
in this place; he is not playing the music of the pipe, like a
shepherd living in the wild, but because he stumbles, I
think, under constraint he utters a far-sounding shout,

---

[203] suppl. Porson

[204] choro tribuit Hermann, Neoptolemo codd.

[209] θρηνεῖ Ll.-J. (γὰρ θρηνεῖ iam Dindorf): γὰρ θροεῖ codd.
plerique

άν, ἢ ναὸς ἄξενον αὐ-
γάζων ὅρμον· προβοᾷ τι δεινόν.

ΦΙΛΟΚΤΗΤΗΣ

ἰὼ ξένοι·
220   τίνες ποτ᾽ ἐς γῆν τήνδε ναυτίλῳ πλάτῃ
κατέσχετ᾽ οὔτ᾽ εὔορμον οὔτ᾽ οἰκουμένην;
ποίας πάτρας ὑμᾶς ἂν ἢ γένους ποτὲ
τύχοιμ᾽ ἂν εἰπών; σχῆμα μὲν γὰρ Ἑλλάδος
στολῆς ὑπάρχει προσφιλεστάτης ἐμοί·
225   φωνῆς δ᾽ ἀκοῦσαι βούλομαι· καὶ μή μ᾽ ὄκνῳ
δείσαντες ἐκπλαγῆτ᾽ ἀπηγριωμένον,
ἀλλ᾽ οἰκτίσαντες ἄνδρα δύστηνον, μόνον,
ἔρημον ὧδε κἄφιλον κακούμενον,
φωνήσατ᾽, εἴπερ ὡς φίλοι προσήκετε.
230   ἀλλ᾽ ἀνταμείψασθ᾽· οὐ γὰρ εἰκὸς οὔτ᾽ ἐμὲ
ὑμῶν ἁμαρτεῖν τοῦτό γ᾽ οὔθ᾽ ὑμᾶς ἐμοῦ.

ΝΕΟΠΤΟΛΕΜΟΣ

ἀλλ᾽, ὦ ξέν᾽, ἴσθι τοῦτο πρῶτον, οὕνεκα
Ἕλληνές ἐσμεν· τοῦτο γὰρ βούλῃ μαθεῖν.

ΦΙΛΟΚΤΗΤΗΣ

ὦ φίλτατον φώνημα· φεῦ τὸ καὶ λαβεῖν
235   πρόσφθεγμα τοιοῦδ᾽ ἀνδρὸς ἐν χρόνῳ μακρῷ.
τίς σ᾽, ὦ τέκνον, κατέσχε, τίς προσήγαγεν
χρεία; τίς ὁρμή; τίς ἀνέμων ὁ φίλτατος;
γέγωνέ μοι πᾶν τοῦθ᾽, ὅπως εἰδῶ τίς εἶ.

or because he descries the ship in her inhospitable anchorage. His cry is fearsome!

Enter PHILOCTETES.

PHILOCTETES

Hail, strangers! Who are you that with the seaman's oar have put in to this land that lacks anchorages and inhabitants? Of what country and race would I be right in saying you were? The manner of your dress is that of Greece, most dear to me. But I would like to hear a voice! Do not shrink from me in fear and be repelled at my wild state, but take pity on an unhappy man, alone, afflicted like this without a companion or a friend, and speak, if indeed you have come as friends! But answer me! It is not right that I should miss this from you or you from me.

NEOPTOLEMUS

Why, stranger, first know this, that we are Greeks! That is what you wish to learn.

PHILOCTETES

O dearest of sounds! Ah, what it is to be addressed by such a man after so long! What need, my son, made you put in, what need brought you here? What was your impulse? Which was the dearest of winds? Tell me all this, so that I may know who you are!

---

²¹⁸ τι Hartung: γάρ τι codd.

²²⁰ ναυτίλῳ πλάτῃ Syp, aZo: κὰκ ποίας πάτρας cett.

²²² del. Radermacher

²²⁸ κακούμενον Brunck: καλούμενον codd.

²³⁶ κατέσχε Ll.-J.: προσέσχε codd.

ΝΕΟΠΤΟΛΕΜΟΣ

ἐγὼ γένος μέν εἰμι τῆς περιρρύτου
240 Σκύρου· πλέω δ' ἐς οἶκον· αὐδῶμαι δὲ παῖς
Ἀχιλλέως, Νεοπτόλεμος. οἶσθ' ἤδη τὸ πᾶν.

ΦΙΛΟΚΤΗΤΗΣ

ὦ φιλτάτου παῖ πατρός, ὦ φίλης χθονός,
ὦ τοῦ γέροντος θρέμμα Λυκομήδους, τίνι
στόλῳ προσέσχες τήνδε γῆν; πόθεν πλέων;

ΝΕΟΠΤΟΛΕΜΟΣ

245 ἐξ Ἰλίου τοι δὴ τανῦν γε ναυστολῶ.

ΦΙΛΟΚΤΗΤΗΣ

πῶς εἶπας; οὐ γὰρ δὴ σύ γ' ἦσθα ναυβάτης
ἡμῖν κατ' ἀρχὴν τοῦ πρὸς Ἴλιον στόλου.

ΝΕΟΠΤΟΛΕΜΟΣ

ἦ γὰρ μετέσχες καὶ σὺ τοῦδε τοῦ πόνου;

ΦΙΛΟΚΤΗΤΗΣ

ὦ τέκνον, οὐ γὰρ οἶσθά μ' ὄντιν' εἰσορᾷς;

ΝΕΟΠΤΟΛΕΜΟΣ

250 πῶς γὰρ κάτοιδ' ὅν γ' εἶδον οὐδεπώποτε;

ΦΙΛΟΚΤΗΤΗΣ

οὐδ' ὄνομ' <ἄρ'> οὐδὲ τῶν ἐμῶν κακῶν κλέος
ἤσθου ποτ' οὐδέν, οἷς ἐγὼ διωλλύμην;

ΝΕΟΠΤΟΛΕΜΟΣ

ὡς μηδὲν εἰδότ' ἴσθι μ' ὧν ἀνιστορεῖς.

PHILOCTETES

NEOPTOLEMUS

By birth I belong to seagirt Skyros; I am sailing home; and I am called the son of Achilles, Neoptolemus. Now you know it all!

PHILOCTETES

Son of the dearest of fathers, of a dear land, nursling of aged Lycomedes,[a] on what errand have you put in to this land? From where are you sailing?

NEOPTOLEMUS

At present it is from Ilium that I am voyaging.

PHILOCTETES

How do you say? Surely you were not our shipmate at the beginning of the voyage to Ilium!

NEOPTOLEMUS

Did you also take part in that labour?

PHILOCTETES

My son, do you not know who it is that you are looking at?

NEOPTOLEMUS

How can I know a man I have never seen before?

PHILOCTETES

Then have you never heard my name or the story of my misfortunes, which have been my torment?

NEOPTOLEMUS

Know that I am ignorant of what you are asking me about!

[a] Lycomedes, king of Skyros, was the father of Neoptolemus' mother, Deidameia.

---

[245] δὴ τανῦν anon. (1810): δῆτα νῦν codd.
[251] suppl. Erfurdt

SOPHOCLES

ΦΙΛΟΚΤΗΤΗΣ

ὦ πόλλ' ἐγὼ μοχθηρός, ὦ πικρὸς θεοῖς,
255 οὗ μηδὲ κληδὼν ὧδ' ἔχοντος οἴκαδε
μηδ' Ἑλλάδος γῆς μηδαμοῦ διῆλθέ που.
ἀλλ' οἱ μὲν ἐκβαλόντες ἀνοσίως ἐμὲ
γελῶσι σῖγ' ἔχοντες, ἡ δ' ἐμὴ νόσος
ἀεὶ τέθηλε κἀπὶ μεῖζον ἔρχεται.
260 ὦ τέκνον, ὦ παῖ πατρὸς ἐξ Ἀχιλλέως,
ὅδ' εἴμ' ἐγώ σοι κεῖνος, ὃν κλύεις ἴσως
τῶν Ἡρακλείων ὄντα δεσπότην ὅπλων,
ὁ τοῦ Ποίαντος παῖς Φιλοκτήτης, ὃν οἱ
δισσοὶ στρατηγοὶ χὠ Κεφαλλήνων ἄναξ
265 ἔρριψαν αἰσχρῶς ὧδ' ἔρημον, ἀγρίᾳ
νόσῳ καταφθίνοντα, τῆς ἀνδροφθόρου
πληγέντ' ἐχίδνης ἀγρίῳ χαράγματι·
ξὺν ᾗ μ' ἐκεῖνοι, παῖ, προθέντες ἐνθάδε
ᾤχοντ' ἔρημον, ἡνίκ' ἐκ τῆς ποντίας
270 Χρύσης κατέσχον δεῦρο ναυβάτῃ στόλῳ.
τότ' ἄσμενοί μ' ὡς εἶδον ἐκ πολλοῦ σάλου
εὕδοντ' ἐπ' ἀκτῆς ἐν κατηρεφεῖ πέτρᾳ,
λιπόντες ᾤχονθ', οἷα φωτὶ δυσμόρῳ
ῥάκη προθέντες βαιὰ καί τι καὶ βορᾶς
275 ἐπωφέλημα σμικρόν, οἷ' αὐτοῖς τύχοι.
οὗ δή, τέκνον, ποίαν μ' ἀνάστασιν δοκεῖς
αὐτῶν βεβώτων ἐξ ὕπνου στῆναι τότε;
ποῖ' ἐκδακρῦσαι, ποῖ' ἀποιμῶξαι κακά;
ὁρῶντα μὲν ναῦς, ἃς ἔχων ἐναυστόλουν,
280 πάσας βεβώσας, ἄνδρα δ' οὐδέν' ἔντοπον,

282

PHILOCTETES

Miserable indeed am I, and hateful to the gods, since no
news of my plight has made its way home or to any part of
Greece! But those who threw me out in unholy fashion
quietly mock me, and my sickness is always flourishing and
is gaining strength. My son, son whose father was Achilles,
I am he whom you have heard to be the master of the
weapons of Heracles, the son of Poeas, Philoctetes, whom
the two generals and the lord of the Cephallenians[a] despi-
cably threw out into this desolation, perishing from a cruel
malady, struck by the cruel sting of the man-slaying ser-
pent. In company with that, my son, they left me here
desolate when they went off, after they had put in here
from Chryse with their fleet. Gladly then they saw me
sleeping on the shore in a rocky cavern after much tossing
from the waves, and went off, leaving me, having put out
for me, as for a poor wretch, a few rags and a little suste-
nance in the way of food; may they get such themselves!
What sort of an awakening from sleep do you think was
mine, my son, when they were gone? What tears do you
imagine I shed, what sorrows I lamented? I who could see
that all the ships with which I had sailed were departed,
and there was no man in the place, no one to support me,

---

[a] Odysseus was king of Ithaca, and the inhabitants of Ithaca and
other neighbouring islands were often called Cephallenians.

---

276 οὖ Kvíčala: σὺ codd.

οὐχ ὅστις ἀρκέσειεν, οὐδ' ὅστις νόσου
κάμνοντι συλλάβοιτο· πάντα δὲ σκοπῶν
ηὕρισκον οὐδὲν πλὴν ἀνιᾶσθαι παρόν,
τούτου δὲ πολλὴν εὐμάρειαν, ὦ τέκνον.

285   ὁ μὲν χρόνος νυν διὰ χρόνου προὔβαινέ μοι,
κᾆδει τι βαιᾷ τῇδ' ὑπὸ στέγῃ μόνον
διακονεῖσθαι· γαστρὶ μὲν τὰ σύμφορα
τόξον τόδ' ἐξηύρισκε, τὰς ὑποπτέρους
βάλλον πελείας· πρὸς δὲ τοῦθ', ὅ μοι βάλοι

290   νευροσπαδὴς ἄτρακτος, αὐτὸς ἂν τάλας
εἰλυόμην, δύστηνον ἐξέλκων πόδα,
πρὸς τοῦτ' ἄν· εἴ τ' ἔδει τι καὶ ποτὸν λαβεῖν,
καί που πάγου χυθέντος, οἷα χείματι,
ξύλον τι θραῦσαι, ταῦτ' ἂν ἐξέρπων τάλας

295   ἐμηχανώμην· εἶτα πῦρ ἂν οὐ παρῆν,
ἀλλ' ἐν πέτροισι πέτρον ἐκτρίβων μόλις
ἔφην' ἄφαντον φῶς, ὃ καὶ σώζει μ' ἀεί.
οἰκουμένη γὰρ οὖν στέγη πυρὸς μέτα
πάντ' ἐκπορίζει πλὴν τὸ μὴ νοσεῖν ἐμέ.

300   φέρ', ὦ τέκνον, νῦν καὶ τὸ τῆς νήσου μάθῃς.
ταύτῃ πελάζει ναυβάτης οὐδεὶς ἑκών·
οὐ γάρ τις ὅρμος ἔστιν, οὐδ' ὅποι πλέων
ἐξεμπολήσει κέρδος, ἢ ξενώσεται.
οὐκ ἐνθάδ' οἱ πλοῖ τοῖσι σώφροσιν βροτῶν.

305   τάχ' οὖν τις ἄκων ἔσχε· πολλὰ γὰρ τάδε
ἐν τῷ μακρῷ γένοιτ' ἂν ἀνθρώπων χρόνῳ·
οὗτοί μ', ὅταν μόλωσιν, ὦ τέκνον, λόγοις
ἐλεοῦσι μέν, καί πού τι καὶ βορᾶς μέρος

or to assist me when I was suffering from my malady!
When I looked all around me, I could find nothing present
but my pain, and of that I had full sufficiency, my son.

So one period of time after another went by for me, and
I had to provide for myself alone under this poor roof. My
stomach's needs this bow found for me, shooting doves on
the wing; and up to what the shaft sped by the bowstring
shot for me, alone in my misery I would crawl, dragging my
wretched foot, right up to that. And if I had to get some
drink also, or perhaps to cut some wood, when ice was on
the ground, as it is in winter, I would struggle along in
misery and manage it; and then there would be no fire!
But by rubbing one stone painfully against another I made
the hidden spark flash out, the thing that has always been
my preservation. So, you see, the dwelling I live in, to-
gether with fire, provides everything, except a cure for my
disease.

Listen, my son, now you must learn about the island!
No sailor comes near here if he can help it; for there is no
harbour, or anywhere where one can sail and trade, or get
hospitality. This is not a place for men of sense to sail to.
Suppose someone is forced to put in, for many such things
can happen in the long history of mankind; these people
when they come show pity in what they say, and sometimes
they have been sorry for me and have given me a little

---

285 νυν Wecklein: δή a: οὖν cett.
291 δύστηνον Canter: -ος codd.

προσέδοσαν οἰκτίραντες, ἤ τινα στολήν·
310 ἐκεῖνο δ' οὐδείς, ἡνίκ' ἂν μνησθῶ, θέλει,
σῶσαί μ' ἐς οἴκους, ἀλλ' ἀπόλλυμαι τάλας
ἔτος τόδ' ἤδη δέκατον ἐν λιμῷ τε καὶ
κακοῖσι βόσκων τὴν ἀδηφάγον νόσον.
τοιαῦτ' Ἀτρεῖδαί μ' ἥ τ' Ὀδυσσέως βία,
315 ὦ παῖ, δεδράκασ'· οἷς Ὀλύμπιοι θεοὶ
δοῖέν ποτ' αὐτοῖς ἀντίποιν' ἐμοῦ παθεῖν.

ΧΟΡΟΣ

ἔοικα κἀγὼ τοῖς ἀφιγμένοις ἴσα
ξένοις ἐποικτίρειν σε, Ποίαντος τέκνον.

ΝΕΟΠΤΟΛΕΜΟΣ

ἐγὼ δὲ καὐτὸς τοῖσδε μάρτυς ἐν λόγοις,
320 ὡς εἴσ' ἀληθεῖς οἶδα, σὺν τυχὼν κακῶν
ἀνδρῶν Ἀτρειδῶν τῆς τ' Ὀδυσσέως βίας.

ΦΙΛΟΚΤΗΤΗΣ

ἦ γάρ τι καὶ σὺ τοῖς πανωλέθροις ἔχεις
ἔγκλημ' Ἀτρείδαις, ὥστε θυμοῦσθαι παθών;

ΝΕΟΠΤΟΛΕΜΟΣ

θυμὸν γένοιτο χειρὶ πληρῶσαί ποτε,
325 ἵν' αἱ Μυκῆναι γνοῖεν ἡ Σπάρτη θ' ὅτι
χἠ Σκῦρος ἀνδρῶν ἀλκίμων μήτηρ ἔφυ.

ΦΙΛΟΚΤΗΤΗΣ

εὖ γ', ὦ τέκνον· τίνος γὰρ ὧδε τὸν μέγαν
χόλον κατ' αὐτῶν ἐγκαλῶν ἐλήλυθας;

---

324 θυμὸν . . . χειρὶ Lambinus: θυμῷ . . . χεῖρα codd.

food, or some clothing; but one thing nobody will do, if I make mention of it, and that is to take me home. No, I have been miserably perishing now for nine years, in hunger and distress, feeding the insatiable disease. That is what the sons of Atreus and the mighty Odysseus have done to me, my son; may the Olympian gods grant that in requital they suffer such things themselves!

CHORUS
I think that I too, like the strangers who came here, feel pity for you, son of Poeas!

NEOPTOLEMUS
And I myself can corroborate your words, knowing that they are true, having like you found that the sons of Atreus and Odysseus are evil men!

PHILOCTETES
Have you also a complaint against the accursed sons of Atreus, so that you are angry at your treatment?

NEOPTOLEMUS
I wish it may be granted to me to satisfy my rage by violence, so that Mycenae and Sparta may know that Scyros also is a mother of valiant men!

PHILOCTETES
Well said, my son! What is the cause of the great anger that leads you to accuse them?

ΝΕΟΠΤΟΛΕΜΟΣ

ὦ παῖ Ποίαντος, ἐξερῶ, μόλις δ' ἐρῶ,

330   ἄγωγ' ὑπ' αὐτῶν ἐξελωβήθην μολών.
ἐπεὶ γὰρ ἔσχε μοῖρ' Ἀχιλλέα θανεῖν —

ΦΙΛΟΚΤΗΤΗΣ

οἴμοι· φράσῃς μοι μὴ πέρα, πρὶν ἂν μάθω
πρῶτον τόδ'· ἦ τέθνηχ' ὁ Πηλέως γόνος;

ΝΕΟΠΤΟΛΕΜΟΣ

τέθνηκεν, ἀνδρὸς οὐδενός, θεοῦ δ' ὕπο,

335   τοξευτός, ὡς λέγουσιν, ἐκ Φοίβου δαμείς.

ΦΙΛΟΚΤΗΤΗΣ

ἀλλ' εὐγενὴς μὲν ὁ κτανών τε χὠ θανών.
ἀμηχανῶ δὲ πότερον, ὦ τέκνον, τὸ σὸν
πάθημ' ἐλέγχω πρῶτον, ἢ κεῖνον στένω.

ΝΕΟΠΤΟΛΕΜΟΣ

οἶμαι μὲν ἀρκεῖν σοί γε καὶ τὰ σ', ὦ τάλας,

340   ἀλγήμαθ', ὥστε μὴ τὰ τῶν πέλας στένειν.

ΦΙΛΟΚΤΗΤΗΣ

ὀρθῶς ἔλεξας. τοιγαροῦν τὸ σὸν φράσον
αὖθις πάλιν μοι πρᾶγμ', ὅτῳ σ' ἐνύβρισαν.

ΝΕΟΠΤΟΛΕΜΟΣ

ἦλθόν με νηὶ ποικιλοστόλῳ μέτα
δῖός τ' Ὀδυσσεὺς χὠ τροφεὺς τοὐμοῦ πατρός,

345   λέγοντες, εἴτ' ἀληθὲς εἴτ' ἄρ' οὖν μάτην,
ὡς οὐ θέμις γίγνοιτ', ἐπεὶ κατέφθιτο
πατὴρ ἐμός, τὰ πέργαμ' ἄλλον ἢ 'μ' ἑλεῖν.
ταῦτ', ὦ ξέν', οὕτως ἐννέποντες οὐ πολὺν

288

PHILOCTETES

NEOPTOLEMUS

Son of Poeas, I will tell you, much as it costs me to tell, the outrage I suffered at their hands when I went there. For when fate caused Achilles to die . . .

PHILOCTETES

Alas! Tell me no more, before I learn this first: is the son of Peleus dead?

NEOPTOLEMUS

He is dead, at the hand of no man, but of a god, shot dead, they say, by Phoebus.

PHILOCTETES

Noble are both the slayer and the slain! But I do not know, my son, whether to ask first about your wrongs or to lament for him.

NEOPTOLEMUS

I think that for you your own griefs are sufficient, poor man, so that you do not need to lament for those of others.

PHILOCTETES

You are right! So tell me again about the matter in which they treated you with insolence!

NEOPTOLEMUS

They came for me in a ship decked with garlands, noble Odysseus and my father's tutor, saying, whether it was true or after all a fiction, that the justice of the gods did not allow, now that my father was dead, that any other except me should take the towers of Troy. Telling this story in this

χρόνον μ᾽ ἐπέσχον μή με ναυστολεῖν ταχύ,
350 μάλιστα μὲν δὴ τοῦ θανόντος ἱμέρῳ,
ὅπως ἴδοιμ᾽ ἄθαπτον· οὐ γὰρ εἰδόμην·
ἔπειτα μέντοι χὠ λόγος καλὸς προσῆν,
εἰ τἀπὶ Τροίᾳ πέργαμ᾽ αἱρήσοιμ᾽ ἰών.
ἦν δ᾽ ἦμαρ ἤδη δεύτερον πλέοντί μοι,
355 κἀγὼ πικρὸν Σίγειον οὐρίῳ πλάτῃ
κατηγόμην· καί μ᾽ εὐθὺς ἐν κύκλῳ στρατὸς
ἐκβάντα πᾶς ἠσπάζετ᾽, ὀμνύντες βλέπειν
τὸν οὐκέτ᾽ ὄντα ζῶντ᾽ Ἀχιλλέα πάλιν.
κεῖνος μὲν οὖν ἔκειτ᾽· ἐγὼ δ᾽ ὁ δύσμορος,
360 ἐπεὶ ᾽δάκρυσα κεῖνον, οὐ μακρῷ χρόνῳ
ἐλθὼν Ἀτρείδας προσφιλῶς, ὡς εἰκὸς ἦν,
τά θ᾽ ὅπλ᾽ ἀπῄτουν τοῦ πατρὸς τά τ᾽ ἄλλ᾽ ὅσ᾽ ἦν.
οἱ δ᾽ εἶπον, οἴμοι, τλημονέστατον λόγον,
"ὦ σπέρμ᾽ Ἀχιλλέως, τἄλλα μὲν πάρεστί σοι
365 πατρῷ᾽ ἑλέσθαι, τῶν δ᾽ ὅπλων κείνων ἀνὴρ
ἄλλος κρατύνει νῦν, ὁ Λαέρτου γόνος."
κἀγὼ ᾽κδακρύσας εὐθὺς ἐξανίσταμαι
ὀργῇ βαρείᾳ, καὶ καταλγήσας λέγω,
"ὦ σχέτλι᾽, ἦ ᾽τολμήσατ᾽ ἀντ᾽ ἐμοῦ τινι
370 δοῦναι τὰ τεύχη τἀμά, πρὶν μαθεῖν ἐμοῦ;"
ὁ δ᾽ εἶπ᾽ Ὀδυσσεύς, πλησίον γὰρ ὢν κυρεῖ,
"ναί, παῖ, δεδώκασ᾽ ἐνδίκως οὗτοι τάδε·
ἐγὼ γὰρ αὔτ᾽ ἔσωσα κἀκεῖνον παρών."
κἀγὼ χολωθεὶς εὐθὺς ἤρασσον κακοῖς
375 τοῖς πᾶσιν, οὐδὲν ἐνδεὲς ποιούμενος,
εἰ τἀμὰ κεῖνος ὅπλ᾽ ἀφαιρήσοιτό με.

way, they did nothing to restrain me from sailing soon,
most of all because of my longing for the dead man, so that
I might see him while yet unburied, for I had never looked
on him. But also there was the splendid promise that if I
went I would take the towers of Troy. It was already the
second day of my voyage, and oars and wind brought me to
hateful Sigeum. At once the whole army surrounded me,
when I landed, and greeted me, swearing that they saw
Achilles, who was no more, alive again. But he lay there;
and I, poor fellow, after I had wept for him, soon came to
the sons of Atreus in friendly fashion, as was natural, and
asked for my father's arms and the other things that had
been his. But they spoke, alas, miserable words, "Seed of
Achilles, you may take your father's other possessions, but
those arms have another master now, the son of Laertes."
Bursting into tears, I at once rose up in grievous anger, and
in bitterness said, "Wretch, have you dared to give my
weapons to anyone but me, before asking me?" And Odys-
seus, who was standing by, said, "Yes, boy, they gave them
to me justly; for I had been there and saved them and
him." And I in anger at once assailed him with every kind
of insult, leaving nothing out, at the thought that he was to
deprive me of my arms. And he, brought to that point—for

---

361 προσφιλῶς R (coni. Bothe): πρὸς φίλους fere cett.
367 'κδακρύσας Zn: δακρύσας cett.

ὁ δ' ἐνθάδ' ἥκων, καίπερ οὐ δύσοργος ὤν,
δηχθεὶς πρὸς ἀξήκουσεν ὧδ' ἠμείψατο·
"οὐκ ἦσθ' ἵν' ἡμεῖς, ἀλλ' ἀπῆσθ' ἵν' οὔ σ' ἔδει.
380 καὶ ταῦτ', ἐπειδὴ καὶ λέγεις θρασυστομῶν,
οὐ μή ποτ' ἐς τὴν Σκῦρον ἐκπλεύσῃς ἔχων."
      τοιαῦτ' ἀκούσας κἀξονειδισθεὶς κακὰ
πλέω πρὸς οἴκους, τῶν ἐμῶν τητώμενος
πρὸς τοῦ κακίστου κἀκ κακῶν Ὀδυσσέως.
385 [κοὐκ αἰτιῶμαι κεῖνον ὡς τοὺς ἐν τέλει·
πόλις γάρ ἐστι πᾶσα τῶν ἡγουμένων
στρατός τε σύμπας· οἱ δ' ἀκοσμοῦντες βροτῶν
διδασκάλων λόγοισι γίγνονται κακοί.]
      λόγος λέλεκται πᾶς· ὁ δ' Ἀτρείδας στυγῶν
390 ἐμοί θ' ὁμοίως καὶ θεοῖς εἴη φίλος.

ΧΟΡΟΣ

ὀρεστέρα παμβῶτι Γᾶ,   στρ.
μᾶτερ αὐτοῦ Διός,
ἃ τὸν μέγαν Πακτωλὸν εὔχρυσον νέμεις,
395 σὲ κἀκεῖ, μᾶτερ πότνι', ἐπηυδώμαν,
ὅτ' ἐς τόνδ' Ἀτρειδᾶν
ὕβρις πᾶσ' ἐχώρει,
ὅτε τὰ πάτρια τεύχεα παρεδίδοσαν,
400 ἰὼ μάκαιρα ταυροκτόνων
λεόντων ἔφεδρε, τῷ Λαρτίου,
σέβας ὑπέρτατον.

385–88 del. Barrett

292

though not easily angered he had been stung by what he had heard—gave me this answer, "You were not where we were, but you were away where you should not have been; and now that you are speaking with a reckless tongue, you shall never sail to Skyros with these arms."

When I heard myself reviled with such insults, I sailed for home, cheated of what was mine by the most evil Odysseus, sprung from evil ancestors. [And I do not blame him so much as the commanders; for the whole city and the entire army belong to the rulers; and it is through the words of those that instruct them that men who lack discipline become evil.]

That is all I have to say; and may he who loathes the sons of Atreus be dear alike to me and to the gods!

CHORUS

Goddess of the mountains, Earth that feeds all, mother of Zeus himself,[a] you who rule the great Pactolus[b] rich in gold, there also, lady mother, I called upon you, when all the insolence of the sons of Atreus was coming against him, when they handed over his father's weapons—ah, blessed one that sits behind bull-slaughtering lions!—an object of reverence sublime, to the son of Lartius!

[a] Cybele, the Phrygian mother of the gods, was often identified with Rhea, mother of Zeus, and with the Earth Goddess.

[b] A river in Lydia, from whose waters gold dust was extracted.

ΦΙΛΟΚΤΗΤΗΣ

ἔχοντες, ὡς ἔοικε, σύμβολον σαφὲς
λύπης πρὸς ἡμᾶς, ὦ ξένοι, πεπλεύκατε,
405 καί μοι προσᾴδεθ' ὥστε γιγνώσκειν ὅτι
ταῦτ' ἐξ Ἀτρειδῶν ἔργα κἀξ Ὀδυσσέως.
ἔξοιδα γάρ νιν παντὸς ἂν λόγου κακοῦ
γλώσσῃ θιγόντα καὶ πανουργίας, ἀφ' ἧς
μηδὲν δίκαιον ἐς τέλος μέλλοι ποεῖν.
410 ἀλλ' οὔ τι τοῦτο θαῦμ' ἔμοιγ', ἀλλ' εἰ παρὼν
Αἴας ὁ μείζων ταῦθ' ὁρῶν ἠνείχετο.

ΝΕΟΠΤΟΛΕΜΟΣ

οὐκ ἦν ἔτι ζῶν, ὦ ξέν'· οὐ γὰρ ἄν ποτε
ζῶντός γ' ἐκείνου ταῦτ' ἐσυλήθην ἐγώ.

ΦΙΛΟΚΤΗΤΗΣ

πῶς εἶπας; ἀλλ' ἦ χοὖτος οἴχεται θανών;

ΝΕΟΠΤΟΛΕΜΟΣ

415 ὡς μηκέτ' ὄντα κεῖνον ἐν φάει νόει.

ΦΙΛΟΚΤΗΤΗΣ

οἴμοι τάλας. ἀλλ' οὐχ ὁ Τυδέως γόνος,
οὐδ' οὑμπολητὸς Σισύφου Λαερτίῳ,
οὐ μὴ θάνωσι· τούσδε γὰρ μὴ ζῆν ἔδει.

ΝΕΟΠΤΟΛΕΜΟΣ

οὐ δῆτ'· ἐπίστω τοῦτό γ'· ἀλλὰ καὶ μέγα
420 θάλλοντές εἰσι νῦν ἐν Ἀργείων στρατῷ.

PHILOCTETES

PHILOCTETES

You have sailed here, strangers, with a pain that commends you to me, and you are in harmony with me, so that I recognise that these are the actions of the sons of Atreus and Odysseus! For I know that he lends his tongue to every evil speech and every villainy that can help him compass a dishonest end. But it is not so much this that surprises me, as that the greater Ajax can have been there and have put up with this.

NEOPTOLEMUS

He was no longer living, stranger; if he had been alive, I should never have been robbed of the arms.

PHILOCTETES

What are you saying? Is he also dead and gone?

NEOPTOLEMUS

Think of him as no longer in the world of light!

PHILOCTETES

Alas for me! But the son of Tydeus,[a] and he who was palmed off on Laertius by Sisyphus,[b] they will never die! For they ought not to be alive!

NEOPTOLEMUS

No, you can be sure of that! But they are now with the Argive army, flourishing.

---

[a] Diomedes, son of Tydeus, was associated with Odysseus in several of his enterprises.

[b] There was a story that Odysseus was not really the son of Laertes, but that the cunning king of Corinth, Sisyphus, was his real father, having seduced his mother Anticleia.

ΦΙΛΟΚΤΗΤΗΣ

<φεῦ·> τί δ'; ὁ παλαιὸς κἀγαθὸς φίλος τ' ἐμός,
Νέστωρ ὁ Πύλιος, ἔστιν; οὗτος γὰρ τάχ' ἂν
κείνων κάκ' ἐξήρυκε, βουλεύων σοφά.

ΝΕΟΠΤΟΛΕΜΟΣ

κεῖνός γε πράσσει νῦν κακῶς, ἐπεὶ θανὼν
425   Ἀντίλοχος αὐτῷ φροῦδος ὃς παρῆν γόνος.

ΦΙΛΟΚΤΗΤΗΣ

οἴμοι, δύ' αὖ τώδ' ἄνδρ' ἔλεξας, οἷν ἐγὼ
ἥκιστ' ἂν ἠθέλησ' ὀλωλότοιν κλύειν.
φεῦ φεῦ· τί δῆτα δεῖ σκοπεῖν, ὅθ' οἵδε μὲν
τεθνᾶσ', Ὀδυσσεὺς δ' ἔστιν αὖ κἀνταῦθ' ἵνα
430   χρῆν ἀντὶ τούτων αὐτὸν αὐδᾶσθαι νεκρόν;

ΝΕΟΠΤΟΛΕΜΟΣ

σοφὸς παλαιστὴς κεῖνος, ἀλλὰ καὶ σοφαὶ
γνῶμαι, Φιλοκτῆτ', ἐμποδίζονται θαμά.

ΦΙΛΟΚΤΗΤΗΣ

φέρ' εἰπὲ πρὸς θεῶν, ποῦ γὰρ ἦν ἐνταῦθά σοι
Πάτροκλος, ὃς σοῦ πατρὸς ἦν τὰ φίλτατα;

ΝΕΟΠΤΟΛΕΜΟΣ

435   χοῦτος τεθνηκὼς ἦν· λόγῳ δέ σ' <ἐν> βραχεῖ
τοῦτ' ἐκδιδάξω. πόλεμος οὐδέν' ἄνδρ' ἑκὼν
αἱρεῖ πονηρόν, ἀλλὰ τοὺς χρηστοὺς ἀεί.

421 suppl. Page
422 τάχ' ἂν Hermann: τάχα GR: τά γε cett.
425 ὃς παρῆν Hermann: ὅσπερ ἦν codd.

296

PHILOCTETES

Alas! But is my old and noble friend Nestor of Pylos alive?
He perhaps might have checked their evildoing by his wise
counsel.

NEOPTOLEMUS

He is now in trouble, since he lost by death Antilochus, the
son who was with him.

PHILOCTETES

Alas, again you have spoken of two men who I should least
have wished to learn were dead! Ah, ah! Where must one
look, when they are dead, and Odysseus is alive, even when
he ought to be pronounced dead instead of them?

NEOPTOLEMUS

He is a cunning wrestler; but even clever plans are some-
times thwarted, Philoctetes.

PHILOCTETES

Come, pray tell me, where was Patroclus, who was the
dearest of all to your father?

NEOPTOLEMUS

He too was dead; in one word I will tell you this: war never
willingly destroys a villain, but always noble men.

---

[426] αὖ τώδ᾽ ἄνδρ᾽ ἔλεξας Blaydes, Jebb: αὔτως δείν᾽ ἔλεξας
codd.

[434] σοῦ Hemsterhuys: σοι codd.

[435] suppl. Erfurdt

ΦΙΛΟΚΤΗΤΗΣ

ξυμμαρτυρῶ σοι· καὶ κατ' αὐτὸ τοῦτό γε
ἀναξίου μὲν φωτὸς ἐξερήσομαι,
440   γλώσσῃ δὲ δεινοῦ καὶ σοφοῦ, τί νῦν κυρεῖ.

ΝΕΟΠΤΟΛΕΜΟΣ

ποίου δὲ τούτου πλήν γ' Ὀδυσσέως ἐρεῖς;

ΦΙΛΟΚΤΗΤΗΣ

οὐ τοῦτον εἶπον, ἀλλὰ Θερσίτης τις ἦν,
ὃς οὐκ ἂν εἵλετ' εἰσάπαξ εἰπεῖν, ὅπου
μηδεὶς ἐῴη· τοῦτον οἶσθ' εἰ ζῶν κυρεῖ;

ΝΕΟΠΤΟΛΕΜΟΣ

445   οὐκ εἶδον αὐτός, ᾐσθόμην δ' ἔτ' ὄντα νιν.

ΦΙΛΟΚΤΗΤΗΣ

ἔμελλ'· ἐπεὶ οὐδέν πω κακόν γ' ἀπώλετο,
ἀλλ' εὖ περιστέλλουσιν αὐτὰ δαίμονες,
καί πως τὰ μὲν πανοῦργα καὶ παλιντριβῆ
χαίρουσ' ἀναστρέφοντες ἐξ Ἅιδου, τὰ δὲ
450   δίκαια καὶ τὰ χρήστ' ἀποστέλλουσ' ἀεί.
ποῦ χρὴ τίθεσθαι ταῦτα, ποῦ δ' αἰνεῖν, ὅταν
τὰ θεῖ' ἐπαθρῶν τοὺς θεοὺς εὕρω κακούς;

ΝΕΟΠΤΟΛΕΜΟΣ

ἐγὼ μέν, ὦ γένεθλον Οἰταίου πατρός,
τὸ λοιπὸν ἤδη τηλόθεν τό τ' Ἴλιον
455   καὶ τοὺς Ἀτρείδας εἰσορῶν φυλάξομαι·
ὅπου δ' ὁ χείρων τἀγαθοῦ μεῖζον σθένει

---

445 αὐτός Burges: -όν codd.
452 ἐπαθρῶν Postgate: ἐπαινῶν codd.

298

PHILOCTETES

PHILOCTETES

I bear you witness; and under that very head I will ask
about the fortunes of a man who is unworthy, but cunning
and skilled in speech.

NEOPTOLEMUS

About whom will you ask other than Odysseus?

PHILOCTETES

I did not mean him, but there was one Thersites, who was
never content to speak once and for all, even when no one
wished to let him talk; do you know if he is living?

NEOPTOLEMUS

I did not see him, but I heard that he was still alive.[a]

PHILOCTETES

He would be! Why, nothing evil has ever perished, but the
gods carefully protect it, and somehow they delight in turn-
ing back from Hades cunning and villainy, while righteous-
ness and valour they are for ever sending away. How can
we account for this, and how can we approve it, when if we
survey the actions of the gods we find that the gods are
evil?

NEOPTOLEMUS

For my part, son of an Oetaean father, for the future I shall
look from far off on Ilium and the sons of Atreus and be
wary of them. Where the worse man has more power than

---

[a] According to the usual story Thersites was dead, having been
killed by Achilles when he mocked him for his grief over the Ama-
zon Penthesileia, whom he (Achilles) had killed in battle.

κἀποφθίνει τὰ χρηστὰ χὠ δειλὸς κρατεῖ,
τούτους ἐγὼ τοὺς ἄνδρας οὐ στέρξω ποτέ·
ἀλλ' ἡ πετραία Σκῦρος ἐξαρκοῦσά μοι
460 ἔσται τὸ λοιπόν, ὥστε τέρπεσθαι δόμῳ.

νῦν δ' εἶμι πρὸς ναῦν. καὶ σύ, Ποίαντος τέκνον,
χαῖρ' ὡς μέγιστα, χαῖρε· καί σε δαίμονες
νόσου μεταστήσειαν, ὡς αὐτὸς θέλεις.
ἡμεῖς δ' ἴωμεν, ὡς ὁπηνίκ' ἂν θεὸς
465 πλοῦν ἡμὶν εἴκῃ, τηνικαῦθ' ὁρμώμεθα.

ΦΙΛΟΚΤΗΤΗΣ

ἤδη, τέκνον, στέλλεσθε;

ΝΕΟΠΤΟΛΕΜΟΣ

καιρὸς γὰρ καλεῖ
πλοῦν μὴ 'ξ ἀπόπτου μᾶλλον ἢ 'γγύθεν σκοπεῖν.

ΦΙΛΟΚΤΗΤΗΣ

πρός νύν σε πατρός, πρός τε μητρός, ὦ τέκνον,
πρός τ' εἴ τί σοι κατ' οἶκόν ἐστι προσφιλές,
470 ἱκέτης ἱκνοῦμαι, μὴ λίπῃς μ' οὕτω μόνον,
ἔρημον ἐν κακοῖσι τοῖσδ' οἵοις ὁρᾷς
ὅσοισί τ' ἐξήκουσας ἐνναίοντά με·
ἀλλ' ἐν παρέργῳ θοῦ με. δυσχέρεια μέν,
ἔξοιδα, πολλὴ τοῦδε τοῦ φορήματος·
475 ὅμως δὲ τλῆθι· τοῖσι γενναίοισί τοι
τό τ' αἰσχρὸν ἐχθρὸν καὶ τὸ χρηστὸν εὐκλεές.
σοὶ δ', ἐκλιπόντι τοῦτ', ὄνειδος οὐ καλόν,
δράσαντι δ', ὦ παῖ, πλεῖστον εὐκλείας γέρας,
ἐὰν μόλω 'γὼ ζῶν πρὸς Οἰταίαν χθόνα.

the better, what is good perishes, and the coward is in
power, the men in that place I will never tolerate. No,
rocky Skyros shall be sufficient for me for the future, so
that I shall be content with home. But now I shall go to the
ship; and you, son of Poeas, farewell, heartily farewell!
And may the gods relieve you of your sickness, just as you
wish yourself. But let us go, so that whenever the god
allows good sailing, we may set off!

PHILOCTETES

Are you departing already, my son?

NEOPTOLEMUS

Yes, to seize our opportunity we must watch out for the
chance to sail from near at hand, not from where we cannot
see.

PHILOCTETES

Now by your father and your mother, my son, and by any-
thing you have at home that is dear to you, I implore you as
a suppliant, do not leave me alone like this, isolated amid
such troubles as you see and all others that you have heard
I live among! Make me a lesser concern; I know well the
discomfort that arises if you take me. But none the less put
up with it! For noble men meanness is detestable and gen-
erosity brings fame! And if you neglect this duty, a
reproach that brings discredit attaches to you, but if you do
it, my son, a great reward in increase in your fame, if I
reach the land of Oeta still alive. Come! The trouble will

---

[457] δειλὸς Brunck: δεινὸς codd.

SOPHOCLES

480 ἴθ'· ἡμέρας τοι μόχθος οὐχ ὅλης μιᾶς.
τόλμησον, ἐμβαλοῦ μ' ὅποι θέλεις ἄγων,
ἐς ἀντλίαν, ἐς πρῷραν, ἐς πρύμναν†, ὅπου
ἥκιστα μέλλω τοὺς ξυνόντας ἀλγυνεῖν.
νεῦσον, πρὸς αὐτοῦ Ζηνὸς ἱκεσίου, τέκνον,
485 πείσθητι, προσπίτνω σε γόνασι, καίπερ ὢν
ἀκράτωρ ὁ τλήμων, χωλός. ἀλλὰ μή μ' ἀφῇς
ἔρημον οὕτω χωρὶς ἀνθρώπων στίβου,
ἀλλ' ἢ πρὸς οἶκον τὸν σὸν ἔκσωσόν μ' ἄγων,
ἢ πρὸς τὰ Χαλκώδοντος Εὐβοίας σταθμά·
490 κἀκεῖθεν οὔ μοι μακρὸς εἰς Οἴτην στόλος
Τραχινίαν τε δεράδα καὶ τὸν εὔροον
Σπερχειὸν ἔσται, πατρί μ' ὡς δείξῃς φίλῳ,
ὃν δὴ παλαιὸν ἐξότου δέδοικ' ἐγὼ
μή μοι βεβήκῃ. πολλὰ γὰρ τοῖς ἱγμένοις
495 ἔστελλον αὐτὸν ἱκεσίους πέμπων λιτάς,
αὐτόστολον πλεύσαντά μ' ἐκσῶσαι δόμους.
ἀλλ' ἢ τέθνηκεν, ἢ τὰ τῶν διακόνων,
ὡς εἰκός, οἶμαι, τοὐμὸν ἐν σμικρῷ μέρος
ποιούμενοι τὸν οἴκαδ' ἤπειγον στόλον.
500   νῦν δ', ἐς σὲ γὰρ πομπόν τε καὐτὸν ἄγγελον
ἥκω, σὺ σῶσον, σύ μ' ἐλέησον, εἰσορῶν
ὡς πάντα δεινὰ κἀπικινδύνως βροτοῖς
κεῖται παθεῖν μὲν εὖ, παθεῖν δὲ θἄτερα.
[χρὴ δ' ἐκτὸς ὄντα πημάτων τὰ δείν' ὁρᾶν,
505 χὤταν τις εὖ ζῇ, τηνικαῦτα τὸν βίον
σκοπεῖν μάλιστα μὴ διαφθαρεὶς λάθῃ.]

302

last less than one whole day. Bring yourself to do it, take
me and put me where you will, in the bilge, on the prow, in
the stern, wherever I am least likely to cause pain to my
companions. Consent! In the name of Zeus the god of
suppliants himself, be persuaded! I fall on my knees
before you, although I am helpless in my misery, lame!
But do not leave me thus deserted, far from the tread of
men, but take me either to your home or to the Euboean
dwelling of Chalcodon—from there I have a short voyage
to Oeta and the ridge of Trachis and the broad stream of
Spercheius—so that you can show me to my father. Long
since I have been afraid that he is gone; for I sent many
messages by those who came, conveying the entreaties of a
suppliant that he should sail in person to fetch me home.
But either he is dead or the messengers, paying small heed
to me, as was natural, hurried home.

But now, since I come to you as one who can bring my
message and myself, save me, take pity on me, seeing that
for mortals all things are full of fear and of the danger that
after good fortune may come evil. [While free from trouble
one must look on what is to be feared, and while pros-
perous, then most of all one must look to one's life in case
ruin should come upon one unawares.]

481–82 fort. ἄγων ... πρύμναν delenda sunt: μ' post πρύμναν
suppl. Bergk
496 πλεύσαντά Syp (coni. Blaydes): πέμψαντά codd.
504–6 del. Reeve

ΧΟΡΟΣ

οἴκτιρ᾽, ἄναξ· πολλῶν ἔλε-   ἀντ.
ξεν δυσοίστων πόνων
ἆθλ᾽, οἷα μηδεὶς τῶν ἐμῶν τύχοι φίλων.
510 εἰ δὲ πικρούς, ἄναξ, ἔχθεις Ἀτρείδας,
ἐγὼ μέν, τὸ κείνων
κακὸν τῷδε κέρδος
515 μέγα τιθέμενος, ἔνθαπερ ἐπιμέμονεν,
ἐπ᾽ εὐστόλου ταχείας νεὼς
πορεύσαιμ᾽ ἂν ἐς δόμους, τὰν θεῶν
νέμεσιν ἐκφυγών.

ΝΕΟΠΤΟΛΕΜΟΣ

ὅρα σὺ μὴ νῦν μέν τις εὐχερὴς παρῇς,
520 ὅταν δὲ πλησθῇς τῆς νόσου ξυνουσίᾳ,
τότ᾽ οὐκέθ᾽ αὑτὸς τοῖς λόγοις τούτοις φανῇς.

ΧΟΡΟΣ

ἥκιστα· τοῦτ᾽ οὐκ ἔσθ᾽ ὅπως ποτ᾽ εἰς ἐμὲ
τοὔνειδος ἕξεις ἐνδίκως ὀνειδίσαι.

ΝΕΟΠΤΟΛΕΜΟΣ

ἀλλ᾽ αἰσχρὰ μέντοι σοῦ γέ μ᾽ ἐνδεέστερον
525 ξένῳ φανῆναι πρὸς τὸ καίριον πονεῖν.
ἀλλ᾽ εἰ δοκεῖ, πλέωμεν, ὁρμάσθω ταχύς·
χἠ ναῦς γὰρ ἄξει κοὐκ ἀπαρνηθήσεται.
μόνον θεοὶ σῴζοιεν ἔκ τε τῆσδε γῆς
ἡμᾶς ὅποι τ᾽ ἐνθένδε βουλοίμεσθα πλεῖν.

---

[509] οἷα Porson: ὅσ(σ)α codd.
[517] post τὰν add. ἐκ codd., del. Hermann

PHILOCTETES

CHORUS

Take pity on him, my lord! He has spoken of the ordeal of
many troubles, hard to bear; may such attend none of my
friends! And if you hate the odious sons of Atreus, my lord,
I would make their evil actions a great benefit for him, and
would convey him home, where he longs to go, upon the
well-appointed swift ship, escaping the righteous anger of
the gods.

NEOPTOLEMUS

Take care that for all the indulgence you show now you do
not appear a different person when you have had enough
of contact with the sickness!

CHORUS

By no means! You will never be able to level this reproach
at me with justice.

NEOPTOLEMUS

Well, it is shameful for me to seem to the stranger less
ready than you are to work to serve his need. If you are
agreeable, let us sail, let him set off in haste; the ship will
carry him and will not refuse! Only may the gods convey us
safely out of this land to wherever we may desire to sail!

ΦΙΛΟΚΤΗΤΗΣ

530　ὦ φίλτατον μὲν ἦμαρ, ἥδιστος δ᾽ ἀνήρ,
　　φίλοι δὲ ναῦται, πῶς ἂν ὑμὶν ἐμφανὴς
　　ἔργῳ γενοίμην, ὥς μ᾽ ἔθεσθε προσφιλῆ.
　　ἴωμεν, ὦ παῖ, προσκύσαντε τὴν ἔσω
　　ἄοικον ἐξοίκησιν, ὥς με καὶ μάθῃς
535　ἀφ᾽ ὧν διέζων, ὥς τ᾽ ἔφυν εὐκάρδιος.
　　οἶμαι γὰρ οὐδ᾽ ἂν ὄμμασιν μόνον θέαν
　　ἄλλον λαβόντα πλὴν ἐμοῦ τλῆναι τάδε·
　　ἐγὼ δ᾽ ἀνάγκῃ προὔμαθον στέργειν κακά.

ΧΟΡΟΣ

　　ἐπίσχετον, σταθῶμεν· ἄνδρε γὰρ δύο,
540　ὁ μὲν νεὼς σῆς ναυβάτης, ὁ δ᾽ ἀλλόθρους,
　　χωρεῖτον, ὧν μαθόντες αὖθις εἴσιτον.

ΕΜΠΟΡΟΣ

　　Ἀχιλλέως παῖ, τόνδε τὸν ξυνέμπορον,
　　ὃς ἦν νεὼς σῆς σὺν δυοῖν ἄλλοιν φύλαξ,
　　ἐκέλευσ᾽ ἐμοί σε ποῦ κυρῶν εἴης φράσαι,
545　ἐπείπερ ἀντέκυρσα, δοξάζων μὲν οὔ,
　　τύχῃ δέ πως πρὸς ταὐτὸν ὁρμισθεὶς πέδου.
　　πλέω γὰρ ὡς ναύκληρος οὐ πολλῷ στόλῳ
　　ἀπ᾽ Ἰλίου πρὸς οἶκον ἐς τὴν εὔβοτρυν
　　Πεπάρηθον, ὡς <δ᾽> ἤκουσα τοὺς ναύτας ὅτι
550　σοὶ πάντες εἶεν συννεναυστοληκότες,
　　ἔδοξέ μοι μὴ σῖγα, πρὶν φράσαιμί σοι,

PHILOCTETES

O dearest of days, and most agreeable of men, O dear sailors, how could I show you by an action what friendship you have made me feel for you! Let us go, my son, when we have saluted the home that is not a home inside, so that you may learn how I contrived to live, and what courage I displayed! I think that no other but me who had even set eyes on it could have endured this; but of necessity I gradually learned to put up with hardships.

CHORUS

Halt, let us stand still! Two men are coming, one a sailor from your ship, the other a foreigner; hear what they can tell us and go in later!

Enter MERCHANT, accompanied by a Sailor.

MERCHANT[a]

Son of Achilles, I told my companion here, who with two others was guarding your ship, to tell me where you were, since I had met them, not expecting to, but having happened to anchor in the same place. For I am a sea-captain, sailing with a small party from Ilium to Peparethus,[b] rich in grapes, and when I heard that all the sailors were members of your crew, I thought that I should not complete my

---

[a] See lines 125 f.

[b] A small island northeast of Skyros, now called Skopelos.

---

534 ἐξοίκησιν Frederking: εἰσοίκησιν fere codd.

536 μόνον Blaydes: μόνην codd.

539 σταθῶμεν Hense: μάθωμεν codd.

546 πέδου Maguinness: πέδον codd.

547 πλέω Reiske: πλέων codd.   549 suppl. Reiske

550 συννεναυστοληκότες Dobree: οἱ νεναυ- codd.

SOPHOCLES

τὸν πλοῦν ποεῖσθαι, προστυχόντι τῶν ἴσων.
οὐδὲν σύ που κάτοισθα τῶν σαυτοῦ πέρι,
ἃ τοῖσιν Ἀργείοισιν ἀμφὶ σοῦ νέα
555 βουλεύματ᾽ ἐστί, κοὐ μόνον βουλεύματα,
ἀλλ᾽ ἔργα δρώμεν᾽, οὐκέτ᾽ ἐξαργούμενα.

ΝΕΟΠΤΟΛΕΜΟΣ

ἀλλ᾽ ἡ χάρις μὲν τῆς προμηθίας, ξένε,
εἰ μὴ κακὸς πέφυκα, προσφιλὴς μενεῖ·
φράσον δὲ τἄργ᾽ ἄλεξας, ὡς μάθω τί μοι
560 νεώτερον βούλευμ᾽ ἀπ᾽ Ἀργείων ἔχεις.

ΕΜΠΟΡΟΣ

φροῦδοι διώκοντές σε ναυτικῷ στόλῳ
Φοῖνίξ θ᾽ ὁ πρέσβυς οἵ τε Θησέως κόροι.

ΝΕΟΠΤΟΛΕΜΟΣ

ὡς ἐκ βίας μ᾽ ἄξοντες ἢ λόγοις πάλιν;

ΕΜΠΟΡΟΣ

οὐκ οἶδ᾽. ἀκούσας δ᾽ ἄγγελος πάρειμί σοι.

ΝΕΟΠΤΟΛΕΜΟΣ

565 ἦ ταῦτα δὴ Φοῖνίξ τε χοὶ ξυνναυβάται
οὕτω καθ᾽ ὁρμὴν δρῶσιν Ἀτρειδῶν χάριν;

ΕΜΠΟΡΟΣ

ὡς ταῦτ᾽ ἐπίστω δρώμεν᾽, οὐ μέλλοντ᾽ ἔτι.

ΝΕΟΠΤΟΛΕΜΟΣ

πῶς οὖν Ὀδυσσεὺς πρὸς τάδ᾽ οὐκ αὐτάγγελος
πλεῖν ἦν ἑτοῖμος; ἢ φόβος τις εἶργέ νιν;

554 σοῦ νέα Auratus: σοῦ 'νεκα fere codd.   559 τἄργ᾽ Dale:
ἅπερ γ᾽ a: ἅπερ cett.   ἄλεξας Dale: ἔλεξας codd.

308

voyage without speaking, but that I should warn you, for proper recompense. You are ignorant, I think, of what concerns yourself, of the new plans that the Argives have concerning you, and not only plans, but actions which are no longer being put off, but are in hand.

NEOPTOLEMUS

Stranger, if I am an honest man, the kindness shown by your forethought shall be remembered gratefully. But tell me of the actions you have spoken of, so that I may learn what new plan proceeding from the Argives you know of!

MERCHANT

They have sailed in pursuit of you—the aged Phoenix[a] and the sons of Theseus!

NEOPTOLEMUS

To bring me back by force or by argument?

MERCHANT

I do not know; but I heard it, and am here to report.

NEOPTOLEMUS

Are Phoenix and his companions doing this with so much eagerness to please the sons of Atreus?

MERCHANT

Know that these things are in process, and are no longer in the future.

NEOPTOLEMUS

Then why was Odysseus not ready to sail and be his own messenger? Did some fear restrain him?

[a] He had been Achilles' tutor; see Homer, *Iliad* 9.

EMΠΟΡΟΣ

570 κεῖνός γ᾽ ἐπ᾽ ἄλλον ἄνδρ᾽ ὁ Τυδέως τε παῖς
ἔστελλον, ἡνίκ᾽ ἐξανηγόμην ἐγώ.

ΝΕΟΠΤΟΛΕΜΟΣ

πρὸς ποῖον αὖ τόνδ᾽ αὐτὸς Οὐδυσσεὺς ἔπλει;

EMΠΟΡΟΣ

ἦν δή τις — ἀλλὰ τόνδε μοι πρῶτον φράσον
τίς ἐστίν· ἂν λέγῃς δὲ μὴ φώνει μέγα.

ΝΕΟΠΤΟΛΕΜΟΣ

575 ὅδ᾽ ἔσθ᾽ ὁ κλεινός σοι Φιλοκτήτης, ξένε.

EMΠΟΡΟΣ

μή νύν μ᾽ ἔρῃ τὰ πλείον᾽, ἀλλ᾽ ὅσον τάχος
ἔκπλει σεαυτὸν ξυλλαβὼν ἐκ τῆσδε γῆς.

ΦΙΛΟΚΤΗΤΗΣ

τί φησιν, ὦ παῖ; τί δὲ κατὰ σκότον ποτὲ
διεμπολᾷ λόγοισι πρός σ᾽ ὁ ναυβάτης;

ΝΕΟΠΤΟΛΕΜΟΣ

580 οὐκ οἶδά πω τί φησι· δεῖ δ᾽ αὐτὸν λέγειν
ἐς φῶς ὃ λέξει, πρὸς σὲ κἀμὲ τούσδε τε.

EMΠΟΡΟΣ

ὦ σπέρμ᾽ Ἀχιλλέως, μή με διαβάλῃς στρατῷ
λέγονθ᾽ ἃ μὴ δεῖ· πόλλ᾽ ἐγὼ κείνων ὕπο
δρῶν ἀντιπάσχω χρηστά θ᾽, οἷ᾽ ἀνὴρ πένης.

---

572 αὖ Dobree: ἂν codd.
578 δὲ Seyffert: με codd.
584 θ᾽ Dobree: γ᾽ fere codd.

PHILOCTETES

MERCHANT

He and the son of Tydeus were on the track of another man when I put out.

NEOPTOLEMUS

Who was this man after whom Odysseus was sailing?

MERCHANT

It was a certain . . . but first tell me who this man is! And in telling me do not speak loud!

NEOPTOLEMUS

This is the renowned Philoctetes, stranger!

MERCHANT

Ask me no more questions, but as soon as possible sail and take yourself away from this land!

PHILOCTETES

What is he saying, my son? What is this transaction that the seaman is carrying on with you in secret?

NEOPTOLEMUS

I do not yet know what he is saying; but he must say what he is going to say openly, to you and me and these men.

MERCHANT

Child of Achilles, do not denounce me to the army for telling what I should not tell! I do many things for them and am rewarded, poor man that I am.

SOPHOCLES

ΝΕΟΠΤΟΛΕΜΟΣ

585 ἐγὼ μὲν αὐτοῖς δυσμενής· οὗτος δέ μοι
φίλος μέγιστος, οὕνεκ' Ἀτρείδας στυγεῖ.
δεῖ δή σ', ἔμοιγ' ἐλθόντα προσφιλῆ, λόγων
κρύψαι πρὸς ἡμᾶς μηδὲν ὧν ἀκήκοας.

ΕΜΠΟΡΟΣ

ὅρα τί ποιεῖς, παῖ.

ΝΕΟΠΤΟΛΕΜΟΣ

σκοπῶ κἀγὼ πάλαι.

ΕΜΠΟΡΟΣ

590 σὲ θήσομαι τῶνδ' αἴτιον.

ΝΕΟΠΤΟΛΕΜΟΣ

ποιοῦ λέγων.

ΕΜΠΟΡΟΣ

λέγω. 'πὶ τοῦτον ἄνδρε τώδ' ὥπερ κλύεις,
ὁ Τυδέως παῖς ἥ τ' Ὀδυσσέως βία,
διώμοτοι πλέουσιν ἦ μὴν ἢ λόγῳ
πείσαντες ἄξειν, ἢ πρὸς ἰσχύος κράτος.
595 καὶ ταῦτ' Ἀχαιοὶ πάντες ἤκουον σαφῶς
Ὀδυσσέως λέγοντος· οὗτος γὰρ πλέον
τὸ θάρσος εἶχε θατέρου δράσειν τάδε.

ΝΕΟΠΤΟΛΕΜΟΣ

τίνος δ' Ἀτρεῖδαι τοῦδ' ἄγαν οὕτω χρόνῳ
τοσῷδ' ἐπεστρέφοντο πράγματος χάριν,
600 ὅν γ' εἶχον ἤδη χρόνιον ἐκβεβληκότες;
τίς ὁ πόθος αὐτοὺς ἵκετ'; ἢ θεῶν βία

PHILOCTETES

NEOPTOLEMUS

I am their enemy; and this man is my great friend, because
he hates the sons of Atreus. Since you have come as a
friend to me, you ought to conceal from us none of the
things that you have heard.

MERCHANT

Be careful what you are doing, my son!

NEOPTOLEMUS

I have been careful all the time.

MERCHANT

I shall hold you responsible for this!

NEOPTOLEMUS

Do so, but speak!

MERCHANT

I will speak! It is for him that the two men I spoke of, the
son of Tydeus and the mighty Odysseus, are sailing, having
sworn to bring him back, either by persuasion or by brute
force. And all the Achaeans heard Odysseus saying this
clearly; for he had more confidence than the other that he
would accomplish this.

NEOPTOLEMUS

But why have the sons of Atreus after so long a time taken
so much trouble to secure one whom long ago they had
thrown out? What reason for wanting him has come to

---

585 αὐτοῖς Blaydes: Ἀτρείδαις codd.
587 λόγων Burges: λόγον codd.

καὶ νέμεσις, αἵπερ ἔργ᾽ ἀμύνουσιν κακά;

ΕΜΠΟΡΟΣ

ἐγώ σε τοῦτ᾽, ἴσως γὰρ οὐκ ἀκήκοας,
πᾶν ἐκδιδάξω. μάντις ἦν τις εὐγενής,
605 Πριάμου μὲν υἱός, ὄνομα δ᾽ ὠνομάζετο
Ἕλενος, ὃν οὗτος νυκτὸς ἐξελθὼν μόνος
ὁ πάντ᾽ ἀκούων αἰσχρὰ καὶ λωβήτ᾽ ἔπη
δόλοις Ὀδυσσεὺς εἷλε· δέσμιόν τ᾽ ἄγων
ἔδειξ᾽ Ἀχαιοῖς ἐς μέσον, θήραν καλήν·
610 ὃς δὴ τά τ᾽ ἄλλ᾽ αὐτοῖσι πάντ᾽ ἐθέσπισεν
καὶ τἀπὶ Τροίᾳ πέργαμ᾽ ὡς οὐ μή ποτε
πέρσοιεν, εἰ μὴ τόνδε πείσαντες λόγῳ
ἄγοιντο νήσου τῆσδ᾽ ἐφ᾽ ἧς ναίει τὰ νῦν.
καὶ ταῦθ᾽ ὅπως ἤκουσ᾽ ὁ Λαέρτου τόκος
615 τὸν μάντιν εἰπόντ᾽, εὐθέως ὑπέσχετο
τὸν ἄνδρ᾽ Ἀχαιοῖς τόνδε δηλώσειν ἄγων·
οἴοιτο μὲν μάλισθ᾽ ἑκούσιον λαβών,
εἰ μὴ θέλοι δ᾽, ἄκοντα· καὶ τούτων κάρα
τέμνειν ἐφεῖτο τῷ θέλοντι μὴ τυχών.
620 ἤκουσας, ὦ παῖ, πάντα· τὸ σπεύδειν δέ σοι
καὐτῷ παραινῶ κεἴ τινος κήδῃ πέρι.

ΦΙΛΟΚΤΗΤΗΣ

οἴμοι τάλας. ἦ κεῖνος, ἡ πᾶσα βλάβη,
ἔμ᾽ εἰς Ἀχαιοὺς ὤμοσεν πείσας στελεῖν;
πεισθήσομαι γὰρ ὧδε κἀξ Ἅιδου θανὼν
625 πρὸς φῶς ἀνελθεῖν, ὥσπερ οὑκείνου πατήρ.

them? Is it the power and the just anger of the gods, who punish wicked deeds?

MERCHANT

I shall explain all this to you, since perhaps you have not heard it! There was a noble prophet, a son of Priam, called Helenus; that man went out alone at night—he of whom shameful and outrageous things are said, Odysseus—and ambushed him, and brought him as a prisoner into the middle of the Achaeans, a splendid prize. He prophesied all other events to them, and told them that they would never take the towers of Troy, unless they persuaded Philoctetes and brought him from the island where he is now living. And when the son of Laertes heard that the prophet had said this, at once he promised the Achaeans that he would bring him and display him to them. He thought he would take him of his own free will, but if he refused, he would capture him against it, and if he failed, he would allow anyone who wished to cut off his head. You have heard it all, my son; and I advise you and anyone you care about to make haste!

PHILOCTETES

Alas for me! Did that man, that utter plague, swear that he would bring me to the Achaeans? I shall as soon be persuaded to return from Hades to the world of light after my death, like his father![a]

[a] See note on line 417; Sisyphus died and escaped from Hades by a trick, only to die again later and remain there.

---

602 αἵπερ Pallis: οἵπερ fere codd.
608 δόλοις Housman: δόλιος codd.

SOPHOCLES

ΕΜΠΟΡΟΣ

οὐκ οἶδ᾽ ἐγὼ ταῦτ᾽· ἀλλ᾽ ἐγὼ μὲν εἶμ᾽ ἐπὶ
ναῦν, σφῷν δ᾽ ὅπως ἄριστα συμφέροι θεός.

ΦΙΛΟΚΤΗΤΗΣ

οὔκουν τάδ᾽, ὦ παῖ, δεινά, τὸν Λαερτίου
ἔμ᾽ ἐλπίσαι ποτ᾽ ἂν λόγοισι μαλθακοῖς
630   δεῖξαι νεὼς ἄγοντ᾽ ἐν Ἀργείοις μέσοις;
οὔ· θᾶσσον ἂν τῆς πλεῖστον ἐχθίστης ἐμοὶ
κλύοιμ᾽ ἐχίδνης, ἥ μ᾽ ἔθηκεν ὧδ᾽ ἄπουν.
ἀλλ᾽ ἔστ᾽ ἐκείνῳ πάντα λεκτά, πάντα δὲ
τολμητά· καὶ νῦν οἶδ᾽ ὁθούνεχ᾽ ἵξεται.
635   ἀλλ᾽, ὦ τέκνον, χωρῶμεν, ὡς ἡμᾶς πολὺ
πέλαγος ὁρίζῃ τῆς Ὀδυσσέως νεώς.
ἴωμεν· ἤ τοι καίριος σπουδὴ πόνου
λήξαντος ὕπνον κἀνάπαυλαν ἤγαγεν.

ΝΕΟΠΤΟΛΕΜΟΣ

οὐκοῦν ἐπειδὰν πνεῦμα τοὐκ πρῴρας ἀνῇ,
640   τότε στελοῦμεν· νῦν γὰρ ἀντιοστατεῖ.

ΦΙΛΟΚΤΗΤΗΣ

ἀεὶ καλὸς πλοῦς ἔσθ᾽, ὅταν φεύγῃς κακά.

ΝΕΟΠΤΟΛΕΜΟΣ

οἶδ᾽· ἀλλὰ κἀκείνοισι ταῦτ᾽ ἐναντία.

ΦΙΛΟΚΤΗΤΗΣ

οὐκ ἔστι λῃσταῖς πνεῦμ᾽ ἐναντιούμενον,
ὅταν παρῇ κλέψαι τε χἁρπάσαι βίᾳ.

---

639 ἀνῇ Lambinus: ἄῃ lrt

316

PHILOCTETES

MERCHANT

I know nothing of this; but I will go to the ship, and may
the god help you as best he may!

Exit MERCHANT.

PHILOCTETES

Is this not shocking, my son, that the son of Laertius should
hope by his cajoling words to bring me and display me in
the middle of the Argives? No! I would sooner listen to
the thing I hate most of all, the serpent that made my foot
thus useless! But he will say anything and dare anything;
and now I know that he will come! My son, let us go, so
that a great expanse of sea may separate us from Odysseus'
ship! Let us go! Make haste when need calls, and you shall
have sleep and rest when the work is over!

NEOPTOLEMUS

Then when the breeze from the prow lets up, we will set
out; for at present it is against us.

PHILOCTETES

It is always good sailing weather when one is escaping from
trouble.

NEOPTOLEMUS

I know; but the wind is against them too.

PHILOCTETES

There is no such thing as an adverse wind for pirates, when
they have a chance to rob and kidnap.

---

642 οἶδ᾽ · ἀλλὰ Doederlein: οὔκ · ἀλλὰ codd.

317

ΝΕΟΠΤΟΛΕΜΟΣ

645 ἀλλ᾽ εἰ δοκεῖ, χωρῶμεν, ἔνδοθεν λαβὼν
ὅτου σε χρεία καὶ πόθος μάλιστ᾽ ἔχει.

ΦΙΛΟΚΤΗΤΗΣ

ἀλλ᾽ ἔστιν ὧν δεῖ, καίπερ οὐ πολλῶν ἄπο.

ΝΕΟΠΤΟΛΕΜΟΣ

τί τοῦθ᾽ ὃ μὴ νεώς γε τῆς ἐμῆς ἔπι;

ΦΙΛΟΚΤΗΤΗΣ

φύλλον τί μοι πάρεστιν, ᾧ μάλιστ᾽ ἀεὶ
650 κοιμῶ τόδ᾽ ἕλκος, ὥστε πραΰνειν πάνυ.

ΝΕΟΠΤΟΛΕΜΟΣ

ἀλλ᾽ ἔκφερ᾽ αὐτό· τί γὰρ ἔτ᾽ ἄλλ᾽ ἐρᾷς λαβεῖν;

ΦΙΛΟΚΤΗΤΗΣ

εἴ μοί τι τόξων τῶνδ᾽ ἀπημελημένον
παρερρύηκεν, ὡς λίπω μή τῳ λαβεῖν.

ΝΕΟΠΤΟΛΕΜΟΣ

ἦ ταῦτα γὰρ τὰ κλεινὰ τόξ᾽ ἃ νῦν ἔχεις;

ΦΙΛΟΚΤΗΤΗΣ

655 ταῦτ᾽, οὐ γὰρ ἄλλ᾽ ἔστ᾽, ἀλλ᾽ ἃ βαστάζω χεροῖν.

ΝΕΟΠΤΟΛΕΜΟΣ

ἆρ᾽ ἔστιν ὥστε κἀγγύθεν θέαν λαβεῖν,
καὶ βαστάσαι με προσκύσαι θ᾽ ὥσπερ θεόν;

645 λαβὼν] λαβεῖν Page
648 ἔπι Auratus: ἔνι codd.
655 ἀλλ᾽ ἔστ᾽, ἀλλ᾽ Seyffert: ἀλλ᾽ ἔσθ᾽, ἀλλ᾽ GR: ἄλλα γ᾽ ἔσθ᾽
a: ἀλλ᾽ ἔσθ᾽ ltz

PHILOCTETES

NEOPTOLEMUS

Well, if you wish, let us go, when you have taken from inside whatever you most need and most desire!

PHILOCTETES

There are things which I need, though my resources are not great.

NEOPTOLEMUS

What thing do you mean that does not exist upon my ship?

PHILOCTETES

I have a herb which I use chiefly every time to lull this wound, so as to make the pain much less.

NEOPTOLEMUS

Why, bring it out! What else do you desire to take?

PHILOCTETES

Any of these arrows that has been carelessly dropped, so that I do not leave it for anyone to pick up.

NEOPTOLEMUS

Is that the famous bow that you are holding?

PHILOCTETES

Yes, I have no other; it is the one I am carrying in my hands.

NEOPTOLEMUS

Is it possible for me to look at it from close, and to hold it and kiss it as though it were a god?

SOPHOCLES

ΦΙΛΟΚΤΗΤΗΣ

σοί γ', ὦ τέκνον, καὶ τοῦτο κάλλο τῶν ἐμῶν
ὁποῖον ἄν σοι ξυμφέρῃ γενήσεται.

ΝΕΟΠΤΟΛΕΜΟΣ

660 καὶ μὴν ἐρῶ γε· τὸν δ' ἔρωθ' οὕτως ἔχω·
εἴ μοι θέμις, θέλοιμ' ἄν· εἰ δὲ μή, πάρες.

ΦΙΛΟΚΤΗΤΗΣ

ὅσιά τε φωνεῖς ἔστι τ', ὦ τέκνον, θέμις,
ὅς γ' ἡλίου τόδ' εἰσορᾶν ἐμοὶ φάος
μόνος δέδωκας, ὃς χθόν' Οἰταίαν ἰδεῖν,
665 ὃς πατέρα πρέσβυν, ὃς φίλους, ὃς τῶν ἐμῶν
ἐχθρῶν μ' ἔνερθεν ὄντ' ἀνέστησας πέρα.
θάρσει, παρέσται ταῦτά σοι καὶ θιγγάνειν
καὶ δόντι δοῦναι κἀξεπεύξασθαι βροτῶν
ἀρετῆς ἕκατι τῶνδ' ἐπιψαῦσαι μόνῳ·
670 εὐεργετῶν γὰρ καὐτὸς αὔτ' ἐκτησάμην.

ΝΕΟΠΤΟΛΕΜΟΣ

οὐκ ἄχθομαί σ' ἰδών τε καὶ λαβὼν φίλον.
ὅστις γὰρ εὖ δρᾶν εὖ παθὼν ἐπίσταται,
παντὸς γένοιτ' ἂν κτήματος κρείσσων φίλος.
χωροῖς ἂν εἴσω.

ΦΙΛΟΚΤΗΤΗΣ

      καὶ σέ γ' εἰσάξω· τὸ γὰρ
675 νοσοῦν ποθεῖ σε ξυμπαραστάτην λαβεῖν.

ΧΟΡΟΣ

λόγῳ μὲν ἐξήκουσ', ὄπωπα δ' οὐ μάλα,   στρ. α'
τὸν πελάταν

320

PHILOCTETES

PHILOCTETES

For *you*, my son, this and any other privilege in my gift shall be granted.

NEOPTOLEMUS

Well, I desire it, but this is the nature of my desire; if it is right for me, I would like it; but if it is not, let it go!

PHILOCTETES

Your words are innocent, and it is right, my son; you alone have given me the power to see the light of the sun, to see the land of Oeta, and my aged father, and my friends, and when I lay at the feet of my enemies you raised me up beyond their reach. Be assured, it shall be granted you to handle it, and to return it to the giver, and to boast that because of your nobility you alone among mortals have laid hands on it; for it was by doing a kindness that I myself acquired it.

NEOPTOLEMUS

I am not sorry to have met you and got you as a friend; for whoever knows how to return a kindness is a friend more precious than any possession. Go inside!

PHILOCTETES

I will bring you too in; for my sickness requires me to get you to stand by me.

CHORUS

I have heard, though I have never seen, how he who drew near to the god's own marriage bed[a] was bound and placed

[a] Ixion.

669 μόνῳ Nauck: μόνον codd.
671–73 Neoptolemo tribuit Doederlein, Philoctetae codd.

321

λέκτρων <σφετέρων> ποτὲ
κατ' ἄμπυκα δὴ δρομάδ' <Ἅιδου>
δέσμιον ὡς ἔλαβεν
παγκρατὴς Κρόνου παῖς·

680 ἄλλον δ' οὔτιν' ἔγωγ' οἶδα κλυὼν οὐδ' ἐσιδὼν μοίρᾳ
τοῦδ' ἐχθίονι συντυχόντα θνατῶν,
ὃς οὔτε τι ῥέξας τιν', οὔτε νοσφίσας,
ἀλλ' ἴσος ἐν ἴσοις ἀνήρ,

685 ὤλλυθ' ὧδ' ἀναξίως.
τόδε <μὰν> θαῦμά μ' ἔχει,
πῶς ποτε πῶς ποτ' ἀμφιπλήκτων
ῥοθίων μόνος κλύων, πῶς
ἄρα πανδάκρυτον οὕτω

690 βιοτὰν κατέσχεν·
ἵν' αὐτὸς ἦν, πρόσουρον οὐκ ἔχων βάσιν,   ἀντ. α'
οὐδέ τιν' ἐγ-
χώρων, κακογείτονα,
παρ' ᾧ στόνον ἀντίτυπον <νό-
σον> βαρυβρῶτ' ἀποκλαύ-

695 σειεν αἱματηρόν·
οὐδ' ὃς θερμοτάταν αἱμάδα κηκιομέναν ἑλκέων
ἐνθήρου ποδὸς ἠπίοισι φύλλοις
κατευνάσειε, <σπασμὸς> εἴ τις ἐμπέσοι,

700 φορβάδος τι γᾶς ἑλών·
εἷρπε δ' ἄλλοτ' ἀλλ<αχ>ᾷ
τότ' ἂν εἰλυόμενος,
παῖς ἄτερ ὡς φίλας τιθήνας,
ὅθεν εὐμάρει' ὑπάρχοι

upon a deadly revolving wheel by the all-mighty son of
Kronos. But there is none other among mortals whom I
have heard of or have looked upon who has met with a
more hateful destiny than this man, who having done noth-
ing to anyone, done no murder, but being a just man
among just men, was perishing thus undeservedly. But at
this I wonder, how, how did he listen alone to the waves
that beat the shore around him, and endure a life so full of
tears?

Where he was alone, having no one walking near him,
nor any inhabitant, a neighbour in his troubles, beside
whom he could have lamented the sickness that cruelly
devoured him, with groans inviting a response; nor any to
lull to sleep with healing herbs the burning flux oozing
from the ulcers of his louse-ridden foot, if a spasm should
come over him, taking something from the nurturing
earth. And he moved this way or that, crawling, like a child
without a loving nurse, searching for his need to be sup-

---

677 <σφετέρων> suppl. Ll.-J.   post ποτὲ add. Διὸς Ἰξίονα
codd.: Διὸς del. Stinton, Ἰξίονα iam Erfurdt
678 <Ἄιδου> ex gr. suppl. Ll.-J.   ἔλαβεν Vater: ἔλαβ' ὁ
codd.
683 οὔτε τι ῥέξας Eustathius: οὔτ' ἔρξας codd.
686 suppl. Ll.-J.   μ' ἔχει Hermann: ἔχει με codd.
691 πρόσουρον Bothe: -ος codd.
694 suppl. Ll.-J.
696 post ὃς add. τὰν codd., del. Erfurdt
699 suppl. Dawe
700 τι Stinton: ἔκ τε codd.   ἑλών Turnebus: ἑλεῖν codd.
701 εἷρπε Bothe: ἕρπει codd.   δ' Hermann: γὰρ codd.
ἀλλαχᾷ Campbell: ἄλλᾳ codd.

705 πόρου, ἁνίκ' ἐξανείη
     δακέθυμος ἄτα·
     οὐ φορβὰν ἱερᾶς γᾶς σπόρον, οὐκ ἄλλων   στρ. β'
     αἴρων τῶν νεμόμεσθ' ἀνέρες ἀλφησταί,
710 πλὴν ἐξ ὠκυβόλων εἴ ποτε τόξων
     πτανοῖς ἰοῖς ἀνύσειε γαστρὶ φορβάν.
     ὦ μελέα ψυχά,
715 ὃς μηδ' οἰνοχύτου πώματος ἥσθη δεκέτει χρόνῳ,
     λεύσσων δ' ὅπου γνοίη στατὸν εἰς ὕδωρ,
     αἰεὶ προσενώμα.
     νῦν δ' ἀνδρῶν ἀγαθῶν παιδὸς ὑπαντήσας   ἀντ. β'
720 εὐδαίμων ἀνύσει καὶ μέγας ἐκ κείνων·
     ὅς νιν ποντοπόρῳ δούρατι, πλήθει
     πολλῶν μηνῶν, πατρίαν ἄγει πρὸς αὐλὰν
725 Μηλιάδων νυμφᾶν,
     Σπερχειοῦ τε παρ' ὄχθας, ἵν' ὁ χάλκασπις ἀνὴρ θεοῖς
     πλάθῃ θεὸς θείῳ πυρὶ παμφαής,
     Οἴτας ὑπὲρ ὄχθων.

NEΟΠΤΟΛΕΜΟΣ

730 ἕρπ', εἰ θέλεις. τί δή ποθ' ὧδ' ἐξ οὐδενὸς
     λόγου σιωπᾷς κἀπόπληκτος ὧδ' ἔχῃ;

ΦΙΛΟΚΤΗΤΗΣ

ἇ ἇ ἇ ἇ.

ΝΕΟΠΤΟΛΕΜΟΣ

τί ἔστιν;

plied, when the plague that devoured his mind abated.

He never gathered food from the sowing of the sacred earth, never the other things that we men who earn our living dispose of, except when with the winged arrows from his swift-shooting bow he could acquire the food he needed. Poor soul, who for ten whole years lacked even the pleasure of the wine cup, and would ever look to find a stagnant pool and make his way to it!

But now he has met the son of noble men, and will attain happiness and greatness through them; and he is bringing him in a ship travelling over the sea, after many months, to the haunts of the nymphs of Malis, native to him, and to the banks of Spercheius, where the man with the brazen shield[a] joined the gods as a god, blazing with fire divine, beyond the hills of Oeta.

NEOPTOLEMUS

Come, pray! Why are you silent like this, although nothing has been said, and stand as though struck dumb?

PHILOCTETES

Ah, ah, ah, ah!

NEOPTOLEMUS

What is the matter?

---

[a] Heracles.

---

705 πόρου Wakefield: -ον l: -ων cett.   ἐξανείη Hermann: ἐξανίησι codd.

711 πτανοῖς ἰοῖς Erfurdt: πτανῶν πτανοῖς codd.

724 πατρίαν Porson: πατρῴαν codd.

726 ὄχθας Hermann: ὄχθαις codd.

728 θεὸς Hermann: πᾶσι codd.

ΦΙΛΟΚΤΗΤΗΣ
οὐδὲν δεινόν. ἀλλ᾽ ἴθ᾽, ὦ τέκνον.

ΝΕΟΠΤΟΛΕΜΟΣ
μῶν ἄλγος ἴσχεις σῆς παρεστώσης νόσου;

ΦΙΛΟΚΤΗΤΗΣ
735 οὐ δῆτ᾽ ἔγωγ᾽, ἀλλ᾽ ἄρτι κουφίζειν δοκῶ.
ὦ θεοί.

ΝΕΟΠΤΟΛΕΜΟΣ
τί τοὺς θεοὺς ὧδ᾽ ἀναστένων καλεῖς;

ΦΙΛΟΚΤΗΤΗΣ
σωτῆρας αὐτοὺς ἠπίους θ᾽ ἡμῖν μολεῖν.
ἆ ἆ ἆ ἆ.

ΝΕΟΠΤΟΛΕΜΟΣ
740 τί ποτε πέπονθας; οὐκ ἐρεῖς, ἀλλ᾽ ὧδ᾽ ἔσῃ
σιγηλός; ἐν κακῷ δέ τῳ φαίνῃ κυρῶν.

ΦΙΛΟΚΤΗΤΗΣ
ἀπόλωλα, τέκνον, κοὐ δυνήσομαι κακὸν
κρύψαι παρ᾽ ὑμῖν, ἀτταταῖ· διέρχεται,
διέρχεται. δύστηνος, ὦ τάλας ἐγώ.
745 ἀπόλωλα, τέκνον· βρύκομαι, τέκνον· παπαῖ,
ἀπαππαπαῖ, παπᾶ παπᾶ παπᾶ παπαῖ.
πρὸς θεῶν, πρόχειρον εἴ τί σοι, τέκνον, πάρα
ξίφος χεροῖν, πάταξον εἰς ἄκρον πόδα·
ἀπάμησον ὡς τάχιστα· μὴ φείσῃ βίου.
750 ἴθ᾽, ὦ παῖ.

PHILOCTETES
Nothing grave. Come, my son!

NEOPTOLEMUS
Are you in pain because your sickness is with you?

PHILOCTETES
No, I think I am just getting better. O gods!

NEOPTOLEMUS
Why do you thus groan and call upon the gods?

PHILOCTETES
I am calling on them to come as preservers and be kind to us. Ah, ah, ah, ah!

NEOPTOLEMUS
What is the matter with you? Will you not tell me, but remain silent as you are? You seem to be in some trouble.

PHILOCTETES
I am lost, my son, I shall not be able to conceal my pain in your company. Ah! It goes through me, it goes through me! O misery, unhappy as I am! I am lost, my son! I am devoured, my son! A-a-a-a-a-h! I beg you, if you have a sword handy, strike at my heel! Lop it off quickly! Do not spare my life! Come, my son!

---

734 σῆς West: τῆς codd.
737 ὦ θεοί Zg (coni. anon. 1810): ἰὼ θεοί cett.   ὦδ' anon.
(1810): οὕτως aZot: om. cett.

SOPHOCLES

ΝΕΟΠΤΟΛΕΜΟΣ
τί δ' ἔστιν οὕτω νεοχμὸν ἐξαίφνης, ὅτου
τοσήνδ' ἰυγὴν καὶ στόνον σαυτοῦ ποῇ;

ΦΙΛΟΚΤΗΤΗΣ
οἶσθ', ὦ τέκνον.

ΝΕΟΠΤΟΛΕΜΟΣ
τί ἔστιν;

ΦΙΛΟΚΤΗΤΗΣ
οἶσθ', ὦ παῖ.

ΝΕΟΠΤΟΛΕΜΟΣ
τί σοί;
οὐκ οἶδα.

ΦΙΛΟΚΤΗΤΗΣ
πῶς οὐκ οἶσθα; παππαπαππαπαῖ.

ΝΕΟΠΤΟΛΕΜΟΣ
755   δεινόν γε τοὐπίσαγμα τοῦ νοσήματος.

ΦΙΛΟΚΤΗΤΗΣ
δεινὸν γὰρ οὐδὲ ῥητόν· ἀλλ' οἴκτιρέ με.

ΝΕΟΠΤΟΛΕΜΟΣ
τί δῆτα δράσω;

ΦΙΛΟΚΤΗΤΗΣ
μή με ταρβήσας προδῷς·
ἥκει γὰρ αὐτὴ διὰ χρόνου, πλάνης ἴσως
ὡς ἐξεπλήσθη, νόσος.

---

752 ποῇ Jebb: ποεῖς codd.
758 αὐτὴ F. W. Schmidt: αὕτη codd. plerique

328

PHILOCTETES

NEOPTOLEMUS

What is this sudden new thing that makes you cry out and
groan so much?

PHILOCTETES

You know, my son!

NEOPTOLEMUS

What is it?

PHILOCTETES

You know, my boy!

NEOPTOLEMUS

What is the matter with you? I do not know.

PHILOCTETES

How can you not know? A-a-a-a-a-h!

NEOPTOLEMUS

The burden of the sickness is grievous!

PHILOCTETES

Grievous indeed, and indescribable!

NEOPTOLEMUS

What shall I do?

PHILOCTETES

Do not take fright and betray me! It has come in person
after a time, perhaps because it is weary of wandering, the
sickness.

ΝΕΟΠΤΟΛΕΜΟΣ

ἰὼ δύστηνε σύ,

760 δύστηνε δῆτα διὰ πόνων πάντων φανείς.
βούλῃ λάβωμαι δῆτα καὶ θίγω τί σου;

ΦΙΛΟΚΤΗΤΗΣ

μὴ δῆτα τοῦτό γ᾽· ἀλλά μοι τὰ τόξ᾽ ἑλὼν
τάδ᾽, ὥσπερ ᾔτου μ᾽ ἀρτίως, ἕως ἀνῇ
765 τὸ πῆμα τοῦτο τῆς νόσου τὸ νῦν παρόν,
σῷζ᾽ αὐτὰ καὶ φύλασσε. λαμβάνει γὰρ οὖν
ὕπνος μ᾽, ὅταν περ τὸ κακὸν ἐξίῃ τόδε·
κοὐκ ἔστι λῆξαι πρότερον· ἀλλ᾽ ἐᾶν χρεὼν
ἔκηλον εὕδειν. ἢν δὲ τῷδε τῷ χρόνῳ
770 μόλωσ᾽ ἐκεῖνοι, πρὸς θεῶν, ἐφίεμαι
ἑκόντα μήτ᾽ ἄκοντα μήτε τῳ τέχνῃ
κείνοις μεθεῖναι ταῦτα, μὴ σαυτόν θ᾽ ἅμα
κἄμ᾽, ὄντα σαυτοῦ πρόστροπον, κτείνας γένῃ.

ΝΕΟΠΤΟΛΕΜΟΣ

θάρσει προνοίας οὕνεκ᾽. οὐ δοθήσεται
775 πλὴν σοί τε κἀμοί· ξὺν τύχῃ δὲ πρόσφερε.

ΦΙΛΟΚΤΗΤΗΣ

ἰδού, δέχου, παῖ· τὸν φθόνον δὲ πρόσκυσον,
μή σοι γενέσθαι πολύπον᾽ αὐτά, μηδ᾽ ὅπως
ἐμοί τε καὶ τῷ πρόσθ᾽ ἐμοῦ κεκτημένῳ.

ΝΕΟΠΤΟΛΕΜΟΣ

ὦ θεοί, γένοιτο ταῦτα νῷν· γένοιτο δὲ
780 πλοῦς οὔριός τε κεὐσταλὴς ὅποι ποτὲ
θεὸς δικαιοῖ χὠ στόλος πορσύνεται.

NEOPTOLEMUS

Ah, unlucky one! Unlucky you are found to be in every
kind of trouble! Do you wish me to take hold of you and
hold you?

PHILOCTETES

No, not that! But take my bow here, as you asked me for it
earlier, and guard it and keep it, until the pain of the sick-
ness that is now upon me shall abate; for sleep takes me,
whenever this trouble is departing, and it cannot stop till
then. You must leave me to sleep peacefully; and if
meanwhile those people come, I beg you not to let them
have it, willingly or unwillingly or in any way, in case you
cause the death both of yourself and me, who am your sup-
pliant.

NEOPTOLEMUS

Be assured as regards the care that I shall take! It shall be
given to no one except you and me; hand it to me, and may
good luck come of it!

PHILOCTETES

There, take it, boy; and kiss it to avert a curse, in case it
should bring trouble upon you, as things were with me and
with him who had it before me.

NEOPTOLEMUS

O gods, grant this to us! And may our voyage be pros-
perous and rapid to wherever the god thinks right and our
mission lies!

---

759 νόσος. ἰὼ Robertson: ἰὼ ἰὼ codd. plerique

ΦΙΛΟΚΤΗΤΗΣ

ἆ ἆ ἆ ἆ.

δέδοικα <δ᾿>, ὦ παῖ, μὴ ἀτελὴς εὐχὴ <τύχῃ>·
στάζει γὰρ αὖ μοι φοίνιον τόδ᾿ ἐκ βυθοῦ
κηκῖον αἷμα, καί τι προσδοκῶ νέον.

785   παπαῖ, φεῦ.
παπαῖ μάλ᾿, ὦ πούς, οἷά μ᾿ ἐργάσῃ κακά.
προσέρπει,
προσέρχεται τόδ᾿ ἐγγύς. οἴμοι μοι τάλας.
ἔχετε τὸ πρᾶγμα· μὴ φύγητε μηδαμῇ.

790   ἀτταταῖ.
ὦ ξένε Κεφαλλήν, εἴθε σοῦ διαμπερὲς
στέρνων ἵκοιτ᾿ ἄλγησις ἥδε. φεῦ, παπαῖ.
παπαῖ μάλ᾿ αὖθις. ὦ διπλοῖ στρατηλάται,
['Αγάμεμνον, ὦ Μενέλαε, πῶς ἂν ἀντ᾿ ἐμοῦ]

795   τὸν ἴσον χρόνον τρέφοιτε τήνδε τὴν νόσον.
ὤμοι μοι.
ὦ θάνατε θάνατε, πῶς ἀεὶ καλούμενος
οὕτω κατ᾿ ἦμαρ οὐ δύνῃ μολεῖν ποτε;
ὦ τέκνον, ὦ γενναῖον, ἀλλὰ συλλαβὼν

800   τῷ Λημνίῳ τῷδ᾿ ἀνακαλουμένῳ πυρὶ
ἔμπρησον, ὦ γενναῖε· κἀγώ τοί ποτε
τὸν τοῦ Διὸς παῖδ᾿ ἀντὶ τῶνδε τῶν ὅπλων,
ἃ νῦν σὺ σῴζεις, τοῦτ᾿ ἐπηξίωσα δρᾶν.
τί φής, παῖ;

805   τί φής; τί σιγᾷς; ποῦ ποτ᾿ ὤν, τέκνον, κυρεῖς;

ΝΕΟΠΤΟΛΕΜΟΣ

ἀλγῶ πάλαι δὴ τἀπὶ σοὶ στένων κακά.

PHILOCTETES

PHILOCTETES

Ah, ah, ah, ah! I am afraid, boy, that your prayer may be
unfulfilled! For again this oozing dark blood is dripping
from the depths, and I am expecting some new trouble. Ah
me, alas! Ah me indeed, my foot, what pains you are caus-
ing me! It is coming, it is advancing closer! Alas for me,
poor wretch! You know what is the matter! Do not run
away, I beg you! A-a-a-a-h! Cephallenian stranger, I wish
this pain would go right through your chest! Ah, ah, alas!
Alas once more! O you two generals, [Agamemnon, O
Menelaus, if only instead of me] may you feed this sickness
for an equal time! Ah me! O death, death, why can you
never come, though I do not cease to call you thus each
day? O my son, O my noble son, take me and burn me with
this fire that is invoked as Lemnian, noble one! I also once
consented to do this to the son of Zeus in return for those
weapons which you now are guarding! What do you say,
boy? What do you say? Why are you silent? Where are
you, my son?

NEOPTOLEMUS

I have been in pain long since, lamenting for your woes.

---

⁷⁸² ἆ quater Philp: ἀλλὰ codd. plerique   suppl. Wunder
⁷⁹² ἵκοιτ' Wakefield: ἔχοιτ' codd.
⁷⁹⁴ del. E. Philipp

333

ΦΙΛΟΚΤΗΤΗΣ

ἀλλ᾽, ὦ τέκνον, καὶ θάρσος ἴσχ᾽· ὡς ἥδε μοι
ὀξεῖα φοιτᾷ καὶ ταχεῖ᾽ ἀπέρχεται.
ἀλλ᾽ ἀντιάζω, μή με καταλίπῃς μόνον.

ΝΕΟΠΤΟΛΕΜΟΣ

810 θάρσει, μενοῦμεν.

ΦΙΛΟΚΤΗΤΗΣ

ἦ μενεῖς;

ΝΕΟΠΤΟΛΕΜΟΣ

σαφῶς φρόνει.

ΦΙΛΟΚΤΗΤΗΣ

οὐ μήν σ᾽ ἔνορκόν γ᾽ ἀξιῶ θέσθαι, τέκνον.

ΝΕΟΠΤΟΛΕΜΟΣ

ὡς οὐ θέμις γ᾽ ἐμοῦστι σοῦ μολεῖν ἄτερ.

ΦΙΛΟΚΤΗΤΗΣ

ἔμβαλλε χειρὸς πίστιν.

ΝΕΟΠΤΟΛΕΜΟΣ

ἐμβάλλω μενεῖν.

ΦΙΛΟΚΤΗΤΗΣ

ἐκεῖσε νῦν μ᾽, ἐκεῖσε —

ΝΕΟΠΤΟΛΕΜΟΣ

ποῖ λέγεις;

ΦΙΛΟΚΤΗΤΗΣ

ἄνω —

PHILOCTETES

PHILOCTETES
But take courage, my son! This sickness of mine returns fiercely and swiftly departs; but, I implore you, do not leave me here alone!

NEOPTOLEMUS
Be assured, we will stay!

PHILOCTETES
Will you indeed stay?

NEOPTOLEMUS
Know it for certain!

PHILOCTETES
Indeed I do not think it right to make you swear an oath, my son.

NEOPTOLEMUS
No, it is not right for me to go without you.

PHILOCTETES
Give me your hand as a pledge!

NEOPTOLEMUS
I pledge myself to stay!

PHILOCTETES
Up there, up there . . .

NEOPTOLEMUS
Where do you mean?

PHILOCTETES
Above . . .

SOPHOCLES

ΝΕΟΠΤΟΛΕΜΟΣ

815 τί παραφρονεῖς αὖ; τί τὸν ἄνω λεύσσεις κύκλον;

ΦΙΛΟΚΤΗΤΗΣ

μέθες μέθες με.

ΝΕΟΠΤΟΛΕΜΟΣ

ποῖ μεθῶ;

ΦΙΛΟΚΤΗΤΗΣ

μέθες ποτέ.

ΝΕΟΠΤΟΛΕΜΟΣ

οὔ φημ' ἐάσειν.

ΦΙΛΟΚΤΗΤΗΣ

ἀπό μ' ὀλεῖς, ἢν προσθίγῃς.

ΝΕΟΠΤΟΛΕΜΟΣ

καὶ δὴ μεθίημ', εἴ τι δὴ πλέον φρονεῖς.

ΦΙΛΟΚΤΗΤΗΣ

ὦ γαῖα, δέξαι θανάσιμόν μ' ὅπως ἔχω·
820 τὸ γὰρ κακὸν τόδ' οὐκέτ' ὀρθοῦσθαί μ' ἐᾷ.

ΝΕΟΠΤΟΛΕΜΟΣ

τὸν ἄνδρ' ἔοικεν ὕπνος οὐ μακροῦ χρόνου
ἕξειν· κάρα γὰρ ὑπτιάζεται τόδε·
ἱδρώς γέ τοί νιν πᾶν καταστάζει δέμας,
μέλαινά τ' ἄκρου τις παρέρρωγεν ποδὸς
825 αἱμορραγὴς φλέψ. ἀλλ' ἐάσωμεν, φίλοι,
ἔκηλον αὐτόν, ὡς ἂν εἰς ὕπνον πέσῃ.

---

818 εἴ τι δὴ Hermann: τί δὲ δὴ a: τί δὴ cett.

336

PHILOCTETES

NEOPTOLEMUS

Why are you delirious once more? Why do you gaze at the sky above?

PHILOCTETES

Let me go, let me go!

NEOPTOLEMUS

Let you go where?

PHILOCTETES

Only let me go!

NEOPTOLEMUS

I say I will not!

PHILOCTETES

You will kill me if you touch me!

NEOPTOLEMUS

Well, I will let you go, since you are now saner!

PHILOCTETES

O Earth, receive me in death, just as I am! This trouble no longer lets me stand upright.

He sinks to the ground.

NEOPTOLEMUS

It seems that sleep will hold him before long; see, his head is falling backwards. Yes, a sweat is pouring over his whole body, and a vein of dark blood has burst out from his heel. Come, let us leave him in peace, my friends, so that he may fall asleep!

SOPHOCLES

ΧΟΡΟΣ

Ὕπν' ὀδύνας ἀδαής, Ὕπνε δ' ἀλγέων,   στρ.
εὐαὴς ἡμῖν ἔλθοις, εὐαίων,
830 εὐαίων, ὦναξ· ὄμμασι δ' ἀντίσχοις
τάνδ' αἴγλαν, ἃ τέταται τανῦν.
ἴθι ἴθι μοι, Παιών.
ὦ τέκνον, ὅρα ποῦ στάσῃ,
ποῖ δὲ βάσῃ,
πῶς δέ σοι τἀντεῦθεν
835 φροντίδος. ὁρᾷς ἤδη.
πρὸς τί μένομεν πράσσειν;
καιρός τοι πάντων γνώμαν ἴσχων
<πολύ τι> πολὺ παρὰ πόδα κράτος ἄρνυται.

ΝΕΟΠΤΟΛΕΜΟΣ

ἀλλ' ὅδε μὲν κλύει οὐδέν, ἐγὼ δ' ὁρῶ οὕνεκα θήραν
840 τήνδ' ἁλίως ἔχομεν τόξων, δίχα τοῦδε πλέοντες.
τοῦδε γὰρ ἡ στέφανος, τοῦτον θεὸς εἶπε κομίζειν.
κομπεῖν δ' ἔργ' ἀτελῆ σὺν ψεύδεσιν αἰσχρὸν ὄνειδος.

ΧΟΡΟΣ

ἀλλά, τέκνον, τάδε μὲν θεὸς ὄψεται·   ἀντ.
ὧν δ' ἂν κἀμείβῃ μ' αὖθις, βαιάν μοι,
845 βαιάν, ὦ τέκνον,
πέμπε λόγων φήμαν·

830 ἀντίσχοις Musgrave: ἀντέχοις codd.
834 σοι Blaydes: μοι codd.
835 ἤδη] εὕδει Herwerden
836 μένομεν Erfurdt: μενοῦμεν codd.
838 suppl. Hermann

CHORUS

Sleep, ignorant of anguish, ignorant of pains, come to us
with gentle breath, come bringing felicity, bringing felicity,
lord! Over his eyes hold this brightness that now extends
before them! Come, come, Healer!

My son, take care where you stand, take care where you
go, and take care regarding your next thinking. You see
already . . . ! Why do we delay to act? The choice of the
right moment, which decides all things, wins a great vic-
tory, one great indeed, by a prompt stroke!

NEOPTOLEMUS

Why, he can hear nothing, but I see that we capture the
bow in vain if we sail without him! It is he who wins the
garland, he whom the god told us to bring; and to boast of
actions incomplete while uttering falsehoods is a shameful
disgrace!

CHORUS

But that, my son, the god will see to. Convey to me briefly,
briefly, my son, a message in reply! The unsleeping sleep

---

842 ἔργ' Blaydes: ἐστ' codd.
844 κἀμείβη Hermann: ἀμείβη codd.

ὡς πάντων ἐν νόσῳ εὐδρακὴς
ὕπνος ἄυπνος λεύσσειν.
ἀλλ' ὅ τι δύνᾳ μάκιστον,
κεῖνο <δή> μοι,
850   κεῖνό <μοι> λαθραίως
ἐξιδοῦ ὅπως πράξεις.
οἶσθα γὰρ ὃν αὐδῶμαι·
εἰ ταὐτᾷ τούτῳ γνώμαν ἴσχεις,
μάλα τοι ἄπορα πυκινοῖς ἐνιδεῖν πάθη.
855   οὖρός τοι, τέκνον, οὖρος· ἁ-   ἐπ.
νὴρ δ' ἀνόμματος, οὐδ' ἔχων ἀρωγάν,
ἐκτέταται νύχιος —
ἀδεὴς ὕπνος ἐσθλός —
860   οὐ χερός, οὐ ποδός, οὔτινος ἄρχων,
ἀλλά τις ὡς Ἀΐδᾳ πάρα κείμενος.
ὅρα, βλέπ' εἰ καίρια
φθέγγῃ· τὸ δ' ἁλώσιμον
ἐμᾷ φροντίδι, παῖ, πόνος
ὁ μὴ φοβῶν κράτιστος.

ΝΕΟΠΤΟΛΕΜΟΣ

865   σιγᾶν κελεύω, μηδ' ἀφεστάναι φρενῶν.
κινεῖ γὰρ ἀνὴρ ὄμμα κἀνάγει κάρα.

ΦΙΛΟΚΤΗΤΗΣ

ὦ φέγγος ὕπνου διάδοχον, τό τ' ἐλπίδων
ἄπιστον οἰκούρημα τῶνδε τῶν ξένων.
οὐ γάρ ποτ', ὦ παῖ, τοῦτ' ἂν ἐξηύχησ' ἐγώ,
870   τλῆναί σ' ἐλεινῶς ὧδε τἀμὰ πήματα

of all men who are sick is quick to see! But the thing you can do that counts for most, that thing, that thing, see to it that in secret you accomplish undetected! You know of whom I speak; if your judgment is the same as his, there are dangers to see in this perplexing even to the subtle.

There is a wind, my son, a wind! The man can see nothing, and has none to help him, as he lies stretched out in darkness—good sleep has no fears—with no control over hand or foot or anything, but like one who lies in Hades. Look, see if your speech suits the moment! The thing my mind can grasp, my son, is that the work attended by no fear is best!

NEOPTOLEMUS

I tell you to be silent, and not to lose your wits! For the man is beginning to see and is raising his head!

PHILOCTETES

O light that succeeds sleep, and watch kept by these strangers that my hopes could not believe in! Never, my son, would I have thought that you would have endured to

---

849 suppl. Hermann
850 suppl. Kuiper   λαθραίως Campbell: λάθρᾳ codd.
853 ταὐτᾷ Dobree: ταυτὰν (sic) codd. plerique
859 ἀδεὴς Reiske: ἀλεὴς codd.
861 τις ὡς Wunder: ὥς τις codd. plerique

341

μεῖναι παρόντα καὶ ξυνωφελοῦντά μοι.
οὔκουν Ἀτρεῖδαι τοῦτ' ἔτλησαν εὐφόρως
οὕτως ἐνεγκεῖν, ἀγαθοὶ στρατηλάται.
ἀλλ' εὐγενὴς γὰρ ἡ φύσις κἀξ εὐγενῶν,

875 ὦ τέκνον, ἡ σή, πάντα ταῦτ' ἐν εὐχερεῖ
ἔθου, βοῆς τε καὶ δυσοσμίας γέμων.
καὶ νῦν ἐπειδὴ τοῦδε τοῦ κακοῦ δοκεῖ
λήθη τις εἶναι κἀνάπαυλα δή, τέκνον,
σύ μ' αὐτὸς ἆρον, σύ με κατάστησον, τέκνον,

880 ἵν', ἡνίκ' ἂν κόπος μ' ἀπαλλάξῃ ποτέ,
ὁρμώμεθ' ἐς ναῦν μηδ' ἐπίσχωμεν τὸ πλεῖν.

ΝΕΟΠΤΟΛΕΜΟΣ

ἀλλ' ἥδομαι μέν σ' εἰσιδὼν παρ' ἐλπίδα
ἀνώδυνον βλέποντα κἀμπνέοντ' ἔτι·
ὡς οὐκέτ' ὄντος γὰρ τὰ συμβόλαιά σου

885 πρὸς τὰς παρούσας ξυμφορὰς ἐφαίνετο.
νῦν δ' αἶρε σαυτόν· εἰ δέ σοι μᾶλλον φίλον,
οἴσουσί σ' οἵδε· τοῦ πόνου γὰρ οὐκ ὄκνος,
ἐπείπερ οὕτω σοί τ' ἔδοξ' ἐμοί τε δρᾶν.

ΦΙΛΟΚΤΗΤΗΣ

αἰνῶ τάδ', ὦ παῖ, καί μ' ἔπαιρ', ὥσπερ νοεῖς·
890 τούτους δ' ἔασον, μὴ βαρυνθῶσιν κακῇ
ὀσμῇ πρὸ τοῦ δέοντος· οὑπὶ νηὶ γὰρ
ἅλις πόνος τούτοισι συνναίειν ἐμοί.

ΝΕΟΠΤΟΛΕΜΟΣ

ἔσται τάδ'· ἀλλ' ἴστω τε καὐτὸς ἀντέχου.

wait with pity throughout my suffering and to help me!
The sons of Atreus did not endure to tolerate this easily,
the noble generals! But since your nature is noble and
sprung from noble ancestors, my son, you made light of
this, though afflicted by my cries and by my evil smell. But
now that this plague seems to forget itself and give me
respite, my son, do you yourself lift me up, do you help me
to stand, so that whenever weariness departs from me we
may start for the ship and not delay our voyage!

NEOPTOLEMUS

I rejoice to see you, beyond all hope, still living and breath-
ing without pain; because in view of the troubles that
attend you your symptoms seemed to show that you were
no more. But now raise yourself up! Or if you prefer these
men will carry you; we do not shrink from labour, since you
and I have determined on this action.

PHILOCTETES

I thank you, my son; raise me up, as you intend! But let
them be, for fear they are irked by the evil smell before the
time; living with me on the ship will be trouble enough for
them!

NEOPTOLEMUS

It shall be so! Stand up, and hold on to me!

---

[872] εὐφόρως Brunck: εὐπόρως codd.

ΦΙΛΟΚΤΗΤΗΣ

θάρσει· τό τοι σύνηθες ὀρθώσει μ᾽ ἔθος.

ΝΕΟΠΤΟΛΕΜΟΣ

895   παπαῖ· τί δῆτ᾽ <ἂν> δρῷμ᾽ ἐγὼ τοὐνθένδε γε;

ΦΙΛΟΚΤΗΤΗΣ

τί δ᾽ ἔστιν, ὦ παῖ; ποῖ ποτ᾽ ἐξέβης λόγῳ;

ΝΕΟΠΤΟΛΕΜΟΣ

οὐκ οἶδ᾽ ὅπῃ χρὴ τἄπορον τρέπειν ἔπος.

ΦΙΛΟΚΤΗΤΗΣ

ἀπορεῖς δὲ τοῦ σύ; μὴ λέγ᾽, ὦ τέκνον, τάδε.

ΝΕΟΠΤΟΛΕΜΟΣ

ἀλλ᾽ ἐνθάδ᾽ ἤδη τοῦδε τοῦ πάθους κυρῶ.

ΦΙΛΟΚΤΗΤΗΣ

900   οὐ δή σε δυσχέρεια τοῦ νοσήματος
ἔπαισεν ὥστε μή μ᾽ ἄγειν ναύτην ἔτι;

ΝΕΟΠΤΟΛΕΜΟΣ

ἅπαντα δυσχέρεια, τὴν αὑτοῦ φύσιν
ὅταν λιπών τις δρᾷ τὰ μὴ προσεικότα.

ΦΙΛΟΚΤΗΤΗΣ

ἀλλ᾽ οὐδὲν ἔξω τοῦ φυτεύσαντος σύ γε
905   δρᾷς οὐδὲ φωνεῖς, ἐσθλὸν ἄνδρ᾽ ἐπωφελῶν.

ΝΕΟΠΤΟΛΕΜΟΣ

αἰσχρὸς φανοῦμαι· τοῦτ᾽ ἀνιῶμαι πάλαι.

ΦΙΛΟΚΤΗΤΗΣ

οὔκουν ἐν οἷς γε δρᾷς· ἐν οἷς δ᾽ αὐδᾷς ὀκνῶ.

---

895 suppl. Schaefer

PHILOCTETES

PHILOCTETES

Do not worry! The force of habit will raise me up.

NEOPTOLEMUS

Ah! What am I to do next?

PHILOCTETES

What is the matter, boy? Where has your talk strayed to?

NEOPTOLEMUS

I do not know where to turn my words in my perplexity!

PHILOCTETES

But what perplexes you? Do not say these things, my son!

NEOPTOLEMUS

But that is the point I have now come to in my trouble!

PHILOCTETES

Surely the thought of how distasteful my sickness is has not come home to you, so that you are no longer taking me on board?

NEOPTOLEMUS

Everything is distasteful, when a man has abandoned his own nature and is doing what is unlike him!

PHILOCTETES

But you are not doing or saying anything unlike your father, in helping a noble man!

NEOPTOLEMUS

I shall be seen to be a traitor; that is what has long been paining me.

PHILOCTETES

Not on account of your actions; but your words frighten me!

SOPHOCLES

ΝΕΟΠΤΟΛΕΜΟΣ

ὦ Ζεῦ, τί δράσω; δεύτερον ληφθῶ κακός,
κρύπτων θ' ἃ μὴ δεῖ καὶ λέγων αἴσχιστ' ἐπῶν;

ΦΙΛΟΚΤΗΤΗΣ

910 ἀνὴρ ὅδ', εἰ μὴ 'γὼ κακὸς γνώμην ἔφυν,
προδούς μ' ἔοικε κἀκλιπὼν τὸν πλοῦν στελεῖν.

ΝΕΟΠΤΟΛΕΜΟΣ

λιπὼν μὲν οὐκ ἔγωγε, λυπηρῶς δὲ μὴ
πέμπω σε μᾶλλον, τοῦτ' ἀνιῶμαι πάλαι.

ΦΙΛΟΚΤΗΤΗΣ

τί ποτε λέγεις, ὦ τέκνον; ὡς οὐ μανθάνω.

ΝΕΟΠΤΟΛΕΜΟΣ

915 οὐδέν σε κρύψω· δεῖ γὰρ ἐς Τροίαν σε πλεῖν
πρὸς τοὺς Ἀχαιοὺς καὶ τὸν Ἀτρειδῶν στόλον.

ΦΙΛΟΚΤΗΤΗΣ

οἴμοι, τί εἶπας;

ΝΕΟΠΤΟΛΕΜΟΣ

μὴ στέναζε, πρὶν μάθῃς.

ΦΙΛΟΚΤΗΤΗΣ

ποῖον μάθημα; τί με νοεῖς δρᾶσαί ποτε;

ΝΕΟΠΤΟΛΕΜΟΣ

σῶσαι κακοῦ μὲν πρῶτα τοῦδ', ἔπειτα δὲ
920 ξὺν σοὶ τὰ Τροίας πεδία πορθῆσαι μολών.

ΦΙΛΟΚΤΗΤΗΣ

καὶ ταῦτ' ἀληθῆ δρᾶν νοεῖς;

PHILOCTETES

NEOPTOLEMUS

O Zeus, what am I to do? Am I to be doubly convicted as a villain, by wrongful silence and by shameful speech?

PHILOCTETES

If my judgment is not misguided, this man is likely to sail away, betraying and deserting me!

NEOPTOLEMUS

It is not the thought that I will desert you, but rather the thought that I will take you on a journey that will cause you grief, that has long pained me.

PHILOCTETES

What are you saying, my son? I do not understand.

NEOPTOLEMUS

I shall hide nothing from you! You must sail to Troy, to the Achaeans and the expedition of the sons of Atreus.

PHILOCTETES

Alas, what have you said?

NEOPTOLEMUS

Do not lament before you have learned all!

PHILOCTETES

Learned what? What do you mean to do to me?

NEOPTOLEMUS

First to save you from this trouble, and then to go with you and conquer the land of Troy.

PHILOCTETES

And is that really what you intend?

ΝΕΟΠΤΟΛΕΜΟΣ

πολλὴ κρατεῖ
τούτων ἀνάγκη· καὶ σὺ μὴ θυμοῦ κλύων.

ΦΙΛΟΚΤΗΤΗΣ

ἀπόλωλα τλήμων, προδέδομαι. τί μ᾽, ὦ ξένε,
δέδρακας; ἀπόδος ὡς τάχος τὰ τόξα μοι.

ΝΕΟΠΤΟΛΕΜΟΣ

925   ἀλλ᾽ οὐχ οἷόν τε· τῶν γὰρ ἐν τέλει κλύειν
τό τ᾽ ἔνδικόν με καὶ τὸ συμφέρον ποεῖ.

ΦΙΛΟΚΤΗΤΗΣ

ὦ πῦρ σὺ καὶ πᾶν δεῖμα καὶ πανουργίας
δεινῆς τέχνημ᾽ ἔχθιστον, οἷά μ᾽ εἰργάσω,
οἷ᾽ ἠπάτηκας· οὐδ᾽ ἐπαισχύνῃ μ᾽ ὁρῶν
930   τὸν προστρόπαιον, τὸν ἱκέτην, ὦ σχέτλιε;
ἀπεστέρηκας τὸν βίον τὰ τόξ᾽ ἑλών.
ἀπόδος, ἱκνοῦμαί σ᾽, ἀπόδος, ἱκετεύω, τέκνον.
πρὸς θεῶν πατρῴων, τὸν βίον με μὴ ἀφέλῃ.
ὤμοι τάλας. ἀλλ᾽ οὐδὲ προσφωνεῖ μ᾽ ἔτι,
935   ἀλλ᾽ ὡς μεθήσων μήποθ᾽, ὧδ᾽ ὁρᾷ πάλιν.
    ὦ λιμένες, ὦ προβλῆτες, ὦ ξυνουσίαι
θηρῶν ὀρείων, ὦ καταρρῶγες πέτραι,
ὑμῖν τάδ᾽, οὐ γὰρ ἄλλον οἶδ᾽ ὅτῳ λέγω,
ἀνακλαίομαι παροῦσι τοῖς εἰωθόσιν,
940   οἷ᾽ ἔργ᾽ ὁ παῖς μ᾽ ἔδρασεν οὑξ Ἀχιλλέως·
ὀμόσας ἀπάξειν οἴκαδ᾽, ἐς Τροίαν μ᾽ ἄγει·
προσθείς τε χεῖρα δεξιάν, τὰ τόξα μου
ἱερὰ λαβὼν τοῦ Ζηνὸς Ἡρακλέους ἔχει,

348

PHILOCTETES

NEOPTOLEMUS

A powerful necessity determines this; do not be angry when you hear it!

PHILOCTETES

I am lost, poor man! I am betrayed! What have you done to me, stranger? Give back my bow at once!

NEOPTOLEMUS

Why, I cannot! Justice and policy cause me to obey those in command.

PHILOCTETES

You fire, you total horror, you hateful masterpiece of dire villainy, what things you have done to me, how you have deceived me! Are you not even ashamed to look upon the suppliant who turned to you, you wretch? By taking my bow you have deprived me of my life! Give it back, I beg you, give it back, I beseech you, my son! By the gods of your fathers, do not take away my life! Alas for me! But he does not even speak to me any longer, but looks away like this, as though he will never let it go.

O harbours, O promontories, O society of mountain beasts, O jagged rocks, to you, for I know no other I can speak to, to my accustomed companions I address my lament at the things the son of Achilles has done to me! Having sworn to take me home, he is taking me to Troy; and having given his right hand as pledge, he has taken and is keeping my sacred bow of Heracles the son of Zeus; and

---

933 με μὴ ἀφέλῃ Elmsley: μή μου 'φέλῃς a: μή μ' ἀφέλῃς cett.

καὶ τοῖσιν Ἀργείοισι φήνασθαι θέλει,
945 ὡς ἄνδρ' ἑλὼν δ' ἰσχυρὸν ἐκ βίας μ' ἄγει.
κοὐκ οἶδ' ἐναίρων νεκρόν, ἢ καπνοῦ σκιάν,
εἴδωλον ἄλλως. οὐ γὰρ ἂν σθένοντά γε
εἷλέν μ'· ἐπεὶ οὐδ' ἂν ὧδ' ἔχοντ', εἰ μὴ δόλῳ.
νῦν δ' ἠπάτημαι δύσμορος. τί χρή με δρᾶν;
950 <ἀλλ'> ἀπόδος. ἀλλὰ νῦν ἔτ' ἐν σαυτοῦ γενοῦ.
τί φῄς; σιωπᾷς. οὐδέν εἰμ' ὁ δύσμορος.

ὦ σχῆμα πέτρας δίπυλον, αὖθις αὖ πάλιν
εἴσειμι πρὸς σὲ ψιλός, οὐκ ἔχων τροφήν·
ἀλλ' αὐανοῦμαι τῷδ' ἐν αὐλίῳ μόνος,
955 οὐ πτηνὸν ὄρνιν, οὐδὲ θῆρ' ὀρειβάτην
τόξοις ἐναίρων τοισίδ', ἀλλ' αὐτὸς τάλας
θανὼν παρέξω δαῖτ' ἀφ' ὧν ἐφερβόμην,
καί μ' οὓς ἐθήρων πρόσθε θηράσουσι νῦν·
φόνον φόνου δὲ ῥύσιον τείσω τάλας
960 πρὸς τοῦ δοκοῦντος οὐδὲν εἰδέναι κακόν.
ὄλοιο — μή πω, πρὶν μάθοιμ', εἰ καὶ πάλιν
γνώμην μετοίσεις· εἰ δὲ μή, θάνοις κακῶς.

ΧΟΡΟΣ

τί δρῶμεν; ἐν σοὶ καὶ τὸ πλεῖν ἡμᾶς, ἄναξ,
ἤδη 'στὶ καὶ τοῖς τοῦδε προσχωρεῖν λόγοις.

ΝΕΟΠΤΟΛΕΜΟΣ

965 ἐμοὶ μὲν οἶκτος δεινὸς ἐμπέπτωκέ τις
τοῦδ' ἀνδρὸς οὐ νῦν πρῶτον, ἀλλὰ καὶ πάλαι.

945 δ" Dindorf: μ' fere codd.
950 suppl. Turnebus

he says he will display me to the Argives, as though he were bringing a strong man whom he had taken by force, and does not know that he is killing a corpse, the shadow of smoke, a mere phantom! Yes, he would never have taken me had I had my strength! Why, he would not have done so even in this condition, except by treachery! But now in my misery I have been deceived. What must I do? Give it back! Even now it is not too late, come to yourself! What do you say? You are silent! I am nothing, miserable one!

O rock with double entrance, once again I shall enter you stripped, without the means of living; but I shall wither away alone in this bivouac, never killing a winged bird or a mountain beast with this bow, but I myself shall die and provide food for those off whom I used to live, and those I used to hunt will now hunt me! And I shall pay for blood with blood, poor fellow, through the act of one who seemed innocent of evil. May you perish—but not yet, before I learn whether you will once more change your decision! If you do not, may you die miserably!

CHORUS

What are we to do? It rests with you, my lord, whether we sail at once or accede to this man's words.

NEOPTOLEMUS

As for me, a strange pity for this man has fallen upon me, not now for the first time, but since long ago.

---

957 ἀφ᾽ Wunder: ὑφ᾽ codd.

SOPHOCLES

ΦΙΛΟΚΤΗΤΗΣ

ἐλέησον, ὦ παῖ, πρὸς θεῶν, καὶ μὴ παρῇς
σαυτὸν βροτοῖς ὄνειδος, ἐκκλέψας ἐμέ.

ΝΕΟΠΤΟΛΕΜΟΣ

οἴμοι, τί δράσω; μή ποτ᾽ ὤφελον λιπεῖν
970 τὴν Σκῦρον· οὕτω τοῖς παροῦσιν ἄχθομαι.

ΦΙΛΟΚΤΗΤΗΣ

οὐκ εἶ κακὸς σύ· πρὸς κακῶν δ᾽ ἀνδρῶν μαθὼν
ἔοικας ἥκειν αἰσχρά. νῦν δ᾽ ἄλλοισι δοὺς
ὅσ᾽ εἰκὸς ἔκπλει, τἄμ᾽ ἐμοὶ μεθεὶς ὅπλα.

ΝΕΟΠΤΟΛΕΜΟΣ

τί δρῶμεν, ἄνδρες;

ΟΔΥΣΣΕΥΣ

  ὦ κάκιστ᾽ ἀνδρῶν, τί δρᾷς;
975 οὐκ εἶ μεθεὶς τὰ τόξα ταῦτ᾽ ἐμοὶ πάλιν;

ΦΙΛΟΚΤΗΤΗΣ

οἴμοι, τίς ἀνήρ; ἆρ᾽ Ὀδυσσέως κλύω;

ΟΔΥΣΣΕΥΣ

Ὀδυσσέως, σάφ᾽ ἴσθ᾽, ἐμοῦ γ᾽, ὃν εἰσορᾷς.

ΦΙΛΟΚΤΗΤΗΣ

οἴμοι· πέπραμαι κἀπόλωλ᾽· ὅδ᾽ ἦν ἄρα
ὁ ξυλλαβών με κἀπονοσφίσας ὅπλων.

ΟΔΥΣΣΕΥΣ

980 ἐγώ, σάφ᾽ ἴσθ᾽, οὐκ ἄλλος· ὁμολογῶ τάδε.

972 ἄλλοισι] ἄλλοις σε Wakefield
973 ὅσ᾽ Wilson: οἷς codd.: οἳ Dindorf τἄμ᾽ ἐμοὶ Platt: τἀμά μοι codd.

352

PHILOCTETES

Have pity on me, boy, I beg you, and do not let yourself become the object of reproach to men by having deceived me!

NEOPTOLEMUS

Alas, what am I to do? I ought never to have left Scyros; such is the grief the situation causes me!

PHILOCTETES

You are not a villain, but you have come here after learning shameful things from men who are. But now give to others what is their due, and sail away, after giving back to me my weapons.

NEOPTOLEMUS

What are we to do, my men?

Enter suddenly ODYSSEUS.

ODYSSEUS

You utter scoundrel, what are you about? Will you not get back, and resign the bow to me!

PHILOCTETES

Alas, what man is this? Do I hear Odysseus?

ODYSSEUS

Odysseus, be sure, me whom you see!

PHILOCTETES

Alas! I am sold and I am ruined! So it was he who captured me and deprived me of my weapons!

ODYSSEUS

I, be sure, and no other! I admit this.

ΦΙΛΟΚΤΗΤΗΣ

ἀπόδος, ἄφες μοι, παῖ, τὰ τόξα.

ΟΔΥΣΣΕΥΣ

τοῦτο μέν,
οὐδ' ἢν θέλῃ, δράσει ποτ'· ἀλλὰ καὶ σὲ δεῖ
στείχειν ἅμ' αὐτοῖς, ἢ βίᾳ στελοῦσί σε.

ΦΙΛΟΚΤΗΤΗΣ

ἔμ', ὦ κακῶν κάκιστε καὶ τολμήστατε,
985   οἵδ' ἐκ βίας ἄξουσιν;

ΟΔΥΣΣΕΥΣ

ἢν μὴ ἕρπῃς ἑκών.

ΦΙΛΟΚΤΗΤΗΣ

ὦ Λημνία χθὼν καὶ τὸ παγκρατὲς σέλας
Ἡφαιστότευκτον, ταῦτα δῆτ' ἀνασχετά,
εἴ μ' οὗτος ἐκ τῶν σῶν ἀπάξεται βίᾳ;

ΟΔΥΣΣΕΥΣ

Ζεύς ἐσθ', ἵν' εἰδῇς, Ζεύς, ὁ τῆσδε γῆς κρατῶν,
990   Ζεύς, ᾧ δέδοκται ταῦθ'· ὑπηρετῶ δ' ἐγώ.

ΦΙΛΟΚΤΗΤΗΣ

ὦ μῖσος, οἷα κἀξανευρίσκεις λέγειν·
θεοὺς προτείνων τοὺς θεοὺς ψευδεῖς τίθης.

ΟΔΥΣΣΕΥΣ

οὔκ, ἀλλ' ἀληθεῖς. ἡ δ' ὁδὸς πορευτέα.

ΦΙΛΟΚΤΗΤΗΣ

οὔ φημ'.

PHILOCTETES

Give it back! Boy, let me have my bow!

ODYSSEUS

That he shall never do, even if he wants to; but you too
must come with it, or they will bring you by force.

PHILOCTETES

Shall they bring me by force, greatest and most impudent
of villains?

ODYSSEUS

If you do not come of your own will!

PHILOCTETES

Land of Lemnos and almighty fire made by Hephaestus,[a]
can this be tolerated, that he shall take me away from your
land by force?

ODYSSEUS

It is Zeus, let me tell you, Zeus, the ruler of this land, Zeus
who has decided this; and I execute his will!

PHILOCTETES

Hateful creature, what things you find to say! By shelter-
ing behind gods you make the gods liars!

ODYSSEUS

No, truth-tellers! And the journey must be made!

PHILOCTETES

I say No!

---

[a] The fire god and craftsman god, Hephaestus, was thought to
have his workshop on Lemnos.

---

992 τίθης Auratus: τιθείς vel τιθεῖς codd.

SOPHOCLES

ΟΔΥΣΣΕΥΣ

ἐγὼ δέ φημι. πειστέον τάδε.

ΦΙΛΟΚΤΗΤΗΣ

995 οἴμοι τάλας. ἡμᾶς μὲν ὡς δούλους σαφῶς
πατὴρ ἄρ᾽ ἐξέφυσεν οὐδ᾽ ἐλευθέρους.

ΟΔΥΣΣΕΥΣ

οὔκ, ἀλλ᾽ ὁμοίους τοῖς ἀριστεῦσιν, μεθ᾽ ὧν
Τροίαν σ᾽ ἑλεῖν δεῖ καὶ κατασκάψαι βίᾳ.

ΦΙΛΟΚΤΗΤΗΣ

οὐδέποτέ γ᾽· οὐδ᾽ ἢν χρῇ με πᾶν παθεῖν κακόν,
1000 ἕως γ᾽ ἂν ᾖ μοι γῆς τόδ᾽ αἰπεινὸν βάθρον.

ΟΔΥΣΣΕΥΣ

τί δ᾽ ἐργασείεις;

ΦΙΛΟΚΤΗΤΗΣ

κρᾶτ᾽ ἐμὸν τόδ᾽ αὐτίκα
πέτρᾳ πέτρας ἄνωθεν αἱμάξω πεσών.

ΟΔΥΣΣΕΥΣ

ξυλλάβετον αὐτόν· μὴ ᾽πὶ τῷδ᾽ ἔστω τάδε.

ΦΙΛΟΚΤΗΤΗΣ

ὦ χεῖρες, οἷα πάσχετ᾽ ἐν χρείᾳ φίλης
1005 νευρᾶς, ὑπ᾽ ἀνδρὸς τοῦδε συνθηρώμεναι.
ὦ μηδὲν ὑγιὲς μηδ᾽ ἐλεύθερον φρονῶν,
οἷ᾽ αὖ μ᾽ ὑπῆλθες, ὥς μ᾽ ἐθηράσω, λαβὼν
πρόβλημα σαυτοῦ παῖδα τόνδ᾽ ἀγνῶτ᾽ ἐμοί,

994 οὔ φημ᾽. Ὀδ. ἐγὼ δὲ Gernhard: οὔ φημ᾽ ἔγωγε codd.

1003 ξυλλάβετον Bernhardy: ξυλλάβετ᾽ codd. plerique: ξυλλάβετέ γ᾽ a

ODYSSEUS

But I say Yes! You must obey!

PHILOCTETES

Alas for me! Clearly my father gave me life as a slave, not as a free man!

ODYSSEUS

No, as a peer of the chieftains with whom you are to take Troy and destroy it!

PHILOCTETES

Never! Not even if I must suffer every evil, so long as I have this high pinnacle of the land!

PHILOCTETES makes a move towards the edge of the cliff.

ODYSSEUS

What do you mean to do?

PHILOCTETES

At once I shall throw myself from the rock and make my head bloody upon the rock below.

ODYSSEUS

Seize him! Let this not be in his power!

Two of the sailors seize PHILOCTETES.

PHILOCTETES

My arms, what things you suffer in the lack of my dear bow, forced together by this man's order! You who have no wholesome or generous thought, how you have crept up on me, how you have trapped me, taking as your screen this boy whom I did not know, too good for you, good enough

---

[1007] οἵ’ αὖ Hermann: οἷόν Zg, v.l. in a, coni. Blaydes: οἷα fere codd.

357

ἀνάξιον μὲν σοῦ, κατάξιον δ' ἐμοῦ,
1010 ὃς οὐδὲν ᾔδει πλὴν τὸ προσταχθὲν ποεῖν,
δῆλος δὲ καὶ νῦν ἐστιν ἀλγεινῶς φέρων
οἷς τ' αὐτὸς ἐξήμαρτεν οἷς τ' ἐγὼ 'παθον.
ἀλλ' ἡ κακὴ σὴ διὰ μυχῶν βλέπουσ' ἀεὶ
ψυχή νιν ἀφυᾶ τ' ὄντα κοὺ θέλονθ' ὅμως
1015 εὖ προὐδίδαξεν ἐν κακοῖς εἶναι σοφόν.
καὶ νῦν ἔμ', ὦ δύστηνε, συνδήσας νοεῖς
ἄγειν ἀπ' ἀκτῆς τῆσδ', ἐν ᾗ με προὐβάλου
ἄφιλον ἐρῆμον ἄπολιν ἐν ζῶσιν νεκρόν.
φεῦ.
ὄλοιο· καίτοι πολλάκις τόδ' ηὐξάμην.
1020 ἀλλ' οὐ γὰρ οὐδὲν θεοὶ νέμουσιν ἡδύ μοι,
σὺ μὲν γέγηθας ζῶν, ἐγὼ δ' ἀλγύνομαι
τοῦτ' αὔθ' ὅτι ζῶ σὺν κακοῖς πολλοῖς τάλας,
γελώμενος πρὸς σοῦ τε καὶ τῶν Ἀτρέως
διπλῶν στρατηγῶν, οἷς σὺ ταῦθ' ὑπηρετεῖς.
1025 καίτοι σὺ μὲν κλοπῇ τε κἀνάγκῃ ζυγεὶς
ἔπλεις ἅμ' αὐτοῖς, ἐμὲ δὲ τὸν πανάθλιον
ἑκόντα πλεύσανθ' ἑπτὰ ναυσὶ ναυβάτην
ἄτιμον ἔβαλον, ὡς σὺ φής, κεῖνοι δὲ σέ.
    καὶ νῦν τί μ' ἄγετε; τί μ' ἀπάγεσθε; τοῦ χάριν;
1030 ὃς οὐδέν εἰμι καὶ τέθνηχ' ὑμῖν πάλαι.
πῶς, ὦ θεοῖς ἔχθιστε, νῦν οὐκ εἰμί σοι
χωλός, δυσώδης; πῶς θεοῖς ἔξεσθ', ὁμοῦ
πλεύσαντος, αἴθειν ἱερά; πῶς σπένδειν ἔτι;
[αὕτη γὰρ ἦν σοι πρόφασις ἐκβαλεῖν ἐμέ.]
1035 κακῶς ὄλοισθ'· ὀλεῖσθε δ' ἠδικηκότες

for me, who knew nothing but that he should obey his orders! And you can see now how he is pained by his crime and by my suffering! But your evil mind looking out from its recesses skilfully taught him, inept pupil and unwilling as he was, how to be cunning in doing evil. And now, you wretch, you mean to tie me up and carry me away from this shore, on which you threw me out, friendless, deserted, citiless, a corpse among the living! Alas! May you perish! Yet I have often prayed for this; but since the gods never grant me any pleasure, you are alive and happy, and I feel pain at the very thought that I am alive with many troubles, mocked by you and by the two generals, sons of Atreus, whom you are serving in this matter. Yet you sailed with them after being kidnapped and compelled, and I, the unfortunate one, had sailed of my own free will with seven ships before they, as you say, but as they say you, threw me out, dishonoured.

And now why are you taking me? Why are you carrying me off? For what reason?—me who am nothing to you and have been dead for you long since. Why, you whom the gods loathe, am I not for you lame, evil-smelling? How, if I sail with you, can you make burnt offerings? How can you still pour libations? [For that was your pretext for throwing me out.] May you perish miserably! And you will

---

[1019] καίτοι Wakefield: καί σοι vel καὶ σὺ codd.

[1032] ἔξεσθ' Pierson: εὔξεσθ' codd.   ὁμοῦ Gγρ: ἐμοῦ codd.

[1034] del. Mollweide

[1035] ὀλεῖσθε Brunck: ὄλοισθε codd.

τὸν ἄνδρα τόνδε, θεοῖσιν εἰ δίκης μέλει.
ἔξοιδα δ᾽ ὡς μέλει γ᾽· ἐπεὶ οὔποτ᾽ ἂν στόλον
ἐπλεύσατ᾽ ἂν τόνδ᾽ οὔνεκ᾽ ἀνδρὸς ἀθλίου—
εἰ μή τι κέντρον θεῖον ἦγ᾽ ὑμᾶς—ἐμοῦ.

1040   ἀλλ᾽, ὦ πατρῷα γῆ θεοί τ᾽ ἐπόψιοι,
τείσασθε τείσασθ᾽ ἀλλὰ τῷ χρόνῳ ποτὲ
ξύμπαντας αὐτούς, εἴ τι κἄμ᾽ οἰκτίρετε.
ὡς ζῶ μὲν οἰκτρῶς, εἰ δ᾽ ἴδοιμ᾽ ὀλωλότας
τούτους, δοκοῖμ᾽ ἂν τῆς νόσου πεφευγέναι.

ΧΟΡΟΣ

1045   βαρύς τε καὶ βαρεῖαν ὁ ξένος φάτιν
τήνδ᾽ εἶπ᾽, Ὀδυσσεῦ, κοὐχ ὑπείκουσαν κακοῖς.

ΟΔΥΣΣΕΥΣ

πόλλ᾽ ἂν λέγειν ἔχοιμι πρὸς τὰ τοῦδ᾽ ἔπη,
εἴ μοι παρείκοι· νῦν δ᾽ ἑνὸς κρατῶ λόγου.
οὗ γὰρ τοιούτων δεῖ, τοιοῦτός εἰμ᾽ ἐγώ·

1050   χὤπου δικαίων κἀγαθῶν ἀνδρῶν κρίσις,
οὐκ ἂν λάβοις μου μᾶλλον οὐδέν᾽ εὐσεβῆ.
νικᾶν γε μέντοι πανταχοῦ χρῄζων ἔφυν,
πλὴν ἐς σέ· νῦν δὲ σοί γ᾽ ἑκὼν ἐκστήσομαι.
ἄφετε γὰρ αὐτόν, μηδὲ προσψαύσητ᾽ ἔτι.

1055   ἐᾶτε μίμνειν. οὐδὲ σοῦ προσχρῄζομεν,
τά γ᾽ ὅπλ᾽ ἔχοντες ταῦτ᾽· ἐπεὶ πάρεστι μὲν
Τεῦκρος παρ᾽ ἡμῖν, τήνδ᾽ ἐπιστήμην ἔχων,
ἐγώ θ᾽, ὃς οἶμαι σοῦ κάκιον οὐδὲν ἂν
τούτων κρατύνειν, μηδ᾽ ἐπιθύνειν χερί.

1060   τί δῆτα σοῦ δεῖ; χαῖρε τὴν Λῆμνον πατῶν.

perish, for the wrong you did this man, if the gods care for justice. And I know that they do care, for otherwise you would never have sailed on this voyage for the sake of a miserable man like me, unless some prompting from the gods had led you to.

O native land and gods that look upon it, punish them, punish all of them, late but surely, if you feel any pity for me! For my life is pitiable; but if I were to see them ruined, I would seem to have escaped my sickness!

CHORUS

Bitter is the stranger and bitter his speech, Odysseus, and one that does not give way before his troubles!

ODYSSEUS

I could say much in answer to his words, if I had time; but as things are I can say one thing only. Where there is need of men like this, I am such a man; but where there is a test for just and noble men, you will find no one more scrupulous than I. But it is my nature always to desire victory . . . except over you! Now I will willingly give way to you!

Yes, let him go, take your hands off him! Let him remain! We have no need of you, now that we have these weapons; for we have with us Teucer, who possesses this skill, and me too; I think I would be no worse a master of these than you, and no worse a hand at aiming arrows. Why do we need you? Walk about Lemnos and fare well!

ἡμεῖς δ' ἴωμεν. καὶ τάχ' ἂν τὸ σὸν γέρας
τιμὴν ἐμοὶ νείμειεν, ἣν σὲ χρῆν ἔχειν.

ΦΙΛΟΚΤΗΤΗΣ

οἴμοι· τί δράσω δύσμορος; σὺ τοῖς ἐμοῖς
ὅπλοισι κοσμηθεὶς ἐν Ἀργείοις φανῇ;

ΟΔΥΣΣΕΥΣ

1065 μή μ' ἀντιφώνει μηδέν, ὡς στείχοντα δή.

ΦΙΛΟΚΤΗΤΗΣ

ὦ σπέρμ' Ἀχιλλέως, οὐδὲ σοῦ φωνῆς ἔτι
γενήσομαι προσφθεγκτός, ἀλλ' οὕτως ἄπει;

ΟΔΥΣΣΕΥΣ

χώρει σύ· μὴ πρόσλευσσε, γενναῖός περ ὤν,
ἡμῶν ὅπως μὴ τὴν τύχην διαφθερεῖς.

ΦΙΛΟΚΤΗΤΗΣ

1070 ἦ καὶ πρὸς ὑμῶν ὧδ' ἔρημος, ὦ ξένοι,
λειφθήσομαι δὴ κοὐκ ἐποικτερεῖτέ με;

ΧΟΡΟΣ

ὅδ' ἐστὶν ἡμῶν ναυκράτωρ ὁ παῖς. ὅσ' ἂν
οὗτος λέγῃ σοι, ταῦτά σοι χἠμεῖς φαμεν.

ΝΕΟΠΤΟΛΕΜΟΣ

ἀκούσομαι μὲν ὡς ἔφυν οἴκτου πλέως
1075 πρὸς τοῦδ'· ὅμως δὲ μείνατ', εἰ τούτῳ δοκεῖ,
χρόνον τοσοῦτον, εἰς ὅσον τά τ' ἐκ νεὼς
στείλωσι ναῦται καὶ θεοῖς εὐξώμεθα.
χοὖτος τάχ' ἂν φρόνησιν ἐν τούτῳ λάβοι
λῴω τιν' ἡμῖν. νὼ μὲν οὖν ὁρμώμεθον,
1080 ὑμεῖς δ', ὅταν καλῶμεν, ὁρμᾶσθαι ταχεῖς.

PHILOCTETES

But let us go; and perhaps they will assign to me as a prize
your treasured possession, which you should have kept.

PHILOCTETES

Alas! What am I to do, unhappy man? Shall you appear
among the Argives flaunting my weapons?

ODYSSEUS

Answer me no longer, as I am departing!

PHILOCTETES

Seed of Achilles, shall I no longer be addressed by you, but
shall you go away like this?

ODYSSEUS

You come with me! Do not look at him, noble as you are,
so that you do not destroy our luck!

PHILOCTETES

Shall I be left here desolate by you also, strangers, and shall
you have no pity for me?

CHORUS

This boy is our captain; what he says to you, we also say to
you.

NEOPTOLEMUS

This man will say that I am too full of pity; but none the less
remain, if he approves, long enough for the sailors to make
preparations on the ship and for us to pray to the gods!
And meanwhile perhaps this man will come to a better way
of thinking with regard to us. So let us set off, and do you
be quick to set off also when we call you!

---

¹⁰⁷¹ λειφθήσομαι δὴ Wakefield: λειφθήσομ' ἤδη codd.

ΦΙΛΟΚΤΗΤΗΣ

ὦ κοίλας πέτρας γύαλον   στρ. α΄
θερμὸν καὶ παγετῶδες, ὥς
σ' οὐκ ἔμελλον ἄρ', ὦ τάλας,
λείψειν οὐδέποτ', ἀλλά μοι
1085 καὶ θνήσκοντι συνείσῃ.
ὤμοι μοί μοι.
ὦ πληρέστατον αὔλιον
λύπας τᾶς ἀπ' ἐμοῦ τάλαν,
τίπτ' αὖ μοι τὸ κατ' ἦμαρ ἔσται;
1090 τοῦ ποτε τεύξομαι
σιτονόμου μέλεος πόθεν ἐλπίδος;
ἴθ' αἱ πρόσθ' ἄνω
πτωκάδες ὀξυτόνου διὰ πνεύματος·
ἅλωσιν οὐκέτ' ἴσχω.

ΧΟΡΟΣ

1095 σύ τοι κατηξίωσας, ὦ βαρύποτμε, κοὐκ
ἄλλοθεν ἁ τύχα ἅδ' ἀπὸ μείζονος·
εὖτέ γε παρὸν φρονῆσαι
1100 λωίονος δαίμονος εἵλου τὸ κάκιον αἰνεῖν.

ΦΙΛΟΚΤΗΤΗΣ

ὦ τλάμων τλάμων ἄρ' ἐγὼ   ἀντ. α΄
καὶ μόχθῳ λωβατός, ὃς ἤ-
δη μετ' οὐδενὸς ὕστερον
ἀνδρῶν εἰσοπίσω τάλας

PHILOCTETES

Exeunt ODYSSEUS *and* NEOPTOLEMUS.

PHILOCTETES

O hollow of the cavernous rock, hot and icy by turns, so I
was not after all destined, poor fellow, to leave you ever,
but you will be with me even at my death! Alas, alas! O
bivouac permeated by my pain, what shall be my daily por-
tion? What hope of obtaining food shall come to me, and
from where, unhappy man? Come, you timorous creatures
in the sky that once feared me, through the piercing
breeze! No longer do I have the power to catch you.

CHORUS

It is you, man whose fate is grievous, who have chosen this;
this fortune has not come to you from one more powerful;
for when it was possible to show good sense, you chose to
approve the worse, rather than the better fate.

PHILOCTETES

Wretched, wretched am I and shattered by my suffering, I
who from now on shall live with no companion and shall

1085 συνείση Reiske: συνοίση codd.

1089 τίπτ᾽ Musgrave: τί ποτ᾽ codd.

1092 ἴθ᾽ αἱ πρόσθ᾽ Hermann: εἴθ᾽ αἰθέρος codd.

1094 ἅλωσιν Jeep: ἕλωσί μ᾽ codd.   οὐκέτ᾽ ἴσχω Dissen: οὐ
γὰρ ἔτ᾽ ἰσχύω codd.

1097 ἁ τύχα ἅδ᾽ Dindorf: ἔχῃ τύχᾳ τᾷδ᾽ codd.

1100 λωίονος Bothe: τοῦ λῴονος codd.   αἰνεῖν Hermann:
ἑλεῖν codd.

1105 ναίων ἐνθάδ᾽ ὀλοῦμαι,
αἰαῖ αἰαῖ,
οὐ φορβὰν ἔτι προσφέρων,
οὐ πτανῶν ἀπ᾽ ἐμῶν ὅπλων
1110 κραταιαῖς μετὰ χερσὶν ἴσχων·
ἀλλά μοι ἄσκοπα
κρυπτά τ᾽ ἔπη δολερᾶς ὑπέδυ φρενός·
ἰδοίμαν δέ νιν,
τὸν τάδε μησάμενον, τὸν ἴσον χρόνον
1115 ἐμὰς λαχόντ᾽ ἀνίας.

ΧΟΡΟΣ

πότμος σε δαιμόνων τάδ᾽, οὐδὲ σέ γε δόλος
ἔσχ᾽ ὑπὸ χειρὸς ἐμᾶς· στυγερὰν ἔχε
1120 δύσποτμον ἀρὰν ἐπ᾽ ἄλλοις.
καὶ γὰρ ἐμοὶ τοῦτο μέλει, μὴ φιλότητ᾽ ἀπώσῃ.

ΦΙΛΟΚΤΗΤΗΣ

οἴμοι μοι, καί που πολιᾶς   στρ. β΄
πόντου θινὸς ἐφήμενος,
1125 γελᾷ μου, χερὶ πάλλων
τὰν ἐμὰν μελέου τροφάν,
τὰν οὐδείς ποτ᾽ ἐβάστασεν.
ὦ τόξον φίλον, ὦ φίλων
χειρῶν ἐκβεβιασμένον,
1130 ἦ που ἐλεινὸν ὁρᾷς, φρένας εἴ τινας
ἔχεις, τὸν Ἡράκλειον
ἄθλιον ὧδέ σοι
οὐκέτι χρησόμενον τὸ μεθύστερον,

perish here, alas, alas, no longer bringing home food, no longer getting it through my winged weapons in my powerful hands. But the unsuspected and deceitful words of a cunning mind beguiled me! And may I see him, him who contrived this scheme, for the same extent of time doomed to my agony!

CHORUS

This is fate sent by the gods; it was not treachery to which I lent a hand that came upon you; direct the hatred of your baneful curse at others! For I am concerned that you shall not reject my friendship.

PHILOCTETES

Alas for me, somewhere by the shore of the gray sea he sits and mocks me, brandishing that which was my livelihood, miserable one, that which no other had held. O beloved bow, bow that was forced out of my loving hands, you look with pity, I think, if you have any feeling, upon the unhappy friend of Heracles who shall never use you any

ἀλλ' ἐν μεταλλαγᾷ <χεροῖν>
1135 πολυμηχάνου ἀνδρὸς ἐρέσσῃ,
ὁρῶν μὲν αἰσχρὰς ἀπάτας,
στυγνόν τε φῶτ' ἐχθοδοπόν,
μυρί' ἀπ' αἰσχρῶν ἀνατέλ-
λονθ' ὃς ἐφ' ἡμῖν κάκ' ἐμήσατ' ἔργων.

ΧΟΡΟΣ

1140 ἀνδρός τοι τὸ μὲν ὂν δίκαιον εἰπεῖν,
εἰπόντος δὲ μὴ φθονερὰν
ἐξῶσαι γλώσσας ὀδύναν.
κεῖνος δ' εἷς ἀπὸ πολλῶν
ταχθεὶς τοῦδ' ἐφημοσύνᾳ
1145 κοινὰν ἤνυσεν ἐς φίλους ἀρωγάν.

ΦΙΛΟΚΤΗΤΗΣ

ὦ πταναὶ θῆραι χαροπῶν τ'   ἀντ. β'
ἔθνη θηρῶν, οὓς ὅδ' ἔχει
χῶρος οὐρεσιβώτας,
φυγᾷ μηκέτ' ἀπ' αὐλίων
1150 ἐλᾶτ'· οὐ γὰρ ἔχω χεροῖν
τὰν πρόσθεν βελέων ἀλκάν,
ὦ δύστανος ἐγὼ τανῦν.
ἀλλ' ἀνέδην — ὅδε χωλὸς ἐρύκομαι,
οὐκέτι φοβητὸς ὑμῖν —
1155 ἕρπετε, νῦν καλὸν
ἀντίφονον κορέσαι στόμα πρὸς χάριν
ἐμᾶς <γε> σαρκὸς αἰόλας.
ἀπὸ γὰρ βίον αὐτίκα λείψω·

more, but you are plied instead in the grasp of a cunning
man, looking on his shameful deceptions and on the loath-
some enemy, who contrived against me innumerable evils
that arise from shameful deeds!

CHORUS

It is the part of a man to argue his own case, and when he
has spoken not to thrust out a hateful tongue and to give
pain! This man was one among many who was ordered by
the other to render a service that helped all their friends.

PHILOCTETES

O my winged prey and tribes of bright-eyed beasts whom
the mountain pastures of this place contain, no longer shall
you rush in flight from your lairs, for my hands no longer
hold the arrows that were once my protection! Unhappy
am I now! But come as you please—I am lame, and you
need no longer fear me—now it is easy to sate your mouths
in revenge upon my quivering flesh! At once I shall

---

¹¹³⁴ suppl. Stinton

¹¹³⁹ ἔργων Blaydes: Ὀδυσσεύς codd.

¹¹⁴⁰ ὃν Kells: εὖ codd.: οἴ Axt

¹¹⁴⁹ μηκέτ᾿ Auratus: μ᾿ οὐκέτ᾿ codd.

¹¹⁵⁰ ἐλᾶτ᾿ Canter: πελᾶτ᾿ codd.

¹¹⁵³ χωλὸς Porson: χῶρος codd.   ἐρύκομαι Blaydes:
ἐρύκεται codd.

¹¹⁵⁷ suppl. Ll.-J.

πόθεν γὰρ ἔσται βιοτά;
1160 τίς ὧδ᾽ ἐν αὔραις τρέφεται,
μηκέτι μηδενὸς κρατύ-
νων ὅσα πέμπει βιόδωρος αἶα;

ΧΟΡΟΣ

πρὸς θεῶν, εἴ τι σέβῃ ξένον, πέλασσον,
εὐνοίᾳ πάσᾳ πελάταν·
1165 ἀλλὰ γνῶθ᾽, εὖ γνῶθ᾽· ἐπὶ σοὶ
κῆρα τάνδ᾽ ἀποφεύγειν.
οἰκτρὰ γὰρ βόσκειν, ἀδαὴς δ᾽
ὀχεῖν μυρίον ἄχθος ᾧ ξυνοικεῖ.

ΦΙΛΟΚΤΗΤΗΣ

πάλιν πάλιν παλαιὸν ἄλ-   ἐπ.
1170 γημ᾽ ὑπέμνασας, ὦ
λῷστε τῶν πρὶν ἐντόπων.
τί μ᾽ ὤλεσας; τί μ᾽ εἴργασαι;

ΧΟΡΟΣ

τί τοῦτ᾽ ἔλεξας;

ΦΙΛΟΚΤΗΤΗΣ

εἰ σὺ τὰν ἐμοὶ
1175 στυγερὰν Τρῳάδα γᾶν μ᾽ ἤλπισας ἄξειν.

ΧΟΡΟΣ

τόδε γὰρ νόῳ κράτιστον.

ΦΙΛΟΚΤΗΤΗΣ

ἀπό νύν με λείπετ᾽ ἤδη.

abandon life; for where shall my living come from? Who can feed like this upon the winds, when he no longer has power over any of the things that the life-giving earth supplies?

CHORUS

I beg you, if you have any regard for your friend, draw near to him; he draws near in all loyalty to you. Come, know it, know it well! It is in your power to escape this deadly fate. For it feeds upon you cruelly, and he who lives with it cannot learn to sustain the countless pains it brings.

PHILOCTETES

Again, again you have reminded me of my ancient pain, O best of those who have been here! Why have you destroyed me? What have you done to me?

CHORUS

Why do you say this?

PHILOCTETES

If you hoped to take me to the detested land of Troy!

CHORUS

This is what I think is best.

PHILOCTETES

Leave me at once!

---

¹¹⁶⁵ ἐπὶ σοὶ Seyffert: ὅτι σοὶ codd.
¹¹⁶⁸ ὀχεῖν Zg, novit sch. L: ἔχειν cett.

ΧΟΡΟΣ

φίλα μοι, φίλα ταῦτα παρήγγει-
λας ἑκόντι τε πράσσειν.
ἴωμεν ἴωμεν
1180   ναὸς ἵν' ἡμῖν τέτακται.

ΦΙΛΟΚΤΗΤΗΣ

μή, πρὸς ἀραίου Διός, ἔλ-
θῃς, ἱκετεύω.

ΧΟΡΟΣ

     μετρίαζ'.

ΦΙΛΟΚΤΗΤΗΣ

ὦ ξένοι,
1185   μείνατε, πρὸς θεῶν.

ΧΟΡΟΣ

     τί θροεῖς;

ΦΙΛΟΚΤΗΤΗΣ

αἰαῖ αἰαῖ,
δαίμων δαίμων· ἀπόλωλ' ὁ τάλας·
ὦ πούς, πούς, τί σ' ἔτ' ἐν βίῳ
τεύξω τῷ μετόπιν, τάλας;
1190   ὦ ξένοι, ἔλθετ' ἐπήλυδες αὖθις.

ΧΟΡΟΣ

τί ῥέξοντες; ἀλλόκοτος
γνώμα τῶν πάρος ἂν προφαίνεις.

1191–92 ἀλλόκοτος γνώμα . . . ἂν Page: -κότῳ -ᾳ . . . ὦν codd.
1192 προφαίνεις Pearson: προὔφαινες Srzt: προὔφηνες LVa

PHILOCTETES

CHORUS

Welcome, welcome is the order you give me; gladly will I do it! Let us go, let us go to our posts on the ship!

PHILOCTETES

Do not go, by Zeus who is invoked in curses, I implore you!

CHORUS

Be reasonable!

PHILOCTETES

Strangers, remain, I beg you!

CHORUS

Why are you calling us?

PHILOCTETES

Alas, alas, my fate, my fate! I am lost, poor man! O foot, foot, what shall I do with you in my remaining life, poor wretch? Strangers, return to be with me once more!

CHORUS

What are we to do? The purpose you put forward is different from your former one.

ΦΙΛΟΚΤΗΤΗΣ

οὔτοι νεμεσητὸν
ἀλύοντα χειμερίῳ
1195 λύπᾳ καὶ παρὰ νοῦν θροεῖν.

ΧΟΡΟΣ

βᾶθί νυν, ὦ τάλαν, ὥς σε κελεύομεν.

ΦΙΛΟΚΤΗΤΗΣ

οὐδέποτ᾽ οὐδέποτ᾽, ἴσθι τόδ᾽ ἔμπεδον,
οὐδ᾽ εἰ πυρφόρος ἀστεροπητὴς
βροντᾶς αὐγαῖς μ᾽ εἶσι φλογίζων.
1200 ἐρρέτω Ἴλιον, οἵ θ᾽ ὑπ᾽ ἐκείνῳ
πάντες ὅσοι τόδ᾽ ἔτλασαν ἐμοῦ ποδὸς
ἄρθρον ἀπῶσαι.
ὦ ξένοι, ἕν γέ μοι εὖχος ὀρέξατε.

ΧΟΡΟΣ

ποῖον ἐρεῖς τόδ᾽ ἔπος;

ΦΙΛΟΚΤΗΤΗΣ

ξίφος, εἴ ποθεν,
1205 ἢ γένυν, ἢ βελέων τι, προπέμψατε.

ΧΟΡΟΣ

ὡς τίνα <δὴ> ῥέξῃς παλάμαν ποτέ;

ΦΙΛΟΚΤΗΤΗΣ

κρᾶτα καὶ ἄρθρ᾽ ἀπὸ πάντα τέμω χερί·
φονᾷ φονᾷ νόος ἤδη.

ΧΟΡΟΣ

1210 τί ποτε;

PHILOCTETES

You cannot resent it if a man distraught by storms of pain
speaks some words that are insane.

CHORUS

Come now, unhappy man, as we direct you!

PHILOCTETES

Never, never, know that for certain, not if the fire-bearing
lord of the lightning comes to consume me in the blaze of
his thunder! May Ilium perish, and all those beneath it
who had the heart to reject my tortured foot! Strangers,
grant me one prayer!

CHORUS

What is it you are going to say?

PHILOCTETES

Hand me a sword, if you have one, or an axe, or an arrow!

CHORUS

So that you can do what deed?

PHILOCTETES

So that I can cut off my head and every limb! To kill, to kill
is now my wish!

CHORUS

Why?

1193 -τόν <μ'> Page
1199 βροντᾶς αὐγαῖς sch.: βρονταῖς αὐταῖς codd.
1203 ante ὦ praebent ἀλλ' codd.: del. Erfurdt
1206 suppl. Hermann

ΦΙΛΟΚΤΗΤΗΣ

πατέρα ματεύων.

ΧΟΡΟΣ

ποῖ γᾶς;

ΦΙΛΟΚΤΗΤΗΣ

ἐς ῞Αιδου.
οὐ γάρ ἐστ᾽ ἐν φάει γ᾽ ἔτι.
ὦ πόλις πόλις πατρία,
πῶς ἂν εἰσίδοιμ᾽
ἄθλιός σ᾽ ἀνήρ,
1215 ὅς γε σὰν λιπὼν ἱερὰν
λιβάδ᾽ ἐχθροῖς ἔβαν Δαναοῖς
ἀρωγός· ἔτ᾽ οὐδέν εἰμι.

[ΧΟΡΟΣ

ἐγὼ μὲν ἤδη καὶ πάλαι νεὼς ὁμοῦ
στείχων ἂν ἦν σοι τῆς ἐμῆς, εἰ μὴ πέλας
1220 Ὀδυσσέα στείχοντα τόν τ᾽ Ἀχιλλέως
γόνον πρὸς ἡμᾶς δεῦρ᾽ ἰόντ᾽ ἐλεύσσομεν.]

ΟΔΥΣΣΕΥΣ

οὐκ ἂν φράσειας ἥντιν᾽ αὖ παλίντροπος
κέλευθον ἕρπεις ὧδε σὺν σπουδῇ ταχύς;

ΝΕΟΠΤΟΛΕΜΟΣ

λύσων ὅσ᾽ ἐξήμαρτον ἐν τῷ πρὶν χρόνῳ.

ΟΔΥΣΣΕΥΣ

1225 δεινόν γε φωνεῖς· ἡ δ᾽ ἁμαρτία τίς ἦν;

PHILOCTETES

To look for my father!

CHORUS

Where?

PHILOCTETES

In Hades! For he is no longer in the world of light. O my city, O my native city, if only I could see you, wretched man that I am, I who left your sacred stream and went to help the Greeks! I am nothing any more!

[CHORUS

I should have been on my way together with my ship long since, were it not that I see Odysseus coming and Achilles' son approaching us.]

Exit PHILOCTETES *into the cave. Enter* ODYSSEUS *and* NEOPTOLEMUS.

ODYSSEUS

Will you not tell me why you are hurrying back in such hot haste?

NEOPTOLEMUS

To put right the wrong I did before!

ODYSSEUS

What you say is dreadful! What did you do wrong?

1213 alterum πόλις suppl. Gleditsch
1214 εἰσίδοιμ' ἄθλιός σ' Dindorf: εἰσίδοιμί σ' ἄθλιός γ' codd.
1218–21 del. Mekler

ΝΕΟΠΤΟΛΕΜΟΣ

ἦν σοὶ πιθόμενος τῷ τε σύμπαντι στρατῷ—

ΟΔΥΣΣΕΥΣ

ἔπραξας ἔργον ποῖον ὧν οὔ σοι πρέπον;

ΝΕΟΠΤΟΛΕΜΟΣ

ἀπάταισιν αἰσχραῖς ἄνδρα καὶ δόλοις ἑλών.

ΟΔΥΣΣΕΥΣ

τὸν ποῖον; ὤμοι· μῶν τι βουλεύῃ νέον;

ΝΕΟΠΤΟΛΕΜΟΣ

1230   νέον μὲν οὐδέν, τῷ δὲ Ποίαντος τόκῳ—

ΟΔΥΣΣΕΥΣ

τί χρῆμα δράσεις; ὥς μ᾽ ὑπῆλθέ τις φόβος.

ΝΕΟΠΤΟΛΕΜΟΣ

παρ᾽ οὖπερ ἔλαβον τάδε τὰ τόξ᾽, αὖθις πάλιν—

ΟΔΥΣΣΕΥΣ

ὦ Ζεῦ, τί λέξεις; οὔ τί που δοῦναι νοεῖς;

ΝΕΟΠΤΟΛΕΜΟΣ

αἰσχρῶς γὰρ αὐτὰ κοὐ δίκῃ λαβὼν ἔχω.

ΟΔΥΣΣΕΥΣ

1235   πρὸς θεῶν, πότερα δὴ κερτομῶν λέγεις τάδε;

ΝΕΟΠΤΟΛΕΜΟΣ

εἰ κερτόμησίς ἐστι τἀληθῆ λέγειν.

1235 δὴ a: om. cett.: σὺ Hermann
1236 <γ᾽> ἐστὶ Herwerden

PHILOCTETES

NEOPTOLEMUS

Obeying you and the entire army—

ODYSSEUS

You did what thing that was not proper for you?

NEOPTOLEMUS

I overcame a man with shameful trickery and deceit.

ODYSSEUS

What man? Alas! Can you be planning some new surprise?

NEOPTOLEMUS

No surprise, but to the son of Poeas—

ODYSSEUS

What are you going to do? A fear steals over me!

NEOPTOLEMUS

From whom I took this bow, once again—

ODYSSEUS

O Zeus, what are you about to say? Surely you do not mean to give it back?

NEOPTOLEMUS

Yes, because I acquired it shamefully and not justly!

ODYSSEUS

I beg you, are you saying this to tease me?

NEOPTOLEMUS

If it is teasing to tell the truth!

ΟΔΥΣΣΕΥΣ
τί φής, Ἀχιλλέως παῖ; τίν' εἴρηκας λόγον;

ΝΕΟΠΤΟΛΕΜΟΣ
δὶς ταὐτὰ βούλῃ καὶ τρὶς ἀναπολεῖν μ' ἔπη;

ΟΔΥΣΣΕΥΣ
ἀρχὴν κλύειν ἂν οὐδ' ἅπαξ ἐβουλόμην.

ΝΕΟΠΤΟΛΕΜΟΣ
1240   εὖ νῦν ἐπίστω πάντ' ἀκηκοὼς λόγον.

ΟΔΥΣΣΕΥΣ
ἔστιν τις ἔστιν ὅς σε κωλύσει τὸ δρᾶν.

ΝΕΟΠΤΟΛΕΜΟΣ
τί φής; τίς ἔσται μ' οὑπικωλύσων τάδε;

ΟΔΥΣΣΕΥΣ
ξύμπας Ἀχαιῶν λάος, ἐν δὲ τοῖς ἐγώ.

ΝΕΟΠΤΟΛΕΜΟΣ
σοφὸς πεφυκὼς οὐδὲν ἐξαυδᾷς σοφόν.

ΟΔΥΣΣΕΥΣ
1245   σὺ δ' οὔτε φωνεῖς οὔτε δρασείεις σοφά.

ΝΕΟΠΤΟΛΕΜΟΣ
ἀλλ' εἰ δίκαια, τῶν σοφῶν κρείσσω τάδε.

ΟΔΥΣΣΕΥΣ
καὶ πῶς δίκαιον, ἅ γ' ἔλαβες βουλαῖς ἐμαῖς,
πάλιν μεθεῖναι ταῦτα;

1245 σοφά Brunck: σοφόν codd.

PHILOCTETES

ODYSSEUS

What are you saying, son of Achilles? What word have you pronounced?

NEOPTOLEMUS

Do you wish me to repeat the same words twice and three times over?

ODYSSEUS

I should rather not have heard it at all, not even once!

NEOPTOLEMUS

Be certain now that you have heard all I have to say!

ODYSSEUS

There is, there is one who shall prevent this action!

NEOPTOLEMUS

What do you mean? Who is there that shall prevent my doing this?

ODYSSEUS

The whole people of the Achaeans, and among them I!

NEOPTOLEMUS

Clever as you are, what you are saying is not clever!

ODYSSEUS

Neither your words nor your intentions are clever!

NEOPTOLEMUS

But if they are right, that is better than being clever!

ODYSSEUS

And how is it right to let go again what you got through my planning?

ΝΕΟΠΤΟΛΕΜΟΣ
τὴν ἁμαρτίαν
αἰσχρὰν ἁμαρτὼν ἀναλαβεῖν πειράσομαι.

ΟΔΥΣΣΕΥΣ
1250 στρατὸν δ᾽ Ἀχαιῶν οὐ φοβῇ, πράσσων τάδε;

ΝΕΟΠΤΟΛΕΜΟΣ
ξὺν τῷ δικαίῳ τὸν σὸν οὐ ταρβῶ <στρατόν.

ΟΔΥΣΣΕΥΣ
× – ∪ – × – ∪ – × – > φόβον.

ΝΕΟΠΤΟΛΕΜΟΣ
ἀλλ᾽ οὐδέ τοι σῇ χειρὶ πείθομαι τὸ δρᾶν.

ΟΔΥΣΣΕΥΣ
οὔ τἄρα Τρωσίν, ἀλλὰ σοὶ μαχούμεθα.

ΝΕΟΠΤΟΛΕΜΟΣ
ἔστω τὸ μέλλον.

ΟΔΥΣΣΕΥΣ
χεῖρα δεξιὰν ὁρᾷς
1255 κώπης ἐπιψαύουσαν;

ΝΕΟΠΤΟΛΕΜΟΣ
ἀλλὰ κἀμέ τοι
ταὐτὸν τόδ᾽ ὄψῃ δρῶντα κοὐ μέλλοντ᾽ ἔτι.

ΟΔΥΣΣΕΥΣ
καίτοι σ᾽ ἐάσω· τῷ δὲ σύμπαντι στρατῷ
λέξω τάδ᾽ ἐλθών, ὅς σε τιμωρήσεται.

PHILOCTETES

NEOPTOLEMUS
The wrong I did was disgraceful, and I shall try to undo it!

ODYSSEUS
And are you not afraid of the army of the Achaeans when
you mean to do this?

NEOPTOLEMUS
With right on my side I am not afraid of your army!

ODYSSEUS
. . . . fear.

NEOPTOLEMUS
I shall disobey you even when you threaten force!

ODYSSEUS
Then we shall fight not with the Trojans, but with you!

NEOPTOLEMUS
Let what will come come!

ODYSSEUS
Do you see my right hand clasping my sword-hilt?

NEOPTOLEMUS
But you will see me doing the same thing and not delaying!

ODYSSEUS
Well, I will let you be! But I shall go and tell this story to
the whole army, which will punish you.

1251 στρατόν Hermann, qui lacunam indicavit: φόβον codd.,
quod in finem v. 1251 b traiecit Jackson

ΝΕΟΠΤΟΛΕΜΟΣ

ἐσωφρόνησας· κἂν τὰ λοίφ᾽ οὕτω φρονῇς,
1260 ἴσως ἂν ἐκτὸς κλαυμάτων ἔχοις πόδα.
σὺ δ᾽, ὦ Ποίαντος παῖ, Φιλοκτήτην λέγω,
ἔξελθ᾽, ἀμείψας τάσδε πετρήρεις στέγας.

ΦΙΛΟΚΤΗΤΗΣ

τίς αὖ παρ᾽ ἄντροις θόρυβος ἵσταται βοῆς;
τί μ᾽ ἐκκαλεῖσθε; τοῦ κεχρημένοι, ξένοι;
1265 ὤμοι· κακὸν τὸ χρῆμα. μῶν τί μοι μέγα
πάρεστε πρὸς κακοῖσι πέμποντες κακόν;

ΝΕΟΠΤΟΛΕΜΟΣ

θάρσει· λόγους δ᾽ ἄκουσον οὓς ἥκω φέρων.

ΦΙΛΟΚΤΗΤΗΣ

δέδοικ᾽ ἔγωγε. καὶ τὰ πρὶν γὰρ ἐκ λόγων
καλῶν κακῶς ἔπραξα, σοῖς πεισθεὶς λόγοις.

ΝΕΟΠΤΟΛΕΜΟΣ

1270 οὔκουν ἔνεστι καὶ μεταγνῶναι πάλιν;

ΦΙΛΟΚΤΗΤΗΣ

τοιοῦτος ἦσθα τοῖς λόγοισι χὤτε μου
τὰ τόξ᾽ ἔκλεπτες, πιστός, ἀτηρὸς λάθρᾳ.

ΝΕΟΠΤΟΛΕΜΟΣ

ἀλλ᾽ οὔ τι μὴν νῦν· βούλομαι δέ σου κλύειν,
πότερα δέδοκταί σοι μένοντι καρτερεῖν,
1275 ἢ πλεῖν μεθ᾽ ἡμῶν.

PHILOCTETES

NEOPTOLEMUS

Very wise of you! If in future you show as much sense, perhaps you will keep your foot out of trouble.

Exit ODYSSEUS.

But you, son of Poeas, I mean Philoctetes, come out, leaving this rocky dwelling!

Enter PHILOCTETES.

PHILOCTETES

What is this new clamour of shouting by the cave? Why do you call me out? What do you need, strangers? Alas! It is something bad! Are you here to bring me some great evil in addition to my others!

NEOPTOLEMUS

Do not be afraid, but listen to the message that I come with!

PHILOCTETES

I am afraid; before also I met with misfortune through your fair words, when they persuaded me.

NEOPTOLEMUS

Is it not possible to change my mind once more?

PHILOCTETES

That is how you were in your words when you stole my bow, persuasive, but in secret deadly.

NEOPTOLEMUS

But not now! But I wish to hear from you whether you have decided to stay here and endure, or to sail with us.

ΦΙΛΟΚΤΗΤΗΣ

παῦε, μὴ λέξῃς πέρα.
μάτην γὰρ ἂν εἴπῃς γε πάντ᾽ εἰρήσεται.

ΝΕΟΠΤΟΛΕΜΟΣ

οὕτω δέδοκται;

ΦΙΛΟΚΤΗΤΗΣ

καὶ πέρα γ᾽ ἴσθ᾽ ἢ λέγω.

ΝΕΟΠΤΟΛΕΜΟΣ

ἀλλ᾽ ἤθελον μὲν ἄν σε πεισθῆναι λόγοις
ἐμοῖσιν· εἰ δὲ μή τι πρὸς καιρὸν λέγων
1280 κυρῶ, πέπαυμαι.

ΦΙΛΟΚΤΗΤΗΣ

πάντα γὰρ φράσεις μάτην·
οὐ γάρ ποτ᾽ εὔνουν τὴν ἐμὴν κτήσῃ φρένα,
ὅστις γ᾽ ἐμοῦ δόλοισι τὸν βίον λαβὼν
ἀπεστέρηκας· κᾆτα νουθετεῖς ἐμὲ
ἐλθών, ἀρίστου πατρὸς ἔχθιστος γεγώς.
1285 ὄλοισθ᾽, Ἀτρεῖδαι μὲν μάλιστ᾽, ἔπειτα δὲ
ὁ Λαρτίου παῖς, καὶ σύ.

ΝΕΟΠΤΟΛΕΜΟΣ

μὴ ᾽πεύξῃ πέρα·
δέχου δὲ χειρὸς ἐξ ἐμῆς βέλη τάδε.

ΦΙΛΟΚΤΗΤΗΣ

πῶς εἶπας; ἆρα δεύτερον δολούμεθα;

ΝΕΟΠΤΟΛΕΜΟΣ

ἀπώμοσ᾽ ἁγνὸν Ζηνὸς ὑψίστου σέβας.

PHILOCTETES

PHILOCTETES

Stop, say no more! For anything you may say will be said in vain.

NEOPTOLEMUS

Is that your decision?

PHILOCTETES

Even more decidedly than I have said it.

NEOPTOLEMUS

Well, I wish you had been persuaded by my words; but if what I am saying is not apposite, I am silent.

PHILOCTETES

All that you say will be in vain; for you will never get me to lend a friendly ear, you who by cunning took and deprived me of my livelihood. And after that you come and lecture me, hateful son of a most noble father! A plague upon you all, most of all upon the sons of Atreus, then upon the son of Lartius, and upon yourself!

NEOPTOLEMUS

Utter no more prayers, but receive from my hand this weapon!

PHILOCTETES

What did you say? Am I being tricked again?

NEOPTOLEMUS

I swear by the sacred majesty of highest Zeus!

---

¹²⁸⁸ ante ἆρα add. οὐκ codd., del. Porson
¹²⁸⁹ ἁγνὸν Wakefield: -οῦ codd.   ὑψίστου VTa, coni. Wakefield: -ιστον cett.

ΦΙΛΟΚΤΗΤΗΣ

1290 ὦ φίλτατ᾽ εἰπών, εἰ λέγεις ἐτήτυμα.

ΝΕΟΠΤΟΛΕΜΟΣ

τοὔργον παρέσται φανερόν. ἀλλὰ δεξιὰν
πρότεινε χεῖρα, καὶ κράτει τῶν σῶν ὅπλων.

ΟΔΥΣΣΕΥΣ

ἐγὼ δ᾽ ἀπαυδῶ γ᾽, ὡς θεοὶ ξυνίστορες,
ὑπέρ τ᾽ Ἀτρειδῶν τοῦ τε σύμπαντος στρατοῦ.

ΦΙΛΟΚΤΗΤΗΣ

1295 τέκνον, τίνος φώνημα, μῶν Ὀδυσσέως,
ἐπῃσθόμην;

ΟΔΥΣΣΕΥΣ

σάφ᾽ ἴσθι· καὶ πέλας γ᾽ ὁρᾷς,
ὅς σ᾽ ἐς τὰ Τροίας πεδί᾽ ἀποστελῶ βίᾳ,
ἐάν τ᾽ Ἀχιλλέως παῖς ἐάν τε μὴ θέλῃ.

ΦΙΛΟΚΤΗΤΗΣ

ἀλλ᾽ οὔ τι χαίρων, ἢν τόδ᾽ ὀρθωθῇ βέλος.

ΝΕΟΠΤΟΛΕΜΟΣ

1300 ἆ, μηδαμῶς, μή, πρὸς θεῶν, μὴ ᾽φῇς βέλος.

ΦΙΛΟΚΤΗΤΗΣ

μέθες με, πρὸς θεῶν, χεῖρα, φίλτατον τέκνον.

ΝΕΟΠΤΟΛΕΜΟΣ

οὐκ ἂν μεθείην.

1300 μὴ ᾽φῇς Meineke: μεθῇς codd.

388

PHILOCTETES

PHILOCTETES
O speaker of welcome words—if your words are true!

NEOPTOLEMUS
The act shall make it clear! Come, put out your right hand
and be master of your weapon!

Enter suddenly ODYSSEUS.

ODYSSEUS
But I forbid it, as the gods are my witnesses, in the name of
the sons of Atreus and the whole army!

PHILOCTETES
My son, whose voice is that? Did I hear Odysseus?

ODYSSEUS
Be sure of it! And you see me near, me who will carry you
to the land of Troy by force, whether Achilles' son wishes it
or not!

PHILOCTETES
*(who with the speed of the great archer puts an arrow to
his bow and levels it at* ODYSSEUS*)*
But not so easily, if this arrow goes straight!

NEOPTOLEMUS
Ah, do not, I beg you, shoot the arrow!

PHILOCTETES
Let go my hand, let go, my dearest boy!

NEOPTOLEMUS
I will not let go!

Exit ODYSSEUS.

SOPHOCLES

ΦΙΛΟΚΤΗΤΗΣ
φεῦ· τί μ᾽ ἄνδρα πολέμιον
ἐχθρόν τ᾽ ἀφείλου μὴ κτανεῖν τόξοις ἐμοῖς;

ΝΕΟΠΤΟΛΕΜΟΣ
ἀλλ᾽ οὔτ᾽ ἐμοὶ καλὸν τόδ᾽ ἐστὶν οὔτε σοί.

ΦΙΛΟΚΤΗΤΗΣ
1305 ἀλλ᾽ οὖν τοσοῦτόν γ᾽ ἴσθι, τοὺς πρώτους στρατοῦ,
τοὺς τῶν Ἀχαιῶν ψευδοκήρυκας, κακοὺς
ὄντας πρὸς αἰχμήν, ἐν δὲ τοῖς λόγοις θρασεῖς.

ΝΕΟΠΤΟΛΕΜΟΣ
εἶέν. τὰ μὲν δὴ τόξ᾽ ἔχεις, κοὐκ ἔσθ᾽ ὅτου
ὀργὴν ἔχοις ἂν οὐδὲ μέμψιν εἰς ἐμέ.

ΦΙΛΟΚΤΗΤΗΣ
1310 ξύμφημι. τὴν φύσιν δ᾽ ἔδειξας, ὦ τέκνον,
ἐξ ἧς ἔβλαστες, οὐχὶ Σισύφου πατρός,
ἀλλ᾽ ἐξ Ἀχιλλέως, ὃς μετὰ ζώντων ὅτ᾽ ἦν
ἤκου᾽ ἄριστα, νῦν δὲ τῶν τεθνηκότων.

ΝΕΟΠΤΟΛΕΜΟΣ
ἥσθην πατέρα τὸν ἀμὸν εὐλογοῦντά σε
1315 αὐτόν τ᾽ ἔμ᾽· ὧν δέ σου τυχεῖν ἐφίεμαι
ἄκουσον. ἀνθρώποισι τὰς μὲν ἐκ θεῶν
τύχας δοθείσας ἔστ᾽ ἀναγκαῖον φέρειν·
ὅσοι δ᾽ ἑκουσίοισιν ἔγκεινται βλάβαις,
ὥσπερ σύ, τούτοις οὔτε συγγνώμην ἔχειν
1320 δίκαιόν ἐστιν οὔτ᾽ ἐποικτίρειν τινά.
σὺ δ᾽ ἠγρίωσαι, κοὔτε σύμβουλον δέχῃ,

1308 ὅτου Turnebus: ὅπου codd.
390

PHILOCTETES

PHILOCTETES

Alas! Why did you prevent me from killing a hated enemy with my bow?

NEOPTOLEMUS

But that would not be honourable for me or for you.

PHILOCTETES

Well, know this much, that the leaders of the army, the false heralds of the Achaeans, are brave with words, but cowardly in battle!

NEOPTOLEMUS

So! You have the bow, and you have no reason to be angry with me or to blame me.

PHILOCTETES

I agree! You showed the nature, my son, of the stock you come from, having not Sisyphus for father, but Achilles, who had the greatest fame while he was among the living and has it now among the dead.

NEOPTOLEMUS

I am glad to hear you praise my father and myself; but hear of the favour which I am asking of you! The fortunes given them by the gods men are obliged to bear; but those who are the prey of damage that is self-inflicted it is wrong that any should be sorry for or pity! You have become savage,

ἐάν τε νουθετῇ τις εὐνοίᾳ λέγων,
στυγεῖς, πολέμιον δυσμενῆ θ᾽ ἡγούμενος.
ὅμως δὲ λέξω· Ζῆνα δ᾽ ὅρκιον καλῶ·
1325 καὶ ταῦτ᾽ ἐπίστω, καὶ γράφου φρενῶν ἔσω.
σὺ γὰρ νοσεῖς τόδ᾽ ἄλγος ἐκ θείας τύχης,
Χρύσης πελασθεὶς φύλακος, ὃς τὸν ἀκαλυφῆ
σηκὸν φυλάσσει κρύφιος οἰκουρῶν ὄφις·
καὶ παῦλαν ἴσθι τῆσδε μή ποτ᾽ ἂν τυχεῖν
1330 νόσου βαρείας, ἕως ἂν αὐτὸς ἥλιος
ταύτῃ μὲν αἴρῃ, τῇδε δ᾽ αὖ δύνῃ πάλιν,
πρὶν ἂν τὰ Τροίας πεδί᾽ ἑκὼν αὐτὸς μόλῃς,
καὶ τῶν παρ᾽ ἡμῖν ἐντυχὼν Ἀσκληπιδῶν
νόσου μαλαχθῇς τῆσδε, καὶ τὰ πέργαμα
1335 ξὺν τοῖσδε τόξοις ξύν τ᾽ ἐμοὶ πέρσας φανῇς.
ὡς δ᾽ οἶδα ταῦτα τῇδ᾽ ἔχοντ᾽ ἐγὼ φράσω.
ἀνὴρ παρ᾽ ἡμῖν ἔστιν ἐκ Τροίας ἁλούς,
Ἕλενος ἀριστόμαντις, ὃς λέγει σαφῶς
ὡς δεῖ γενέσθαι ταῦτα· καὶ πρὸς τοῖσδ᾽ ἔτι,
1340 ὡς ἔστ᾽ ἀνάγκη τοῦ παρεστῶτος θέρους
Τροίαν ἁλῶναι πᾶσαν· ἢ δίδωσ᾽ ἑκὼν
κτείνειν ἑαυτόν, ἢν τάδε ψευσθῇ λέγων.
ταῦτ᾽ οὖν ἐπεὶ κάτοισθα, συγχώρει θέλων.
καλὴ γὰρ ἡ ᾽πίκτησις, Ἑλλήνων ἕνα
1345 κριθέντ᾽ ἄριστον, τοῦτο μὲν παιωνίας
ἐς χεῖρας ἐλθεῖν, εἶτα τὴν πολύστονον
Τροίαν ἑλόντα κλέος ὑπέρτατον λαβεῖν.

1329 ἂν τυχεῖν Porson: ἐντυχεῖν codd.
1337 παρ᾽ Elmsley: γὰρ codd.

and will not accept a counsellor, and if anyone tries to teach you, speaking with good will, you turn your back on him, thinking him an enemy and an ill-wisher. But all the same I will speak, and I call on Zeus the guarantor of oaths! Know this, and write it down inside your mind! You acquired this painful sickness through an event caused by the gods, when you came near to the guardian of Chryse, who protects the roofless sanctuary, the snake that keeps watch unseen. And know that you will never have respite from grievous sickness, so long as the sun rises in one quarter and sets again in another, before you come of your own will to the land of Troy, and meeting the sons of Asclepius that are with us you are relieved of this malady, and with this bow and with me you are revealed as the conqueror of the towers. I will tell you how I know that this is so! There is a man with us who was taken prisoner from Troy, Helenus, the noble prophet, who tells us beyond doubt that this is bound to happen; and in addition, that it is fated that Troy be entirely taken during the present summer; and if he is found to be telling lies, he gives us permission to kill him. Then since you know this, give your willing consent! It is a glorious addition to be reckoned the noblest of all the Greeks, and first to come to healing hands, and second to take Troy, the cause of so much mourning, and win the highest fame!

ΦΙΛΟΚΤΗΤΗΣ

ὦ στυγνὸς αἰών, τί μ' ἔτι δῆτ' ἔχεις ἄνω
βλέποντα, κοὐκ ἀφῆκας εἰς Ἅιδου μολεῖν;
1350 οἴμοι, τί δράσω; πῶς ἀπιστήσω λόγοις
τοῖς τοῦδ', ὃς εὔνους ὢν ἐμοὶ παρῄνεσεν;
ἀλλ' εἰκάθω δῆτ'; εἶτα πῶς ὁ δύσμορος
ἐς φῶς τάδ' ἔρξας εἶμι; τῷ προσήγορος;
πῶς, ὦ τὰ πάντ' ἰδόντες ἀμφ' ἐμοὶ κύκλοι,
1355 ταῦτ' ἐξανασχήσεσθε, τοῖσιν Ἀτρέως
ἐμὲ ξυνόντα παισίν, οἵ μ' ἀπώλεσαν;
πῶς τῷ πανώλει παιδὶ τῷ Λαερτίου;
οὐ γάρ με τἄλγος τῶν παρελθόντων δάκνει,
ἀλλ' οἷα χρὴ παθεῖν με πρὸς τούτων ἔτι
1360 δοκῶ προλεύσσειν. οἷς γὰρ ἡ γνώμη κακῶν
μήτηρ γένηται, κἄλλα φιτεύει κακά.
καὶ σοῦ δ' ἔγωγε θαυμάσας ἔχω τόδε·
χρῆν γάρ σε μήτ' αὐτόν ποτ' ἐς Τροίαν μολεῖν,
ἡμᾶς τ' ἀπείργειν· οἵδε σου καθύβρισαν,
1365 πατρὸς γέρας συλῶντες. εἶτα τοῖσδε σὺ
εἶ ξυμμαχήσων, κἄμ' ἀναγκάζεις τόδε;
μὴ δῆτα, τέκνον· ἀλλ' ἅ μοι ξυνώμοσας,
πέμψον πρὸς οἴκους· καὐτὸς ἐν Σκύρῳ μένων
ἔα κακῶς αὐτοὺς ἀπόλλυσθαι κακούς.
1370 χοὔτω διπλῆν μὲν ἐξ ἐμοῦ κτήσῃ χάριν,
διπλῆν δὲ πατρός· κοὐ κακοὺς ἐπωφελῶν
δόξεις ὅμοιος τοῖς κακοῖς πεφυκέναι.

1361 κἄλλα Cavallin: τἄλλα codd.: πάντα Reiske

PHILOCTETES

O hateful life, why do you still keep me alive above the ground, and have not let me depart to Hades? Alas, what am I to do? How am I to disbelieve the words of this man, who gave me advice for my own good? But am I to give in? Then how can I come into men's sight, unhappy one, after doing this? Who will speak to me? How can you, eyes that have witnessed all that has taken place around me, put up with this, my being with the sons of Atreus, who were my ruin? How can I be with the accursed son of Laertius? It is not the pain of the past that stings me, but the sufferings still in store for me at their hands that I seem to foresee; for when men's mind has once become the mother of evil deeds, it begets yet more evil. And I wonder at this in you; for you ought not to go to Troy yourself, and you ought to keep me away from it. These men insulted you when they robbed you of your father's treasure; after that will you go and fight on their side, and compel me to do the same? Never, my son! But as you swore to do, take me home, and remain yourself in Scyros and allow these miserable men to perish miserably. In this way you will win double gratitude from me, and double gratitude from my father; and you will not through helping evildoers seem to have a nature such as theirs.

---

¹³⁶⁴ οἶδε Ll.-J.: οἵ τε codd.

¹³⁶⁵ inter συλῶντες et εἶτα add. οἳ τὸν ἄθλιον | Αἴανθ᾽ ὅπλων σοῦ πατρὸς ὕστερον δίκῃ Ὀδυσσέως ἔκριναν codd., del. Brunck

ΝΕΟΠΤΟΛΕΜΟΣ

λέγεις μὲν εἰκότ᾽, ἀλλ᾽ ὅμως σε βούλομαι
θεοῖς τε πιστεύσαντα τοῖς τ᾽ ἐμοῖς λόγοις
1375 φίλου μετ᾽ ἀνδρὸς τοῦδε τῆσδ᾽ ἐκπλεῖν χθονός.

ΦΙΛΟΚΤΗΤΗΣ

ἦ πρὸς τὰ Τροίας πεδία καὶ τὸν Ἀτρέως
ἔχθιστον υἱὸν τῷδε δυστήνῳ ποδί;

ΝΕΟΠΤΟΛΕΜΟΣ

πρὸς τοὺς μὲν οὖν σε τήνδε τ᾽ ἔμπυον βάσιν
παύσοντας ἄλγους κἀποσώσοντας νόσου.

ΦΙΛΟΚΤΗΤΗΣ

1380 ὦ δεινὸν αἶνον αἰνέσας, τί φῂς ποτε;

ΝΕΟΠΤΟΛΕΜΟΣ

ἃ σοί τε κἀμοὶ λῷσθ᾽ ὁρῶ τελούμενα.

ΦΙΛΟΚΤΗΤΗΣ

καὶ ταῦτα λέξας οὐ καταισχύνῃ θεούς;

ΝΕΟΠΤΟΛΕΜΟΣ

πῶς γάρ τις αἰσχύνοιτ᾽ ἂν ὠφελῶν φίλους;

ΦΙΛΟΚΤΗΤΗΣ

λέγεις δ᾽ Ἀτρείδαις ὄφελος, ἢ ᾽π᾽ ἐμοὶ τόδε;

ΝΕΟΠΤΟΛΕΜΟΣ

1385 σοί που φίλος γ᾽ ὤν· χὠ λόγος τοιόσδε μου.

ΦΙΛΟΚΤΗΤΗΣ

πῶς, ὅς γε τοῖς ἐχθροῖσί μ᾽ ἐκδοῦναι θέλεις;

1379 κἀποσώσοντας Heath: -σώζοντας codd.
1381 λῷσθ᾽ Dindorf: κάλ᾽ a: καλῶς cett.

PHILOCTETES

NEOPTOLEMUS

What you say is sensible, but none the less I wish you to put your trust in the gods and in my words, and sail from this land together with me your friend.

PHILOCTETES

To the land of Troy and to the hateful son of Atreus with this miserable foot?

NEOPTOLEMUS

No, to those who will rescue you and this suppurating foot from pain and save you from your sickness!

PHILOCTETES

What are you saying, you who give terrible advice?

NEOPTOLEMUS

What I see is best for you and me if it is accomplished.

PHILOCTETES

And when you say that, have you no shame before the gods?

NEOPTOLEMUS

Why should one be ashamed at helping one's friends?

PHILOCTETES

Do you say this to help the sons of Atreus, or is this for me?

NEOPTOLEMUS

For you, of course, since I am your friend; and that is what I say.

PHILOCTETES

How so, if you wish to hand me over to my enemies?

1383 ὠφελῶν φίλους Buttmann: ὠφελούμενος codd.
1386 ἐχθροῖσί μ' Valckenaer: ἐχθροῖσιν codd.

ΝΕΟΠΤΟΛΕΜΟΣ

ὦ τᾶν, διδάσκου μὴ θρασύνεσθαι κακοῖς.

ΦΙΛΟΚΤΗΤΗΣ

ὀλεῖς με, γιγνώσκω σε, τοῖσδε τοῖς λόγοις.

ΝΕΟΠΤΟΛΕΜΟΣ

οὔκουν ἔγωγε· φημὶ δ᾽ οὔ σε μανθάνειν.

ΦΙΛΟΚΤΗΤΗΣ

1390   ἐγὼ οὐκ Ἀτρείδας ἐκβαλόντας οἶδά με;

ΝΕΟΠΤΟΛΕΜΟΣ

ἀλλ᾽ ἐκβαλόντες εἰ πάλιν σώσουσ᾽ ὅρα.

ΦΙΛΟΚΤΗΤΗΣ

οὐδέποθ᾽ ἑκόντα γ᾽ ὥστε τὴν Τροίαν ἰδεῖν.

ΝΕΟΠΤΟΛΕΜΟΣ

τί δῆτ᾽ ἂν ἡμεῖς δρῷμεν, εἰ σέ γ᾽ ἐν λόγοις
πείσειν δυνησόμεσθα μηδὲν ὧν λέγω;
1395   ὥρα ᾽στ᾽ ἐμοὶ μὲν τῶν λόγων λῆξαι, σὲ δὲ
ζῆν, ὥσπερ ἤδη ζῇς, ἄνευ σωτηρίας.

ΦΙΛΟΚΤΗΤΗΣ

ἔα με πάσχειν ταῦθ᾽ ἅπερ παθεῖν με δεῖ·
ἃ δ᾽ ᾔνεσάς μοι δεξιᾶς ἐμῆς θιγών,
πέμπειν πρὸς οἴκους, ταῦτά μοι πρᾶξον, τέκνον,
1400   καὶ μὴ βράδυνε μηδ᾽ ἐπιμνησθῇς ἔτι
Τροίας· ἅλις γάρ μοι τεθρύληται λόγος.

1390 ἐγὼ Hermann: ἔγωγ᾽ codd.
1395 ὥρα ᾽στ᾽ ἐμοὶ Bergk: ὡς ὥρα ἔστ(α)ι ᾽μοι z: ὡς ῥᾷστ᾽ ἐμοὶ
cett.

398

PHILOCTETES

NEOPTOLEMUS
Sir, learn not to be arrogant in your misfortunes!

PHILOCTETES
You will be my ruin, I know it, with this talk!

NEOPTOLEMUS
Not I! But I say you do not understand!

PHILOCTETES
Do I not know it was the sons of Atreus who threw me out?

NEOPTOLEMUS
Well, see if, having thrown you out, they will not now save you!

PHILOCTETES
Never, if I must of my own will look upon Troy!

NEOPTOLEMUS
What am I to do, if nothing I can say will persuade you? It is time for me to stop talking, and for you to go on living, as you are living, without deliverance.

PHILOCTETES
Allow me to suffer what it is my fate to suffer! But do for me what you swore, clasping my right hand, that you would do: escort me home! And do not delay or make further mention of Troy; for me, enough words have been spoken.

1401 τεθρύληται Aristobulus Apostolides, coni. Hermann: τεθρήνηται cett.   λόγος Ka: λόγοις LVrzt: γόοις γρ in LraT

399

SOPHOCLES

ΝΕΟΠΤΟΛΕΜΟΣ

εἰ δοκεῖ, στείχωμεν.

ΦΙΛΟΚΤΗΤΗΣ

ὦ γενναῖον εἰρηκὼς ἔπος.

ΝΕΟΠΤΟΛΕΜΟΣ

ἀντέρειδέ νυν βάσιν σήν.

ΦΙΛΟΚΤΗΤΗΣ

εἰς ὅσον γ᾽ ἐγὼ σθένω.

ΝΕΟΠΤΟΛΕΜΟΣ

αἰτίαν δὲ πῶς Ἀχαιῶν φεύξομαι;

ΦΙΛΟΚΤΗΤΗΣ

μὴ φροντίσῃς.

ΝΕΟΠΤΟΛΕΜΟΣ

1405   τί γάρ, ἐὰν πορθῶσι χώραν τὴν ἐμήν;

ΦΙΛΟΚΤΗΤΗΣ

ἐγὼ παρὼν —

ΝΕΟΠΤΟΛΕΜΟΣ

τίνα προσωφέλησιν ἔρξεις;

ΦΙΛΟΚΤΗΤΗΣ

βέλεσι τοῖς Ἡρακλέοις —

ΝΕΟΠΤΟΛΕΜΟΣ

πῶς λέγεις;

1402-3 del. Dawe
1402 εἰ δοκεῖ del. Porson
1406 Ἡρακλέοις Wackernagel: -είοις codd.: -έους Brunck

400

PHILOCTETES

NEOPTOLEMUS

If you wish, let us depart!

PHILOCTETES

O speaker of a noble word!

NEOPTOLEMUS

Plant your steps firmly after mine!

PHILOCTETES

To the best of my strength!

NEOPTOLEMUS

But how shall I escape blame from the Achaeans?

PHILOCTETES

Do not think about it!

NEOPTOLEMUS

What if they ravage my country?

PHILOCTETES

I will be there—

NEOPTOLEMUS

What will you do to help?

PHILOCTETES

And with the arrows of Heracles—

NEOPTOLEMUS

What do you mean?

ΦΙΛΟΚΤΗΤΗΣ

εἴρξω πελάζειν [σῆς πάτρας].

ΝΕΟΠΤΟΛΕΜΟΣ

[ἀλλ' εἰ < ∪ –
– ∪ > δρᾷς ταῦθ' ὥσπερ αὐδᾷς,] στεῖχε προσκύσας
χθόνα.

ΗΡΑΚΛΗΣ

μήπω γε, πρὶν ἂν τῶν ἡμετέρων
1410 ἀΐῃς μύθων, παῖ Ποίαντος·
φάσκειν δ' αὐδὴν τὴν Ἡρακλέους
ἀκοῇ τε κλύειν λεύσσειν τ' ὄψιν.
τὴν σὴν δ' ἥκω χάριν οὐρανίας
ἕδρας προλιπών,
1415 τὰ Διός τε φράσων βουλεύματά σοι,
κατερητύσων θ' ὁδὸν ἣν στέλλῃ·
σὺ δ' ἐμῶν μύθων ἐπάκουσον.
καὶ πρῶτα μέν σοι τὰς ἐμὰς λέξω τύχας,
ὅσους πονήσας καὶ διεξελθὼν πόνους
1420 ἀθάνατον ἀρετὴν ἔσχον, ὡς πάρεσθ' ὁρᾶν.
καὶ σοί, σάφ' ἴσθι, τοῦτ' ὀφείλεται παθεῖν,
ἐκ τῶν πόνων τῶνδ' εὐκλεᾶ θέσθαι βίον.
ἐλθὼν δὲ σὺν τῷδ' ἀνδρὶ πρὸς τὸ Τρωικὸν
πόλισμα πρῶτον μὲν νόσου παύσῃ λυγρᾶς,
1425 ἀρετῇ τε πρῶτος ἐκκριθεὶς στρατεύματος,
Πάριν μέν, ὃς τῶνδ' αἴτιος κακῶν ἔφυ,

1407-8 σῆς ... αὐδᾷς del. Dindorf   ἀλλ' <εἰ δοκεῖ ταῦτα>
δρᾶν ὅπωσπερ αὐδᾷς Porson

PHILOCTETES

PHILOCTETES
I will prevent them from coming near [your country].

NEOPTOLEMUS
[But if . . . you do this as you say you will] Come, when you have kissed the ground!

HERACLES appears on the top of the stage building.

HERACLES
Not yet, before you have listened to my words, son of Poeas; and say that your ears hear and your eyes view the form of Heracles. For your sake I have come, leaving my home in heaven, to tell you of the plans of Zeus, and to restrain you from the voyage on which you are embarking. Do you listen to my words!

And first I will tell you of my fortunes, of how many labours I endured to go through to win eternal glory, as you can see. For you too, know it for sure, destiny is the same, after these sufferings to make your life glorious. You shall go with this man to the city of Troy and first be cured of your grim sickness. And you shall be judged first of the army in valour, depriving of life Paris, who was the cause of

τόξοισι τοῖς ἐμοῖσι νοσφιεῖς βίου,
πέρσεις τε Τροίαν, σκῦλά τ᾽ ἐς μέλαθρα σὰ
πέμψεις, ἀριστεῖ᾽ ἐκλαβὼν στρατεύματος,
1430 Ποίαντι πατρὶ πρὸς πάτρας Οἴτης πλάκα.
ἃ δ᾽ ἂν λάβῃς σὺ σκῦλα τοῦδε τοῦ στρατοῦ,
τόξων ἐμῶν μνημεῖα πρὸς πυρὰν ἐμὴν
κόμιζε. καὶ σοὶ ταῦτ᾽, Ἀχιλλέως τέκνον,
παρήνεσ᾽· οὔτε γὰρ σὺ τοῦδ᾽ ἄτερ σθένεις
1435 ἑλεῖν τὸ Τροίας πεδίον οὔθ᾽ οὗτος σέθεν·
ἀλλ᾽ ὡς λέοντε συννόμω φυλάσσετον
οὗτος σὲ καὶ σὺ τόνδ᾽. ἐγὼ δ᾽ Ἀσκληπιὸν
παυστῆρα πέμψω σῆς νόσου πρὸς Ἴλιον.
τὸ δεύτερον γὰρ τοῖς ἐμοῖς αὐτὴν χρεὼν
1440 τόξοις ἁλῶναι. τοῦτο δ᾽ ἐννόειθ᾽, ὅταν
πορθῆτε γαῖαν, εὐσεβεῖν τὰ πρὸς θεούς·
ὡς τἆλλα πάντα δεύτερ᾽ ἡγεῖται πατὴρ
Ζεύς. οὐ γὰρ ηὑσέβεια συνθνήσκει βροτοῖς·
κἂν ζῶσι κἂν θάνωσιν, οὐκ ἀπόλλυται.

ΦΙΛΟΚΤΗΤΗΣ

1445 ὦ φθέγμα ποθεινὸν ἐμοὶ πέμψας,
χρόνιός τε φανείς,
οὐκ ἀπιθήσω τοῖς σοῖς μύθοις.

ΝΕΟΠΤΟΛΕΜΟΣ

κἀγὼ γνώμην ταύτῃ τίθεμαι.

1440 ἐννόειθ᾽ Elmsley: ἐννοεῖς VTa: ἐννοεῖσθ᾽ cett.
1443 οὐ Gataker: ἡ codd.   ηὑσέβεια Dawes: εὐ- codd.
1448 γνώμην Lambinus: -ῃ codd.

404

these troubles, and taking Troy, and bringing the spoils to your abode, receiving the greatest prize of the army, for your father Poeas to the topmost plain of Oeta, your native place. The spoils you receive from this expedition you must bring to my pyre as a memorial of my bow. And to you I give the same counsel, son of Achilles; for you have not the strength to conquer the land of Troy without him, neither has he without you; but guard each other like two companion lions! And I will send Asclepius to Ilium to put an end to your disease. For it is fated to be taken once again by the aid of this bow. But remember when you conquer the land to show reverence to the gods; for all things come after this in the mind of Zeus my father. For reverence for the gods does not die along with mortals; whether they live or die, it never perishes.

PHILOCTETES

O you who have brought to me a voice I longed for, you who have appeared at last, I will not disobey your orders!

NEOPTOLEMUS

I too make the same decision!

ΗΡΑΚΛΗΣ

μή νυν χρόνιοι μέλλετε πράσσειν.
1450 ὅδ᾽ ἐπείγει γὰρ
καιρὸς καὶ πλοῦς κατὰ πρύμναν.

ΦΙΛΟΚΤΗΤΗΣ

φέρε νῦν στείχων χώραν καλέσω.
χαῖρ᾽, ὦ μέλαθρον ξύμφρουρον ἐμοί,
Νύμφαι τ᾽ ἔνυδροι λειμωνιάδες,
1455 καὶ κτύπος ἄρσην πόντου προβολῆς,
οὗ πολλάκι δὴ τοὐμὸν ἐτέγχθη
κρᾶτ᾽ ἐνδόμυχον πληγῇσι νότου,
πολλὰ δὲ φωνῆς τῆς ἡμετέρας
Ἑρμαῖον ὄρος παρέπεμψεν ἐμοὶ
1460 στόνον ἀντίτυπον χειμαζομένῳ.
νῦν δ᾽, ὦ κρῆναι Λύκιόν τε ποτόν,
λείπομεν ὑμᾶς, λείπομεν ἤδη,
δόξης οὔ ποτε τῆσδ᾽ ἐπιβάντες.
χαῖρ᾽, ὦ Λήμνου πέδον ἀμφίαλον,
1465 καί μ᾽ εὐπλοίᾳ πέμψον ἀμέμπτως,
ἔνθ᾽ ἡ μεγάλη Μοῖρα κομίζει,
γνώμη τε φίλων χὠ πανδαμάτωρ
δαίμων, ὃς ταῦτ᾽ ἐπέκρανεν.

ΧΟΡΟΣ

χωρῶμεν δὴ πάντες ἀολλεῖς,
1470 Νύμφαις ἁλίαισιν ἐπευξάμενοι
νόστου σωτῆρας ἱκέσθαι.

PHILOCTETES

HERACLES

Then do not delay action for long! For the moment for sailing is hurrying you on, with the wind at the stern.

PHILOCTETES

Come now, as I depart I will call upon the land! Farewell, home that shared my watches, and water nymphs of the meadows, and strong sound of sea beating on the promontory, where often my head was drenched inside my cave by the battering of the wind, and often the mountain of Hermes brought back to me a groan answering my voice as the storm assailed me! But now, springs and Lycian well, we are leaving you, we are leaving now, though we had never dared to trust this hope. Farewell, seagirt land of Lemnos, and waft me on a peaceful voyage that I cannot complain of, to where mighty Fate is taking me, and the will of my friends and the all-subduing god who has decreed this!

CHORUS

Let us depart all together, with a prayer to the sea nymphs that they may come to bring us safely home.

1450-51 ὅδ᾽ ἐπείγει γάρ huc traiecit Burges: post πλοῦς habent codd.

1455 προβολῆς Hermann: προβολὴς Zo: προβλής cett.

OEDIPUS AT COLONUS

ΤΑ ΤΟΥ ΔΡΑΜΑΤΟΣ ΠΡΟΣΩΠΑ

Οἰδίπους
Ἀντιγόνη
Ξένος
Χορὸς Ἀττικῶν γερόντων
Ἰσμήνη
Θησεύς
Κρέων
Πολυνείκης
Ἄγγελος

Oedipus
Antigone
Peasant
Chorus of Elders of Colonus
Ismene
Theseus
Creon
Polynices
Messenger

Scene: The deme of Colonus, in the country, near Athens.

ΟΙΔΙΠΟΥΣ ΕΠΙ ΚΟΛΩΝΩΙ

ΟΙΔΙΠΟΥΣ

Τέκνον τυφλοῦ γέροντος Ἀντιγόνη, τίνας
χώρους ἀφίγμεθ᾽ ἢ τίνων ἀνδρῶν πόλιν;
τίς τὸν πλανήτην Οἰδίπουν καθ᾽ ἡμέραν
τὴν νῦν σπανιστοῖς δέξεται δωρήμασιν,
5   σμικρὸν μὲν ἐξαιτοῦντα, τοῦ σμικροῦ δ᾽ ἔτι
μεῖον φέροντα, καὶ τόδ᾽ ἐξαρκοῦν ἐμοί;
στέργειν γὰρ αἱ πάθαι με χὠ χρόνος ξυνὼν
μακρὸς διδάσκει καὶ τὸ γενναῖον τρίτον.
ἀλλ᾽, ὦ τέκνον, θάκησιν εἴ τινα βλέπεις
10   ἢ πρὸς βεβήλοις ἢ πρὸς ἄλσεσιν θεῶν,
στῆσόν με κἀξίδρυσον, ὡς πυθώμεθα
ὅπου ποτ᾽ ἐσμέν· μανθάνειν γὰρ ἥκομεν
ξένοι πρὸς ἀστῶν, ἃν δ᾽ ἀκούσωμεν τελεῖν.

⁹ θάκησιν Zacharias Callierges, coni. Seidler: θάκοισιν cett.
¹⁰ prius ἢ πρὸς] χώροις Hartung

OEDIPUS AT COLONUS

The scene is a rural setting, near the sacred grove of the Eumenides at Colonus, northwest of Athens. Somewhere in the middle of the stage a rock, which can be used as a seat, is visible; the grove is bounded by a low ridge of rock, and one could sit upon its edge. On the stage can be seen the statue of the hero Colonus. Enter OEDIPUS *and* ANTIGONE.

OEDIPUS

Child of a blind old man, Antigone, to what regions, or to what men's city have we come? Who on this day shall receive Oedipus the wanderer with scanty gifts? I ask for little, and I get even less, but for me that is sufficient; for my sufferings, and the time that has long been my companion, and thirdly my nobility teach me to be content with it. But come, my child, if you see any seat, either near ground unconsecrated or near the precincts of the gods, stop me and let me sit there, so that we may find out where we are; for we have come as strangers, and must learn from the citizens and do as they tell us.

---

[11] πυθώμεθα Brunck: -οίμεθα codd.

ΑΝΤΙΓΟΝΗ

πάτερ ταλαίπωρ' Οἰδίπους, πύργοι μὲν οἳ
15 πόλιν στέφουσιν, ὡς ἀπ' ὀμμάτων, πρόσω·
χῶρος δ' ὅδ' ἱερός, ὡς σάφ' εἰκάσαι, βρύων
δάφνης, ἐλαίας, ἀμπέλου· πυκνόπτεροι δ'
εἴσω κατ' αὐτὸν εὐστομοῦσ' ἀηδόνες·
οὗ κῶλα κάμψον τοῦδ' ἐπ' ἀξέστου πέτρου·
20 μακρὰν γὰρ ὡς γέροντι προὐστάλης ὁδόν.

ΟΙΔΙΠΟΥΣ

κάθιζέ νύν με καὶ φύλασσε τὸν τυφλόν.

ΑΝΤΙΓΟΝΗ

χρόνου μὲν οὕνεκ' οὐ μαθεῖν με δεῖ τόδε.

ΟΙΔΙΠΟΥΣ

ἔχεις διδάξαι δή μ' ὅποι καθέσταμεν ;

ΑΝΤΙΓΟΝΗ

τὰς γοῦν Ἀθήνας οἶδα, τὸν δὲ χῶρον οὔ.

ΟΙΔΙΠΟΥΣ

25 πᾶς γάρ τις ηὔδα τοῦτό γ' ἡμὶν ἐμπόρων.

ΑΝΤΙΓΟΝΗ

ἀλλ' ὅστις ὁ τόπος ἦ μάθω μολοῦσά ποι ;

ΟΙΔΙΠΟΥΣ

ναί, τέκνον, εἴπερ ἐστί γ' ἐξοικήσιμος.

ΑΝΤΙΓΟΝΗ

ἀλλ' ἐστὶ μὴν οἰκητός· οἴομαι δὲ δεῖν
οὐδέν· πέλας γὰρ ἄνδρα τόνδε νῷν ὁρῶ.

ANTIGONE

Unhappy father, Oedipus, the walls that surround the city
look to be far off; and this place is sacred, one can easily
guess, with the bay, the olive, and the vine growing every-
where; and inside it many feathered nightingales make
their music. Relax your limbs here on this unhewn rock;
for you have gone a long way for an aged man.

OEDIPUS

Then seat me here and guard me, blind as I am!

ANTIGONE

After so long, you do not need to tell me that!

She seats OEDIPUS *upon the rock in the middle of the
stage.*

OEDIPUS

Can you explain to me where it is we are?

ANTIGONE

I know that it is Athens, but I do not know what place.

OEDIPUS

Yes, all the people on the road told us that much.

ANTIGONE

But shall I go and discover what place it is?

OEDIPUS

Yes, my child, if indeed it can be lived in.

ANTIGONE

Why, it is lived in! But I think there is no need to go, for I
see a man here near us.

---

[15] στέφουσιν Wakefield: στέγουσιν codd.
[25] τοῦτό γ' Aristobulus Apostolides: τοῦτον cett.

ΟΙΔΙΠΟΥΣ

30 ἢ δεῦρο προστείχοντα κἀξωρμημένον;

ΑΝΤΙΓΟΝΗ

καὶ δὴ μὲν οὖν παρόντα· χὠ τι σοι λέγειν
εὔκαιρόν ἐστιν, ἔννεφ᾽, ὡς ἀνὴρ ὅδε.

ΟΙΔΙΠΟΥΣ

ὦ ξεῖν᾽, ἀκούων τῆσδε τῆς ὑπέρ τ᾽ ἐμοῦ
αὐτῆς θ᾽ ὁρώσης οὕνεχ᾽ ἡμὶν αἴσιος
35 σκοπὸς προσήκεις ὧν ἀδηλοῦμεν φράσαι —

ΞΕΝΟΣ

πρὶν νῦν τὰ πλείον᾽ ἱστορεῖν, ἐκ τῆσδ᾽ ἕδρας
ἔξελθ᾽· ἔχεις γὰρ χῶρον οὐχ ἁγνὸν πατεῖν.

ΟΙΔΙΠΟΥΣ

τίς δ᾽ ἔσθ᾽ ὁ χῶρος; τοῦ θεῶν νομίζεται;

ΞΕΝΟΣ

ἄθικτος οὐδ᾽ οἰκητός. αἱ γὰρ ἔμφοβοι
40 θεαί σφ᾽ ἔχουσι, Γῆς τε καὶ Σκότου κόραι.

ΟΙΔΙΠΟΥΣ

τίνων τὸ σεμνὸν ὄνομ᾽ ἂν εὐξαίμην κλυών;

ΞΕΝΟΣ

τὰς πάνθ᾽ ὁρώσας Εὐμενίδας ὅ γ᾽ ἐνθάδ᾽ ἂν
εἴποι λεώς νιν· ἄλλα δ᾽ ἀλλαχοῦ καλά.

30 κἀξωρμημένον J. F. Davies: κἀξορμώμενον codd.
35 ὧν Elmsley: τῶν codd.
42 ἂν Vauvilliers: ὧν codd.

OEDIPUS

Is he advancing in this direction?

Enter PEASANT.

ANTIGONE

No, he is already here! Say whatever the moment calls for, since the man is present!

OEDIPUS

Stranger, hearing from this girl, who sees for me as well as for herself, that you have come to inquire at the right moment to resolve our doubts . . .

PEASANT

Before you ask me any more questions, leave this seat! The ground you occupy cannot be trodden without pollution!

OEDIPUS

But what is the place? To which of the gods is it thought to belong?

PEASANT

It is inviolable, and not inhabited; for it belongs to the dread goddesses, daughters of Earth and Darkness.

OEDIPUS

Who are they to whom I shall pray when I have heard their awful name?

PEASANT

The people here call them the all-seeing Eumenides; but different names are right in different places.[a]

---

[a] The Erinyes were also called the Eumenides (= The Kindly Ones) and the Semnai Theai (= The Dread Goddesses).

ΟΙΔΙΠΟΥΣ

ἀλλ᾽ ἵλεῳ μὲν τὸν ἱκέτην δεξαίατο·
45 ὡς οὐχ ἕδρας γε τῆσδ᾽ ἂν ἐξέλθοιμ᾽ ἔτι.

ΞΕΝΟΣ

τί δ᾽ ἐστὶ τοῦτο;

ΟΙΔΙΠΟΥΣ

ξυμφορᾶς ξύνθημ᾽ ἐμῆς.

ΞΕΝΟΣ

ἀλλ᾽ οὐδ᾽ ἐμοί τοι τοὐξανιστάναι πόλεως
δίχ᾽ ἐστὶ θάρσος, πρίν γ᾽ ἂν ἐνδείξω τί δρᾷς.

ΟΙΔΙΠΟΥΣ

πρός νυν θεῶν, ὦ ξεῖνε, μή μ᾽ ἀτιμάσῃς,
50 τοιόνδ᾽ ἀλήτην, ὧν σε προστρέπω φράσαι.

ΞΕΝΟΣ

σήμαινε, κοὐκ ἄτιμος ἔκ γ᾽ ἐμοῦ φανῇ.

ΟΙΔΙΠΟΥΣ

τίς ἔσθ᾽ ὁ χῶρος δῆτ᾽ ἐν ᾧ βεβήκαμεν;

ΞΕΝΟΣ

ὅσ᾽ οἶδα κἀγὼ πάντ᾽ ἐπιστήσῃ κλυών.
χῶρος μὲν ἱερὸς πᾶς ὅδ᾽ ἔστ᾽· ἔχει δέ νιν
55 σεμνὸς Ποσειδῶν· ἐν δ᾽ ὁ πυρφόρος θεὸς
Τιτὰν Προμηθεύς· ὃν δ᾽ ἐπιστείβεις τόπον
χθονὸς καλεῖται τῆσδε χαλκόπους ὁδός,

---

44 τὸν ed. Londiniensis a. 1747: τόνδ᾽ codd.
45 ὡς Vauvilliers: ὥστ᾽ codd.   γε Musgrave: γῆς codd.
47 ἐμοί τοι Seidler: ἐμόν τοι lR: μέντοι a

418

OEDIPUS

May they receive a suppliant graciously, for I shall never
again leave this seat!

PEASANT

But what does this mean?

OEDIPUS

It is the token of my destiny!

PEASANT

Well, I cannot even dare to turn you out without orders
from the city, before I report what you are doing.

OEDIPUS

I pray you, stranger, do not refuse me, though I am such a
vagrant as you see, the knowledge which I beg of you!

PEASANT

Tell me what it is, and no refusal shall come from me!

OEDIPUS

What is this place which we have entered?

PEASANT

You shall hear and learn all that I know! All of this place is
sacred, and it belongs to the dread Poseidon; and the fire-
bearing god, the Titan Prometheus, too is here; and the
spot where you are treading is called the Brazen-footed

ἔρεισμ' Ἀθηνῶν· οἱ δὲ πλησίοι γύαι
τόνδ' ἱππότην Κολωνὸν εὔχονται σφίσιν
60 ἀρχηγὸν εἶναι, καὶ φέρουσι τοὔνομα
τὸ τοῦδε κοινὸν πάντες ὠνομασμένοι.
τοιαῦτά σοι ταῦτ' ἐστίν, ὦ ξέν', οὐ λόγοις
τιμώμεν', ἀλλὰ τῇ ξυνουσίᾳ πλέον.

ΟΙΔΙΠΟΥΣ

ἦ γάρ τινες ναίουσι τούσδε τοὺς τόπους;

ΞΕΝΟΣ

65 καὶ κάρτα, τοῦδε τοῦ θεοῦ γ' ἐπώνυμοι.

ΟΙΔΙΠΟΥΣ

ἄρχει τις αὐτῶν, ἢ 'πὶ τῷ πλήθει λόγος;

ΞΕΝΟΣ

ἐκ τοῦ κατ' ἄστυ βασιλέως τάδ' ἄρχεται.

ΟΙΔΙΠΟΥΣ

οὗτος δὲ τίς λόγῳ τε καὶ σθένει κρατεῖ;

ΞΕΝΟΣ

Θησεὺς καλεῖται, τοῦ πρὶν Αἰγέως τόκος.

ΟΙΔΙΠΟΥΣ

70 ἆρ' ἄν τις αὐτῷ πομπὸς ἐξ ὑμῶν μόλοι;

ΞΕΝΟΣ

ὡς πρὸς τί; λέξων ἢ καταρτύσων τί σοι;

ΟΙΔΙΠΟΥΣ

ὡς ἂν προσαρκῶν σμικρὰ κερδάνῃ μέγα.

---

[71] τί σοι Ll.-J.: μόλοι lzt

420

Threshold of this land, the bulwark of Athens; and the neighbouring acres boast that their founder is the horseman Colonus here,[a] whose name is borne by their community. That is the story, stranger; it has no honour in legend, but rather in the minds of us who live with it.

OEDIPUS

So are there people that live in these places?

PEASANT

Indeed there are, those that take their name from this god!

OEDIPUS

Have they a ruler, or does the people have the say?

PEASANT

This place is ruled by the king in the city.

OEDIPUS

And who has power by his speech and by his strength?

PEASANT

He is called Theseus, son of the old king Aegeus.

OEDIPUS

Could an envoy go from you to him?

PEASANT

For what purpose? With a message, or to arrange something for you?

OEDIPUS

So that by doing a small service he may make a great gain.

[a] He points to the statue.

SOPHOCLES

ΞΕΝΟΣ

καὶ τίς πρὸς ἀνδρὸς μὴ βλέποντος ἄρκεσις;

ΟΙΔΙΠΟΥΣ

ὅσ᾽ ἂν λέγωμεν πάνθ᾽ ὁρῶντα λέξομεν.

ΞΕΝΟΣ

75 οἶσθ᾽, ὦ ξέν᾽, ὡς νῦν μὴ σφαλῇς; ἐπείπερ εἶ
γενναῖος, ὡς ἰδόντι, πλὴν τοῦ δαίμονος,
αὐτοῦ μέν᾽, οὗπερ κἀφάνης, ἕως ἐγὼ
τοῖς ἐνθάδ᾽ αὐτοῦ μὴ κατ᾽ ἄστυ δημόταις
λέξω τάδ᾽ ἐλθών. οἵδε γὰρ κρινοῦσί σοι
80 εἰ χρή σε μίμνειν, ἢ πορεύεσθαι πάλιν.

ΟΙΔΙΠΟΥΣ

ὦ τέκνον, ἦ βέβηκεν ἡμὶν ὁ ξένος;

ΑΝΤΙΓΟΝΗ

βέβηκεν, ὥστε πᾶν ἐν ἡσύχῳ, πάτερ,
ἔξεστι φωνεῖν, ὡς ἐμοῦ μόνης πέλας.

ΟΙΔΙΠΟΥΣ

ὦ πότνιαι δεινῶπες, εὗτε νῦν ἕδρας
85 πρώτων ἐφ᾽ ὑμῶν τῆσδε γῆς ἔκαμψ᾽ ἐγώ,
Φοίβῳ τε κἀμοὶ μὴ γένησθ᾽ ἀγνώμονες,
ὅς μοι, τὰ πόλλ᾽ ἐκεῖν᾽ ὅτ᾽ ἐξέχρη κακά,
ταύτην ἔλεξε παῦλαν ἐν χρόνῳ μακρῷ,
ἐλθόντι χώραν τερμίαν, ὅπου θεῶν
90 σεμνῶν ἕδραν λάβοιμι καὶ ξενόστασιν,
ἐνταῦθα κάμψειν τὸν ταλαίπωρον βίον,
κέρδη μὲν οἰκήσαντα τοῖς δεδεγμένοις,
ἄτην δὲ τοῖς πέμψασιν, οἵ μ᾽ ἀπήλασαν·

PEASANT

And what help can be given by a man who cannot see?

OEDIPUS

All the words I utter shall have sight!

PEASANT

You know, stranger, so that you do not come to harm—for you are noble, judging by your looks, leaving aside your fortune—stay here, in the place where you first appeared, till I go and speak of this to the men of the deme here, not those in the city; for they will decide whether you are to stay here, or must set off again.

Exit PEASANT.

OEDIPUS

My child, has the stranger left?

ANTIGONE

He has, so that you can say everything in peace, father, since I alone am near.

OEDIPUS

(*in prayer to the Eumenides*) Ladies of dread aspect, since the first place I have drawn near to in this country is your seat, show sympathy for Phoebus and for me! For he told me, when he predicted all that evil, that this should be my respite after long years, when I came to the land that was my final bourne, where I should find a seat of the dread goddesses and a shelter, I should there reach the goal of my long-suffering life, bringing advantage by my settlement to those who had received me, and ruin to those who

---

⁷⁸ τοῖς Turnebus: τοῖσδ' codd.

σημεῖα δ᾽ ἥξειν τῶνδέ μοι παρηγγύα,
95 ἢ σεισμόν, ἢ βροντήν τιν᾽, ἢ Διὸς σέλας.
ἔγνωκα μέν νυν ὥς με τήνδε τὴν ὁδὸν
οὐκ ἔσθ᾽ ὅπως οὐ πιστὸν ἐξ ὑμῶν πτερὸν
ἐξήγαγ᾽ ἐς τόδ᾽ ἄλσος. οὐ γὰρ ἄν ποτε
πρώταισιν ὑμῖν ἀντέκυρσ᾽ ὁδοιπορῶν,
100 νήφων ἀοίνοις, κἀπὶ σεμνὸν ἑζόμην
βάθρον τόδ᾽ ἀσκέπαρνον. ἀλλά μοι, θεαί,
βίου κατ᾽ ὀμφὰς τὰς Ἀπόλλωνος δότε
πέρασιν ἤδη καὶ καταστροφήν τινα,
εἰ μὴ δοκῶ τι μειόνως ἔχειν, ἀεὶ
105 μόχθοις λατρεύων τοῖς ὑπερτάτοις βροτῶν.
ἴτ᾽, ὦ γλυκεῖαι παῖδες ἀρχαίου Σκότου,
ἴτ᾽, ὦ μεγίστης Παλλάδος καλούμεναι
πασῶν Ἀθῆναι τιμιωτάτη πόλις,
οἰκτίρατ᾽ ἀνδρὸς Οἰδίπου τόδ᾽ ἄθλιον
110 εἴδωλον· οὐ γὰρ δὴ τό γ᾽ ἀρχαῖον δέμας.

ΑΝΤΙΓΟΝΗ

σίγα. πορεύονται γὰρ οἵδε δή τινες
χρόνῳ παλαιοί, σῆς ἕδρας ἐπίσκοποι.

ΟΙΔΙΠΟΥΣ

σιγήσομαί τε καὶ σύ μ᾽ ἐξ ὁδοῦ 'κποδὼν
κρύψον κατ᾽ ἄλσος, τῶνδ᾽ ἕως ἂν ἐκμάθω
115 τίνας λόγους ἐροῦσιν. ἐν γὰρ τῷ μαθεῖν
ἔνεστιν ηὐλάβεια τῶν ποιουμένων.

ΧΟΡΟΣ

ὅρα. τίς ἄρ᾽ ἦν; ποῦ ναίει;   στρ. α´
ποῦ κυρεῖ ἐκτόπιος συθεὶς ὁ πάντων,

had sent me, who had driven me away. And he promised
that signs of this would come, an earthquake or thunder or
the lightning of Zeus. I knew that surely it was a
trustworthy omen sent by you that brought me to this
grove, for never otherwise would you have been the first
that I encountered in my travel, coming sober to you who
drink no wine, nor would I have taken my seat upon this
venerable unhewn pedestal. Come, goddesses, in accor-
dance with Apollo's sacred word, grant to me a passage and
a conclusion of my life, if I do not seem too low, being ever
a slave to the worst sufferings of any man! Come, delight-
ful daughters of ancient Darkness! Come, Athens, called
the city of greatest Pallas, city most honoured of them all!
Take pity on this miserable ghost of the man Oedipus, for
this is not the form that once was mine!

ANTIGONE

Be silent! For here come some men advanced in age, to
spy out your seat!

OEDIPUS

I will be silent, and do you hide me in the grove, away from
the road, until I know what words they will utter; for if we
are to act cautiously we must find out!

Enter the CHORUS of old men of Colonus.

CHORUS

Look! Who was he, then? Where is he? Where has he
rushed to out of the way, the man most impudent of all, of

---

[113] ἐξ ὁδοῦ 'κποδὼν Tournier: ἐξ ὁδοῦ πόδα codd.

120 ὁ πάντων ἀκορέστατος·
προσδέρκου, προσφθέγγου,
προσπεύθου πανταχᾷ. πλανάτας,
πλανάτας τις ὁ πρέσβυς, οὐδ᾽

125 ἔγχωρος· προσέβα γὰρ οὐκ
ἄν ποτ᾽ ἀστιβὲς ἄλσος ἐς
τᾶνδ᾽ ἀμαιμακετᾶν κορᾶν,
ἇς τρέμομεν λέγειν,

130 καὶ παραμειβόμεσθ᾽ ἀδέρκτως,
ἀφώνως, ἀλόγως τὸ τᾶς
εὐφήμου στόμα φροντίδος
ἱέντες· τὰ δὲ νῦν τιν᾽ ἥκειν
λόγος οὐδὲν ἄζονθ᾽,

135 ὃν ἐγὼ λεύσσων περὶ πᾶν οὔπω
δύναμαι τέμενος
γνῶναι ποῦ μοί ποτε ναίει.

ΟΙΔΙΠΟΥΣ

ὅδ᾽ ἐκεῖνος ἐγώ· φωνῇ γὰρ ὁρῶ,
τὸ φατιζόμενον.

ΧΟΡΟΣ

140 ἰὼ ἰώ,
δεινὸς μὲν ὁρᾶν, δεινὸς δὲ κλύειν.

ΟΙΔΙΠΟΥΣ

μή μ᾽, ἱκετεύω, προσίδητ᾽ ἄνομον.

ΧΟΡΟΣ

Ζεῦ ἀλεξῆτορ, τίς ποθ᾽ ὁ πρέσβυς;

all? Look, speak out, enquire everywhere! The old man is a wanderer, a wanderer, not a native! Else he would never have come to the inviolable grove of these awful maidens, whom we are afraid to name, and whom we pass without looking, without sound, without speech, moving our lips in respectful silence. But now they say that one has come who shows no reverence; but as I look about the whole precinct I cannot yet see where he may be!

CHORUS

OEDIPUS

I who am here am he; for I see with my voice, as they say!

CHORUS

Ah, ah! He is terrible to see and terrible to hear!

OEDIPUS

Do not look on me, I beg you, as a lawless one!

CHORUS

Zeus our protector, who is the old man?

---

121 ante προσδέρκου add. λεύσ(σ)ατ᾽ (λεύσσετ᾽ zt) codd., del. Dawe

125 ἔγχωρος Bothe: -ιος codd.

ΟΙΔΙΠΟΥΣ

οὐ πάνυ μοίρας εὐδαιμονίσαι
145 πρώτης, ὦ τῆσδ᾽ ἔφοροι χώρας.
δηλῶ δ᾽· οὐ γὰρ ἂν ὧδ᾽ ἀλλοτρίοις
ὄμμασιν εἷρπον
κἀπὶ σμικροῖς μέγας ὥρμουν.

ΧΟΡΟΣ

150 ἐή· ἀλαῶν ὀμμάτων   ἀντ. α´
ἆρα καὶ ἦσθα φυτάλμιος; δυσαίων
μακραίων θ᾽, ὅσ᾽ ἐπεικάσαι.
ἀλλ᾽ οὐ μὰν ἔν γ᾽ ἐμοὶ
155 προσθήσεις τάσδ᾽ ἀράς. περᾷς γάρ,
περᾷς· ἀλλ᾽ ἵνα τῷδ᾽ ἐν ἀ-
φθέγκτῳ μὴ προπέσῃς νάπει
ποιάεντι, κάθυδρος οὗ
κρατὴρ μειλιχίων ποτῶν
160 ῥεύματι συντρέχει,
τῶν, ξένε πάμμορ᾽ — εὖ φύλαξαι —
μετάσταθ᾽, ἀπόβαθι. πολ-
λὰ κέλευθος ἐρατύοι·
165 κλύεις, ὦ πολύμοχθ᾽ ἀλᾶτα;
λόγον εἴ τιν᾽ οἴσεις
πρὸς ἐμὰν λέσχαν, ἀβάτων ἀποβάς,
ἵνα πᾶσι νόμος
φώνει· πρόσθεν δ᾽ ἀπερύκου.

ΟΙΔΙΠΟΥΣ

170 θύγατερ, ποῖ τις φροντίδος ἔλθῃ;

428

OEDIPUS

Not one with a fortune you can envy him, guardians of this
land! And I will prove it; for else I should not be moving
with another's eyes and be anchored, great as I am, upon a
small person.

CHORUS

Ah! Were you even blind from birth? Yours has been a sad
life and a long one, it would seem! But you shall not bring
down these curses upon me! For you go too far, too far!
But so that you do not burst into this grassy glade, where
no word must be spoken, where the bowl of water runs
together with the stream of liquid honey ... from there,
hapless stranger—take care! —stand away, depart! Let a
great distance separate you! Do you hear me, long-
suffering wanderer? If you have any word to say in con-
verse with me, stand away from the forbidden ground and
speak where it is lawful for all! But till then, refrain!

OEDIPUS

Daughter, which way should our thoughts go?

---

152 θ᾽, ὅσ᾽ Bothe: θ᾽ ὡς r: τέ θ᾽ ὡς La
157 προπέσῃς Hermann: προσπέσῃς codd.
164 ἐρατύοι Musgrave: -ει codd.

ΑΝΤΙΓΟΝΗ

ὦ πάτερ, ἀστοῖς ἴσα χρὴ μελετᾶν,
εἴκοντας ἃ δεῖ κἀκούοντας.

ΟΙΔΙΠΟΥΣ

πρόσθιγέ νύν μου.

ΑΝΤΙΓΟΝΗ

ψαύω καὶ δή.

ΟΙΔΙΠΟΥΣ

ὦ ξεῖνοι, μὴ δῆτ' ἀδικηθῶ,
175   σοὶ πιστεύσας, μεταναστάς.

ΧΟΡΟΣ

οὔ τοι μήποτέ σ' ἐκ τῶνδ' ἑδράνων, ὦ γέρον,
    ἄκοντά τις ἄξει.   στρ. β'

ΟΙΔΙΠΟΥΣ

ἔτ' οὖν;

ΧΟΡΟΣ

    ἔτι βαῖνε πόρσω.

ΟΙΔΙΠΟΥΣ

180   ἔτι;

ΧΟΡΟΣ

    προβίβαζε, κούρα,
πόρσω· σὺ γὰρ ἀίεις.

ΑΝΤΙΓΟΝΗ

ἕπεο μάν, ἕπε' ὧδ' ἀμαυ-
ρῷ κώλῳ, πάτερ, ᾷ σ' ἄγω.

ANTIGONE

Father, we should share the concerns of the citizens, giving way and obeying when we must.

OEDIPUS

Take hold of me, then!

ANTIGONE

See, I am touching you!

OEDIPUS

Strangers, let me suffer no wrong, if I move, having trust in you!

CHORUS

Never shall anyone take you from this place of rest, old man, against your will!

OEDIPUS

Further, then?

CHORUS

Come further forward!

OEDIPUS

Further?

CHORUS

Lead him forward, maiden, for you can understand!

ANTIGONE

Follow, follow me this way with your unseeing steps, father, where I lead you!

---

[172] κἀκούοντας Musgrave: κοὐκ ἀκούοντας Lra
[175] ante μεταναστάς add. καὶ codd., del. Hermann
[178] post ἔτ᾽ οὖν; add. ἔτι προβῶ; codd., del. Bothe

<ΟΙΔΙΠΟΥΣ

— — — —

ΑΝΤΙΓΟΝΗ

o o – ◡◡ – ◡ –
o o – ◡◡ – ◡ –

ΟΙΔΙΠΟΥΣ

o o – ◡◡ – – >

ΧΟΡΟΣ

τόλμα ξεῖνος ἐπὶ ξένας,
185   ὦ τλάμων, ὅ τι καὶ πόλις
τέτροφεν ἄφιλον ἀποστυγεῖν
καὶ τὸ φίλον σέβεσθαι.

ΟΙΔΙΠΟΥΣ

ἄγε νυν σύ με, παῖς,
ἵν’ ἂν εὐσεβίας ἐπιβαίνοντες
190   τὸ μὲν εἴποιμεν, τὸ δ’ ἀκούσαιμεν,
καὶ μὴ χρείᾳ πολεμῶμεν.

ΧΟΡΟΣ

αὐτοῦ· μηκέτι τοῦδ’ αὐτοπέτρου βήματος ἔξω
πόδα κλίνῃς.   ἀντ. β΄

ΟΙΔΙΠΟΥΣ

οὕτως;

ΧΟΡΟΣ

ἅλις, ὡς ἀκούεις.

ΟΙΔΙΠΟΥΣ

195   ἦ ἐσθῶ;

One line of OEDIPUS, two lines of ANTIGONE, and again one line of OEDIPUS are lost.

CHORUS

You are a stranger, poor man, in a strange land; bring yourself to loathe what the city is accustomed to dislike and to respect what it holds dear!

OEDIPUS

Lead me, then, daughter, so that we may tread where piety dictates, speaking and listening to others, and may not be at war with necessity!

ANTIGONE slowly leads OEDIPUS to the ledge of rock that bounds the grove.

CHORUS

Here! Do not incline your steps beyond this ledge of native rock!

OEDIPUS

Like this?

CHORUS

Enough, as I tell you!

OEDIPUS

Shall I sit down?

---

[183] post hunc v. lacunam statuit Hermann, ante 182 et post 183 Jebb
[188] παῖς Musgrave: παῖ codd.
[192] αὐτοπέτρου Musgrave: ἀντιπέτρου codd.

433

ΧΟΡΟΣ

λέχριός γ' ἐπ' ἄκρου
λάου βραχὺς ὀκλάσας.

ΑΝΤΙΓΟΝΗ

πάτερ, ἐμὸν τόδ'· ἐν ἡσυχαί-
199 ᾳ βάσει βάσιν ἅρμοσαι —

ΟΙΔΙΠΟΥΣ

198 ἰώ μοί μοι.

ΑΝΤΙΓΟΝΗ

200 γεραὸν ἐς χέρα σῶμα σὸν
προκλίνας φιλίαν ἐμάν.

ΟΙΔΙΠΟΥΣ

ὤμοι δύσφρονος ἄτας.

ΧΟΡΟΣ

ὦ τλάμων, ὅτε νῦν χαλᾷς,
αὔδασον, τίς ἔφυς βροτῶν;
205 τίς ὁ πολύπονος ἄγῃ; τίν' ἂν
σοῦ πατρίδ' ἐκπυθοίμαν;

ΟΙΔΙΠΟΥΣ

ὦ ξένοι, ἀπόπολις· ἀλλὰ μή —   ἐπ.

ΧΟΡΟΣ

τί τόδ' ἀπεννέπεις, γέρον;

ΟΙΔΙΠΟΥΣ

210 μὴ μή μ' ἀνέρῃ τίς εἰ-
μι, μηδ' ἐξετάσῃς πέρα ματεύων.

CHORUS

Yes, move sideways and crouch low down on the edge of the rock!

ANTIGONE

Father, this is for me to do! Peacefully follow step with step . . .

OEDIPUS

Ah me!

ANTIGONE

. . . leaning your aged body upon my loving arm!

OEDIPUS

Alas for my ruinous affliction.

OEDIPUS *takes his seat upon the ledge.*

CHORUS

Unhappy one, since now you are at ease, tell us who among men you are? Who is conducted in so much pain? What country can we learn to be your fatherland?

OEDIPUS

Strangers, I am an exile; but do not . . .

CHORUS

What are you forbidding us to say, old man?

OEDIPUS

Do not, do not ask me who I am! Do not question me, enquiring further!

198-9 trsp. Hermann

205 τίν' ἂν Vauvilliers: τίνα codd.

208 ἀπόπολις Ebeling: ἀπόπτολις codd.

ΧΟΡΟΣ

τί δέ;

ΟΙΔΙΠΟΥΣ

δεινὰ φύσις.

ΧΟΡΟΣ

αὔδα.

ΟΙΔΙΠΟΥΣ

τέκνον, ὤμοι, τί γεγώνω;

ΧΟΡΟΣ

τίνος εἶ σπέρματος, <ὦ>
215 ξένε, φώνει, πατρόθεν;

ΟΙΔΙΠΟΥΣ

ὤμοι ἐγώ, τί πάθω, τέκνον ἐμόν;

ΧΟΡΟΣ

λέγ', ἐπείπερ ἐπ' ἔσχατα βαίνεις.

ΟΙΔΙΠΟΥΣ

ἀλλ' ἐρῶ· οὐ γὰρ ἔχω κατακρυφάν.

ΧΟΡΟΣ

μακρὰ μέλλεται· ἀλλὰ τάχυνε.

ΟΙΔΙΠΟΥΣ

220 Λαΐου ἴστε τιν' —

ΧΟΡΟΣ

ὤ· ἰοὺ ἰού.

212 τί δέ; Elmsley: τί τόδε; codd.
214 suppl. Heath

CHORUS

Why?

OEDIPUS

Terrible was my birth!

CHORUS

Speak!

OEDIPUS

My child, alas, what am I to say?

CHORUS

Tell us from what seed you come, stranger, on your father's
side!

OEDIPUS

Alack, what is to become of me, my child?

CHORUS

Tell us, seeing that you are driven to the brink!

OEDIPUS

Well, I will speak; for I have no means of hiding it!

CHORUS

The delay is long; make haste!

OEDIPUS

Do you know of a son of Laius . . . ?

CHORUS

Oh! Ah, ah!

---

²¹⁷ choro tribuit R. Meridor, Antigonae codd.
²¹⁹ μέλλεται Ll.-J.: μέλλετ᾽ Laz
²²⁰ post τιν᾽ add. ἀπόγονον codd., del. Reisig

ΟΙΔΙΠΟΥΣ

τό τε Λαβδακιδᾶν γένος;

ΧΟΡΟΣ

ὦ Ζεῦ.

ΟΙΔΙΠΟΥΣ

ἄθλιον Οἰδιπόδαν;

ΧΟΡΟΣ

σὺ γὰρ ὅδ' εἶ;

ΟΙΔΙΠΟΥΣ

δέος ἴσχετε μηδὲν ὅσ' αὐδῶ.

ΧΟΡΟΣ

ἰὼ ὦ ὤ.

ΟΙΔΙΠΟΥΣ

δύσμορος.

ΧΟΡΟΣ

ὦ ὤ.

ΟΙΔΙΠΟΥΣ

225 θύγατερ, τί ποτ' αὐτίκα κύρσει;

ΧΟΡΟΣ

ἔξω πόρσω βαίνετε χώρας.

ΟΙΔΙΠΟΥΣ

ἃ δ' ὑπέσχεο ποῖ καταθήσεις;

ΧΟΡΟΣ

οὐδενὶ μοιριδία τίσις ἔρχεται
230 ὧν προπάθῃ τὸ τίνειν· ἀπάτα δ' ἀπά-

438

OEDIPUS

. . . and of the race of the Labdacids?

CHORUS

O Zeus!

OEDIPUS

. . . the unhappy Oedipus?

CHORUS

Why, are you he?

OEDIPUS

Have no fear at any of my words!

CHORUS

Ah! Oh, oh!

OEDIPUS

Miserable am I!

CHORUS

Oh, oh!

OEDIPUS

Daughter, what will happen now?

CHORUS

Go far away, out of the country!

OEDIPUS

But your promises . . . how will you redeem them?

CHORUS

Fate punishes no man who is avenging what he has first suffered, and deception that matches other deceptions

ταῖς ἑτέραις ἑτέρα παραβαλλομέ-
να πόνον, οὐ χάριν, ἀντιδίδωσιν ἔ-
χειν. σὺ δὲ τῶνδ' ἑδράνων πάλιν ἔκτοπος
αὖθις ἄφορμος ἐμᾶς χθονὸς ἔκθορε,
235 μή τι πέρα χρέος
ἐμᾷ πόλει προσάψῃς.

ΑΝΤΙΓΟΝΗ

ὦ ξένοι αἰδόφρονες,
ἀλλ' ἐπεὶ γεραὸν πατέρα
τόνδ' ἐμὸν οὐκ ἀνέτλατ' ἔργων
240 ἀκόντων ἀίοντες αὐδάν,
ἀλλ' ἐμὲ τὰν μελέαν, ἱκετεύομεν,
ὦ ξένοι, οἰκτίραθ', ἃ
πατρὸς ὑπὲρ τοῦ τλάμονος ἄντομαι,
ἄντομαι οὐκ ἀλαοῖς προσορωμένα
245 ὄμμα σὸν ὄμμασιν, ὥς τις ἀφ' αἵματος
ὑμετέρου προφανεῖσα, τὸν ἄθλιον
αἰδοῦς κῦρσαι· ἐν ὑμῖν ὡς θεῷ
κείμεθα τλάμονες· ἀλλ' ἴτε, νεύσατε
τὰν ἀδόκητον χάριν,
250 πρός σ' ὅ τι σοι φίλον οἴκοθεν ἄντομαι,
ἢ τέκνον, ἢ λέχος, ἢ χρέος, ἢ θεός.
οὐ γὰρ ἴδοις ἂν ἀθρῶν βροτὸν ὅστις ἄν,
εἰ θεὸς ἄγοι,
ἐκφυγεῖν δύναιτο.

237-57 a quibusdam deleri testatur sch.
243 τοῦ τλάμονος Hense: τοῦ μόνου La: τοὐμοῦ rzt

gives in return not gratitude, but pain; and do you leave this seat and hasten away from my country, for fear you may fasten some heavier burden on my city!

ANTIGONE

Strangers of respectful mind, since you have not borne with my aged father here, having heard of the things he did unwittingly, yet pity my unhappy self, I beseech you, strangers, when I appeal to you on behalf of my poor father. I appeal to you, looking upon your eyes with eyes that are not blind, appearing as though I came from your own blood, that the miserable man may meet with respect! We are in your hands, as though you were a god. Come, grant the unhoped-for favour, I beseech you by whatever you hold dear, be it a child or a wife or a possession or a god! For however hard you look, you will not discern a mortal who, when a god drives him, can escape!

---

247 post ὑμῖν add. γὰρ codd., del. Brunck
250 οἴκοθεν Elmsley: ἐκ σέθεν Lrat
251 λέχος Reiske: λόγος codd.
253 post ἄγοι add. <σφ'> Dawe

SOPHOCLES

ΧΟΡΟΣ

ἀλλ' ἴσθι, τέκνον Οἰδίπου, σέ τ' ἐξ ἴσου
255 οἰκτίρομεν καὶ τόνδε συμφορᾶς χάριν·
τὰ δ' ἐκ θεῶν τρέμοντες οὐ σθένοιμεν ἂν
φωνεῖν πέρα τῶν πρὸς σὲ νῦν εἰρημένων.

ΟΙΔΙΠΟΥΣ

τί δῆτα δόξης, ἢ τί κληδόνος καλῆς
μάτην ῥεούσης ὠφέλημα γίγνεται,
260 εἰ τάς γ' Ἀθήνας φασὶ θεοσεβεστάτας
εἶναι, μόνας δὲ τὸν κακούμενον ξένον
σῴζειν οἵας τε καὶ μόνας ἀρκεῖν ἔχειν;
κἄμοιγε ποῦ ταῦτ' ἐστίν, οἵτινες βάθρων
ἐκ τῶνδέ μ' ἐξάραντες εἶτ' ἐλαύνετε,
265 ὄνομα μόνον δείσαντες; οὐ γὰρ δὴ τό γε
σῶμ' οὐδὲ τἄργα τἄμ'· ἐπεὶ τά γ' ἔργα με
πεπονθότ' ἴσθι μᾶλλον ἢ δεδρακότα,
εἴ σοι τὰ μητρὸς καὶ πατρὸς χρείη λέγειν,
ὧν οὕνεκ' ἐκφοβῇ με· τοῦτ' ἐγὼ καλῶς
270 ἔξοιδα. καίτοι πῶς ἐγὼ κακὸς φύσιν,
ὅστις παθὼν μὲν ἀντέδρων, ὥστ' εἰ φρονῶν
ἔπρασσον, οὐδ' ἂν ὧδ' ἐγιγνόμην κακός;
νῦν δ' οὐδὲν εἰδὼς ἱκόμην ἵν' ἱκόμην,
ὑφ' ὧν δ' ἔπασχον, εἰδότων ἀπωλλύμην.
275   ἀνθ' ὧν ἱκνοῦμαι πρὸς θεῶν ὑμᾶς, ξένοι,
ὥσπερ με κἀνεστήσαθ' ὧδε σώσατε,
καὶ μὴ θεοὺς τιμῶντες εἶτα τοὺς θεοὺς
ποιεῖσθ' ἀμαυροὺς μηδαμῶς· ἡγεῖσθε δὲ

CHORUS

Why, know, child of Oedipus, that we pity you and him
equally for your fortune; but for fear of what may come
from the gods we could not find the strength to say more
than has now been said to you.

OEDIPUS

What help comes from fame, or from a fine reputation that
flows away in vain, seeing that Athens, they say, has most
reverence for the gods, and alone can protect the afflicted
stranger, and alone can give him aid? How is this the case
with me, when you have made me rise up from these
ledges and are driving me away, simply from fear of my
name? For it is not my person or my actions that you fear;
why, know that my actions consisted in suffering rather
than in doing, if I must speak of the matter of my mother
and my father, on account of which you are afraid of me!
This I know for sure! Yet in my nature how am I evil, I who
struck back when I had been struck, so that if I had acted
knowingly, not even then would I have been evil? But as it
is I got to where I came to in all ignorance; but those who
have ill used me knowingly destroyed me.

Because of this I implore you by the gods, strangers;
just as you raised me up, even so preserve me, and in no
wise honour the gods, but then consign them to darkness!

---

²⁶⁰ γ' Janus Lascaris: τ' codd.

^{266–67} με . . . ἴσθι Hertel: μου . . . ἐστὶ codd.

²⁷⁸ ποιεῖσθ' ἀμαυροὺς Fraenkel: μώρους ποιεῖσθε KR: μωροὺς π.
Q: μοίραις π. La

443

βλέπειν μὲν αὐτοὺς πρὸς τὸν εὐσεβῆ βροτῶν,
280 βλέπειν δὲ πρὸς τοὺς δυσσεβεῖς, φυγὴν δέ του
μήπω γενέσθαι φωτὸς ἀνοσίου ποτέ.
ξὺν οἷς σὺ μὴ κάλυπτε τὰς εὐδαίμονας
ἔργοις Ἀθήνας ἀνοσίοις ὑπηρετῶν.
ἀλλ' ὥσπερ ἔλαβες τὸν ἱκέτην ἐχέγγυον,
285 ῥύου με κἀκφύλασσε· μηδέ μου κάρα
τὸ δυσπρόσοπτον εἰσορῶν ἀτιμάσῃς.
ἥκω γὰρ ἱερὸς εὐσεβής τε καὶ φέρων
ὄνησιν ἀστοῖς τοῖσδ'· ὅταν δ' ὁ κύριος
παρῇ τις, ὑμῶν ὅστις ἐστὶν ἡγεμών,
290 τότ' εἰσακούων πάντ' ἐπιστήσῃ· τὰ δὲ
μεταξὺ τούτου μηδαμῶς γίγνου κακός.

ΧΟΡΟΣ
ταρβεῖν μέν, ὦ γεραιέ, τἀνθυμήματα
πολλή 'στ' ἀνάγκη τἀπὸ σοῦ· λόγοισι γὰρ
οὐκ ὠνόμασται βραχέσι. τοὺς δὲ τῆσδε γῆς
295 ἄνακτας ἀρκεῖ ταῦτά μοι διειδέναι.

ΟΙΔΙΠΟΥΣ
καὶ ποῦ 'σθ' ὁ κραίνων τῆσδε τῆς χώρας, ξένοι;

ΧΟΡΟΣ
πατρῷον ἄστυ γῆς ἔχει· σκοπὸς δέ νιν,
ὃς κἀμὲ δεῦρ' ἔπεμψεν, οἴχεται στελῶν.

ΟΙΔΙΠΟΥΣ
ἦ καὶ δοκεῖτε τοῦ τυφλοῦ τιν' ἐντροπὴν
300 ἢ φροντίδ' ἕξειν, αὐτὸν ὥστ' ἐλθεῖν πέλας;

But believe that they look upon the mortal who shows reverence, and look upon the impious, and that no unholy fellow has ever yet escaped! With their aid do not cloud the fame of fortunate Athens by lending aid to unholy actions; but as you received the suppliant under a pledge, so protect and guard me, and do not dishonour me when you behold my unsightly face! For I come sacred and reverent, and I bring advantage to the citizens here; and when the man with power comes, whoever is your leader, then he shall hear and know all; but until then do you by no means be cruel!

CHORUS

There is every necessity, aged man, to regard with awe the thoughts that come from you, for they have been expressed in no light words; and I am content that the rulers of this land should decide this matter.

OEDIPUS

And where is the ruler of this land, strangers?

CHORUS

He is in the city of the fathers of the land, and a messenger, the same that brought me here, has gone to fetch him.

OEDIPUS

Do you truly think that he will show any thought or any regard for the blind man, so as to come near in person?

---

281 ποτέ Tournier et Desrousseaux: βροτῶν codd.

300 αὐτὸν ὥστ᾽ Porson: ἀπόνως τ᾽ Lat: ἀπόντ᾽ r

ΧΟΡΟΣ

καὶ κάρθ᾽, ὅταν περ τοὔνομ᾽ αἴσθηται τὸ σόν.

ΟΙΔΙΠΟΥΣ

τίς δ᾽ ἔσθ᾽ ὁ κείνῳ τοῦτο τοὔπος ἀγγελῶν;

ΧΟΡΟΣ

μακρὰ κέλευθος· πολλὰ δ᾽ ἐμπόρων ἔπη
φιλεῖ πλανᾶσθαι, τῶν ἐκεῖνος ἀίων,
305 θάρσει, παρέσται. πολὺ γάρ, ὦ γέρον, τὸ σὸν
ὄνομα διήκει πάντας, ὥστε κεἰ βραδὺς
εὕδει, κλυών σου δεῦρ᾽ ἀφίξεται ταχύς.

ΟΙΔΙΠΟΥΣ

ἀλλ᾽ εὐτυχὴς ἵκοιτο τῇ θ᾽ αὑτοῦ πόλει
ἐμοί τε· τίς γὰρ ἐσθλὸς οὐχ αὑτῷ φίλος;

ΑΝΤΙΓΟΝΗ

310 ὦ Ζεῦ, τί λέξω; ποῖ φρενῶν ἔλθω, πάτερ;

ΟΙΔΙΠΟΥΣ

τί δ᾽ ἔστι, τέκνον Ἀντιγόνη;

ΑΝΤΙΓΟΝΗ

γυναῖχ᾽ ὁρῶ
στείχουσαν ἡμῶν ἆσσον, Αἰτναίας ἐπὶ
πώλου βεβῶσαν· κρατὶ δ᾽ ἡλιοστερὴς
κυνῆ πρόσωπα Θεσσαλίς νιν ἀμπέχει.
315 τί φωνῶ;
ἆρ᾽ ἔστιν; ἆρ᾽ οὐκ ἔστιν; ἢ γνώμη πλανᾷ;
καὶ φημὶ κἀπόφημι κοὐκ ἔχω τί φῶ.
τάλαινα,

446

CHORUS

Indeed he will, when he hears your name!

OEDIPUS

And who shall bring that message to him?

CHORUS

The distance is great; but much talk of travellers circulates; and when he has heard it, be assured, he will be here. For your name, aged man, has spread greatly to all, so that even if he sleeps and moves slowly, when he hears of you he will be quick to arrive.

OEDIPUS

May his coming be fortunate for his city and for me! For what noble man is not a friend to himself?

ANTIGONE

O Zeus, what am I to say? What am I to think, father?

OEDIPUS

What is the matter, Antigone my child?

ANTIGONE

I see a woman coming near to us, mounted upon an Etnean colt; and a Thessalian sunhat on her head hides her face. What am I to say? Is it, or is it not? Are my thoughts wandering? I say yes and I say no, and I do not know what

---

315 φωνῶ Meineke: φῶ codd.

οὐκ ἔστιν ἄλλη. φαιδρὰ γοῦν ἀπ' ὀμμάτων
320 σαίνει με προστείχουσα· σημαίνει δ' ὅτι
μόνης τόδ' ἐστί, δῆλον, Ἰσμήνης κάρα.

ΟΙΔΙΠΟΥΣ

πῶς εἶπας, ὦ παῖ;

ΑΝΤΙΓΟΝΗ
παῖδα σήν, ἐμὴν δ' ὁρᾶν
ὅμαιμον· αὐδῇ δ' αὐτίκ' ἔξεστιν μαθεῖν.

ΙΣΜΗΝΗ

ὦ δισσὰ πατρὸς καὶ κασιγνήτης ἐμοὶ
325 ἥδιστα προσφωνήμαθ', ὡς ὑμᾶς μόλις
εὑροῦσα λύπῃ δεύτερον μόλις βλέπω.

ΟΙΔΙΠΟΥΣ

ὦ τέκνον, ἥκεις;

ΙΣΜΗΝΗ
ὦ πάτερ δύσμορφ' ὁρᾶν.

ΟΙΔΙΠΟΥΣ

τέκνον, πέφηνας;

ΙΣΜΗΝΗ
οὐκ ἄνευ μόχθου γ' ἐμοῦ.

ΟΙΔΙΠΟΥΣ

πρόσψαυσον, ὦ παῖ.

ΙΣΜΗΝΗ
θιγγάνω δυοῖν ὁμοῦ.

---

327 δύσμορφ' Bücheler: δύσμοιρ' a: δύσμορ' cett.
328 γ' ἐμοῦ K: γέ μοι cett.

448

to say! Poor creature, it is no other! Yes, as she approaches she greets me with a smile, and indicates, it is clear, that this can only be Ismene!

OEDIPUS

What did you say, my child?

ANTIGONE

That I see your daughter and my sister; and now we can know her by her voice!

Enter ISMENE accompanied by a servant.

ISMENE

Father and sister, two persons most delightful to address, how hard it has been to find you and how hard it is to look at you, such is my pain!

OEDIPUS

Child, have you come?

ISMENE

O father, a sorry sight to see!

OEDIPUS

Child, have you appeared?

ISMENE

Not without trouble for me!

OEDIPUS

Touch me, my daughter!

ISMENE

I touch you both together!

ΟΙΔΙΠΟΥΣ

330 ὦ σπέρμ᾽ ὅμαιμον.

ΙΣΜΗΝΗ
ὦ δυσάθλιαι τροφαί.

ΟΙΔΙΠΟΥΣ
ἦ τῆσδε κἀμοῦ;

ΙΣΜΗΝΗ
δυσμόρου τ᾽ ἐμοῦ τρίτης.

ΟΙΔΙΠΟΥΣ
τέκνον, τί δ᾽ ἦλθες;

ΙΣΜΗΝΗ
σῇ, πάτερ, προμηθίᾳ.

ΟΙΔΙΠΟΥΣ
πότερα πόθοισι;

ΙΣΜΗΝΗ
καὶ λόγων γ᾽ αὐτάγγελος,
ξὺν ᾧπερ εἶχον οἰκετῶν πιστῷ μόνῳ.

ΟΙΔΙΠΟΥΣ
335 οἱ δ᾽ αὐθόμαιμοι ποῦ νεανίαι πονεῖν;

ΙΣΜΗΝΗ
εἴσ᾽ οὗπέρ εἰσι· δεινὰ τἀν κείνοις τανῦν.

ΟΙΔΙΠΟΥΣ
ὦ πάντ᾽ ἐκείνω τοῖς ἐν Αἰγύπτῳ νόμοις
φύσιν κατεικασθέντε καὶ βίου τροφάς·

---

[330] post 327 habent codd., corr. Musgrave

OEDIPUS

Ah, children, sisters!

ISMENE

Ah, unhappy state!

OEDIPUS

Do you mean hers and mine?

ISMENE

Yes, and my own, unhappy as I am!

OEDIPUS

Child, why have you come?

ISMENE

Out of concern for you, father!

OEDIPUS

Was it that you missed me?

ISMENE

Yes, and I have news to bring you, together with the only
faithful servant that I had!

OEDIPUS

But where are the young men, your brothers, to take their
share of trouble?

ISMENE

They are where they are; things are now grim for them.

OEDIPUS

Those two conform altogether to the customs that prevail
in Egypt in their nature and the nurture of their lives! For

---

³³¹ τ' Markland: δ' codd.
³³⁶ τὰν κείνοις Schaefer e sch.L: δ' ἐν κείνοις LpcKra: τἀκεί-
νοις zt

SOPHOCLES

ἐκεῖ γὰρ οἱ μὲν ἄρσενες κατὰ στέγας
340 θακοῦσιν ἱστουργοῦντες, αἱ δὲ σύννομοι
τἄξω βίου τροφεῖα πορσύνουσ' ἀεί.
σφῷν δ', ὦ τέκν', οὓς μὲν εἰκὸς ἦν πονεῖν τάδε,
κατ' οἶκον οἰκουροῦσιν ὥστε παρθένοι,
σφὼ δ' ἀντ' ἐκείνοιν τἀμὰ δυστήνου κακὰ
345 ὑπερπονεῖτον. ἡ μὲν ἐξ ὅτου νέας
τροφῆς ἔληξε καὶ κατίσχυσεν δέμας,
ἀεὶ μεθ' ἡμῶν δύσμορος πλανωμένη,
γεροντἀγωγεῖ. πολλὰ μὲν κατ' ἀγρίαν
ὕλην ἄσιτος νηλίπους τ' ἀλωμένη,
350 πολλοῖσι δ' ὄμβροις ἡλίου τε καύμασι
μοχθοῦσα τλήμων δεύτερ' ἡγεῖται τὰ τῆς
οἴκοι διαίτης, εἰ πατὴρ τροφὴν ἔχοι.
σὺ δ', ὦ τέκνον, πρόσθεν μὲν ἐξίκου πατρὶ
μαντεῖ' ἄγουσα πάντα, Καδμείων λάθρᾳ,
355 ἃ τοῦδ' ἐχρήσθη σώματος, φύλαξ δέ μοι
πιστὴ κατέστης, γῆς ὅτ' ἐξηλαυνόμην·
νῦν δ' αὖ τίν' ἥκεις μῦθον, Ἰσμήνη, πατρὶ
φέρουσα; τίς σ' ἐξῆρεν οἴκοθεν στόλος;
ἥκεις γὰρ οὐ κενή γε, τοῦτ' ἐγὼ σαφῶς
360 ἔξοιδα· μή που δεῖμ' ἐμοὶ φέρουσά τι;

ΙΣΜΗΝΗ

ἐγὼ τὰ μὲν παθήμαθ' ἅπαθον, πάτερ,
ζητοῦσα τὴν σὴν ποῦ κατοικοίης τροφήν,
παρεῖσ' ἐάσω. δὶς γὰρ οὐχὶ βούλομαι
πονοῦσά τ' ἀλγεῖν καὶ λέγουσ' αὖθις πάλιν.

there the males sit in their houses working at the loom, and
their consorts provide the necessities of life out of doors.
And in your case, my children, those who ought to perform
this labour sit at home and keep the house like maidens,
and you two in their place bear the burdens of your
unhappy father's sorrows. The one has wandered, poor
creature, with me, ever since she ceased to be cared for as
a child and attained her strength, guiding an aged man.
Straying often through the wild jungle without food or
footwear, and vexed often by the rain and by the scorching
sun, the unhappy one gives second place to her home com-
forts, if her father can be cared for. And you, my child,
came earlier, unbeknown to the Cadmeans, bringing to
your father all the prophecies that had been uttered with
regard to this person, and you were my faithful guardian
when I was driven from the land. And now what news have
you come bringing to your father, Ismene? What mission
has sent you forth from home? For you have not come
empty-handed, that much I know for certain; can you be
bringing me some cause for fear?

The sufferings I endured, father, while I looked for the
place where you had settled to maintain yourself I shall
pass over and let go; for I do not wish to endure the double
pain of suffering them and then going over them once

SOPHOCLES

365 ἃ δ' ἀμφὶ τοῖν σοῖν δυσμόροιν παίδοιν κακὰ
νῦν ἐστι, ταῦτα σημανοῦσ' ἐλήλυθα.
πρὶν μὲν γὰρ αὐτοῖς ἤρεσεν Κρέοντί τε
θρόνους ἐᾶσθαι μηδὲ χραίνεσθαι πόλιν,
λόγῳ σκοποῦσι τὴν πάλαι γένους φθοράν,
370 οἷα κατέσχε τὸν σὸν ἄθλιον δόμον·
νῦν δ' ἐκ θεῶν του κἀξ ἀλειτηροῦ φρενὸς
εἰσῆλθε τοῖν τρὶς ἀθλίοιν ἔρις κακή,
ἀρχῆς λαβέσθαι καὶ κράτους τυραννικοῦ.
χὠ μὲν νεάζων καὶ χρόνῳ μείων γεγὼς
375 τὸν πρόσθε γεννηθέντα Πολυνείκη θρόνων
ἀποστερίσκει κἀξελήλακεν πάτρας.
ὁ δ', ὡς καθ' ἡμᾶς ἐσθ' ὁ πληθύων λόγος,
τὸ κοῖλον Ἄργος βὰς φυγάς, προσλαμβάνει
κῆδός τε καινὸν καὶ ξυνασπιστὰς φίλους,
380 ὡς αὐτίκ' αὐτὸς ἢ τὸ Καδμείων πέδον
τιμῇ καθέξων, ἢ πρὸς οὐρανὸν βιβῶν.
ταῦτ' οὐκ ἀριθμός ἐστιν, ὦ πάτερ, λόγων,
ἀλλ' ἔργα δεινά· τοὺς δὲ σοὺς ὅπῃ θεοὶ
πόνους κατοικτιοῦσιν οὐκ ἔχω μαθεῖν.

ΟΙΔΙΠΟΥΣ

385 ἤδη γὰρ ἔσχες ἐλπίδ' ὡς ἐμοῦ θεοὺς
ὥραν τιν' ἕξειν, ὥστε σωθῆναί ποτε;

ΙΣΜΗΝΗ

ἔγωγε τοῖς νῦν, ὦ πάτερ, μαντεύμασιν.

ΟΙΔΙΠΟΥΣ

ποίοισι τούτοις; τί δὲ τεθέσπισται, τέκνον;

more. But I have come to tell you of the evils that now
afflict your two unhappy sons. At first they agreed that the
throne should be left to Creon and pollution of the city
avoided, considering the nature of the ancient ruin of the
family that oppressed your miserable house. But now by
the action of one of the gods and of their own accursed
minds there has come upon the thrice-unhappy ones an
evil rivalry to grasp at dominion and at royal power. The
younger son, inferior in age, is depriving the first-born,
Polynices, of the throne and has chased him from his coun-
try; and he, according to the story that prevails, has gone in
exile to low-lying Argos and has acquired a new marriage
and friends who will bear arms with him, resolved either to
occupy the Cadmean earth in honour or to mount up to
heaven. This is not a mere heap of words, father, but terri-
ble actions; and when the gods will take pity on your sor-
rows I cannot discover.

OEDIPUS

Have you then attained the hope that the gods would pay
some heed to me, so that I might some day be saved?

ISMENE

Yes, father, from the latest prophecies.

OEDIPUS

What are these? What have the oracles pronounced, my
child?

---

367 ἤρεσεν Bergk: ἦν ἔρις codd.
380 αὐτὸς Nauck: Ἄργος codd.

ΙΣΜΗΝΗ

σὲ τοῖς ἐκεῖ ζητητὸν ἀνθρώποις ποτὲ
390 θανόντ' ἔσεσθαι ζῶντά τ' εὐσοίας χάριν.

ΟΙΔΙΠΟΥΣ

τίς δ' ἂν τοιοῦδ' ὑπ' ἀνδρὸς εὖ πράξειεν ἄν;

ΙΣΜΗΝΗ

ἐν σοὶ τὰ κείνων φασὶ γίγνεσθαι κράτη.

ΟΙΔΙΠΟΥΣ

ὅτ' οὐκέτ' εἰμί, τηνικαῦτ' ἄρ' εἴμ' ἀνήρ;

ΙΣΜΗΝΗ

νῦν γὰρ θεοί σ' ὀρθοῦσι, πρόσθε δ' ὤλλυσαν.

ΟΙΔΙΠΟΥΣ

395 γέροντα δ' ὀρθοῦν φλαῦρον ὃς νέος πέσῃ.

ΙΣΜΗΝΗ

καὶ μὴν Κρέοντά γ' ἴσθι σοι τούτων χάριν
ἥξοντα βαιοῦ κοὐχὶ μυρίου χρόνου.

ΟΙΔΙΠΟΥΣ

ὅπως τί δράσῃ, θύγατερ; ἑρμήνευέ μοι.

ΙΣΜΗΝΗ

ὥς σ' ἄγχι γῆς στήσωσι Καδμείας, ὅπως
400 κρατῶσι μὲν σοῦ, γῆς δὲ μὴ 'μβαίνῃς ὅρων.

ΟΙΔΙΠΟΥΣ

ἡ δ' ὠφέλησις τίς θύρασι κειμένου;

390 εὐσοίας Suda s.v., sch. L: εὐνοίας codd.
401 θύρασι Elmsley: θύραισι codd.

456

ISMENE

That you shall one day be sought by the people there in death and in life for their preservation's sake.

OEDIPUS

And who could obtain success through such a man?

ISMENE

They say that their power will depend on you.

OEDIPUS

When I no longer exist, am I then a man?

ISMENE

Yes, for now the gods are lifting you up, though earlier they destroyed you.

OEDIPUS

But it is a poor thing to uplift when he is old a man who has fallen when he was young!

ISMENE

Yet know that because of this Creon will come to you not after a long time, but soon.

OEDIPUS

To do what, my daughter? Explain to me!

ISMENE

So that they can establish you near the Cadmean land, where they can control you without your entering its bounds.

OEDIPUS

But what help do they get from my being outside their country?

457

ΙΣΜΗΝΗ

κείνοις ὁ τύμβος δυστυχῶν ὁ σὸς βαρύς.

ΟΙΔΙΠΟΥΣ

κἄνευ θεοῦ τις τοῦτό γ᾽ ἂν γνώμῃ μάθοι.

ΙΣΜΗΝΗ

τούτου χάριν τοίνυν σε προσθέσθαι πέλας
405 χώρας θέλουσι, μηδ᾽ ἵν᾽ ἂν σαυτοῦ κρατοῖς.

ΟΙΔΙΠΟΥΣ

ἦ καὶ κατασκιῶσι Θηβαίᾳ κόνει;

ΙΣΜΗΝΗ

ἀλλ᾽ οὐκ ἐᾷ τοὐμφυλον αἷμά γ᾽, ὦ πάτερ.

ΟΙΔΙΠΟΥΣ

οὐκ ἄρ᾽ ἐμοῦ γε μὴ κρατήσωσίν ποτε.

ΙΣΜΗΝΗ

ἔσται ποτ᾽ ἆρα τοῦτο Καδμείοις βάρος.

ΟΙΔΙΠΟΥΣ

410 ποίας φανείσης, ὦ τέκνον, συναλλαγῆς;

ΙΣΜΗΝΗ

τῆς σῆς ὑπ᾽ ὀργῆς, σοῖς ὅτ᾽ ἀντῶσιν τάφοις.

ΟΙΔΙΠΟΥΣ

ἃ δ᾽ ἐννέπεις, κλυοῦσα τοῦ λέγεις, τέκνον;

405 κρατοῖς Brunck: κρατῇς codd.
407 γ᾽ Blaydes: σ᾽ codd.
411 ὅτ᾽ ἀντῶσιν Ll.-J.: ὅταν στῶσιν codd.

ISMENE

If things go wrong with it, your tomb will cause them trouble.

OEDIPUS

Even without a god to tell one, one might know that by guessing.

ISMENE

Then that is why they wish to place you near them, and not where you would be your own master.

OEDIPUS

Will they even shroud my body in Theban soil?

ISMENE

But the shedding of kindred blood does not allow it, father!

OEDIPUS

Then they shall never gain power over me!

ISMENE

Then that will weigh heavily on the Cadmeans!

OEDIPUS

When what conjunction of events has appeared, my child?

ISMENE

Through your anger, when they come up against your tomb!

OEDIPUS

But from whom did you learn what you are telling me, my child?

SOPHOCLES

ΙΣΜΗΝΗ
ἀνδρῶν θεωρῶν Δελφικῆς ἀφ' ἑστίας.

ΟΙΔΙΠΟΥΣ
καὶ ταῦτ' ἐφ' ἡμῖν Φοῖβος εἰρηκὼς κυρεῖ;

ΙΣΜΗΝΗ
415 ὥς φασιν οἱ μολόντες ἐς Θήβης πέδον.

ΟΙΔΙΠΟΥΣ
παίδων τις οὖν ἤκουσε τῶν ἐμῶν τάδε;

ΙΣΜΗΝΗ
ἄμφω γ' ὁμοίως, κἀξεπίστασθον καλῶς.

ΟΙΔΙΠΟΥΣ
κᾆθ' οἱ κάκιστοι τῶνδ' ἀκούσαντες πάρος
τοὐμοῦ πόθου προὔθεντο τὴν τυραννίδα;

ΙΣΜΗΝΗ
420 ἀλγῶ κλύουσα ταῦτ' ἐγώ, φέρω δ' ὅμως.

ΟΙΔΙΠΟΥΣ
ἀλλ' οἱ θεοί σφιν μήτε τὴν πεπρωμένην
ἔριν κατασβέσειαν, ἐν δ' ἐμοὶ τέλος
αὐτοῖν γένοιτο τῆσδε τῆς μάχης πέρι,
ἧς νῦν ἔχονται κἀπαναίρονται δόρυ·
425 ὡς οὔτ' ἂν ὃς νῦν σκῆπτρα καὶ θρόνους ἔχει
μείνειεν, οὔτ' ἂν οὑξεληλυθὼς πάλιν
ἔλθοι ποτ' αὖθις· οἵ γε τὸν φύσαντ' ἐμὲ
οὕτως ἀτίμως πατρίδος ἐξωθούμενον
οὐκ ἔσχον οὐδ' ἤμυναν, ἀλλ' ἀνάστατος
430 αὐτοῖν ἐπέμφθην κἀξεκηρύχθην φυγάς.

460

ISMENE

From men who had gone as envoys, from the Pythian hearth.[a]

OEDIPUS

And did Phoebus really say this regarding me?

ISMENE

So say those who returned to the land of Thebes.

OEDIPUS

Then did either of my sons hear this?

ISMENE

Yes, both alike, and they are well aware of it.

OEDIPUS

And then after they had heard this did the villains put the kingship before the wish to be with me?

ISMENE

I feel pain at hearing this, but still I must endure it.

OEDIPUS

Well may the gods not extinguish their destined quarrel, and may the decision be granted to me in respect of this battle on which they are now set, lifting their spears, so that he who now holds the sceptre and the throne may not remain, and he who has gone away may never return, seeing that when I their father was so shamefully extruded from the land they did not prevent it or defend me, but I was uprooted and sent away by them and was proclaimed

[a] The Delphic oracle.

---

424 κἀπαναίρονται Hermann: -οῦνται codd.

εἴποις ἂν ὡς θέλοντι τοῦτ' ἐμοὶ τότε
πόλις τὸ δῶρον εἰκότως κατήνεσεν;
οὐ δῆτ', ἐπεί τοι τὴν μὲν αὐτίχ' ἡμέραν,
ὁπηνίκ' ἔζει θυμός, ἥδιστον δέ μοι
435   τὸ κατθανεῖν ἦν καὶ τὸ λευσθῆναι πέτροις,
οὐδεὶς ἔρωτ' ἐς τόνδ' ἐφαίνετ' ὠφελῶν·
χρόνῳ δ', ὅτ' ἤδη πᾶς ὁ μόχθος ἦν πέπων,
κἀμάνθανον τὸν θυμὸν ἐκδραμόντα μοι
μείζω κολαστὴν τῶν πρὶν ἡμαρτημένων,
440   τὸ τηνίκ' ἤδη τοῦτο μὲν πόλις βίᾳ
ἤλαυνέ μ' ἐκ γῆς χρόνιον, οἱ δ' ἐπωφελεῖν,
οἱ τοῦ πατρός, τῷ πατρὶ δυνάμενοι, τὸ δρᾶν
οὐκ ἠθέλησαν, ἀλλ' ἔπους σμικροῦ χάριν
φυγάς σφιν ἔξω πτωχὸς ἠλώμην ἀεί·
445   ἐκ ταῖνδε δ', οὔσαιν παρθένοιν, ὅσον φύσις
δίδωσιν αὐταῖν, καὶ τροφὰς ἔχω βίου
καὶ γῆς ἄδειαν καὶ γένους ἐπάρκεσιν·
τὼ δ' ἀντὶ τοῦ φύσαντος εἱλέσθην θρόνους
καὶ σκῆπτρα κραίνειν καὶ τυραννεύειν χθονός.
450   ἀλλ' οὔ τι μὴ λάχωσι τοῦδε συμμάχου,
οὐδέ σφιν ἀρχῆς τῆσδε Καδμείας ποτὲ
ὄνησις ἥξει· τοῦτ' ἐγῷδα, τῆσδέ τε
μαντεῖ' ἀκούων, συννοῶν τε θέσφατα
παλαίφαθ' ἁμοὶ Φοῖβος ἤνυσέν ποτε.
455   πρὸς ταῦτα καὶ Κρέοντα πεμπόντων ἐμοῦ
μαστῆρα, κεἴ τις ἄλλος ἐν πόλει σθένει.
ἐὰν γὰρ ὑμεῖς, ὦ ξένοι, θέλητ' ἐμοὶ
σὺν ταῖσδε ταῖς σεμναῖσι δημούχοις θεαῖς

an exile! Would you say that the city granted this gift to me properly, according to my wish? No, since on that very day, when my passion was still blazing, and it was my dearest wish to be stoned to death with rocks, no one came forward to help me realise that desire; but after a time, when my suffering had grown milder, and I had come to realise that my anger had gone too far in punishing my former errors, at that time the city drove me out by force, after many years, and my sons, who could have helped their father, refused to act, but for the want of a brief word I went off into exile, wandering for ever. And it is from these two, who are maidens, that so far as their nature allows I have sustenance and a safe place to live and help from my family. But those two chose instead of their father to wield the sceptre and to be monarchs of the land! But they shall get nothing from me as an ally, neither shall they ever have benefit from this Cadmean kingship; that I know, from hearing this girl's prophecies, and from interpreting the ancient oracles which Phoebus has at last fulfilled.

In the face of that let them send Creon to look for me, and any other who is powerful in the city! For if you, strangers, are willing with the aid of these awesome

---

[436] ἔρωτ' ἐς τόνδ' Blaydes: ἔρωτος τοῦδ' fere codd.

[451] οὐδέ Hermann: οὔτε fere codd.

[453] τε θέσφατα Heimsoeth: τά τ' ἐξ ἐμοῦ codd.

[458] σὺν ταῖσδε Canter: πρὸς ταῖσι L: σὺν ταῖσι L s.l., razt

ἀλκὴν ποεῖσθαι, τῇδε μὲν πόλει μέγαν
460 σωτῆρ' ἀρεῖσθε, τοῖς δ' ἐμοῖς ἐχθροῖς πόνους.

ΧΟΡΟΣ

ἐπάξιος μέν, Οἰδίπους, κατοικτίσαι,
αὐτός τε παῖδές θ' αἵδ'· ἐπεὶ δὲ τῆσδε γῆς
σωτῆρα σαυτὸν τῷδ' ἐπεμβάλλεις λόγῳ,
παραινέσαι σοι βούλομαι τὰ σύμφορα.

ΟΙΔΙΠΟΥΣ

465 ὦ φίλταθ', ὡς νῦν πᾶν τελοῦντι προξένει.

ΧΟΡΟΣ

θοῦ νῦν καθαρμὸν τῶνδε δαιμόνων, ἐφ' ἃς
τὸ πρῶτον ἵκου καὶ κατέστειψας πέδον.

ΟΙΔΙΠΟΥΣ

τρόποισι ποίοις; ὦ ξένοι, διδάσκετε.

ΧΟΡΟΣ

πρῶτον μὲν ἱερὰς ἐξ ἀειρύτου χοὰς
470 κρήνης ἔνεγκοῦ, δι' ὁσίων χειρῶν θιγών.

ΟΙΔΙΠΟΥΣ

ὅταν δὲ τοῦτο χεῦμ' ἀκήρατον λάβω;

ΧΟΡΟΣ

κρατῆρές εἰσιν, ἀνδρὸς εὔχειρος τέχνη,
ὧν κρᾶτ' ἔρεψον καὶ λαβὰς ἀμφιστόμους.

ΟΙΔΙΠΟΥΣ

θαλλοῖσιν, ἢ κρόκαισιν, ἢ ποίῳ τρόπῳ;

goddesses of your deme to give me protection, you will acquire a great preserver for this city, and cause trouble for my enemies!

CHORUS

You deserve pity, Oedipus, both yourself and these your daughters; and since by this speech you offer yourself as a protector for this land, I wish to give you advice that will benefit you.

OEDIPUS

Dearest sir, speak out as host, for I will do all that you demand!

CHORUS

Perform now a purification for these deities, to whom you first came and whose ground you have trodden!

OEDIPUS

In what fashion, strangers? Explain to me!

CHORUS

First bring sacred libations from an ever-flowing stream, touching them with hands that are pure!

OEDIPUS

And when I have obtained this untainted liquid?

CHORUS

There are basins, the work of a skilled artist; crown their tops and the handles on both sides!

OEDIPUS

With branches, or with woollen cloths, or in what fashion?

ΧΟΡΟΣ

475 οἷος νεώρους νεοπόκῳ μαλλῷ λαβών.

ΟΙΔΙΠΟΥΣ

εἶεν· τὸ δ' ἔνθεν ποῖ τελευτῆσαί με χρή;

ΧΟΡΟΣ

χοὰς χέασθαι στάντα πρὸς πρώτην ἕω.

ΟΙΔΙΠΟΥΣ

ἦ τοῖσδε κρωσσοῖς οἷς λέγεις χέω τάδε;

ΧΟΡΟΣ

τρισσάς γε πηγάς· τὸν τελευταῖον δ' ὅλον —

ΟΙΔΙΠΟΥΣ

480 τοῦ τόνδε πλήσας; προσδίδασκε καὶ τόδε.

ΧΟΡΟΣ

ὕδατος, μελίσσης· μηδὲ προσφέρειν μέθυ.

ΟΙΔΙΠΟΥΣ

ὅταν δὲ τούτων γῆ μελάμφυλλος τύχῃ;

ΧΟΡΟΣ

τρὶς ἐννέ' αὐτῇ κλῶνας ἐξ ἀμφοῖν χεροῖν
τιθεὶς ἐλαίας τάσδ' ἐπεύχεσθαι λιτάς —

ΟΙΔΙΠΟΥΣ

485 τούτων ἀκοῦσαι βούλομαι· μέγιστα γάρ.

---

475 νεώρους Musgrave: νεαρᾶς codd.: γε νεαρᾶς Heath   νεο-
πόκῳ Canter: οἰνεοτόκῳ lr: οἰοπόκῳ l s.l., zt
480 προσδίδασκε Ll.-J.: θῶ; δίδασκε Lra

CHORUS

With the newly sheared fleece of a young lamb that you must take.

OEDIPUS

So be it! And then how must I make an end?

CHORUS

You must pour a libation, taking your stand facing the first morning light.

OEDIPUS

Must I pour it with these buckets that you speak of?

CHORUS

Yes, three streams; and the last one altogether . . .

OEDIPUS

What must I fill it with? Tell me that too!

CHORUS

Water, and honey; but do not add wine!

OEDIPUS

And when the land black with leaves has received this?

CHORUS

Place there three times nine twigs of olive wood and utter these prayers . . .

OEDIPUS

This I wish to hear, for it is most important!

SOPHOCLES

ΧΟΡΟΣ

ὥς σφας καλοῦμεν Εὐμενίδας, ἐξ εὐμενῶν
στέρνων δέχεσθαι τὸν ἱκέτην σωτηρίους
αἰτοῦ σύ τ' αὐτὸς κεἴ τις ἄλλος ἀντὶ σοῦ,
ἄπυστα φωνῶν μηδὲ μηκύνων βοήν.
490 ἔπειτ' ἀφέρπειν ἄστροφος. καὶ ταῦτά σοι
δράσαντι θαρσῶν ἂν παρασταίην ἐγώ,
ἄλλως δὲ δειμαίνοιμ' ἄν, ὦ ξέν', ἀμφὶ σοί.

ΟΙΔΙΠΟΥΣ

ὦ παῖδε, κλύετον τῶνδε προσχώρων ξένων;

ΙΣΜΗΝΗ

ἠκούσαμέν τε χὤ τι δεῖ πρόστασσε δρᾶν.

ΟΙΔΙΠΟΥΣ

495 ἐμοὶ μὲν οὐχ ὁδωτά· λείπομαι γὰρ ἐν
τῷ μὴ δύνασθαι μηδ' ὁρᾶν, δυοῖν κακοῖν·
σφῷν δ' ἡτέρα μολοῦσα πραξάτω τάδε.
ἀρκεῖν γὰρ οἶμαι κἀντὶ μυρίων μίαν
ψυχὴν τάδ' ἐκτίνουσαν, ἢν εὔνους παρῇ.
500 ἀλλ' ἐν τάχει τι πράσσετον· μόνον δέ με
μὴ λείπετ'. οὐ γὰρ ἂν σθένοι τοὐμὸν δέμας
ἔρημον ἕρπειν οὐδ' ὑφηγητοῦ δίχα.

ΙΣΜΗΝΗ

ἀλλ' εἶμ' ἐγὼ τελοῦσα· τὸν τόπον δ' ἵνα
χρῆσταί μ' ἐφευρεῖν, τοῦτο βούλομαι μαθεῖν.

ΧΟΡΟΣ

505 τοὐκεῖθεν ἄλσους, ὦ ξένη, τοῦδ'. ἢν δέ του
σπάνιν τιν' ἴσχῃς, ἔστ' ἔποικος, ὃς φράσει.

468

CHORUS

That as we call them the Kindly Ones, they may receive the
suppliant with kindly hearts, protecting him; do you ask
this yourself and any other on your behalf, speaking low
and not crying out aloud. Then depart without turning
round; and if you do this, I would stand beside you with
confidence; but if not, stranger, I would be afraid for you!

OEDIPUS

Daughters, do you hear the words of these strangers who
are natives?

ISMENE

We have listened, and do you instruct us as to what to do!

OEDIPUS

I cannot go, for I fall short for lack of strength and of vision,
two afflictions; but let one of you go and perform these
actions, for I believe that one living creature can suffice to
make this payment even for countless numbers, coming to
the shrine in sincerity. Come, take action quickly! But do
not leave me alone; for my body has not the strength to
move unaccompanied or without a guide.

ISMENE

I will go and will carry out the rite! But I wish to be told
where I must perform the duty.

CHORUS

On the other side of the grove, stranger; and if there is any-
thing you need, there is a man who lives there who will
instruct you.

---

487 σωτηρίους Bake: -ιον codd.
502 δίχα Hermann: δ’ ἄνευ Lra

ΙΣΜΗΝΗ

χωροῖμ' ἂν ἐς τόδ'· Ἀντιγόνη, σὺ δ' ἐνθάδε
φύλασσε πατέρα τόνδε· τοῖς τεκοῦσι γὰρ
οὐδ' εἰ πονῇ τις, δεῖ πόνου μνήμην ἔχειν.

ΧΟΡΟΣ

510   δεινὸν μὲν τὸ πάλαι κείμενον ἤδη κακόν, ὦ
      ξεῖν', ἐπεγείρειν·   στρ. α΄
  ὅμως δ' ἔραμαι πυθέσθαι —

ΟΙΔΙΠΟΥΣ

τί τοῦτο;

ΧΟΡΟΣ

τᾶς δειλαίας ἀπόρου φανείσας
ἀλγηδόνος, ᾷ ξυνέστας.

ΟΙΔΙΠΟΥΣ

515   μὴ πρὸς ξενίας ἀνοίξῃς
  τᾶς σᾶς ἃ πέπονθ' ἀναιδῶς.

ΧΟΡΟΣ

τό τοι πολὺ καὶ μηδαμὰ λῆγον
χρῄζω, ξεῖν', ὀρθὸν ἄκουσμ' ἀκοῦσαι.

ΟΙΔΙΠΟΥΣ

ὤμοι.

ΧΟΡΟΣ

στέρξον, ἱκετεύω.

ΟΙΔΙΠΟΥΣ

φεῦ φεῦ.

ISMENE

I will go and do it! Antigone, stay here and guard our father; when one takes trouble for a parent, one must not remember that it is trouble!

Exit ISMENE.

CHORUS

It is dreadful, stranger, to reawaken evil long laid to rest; but none the less I long to learn . . .

OEDIPUS

What is this?

CHORUS

Of that grievous pain, appearing irresistibly, with which you came to grips.

OEDIPUS

In the name of hospitality, do not ruthlessly lay bare my sufferings!

CHORUS

The story is spread widely and never ceases; and I wish, stranger, to hear it truly told.

OEDIPUS

Alas!

CHORUS

Bear with me, I beg you!

OEDIPUS

Woe, woe!

---

⁵¹⁶ ἃ πέπονθ' Reisig: πέπονθ' ἔργ' codd.   ἀναιδῶς Ll.-J.: ἀναιδῆ codd.
⁵¹⁸ ξεῖν' Reisig: ξέν' codd.

ΧΟΡΟΣ

520 πείθου· κἀγὼ γὰρ ὅσον σὺ προσχρῄζεις.

ΟΙΔΙΠΟΥΣ

ἤνεγκον κακότατ', ὦ ξένοι, ἤνεγκον ἑκὼν μέν,
   θεὸς ἴστω·   ἀντ. α'
τούτων δ' αὐθαίρετον οὐδέν.

ΧΟΡΟΣ

ἀλλ' ἐς τί;

ΟΙΔΙΠΟΥΣ

525 κακᾷ μ' εὐνᾷ πόλις οὐδὲν ἴδριν
γάμων ἐνέδησεν ἄτᾳ.

ΧΟΡΟΣ

ἦ μητρόθεν, ὡς ἀκούω,
δυσώνυμα λέκτρ' ἐπλήσω;

ΟΙΔΙΠΟΥΣ

ὤμοι, θάνατος μὲν τάδ' ἀκούειν,
530 ὦ ξεῖν'· αὗται δὲ δύ' ἐξ ἐμοῦ <μὲν> —

ΧΟΡΟΣ

πῶς φής;

ΟΙΔΙΠΟΥΣ

παῖδε, δύο δ' ἄτα —

ΧΟΡΟΣ

ὦ Ζεῦ.

---

521 ἑκὼν Bothe: ἄκων codd.
525 ἴδριν Mudge: -ις codd.

CHORUS

Be persuaded, for I grant all that you desire!

OEDIPUS

I endured evil, strangers, I endured it, by my own will, let the god be witness! But none of these things was my own choice!

CHORUS

But for what purpose?

OEDIPUS

By an evil wedlock the city bound me, in all ignorance, to the ruin caused by my marriage.

CHORUS

Was it your mother, as I am told, who shared your ill-famed bed?

OEDIPUS

Alas, it is death to hear this, stranger! But these two girls, sprung from me . . .

CHORUS

How do you say?

OEDIPUS

. . . two curses . . .

CHORUS

O Zeus!

---

530 suppl. Elmsley
531 παῖδε Elmsley: -ες codd.

ΟΙΔΙΠΟΥΣ

ματρὸς κοινᾶς ἀπέβλαστον ὠδῖνος.

ΧΟΡΟΣ

σοί γ᾽ ἆρ᾽ ἀπόγονοί τ᾽ εἰσὶ καὶ — στρ. β'

ΟΙΔΙΠΟΥΣ

535 κοιναί γε πατρὸς ἀδελφεαί.

ΧΟΡΟΣ

ἰώ.

ΟΙΔΙΠΟΥΣ

ἰὼ δῆτα μυ-
ρίων γ᾽ ἐπιστροφαὶ κακῶν.

ΧΟΡΟΣ

ἔπαθες —

ΟΙΔΙΠΟΥΣ

ἔπαθον ἄλαστ᾽ ἔχειν.

ΧΟΡΟΣ

ἔρεξας —

ΟΙΔΙΠΟΥΣ

οὐκ ἔρεξα.

ΧΟΡΟΣ

τί γάρ;

ΟΙΔΙΠΟΥΣ

ἐδεξάμην

540 δῶρον, ὃ μήποτ᾽ ἐγὼ ταλακάρδιος
ἐπωφελήσας ὄφελον ἐξελέσθαι.

OEDIPUS

. . . were born from the labour of my mother!

CHORUS

So to you they are daughters and also . . .

OEDIPUS

Yes, sisters to their father!

CHORUS

Ah!

OEDIPUS

Ah, evils innumerable come back upon me!

CHORUS

You suffered . . .

OEDIPUS

I suffered woes unforgettable!

CHORUS

You did . . .

OEDIPUS

I never did . . .

CHORUS

How so?

OEDIPUS

I received a special gift after the service I had rendered that I, miserable one, should never have accepted!

---

534 σοί γ' ἆρ' Ll.-J.: σοί τ' ἆρ' K: σαί τ' ἆρ' Lra   ἀπόγονοί τ' εἰσὶ Bothe: εἰσὶν ἀπόγονοι Lrzt: εἴσ' ἀπόγονοι Ka
541 ἐπωφελήσας Meineke: -έλησα codd.   ὄφελον Rauchenstein: πόλεως codd.

ΧΟΡΟΣ

δύστανε, τί γάρ; ἔθου φόνον —   ἀντ. β΄

ΟΙΔΙΠΟΥΣ

τί τοῦτο; τί δ᾽ ἐθέλεις μαθεῖν;

ΧΟΡΟΣ

πατρός;

ΟΙΔΙΠΟΥΣ

παπαῖ, δευτέραν
ἔπαισας, ἐπὶ νόσῳ νόσον.

ΧΟΡΟΣ

545   ἔκανες —

ΟΙΔΙΠΟΥΣ

ἔκανον. ἔχει δέ μοι —

ΧΟΡΟΣ

τί τοῦτο;

ΟΙΔΙΠΟΥΣ

πρὸς δίκας τι.

ΧΟΡΟΣ

τί γάρ;

ΟΙΔΙΠΟΥΣ

ἐγὼ φράσω·
ἄτᾳ ἁλοὺς ἐφόνευσ᾽ ἀπό τ᾽ ὤλεσα,
νόμῳ δὲ καθαρός· ἄιδρις ἐς τόδ᾽ ἦλθον.

547 ἄτᾳ Ll.-J.: καὶ γὰρ codd.   ἁλοὺς Hermann: ἄλλους codd.
ἀπό τ᾽ ὤλεσα Platt: καὶ ἀπώλεσα codd.

CHORUS

Unhappy one, what then? You murdered . . .

OEDIPUS

What is this? What do you wish to learn?

CHORUS

. . . your father?

OEDIPUS

Woe! You have struck me a second blow, anguish upon anguish!

CHORUS

You killed . . .

OEDIPUS

I killed, but I have . . .

CHORUS

What is this?

OEDIPUS

. . . a plea in my defence!

CHORUS

What plea?

OEDIPUS

I will explain! I murdered and slaughtered as the victim of the power that sent me mad, but according to the law I am clean! It was in ignorance that I came to this!

---

[548] νόμῳ] νόῳ Karsten

ΧΟΡΟΣ

καὶ μὴν ἄναξ ὅδ' ἡμὶν Αἰγέως γόνος
550 Θησεὺς κατ' ὀμφὴν σὴν ἀποσταλεὶς πάρα.

ΘΗΣΕΥΣ

πολλῶν ἀκούων ἔν τε τῷ πάρος χρόνῳ
τὰς αἱματηρὰς ὀμμάτων διαφθορὰς
ἔγνωκά σ', ὦ παῖ Λαΐου, τανῦν θ' ὁδοῖς
ἐν ταῖσδε λεύσσων μᾶλλον ἐξεπίσταμαι.
555 σκευή τε γάρ σε καὶ τὸ δύστηνον κάρα
δηλοῦτον ἡμῖν ὄνθ' ὃς εἶ, καί σ' οἰκτίσας
θέλω 'περέσθαι, δύσμορ' Οἰδίπους, τίνα
πόλεως ἐπέστης προστροπὴν ἐμοῦ τ' ἔχων,
αὐτός τε χἠ σὴ δύσμορος παραστάτις.
560 δίδασκε· δεινὴν γάρ τιν' ἂν πρᾶξιν τύχοις
λέξας ὁποίας ἐξαφισταίμην ἐγώ·
ὃς οἶδά γ' αὐτὸς ὡς ἐπαιδεύθην ξένος,
ὥσπερ σύ, χὡς εἷς πλεῖστ' ἀνὴρ ἐπὶ ξένης
ἤθλησα κινδυνεύματ' ἐν τὠμῷ κάρᾳ,
565 ὥστε ξένον γ' ἂν οὐδέν' ὄνθ', ὥσπερ σὺ νῦν,
ὑπεκτραποίμην μὴ οὐ συνεκσῴζειν· ἐπεὶ
ἔξοιδ' ἀνὴρ ὢν χὤτι τῆς εἰς αὔριον
οὐδὲν πλέον μοι σοῦ μέτεστιν ἡμέρας.

ΟΙΔΙΠΟΥΣ

Θησεῦ, τὸ σὸν γενναῖον ἐν σμικρῷ λόγῳ
570 παρῆκεν ὥστε βραχέ' ἐμοὶ δεῖσθαι φράσαι.
σὺ γάρ μ' ὅς εἰμι κἀφ' ὅτου πατρὸς γεγὼς
καὶ γῆς ὁποίας ἦλθον, εἰρηκὼς κυρεῖς·

OEDIPUS AT COLONUS

CHORUS

See, here is our king, the son of Aegeus, who was sum-
moned according to your words!

Enter THESEUS.

THESEUS

Having heard from many in time past of your bloody des-
truction of your eyes, I have recognised you, son of Laius,
and now that I see you after this journey I am yet more cer-
tain; for your clothing and your stricken face make it clear
to me that you are who you are; and in pity for you,
Oedipus, I wish to ask you what request of the city and of
me you have come to make, you and your unfortunate
companion. Tell me! For you would need to speak of a
terrible fortune indeed for me to turn away from it! I have
not forgotten that I myself was brought up in exile, as you
were, and that in my exile I struggled against such dangers
to my life as no other man has met with; so that I would
never turn aside from helping to rescue any exile such as
you, since I know that I am a man, and that I have no
greater share in tomorrow than you have.

OEDIPUS

Theseus, your nobility has in a short speech left but little
for me say! For you have said rightly who I am and who
was my father and what land I have come from; so that

---

550 ἀποσταλεὶς Turnebus: ἀπεστάλη codd.

554 λεύσσων Nauck: ἀκούων codd.

557 'περέσθαι Reisig: σ' ἐρέσθαι zt: τι ἐρέσθαι LacKra

563 χὠς εἷς Blomfield: χὦστις codd.

565 γ' ἂν Vauvilliers: γὰρ codd.

ὥστ' ἐστί μοι τὸ λοιπὸν οὐδὲν ἄλλο πλὴν
εἰπεῖν ἃ χρῄζω, χὠ λόγος διοίχεται.

ΘΗΣΕΥΣ

575   τοῦτ' αὐτὸ νῦν δίδασχ', ὅπως ἂν ἐκμάθω.

ΟΙΔΙΠΟΥΣ

δώσων ἱκάνω τοὐμὸν ἄθλιον δέμας
σοί, δῶρον οὐ σπουδαῖον εἰς ὄψιν· τὰ δὲ
κέρδη παρ' αὐτοῦ κρείσσον' ἢ μορφὴ καλή.

ΘΗΣΕΥΣ

ποῖον δὲ κέρδος ἀξιοῖς ἥκειν φέρων;

ΟΙΔΙΠΟΥΣ

580   χρόνῳ μάθοις ἄν, οὐχὶ τῷ παρόντι που.

ΘΗΣΕΥΣ

ποίῳ γὰρ ἡ σὴ προσφορὰ δηλώσεται;

ΟΙΔΙΠΟΥΣ

ὅταν θάνω 'γὼ καὶ σύ μου ταφεὺς γένῃ.

ΘΗΣΕΥΣ

τὰ λοίσθι' αἰτῇ τοῦ βίου, τὰ δ' ἐν μέσῳ
ἢ λῆστιν ἴσχεις ἢ δι' οὐδενὸς ποῇ.

ΟΙΔΙΠΟΥΣ

585   ἐνταῦθα γάρ μοι κεῖνα συγκομίζεται.

ΘΗΣΕΥΣ

ἀλλ' ἐν βραχεῖ δὴ τήνδε μ' ἐξαιτῇ χάριν.

ΟΙΔΙΠΟΥΣ

ὅρα γε μήν· οὐ σμικρός, οὔχ, ἀγὼν ὅδε.

there is nothing left for me but to say what I desire, and the words are at an end.

THESEUS

Explain that very thing, so that I can learn it all!

OEDIPUS

I come to offer you the gift of my miserable body, not much to look at, but the benefits that will come from it are better than good looks.

THESEUS

And what is the benefit that you claim that you have come bringing?

OEDIPUS

You will learn in time, but not, I think, at present.

THESEUS

At what time, then, will your offering be revealed?

OEDIPUS

When I die and you give me burial.

THESEUS

Your request touches the last things in life, and what comes in between you have forgotten or you count as nothing.

OEDIPUS

Yes, because these other things are comprised in that.

THESEUS

Why, the favour that you ask of me is in brief compass!

OEDIPUS

But take care! This is no small conflict, no!

ΘΗΣΕΥΣ

πότερα τὰ τῶν σῶν ἐκγόνων ἢ τοῦ λέγεις;

ΟΙΔΙΠΟΥΣ

κεῖνοι βαδίζειν κεῖσ' ἀναγκάσουσί με.

ΘΗΣΕΥΣ

590   ἀλλ' εἰ θέλοντά γ', οὐδὲ σοὶ φεύγειν καλόν.

ΟΙΔΙΠΟΥΣ

ἀλλ' οὐδ', ὅτ' αὐτὸς ἤθελον, παρίεσαν.

ΘΗΣΕΥΣ

ὦ μῶρε, θυμὸς δ' ἐν κακοῖς οὐ ξύμφορον.

ΟΙΔΙΠΟΥΣ

ὅταν μάθῃς μου, νουθέτει, τανῦν δ' ἔα.

ΘΗΣΕΥΣ

διδάσκ'. ἄνευ γνώμης γὰρ οὔ με χρὴ ψέγειν.

ΟΙΔΙΠΟΥΣ

595   πέπονθα, Θησεῦ, δεινὰ πρὸς κακοῖς κακά.

ΘΗΣΕΥΣ

ἦ τὴν παλαιὰν ξυμφορὰν γένους ἐρεῖς;

ΟΙΔΙΠΟΥΣ

οὐ δῆτ'· ἐπεὶ πᾶς τοῦτό γ' Ἑλλήνων θροεῖ.

ΘΗΣΕΥΣ

τί γὰρ τὸ μεῖζον ἢ κατ' ἄνθρωπον νοσεῖς;

588 ἢ τοῦ Bake: ἢ 'μοῦ codd.
589 βαδίζειν Maehly: κομίζειν codd.
594 ψέγειν Bergk: λέγειν codd.

THESEUS

Do your words concern your sons, or whom?

OEDIPUS

They will try to compel me to go there.

THESEUS

But if they wish you to go willingly, it is not right for you to remain in exile.

OEDIPUS

But they did not allow me to remain when I myself wished to do so!

THESEUS

Foolish man, anger brings no advantage when one is in trouble!

OEDIPUS

When I have told you all, reprove me, but now refrain!

THESEUS

Instruct me, for I ought not to rebuke you without having judged the matter!

OEDIPUS

I have suffered, Theseus, cruel wrong upon wrong!

THESEUS

Will you speak of the ancient misfortune of your family?

OEDIPUS

No, for every Greek talks of that!

THESEUS

Then what is the affliction greater than man can bear from which you suffer?

ΟΙΔΙΠΟΥΣ

οὕτως ἔχει μοι· γῆς ἐμῆς ἀπηλάθην
600   πρὸς τῶν ἐμαυτοῦ σπερμάτων· ἔστιν δέ μοι
πάλιν κατελθεῖν μήποθ᾽, ὡς πατροκτόνῳ.

ΘΗΣΕΥΣ

πῶς δῆτά σ᾽ ἂν πεμψαίαθ᾽, ὥστ᾽ οἰκεῖν δίχα;

ΟΙΔΙΠΟΥΣ

τὸ θεῖον αὐτοὺς ἐξαναγκάσει στόμα.

ΘΗΣΕΥΣ

ποῖον πάθος δείσαντας ἐκ χρηστηρίων;

ΟΙΔΙΠΟΥΣ

605   ὅτι σφ᾽ ἀνάγκη τῇδε πληγῆναι χθονί.

ΘΗΣΕΥΣ

καὶ πῶς γένοιτ᾽ ἂν τἀμὰ κἀκ κείνων πικρά;

ΟΙΔΙΠΟΥΣ

ὦ φίλτατ᾽ Αἰγέως παῖ, μόνοις οὐ γίγνεται
θεοῖσι γῆρας οὐδὲ κατθανεῖν ποτε,
τὰ δ᾽ ἄλλα συγχεῖ πάνθ᾽ ὁ παγκρατὴς χρόνος.
610   φθίνει μὲν ἰσχὺς γῆς, φθίνει δὲ σώματος,
θνήσκει δὲ πίστις, βλαστάνει δ᾽ ἀπιστία,
καὶ πνεῦμα ταὐτὸν οὔποτ᾽ οὔτ᾽ ἐν ἀνδράσιν
φίλοις βέβηκεν οὔτε πρὸς πόλιν πόλει.
τοῖς μὲν γὰρ ἤδη, τοῖς δ᾽ ἐν ὑστέρῳ χρόνῳ
615   τὰ τερπνὰ πικρὰ γίγνεται καὖθις φίλα.
καὶ ταῖσι Θήβαις εἰ τανῦν εὐημερεῖ
καλῶς τὰ πρὸς σέ, μυρίας ὁ μυρίος

OEDIPUS

This is how it is with me: I was driven from my country by
my own offspring, and I can never return, because I killed
my father.

THESEUS

How then can they bring you there, if you must live apart
from them?

OEDIPUS

The voice of the god will compel them to it.

THESEUS

What disaster will the oracles cause them to fear?

OEDIPUS

Because it is fated that they are to be struck down in this
land.

THESEUS

And how can they also cause bitterness for me?

OEDIPUS

Dearest son of Aegeus, for the gods alone there is no old
age and no death ever, but all other things are submerged
by all-powerful time! The strength of the country perishes,
so does the strength of the body, loyalty dies and disloyalty
comes into being, and the same spirit never remains
between friends or between cities, since for some people
now and for others in the future happy relations turn
bitter, and again friendship is restored. And if now all is
sunny weather between Thebes and you, time as it passes

---

606 τἀμὰ κἀκ κείνων Ll.-J.: τἀμὰ κἀκείνων codd.
617 τὰ ed. Londin. a. 1722: τε codd.

χρόνος τεκνοῦται νύκτας ἡμέρας τ᾽ ἰών,
ἐν αἷς τὰ νῦν ξύμφωνα δεξιώματα
620 δόρει διασκεδῶσιν ἐκ σμικροῦ λόγου·
ἵν᾽ οὑμὸς εὕδων καὶ κεκρυμμένος νέκυς
ψυχρός ποτ᾽ αὐτῶν θερμὸν αἷμα πίεται,
εἰ Ζεὺς ἔτι Ζεὺς χὠ Διὸς Φοῖβος σαφής.
ἀλλ᾽ οὐ γὰρ αὐδᾶν ἡδὺ τἀκίνητ᾽ ἔπη,
625 ἔα μ᾽ ἐν οἷσιν ἠρξάμην, τὸ σὸν μόνον
πιστὸν φυλάσσων· κοὔποτ᾽ Οἰδίπουν ἐρεῖς
ἀχρεῖον οἰκητῆρα δέξασθαι τόπων
τῶν ἐνθάδ᾽, εἴπερ μὴ θεοὶ ψεύδουσί με.

ΧΟΡΟΣ

ἄναξ, πάλαι καὶ ταῦτα καὶ τοιαῦτ᾽ ἔπη
630 γῇ τῇδ᾽ ὅδ᾽ ἁνὴρ ὡς τελῶν ἐφαίνετο.

ΘΗΣΕΥΣ

τίς δῆτ᾽ ἂν ἀνδρὸς εὐμένειαν ἐκβάλοι
τοιοῦδ᾽, ὅτῳ πρῶτον μὲν ἡ δορύξενος
κοινὴ παρ᾽ ἡμῖν αἰέν ἐστιν ἑστία;
ἔπειτα δ᾽ ἱκέτης δαιμόνων ἀφιγμένος
635 γῇ τῇδε κἀμοὶ δασμὸν οὐ σμικρὸν τίνει.
ἁγὼ σέβας θεὶς οὔποτ᾽ ἐκβαλῶ χάριν
τὴν τοῦδε, χώρᾳ δ᾽ ἔμπολιν κατοικιῶ.
εἰ δ᾽ ἐνθάδ᾽ ἡδὺ τῷ ξένῳ μίμνειν, σέ νιν
τάξω φυλάσσειν, εἴτ᾽ ἐμοῦ στείχειν μέτα.
640 τί δ᾽ ἡδὺ τούτων, Οἰδίπους, δίδωμί σοι
κρίναντι χρῆσθαι· τῇδε γὰρ ξυνοίσομαι.

brings forth countless nights and days in which they shall
shatter with the spear the present harmonious pledges for
a petty reason. Then shall my dead body, sleeping and
buried, cold as it is, drink their warm blood, if Zeus is still
Zeus and his son Phoebus speaks the truth! But since
there is no pleasure in speaking words that should not be
touched on, leave me in the course I have begun, but only
keep your word, and you shall never say that Oedipus
whom you received into these regions was a useless
inmate, if the gods do not deceive me!

CHORUS

Lord, from the first it has been clear that this man would
discharge this promise and other such promises for this
country.

THESEUS

Who could reject the good will of such a man? First, the
hearth of an ally is always open to him, by natural right,
with us; and, second, he has come as a suppliant of the
gods, and is paying no small reward to this country and to
me. For these things I have respect, and I shall never
reject his kindness, but shall settle him in the country as a
dweller in the city. If it is the stranger's pleasure to remain
here, I shall appoint you to guard him; or he could go with
me. Oedipus, I offer you the choice of whichever course
pleases you; for I shall abide by it.

---

636 σέβας θεὶς Mekler: σὲ βιασθεὶς K: σεβισθεὶς Lra: σεβασθεὶς zt
637 ἔμπολιν Musgrave: ἔμπαλιν codd.
640 τί δ’ Fraenkel: τόδ’ codd.

ΟΙΔΙΠΟΥΣ

ὦ Ζεῦ, διδοίης τοῖσι τοιούτοισιν εὖ.

ΘΗΣΕΥΣ

τί δῆτα χρήζεις ; ἢ δόμους στείχειν ἐμούς ;

ΟΙΔΙΠΟΥΣ

εἴ μοι θέμις γ᾽ ἦν. ἀλλ᾽ ὁ χῶρός ἐσθ᾽ ὅδε —

ΘΗΣΕΥΣ

645   ἐν ᾧ τί πράξεις ; οὐ γὰρ ἀντιστήσομαι.

ΟΙΔΙΠΟΥΣ

ἐν ᾧ κρατήσω τῶν ἔμ᾽ ἐκβεβληκότων.

ΘΗΣΕΥΣ

μέγ᾽ ἂν λέγοις δώρημα τῆς ξυνουσίας.

ΟΙΔΙΠΟΥΣ

εἰ σοί γ᾽ ἅπερ φῂς ἐμμενεῖ τελοῦντί μοι.

ΘΗΣΕΥΣ

θάρσει τὸ τοῦδέ γ᾽ ἀνδρός· οὔ σε μὴ προδῶ.

ΟΙΔΙΠΟΥΣ

650   οὔτοι σ᾽ ὑφ᾽ ὅρκου γ᾽ ὡς κακὸν πιστώσομαι.

ΘΗΣΕΥΣ

οὔκουν πέρα γ᾽ ἂν οὐδὲν ἢ λόγῳ φέροις.

ΟΙΔΙΠΟΥΣ

πῶς οὖν ποήσεις ;

ΘΗΣΕΥΣ

τοῦ μάλιστ᾽ ὄκνος σ᾽ ἔχει ;

OEDIPUS

O Zeus, give good fortune to such men as this!

THESEUS

What is your wish? To go to my palace?

OEDIPUS

If it were right for me to do so; but this is the place . . .

THESEUS

Where you shall do what? I shall not oppose it!

OEDIPUS

In which I shall overcome those who threw me out.

THESEUS

The gift of your presence that you speak of is a great one.

OEDIPUS

Yes, if you abide by your pledge and you discharge it for me.

THESEUS

Have no fears regarding me! I shall never betray you.

OEDIPUS

I shall not bind you with an oath, as though you were dishonest.

THESEUS

You would receive nothing more than by my word.

OEDIPUS

How then will you act?

THESEUS

What are you most afraid of?

ΟΙΔΙΠΟΥΣ

ἥξουσιν ἄνδρες—

ΘΗΣΕΥΣ
ἀλλὰ τοῖσδ' ἔσται μέλον.

ΟΙΔΙΠΟΥΣ

ὅρα με λείπων—

ΘΗΣΕΥΣ
μὴ δίδασχ' ἃ χρή με δρᾶν.

ΟΙΔΙΠΟΥΣ

655   ὀκνοῦντ' ἀνάγκη—

ΘΗΣΕΥΣ
τοὐμὸν οὐκ ὀκνεῖ κέαρ.

ΟΙΔΙΠΟΥΣ

οὐκ οἶσθ' ἀπειλὰς—

ΘΗΣΕΥΣ
οἶδ' ἐγώ σε μή τινα
ἐνθένδ' ἀπάξοντ' ἄνδρα πρὸς βίαν ἐμοῦ.
[πολλαὶ δ' ἀπειλαὶ πολλὰ δὴ μάτην ἔπη
θυμῷ κατηπείλησαν· ἀλλ' ὁ νοῦς ὅταν
660   αὑτοῦ γένηται, φροῦδα τἀπειλήματα.]
κείνοις δ' ἴσως κεἰ δείν' ἐπερρώσθη λέγειν
τῆς σῆς ἀγωγῆς, οἶδ' ἐγώ, φανήσεται
μακρὸν τὸ δεῦρο πέλαγος οὐδὲ πλώσιμον.
θαρσεῖν μὲν οὖν ἔγωγε κἄνευ τῆς ἐμῆς
665   γνώμης ἐπαινῶ, Φοῖβος εἰ προύπεμψέ σε·
ὅμως δὲ κἀμοῦ μὴ παρόντος οἶδ' ὅτι
τοὐμὸν φυλάξει σ' ὄνομα μὴ πάσχειν κακῶς.

OEDIPUS

Men will come . . .

THESEUS

But these men will attend to them.

OEDIPUS

Take care that when you leave me . . .

THESEUS

Do not teach me what I ought to do!

OEDIPUS

I must feel anxious . . .

THESEUS

My heart feels no anxiety.

OEDIPUS

You do not know of the threats . . .

THESEUS

I know that no man shall carry you away from here against
my will! [Many threats have taken the form of many angry
words; but when the mind is in control of itself, threats
vanish.] And even if these men have spoken with much
confidence of taking you away, the sea they would have to
cross will appear wide, I know, and hard to sail over. So I
would advise you to be confident, even apart from my deci-
sion, if it was Phoebus who sent you; and none the less I
know that even when I am absent my name will guard you
from ill-treatment.

Exit THESEUS.

658-60 del. Wecklein

ΧΟΡΟΣ

εὐίππου, ξένε, τᾶσδε χώ-   στρ. α΄
ρας ἵκου τὰ κράτιστα γᾶς ἔπαυλα,
670 τὸν ἀργῆτα Κολωνόν, ἔνθ᾽
ἁ λίγεια μινύρεται
θαμίζουσα μάλιστ᾽ ἀη-
δὼν χλωραῖς ὑπὸ βάσσαις,
τὸν οἰνωπὸν ἔχουσα κισ-
675 σὸν καὶ τὰν ἄβατον θεοῦ
φυλλάδα μυριόκαρπον ἀνήλιον
ἀνήνεμόν τε πάντων
χειμώνων· ἵν᾽ ὁ βακχιώ-
τας ἀεὶ Διόνυσος ἐμβατεύει
680 θείαις ἀμφιπολῶν τιθήναις.
θάλλει δ᾽ οὐρανίας ὑπ᾽ ἄ-   ἀντ. α΄
χνας ὁ καλλίβοτρυς κατ᾽ ἦμαρ αἰεὶ
νάρκισσος, μεγάλαιν θεαῖν
ἀρχαῖον στεφάνωμ᾽, ὅ τε
685 χρυσαυγὴς κρόκος· οὐδ᾽ ἄυ-
πνοι κρῆναι μινύθουσιν
Κηφισοῦ νομάδες ῥεέ-
θρων, ἀλλ᾽ αἰὲν ἐπ᾽ ἤματι
ὠκυτόκος πεδίων ἐπινίσεται
690 ἀκηράτῳ ξὺν ὄμβρῳ
στερνούχου χθονός· οὐδὲ Μου-
σᾶν χοροί νιν ἀπεστύγησαν, οὐδ᾽ αὖθ᾽
ἁ χρυσάνιος Ἀφροδίτα.

CHORUS

In this country of fine horses, stranger, you have come to
the choicest rural dwellings, to white Colonus, where the
melodious nightingale most likes to stay and sing her song
beneath the green glades, living amid the wine-dark ivy
and the inviolable leafage of the goddess, rich in fruit,
never vexed by the sun or by the wind of many winters,
where the reveller Dionysus ever treads the ground, in
company with his divine nurses.[a]

And there flourishes ever day by day, fed by dew from
heaven, the narcissus with its lovely clusters, the ancient
crown of the two great goddesses,[b] and the crocus that
gleams with gold; nor are the sleepless streams that flow
from the waters of Cephisus diminished, but ever each day
the river, quick to bring crops to birth, flows over the plains
of the broad-breasted earth with moisture free from stain.
Nor is this place rejected by the choruses of the Muses, nor
by Aphrodite of the golden reins.

[a] The Maenads.
[b] Demeter and Persephone.

---

674 οἰνωπὸν ἔχουσα Erfurdt: οἴνωπ᾽ ἀνέχουσα vel sim. codd.
692–93 οὐδ᾽ αὖθ᾽ ἁ Ll.-J.: οὐδ᾽ αὖ ἁ t: οὐδ᾽ αὖ L: οὐδ᾽ ἁ rz: οὐδὲ ἁ
Wilamowitz

695   ἔστιν δ' οἷον ἐγὼ γᾶς 'Ασίας οὐκ
          ἐπακούω,   στρ. β'
      οὐδ' ἐν τᾷ μεγάλᾳ Δωρίδι νάσῳ Πέλοπος
          πώποτε βλαστὸν
      φύτευμ' ἀχείρωτον αὐτοποιόν,
      ἐγχέων φόβημα δαΐων,
700   ὃ τᾷδε θάλλει μέγιστα χώρᾳ,
      γλαυκᾶς παιδοτρόφου φύλλον ἐλαίας.
      τὸ μέν τις οὐ νεαρὸς οὐδὲ γήρᾳ
      συνναίων ἁλιώσει χερὶ πέρσας·
      ὁ δ' αἰὲν ὁρῶν κύκλος
705   λεύσσει νιν Μορίου Διὸς
      χἀ γλαυκῶπις 'Αθάνα.
      ἄλλον δ' αἶνον ἔχω ματροπόλει τᾷδε
          κράτιστον,   ἀντ. β'
710   δῶρον τοῦ μεγάλου δαίμονος, εἰπεῖν, <χθονὸς>
          αὔχημα μέγιστον,
      εὔιππον, εὔπωλον, εὐθάλασσον.
      ὦ παῖ Κρόνου, σὺ γάρ νιν ἐς
      τόδ' εἷσας αὔχημ', ἄναξ Ποσειδάν,
      ἵπποισιν τὸν ἀκεστῆρα χαλινὸν
715   πρώταισι ταῖσδε κτίσας ἀγυιαῖς.
      ἁ δ' εὐήρετμος ἔκπαγλα χοροῖσιν
      παραπετομένα πλάτα
      θρώσκει τᾶν ἑκατομπόδων
      Νηρῇδων ἀκόλουθος.

And there is something I have not heard to have grown ever in the land of Asia, or in the great Dorian island of Pelops, a tree not planted by men's hands, but self-created, a terror to the spears of enemies, that flourishes most greatly in this land, the leaf of the gray-green nurturer of children, the olive. This shall no young man nor any that dwells with old age destroy and bring to nothing; for it is looked upon by the ever-seeing eye of Zeus Morios and by gray-eyed Athena.

And I can utter another great word of praise for this my mother city, a gift of the great god, a pride of the land supreme, the might of horses, the might of colts, the might of the sea. Son of Kronos, it was you who enthroned the city in this pride, lord Poseidon, creating first in these roads the bridle that tames horses. And the skilfully plied oar flies splendidly along, racing after the dances of the Nereids' hundred feet.

---

[702] οὐ Porson: οὔτε Lrat   οὐδὲ Jebb: οὔτε codd.

[703] συνναίων Blaydes: σημαίνων codd.

[704] δ' Ritschl: γὰρ codd.   αἰὲν ὁρῶν Hermann: εἰς αἰὲν ὁρῶν Lr: εἰσορῶν a

[710] suppl. Porson

[716] ἔκπαγλα χοροῖσιν Ll.-J.: ἔκπαγλ' ἁλία χερσὶ codd.

[717] παραπετομένα Ll.-J.: παραπτομένα Lraz

[718] τᾶν Platt: τῶν codd.

SOPHOCLES

ΑΝΤΙΓΟΝΗ

720 ὦ πλεῖστ᾽ ἐπαίνοις εὐλογούμενον πέδον,
νῦν σοὶ τὰ λαμπρὰ ταῦτα δεῖ φαίνειν ἔπη.

ΟΙΔΙΠΟΥΣ

τί δ᾽ ἔστιν, ὦ παῖ, καινόν;

ΑΝΤΙΓΟΝΗ

ἆσσον ἔρχεται
Κρέων ὅδ᾽ ἡμῖν οὐκ ἄνευ πομπῶν, πάτερ.

ΟΙΔΙΠΟΥΣ

ὦ φίλτατοι γέροντες, ἐξ ὑμῶν ἐμοὶ
725 φαίνοιτ᾽ ἂν ἤδη τέρμα τῆς σωτηρίας.

ΧΟΡΟΣ

θάρσει, παρέσται· καὶ γὰρ εἰ γέρων ἐγώ,
τὸ τῆσδε χώρας οὐ γεγήρακε σθένος.

ΚΡΕΩΝ

ἄνδρες χθονὸς τῆσδ᾽ εὐγενεῖς οἰκήτορες,
ὁρῶ τιν᾽ ὑμᾶς ὀμμάτων εἰληφότας
730 φόβον νεώρη τῆς ἐμῆς ἐπεισόδου·
ὃν μήτ᾽ ὀκνεῖτε μήτ᾽ ἀφῆτ᾽ ἔπος κακόν.
ἥκω γὰρ οὐχ ὡς δρᾶν τι βουληθείς, ἐπεὶ
γέρων μέν εἰμι, πρὸς πόλιν δ᾽ ἐπίσταμαι
σθένουσαν ἥκων, εἴ τιν᾽ Ἑλλάδος, μέγα.
735 ἀλλ᾽ ἄνδρα τόνδε τηλικόσθ᾽ ἀπεστάλην
πείσων ἕπεσθαι πρὸς τὸ Καδμείων πέδον,
οὐκ ἐξ ἑνὸς στείλαντος, ἀλλ᾽ ἀστῶν ὑπὸ
πάντων κελευσθείς, οὕνεχ᾽ ἧκέ μοι γένει
τὰ τοῦδε πενθεῖν πήματ᾽ εἰς πλεῖστον πόλεως.

496

ANTIGONE

O land most of all others eulogised with praise, now you
must show that these shining words are true!

OEDIPUS

What new thing is this, my daughter?

ANTIGONE

Creon is drawing near to us, not without an escort, father!

OEDIPUS

Dearest elders, now may you show to me the final bourne
of safety!

CHORUS

Do not be afraid, it shall be there! For even if I am old, the
strength of this land has not grown aged.

Enter CREON, *with his escort.*

CREON

Men who are the noble dwellers in this land, I see in your
eyes a fear newly caused by my arrival! But do not be
alarmed by it, nor let fall a hostile word! For I have not
come intending any action, since I am old, and I know that
I have come to a city that has great power, if any has in
Greece. But I set out, old as I am, to persuade this man to
accompany me to the land of the Cadmeans; it is not one
man only who has sent me, but all the citizens who com-
manded me, because family ties caused me to mourn his
sorrows most in all the city.

497

740   ἀλλ', ὦ ταλαίπωρ' Οἰδίπους, κλυὼν ἐμοῦ
ἱκοῦ πρὸς οἴκους. πᾶς σε Καδμείων λεὼς
καλεῖ δικαίως, ἐκ δὲ τῶν μάλιστ' ἐγώ·
[ὅσῳπερ, εἰ μὴ πλεῖστον ἀνθρώπων ἔφυν]
μάλιστα δ' ἀλγῶ τοῖσι σοῖς κακοῖς, γέρον,
745   ὁρῶν σε τὸν δύστηνον ὄντα μὲν ξένον,
ἀεὶ δ' ἀλήτην κἀπὶ προσπόλου μιᾶς
βιοστερῆ χωροῦντα, τὴν ἐγὼ τάλας
οὐκ ἄν ποτ' ἐς τοσοῦτον αἰκίας πεσεῖν
ἔδοξ', ὅσον πέπτωκεν ἥδε δύσμορος,
750   ἀεί σε κηδεύουσα καὶ τὸ σὸν κάρα
πτωχῷ διαίτῃ, τηλικοῦτος, οὐ γάμων
ἔμπειρος, ἀλλὰ τοὐπιόντος ἁρπάσαι.

      ἆρ' ἄθλιον τοὔνειδος, ὦ τάλας ἐγώ,
ὠνείδισ' ἐς σὲ κἀμὲ καὶ τὸ πᾶν γένος;
755   ἀλλ' οὐ γὰρ ἔστι τἀμφανῆ κρύπτειν, σὺ νῦν
πρὸς θεῶν πατρῴων, Οἰδίπους, πεισθεὶς ἐμοὶ
†κρύψον† θελήσας ἄστυ καὶ δόμους μολεῖν
τοὺς σοὺς πατρῴους, τήνδε τὴν πόλιν φίλως
εἰπών· ἐπαξία γάρ· ἡ δ' οἴκοι πλέον
760   δίκη σέβοιτ' ἄν, οὖσα σὴ πάλαι τροφός.

ΟΙΔΙΠΟΥΣ

    ὦ πάντα τολμῶν κἀπὸ παντὸς ἂν φέρων
λόγου δικαίου μηχάνημα ποικίλον,
τί ταῦτα πειρᾷ κἀμὲ δεύτερον θέλεις
ἑλεῖν, ἐν οἷς μάλιστ' ἂν ἀλγοίην ἁλούς;
765   πρόσθεν τε γάρ με τοῖσιν οἰκείοις κακοῖς

Come, long-suffering Oedipus, listen to me and come home! The whole people of Cadmus summons you, with good reason, and I most of all [inasmuch as, if I am not the very worst of men, I] grieve at your sorrows, aged man, seeing that in your misery you are an exile, and ever wander in indigence with but one attendant. Never would I have thought that this poor girl could fall to such a depth of misery as that to which she has fallen, always caring for you and for your person, living like a beggar, at her age, ignorant of wedlock, but at the mercy of a chance comer!

Is not the reproach bitter that I have levelled, woe is me, at you and at myself and at all our family? But since one cannot hide what is manifest, do you now, Oedipus, in the name of the gods of your fathers let me persuade you and yield, consenting to return to the town and to the home of your fathers, saying a kind farewell to this city, for she deserves it; but your home city should in justice be reverenced more, since she reared you long ago.

OEDIPUS

You who would stop at nothing and would extract a cunning scheme from any just plea, why do you make this attempt? Why do you try once more to catch me in the trap that would most pain me if you caught me? In time

---

499

νοσοῦνθ᾽, ὅτ᾽ ἦν μοι τέρψις ἐκπεσεῖν χθονός,
οὐκ ἤθελες θέλοντι προσθέσθαι χάριν,
ἀλλ᾽ ἡνίκ᾽ ἤδη μεστὸς ἦ θυμούμενος,
καὶ τοὐν δόμοισιν ἦν διαιτᾶσθαι γλυκύ,
770 τότ᾽ ἐξεώθεις κἀξέβαλλες, οὐδέ σοι
τὸ συγγενὲς τοῦτ᾽ οὐδαμῶς τότ᾽ ἦν φίλον·
νῦν τ᾽ αὖθις, ἡνίκ᾽ εἰσορᾷς πόλιν τέ μοι
ξυνοῦσαν εὔνουν τήνδε καὶ γένος τὸ πᾶν,
πειρᾷ μετασπᾶν, σκληρὰ μαλθακῶς λέγων.
775 καὶ τίς τοσαύτη τέρψις, ἄκοντας φιλεῖν;
ὥσπερ τις εἴ σοι λιπαροῦντι μὲν τυχεῖν
μηδὲν διδοίη μηδ᾽ ἐπαρκέσαι θέλοι,
πλήρη δ᾽ ἔχοντι θυμὸν ὧν χρῄζοις, τότε
δωροῖθ᾽, ὅτ᾽ οὐδὲν ἡ χάρις χάριν φέροι·
780 ἆρ᾽ ἂν ματαίου τῆσδ᾽ ἂν ἡδονῆς τύχοις;
τοιαῦτα μέντοι καὶ σὺ προσφέρεις ἐμοί,
λόγῳ μὲν ἐσθλά, τοῖσι δ᾽ ἔργοισιν κακά.
φράσω δὲ καὶ τοῖσδ᾽, ὥς σε δηλώσω κακόν.
ἥκεις ἔμ᾽ ἄξων, οὐχ ἵν᾽ ἐς δόμους ἄγῃς,
785 ἀλλ᾽ ὡς πάραυλον οἰκίσῃς, πόλις δέ σοι
κακῶν ἄνατος τῆσδ᾽ ἀπαλλαχθῇ χθονός.
οὐκ ἔστι σοι ταῦτ᾽, ἀλλά σοι τάδ᾽ ἔστ᾽, ἐκεῖ
χώρας ἀλάστωρ οὑμὸς ἐνναίων ἀεί·
ἔστιν δὲ παισὶ τοῖς ἐμοῖσι τῆς ἐμῆς
790 χθονὸς λαχεῖν τοσοῦτον, ἐνθανεῖν μόνον.
ἆρ᾽ οὐκ ἄμεινον ἢ σὺ τἀν Θήβαις φρονῶ;
πολλῷ γ᾽, ὅσῳπερ κἀκ σαφεστέρων κλύω,
Φοίβου τε καὐτοῦ Ζηνός, ὃς κείνου πατήρ.
τὸ σὸν δ᾽ ἀφῖκται δεῦρ᾽ ὑπόβλητον στόμα,

past when I was suffering from my private griefs, and it was my desire to be sent out of the land, you refused to grant me the favour I desired, but when I had had enough of my passion, and it was my wish to live at home, then you pushed me out and drove me into exile, caring not at all at that time for the kinship you now talk of! And now once more, when you see this city and all its people kindly to me as a resident, you try to tear me away, saying hard things in soft words. Why is it so delightful to be kind to men against their will? It is as though someone gave you nothing and refused his aid when you were imploring him to give, and when you had your fill of what you wished for gave to you, at a time when his kindness brought no kindness. Would not your pleasure then be useless? But that is the nature of what you offer me, sounding good, but in essence bad. And I shall explain it to these men also, so that I can prove you are a villain! You have come to fetch me, not so as to take me home, but so that you can settle me near the country, and that your city can escape the harm that threatens it from this land. You shall not have that, but you shall have this, my vengeful spirit ever dwelling here; and my sons can inherit this much only of my country, enough to die in!

Do I not understand better than you do what is afoot in Thebes? Far better, insomuch as I have learned from truer informants, from Phoebus and from Zeus himself who is his father. Your untruthful mouth has come here

---

769 post hunc v. iterant v. 438 codd., del. Valckenaer

775 καὶ τίς τοσαύτη Blaydes: καίτοι τοσαύτη lra: καίτοι τίς αὕτη Kzt

786 τῆσδ' Scaliger: τῶνδ' codd.

792 κἀκ Doederlein: καὶ ra: ἐκ lzt

795 πολλὴν ἔχον στόμωσιν· ἐν δὲ τῷ λέγειν
κάκ' ἂν λάβοις τὰ πλείον' ἢ σωτήρια.
ἀλλ' οἶδα γάρ σε ταῦτα μὴ πείθων, ἴθι·
ἡμᾶς δ' ἔα ζῆν ἐνθάδ'· οὐ γὰρ ἂν κακῶς
οὐδ' ὧδ' ἔχοντες ζῶμεν, εἰ τερποίμεθα.

ΚΡΕΩΝ

800 πότερα νομίζεις δυστυχεῖν ἔμ' ἐς τὰ σά,
ἢ σ' ἐς τὰ σαυτοῦ μᾶλλον ἐν τῷ νῦν λόγῳ;

ΟΙΔΙΠΟΥΣ

ἐμοὶ μέν ἐσθ' ἥδιστον, εἰ σὺ μήτ' ἐμὲ
πείθειν οἷός τ' εἶ μήτε τούσδε τοὺς πέλας.

ΚΡΕΩΝ

ὦ δύσμορ', οὐδὲ τῷ χρόνῳ φύσας φανῇ
805 φρένας ποτ', ἀλλὰ λῦμα τῷ γήρᾳ τρέφῃ;

ΟΙΔΙΠΟΥΣ

γλώσσῃ σὺ δεινός· ἄνδρα δ' οὐδέν' οἶδ' ἐγὼ
δίκαιον ὅστις ἐξ ἅπαντος εὖ λέγει.

ΚΡΕΩΝ

χωρὶς τό τ' εἰπεῖν πολλὰ καὶ τὸ καίρια.

ΟΙΔΙΠΟΥΣ

ὡς δὴ σὺ βραχέα, ταῦτα δ' ἐν καιρῷ λέγεις.

ΚΡΕΩΝ

810 οὐ δῆθ' ὅτῳ γε νοῦς ἴσος καὶ σοὶ πάρα.

ΟΙΔΙΠΟΥΣ

ἄπελθ', ἐρῶ γὰρ καὶ πρὸ τῶνδε, μηδέ με
φύλασσ' ἐφορμῶν ἔνθα χρὴ ναίειν ἐμέ.

with much mouthing, but by your speeches you will get more of harm than of protection! But I know that I cannot convince you; go, and leave me to live here; for I shall not live badly, even as I am, if I am contented with my life.

CREON

Do you believe I suffer more through your actions, or that you suffer more by your own in this discussion?

OEDIPUS

I am best pleased if you fail to persuade either me or these men here.

CREON

Unhappy man, shall you never be seen to have acquired sense with years, but does your old age sustain you as a blight?

OEDIPUS

You are clever with your tongue; but I know no righteous man who speaks well in every cause.

CREON

Speaking much is not the same as speaking rightly!

OEDIPUS

So you speak briefly but to the point!

CREON

Not for one who has a mind like yours!

OEDIPUS

Go—I will speak for these men as well as for myself—and do not stay here watching over me in the place where I must live!

SOPHOCLES

ΚΡΕΩΝ

μαρτύρομαι τούσδ᾽, οὐ σέ, πρὸς δὲ τοὺς φίλους
οἷ᾽ ἀνταμείβῃ ῥήματ᾽· ἢν δ᾽ ἕλω ποτέ —

ΟΙΔΙΠΟΥΣ

815 τίς δ᾽ ἄν με τῶνδε συμμάχων ἕλοι βίᾳ;

ΚΡΕΩΝ

ἦ μὴν σὺ κἄνευ τοῦδε λυπηθεὶς ἔσῃ.

ΟΙΔΙΠΟΥΣ

ποίῳ σὺν ἔργῳ τοῦτ᾽ ἀπειλήσας ἔχεις;

ΚΡΕΩΝ

παίδοιν δυοῖν σοι τὴν μὲν ἀρτίως ἐγὼ
ξυναρπάσας ἔπεμψα, τὴν δ᾽ ἄξω τάχα.

ΟΙΔΙΠΟΥΣ

820 οἴμοι.

ΚΡΕΩΝ

τάχ᾽ ἕξεις μᾶλλον οἰμώζειν τάδε.

ΟΙΔΙΠΟΥΣ

τὴν παῖδ᾽ ἔχεις;

ΚΡΕΩΝ

καὶ τήνδε γ᾽ οὐ μακροῦ χρόνου.

ΟΙΔΙΠΟΥΣ

ἰὼ ξένοι. τί δράσετ᾽; ἦ προδώσετε,
κοὐκ ἐξελᾶτε τὸν ἀσεβῆ τῆσδε χθονός;

---

814 δ᾽ Musgrave: σ᾽ codd.
816 τοῦδε Musgrave: τῶνδε codd.
821 Κρ. καὶ τήνδε Jebb: μου; Κρ. τήνδε codd.

CREON

I call on these men, not on you, and also on my friends
here, to be witnesses of your answers; and if I ever catch
you . . .

OEDIPUS

But who could catch me against the will of these allies?

CREON

I swear that even without that happening you shall suffer
pain!

OEDIPUS

What action is implied by the threat that you have uttered?

CREON

One of your two daughters I have already captured and
sent away, and I shall soon take away the other!

OEDIPUS

Alas!

CREON

You shall soon have greater cause to say Alas!

OEDIPUS

Do you hold my daughter?

CREON

Yes, and I shall soon hold this one also!

OEDIPUS

Ah, my guest-friends! What shall you do? Shall you betray
me, and not drive the impious man from this land?

SOPHOCLES

ΧΟΡΟΣ

χώρει, ξέν', ἔξω θᾶσσον· οὔτε γὰρ τανῦν
825 δίκαια πράσσεις οὔτε πρόσθεν εἴργασαι.

ΚΡΕΩΝ

ὑμῖν ἂν εἴη τήνδε καιρὸς ἐξάγειν
ἄκουσαν, εἰ θέλουσα μὴ πορεύσεται.

ΑΝΤΙΓΟΝΗ

οἴμοι τάλαινα, ποῖ φύγω; ποίαν λάβω
θεῶν ἄρηξιν ἢ βροτῶν;

ΧΟΡΟΣ

τί δρᾷς, ξένε;

ΚΡΕΩΝ

830 οὐχ ἅψομαι τοῦδ' ἀνδρός, ἀλλὰ τῆς ἐμῆς.

ΟΙΔΙΠΟΥΣ

ὦ γῆς ἄνακτες.

ΧΟΡΟΣ

ὦ ξέν', οὐ δίκαια δρᾷς.

ΚΡΕΩΝ

δίκαια.

ΧΟΡΟΣ

πῶς δίκαια;

ΚΡΕΩΝ

τοὺς ἐμοὺς ἄγω.

ΟΙΔΙΠΟΥΣ

ἰὼ πόλις.   στρ.

506

CHORUS

Go away at once, stranger! Neither your present nor your past actions have been righteous!

CREON

(to his escort) It is the moment for you to take this girl away, if she will not go willingly!

ANTIGONE

Ah me, where can I escape to? What help can I get from gods or men?

CHORUS

What are you doing, stranger?

CREON

I shall not touch this man, but only her, who belongs to me!

OEDIPUS

O lords of the land!

CHORUS

Stranger, what you are doing is wrong!

CREON

It is right!

CHORUS

How can it be right?

CREON

I am taking those who are mine!

OEDIPUS

I call on the city!

---

825 οὔτε Koen: οὔθ᾽ ἃ codd.
833 Oedipodi tribuit Wunder, Antigonae codd.

ΧΟΡΟΣ

835 τί δρᾷς, ὦ ξέν'; οὐκ ἀφήσεις; τάχ' ἐς βάσανον
 εἶ χερῶν.

ΚΡΕΩΝ

εἴργου.

ΧΟΡΟΣ

  σοῦ μὲν οὔ, τάδε γε μωμένου.

ΚΡΕΩΝ

πόλει μαχῇ γάρ, εἴ τι πημανεῖς ἐμέ.

ΟΙΔΙΠΟΥΣ

οὐκ ἠγόρευον ταῦτ' ἐγώ;

ΧΟΡΟΣ

    μέθες χεροῖν
τὴν παῖδα θᾶσσον.

ΚΡΕΩΝ

   μὴ 'πίτασσ' ἃ μὴ κρατεῖς.

ΧΟΡΟΣ

840 χαλᾶν λέγω σοι.

ΚΡΕΩΝ

   σοὶ δ' ἔγωγ' ὁδοιπορεῖν.

ΧΟΡΟΣ

προβᾶθ' ὧδε, βᾶτε βᾶτ', ἔντοποι.
πόλις ἐναίρεται, πόλις ἐμά, σθένει.
προβᾶθ' ὧδέ μοι.

ΑΝΤΙΓΟΝΗ

ἀφέλκομαι δύστηνος, ὦ ξένοι ξένοι.

CHORUS

What are you doing, stranger? Will you not let her go?
Soon you will come to a trial of strength.

CREON

Stand back!

CHORUS

Not from you, when this is your plan!

CREON

Yes, you will be fighting with my city, if you do me any
harm!

OEDIPUS

Did I not say it would be so?

CHORUS

Let go the girl at once!

CREON

Do not give orders where you have no power!

CHORUS

I tell you to let go!

CREON

And I tell you to be off!

CHORUS

Forward this way, forward, forward, men of the place! The
city, my city, is being destroyed by violence! Forward this
way, I beg!

ANTIGONE

I am being dragged away, poor creature, hosts, my hosts!

---

⁸³⁷ Creonti tribuit Reisig, Oedipodi codd.   μαχῇ . . .
πημανεῖς Porson: μάχη . . . πημαίνεις codd.
    ⁸⁴² ἐναίρεται] fort. ἐπαίρεται

ΟΙΔΙΠΟΥΣ

845 ποῦ, τέκνον, εἶ μοι;

ΑΝΤΙΓΟΝΗ
πρὸς βίαν πορεύομαι.

ΟΙΔΙΠΟΥΣ
ὄρεξον, ὦ παῖ, χεῖρας.

ΑΝΤΙΓΟΝΗ
ἀλλ' οὐδὲν σθένω.

ΚΡΕΩΝ
οὐκ ἄξεθ' ὑμεῖς;

ΟΙΔΙΠΟΥΣ
ὦ τάλας ἐγώ, τάλας.

ΚΡΕΩΝ
οὔκουν ποτ' ἐκ τούτοιν γε μὴ σκήπτροιν ἔτι
ὁδοιπορήσῃς· ἀλλ' ἐπεὶ νικᾶν θέλεις
850 πατρίδα τε τὴν σὴν καὶ φίλους, ὑφ' ὧν ἐγὼ
ταχθεὶς τάδ' ἔρδω, καὶ τύραννος ὢν ὅμως,
νίκα. χρόνῳ γάρ, οἶδ' ἐγώ, γνώσῃ τάδε,
ὁθούνεκ' αὐτὸς αὑτὸν οὔτε νῦν καλὰ
δρᾷς οὔτε πρόσθεν εἰργάσω, βίᾳ φίλων
855 ὀργῇ χάριν δούς, ἥ σ' ἀεὶ λυμαίνεται.

ΧΟΡΟΣ
ἐπίσχες αὐτοῦ, ξεῖνε.

ΚΡΕΩΝ
μὴ ψαύειν λέγω.

OEDIPUS

My child, where are you?

ANTIGONE

I am forced away!

OEDIPUS

Stretch out your hands, my daughter!

ANTIGONE

But I have not the strength!

CREON

Will you not take her away?

OEDIPUS

Wretched, wretched am I!

CREON

Then you shall never more walk with the aid of these two props! But since you wish for victory over your country and your friends, at whose order I am doing this, king though I am, win your victory! For in time, I know it, you shall realise this, that neither what you are doing now nor what you did before was right, since you yielded to your anger, which has always been your ruin.

CHORUS

Stop where you are, stranger!

CREON

I tell you, do not touch me!

ΧΟΡΟΣ

οὔτοι σ᾽ ἀφήσω, τῶνδέ γ᾽ ἐστερημένος.

ΚΡΕΩΝ

καὶ μεῖζον ἆρα ῥύσιον πόλει τάχα
θήσεις· ἐφάψομαι γὰρ οὐ ταύταιν μόναιν.

ΧΟΡΟΣ

860   ἀλλ᾽ ἐς τί τρέψῃ;

ΚΡΕΩΝ

τόνδ᾽ ἀπάξομαι λαβών.

ΧΟΡΟΣ

δεινὸν λέγεις.

ΚΡΕΩΝ

καὶ τοῦτο νῦν πεπράξεται,
ἢν μή μ᾽ ὁ κραίνων τῆσδε γῆς ἀπειργάθῃ.

ΟΙΔΙΠΟΥΣ

ὦ φθέγμ᾽ ἀναιδές, ἦ σὺ γὰρ ψαύσεις ἐμοῦ;

ΚΡΕΩΝ

αὐδῶ σιωπᾶν.

ΟΙΔΙΠΟΥΣ

μὴ γὰρ αἵδε δαίμονες
865   θεῖέν μ᾽ ἄφωνον τῆσδε τῆς ἀρᾶς ἔτι,
ὅς γ᾽, ὦ κάκιστε, φίλιον ὄμμ᾽ ἀποσπάσας
πρὸς ὄμμασιν τοῖς πρόσθεν ἐξοίχῃ βίᾳ.
τοιγὰρ σὲ καὐτὸν καὶ γένος τὸ σὸν θεῶν
ὁ πάντα λεύσσων Ἥλιος δοίη βίον
870   τοιοῦτον οἷον κἀμὲ γηρᾶναί ποτε.

CHORUS

I shall not let you go, since you have robbed me of these
two!

CREON

Then you shall soon pay a greater price to the city; for I
shall not lay hands on these two only!

CHORUS

Why, to what will you resort?

CREON

I shall seize this man and take him off!

CHORUS

What you say is shocking!

CREON

This too shall be done, unless the king of this country
prevents me![a]

OEDIPUS

O shameless voice, will you indeed lay hands on me?

CREON

I tell you to be silent!

OEDIPUS

No, may the goddesses here no longer check the curse that
is on my lips, on you, you villain, who have snatched from
me by violence the beloved eye I had, gone like the eyes I
had already lost! Therefore may the all-seeing Sun grant
that your old age is like mine!

[a] Creon speaks ironically; not surprisingly, he assumes that the
king is nowhere near.

---

^{865} $\tau\hat{\eta}s$ ed. Lond. a. 1747: $\gamma\hat{\eta}s$ codd.
^{866} γ' Blaydes: μ' codd. $\phi\ell\lambda\iota\omicron\nu$ Meineke: $\psi\iota\lambda\grave{\omicron}\nu$ codd.

ΚΡΕΩΝ
ὁρᾶτε ταῦτα, τῆσδε γῆς ἐγχώριοι;

ΟΙΔΙΠΟΥΣ
ὁρῶσι κἀμὲ καὶ σέ, καὶ φρονοῦσ᾽ ὅτι
ἔργοις πεπονθὼς ῥήμασίν σ᾽ ἀμύνομαι.

ΚΡΕΩΝ
οὔτοι καθέξω θυμόν, ἀλλ᾽ ἄξω βίᾳ
875 κεἰ μοῦνός εἰμι τόνδε κεἰ χρόνῳ βραδύς.

ΟΙΔΙΠΟΥΣ
ἰὼ τάλας.   ἀντ.

ΧΟΡΟΣ
ὅσον λῆμ᾽ ἔχων ἀφίκου, ξέν᾽, εἰ τάδε δοκεῖς
  τελεῖν.

ΚΡΕΩΝ
δοκῶ.

ΧΟΡΟΣ
  τάνδ᾽ ἄρ᾽ οὐκέτι νέμω πόλιν.

ΚΡΕΩΝ
880 τοῖς τοι δικαίοις χὼ βραχὺς νικᾷ μέγαν.

ΟΙΔΙΠΟΥΣ
ἀκούεθ᾽ οἷα φθέγγεται;

ΧΟΡΟΣ
         τά γ᾽ οὐ τελεῖ
<Ζεύς μοι ξυνίστω.>

ΚΡΕΩΝ
         Ζεύς γ᾽ ἂν εἰδείη, σὺ δ᾽ οὔ.

CREON

Do you see this, natives of this land?

OEDIPUS

They see me and you, and they are aware that I have suffered in actions and defend myself against you only in words.

CREON

I shall no longer restrain my anger, but shall carry this man away, even if I am alone and am made slow by age!

OEDIPUS

Ah, misery!

CHORUS

What insolence you have come here with, stranger, if you think you will accomplish this!

CREON

I think I shall!

CHORUS

Then I no longer consider this a city!

CREON

With the aid of justice even the small man vanquishes the great man!

OEDIPUS

Hear the words he utters!

CHORUS

He shall not accomplish this, Zeus be my witness!

CREON

Zeus would know, but you do not!

---

^{875} alterum κεὶ Page: καὶ codd. ^{882} suppl. Jebb   γ'
Hartung: ταῦτ' codd.

ΧΟΡΟΣ

ἆρ᾽ οὐχ ὕβρις τάδ᾽;

ΚΡΕΩΝ

ὕβρις, ἀλλ᾽ ἀνεκτέα.

ΧΟΡΟΣ

ἰὼ πᾶς λεώς, ἰὼ γᾶς πρόμοι,
885   μόλετε σὺν τάχει, μόλετ᾽· ἐπεὶ πέραν
περῶσ᾽ <οἵδε> δή.

ΘΗΣΕΥΣ

τίς ποθ᾽ ἡ βοή; τί τοὖργον; ἐκ τίνος φόβου
ποτὲ
βουθυτοῦντά μ᾽ ἀμφὶ βωμὸν ἔσχετ᾽ ἐναλίῳ θεῷ
τοῦδ᾽ ἐπιστάτῃ Κολωνοῦ; λέξαθ᾽, ὡς εἰδῶ
τὸ πᾶν,
890   οὗ χάριν δεῦρ᾽ ᾖξα θᾶσσον ἢ καθ᾽ ἡδονὴν ποδός.

ΟΙΔΙΠΟΥΣ

ὦ φίλτατ᾽, ἔγνων γὰρ τὸ προσφώνημά σου,
πέπονθα δεινὰ τοῦδ᾽ ὑπ᾽ ἀνδρὸς ἀρτίως.

ΘΗΣΕΥΣ

τὰ ποῖα ταῦτα; τίς δ᾽ ὁ πημήνας; λέγε.

ΟΙΔΙΠΟΥΣ

Κρέων ὅδ᾽, ὃν δέδορκας, οἴχεται τέκνων
895   ἀποσπάσας μου τὴν μόνην ξυνωρίδα.

ΘΗΣΕΥΣ

πῶς εἶπας;

CHORUS

Is this not outrage?

CREON

Outrage, but you must put up with it!

CHORUS

I call on all the people, I call on the chieftains of the land!
Come swiftly, come! For these men are going too far!

Enter, suddenly, THESEUS, *followed by retainers.*

THESEUS

What is this cry for help? What is the matter? What were
you afraid of when you stopped me sacrificing oxen at the
altar to the god of the sea, the protector of Colonus here?
Tell me, so that I know all, why I have rushed here faster
than was easy for my feet!

OEDIPUS

My dear friend, for I recognise your voice, I have just suf-
fered awful treatment from this man.

THESEUS

What was that? Who has given you pain? Tell me!

OEDIPUS

Creon here, whom you see, has taken from me my only
pair of children.

THESEUS

What are you saying?

---

[886] suppl. Elmsley

ΟΙΔΙΠΟΥΣ

οἷα καὶ πέπονθ' ἀκήκοας.

ΘΗΣΕΥΣ

οὔκουν τις ὡς τάχιστα προσπόλων μολὼν
πρὸς τούσδε βωμοὺς πάντ' ἀναγκάσει λεὼν
ἄνιππον ἱππότην τε θυμάτων ἄπο
900 σπεύδειν ἀπὸ ρυτῆρος, ἔνθα δίστομοι
μάλιστα συμβάλλουσιν ἐμπόρων ὁδοί,
ὡς μὴ παρέλθωσ' αἱ κόραι, γέλως δ' ἐγὼ
ξένῳ γένωμαι τῷδε, χειρωθεὶς βίᾳ;
ἴθ', ὡς ἄνωγα, σὺν τάχει. τοῦτον δ' ἐγώ,
905 εἰ μὲν δι' ὀργῆς ἧκον, ἧς ὅδ' ἄξιος,
ἄτρωτον οὐ μεθῆκ' ἂν ἐξ ἐμῆς χερός·
νῦν δ' οὕσπερ αὐτὸς τοὺς νόμους εἰσῆλθ' ἔχων,
τούτοισι κοὐκ ἄλλοισιν ἁρμοσθήσεται.
οὐ γάρ ποτ' ἔξει τῆσδε τῆς χώρας, πρὶν ἂν
910 κείνας ἐναργεῖς δεῦρό μοι στήσῃς ἄγων·
ἐπεὶ δέδρακας οὔτ' ἐμοῦ καταξία
οὔθ' ὧν πέφυκας αὐτὸς οὔτε σῆς χθονός,
ὅστις δίκαι' ἀσκοῦσαν εἰσελθὼν πόλιν
κἄνευ νόμου κραίνουσαν οὐδέν, εἶτ' ἀφεὶς
915 τὰ τῆσδε τῆς γῆς κύρι' ὧδ' ἐπεσπεσὼν
ἄγεις θ' ἃ χρῄζεις καὶ παρίστασαι βίᾳ·
καί μοι πόλιν κένανδρον ἢ δούλην τινὰ
ἔδοξας εἶναι, κἄμ' ἴσον τῷ μηδενί.
    καίτοι σε Θῆβαί γ' οὐκ ἐπαίδευσαν κακόν·
920 οὐ γὰρ φιλοῦσιν ἄνδρας ἐκδίκους τρέφειν,

518

OEDIPUS

You have heard what I have suffered!

THESEUS

Will not one of my attendants go with all speed to these
altars and compel all the people, on foot and on horse, to
leave the sacrifices and make haste with slack rein just to
the point where the two highways come together, so that
the girls do not pass through first, and I am made to look
foolish by this stranger, being worsted by violence? Go, as
I bid you, quickly! As for this man, if I were as angry with
him as he deserves, I would not have let him go un-
wounded by my hand; but as it is he shall be disciplined
according to the laws he himself has brought with him, and
to no others. For you shall never depart from this country,
until you have brought these girls and set them here in my
sight; for your actions are a disgrace to me, and to your own
nature, and to your country, seeing that you came to a city
that abides by justice and decides everything according to
the law and then flouted this land's authorities when you
made your incursion to take away all that you wished and
subjugate it by force. You thought my city had no men or
was enslaved, and I counted for nothing!

Yet it is not Theban training that made you evil; it is not
their way to breed unrighteous men, nor would they praise

---

896 καὶ Jebb: περ codd.
907 οὕσπερ Reiske: ὥσπερ codd.
911 κατάξια Elmsley: -ίως codd.

SOPHOCLES

οὐδ' ἄν σ' ἐπαινέσειαν, εἰ πυθοίατο
συλῶντα τἀμὰ καὶ τὰ τῶν θεῶν, βίᾳ
ἄγοντα φωτῶν ἀθλίων ἱκτήρια.
οὔκουν ἔγωγ' ἂν σῆς ἐπεμβαίνων χθονός,
925   οὐδ' εἰ τὰ πάντων εἶχον ἐνδικώτατα,
ἄνευ γε τοῦ κραίνοντος, ὅστις ἦν, χθονὸς
οὔθ' εἷλκον οὔτ' ἂν ἦγον, ἀλλ' ἠπιστάμην
ξένον παρ' ἀστοῖς ὡς διαιτᾶσθαι χρεών.
σὺ δ' ἀξίαν οὐκ οὖσαν αἰσχύνεις πόλιν
930   τὴν αὐτὸς αὑτοῦ, καί σ' ὁ πληθύων χρόνος
γέρονθ' ὁμοῦ τίθησι καὶ τοῦ νοῦ κενόν.
    εἶπον μὲν οὖν καὶ πρόσθεν, ἐννέπω δὲ νῦν,
τὰς παῖδας ὡς τάχιστα δεῦρ' ἄγειν τινά,
εἰ μὴ μέτοικος τῆσδε τῆς χώρας θέλεις
935   εἶναι βίᾳ τε κοὐχ ἑκών· καὶ ταῦτά σοι
τοῦ νοῦ θ' ὁμοίως κἀπὸ τῆς γλώσσης λέγω.

ΧΟΡΟΣ

ὁρᾷς ἵν' ἥκεις, ὦ ξέν'; ὡς ἀφ' ὧν μὲν εἶ
φαίνῃ δίκαιος, δρῶν δ' ἐφευρίσκῃ κακά.

ΚΡΕΩΝ

ἐγὼ οὔτ' ἄνανδρον τήνδε τὴν πόλιν λέγω,
940   ὦ τέκνον Αἰγέως, οὔτ' ἄβουλον, ὡς σὺ φής,
τοὔργον τόδ' ἐξέπραξα, γιγνώσκων δ' ὅτι
οὐδείς ποτ' αὐτοῖς τῶν ἐμῶν ἂν ἐμπέσοι
ζῆλος ξυναίμων, ὥστ' ἐμοῦ τρέφειν βίᾳ.
ἤδη δ' ὁθούνεκ' ἄνδρα καὶ πατροκτόνον
945   κἄναγνον οὐ δεξοίατ', οὐδ' ὅτῳ γάμου
ξυνόντ' ἐφηυρέθησαν ἀνοσίου τέκνα.

520

you if they knew that you were plundering my property
and that of the gods, carrying off by force unhappy people
who are suppliants. I would never have entered your coun-
try, even in the justest of all causes, without the consent of
the ruler of the land, whoever he was, and have dragged
people off; I would have known how a stranger must con-
duct himself in relations with the citizens. But you are dis-
gracing your own city, which does not deserve it, and
advancing years as they make you old are also depriving
you of sense.

I said earlier and I say now that someone must at once
bring the girls here, unless you wish to become a resident
here by force and against your will; and what I say to you
comes from my mind as well as from my tongue!

CHORUS

You see where you have come to, stranger? Your ancestry
makes you seem honest, but you are caught out doing
wrong!

CREON

I do not say your city has no men, son of Aegeus, nor was
my action rash, as you say, but I knew that no desire for my
relations would so fall upon your people that they would
keep them here against my will. I knew, too, that they
would not receive a parricide and a man impure, nor one in
whose company were found the children of an unholy

---

931 fort. κενοῖ

936 τοῦ νοῦ Meineke: τῷ νῷ codd. plerique

945–46 γάμου ξυνόντ᾽ ἐφηυρέθησαν ἀνοσίου τέκνα Ll.-J.: γάμοι
ξυνόντες ηὑρέθησαν ἀνόσιοι τέκνων fere codd.

521

τοιοῦτον αὐτοῖς Ἄρεος εὔβουλον πάγον
ἐγὼ ξυνῄδη χθόνιον ὄνθ᾽, ὃς οὐκ ἐᾷ
τοιούσδ᾽ ἀλήτας τῇδ᾽ ὁμοῦ ναίειν πόλει·
950 ᾧ πίστιν ἴσχων τήνδ᾽ ἐχειρούμην ἄγραν.
καὶ ταῦτ᾽ ἂν οὐκ ἔπρασσον, εἰ μή μοι πικρὰς
αὐτῷ τ᾽ ἀρὰς ἠρᾶτο καὶ τὠμῷ γένει·
ἀνθ᾽ ὧν πεπονθὼς ἠξίουν τάδ᾽ ἀντιδρᾶν.
[θυμοῦ γὰρ οὐδὲν γῆράς ἐστιν ἄλλο πλὴν
955 θανεῖν· θανόντων δ᾽ οὐδὲν ἄλγος ἅπτεται.]
    πρὸς ταῦτα πράξεις οἷον ἂν θέλῃς· ἐπεὶ
ἐρημία με, κεἰ δίκαι᾽ ὅμως λέγω,
σμικρὸν τίθησι· πρὸς δὲ τὰς πράξεις ἔτι,
καὶ τηλικόσδ᾽ ὤν, ἀντιδρᾶν πειράσομαι.

ΟΙΔΙΠΟΥΣ

960 ὦ λῆμ᾽ ἀναιδές, τοῦ καθυβρίζειν δοκεῖς,
πότερον ἐμοῦ γέροντος, ἢ σαυτοῦ, τόδε;
ὅστις φόνους μοι καὶ γάμους καὶ συμφορὰς
τοῦ σοῦ διῆκας στόματος, ἃς ἐγὼ τάλας
ἤνεγκον ἄκων· θεοῖς γὰρ ἦν οὕτω φίλον,
965 τάχ᾽ ἄν τι μηνίουσιν ἐς γένος πάλαι.
ἐπεὶ καθ᾽ αὑτόν γ᾽ οὐκ ἂν ἐξεύροις ἐμὲ
ἁμαρτίας ὄνειδος οὐδὲν ἀνθ᾽ ὅτου
τάδ᾽ εἰς ἐμαυτὸν τοὺς ἐμούς θ᾽ ἡμάρτανον.
ἐπεὶ δίδαξον, εἴ τι θέσφατον πατρὶ
970 χρησμοῖσιν ἱκνεῖθ᾽ ὥστε πρὸς παίδων θανεῖν,
πῶς ἂν δικαίως τοῦτ᾽ ὀνειδίζοις ἐμοί,
ὃς οὔτε βλάστας πω γενεθλίους πατρός,

marriage. Such is the wisdom of the council of the hill of
Ares, which I knew was in their land, one which does not
permit such wanderers to live together with this city. In
this knowledge I put my trust when I secured this prey;
and I would not have done so, had not he called down
bitter curses on me and on my family. For this treatment I
thought it right to make this return. [For anger knows no
old age, till death; and no pain afflicts the dead.]

In the face of that you may do what you will, since even
if my plea is just, I am alone and powerless; but in response
to what you do, old as I am, I shall one day attempt to act.

OEDIPUS

O shameless insolence, do you think you are doing outrage
against my old age, or your own, you who have prated of
killings and marriages and disasters which I endured
unwittingly, for it was the pleasure of the gods, who
perhaps had long felt anger against my family. For in
myself you could not find any fault to reproach me with, on
account of which I committed these crimes against myself
and against my own. Why, tell me, if a prophecy came to
my father from an oracle that he should die at his chil-
dren's hands, how could you justly make that a reproach
to me, whom no father had begotten, no mother conceived,

---

948 χθόνιον] χρόνιον Bergk
954–55 del. Blaydes
958 ἔτι Ll.-J.: ὅμως codd.
966 κατ' αὐτόν . . . ἐμὲ Wecklein: καθ' αὑτόν . . . ἐμοὶ codd.

SOPHOCLES

οὐ μητρὸς εἶχον, ἀλλ᾽ ἀγέννητος τότ᾽ ἦ;
εἰ δ᾽ αὖ φανεὶς δύστηνος, ὡς ἐγὼ ᾽φάνην,
975 ἐς χεῖρας ἦλθον πατρὶ καὶ κατέκτανον,
μηδὲν ξυνιεὶς ὧν ἔδρων εἰς οὕς τ᾽ ἔδρων,
πῶς ἂν τό γ᾽ ἆκον πρᾶγμ᾽ ἂν εἰκότως ψέγοις;
μητρὸς δέ, τλῆμον, οὐκ ἐπαισχύνη γάμους
οὔσης ὁμαίμου σῆς μ᾽ ἀναγκάζων λέγειν
980 οἵους ἐρῶ τάχ᾽· οὐ γὰρ οὖν σιγήσομαι,
σοῦ γ᾽ ἐς τόδ᾽ ἐξελθόντος, ἀνόσιον στόμα.
ἔτικτε γάρ μ᾽ ἔτικτεν, ὤμοι μοι κακῶν,
οὐκ εἰδότ᾽ οὐκ εἰδυῖα, καὶ τεκοῦσά με
αὑτῆς ὄνειδος παῖδας ἐξέφυσέ μοι.
985 ἀλλ᾽ ἓν γὰρ οὖν ἔξοιδα, σὲ μὲν ἑκόντ᾽ ἐμὲ
κείνην τε ταῦτα δυσστομεῖν· ἐγὼ δέ νιν
ἄκων τ᾽ ἔγημα, φθέγγομαί τ᾽ ἄκων τάδε.
ἀλλ᾽ οὐ γὰρ οὔτ᾽ ἐν τοῖσδ᾽ ἀκούσομαι κακὸς
γάμοισιν οὔθ᾽ οὓς αἰὲν ἐμφορεῖς σύ μοι
990 φόνους πατρῴους ἐξονειδίζων πικρῶς.
ἓν γάρ μ᾽ ἄμειψαι μοῦνον ὧν σ᾽ ἀνιστορῶ·
εἴ τίς σε τὸν δίκαιον αὐτίκ᾽ ἐνθάδε
κτείνοι παραστάς, πότερα πυνθάνοι᾽ ἂν εἰ
πατήρ σ᾽ ὁ καίνων, ἢ τίνοι᾽ ἂν εὐθέως;
995 δοκῶ μέν, εἴπερ ζῆν φιλεῖς, τὸν αἴτιον
τίνοι᾽ ἄν, οὐδὲ τοὐνδικον περιβλέποις.
τοιαῦτα μέντοι καὐτὸς εἰσέβην κακά,
θεῶν ἀγόντων· ὥστ᾽ ἐγὼ οὐδὲ τὴν πατρὸς
ψυχὴν ἂν οἶμαι ζῶσαν ἀντειπεῖν ἐμοί.
1000 σὺ δ᾽, εἰ γὰρ οὐ δίκαιος, ἀλλ᾽ ἅπαν καλὸν

524

but who was still unborn? And if after I unhappily came
to being, as I did, I came to blows with my father and killed
him, altogether ignorant of what I was doing and to whom
I was doing it, how can you reasonably find fault with an
action done unwittingly? And are you not ashamed, you
wretch, of forcing me to speak of my marriage with my
mother, seeing that she was your sister, when it was such
as I shall now describe; for I shall not keep silent, now
that you have gone so far, unholy mouth! Yes, she bore
me, she bore me, alas for my sorrows, and neither of us
knew it, and after she had borne me she brought forth
children for me to my shame! But one thing I know for
certain, that your abuse of her and me is uttered deli-
berately; but my marriage with her and my present words
about it were not willed by me. No, neither this marriage
nor the killing of my father, which you never cease to cast
in my teeth with bitter reproaches, shall prove me to be
evil. Of all my questions, answer me just one! If here and
now a man stood near you, the righteous one, and tried to
kill you, would you ask if the would-be killer was your
father, or would you strike back at once? I think that if you
value life you would strike back at the guilty one, and
would not consider whether it was just or no. But these
were the sorrows into which I entered, led by the gods, so
that I do not think that even my father's spirit, if it came to
life, could contradict me. But you, since you are not a
righteous man, but think it proper to say anything, speak-

λέγειν νομίζων, ῥητὸν ἄρρητόν τ' ἔπος,
τοιαῦτ' ὀνειδίζεις με τῶνδ' ἐναντίον.

κ αί σοι τὸ Θησέως ὄμμα θωπεῦσαι φίλον,
καὶ τὰς Ἀθήνας, ὡς κατῴκηνται καλῶς·
1005 κᾆθ' ὧδ' ἐπαινῶν πολλὰ τοῦδ' ἐκλανθάνη,
ὁθούνεκ' εἴ τις γῇ θεοὺς ἐπίσταται
τιμαῖς σεβίζειν, ἥδε τῷδ' ὑπερφέρει,
ἀφ' ἧς σὺ κλέψας τὸν ἱκέτην γέροντ' ἐμὲ
αὐτόν τ' ἐχειροῦ τὰς κόρας τ' οἴχῃ λαβών.
1010 ἀνθ' ὧν ἐγὼ νῦν τάσδε τὰς θεὰς ἐμοὶ
καλῶν ἱκνοῦμαι καὶ κατασκήπτω λιταῖς
ἐλθεῖν ἀρωγοὺς ξυμμάχους θ', ἵν' ἐκμάθῃς
οἵων ὑπ' ἀνδρῶν ἥδε φρουρεῖται πόλις.

ΧΟΡΟΣ

ὁ ξεῖνος, ὦναξ, χρηστός· αἱ δὲ συμφοραὶ
1015 αὐτοῦ πανώλεις, ἄξιαι δ' ἀμυναθεῖν.

ΘΗΣΕΥΣ

ἅλις λόγων· ὡς οἱ μὲν ἐξηρπασμένοι
σπεύδουσιν, ἡμεῖς δ' οἱ παθόντες ἕσταμεν.

ΚΡΕΩΝ

τί δῆτ' ἀμαυρῷ φωτὶ προστάσσεις ποεῖν;

ΘΗΣΕΥΣ

1019 ὁδοῦ κατάρχειν τῆς ἐκεῖ, πομπὸν δ' ἐμὲ
1028 κοὐκ ἄλλον ἕξεις ἐς τόδ'· ἔξοιδά σε
οὐ ψιλὸν οὐδ' ἄσκευον ἐς τοσήνδ' ὕβριν
1030 ἥκοντα τόλμης τῆς παρεστώσης τανῦν,
ἀλλ' ἔσθ' ὅτῳ σὺ πιστὸς ὢν ἔδρας τάδε.

able and unspeakable alike, reproach me with such things in these men's presence!

And you are glad to flatter Theseus to his face, and to flatter Athens and its government; and then amid all these praises you forget this, that if any country knows how to reverence the gods with honours, this one excels in that respect; and it is from that country that you snatch me, an aged man, a suppliant, and have maltreated me and carried off my daughters! On account of this I now call on these goddesses in supplication and charge them with prayers to come as my helpers and allies, so that you may learn the nature of the men who guard this city!

CHORUS

My lord, the stranger is a good man! His fortune has been ruinous, but is such that we should defend him.

THESEUS

Enough of talk! The abductors are making haste, and we the victims are standing still!

CREON

What order have you for a helpless man?

THESEUS

You must show the way there, and you shall have me and no other escort in that, for I know that you would not have ventured on such insolence as your present daring reveals if you had lacked men and weapons, but you trusted in something when you began such an action. I must

---

1003 ὄμμα K: ὄνομα cett.   φίλον Tournier: καλόν codd.
1007 τιμαῖς Turnebus: τιμὰς codd.
1028–33 post 1019 traiecit Housman

ἃ δεῖ μ' ἀθρῆσαι, μηδὲ τήνδε τὴν πόλιν
1033 ἑνὸς ποῆσαι φωτὸς ἀσθενεστέραν,
1020 χωρεῖν δ' ἵν', εἰ μὲν ἐν τόποισι τοῖσδ' ἔχεις
τὰς παῖδας ἡμῖν, αὐτὸς ἐκδείξῃς ἐμοί·
εἰ δ' ἐγκρατεῖς φεύγουσιν, οὐδὲν δεῖ πονεῖν·
ἄλλοι γὰρ οἱ σπεύσοντες, οὓς οὐ μή ποτε
χώρας φυγόντες τῇσδ' ἐπεύξωνται θεοῖς.
1025 ἀλλ' ἐξυφηγοῦ· γνῶθι δ' ὡς ἔχων ἔχῃ
καί σ' εἷλε θηρῶνθ' ἡ τύχη· τὰ γὰρ δόλῳ
1027 τῷ μὴ δικαίῳ κτήματ' οὐχὶ σῴζεται.
1034 νοεῖς τι τούτων, ἢ μάτην τὰ νῦν τέ σοι
1035 δοκεῖ λελέχθαι χὤτε ταῦτ' ἐμηχανῶ;

ΚΡΕΩΝ

οὐδὲν σὺ μεμπτὸν ἐνθάδ' ὢν ἐρεῖς ἐμοί·
οἴκοι δὲ χἠμεῖς εἰσόμεσθ' ἃ χρὴ ποεῖν.

ΘΗΣΕΥΣ

χωρῶν ἀπείλει νῦν· σὺ δ' ἡμίν, Οἰδίπους,
ἔκηλος αὐτοῦ μίμνε, πιστωθεὶς ὅτι,
1040 ἢν μὴ θάνω 'γὼ πρόσθεν, οὐχὶ παύσομαι
πρὶν ἄν σε τῶν σῶν κύριον στήσω τέκνων.

ΟΙΔΙΠΟΥΣ

ὄναιο, Θησεῦ, τοῦ τε γενναίου χάριν
καὶ τῆς πρὸς ἡμᾶς ἐνδίκου προμηθίας.

ΧΟΡΟΣ

εἴην ὅθι δαΐων   στρ. α´
1045 ἀνδρῶν τάχ' ἐπιστροφαὶ
τὸν χαλκοβόαν Ἄρη

528

look to this, and not render this city weaker than a single man, but come to the place where, if you have the girls in this region, you yourself may show them to me! But if your men are escaping with them in their power, we have no trouble; for there are others who will make haste, whom you shall never escape to thank the gods in prayer. Come, show the way! Know that the captor is captured and in the event the hunter has become the prey, for what is gained by unrighteous cunning is not kept. Have you any understanding of this, or have these words and those that were uttered when you hatched this plot been spoken in vain?

CREON

While you are here nothing that you say to me can be faulted; but at home we too shall know what we must do!

THESEUS

Utter your threats, but now go! But do you, Oedipus, remain here in peace, in the assurance that, if I do not die first, I shall not rest till I have placed your children in your hands!

OEDIPUS

May you be blessed, Theseus, for your nobility and for the righteous concern that you have shown for us!

Exeunt THESEUS and retainers, taking CREON.

CHORUS

I wish I were where the enemy will soon wheel about and join the brazen din of battle, either by the shore dear to

---

1021 ἡμῖν Elmsley: ἡμῶν codd.
1023 σπεύσοντες Meineke: σπεύδοντες codd.

μείξουσιν, ἢ πρὸς Πυθίαις
ἢ λαμπάσιν ἀκταῖς,
1050 οὗ πότνιαι σεμνὰ τιθηνοῦνται τέλη
θνατοῖσιν, ὧν καὶ χρυσέα
κλῂς ἐπὶ γλώσσᾳ βέβα-
κε προσπόλων Εὐμολπιδᾶν·
ἔνθ' οἶμαι τὸν ἐγρεμάχαν
1055 Θησέα καὶ τὰς διστόλους
ἀδμῆτας ἀδελφὰς
αὐτάρκει τάχ' ἐμμείξειν βοᾷ
τούσδ' ἀνὰ χώρους·
ἦ που τὸν ἐφέσπερον   ἀντ. α′
1060 πέτρας νιφάδος πελῶσ'
Οἰάτιδος ἐκ νομοῦ
πώλοισιν ἢ ῥιμφαρμάτοις
φεύγοντες ἁμίλλαις.
1065 ἁλώσεται· δεινὸς ὁ προσχώρων Ἄρης,
δεινὰ δὲ Θησειδᾶν ἀκμά.
πᾶς γὰρ ἀστράπτει χαλι-
νός, πᾶσα δ' ὁρμᾶται †κατ'
ἀμπυκτήρια φάλαρα πώλων†
1070 ἄμβασις, οἳ τὰν ἱππίαν
τιμῶσιν Ἀθάναν
καὶ τὸν πόντιον γαιάοχον
Ῥέας φίλον υἱόν.
ἔρδουσιν ἢ μέλλουσιν; ὡς   στρ. β′
1075 προμνᾶταί τί μοι
γνώμα τάχ' ἀνδώσειν

Apollo[a] or by the torch-lit shore where the divine ladies nurse the august rites for mortals on whose tongues rests the golden key of the attendant sons of Eumolpus![b] Here, I think, Theseus the arouser of battle shall grant to the virgin sisters also all-sufficient aid within these regions!

They are drawing near, I think, to the place west of the snow-white rock,[c] from the pastures of the deme of Oea, fleeing on horses or in swiftly racing chariots. He shall be taken! Powerful is the strength in battle of the natives, terrible the might of Theseus' men! For every bridle is flashing, and every mounted follower makes haste with his rein loose, all they who honour Athena, lady of horses, and him of the sea,[d] the girdler of earth, Rhea's dear son!

Are they in action, or do they delay? My mind prophesies to me that the sufferings of the girls who have

---

[a] Daphnae, where there was a temple of Apollo.

[b] Eleusis; the Eumolpids were an Athenian family that held a hereditary priesthood there.

[c] Probably Mount Aigaleos.

[d] Poseidon.

1050 σεμνὰ Valckenaer: -αὶ codd.
1068 κατ'] καθεῖσ' Schneidewin: χαλῶσ' Hermann
1069 ἀμπυκτήρι᾽ ἀντιπάλων Pearson
1076 ἀνδώσειν] ἐνδώσειν interpretatio ap. sch. L

531

τᾶν δεινὰ τλασᾶν, δεινὰ δ' εὑ-
ρουσᾶν πρὸς αὐθαίμων πάθη.
τελεῖ τελεῖ Ζεύς τι κατ' ἦμαρ.
1080 μάντις εἴμ' ἐσθλῶν ἀγώνων.
εἴθ' ἀελλαία ταχύρρωστος πελειὰς
αἰθερίας νεφέλας κύρσαιμ' ἄνωθ' ἀγώνων
αἰωρήσασα τοὐμὸν ὄμμα.
1085 ἰὼ θεῶν πάνταρχε παντ-   ἀντ. β'
όπτα Ζεῦ, πόροις
γᾶς τᾶσδε δαμούχοις
σθένει 'πινικείῳ τὸν εὔ-
αγρον τελειῶσαι λόχον,
1090 σεμνά τε παῖς Παλλὰς Ἀθάνα,
καὶ τὸν ἀγρευτὰν Ἀπόλλω
καὶ κασιγνήταν πυκνοστίκτων ὀπαδὸν
ὠκυπόδων ἐλάφων στέργω διπλᾶς ἀρωγὰς
1095 μολεῖν γᾷ τᾷδε καὶ πολίταις.

ὦ ξεῖν' ἀλῆτα, τὸν σκοπὸν μὲν οὐκ ἐρεῖς
ὡς ψευδόμαντις· τὰς κόρας γὰρ εἰσορῶ
τάσδ' ἆσσον αὖθις ὧδε προσπολουμένας.

ΟΙΔΙΠΟΥΣ
ποῦ ποῦ; τί φής; πῶς εἶπας;

ΑΝΤΙΓΟΝΗ
ὦ πάτερ πάτερ,
1100 τίς ἂν θεῶν σοι τόνδ' ἄριστον ἄνδρ' ἰδεῖν
δοίη, τὸν ἡμᾶς δεῦρο προσπέμψαντά σοι;

endured grievous things, and have had grievous treatment from their kindred, will soon abate. This day, this day Zeus will fulfil some purpose! I predict a victory in the struggle! I wish I were a wind-swift strong-winged dove, gazing from a lofty cloud upon the contest!

Ah, lord supreme of the gods, all-seeing Zeus, grant to the guardians of this land's people in their ambush to seize the prey with victorious might, you and your august daughter Pallas Athene! And I call upon the hunter Apollo and his sister, follower of dappled swift-footed deer, to come giving the aid of both to this land and to its citizens!

Wandering stranger, you shall not say that your guardian proved a false prophet! For I see these girls being escorted back this way by their attendants!

OEDIPUS

Where, where? What are you saying?

Enter ANTIGONE *and* ISMENE *with* THESEUS.

ANTIGONE

O father, father, which of the gods could grant that you could see this noblest of men, who has brought us here to you?

1077–78 τᾶν ... τλασᾶν ... εὑρουσᾶν sch.: τὰν ... τλᾶσαν ... εὑροῦσαν codd.

1078 πρὸς αὐθαίμων Bothe: πρὸς αὐθομαίμων codd.

1083 ἄνωθ' Hermann: αὐτῶν δ' codd.

1084 αἰωρήσασα Dindorf: θεωρήσασα codd.

1085–86 ἰὼ ... πόροις Jebb: ἰὼ Ζεῦ πάνταρχε θεῶν παντόπτα πόροις codd.

1088 σθένει huc revocavit Hermann: ante τὸν codd.

1096 τὸν σκοπὸν Elmsley: τῷ σκοπῷ codd.

ΟΙΔΙΠΟΥΣ

ὦ τέκνον, ἦ πάρεστον;

ΑΝΤΙΓΟΝΗ

αἵδε γὰρ χέρες
Θησέως ἔσωσαν φιλτάτων τ' ὀπαόνων.

ΟΙΔΙΠΟΥΣ

προσέλθετ', ὦ παῖ, πατρί, καὶ τὸ μηδαμὰ
1105 ἐλπισθὲν ἥξειν σῶμα βαστάσαι δότε.

ΑΝΤΙΓΟΝΗ

αἰτεῖς ἃ τεύξῃ· σὺν πόθῳ γὰρ ἡ χάρις.

ΟΙΔΙΠΟΥΣ

ποῦ δῆτα, ποῦ 'στον;

ΑΝΤΙΓΟΝΗ

αἵδ' ὁμοῦ πελάζομεν.

ΟΙΔΙΠΟΥΣ

ὦ φίλτατ' ἔρνη.

ΑΝΤΙΓΟΝΗ

τῷ τεκόντι πᾶν φίλον.

ΟΙΔΙΠΟΥΣ

ὦ σκῆπτρα φωτός —

ΑΝΤΙΓΟΝΗ

δυσμόρου γε δύσμορα.

ΟΙΔΙΠΟΥΣ

1110 ἔχω τὰ φίλτατ', οὐδ' ἔτ' ἂν πανάθλιος
θανὼν ἂν εἴην σφῷν παρεστώσαιν ἐμοί.

OEDIPUS

My child, are you both here?

ANTIGONE

Yes, these hands of Theseus and his dearest attendants have saved us!

OEDIPUS

Come near to your father, daughter, and allow me to hold the body that I never dared to hope would return!

ANTIGONE

You ask for a thing that will be granted you; the favour that you ask is what we long for!

OEDIPUS

Where, where are you?

ANTIGONE

We are coming near to you together!

OEDIPUS

My dearest offspring!

ANTIGONE

To a parent every child is dear!

OEDIPUS

Staves that support a man . . .

ANTIGONE

Sad staves of a sad man!

OEDIPUS

I have what is dearest to me, and now I should not be entirely miserable if I died while you two stand by me!

1109 γε ed. Lond. a. 1747: τε codd.

ἐρείσατ᾽, ὦ παῖ, πλευρὸν ἀμφιδέξιον
ἐμφύντε τῷ φύσαντι, κἀναπαύσατον
τὸν πρόσθ᾽ ἐρῆμον τοῦδε δυστήνου πλάνου.
1115 καί μοι τὰ πραχθέντ᾽ εἴπαθ᾽ ὡς βράχιστ᾽, ἐπεὶ
ταῖς τηλικαῖσδε σμικρὸς ἐξαρκεῖ λόγος.

ΑΝΤΙΓΟΝΗ

ὅδ᾽ ἔσθ᾽ ὁ σώσας· τοῦδε χρὴ κλύειν, πάτερ,
οὗ κἄστι τοὔργον· τοὐμὸν <ὧδ᾽> ἔσται βραχύ.

ΟΙΔΙΠΟΥΣ

ὦ ξεῖνε, μὴ θαύμαζε, πρὸς τὸ λιπαρὲς
1120 τέκν᾽ εἰ φανέντ᾽ ἄελπτα μηκύνω λόγον.
ἐπίσταμαι γὰρ τήνδε τὴν ἐς τάσδε μοι
τέρψιν παρ᾽ ἄλλου μηδενὸς πεφασμένην.
σὺ γάρ νιν ἐξέσωσας, οὐκ ἄλλος βροτῶν.
καί σοι θεοὶ πόροιεν ὡς ἐγὼ θέλω,
1125 αὐτῷ τε καὶ γῇ τῇδ᾽· ἐπεὶ τό γ᾽ εὐσεβὲς
μόνοις παρ᾽ ὑμῖν ηὗρον ἀνθρώπων ἐγὼ
καὶ τοὐπιεικὲς καὶ τὸ μὴ ψευδοστομεῖν.
εἰδὼς δ᾽ ἀμύνω τοῖσδε τοῖς λόγοις τάδε.
ἔχω γὰρ ἅχω διὰ σὲ κοὐκ ἄλλον βροτῶν.
1130 καί μοι χέρ᾽, ὦναξ, δεξιὰν ὄρεξον, ὡς
ψαύσω φιλήσω τ᾽, εἰ θέμις, τὸ σὸν κάρα.
  καίτοι τί φωνῶ; πῶς σ᾽ ἂν ἄθλιος γεγὼς
θιγεῖν θελήσαιμ᾽ ἀνδρὸς ᾧ τίς οὐκ ἔνι
κηλὶς κακῶν ξύνοικος; οὐκ ἔγωγέ σε,
1135 οὐδ᾽ οὖν ἐάσω. τοῖς γὰρ ἐμπείροις βροτῶν
μόνοις οἷόν τε συνταλαιπωρεῖν τάδε.
σὺ δ᾽ αὐτόθεν μοι χαῖρε καὶ τὰ λοιπά μου

536

Grow one with your father, daughter, each of you pressing
to a side of me, and give repose to one who was made deso-
late by that unhappy wandering! Tell me what was done as
briefly as you can, since for girls of your age few words
suffice!

ANTIGONE

Here is the one who saved us! You must hear him, father,
to whom the deed belongs! What I say shall be as brief as
that!

OEDIPUS

Stranger, do not be surprised at my speaking at length,
insistently, to my children who have appeared beyond all
hope! For I know that the delight I feel in these has come
to me from none other than you; for it is you that saved
them, no other among mortals. And may the gods grant
you what I desire, for yourself and for this country, since I
have found in you alone among mankind piety and fairness
and the absence of lying speech! With knowledge I repay
these things with these words, for I have what I have
through you and through no other mortal. Stretch out your
right hand to me, king, so that I may touch it and may kiss
your face, if it is permitted!

Yet what am I saying? How could I, who was born to
misery, wish you to touch a man in whom every taint of
evils dwells? I cannot wish it, neither can I allow you to do
it! Only those mortals who have experienced these things
can share this misery! Receive my salutation where you

ἐμφύντε Mudge: ἐμφῦτε a: ἐμφῦσα fere cett.
1114 τὸν πρόσθ' ἐρῆμον Sehrwald: τοῦ πρόσθ' ἐρήμου codd.
1118 οὗ κἄστι Wex: καί σοί τε codd.   suppl. Livineius
1121 τὴν Musgrave: σὴν codd.   1132 σ' Hermann: δ' codd.

μέλου δικαίως, ὥσπερ ἐς τόδ᾽ ἡμέρας.

ΘΗΣΕΥΣ

οὔτ᾽ εἴ τι μῆκος τῶν λόγων ἔθου πλέον,
1140 τέκνοισι τερφθεὶς τοῖσδε, θαυμάσας ἔχω,
οὐδ᾽ εἰ πρὸ τοὐμοῦ προὔλαβες τὰ τῶνδ᾽ ἔπη.
βάρος γὰρ ἡμᾶς οὐδὲν ἐκ τούτων ἔχει.
οὐ γὰρ λόγοισι τὸν βίον σπουδάζομεν
λαμπρὸν ποεῖσθαι μᾶλλον ἢ τοῖς δρωμένοις.
1145 δείκνυμι δ᾽· ὧν γὰρ ὤμοσ᾽ οὐκ ἐψευσάμην
οὐδέν σε, πρέσβυ. τάσδε γὰρ πάρειμ᾽ ἄγων
ζώσας, ἀκραιφνεῖς τῶν κατηπειλημένων.
χὤπως μὲν ἀγὼν ᾑρέθη τί δεῖ μάτην
κομπεῖν, ἅ γ᾽ εἴσῃ καὐτὸς ἐκ ταύταιν ξυνών;
1150 λόγος δ᾽ ὃς ἐμπέπτωκεν ἀρτίως ἐμοὶ
στείχοντι δεῦρο, συμβαλοῦ γνώμην, ἐπεὶ
σμικρὸς μὲν εἰπεῖν, ἄξιος δὲ θαυμάσαι.
πρᾶγος δ᾽ ἀτίζειν οὐδὲν ἄνθρωπον χρεών.

ΟΙΔΙΠΟΥΣ

τί δ᾽ ἔστι, τέκνον Αἰγέως; δίδασκέ με,
1155 ὡς μὴ εἰδότ᾽ αὐτὸν μηδὲν ὧν σὺ πυνθάνῃ.

ΘΗΣΕΥΣ

φασίν τιν᾽ ἡμῖν ἄνδρα, σοὶ μὲν ἔμπολιν
οὐκ ὄντα, συγγενῆ δέ, προσπεσόντα πως
βωμῷ καθῆσθαι τῷ Ποσειδῶνος, παρ᾽ ᾧ
θύων ἔκυρον ἡνίχ᾽ ὡρμώμην ἐγώ.

ΟΙΔΙΠΟΥΣ

1160 ποδαπόν; τί προσχρῄζοντα τῷ θακήματι;

538

stand, and for the future take care of me with justice, as
you have up to this time!

THESEUS

I am not surprised that you have spoken at some length, in
your delight over your daughters, nor that you spoke to
them before you spoke to me; for this causes no pain to me,
since I strive to give my life lustre not through words but
through actions. And I can prove it, for I have failed to
keep none of the oaths I swore to you, aged man; I am here
bringing these girls alive, unscathed after the threats
against them. And as to how the fight was won, why should
I vainly boast of what you will hear yourself from them,
being in their company?

But contribute your opinion regarding a request that
has lately come to my ears on my way here, a thing one can
relate briefly, but one that occasions surprise; a human
being should take no matter lightly.

OEDIPUS

What is it, son of Aegeus? Explain it to me, since I know
nothing of what you ask about.

THESEUS

They tell me that a man, not an inhabitant of your city, but
a relation, has come as a suppliant and is sitting by the altar
of Poseidon, at which I was sacrificing when I set off.

OEDIPUS

Where did he come from? What desire provoked his sup-
plication?

  1148 ἀγὼν Heath: ἀγὼν οὗτος codd.: ἄγων Nauck   μάτην
del. Livineius   1153 ἄνθρωπον Markland: -ῳ r: -ων cett.

ΘΗΣΕΥΣ

οὐκ οἶδα πλὴν ἕν· σοῦ γάρ, ὡς λέγουσί μοι,
βραχύν τιν᾽ αἰτεῖ μῦθον οὐκ ὄγκου πλέων.

ΟΙΔΙΠΟΥΣ

ποῖόν τιν᾽; οὐ γὰρ ἧδ᾽ ἕδρα σμικροῦ λόγου.

ΘΗΣΕΥΣ

σοὶ φασὶν αὐτὸν ἐς λόγους μολεῖν μόνον
1165 αἰτεῖν ἀπελθεῖν <τ᾽> ἀσφαλῶς τῆς δεῦρ᾽ ὁδοῦ.

ΟΙΔΙΠΟΥΣ

τίς δῆτ᾽ ἂν εἴη τήνδ᾽ ὁ προσθακῶν ἕδραν;

ΘΗΣΕΥΣ

ὅρα κατ᾽ Ἄργος εἴ τις ὑμὶν ἐγγενὴς
ἔσθ᾽, ὅστις ἄν σου τοῦτο προσχρῄζοι τυχεῖν.

ΟΙΔΙΠΟΥΣ

ὦ φίλτατε, σχὲς οὗπερ εἶ.

ΘΗΣΕΥΣ

τί δ᾽ ἔστι σοι;

ΟΙΔΙΠΟΥΣ

1170 μή μου δεηθῇς —

ΘΗΣΕΥΣ

πράγματος ποίου; λέγε.

ΟΙΔΙΠΟΥΣ

ἔξοιδ᾽ ἀκούων τῶνδ᾽ ὅς ἐσθ᾽ ὁ προστάτης.

1164 μολεῖν μόνον Ll.-J. post Heimsoeth: ἐλθεῖν μολόντ᾽ codd.:
ἐλθεῖν μόνον Vauvilliers

THESEUS

I only know one thing; he is asking for a brief word with
you, they tell me, of no special moment.

OEDIPUS

What kind of word? To sit in supplication is a matter of
much weight.

THESEUS

They say he wishes only to speak with you and to return
unharmed from his journey here.

OEDIPUS

Who can he be, the man who sits making this supplication?

THESEUS

Consider whether you have any relative in Argos, who
might ask this favour of you!

OEDIPUS

Dear friend, stay where you are!

THESEUS

What is the matter with you?

OEDIPUS

Do not ask of me . . .

THESEUS

What thing? Tell me!

OEDIPUS

I know well, from hearing it from these, who the suppliant
is.

1165 suppl. Heath
1169 σχὲς Heath: ἴσχες Lrz: ἐπίσχες a

ΘΗΣΕΥΣ

καὶ τίς ποτ᾽ ἐστίν, ὅν γ᾽ ἐγὼ ψέξαιμί τι;

ΟΙΔΙΠΟΥΣ

παῖς οὑμός, ὦναξ, στυγνός, οὗ λόγων ἐγὼ
ἄλγιστ᾽ ἂν ἀνδρῶν ἐξανασχοίμην κλύων.

ΘΗΣΕΥΣ

1175 τί δ᾽; οὐκ ἀκούειν ἔστι, καὶ μὴ δρᾶν ἃ μὴ
χρῄζεις; τί σοι τοῦδ᾽ ἐστὶ λυπηρὸν κλύειν;

ΟΙΔΙΠΟΥΣ

ἔχθιστον, ὦναξ, φθέγμα τοῦθ᾽ ἥκει πατρί·
καὶ μή μ᾽ ἀνάγκῃ προσβάλῃς τάδ᾽ εἰκαθεῖν.

ΘΗΣΕΥΣ

ἀλλ᾽ εἰ τὸ θάκημ᾽ ἐξαναγκάζει σκόπει·
1180 μή σοι πρόνοι᾽ ᾖ τοῦ θεοῦ φυλακτέα.

ΑΝΤΙΓΟΝΗ

πάτερ, πιθοῦ μοι, κεἰ νέα παραινέσω.
τὸν ἄνδρ᾽ ἔασον τόνδε τῇ θ᾽ αὑτοῦ φρενὶ
χάριν παρασχεῖν τῷ θεῷ θ᾽ ἃ βούλεται,
καὶ νῷν ὕπεικε τὸν κασίγνητον μολεῖν.
1185 οὐ γάρ σε, θάρσει, πρὸς βίαν παρασπάσει
γνώμης ἃ μή σοι συμφέροντα λέξεται.
λόγων δ᾽ ἀκοῦσαι τίς βλάβη; τά τοι κακῶς
ηὑρημέν᾽ ἔργα τῷ λόγῳ μηνύεται.
ἔφυσας αὐτόν· ὥστε μηδὲ δρῶντά σε
1190 τὰ τῶν κακίστων δυσσεβέστατ᾽, ὦ πάτερ,
θέμις σέ γ᾽ εἶναι κεῖνον ἀντιδρᾶν κακῶς.
αἰδοῦ νιν. εἰσὶ χἀτέροις γοναὶ κακαὶ

THESEUS

And who is the man with whom I should find fault?

OEDIPUS

My hateful son, king, whose speech would be more painful
for me to hear than any man's!

THESEUS

Why, is it not possible to listen, but not to do what you do
not wish to do? Why is it painful for you to give this man a
hearing?

OEDIPUS

This man's voice, king, is most hateful to his father; do not
constrain me to grant this concession!

THESEUS

But consider whether his suppliant posture does not oblige
you; perhaps you ought to maintain respect towards the
god.

ANTIGONE

Father, let me persuade you, even though I am young to
give advice! Allow this man to give this satisfaction to his
own mind and to give the god his wish, and yield to us in
letting our brother come! For words to your disadvantage
that he speaks will not, be assured, force you from your
judgment. And what harm is there in listening to what he
says? Actions evilly devised are exposed by words! You are
his father, so that even if he had committed against you the
most impious crimes of any villain, it would not be right for
you to return evil for evil. Show him mercy! Other men

---

¹¹⁷⁶ τοῦδ' Elmsley: τοῦτ' codd.   ¹¹⁸⁷ κακῶς Hermann:
καλῶς Lrat   ¹¹⁸⁹ μηδὲ Dawes: μήτε codd.
¹¹⁹⁰ δυσσεβέστατ' ὦ Dawes: -εστάτων codd.
¹¹⁹² αἰδοῦ νιν Jebb: ἀλλ' αὐτὸν vel αὑτὸν codd.

543

καὶ θυμὸς ὀξύς, ἀλλὰ νουθετούμενοι
φίλων ἐπῳδαῖς ἐξεπᾴδονται φύσιν.
1195 σὺ δ᾽ εἰς ἐκεῖνα, μὴ τὰ νῦν, ἀποσκόπει
πατρῷα καὶ μητρῷα πήμαθ᾽ ἅπαθες,
κἂν κεῖνα λεύσσῃς, οἶδ᾽ ἐγώ, γνώσῃ κακοῦ
θυμοῦ τελευτὴν ὡς κακὴ προσγίγνεται.
ἔχεις γὰρ οὐχὶ βαιὰ τἀνθυμήματα,
1200 τῶν σῶν ἀδέρκτων ὀμμάτων τητώμενος.
ἀλλ᾽ ἡμὶν εἶκε. λιπαρεῖν γὰρ οὐ καλὸν
δίκαια προσχρήζουσιν, οὐδ᾽ αὐτὸν μὲν εὖ
πάσχειν, παθόντα δ᾽ οὐκ ἐπίστασθαι τίνειν.

ΟΙΔΙΠΟΥΣ

τέκνον, βαρεῖαν ἡδονὴν νικᾶτέ με
1205 λέγοντες· ἔστω δ᾽ οὖν ὅπως ὑμῖν φίλον.
μόνον, ξέν᾽, εἴπερ κεῖνος ὧδ᾽ ἐλεύσεται,
μηδεὶς κρατείτω τῆς ἐμῆς ψυχῆς ποτε.

ΘΗΣΕΥΣ

ἅπαξ τὰ τοιαῦτ᾽, οὐχὶ δὶς χρῄζω κλυεῖν,
ὦ πρέσβυ. κομπεῖν δ᾽ οὐχὶ βούλομαι· σὺ δ᾽ ὢν
1210 σῶς ἴσθ᾽, ἐάν περ κἀμέ τις σῴζῃ θεῶν.

ΧΟΡΟΣ

ὅστις τοῦ πλέονος μέρους   στρ.
χρῄζει τοῦ μετρίου παρεὶς
ζώειν, σκαιοσύναν φυλάσ-
σων ἐν ἐμοὶ κατάδηλος ἔσται.
1215 ἐπεὶ πολλὰ μὲν αἱ μακραὶ
ἁμέραι κατέθεντο δὴ
λύπας ἐγγυτέρω, τὰ τέρ-

also have evil children and a swift temper, but they let themselves be charmed by the admonitions of their friends. Think not of the present, but of the past, of the sufferings you endured because of your father and your mother, and if you look on them, I know, you will realise how evil is the result of evil passion! For you have no trivial reminders, being deprived of the sight of your eyes! Come, yield to us! It is not right that those whose wish is good should have to implore, nor to fail to make return for the kindnesses one has received.

OEDIPUS

My child, your words overcome me, giving a pleasure that costs me dear! But let it be as you wish! Only, stranger, if that man comes here, let no one ever get control over my life!

THESEUS

I wish to hear such words only once, aged man, and not twice! I do not wish to boast, but know that you are safe, if one of the gods keeps me safe!

Exit THESEUS.

CHORUS

Whoever desires a greater share of life, not content with a moderate portion, is guarding, it is clear to me, a mistaken view. For the long days lay up, you can see, many things closer to pain, and you cannot see where pleasure lies,

---

1197 **λεύσσῃς** Pierson: **λύσῃς** codd.
1199 **βαιὰ** Musgrave: **βίαια** codd.
1209 **σὺ δ' ὢν** Dindorf: **σὺ δὲ** codd.
1210 **σῶς** Scaliger: **σῶν** codd.
1212 **παρεὶς**] **πέρα** Schneidewin

πόντα δ' οὐκ ἂν ἴδοις ὅπου,
ὅταν τις ἐς πλέον πέσῃ
1220 τοῦ δέοντος· ὁ δ' ἐπίκουρος ἰσοτέλεστος,
Ἄϊδος ὅτε μοῖρ' ἀνυμέναιος
ἄλυρος ἄχορος ἀναπέφηνε,
θάνατος ἐς τελευτάν.

μὴ φῦναι τὸν ἅπαντα νι-   ἀντ.
1225 κᾷ λόγον· τὸ δ', ἐπεὶ φανῇ,
βῆναι κεῖθεν ὅθεν περ ἥ-
κει πολὺ δεύτερον ὡς τάχιστα.
ὡς εὖτ' ἂν τὸ νέον παρῇ
1230 κούφας ἀφροσύνας φέρον,
τίς πλαγὰ πολύμοχθος ἔ-
ξω; τίς οὐ καμάτων ἔνι;
φόνοι, στάσεις, ἔρις, μάχαι
1235 καὶ φθόνος· τό τε κατάμεμπτον ἐπιλέλογχε
πύματον ἀκρατὲς ἀπροσόμιλον
γῆρας ἄφιλον, ἵνα πρόπαντα
κακὰ κακῶν ξυνοικεῖ.

ἐν ᾧ τλάμων ὅδ' — οὐκ ἐγὼ μόνος —   ἐπ.
1240 πάντοθεν βόρειος ὥς τις ἀκτὰ
κυματοπλὴξ χειμερία κλονεῖται,
ὡς καὶ τόνδε κατ' ἄκρας
δειναὶ κυματοαγεῖς
ἆται κλονέουσιν ἀεὶ ξυνοῦσαι,
1245 αἱ μὲν ἀπ' ἀελίου δυσμᾶν,
αἱ δ' ἀνατέλλοντος,
αἱ δ' ἀνὰ μέσσαν ἀκτῖν',
αἱ δ' ἐννυχιᾶν ἀπὸ Ῥιπᾶν.

when anyone falls into more of life than he needs; but the deliverer brings an end for all alike, when the doom of Hades, with no wedding song, no lyre, no dances, is revealed, death at the last.

Not to be born comes first by every reckoning; and once one has appeared, to go back to where one came from as soon as possible is the next best thing. For while youth is with one, carrying with it light-headed thoughtlessnesses, what painful blow is far away? What hardship is not near? Murders, civil strife, quarrels, battles, and resentment! And the next place, at the end, belongs to much-dispraised old age, powerless, unsociable, friendless, where all evils of evils are our neighbours.

In this the unhappy man here—not I alone—is battered from all sides, like a cape facing north, in storms buffeted by the winds. Even so is this man also battered over the head by grim waves of ruin breaking over him that never leave him, some from where the sun goes down, some from where it rises, and others from the mountains of the north, shrouded in night.

[1220] δέοντος Reiske: θέλοντος codd.   ὁ δ' Hermann: οὐδ' codd.

[1226] fort. κεῖσέ γ' ὅθεν

[1231] πλαγὰ Herwerden; πλάγχθη fere codd.

[1234-35] φόνοι et φθόνος traiecit Faehse

[1242] ὡς] ὣς Brunck

SOPHOCLES

ΑΝΤΙΓΟΝΗ

καὶ μὴν ὅδ' ἡμῖν, ὡς ἔοικεν, ὁ ξένος·
1250 ἀνδρῶν γε μοῦνος, ὦ πάτερ, δι' ὄμματος
ἀστακτὶ λείβων δάκρυον ὧδ' ὁδοιπορεῖ.

ΟΙΔΙΠΟΥΣ

τίς οὗτος;

ΑΝΤΙΓΟΝΗ

ὅνπερ καὶ πάλαι κατείχομεν
γνώμῃ, πάρεστι δεῦρο Πολυνείκης ὅδε.

ΠΟΛΥΝΕΙΚΗΣ

οἴμοι, τί δράσω; πότερα τἀμαυτοῦ κακὰ
1255 πρόσθεν δακρύσω, παῖδες, ἢ τὰ τοῦδ' ὁρῶν
πατρὸς γέροντος; ὃν ξένης ἐπὶ χθονὸς
σὺν σφῷν ἐφηύρηκ' ἐνθάδ' ἐκβεβλημένον
ἐσθῆτι σὺν τοιᾷδε, τῆς ὁ δυσφιλὴς
γέρων γέροντι συγκατῴκηκεν πίνος
1260 πλευρὰν μαραίνων, κρατὶ δ' ὀμματοστερεῖ
κόμη δι' αὔρας ἀκτένιστος ᾄσσεται·
ἀδελφὰ δ', ὡς ἔοικε, τούτοισιν φορεῖ
τὰ τῆς ταλαίνης νηδύος θρεπτήρια.
ἀγὼ πανώλης ὄψ' ἄγαν ἐκμανθάνω·
1265 καὶ μαρτυρῶ κάκιστος ἀνθρώπων τροφαῖς
ταῖς σαῖσιν ἥκειν· τἀμὰ μὴ 'ξ ἄλλων πύθῃ.
ἀλλ' ἔστι γὰρ καὶ Ζηνὶ σύνθακος θρόνων
Αἰδὼς ἐπ' ἔργοις πᾶσι, καὶ πρὸς σοί, πάτερ,
παρασταθήτω. τῶν γὰρ ἡμαρτημένων
1270 ἄκη μέν ἐστι, προσφορὰ δ' οὐκ ἔστ' ἔτι.

548

ANTIGONE

Why, here, it seems, is the stranger! Without companions,
father, he is coming this way, with tears streaming from his
eyes.

OEDIPUS

Who is this?

ANTIGONE

The man who for some time has occupied our thoughts,
Polynices has come here!

Enter POLYNICES.

POLYNICES

Alas, what am I to do? Shall I first weep for my own sor-
rows, girls, or for those of my aged father which are before
my eyes? I have found him here in a foreign land with you,
cast out, dressed in this fashion; its distasteful dirt, ancient
itself, has settled on the ancient man, rotting his flesh, and
on his sightless head the uncombed hair flutters in the
breeze; and these things are matched by the food he car-
ries to fill his miserable stomach. Wretch that I am, I am
learning this too late! And I admit that I am the worst of
men in regard to your support; do not ask others, but hear
this from me! But since Mercy shares the throne of Zeus
with regard to all his actions, let her stand by you also,
father! For my crimes can be atoned for, but cannot be
augmented.

1259 πίνος Scaliger: πόνος codd.
1266 τἀμὰ Reiske: τἄλλα codd.

SOPHOCLES

τί σιγᾷς;
φώνησον, ὦ πάτερ, τι· μή μ' ἀποστραφῇς.
οὐδ' ἀνταμείβῃ μ' οὐδέν; ἀλλ' ἀτιμάσας
πέμψεις ἄναυδος, οὐδ' ἃ μηνίεις φράσας;
1275 ὦ σπέρματ' ἀνδρὸς τοῦδ', ἐμαὶ δ' ὁμαίμονες,
πειράσατ' ἀλλ' ὑμεῖς γε κινῆσαι πατρὸς
τὸ δυσπρόσοιστον κἀπροσήγορον στόμα,
ὡς μή μ' ἄτιμον, τοῦ θεοῦ γε προστάτην,
οὕτως ἀφῇ με μηδὲν ἀντειπὼν ἔπος.

ΑΝΤΙΓΟΝΗ

1280 λέγ', ὦ ταλαίπωρ', αὐτὸς ὢν χρείᾳ πάρει.
τὰ πολλὰ γάρ τοι ῥήματ' ἢ τέρψαντά τι,
ἢ δυσχεράναντ', ἢ κατοικτίσαντά πως,
παρέσχε φωνὴν τοῖς ἀφωνήτοις τινά.

ΠΟΛΥΝΕΙΚΗΣ

ἀλλ' ἐξερῶ· καλῶς γὰρ ἐξηγῇ σύ μοι·
1285 πρῶτον μὲν αὐτὸν τὸν θεὸν ποιούμενος
ἀρωγόν, ἔνθεν μ' ὧδ' ἀνέστησεν μολεῖν
ὁ τῆσδε τῆς γῆς κοίρανος, διδοὺς ἐμοὶ
λέξαι τ' ἀκοῦσαί τ' ἀσφαλεῖ σὺν ἐξόδῳ.
καὶ ταῦτ' ἀφ' ὑμῶν, ὦ ξένοι, βουλήσομαι
1290 καὶ ταῦνδ' ἀδελφαῖν καὶ πατρὸς κυρεῖν ἐμοί.
    ἃ δ' ἦλθον ἤδη σοι θέλω λέξαι, πάτερ·
γῆς ἐκ πατρῴας ἐξελήλαμαι φυγάς,
τοῖς σοῖς πάναρχος οὕνεκ' ἐνθακεῖν θρόνοις
γονῇ πεφυκὼς ἠξίουν γεραιτέρᾳ.

Why are you silent? Say some word, father! Do not
turn away from me! Do you not even return me any
answer, but will you send me away in dishonour without a
word, not even explaining why you are angry? Children of
this man and sisters of mine, do you at least try to move my
father's lips, hard to approach and to address, so that he
may not send off without honour me who am protected by
the god, without speaking any word in answer!

ANTIGONE

Tell him yourself, poor brother, what it is you need! For
abundance of words, bringing either delight or annoyance,
or arousing pity, can sometimes lend a voice to those who
are speechless.

POLYNICES

Well, I will speak, for your advice is good, first making the
god himself my helper, the god from whose altar the king
of this land raised me up to come here, granting me the
right to converse and a safe-conduct back. And I hope to
receive these things from you, strangers, and from these
my sisters and from my father.

But now I wish to tell you why I came here, father! I
have been driven from my native land and into exile,
because I claimed that by the right of the first-born I
should sit upon the throne and exercise full power. For

1279 ἀφῇ με Dindorf: μ' ἀφῇ γε Lazt: ἀφῇ γε r
1291 θέλω] an θέλων, puncto post πάτερ deleto?
1293 πάναρχος Fraenkel: πανάρχοις codd.

1295 ἀνθ' ὧν μ' Ἐτεοκλῆς, ὢν φύσει νεώτερος,
γῆς ἐξέωσεν, οὔτε νικήσας λόγῳ
οὔτ' εἰς ἔλεγχον χειρὸς οὐδ' ἔργου μολών,
πόλιν δὲ πείσας. ὧν ἐγὼ μάλιστα μὲν
τὴν σὴν Ἐρινὺν αἰτίαν εἶναι λέγω.
1300 [ἔπειτα κἀπὸ μάντεων ταύτῃ κλύω.]
ἐπεὶ γὰρ ἦλθον Ἄργος ἐς τὸ Δωρικόν,
λαβὼν Ἄδραστον πενθερόν, ξυνωμότας
ἔστησ' ἐμαυτῷ γῆς ὅσοιπερ Ἀπίας
πρῶτοι καλοῦνται καὶ τετίμηνται δορί,
1305 ὅπως τὸν ἑπτάλογχον ἐς Θήβας στόλον
ξὺν τοῖσδ' ἀγείρας ἢ θάνοιμι πανδίκως,
ἢ τοὺς τάδ' ἐκπράξαντας ἐκβάλοιμι γῆς.
εἶέν· τί δῆτα νῦν ἀφιγμένος κυρῶ;
σοὶ προστροπαίους, ὦ πάτερ, λιτὰς ἔχων,
1310 αὐτός τ' ἐμαυτοῦ ξυμμάχων τε τῶν ἐμῶν,
οἳ νῦν σὺν ἑπτὰ τάξεσιν σὺν ἑπτά τε
λόγχαις τὸ Θήβης πεδίον ἀμφεστᾶσι πᾶν·
οἷος δορυσσοῦς Ἀμφιάρεως, τὰ πρῶτα μὲν
δόρει κρατύνων, πρῶτα δ' οἰωνῶν ὁδοῖς·
1315 ὁ δεύτερος δ' Αἰτωλὸς Οἰνέως τόκος
Τυδεύς· τρίτος δ' Ἐτέοκλος, Ἀργεῖος γεγώς·
τέταρτον Ἱππομέδοντ' ἀπέστειλεν πατὴρ
Ταλαός· ὁ πέμπτος δ' εὔχεται κατασκαφῇ
Καπανεὺς τὸ Θήβης ἄστυ δῃώσειν τάχα.
1320 ἕκτος δὲ Παρθενοπαῖος Ἀρκὰς ὄρνυται,

this Eteocles, who is younger, expelled me from the land; he did not vanquish me in argument or come to the test of strength and action, but persuaded the city. Of this I think that the chief cause was your Erinys[;[a] also I have heard this kind of thing from prophets]. For after I had come to Dorian Argos, I got Adrastus[b] as my father-in-law, and established as sworn allies all who are called the first in the Apian land[c] and are honoured for their valour, so that with their aid I could muster the expedition against Thebes with seven spears and either die in a just cause or expel from the land those who had done this.

So be it! Why have I now come here? I have come to entreat you as a suppliant, father, on behalf of myself and my allies, who now with seven companies and seven spears surround all the land of Thebes. They are men such as the spear-brandishing Amphiaraus,[d] first in martial valour and first in interpreting the ways of birds. The second is the Aetolian Tydeus, the son of Oeneus; the third is Eteoclus, Argive by birth; the fourth is Hippomedon, sent by his father Talaus; the fifth is Capaneus,[e] who boasts that he will soon destroy the city of Thebes, burning it to the ground; the sixth is Parthenopaeus, rushing forth,[the

[a] The Erinys brought upon him by his father's curse.

[b] King of Argos.

[c] The Peloponnese.

[d] See *Electra* 837 f.

[e] See *Antigone* 131 f.

1297 οὐδ' Hermann: οὔτ' codd.

1300 del. Reeve

1310 τ' Reiske: γ' codd.

SOPHOCLES

ἐπώνυμος τῆς πρόσθεν ἀδμήτης [χρόνῳ
μητρὸς λοχευθείς, πιστὸς Ἀταλάντης] γόνος ·
ἐγὼ δ᾽ ὁ σός, κεἰ μὴ σός, ἀλλὰ τοῦ κακοῦ
πότμου φυτευθείς, σός γέ τοι καλούμενος,
1325   ἄγω τὸν Ἄργους ἄφοβον ἐς Θήβας στρατόν.

οἵ σ᾽ ἀντὶ παίδων τῶνδε καὶ ψυχῆς, πάτερ,
ἱκετεύομεν ξύμπαντες ἐξαιτούμενοι
μῆνιν βαρεῖαν εἰκαθεῖν ὁρμωμένῳ
τῷδ᾽ ἀνδρὶ τοὐμοῦ πρὸς κασιγνήτου τίσιν,
1330   ὅς μ᾽ ἐξέωσε κἀπεσύλησεν πάτρας.
εἰ γάρ τι πιστόν ἐστιν ἐκ χρηστηρίων,
οἷς ἂν σὺ προσθῇ, τοῖσδ᾽ ἔφασκ᾽ εἶναι κράτος.
πρός νύν σε κρηνῶν, πρὸς θεῶν ὁμογνίων
αἰτῶ πιθέσθαι καὶ παρεικαθεῖν, ἐπεὶ
1335   πτωχοὶ μὲν ἡμεῖς καὶ ξένοι, ξένος δὲ σύ·
ἄλλους δὲ θωπεύοντες οἰκοῦμεν σύ τε
κἀγώ, τὸν αὐτὸν δαίμον᾽ ἐξειληχότες.
ὁ δ᾽ ἐν δόμοις τύραννος, ὦ τάλας ἐγώ,
κοινῇ καθ᾽ ἡμῶν ἐγγελῶν ἁβρύνεται·
1340   ὅν, εἰ σὺ τῇμῇ ξυμπαραστήσῃ φρενί,
βραχεῖ σὺν ὄγκῳ καὶ πόνῳ διασκεδῶ.
ὥστ᾽ ἐν δόμοισι τοῖσι σοῖς στήσω σ᾽ ἄγων,
στήσω δ᾽ ἐμαυτόν, κεῖνον ἐκβαλὼν βίᾳ.
καὶ ταῦτα σοῦ μὲν ξυνθέλοντος ἔστι μοι
1345   κομπεῖν, ἄνευ σοῦ δ᾽ οὐδὲ σωθῆναι σθένω.

ΧΟΡΟΣ

τὸν ἄνδρα, τοῦ πέμψαντος οὕνεκ᾽, Οἰδίπους,
εἰπὼν ὁποῖα ξύμφορ᾽ ἔκπεμψαι πάλιν.

trusty] son of her who was formerly virgin, who takes his name from her [, Atalanta who in the end gave birth]. And I, your son, who even if I am not your son, but the child of evil destiny, am at least called yours, lead the fearless army of Argos to Thebes.

We all now beseech you in supplication, by your daughters and by your life, father, to renounce your grievous anger in favour of myself, as I set out to take vengeance on my brother, who drove me out and robbed me of my country. For if any credit can be given to oracles, they said that whichever side you joined would prevail. Now in the name of the fountains and the gods of our race I beg you to be persuaded and to give way, father, for we are beggars and strangers, and you are a stranger. You and I both live on the charity of others, since we have a fate that is the same; and the tyrant at home, woe is me, delights in mocking us both together. If you will stand by my purpose, with small trouble and toil I will destroy him, so that I shall bring you and set you up in your own house, and shall set up myself, expelling him by force. If you will the same as I, these things are mine to boast of; but without you I have not the strength even to come off safely.

For the sake of him that sent him, Oedipus, say whatever is expedient and send the man away again!

1321–22 χρόνῳ . . . 'Αταλάντης om. r, del. Gratwick
1323 δ' ὁ Brunck: δὲ codd.

ΟΙΔΙΠΟΥΣ

ἀλλ' εἰ μέν, ἄνδρες τῆσδε δημοῦχοι χθονός,
μὴ 'τύγχαν' αὐτὸν δεῦρο προσπέμψας ἐμοὶ
1350 Θησεύς, δικαιῶν ὥστ' ἐμοῦ κλυεῖν λόγους,
οὔ τἄν ποτ' ὀμφῆς τῆς ἐμῆς ἐπῄσθετο·
νῦν δ' ἀξιωθεὶς εἶσι κἀκούσας γ' ἐμοῦ
τοιαῦθ' ἃ τὸν τοῦδ' οὔ ποτ' εὐφρανεῖ βίον·
ὅς γ', ὦ κάκιστε, σκῆπτρα καὶ θρόνους ἔχων,
1355 ἃ νῦν ὁ σὸς ξύναιμος ἐν Θήβαις ἔχει,
τὸν αὐτὸς αὑτοῦ πατέρα τόνδ' ἀπήλασας
κἄθηκας ἄπολιν καὶ στολὰς ταύτας φορεῖν,
ἃς νῦν δακρύεις εἰσορῶν, ὅτ' ἐν κλόνῳ
ταὐτῷ βεβηκὼς τυγχάνεις κακῶν ἐμοί.
1360 οὐ κλαυτὰ δ' ἐστίν, ἀλλ' ἐμοὶ μὲν οἰστέα
τάδ' ἕωσπερ ἂν ζῶ, σοῦ φονέως μεμνημένῳ·
σὺ γάρ με μόχθῳ τῷδ' ἔθηκας ἔντροφον,
σύ μ' ἐξέωσας, ἐκ σέθεν δ' ἀλώμενος
ἄλλους ἐπαιτῶ τὸν καθ' ἡμέραν βίον.
1365 εἰ δ' ἐξέφυσα τάσδε μὴ 'μαυτῷ τροφοὺς
τὰς παῖδας, ἦ τἂν οὐκ ἂν ἦ, τὸ σὸν μέρος·
νῦν δ' αἵδε μ' ἐκσώζουσιν, αἵδ' ἐμαὶ τροφοί,
αἵδ' ἄνδρες, οὐ γυναῖκες, ἐς τὸ συμπονεῖν·
ὑμεῖς δ' ἀπ' ἄλλου κοὐκ ἐμοῦ πεφύκατον.
1370 τοιγάρ σ' ὁ δαίμων εἰσορᾷ μὲν οὔ τί πω
ὡς αὐτίκ', εἴπερ οἵδε κινοῦνται λόχοι
πρὸς ἄστυ Θήβης. οὐ γὰρ ἔσθ' ὅπως πόλιν
κείνην ἐρείψεις, ἀλλὰ πρόσθεν αἵματι
πεσῇ μιανθεὶς χὠ ξύναιμος ἐξ ἴσου.

OEDIPUS

Men who are guardians of the people of this land, if it were not Theseus who had sent him here to me, judging it right for him to hear me speak, he would never have heard my voice; but now he shall depart having had this privilege, and having heard from me things that shall in no way gladden his life! You are the one, villain, who when you held the sceptre and the throne that are now held by your brother in Thebes, drove away your own father here, and made him cityless, wearing such clothes as these, which now you weep when you behold, now that you stand in the same turmoil of troubles as I. There is no cause for tears, but I must bear this while I live, remembering you as my murderer; for it was you who put me on this diet of misery, you who thrust me out, you who caused me to wander begging others for my daily sustenance! And if I had not begotten these daughters to attend me, I would not be living, for all you did for me. But as it is they preserve me, they are my nurses, they are men, not women, when it comes to working for me; but you are sons of some other, and no sons of mine.

Therefore does the god look upon you, not yet as he soon shall, if these squadrons move towards the city of Thebes; for you shall never destroy the city, but first you shall fall, polluted by bloodshed, and your brother also.

1358 κλόνῳ Martin: πόνῳ codd.
1361 μεμνημένῳ Blaydes: -ένου A: -ένος cett.
1373 ἐρείψεις Turnebus: ἐρεῖ τις codd.

1375 τοιάσδ' ἀρὰς σφῷν πρόσθε τ' ἐξανῆκ' ἐγὼ
νῦν τ' ἀνακαλοῦμαι ξυμμάχους ἐλθεῖν ἐμοί,
ἵν' ἀξιῶτον τοὺς φυτεύσαντας σέβειν,
καὶ μὴ 'ξατιμάζητον, εἰ τυφλοῦ πατρὸς
τοιῶδ' ἔφυτον. αἵδε γὰρ τάδ' οὐκ ἔδρων.

1380 τοιγὰρ τὸ σὸν θάκημα καὶ τοὺς σοὺς θρόνους
κρατοῦσιν, εἴπερ ἐστὶν ἡ παλαίφατος
Δίκη ξύνεδρος Ζηνὸς ἀρχαίοις νόμοις.

σὺ δ' ἔρρ' ἀπόπτυστός τε κἀπάτωρ ἐμοῦ,
κακῶν κάκιστε, τάσδε συλλαβὼν ἀράς,

1385 ἅς σοι καλοῦμαι, μήτε γῆς ἐμφυλίου
δόρει κρατῆσαι μήτε νοστῆσαί ποτε
τὸ κοῖλον Ἄργος, ἀλλὰ συγγενεῖ χερὶ
θανεῖν κτανεῖν θ' ὑφ' οὗπερ ἐξελήλασαι.
τοιαῦτ' ἀρῶμαι, καὶ καλῶ τὸ Ταρτάρου

1390 στυγνὸν πατρῷον ἔρεβος, ὥς σ' ἀποικίσῃ,
καλῶ δὲ τάσδε δαίμονας, καλῶ δ' Ἄρη
τὸν σφῷν τὸ δεινὸν μῖσος ἐμβεβληκότα.
καὶ ταῦτ' ἀκούσας στεῖχε, κἀξάγγελλ' ἰὼν
καὶ πᾶσι Καδμείοισι τοῖς σαυτοῦ θ' ἅμα

1395 πιστοῖσι συμμάχοισιν, οὕνεκ' Οἰδίπους
τοιαῦτ' ἔνειμε παισὶ τοῖς αὑτοῦ γέρα.

ΧΟΡΟΣ

Πολύνεικες, οὔτε ταῖς παρελθούσαις ὁδοῖς
ξυνήδομαί σοι, νῦν τ' ἴθ' ὡς τάχος πάλιν.

1389 τὸ Hermann: τοῦ codd. plerique

558

Such are the curses which I pronounced upon you in the past and which I now call to come and fight beside me, so that you two may learn respect for your begetters, and not dishonour them, even if the father that begot such men is blind; for these girls did not do this! Therefore these curses overcome your supplication and your thrones, if Justice sits of old beside the throne of Zeus according to the ancient laws.

Be off, spat upon by me who am no more your father, villain of villains, taking with you these curses which I call down upon you, so that you shall never conquer in war your native land nor ever return to low-lying Argos, but shall perish by your brother's hand and kill him who drove you out! Such is my curse, and I call upon the hateful paternal darkness of Tartarus to give you a new home, and I call upon these goddesses, and upon the war god, who injected this grim hatred into your minds! Now that you have heard this, depart, and go tell all the Cadmeans and your own trusty allies too that such are the prizes which Oedipus has bestowed upon his sons!

CHORUS

Polynices, I take no pleasure in your former journeys, and now return with all speed!

SOPHOCLES

ΠΟΛΥΝΕΙΚΗΣ

οἴμοι κελεύθου τῆς τ' ἐμῆς δυσπραξίας
1400 οἴμοι δ' ἑταίρων· οἷον ἆρ' ὁδοῦ τέλος
Ἄργους ἀφωρμήθημεν, ὦ τάλας ἐγώ,
τοιοῦτον οἷον οὐδὲ φωνῆσαί τινι
ἔξεσθ' ἑταίρων, οὐδ' ἀποστρέψαι πάλιν,
ἀλλ' ὄντ' ἄναυδον τῇδε συγκῦρσαι τύχῃ.
1405 ὦ τοῦδ' ὅμαιμοι παῖδες, ἀλλ' ὑμεῖς, ἐπεὶ
τὰ σκληρὰ πατρὸς κλύετε ταῦτ' ἀρωμένου,
μή τοί με πρὸς θεῶν σφώ γ', ἐὰν αἱ τοῦδ' ἀραὶ
πατρὸς τελῶνται καί τις ὑμὶν ἐς δόμους
νόστος γένηται, μή μ' ἀτιμάσητέ γε,
1410 ἀλλ' ἐν τάφοισι θέσθε κἀν κτερίσμασιν.
καὶ σφῶν ὁ νῦν ἔπαινος, ὃν κομίζετον
τοῦδ' ἀνδρὸς οἷς πονεῖτον, οὐκ ἐλάσσονα
ἔτ' ἄλλον οἴσει τῆς ἐμῆς ὑπουργίας.

ΑΝΤΙΓΟΝΗ

Πολύνεικες, ἱκετεύω σε πεισθῆναί τί μοι.

ΠΟΛΥΝΕΙΚΗΣ

1415 ὦ φιλτάτη, τὸ ποῖον, Ἀντιγόνη; λέγε.

ΑΝΤΙΓΟΝΗ

στρέψας στράτευμ' ἐς Ἄργος ὡς τάχιστ' ἄγε,
καὶ μὴ σέ τ' αὐτὸν καὶ πόλιν διεργάσῃ.

ΠΟΛΥΝΕΙΚΗΣ

ἀλλ' οὐχ οἷόν τε. πῶς γὰρ αὖθις αὖ πάλιν
στράτευμ' ἄγοιμ' <ἂν> ταὐτὸν εἰσάπαξ τρέσας;

¹⁴⁰² τινι ed. Lond. a. 1747: τινα codd.

560

POLYNICES

Alas for my coming and for my disaster, and alas for my
companions! What an end has come of our march from
Argos—wretched am I—such an end as I cannot even
speak of to any of my companions, nor can I turn back, but
in silence I must meet with this fate! My sisters, daughters
of this man, since you hear my father pronounce this cruel
curse, do not you at least, I beg you, if my father's curses
are fulfilled and you somehow return home, do not you
dishonour me, but place me in my tomb with funeral rites.
And to the praise you have already earned, which you are
acquiring by your labours for this man, shall be added
further and no lesser praise because of the service you shall
render me.

ANTIGONE

Polynices, I beg you to let me persuade you in a certain
matter!

POLYNICES

Dearest Antigone, what is it? Tell me!

ANTIGONE

Turn back your army at once to Argos, and do not destroy
yourself and the city!

POLYNICES

Why, that cannot be! For how could I bring back the army
again, when I had once shown cowardice?

1406 ταῦτ' Sehrwald: τοῦδ' codd.
1407 σφώ γ' ἐὰν Elmsley: σφῷν γ' ἂν fere codd.
1416 στρέψας A. Y. Campbell: στρέψαι codd.   τάχιστ' ἄγε
Badham et Blaydes: τάχιστά γε codd.
1417 σέ τ' αὐτὸν Brunck: σεαυτὸν r: σέ γ' αὐτὸν cett.
1419 suppl. Toup

SOPHOCLES

ΑΝΤΙΓΟΝΗ

1420 τί δ' αὖθις, ὦ παῖ, δεῖ σε θυμοῦσθαι; τί σοι
πάτραν κατασκάψαντι κέρδος ἔρχεται;

ΠΟΛΥΝΕΙΚΗΣ

αἰσχρὸν τὸ φεύγειν, καὶ τὸ πρεσβεύοντ' ἐμὲ
οὕτω γελᾶσθαι τοῦ κασιγνήτου πάρα.

ΑΝΤΙΓΟΝΗ

ὁρᾷς τὰ τοῦδ' οὖν ὡς ἐς ὀρθὸν ἐκφέρεις
1425 μαντεύμαθ', ὃς σφῷν θάνατον ἐξ ἀμφοῖν θροεῖ;

ΠΟΛΥΝΕΙΚΗΣ

χρῄζει γάρ· ἡμῖν δ' οὐχὶ συγχωρητέα;

ΑΝΤΙΓΟΝΗ

οἴμοι τάλαινα· τίς δὲ τολμήσει κλυὼν
τὰ τοῦδ' ἔπεσθαι τἀνδρός, οἷ' ἐθέσπισεν;

ΠΟΛΥΝΕΙΚΗΣ

οὐδ' ἀγγελοῦμεν φλαῦρ'· ἐπεὶ στρατηλάτου
1430 χρηστοῦ τὰ κρείσσω μηδὲ τἀνδεᾶ λέγειν.

ΑΝΤΙΓΟΝΗ

οὕτως ἄρ', ὦ παῖ, ταῦτά σοι δεδογμένα;

ΠΟΛΥΝΕΙΚΗΣ

καὶ μή μ' ἐπίσχῃς γ'· ἀλλ' ἐμοὶ μὲν ἥδ' ὁδὸς
ἔσται μέλουσα δύσποτμός τε καὶ κακὴ
πρὸς τοῦδε πατρὸς τῶν τε τοῦδ' Ἐρινύων.
1435 σφῷν δ' εὖ διδοίη Ζεύς, τάδ' εἰ τελεῖτέ μοι.

562

ANTIGONE

Why must you be angry once more, brother? What profit
do you gain by the ruin of your country?

POLYNICES

To run away is shameful, and it is shameful for me, the
senior, to be mocked like this by my brother!

ANTIGONE

Then do you see how you are fulfilling the prophecies of
this man, who declared that you should die at one another's
hands?

POLYNICES

Yes, that is his wish; and must we not comply?

ANTIGONE

Ah me, unhappy one! And who shall dare to follow, when
he has heard the prophecies this man has uttered?

POLYNICES

We shall not even report bad news; for it is the duty of a
good commander to tell the better news, and not that
which falls short.

ANTIGONE

Then is your mind made up after this fashion, brother?

POLYNICES

Yes, and do not delay me! My work shall be to see to this
march, ill-fated and evil as it has been made by my father
here and his Erinyes. But to you may Zeus give good for-
tune, if you discharge the duties I have asked for me [in

1424 ἐκφέρεις Tyrwhitt: ἐκφέρει codd.
1426 interrogationis notam posuit Ferrari
1435 εὖ διδοίη Burges: εὐοδοίη codd.

[θανόντ᾽ ἐπεὶ οὔ μοι ζῶντί γ᾽ αὖθις ἕξετον.]
μέθεσθε δ᾽ ἤδη, χαίρετόν τ᾽. οὐ γάρ μ᾽ ἔτι
βλέποντ᾽ ἐσόψεσθ᾽ αὖθις.

ΑΝΤΙΓΟΝΗ
ὦ τάλαιν᾽ ἐγώ.

ΠΟΛΥΝΕΙΚΗΣ
μή τοί μ᾽ ὀδύρου.

ΑΝΤΙΓΟΝΗ
καὶ τίς ἄν σ᾽ ὁρμώμενον
1440   ἐς προὖπτον Ἅιδην οὐ καταστένοι, κάσι;

ΠΟΛΥΝΕΙΚΗΣ
εἰ χρή, θανοῦμαι.

ΑΝΤΙΓΟΝΗ
μὴ σύ γ᾽, ἀλλ᾽ ἐμοὶ πιθοῦ.

ΠΟΛΥΝΕΙΚΗΣ
μὴ πεῖθ᾽ ἃ μὴ δεῖ.

ΑΝΤΙΓΟΝΗ
δυστάλαινά τἄρ᾽ ἐγώ,
εἴ σου στερηθῶ.

ΠΟΛΥΝΕΙΚΗΣ
ταῦτα δ᾽ ἐν τῷ δαίμονι
καὶ τῇδε φῦναι χἀτέρᾳ. σφῷν δ᾽ οὖν ἐγὼ
1445   θεοῖς ἀρῶμαι μή ποτ᾽ ἀντῆσαι κακῶν·
ἀνάξιαι γὰρ πᾶσίν ἐστε δυστυχεῖν.

ΧΟΡΟΣ
νέα τάδε νεόθεν ἦλθέ μοι   στρ. α´
<νέα> βαρύποτμα κακὰ παρ᾽ ἀλαοῦ ξένου,

564

death, since you will not be able to in life]. But now let go
of me, and farewell! For you will never again see me living!

ANTIGONE

Miserable am I!

POLYNICES

Do not lament for me!

ANTIGONE

And who would not weep for you, brother, seeing you set-
ting out for certain death?

POLYNICES

I shall die if I must!

ANTIGONE

Never, but do as I wish!

POLYNICES

Do not try to persuade me when you must not!

ANTIGONE

Then woe is me indeed, if I am to be deprived of you!

POLYNICES

These things depend on fate, to go one way or the other.
Well, I pray to the gods that you two may never meet with
evil; for all men know that you do not deserve misfortune.

Exit POLYNICES.

CHORUS

New evils have come from a new source, bringing a
grievous fate, from the blind stranger, unless destiny is

1436 del. Burges et Dindorf
1449 suppl. Hermann

1450 εἴ τι μοῖρα μὴ κιγχάνει.
ματᾶν γὰρ οὐδὲν ἀξίω-
μα δαιμόνων ἔχω φράσαι.
ὁρᾷ δ᾽ ὁρᾷ πάντ᾽ ἀεὶ
χρόνος, στρέφων μὲν ἕτερα,
1455 τὰ δὲ παρ᾽ ἦμαρ αὖθις αὔξων ἄνω.
ἔκτυπεν αἰθήρ, ὦ Ζεῦ.

ΟΙΔΙΠΟΥΣ

ὦ τέκνα τέκνα, πῶς ἄν, εἴ τις ἔντοπος,
τὸν πάντ᾽ ἄριστον δεῦρο Θησέα πόροι;

ΑΝΤΙΓΟΝΗ

πάτερ, τί δ᾽ ἐστὶ τἀξίωμ᾽ ἐφ᾽ ᾧ καλεῖς;

ΟΙΔΙΠΟΥΣ

1460 Διὸς πτερωτὸς ἥδε μ᾽ αὐτίκ᾽ ἄξεται
βροντὴ πρὸς Ἅιδην. ἀλλὰ πέμψαθ᾽ ὡς τάχος.

ΧΟΡΟΣ

ἴδε μάλα· μέγας ἐρείπεται   ἀντ. α΄
κτύπος ἄφατος ὅδε διόβολος, ἐς δ᾽ ἄκραν
1465 δεῖμ᾽ ὑπῆλθε κρατὸς φόβαν.
ἔπταξα θυμόν· οὐρανὸν
γὰρ ἀστραπὰ φλέγει πάλιν.
τί μάν; ἀφήσει βέλος;
δέδια τόδ᾽· οὐ γὰρ ἅλιον
1470 ἀφορμᾷ ποτ᾽, οὐδ᾽ ἄνευ ξυμφορᾶς,
ὦ μέγας αἰθήρ, ὦ Ζεῦ.

finding its goal. For I cannot say that any purpose of the
gods is vain. Time sees, sees always all things, overthrow-
ing some and causing others in turn to rise up next day.
The sky has sounded forth! O Zeus!

OEDIPUS

Children,. children, if anyone is here, could he bring here
Theseus, in all ways best of men?

ANTIGONE

Father, what is the purpose that leads you to summon him?

OEDIPUS

This is the winged thunder of Zeus, that will soon carry me
to Hades; come, bring him here at once!

CHORUS

Look now! Hear, a great crash, unspeakable, sent by Zeus,
resounds, and terror spreads to the very ends of the hairs of
my head! My spirit cowers, for again lightning blazes in the
sky! What can this be? Will he cast his bolt? I dread this;
for it never shoots forth for nothing, nor without catas-
trophe. O vast sky! O Zeus!

[1451] ματᾶν Heimsoeth: μάτην codd.

[1453] δ' post prius ὁρᾷ inseruit Bergk   πάντ' Dindorf:
ταῦτ' codd.

[1454] στρέφων Hartung: ἐπεὶ codd.

[1455] τὰ δὲ παρ' ἦμαρ Canter e sch.: τάδε πήματ' codd. plerique

[1466] οὐρανὸν Meineke: οὐρανία codd.: οὐλία Maas

[1468] βέλος Abresch: τέλος codd.

[1470] οὐδ' Heath: οὐκ codd.

ΟΙΔΙΠΟΥΣ

ὦ παῖδες, ἥκει τῷδ' ἐπ' ἀνδρὶ θέσφατος
βίου τελευτή, κοὐκέτ' ἔστ' ἀποστροφή.

ΑΝΤΙΓΟΝΗ

πῶς οἶσθα; τῷ δὲ τοῦτο συμβαλὼν ἔχεις;

ΟΙΔΙΠΟΥΣ

1475 καλῶς κάτοιδ' · ἀλλ' ὡς τάχιστά μοι μολὼν
ἄνακτα χώρας τῆσδέ τις πορευσάτω.

ΧΟΡΟΣ

ἔα ἔα, ἰδοὺ μάλ' αὖ-   στρ. β'
θις · ἀμφίσταται διαπρύσιος ὄτοβος.
1480 ἵλαος, ὦ δαίμων, ἵλαος, εἴ τι γᾷ
ματέρι τυγχάνεις ἀφεγγὲς φέρων.
ἐναισίου δὲ σοῦ τύχοι-
μι, μηδ' ἄλαστον ἄνδρ' ἰδὼν
ἀκερδῆ χάριν μετάσχοιμί πως.
1485 Ζεῦ ἄνα, σοὶ φωνῶ.

ΟΙΔΙΠΟΥΣ

ἆρ' ἐγγὺς ἀνήρ; ἆρ' ἔτ' ἐμψύχου, τέκνα,
κιχήσεταί μου καὶ κατορθοῦντος φρένα;

ΑΝΤΙΓΟΝΗ

τί δ' ἂν θέλοις τὸ πιστὸν ἐμφῦναι φρενί;

ΟΙΔΙΠΟΥΣ

ἀνθ' ὧν ἔπασχον εὖ τελεσφόρον χάριν
1490 δοῦναί σφιν, ἥνπερ τυγχάνων ὑπεσχόμην.

OEDIPUS

Children, the end of life that was prophesied has come
upon this man, and there is no way of putting it off!

ANTIGONE

How do you know? What leads you to this knowledge?

OEDIPUS

I know it well; but let someone go as quickly as he can and
bring here the monarch of the land!

CHORUS

Ah, ah! See once more! A din resounds all around us!
Kindly, O god, kindly be your coming, if you are bringing
something wrapped in darkness to the earth our mother!
May I encounter you in auspicious mood, and may my see-
ing of an accursed man not bring me a return that is no
gain! Lord Zeus, it is to you I speak!

OEDIPUS

Is the man near? Will he find me still living, and of sound
mind, my children?

ANTIGONE

Why are you wishing for your mind to be trustworthy?

OEDIPUS

In return for my kind treatment I wish to make him the
requital that I promised when I received them.

1474 Antigonae tribuit Turnebus, choro codd.
1482 σοῦ τύχοιμι Cobet: συντύχοιμι codd.
1488 Antigonae tribuit Turnebus, choro codd.

ΧΟΡΟΣ

ἰὼ ἰώ, παῖ, βᾶθι βᾶθ᾽,   ἀντ. β΄
†εἴτ᾽ ἄκραν ἐπὶ† γύαλον ἐναλίῳ
Ποσειδανίῳ θεῷ τυγχάνεις
1495 βούθυτον ἑστίαν ἁγίζων, ἱκοῦ.
ὁ γὰρ ξένος σε καὶ πόλι-
σμα καὶ φίλους ἐπαξιοῖ
δικαίαν χάριν παρασχεῖν παθών.
<σπεῦσον>, ἄισσ᾽, ὦναξ.

ΘΗΣΕΥΣ

1500 τίς αὖ παρ᾽ ὑμῶν κοινὸς ἠχεῖται κτύπος,
σαφὴς μὲν αὐτῶν, ἐμφανὴς δὲ τοῦ ξένου;
μή τις Διὸς κεραυνός, ἤ τις ὀμβρία
χάλαζ᾽ ἐπιρράξασα; πάντα γὰρ θεοῦ
τοιαῦτα χειμάζοντος εἰκάσαι πάρα.

ΟΙΔΙΠΟΥΣ

1505 ἄναξ, ποθοῦντι προὐφάνης, καί σοι θεῶν
τύχην τις ἐσθλὴν τῆσδ᾽ ἔθηκε τῆς ὁδοῦ.

ΘΗΣΕΥΣ

τί δ᾽ ἐστίν, ὦ παῖ Λαΐου, νέορτον αὖ;

ΟΙΔΙΠΟΥΣ

ῥοπὴ βίου μοι· καί σ᾽ ἅπερ ξυνῄνεσα
θέλω πόλιν τε τήνδε μὴ ψεύσας θανεῖν.

ΘΗΣΕΥΣ

1510 ἐν τῷ δὲ κεῖσαι τοῦ μόρου τεκμηρίῳ;

CHORUS

Oh! Oh! My son, come, come! Leave the recess among the high rocks where you are hallowing with sacrifice of oxen the altar for the god Poseidon, come! For the stranger makes demand of you and of the city and of his friends, wishing to give a fair requital for his treatment. Make haste, come rushing, king!

Enter THESEUS.

THESEUS

What is this din that resounds from all of you together, clearly from yourselves, manifestly from the stranger? Is it some thunder from Zeus, or a shower of rain clattering down? For when the god sends such stormy weather, one may make any guess!

OEDIPUS

King, your appearance is welcome, and some one of the gods has made good fortune for you in this coming!

THESEUS

What has happened now, son of Laius?

OEDIPUS

The scale of my life is turning, and I do not wish to die leaving my promises to you and to the city unfulfilled.

THESEUS

But what sign of your demise has come to you?

1492–93 fort. ἴθ' ἀκρᾶν πετρᾶν λίπε γύαλον ἐν ᾧ

1494 Ποσειδανίῳ Seidler: Ποσειδαωνίῳ codd. plerique

1498 παθών r: ὧν εὖ πάθοι K: παθῶν cett.

1499 <σπεῦσον> t: om. cett.

1506 τῆσδ' ἔθηκε Heath: θῆκε τῆσδε codd.

ΟΙΔΙΠΟΥΣ

αὐτοὶ θεοὶ κήρυκες ἀγγέλλουσί μοι,
ψεύδοντες οὐδὲν σημάτων προκειμένων.

ΘΗΣΕΥΣ

πῶς εἶπας, ὦ γεραιέ, δηλοῦσθαι τάδε;

ΟΙΔΙΠΟΥΣ

δῖαί τε βρονταὶ διατελεῖς τὰ πολλά τε
1515 στράψαντα χειρὸς τῆς ἀνικήτου βέλη.

ΘΗΣΕΥΣ

πείθεις με· πολλὰ γάρ σε θεσπίζονθ᾽ ὁρῶ
κοὐ ψευδόφημα· χὦ τι χρὴ ποεῖν λέγε.

ΟΙΔΙΠΟΥΣ

ἐγὼ διδάξω, τέκνον Αἰγέως, ἅ σοι
γήρως ἄλυπα τῇδε κείσεται πόλει.
1520 χῶρον μὲν αὐτὸς αὐτίκ᾽ ἐξηγήσομαι,
ἄθικτος ἡγητῆρος, οὗ με χρὴ θανεῖν.
τοῦτον δὲ φράζε μήποτ᾽ ἀνθρώπων τινί,
μήθ᾽ οὗ κέκευθε μήτ᾽ ἐν οἷς κεῖται τόποις·
ὥς σοι πρὸ πολλῶν ἀσπίδων ἀλκὴν ὅδε
1525 δορός τ᾽ ἐπακτοῦ γειτόνων ἀεὶ τιθῇ.
ἃ δ᾽ ἐξάγιστα μηδὲ κινεῖται λόγῳ
αὐτὸς μαθήσῃ, κεῖσ᾽ ὅταν μόλῃς μόνος·
ὡς οὔτ᾽ ἂν ἀστῶν τῶνδ᾽ ἂν ἐξείποιμί τῳ
οὔτ᾽ ἂν τέκνοισι τοῖς ἐμοῖς, στέργων ὅμως.
1530 ἀλλ᾽ αὐτὸς αἰεὶ σῷζε, χὦταν ἐς τέλος
τοῦ ζῆν ἀφικῇ, τῷ προφερτάτῳ μόνῳ
σήμαιν᾽, ὁ δ᾽ αἰεὶ τὠπιόντι δεικνύτω.

OEDIPUS

The gods themselves are the heralds who announce it to
me, not failing to give any of the signs appointed.

THESEUS

How do you say this is being made clear, aged man?

OEDIPUS

The continuous thunderings of Zeus and the many bolts
that have flashed from the unconquerable hand!

THESEUS

You convince me; for I have seen you utter many prophe-
cies, and they have not been false. Tell me what I must do!

OEDIPUS

I will explain, son of Aegeus, what things are laid up for
your city, invulnerable to passing time! I myself, with no
guide to lay a hand on me, shall now show you the place
where I must die. Do not ever reveal to any human being
either where it is concealed or the region in which it lies;
for its perpetual nearness renders to you a protection
stronger than many shields or spears brought in from out-
side! But the things that are taboo and that speech must
not disturb you yourself shall learn, when you go there
alone; for I would not reveal them to any of these citizens,
nor to my children, much though I love them. But do you
always guard them, and when you come to the end of life,
indicate them only to him who is foremost, and let that
man reveal them each time to his successor! In this way

1514 δίαί τε Housman: αἱ πολλὰ azt: αἱ πολλαὶ lrV
1515 στράψαντα Pierson: idem K, nisi quod a- in fine v. 1514
habet: στρέψαντα cett.

χοὔτως ἀδῇον τήνδ' ἐνοικήσεις πόλιν
σπαρτῶν ἀπ' ἀνδρῶν· αἱ δὲ μυρίαι πόλεις,
1535   κἂν εὖ τις οἰκῇ, ῥᾳδίως καθύβρισαν.
θεοὶ γὰρ εὖ μέν, ὀψὲ δ' εἰσορῶσ', ὅταν
τὰ θεῖ' ἀφείς τις ἐς τὸ μαίνεσθαι τραπῇ·
ὃ μὴ σύ, τέκνον Αἰγέως, βούλου παθεῖν.
    τὰ μὲν τοιαῦτ' οὖν εἰδότ' ἐκδιδάσκομεν.
1540   χῶρον δ', ἐπείγει γάρ με τοὐκ θεοῦ παρόν,
στείχωμεν ἤδη, μηδ' ἔτ' ἐντρεπώμεθα.
ὦ παῖδες, ὧδ' ἕπεσθ'. ἐγὼ γὰρ ἡγεμὼν
σφῷν αὖ πέφασμαι καινός, ὥσπερ σφὼ πατρί.
χωρεῖτε, καὶ μὴ ψαύετ', ἀλλ' ἐᾶτέ με
1545   αὐτὸν τὸν ἱερὸν τύμβον ἐξευρεῖν, ἵνα
μοῖρ' ἀνδρὶ τῷδε τῇδε κρυφθῆναι χθονί.
τῇδ', ὧδε, τῇδε βᾶτε· τῇδε γάρ μ' ἄγει
Ἑρμῆς ὁ πομπὸς ἥ τε νερτέρα θεός.
ὦ φῶς ἀφεγγές, πρόσθε πού ποτ' ἦσθ' ἐμόν,
1550   νῦν δ' ἔσχατόν σου τοὐμὸν ἅπτεται δέμας.
ἤδη γὰρ ἕρπω τὸν τελευταῖον βίον
κρύψων παρ' Ἅιδην. ἀλλά, φίλτατε ξένων,
αὐτός τε χώρα θ' ἥδε πρόσπολοί τε σοὶ
εὐδαίμονες γένοισθε, κἀπ' εὐπραξίᾳ
1555   μέμνησθέ μου θανόντος εὐτυχεῖς ἀεί.

                    ΧΟΡΟΣ

εἰ θέμις ἐστί μοι τὰν ἀφανῆ θεὸν   στρ.
καὶ σὲ λιταῖς σεβίζειν,
ἐννυχίων ἄναξ, Αἰδωνεῦ

574

the city you live in shall never be ravaged by the men sprung from the sowing.[a] For countless cities, even though well governed, easily slip into insolence. For the gods see it clearly, though late, when anyone lets go religion and turns to madness. Do you, son of Aegeus, never wish to suffer that!

These things that I am teaching you you know already. But let us go now to the place, for the power of the god is present, hurrying me on, and let us no longer hesitate! Daughters, follow me this way! For I am now revealed to you as guide, as formerly you used to guide your father. Come, and do not touch me, but let me myself find out the sacred tomb where it is fated for this man to be hidden in this earth! This way, thus, this way! For it is this way that I am led by the escorting Hermes and by the goddess below. O light without a glimmer, formerly you were mine, but now my body feels you for the final time! For now I am setting off to conceal in Hades the finish of my life. Come, dearest of strangers, may you have good fortune, yourself and this land and your attendants, and in prosperity remember me when I am dead for your success for ever!

Exeunt OEDIPUS, *his daughters, and* THESEUS.

CHORUS

If it is right for me to reverence with prayers the goddess in darkness and yourself, lord of those who dwell in night,

---

[a] Some, at least, of the Thebans were thought to be descended from the giants who sprang from the dragon's teeth sowed by the founder of the city, Cadmus.

1541 μηδ' ἔτ' Reisig: μηδέ γ' fere codd.

1560 Ἀϊδωνεῦ, λίσσομαι
ἐπιπόνως μήτ' ἐπὶ βαρυαχεῖ
ξένον ἐξανύσαι
μόρῳ τὰν παγκευθῆ κάτω νεκρῶν πλάκα
καὶ Στύγιον δόμον.

1565 πολλῶν γὰρ ἂν καὶ μάταν
πημάτων ἱκνουμένων
πάλιν σφε δαίμων δίκαιος αὔξοι.
ὦ χθόνιαι θεαί, σῶμά τ' ἀνικάτου   ἀντ.
θηρός, ὃν ἐν πύλαισι

1570 ταῖσι πολυξένοις εὐνᾶσθαι
κνυζεῖσθαί τ' ἐξ ἄντρων
ἀδάματον φύλακα παρ' Ἀΐδᾳ
λόγος αἰὲν ἔχει.
τόν, ὦ Γᾶς παῖ καὶ Ταρτάρου, κατεύχομαι

1575 ἐν καθαρῷ βῆναι
ὁρμωμένῳ νερτέρας
τῷ ξένῳ νεκρῶν πλάκας·
σέ τοι κικλήσκω τὸν αἰὲν ὕπνον.

                    ΑΓΓΕΛΟΣ

ἄνδρες πολῖται, ξυντομωτάτως μὲν ἂν

1580 τύχοιμι λέξας Οἰδίπουν ὀλωλότα·
ἃ δ' ἦν τὰ πραχθέντ' οὔθ' ὁ μῦθος ἐν βραχεῖ
φράσαι πάρεστιν οὔτε τἄργ' ὅσ' ἦν ἐκεῖ.

1561 ἐπιπόνως Ll.-J. post Jebb: μήτ' ἐπίπονα raz: μήτ' ἐπιπόνω
LV
1562 ἐξανύσαι Vauvilliers (κατανύσαι sch.): ἐκτανύσαι codd.
1563 νεκρῶν t: νεκύων cett.

Aidoneus, Aidoneus,[a] I pray that the stranger may arrive at the plain of the dead that holds all below and at the house of Styx without pain and with no grievous fate! For after many futile troubles have beset him, once more a just god would be exalting him.

O goddesses of earth,[b] and you, form of the invincible beast which, fame ever tells us, have your bed and growl from your cave in the gates passed through by many strangers, a guardian not to be subdued in Hades![c] I pray, child of Earth and Tartarus,[d] that he may walk clear when the stranger comes to the plains of the dead below. On you I call, who are eternal sleep!

Enter MESSENGER.

MESSENGER

Men of the city, the briefest way to tell my news would be to say that Oedipus is dead! But to tell in few words what happened neither the words nor the actions that took place there permit.

[a] A name for Hades; the names of Hades and Persephone, and other chthonic powers, were not often spoken.

[b] Demeter and Persephone were the chief goddesses of earth, but other powers, such as the Erinyes, might also be in mind.

[c] Cerberus.

[d] Death.

1567 σφε Reiske: σε codd.
1570 ταῖσι Bergk: φασὶ codd.   πολυξένοις Musgrave: πολυξέστοις codd.
1572 ἀδάματον Brunck: -αστον fere codd.
1574 τόν Hermann: ὅν codd.
1578 αἰὲν ὕπνον Ll.-J.: αἰένυπνον codd.

ΧΟΡΟΣ

ὄλωλε γὰρ δύστηνος;

ΑΓΓΕΛΟΣ

ὡς λελοιπότα
κεῖνον τὸν ἀεὶ βίοτον ἐξεπίστασο.

ΧΟΡΟΣ

1585 πῶς; ἆρα θείᾳ κἀπόνῳ τάλας τύχῃ;

ΑΓΓΕΛΟΣ

τοῦτ' ἐστὶν ἤδη κἀποθαυμάσαι πρέπον.
ὡς μὲν γὰρ ἐνθένδ' εἷρπε, καὶ σύ που παρὼν
ἔξοισθ', ὑφ' ἡγητῆρος οὐδενὸς φίλων,
ἀλλ' αὐτὸς ἡμῖν πᾶσιν ἐξηγούμενος·
1590 ἐπεὶ δ' ἀφῖκτο τὸν καταρράκτην ὁδὸν
χαλκοῖς βάθροισι γῆθεν ἐρριζωμένον,
ἔστη κελεύθων ἐν πολυσχίστων μιᾷ,
κοίλου πέλας κρατῆρος, οὗ τὰ Θησέως
Περίθου τε κεῖται πίστ' ἀεὶ ξυνθήματα·
1595 ἀφ' οὗ μέσος στὰς τοῦ τε Θορικίου πέτρου
κοίλης τ' ἀχέρδου κἀπὶ λαΐνου τάφου
καθέζετ'· εἶτ' ἔλυσε δυσπινεῖς στολάς.
κἄπειτ' ἀΰσας παῖδας ἠνώγει ῥυτῶν
ὑδάτων ἐνεγκεῖν λουτρὰ καὶ χοάς ποθεν·
1600 τὼ δ' εὐχλόου Δήμητρος εἰς προσόψιον
πάγον μολούσα τάσδ' ἐπιστολὰς πατρὶ
ταχεῖ 'πόρευσαν ξὺν χρόνῳ, λουτροῖς τέ νιν
ἐσθῆτί τ' ἐξήσκησαν ᾗ νομίζεται.

CHORUS

Is the poor man dead indeed?

MESSENGER

Be assured that that man has left our ordinary life!

CHORUS

How did it happen? Did the poor man die in a godsent and painless fashion?

MESSENGER

The matter now is something we may wonder at! For how he left here you know well, since you were present, with none of his friends to guide him, but himself giving directions to us all. But when he came to the threshold that plunges down, rooted in the earth with brazen steps,[a] he stopped in one of many branching paths, near to the hollow basin, where lies the covenant of Perithus[b] and Theseus, ever to be trusted. Between this and the Thorician[c] rock he took his stand, and sat down by the hollow pear tree and the tomb of stone; then he undid his filthy garments. Next he called upon his daughters, telling them to bring water for washing and libation from a running stream somewhere. And they went to the hill of verdant Demeter that was in view and discharged these duties swiftly for their father, and gave him the bath and the raiment that is cus-

---

[a] See lines 56 f above.

[b] The friend of Theseus, usually called Peirithous.

[c] Thoricus was a town in Attica, thought to be called after a hero of the same name.

1592 πολυσχίστων Heath: -ίστῳ codd.
1595 ἀφ' οὗ Brunck: ἐφ' οὗ codd.   μέσος Brunck: μέσου codd.   1596 κἀπὶ K, coni. Canter: κἀπὸ codd.

ἐπεὶ δὲ πᾶσαν ἔσχε δρῶντος ἡδονὴν
1605   κοὐκ ἦν ἔτ' οὐδὲν ἀργὸν ὧν ἐφίετο,
κτύπησε μὲν Ζεὺς χθόνιος, αἱ δὲ παρθένοι
ῥίγησαν, ὡς ἤκουσαν· ἐς δὲ γούνατα
πατρὸς πεσοῦσαι 'κλαιον οὐδ' ἀνίεσαν
στέρνων ἀραγμοὺς οὐδὲ παμμήκεις γόους.
1610   ὁ δ' ὡς ἀκούει φθόγγον ἐξαίφνης πικρόν,
πτύξας ἐπ' αὐταῖς χεῖρας εἶπεν, "ὦ τέκνα,
οὐκ ἔστ' ἔθ' ὑμῖν τῆδ' ἐν ἡμέρᾳ πατήρ.
ὄλωλε γὰρ δὴ πάντα τἀμά, κοὐκέτι
τὴν δυσπόνητον ἕξετ' ἀμφ' ἐμοὶ τροφήν·
1615   σκληρὰν μέν, οἶδα, παῖδες· ἀλλ' ἓν γὰρ μόνον
τὰ πάντα λύει ταῦτ' ἔπος μοχθήματα.
τὸ γὰρ φιλεῖν οὐκ ἔστιν ἐξ ὅτου πλέον
ἢ τοῦδε τἀνδρὸς ἔσχεθ', οὗ τητώμεναι
τὸ λοιπὸν ἤδη τὸν βίον διάξετον."
1620   τοιαῦτ' ἐπ' ἀλλήλοισιν ἀμφικείμενοι
λύγδην ἔκλαιον πάντες. ὡς δὲ πρὸς τέλος
γόων ἀφίκοντ' οὐδ' ἔτ' ὠρώρει βοή,
ἦν μὲν σιωπή, φθέγμα δ' ἐξαίφνης τινὸς
θώυξεν αὐτόν, ὥστε πάντας ὀρθίας
1625   στῆσαι φόβῳ δείσαντας εὐθέως τρίχας·
καλεῖ γὰρ αὐτὸν πολλὰ πολλαχῇ θεός·
"ὦ οὗτος οὗτος, Οἰδίπους, τί μέλλομεν
χωρεῖν; πάλαι δὴ τἀπὸ σοῦ βραδύνεται."
ὁ δ' ὡς ἐπῄσθετ' ἐκ θεοῦ καλούμενος,
1630   αὐδᾷ μολεῖν οἱ γῆς ἄνακτα Θησέα.
κἀπεὶ προσῆλθεν, εἶπεν, "ὦ φίλον κάρα,

tomary. But when he had got all the pleasure belonging to a doer, and none of his commands had been left unfulfilled, Zeus of the earth thundered, and the maidens shuddered when they heard it. Falling by their father's knees, they wept, and did not cease to beat their breasts and to cry out at length. But when he heard the sudden bitter sound, he opened his arms to them, and said, "My children, on this day your father is no more! For everything is at an end for me, and no longer shall you have the irksome task of caring for me. It was hard, I know, my daughters; but a single word dissolves all these hardships. For from none did you have love more than from this man, without whom you will now spend the remainder of your lives."

Thus, clinging closely to each other, all of them sobbed; but when they came to the end of their lamenting, and no sound still rose up, there was silence, and suddenly the voice of someone hailed him, so that the hair of all stood upright suddenly in terror. For the god called him often and from many places: "You there, Oedipus, why do we wait to go? You have delayed too long!" But when he realised that the god was calling him, he told the king of the country, Theseus, to come to him. And when he had approached, he said, "My dear friend, pray give the ancient

---

1604 πᾶσαν ἔσχε Ll.-J.: παντὸς εἶχε codd.
1619 τὸν βίον Elmsley: βίοτον codd. plerique
1625 εὐθέως Dindorf: ἐξαίφνης codd.

SOPHOCLES

δός μοι χερὸς σῆς πίστιν ἀρχαίαν τέκνοις,
ὑμεῖς τε, παῖδες, τῷδε· καὶ καταίνεσον
μήποτε προδώσειν τάσδ' ἑκών, τελεῖν δ' ὅσ' ἂν
1635 μέλλῃς φρονῶν εὖ ξυμφέροντ' αὐταῖς ἀεί."
ὁ δ', ὡς ἀνὴρ γενναῖος, οὐκ οἴκτου μέτα
κατήνεσεν τάδ' ὅρκιος δράσειν ξένῳ.
ὅπως δὲ ταῦτ' ἔδρασεν, εὐθὺς Οἰδίπους
ψαύσας ἀμαυραῖς χερσὶν ὧν παίδων λέγει,
1640 "ὦ παῖδε, τλάσας χρὴ †τὸ γενναῖον φέρειν†
χωρεῖν τόπων ἐκ τῶνδε, μηδ' ἃ μὴ θέμις
λεύσσειν δικαιοῦν, μηδὲ φωνούντων κλύειν.
ἀλλ' ἕρπεθ' ὡς τάχιστα· πλὴν ὁ κύριος
Θησεὺς παρέστω μανθάνειν τὰ δρώμενα."
1645   τοσαῦτα φωνήσαντος εἰσηκούσαμεν
ξύμπαντες· ἀστακτεὶ δὲ σὺν ταῖς παρθένοις
στένοντες ὡμαρτοῦμεν. ὡς δ' ἀπήλθομεν,
χρόνῳ βραχεῖ στραφέντες, ἐξαπείδομεν
τὸν ἄνδρα τὸν μὲν οὐδαμοῦ παρόντ' ἔτι,
1650 ἄνακτα δ' αὐτὸν ὀμμάτων ἐπίσκιον
χεῖρ' ἀντέχοντα κρατός, ὡς δεινοῦ τινος
φόβου φανέντος οὐδ' ἀνασχετοῦ βλέπειν.
ἔπειτα μέντοι βαιὸν οὐδὲ σὺν λόγῳ
ὁρῶμεν αὐτὸν γῆν τε προσκυνοῦνθ' ἅμα
1655 καὶ τὸν θεῶν Ὄλυμπον ἐν ταὐτῷ χρόνῳ.
μόρῳ δ' ὁποίῳ κεῖνος ὤλετ' οὐδ' ἂν εἷς
θνητῶν φράσειε πλὴν τὸ Θησέως κάρα.
οὐ γάρ τις αὐτὸν οὔτε πυρφόρος θεοῦ
κεραυνὸς ἐξέπραξεν οὔτε ποντία

pledge of a handclasp to my children, and do you, daughters, give the same to him! And promise that you will never willingly betray them, and that you will always accomplish kindly all that will do them good."

And he like a noble man, without lamenting promised upon oath that he would do this for the stranger. And when he had done this, at once Oedipus laid his feeble hands upon his children and said, "Daughters, you must bear this with a noble mind and depart from these regions, and not claim to look upon what may not be seen, or to hear such speech. Come, go with all speed! Only let him who is responsible, Theseus, be here to learn what is being done!"

We all heard him speak these words; and we accompanied the maidens, with floods of tears. And when we had departed, after a short time we turned around, and could see that the man was no longer there, and the king was holding his hand before his face to shade his eyes, as though some terrifying sight, which he could not bear to look on, had been presented. But then after a moment, with no word spoken, we saw him salute the earth and the sky, home of the gods, at the same moment. But by what death that man perished none among mortals could tell but Theseus. For no fiery thunderbolt of the god made

---

1640 τὸ γενναῖον suspectum: τόδ᾽ εὐγενεῖ φρενί Maehly

1644 μανθάνειν Reiske: -ων codd.

1653 λόγῳ Wilson: χρόνῳ codd.

1655 χρόνῳ Blaydes: λόγῳ codd.

1660 θύελλα κινηθεῖσα τῷ τότ᾽ ἐν χρόνῳ,
ἀλλ᾽ ἤ τις ἐκ θεῶν πομπός, ἢ τὸ νερτέρων
εὔνουν διαστὰν γῆς ἀλάμπετον βάθρον.
ἀνὴρ γὰρ οὐ στενακτὸς οὐδὲ σὺν νόσοις
ἀλγεινὸς ἐξεπέμπετ᾽, ἀλλ᾽ εἴ τις βροτῶν
1665 θαυμαστός. εἰ δὲ μὴ δοκῶ φρονῶν λέγειν,
οὐκ ἂν παρείμην οἷσι μὴ δοκῶ φρονεῖν.

ΧΟΡΟΣ

ποῦ δ᾽ αἵ τε παῖδες χοἰ προπέμψαντες φίλων;

ΑΓΓΕΛΟΣ

αἵδ᾽ οὐχ ἑκάς· γόων γὰρ οὐκ ἀσήμονες
φθόγγοι σφε σημαίνουσι δεῦρ᾽ ὁρμωμένας.

ΑΝΤΙΓΟΝΗ

1670 αἰαῖ, φεῦ· ἔστιν, ἔστι νῶν δὴ   στρ. α΄
οὐ τὸ μέν, ἄλλο δὲ μή, πατρὸς ἔμφυτον
ἄλαστον αἷμα δυσμόροιν στενάζειν,
ᾧτινι τὸν πολὺν
ἄλλοτε μὲν πόνον ἔμπεδον εἴχομεν,
1675 ἐν πυμάτῳ δ᾽ ἀλόγιστα παροίσομεν,
ἰδόντε καὶ παθούσα.

ΧΟΡΟΣ

τί δ᾽ ἔστιν;

ΑΝΤΙΓΟΝΗ

ἔστιν μὲν εἰκάσαι, φίλοι.

ΧΟΡΟΣ

βέβηκεν;

584

away with him, nor any whirlwind rising up from the sea at that time; but either some escort come from the gods or the unlighted foundation of the earth that belongs to those below, opening in kindness. For the man was taken away with no lamentations, and by no painful disease, but, if any among mortals, by a miracle. And if anyone thinks I speak foolishly, I would not beg for the credence of those who think I am a fool.

CHORUS

And where are the girls and those friends who escorted them?

MESSENGER

They are not far off; for audible sounds of lamentation show that they are coming this way.

Enter ANTIGONE and ISMENE.

ANTIGONE

Alas, alack! It is for us, it is for us to lament in all fullness for the accursed blood from our father that is in us, unhappy pair; our father for whom we endured continual pain, and at the last we shall carry away from him things beyond reason that we have seen and suffered.

CHORUS

What is it?

ANTIGONE

We can but guess, my friends!

CHORUS

He is gone?

---

¹⁶⁷⁶ παθοῦσα] παθόντε Brunck

ΑΝΤΙΓΟΝΗ

ὡς μάλιστ᾽ ἂν ἐν πόθῳ λάβοις.
τί γάρ; ὅτῳ μήτ᾽ Ἄρης
1680 μήτε πόντος ἀντέκυρσεν,
ἄσκοποι δὲ πλάκες ἔμαρψαν
ἐν ἀφανεῖ τινι μόρῳ φερόμενον.
τάλαινα, νῷν δ᾽ ὀλεθρία
νὺξ ἐπ᾽ ὄμμασιν βέβακε·
1685 πῶς γὰρ ἢ τιν᾽ ἀπίαν
γᾶν ἢ πόντιον
κλύδων᾽ ἀλώμεναι βίου
δύσοιστον ἕξομεν τροφάν;

ΙΣΜΗΝΗ

οὐ κάτοιδα. κατά με φόνιος
1690 Ἀΐδας ἕλοι πατρὶ
ξυνθανεῖν γεραιῷ
τάλαιναν, ὡς ἔμοιγ᾽ ὁ μέλ-
λων βίος οὐ βιωτός.

ΧΟΡΟΣ

ὦ διδύμα τέκνων ἀρί-
στα, τὸ θεοῦ καλῶς φέρειν,
1695 μηδ᾽ ἔτ᾽ ἄγαν φλέγεσθον· οὔ-
τοι κατάμεμπτ᾽ ἔβητον.

ΑΝΤΙΓΟΝΗ

πόθος <τοι> καὶ κακῶν ἄρ᾽ ἦν τις.   ἀντ. α΄
καὶ γὰρ ὃ μηδαμὰ δὴ φίλον ἦν φίλον,
ὁπότε γε καὶ τὸν ἐν χεροῖν κατεῖχον.

ANTIGONE

Just as one might desire! Yes, indeed, for neither the war
god nor the sea came against him, but the immeasurable
plains took him, carried away in a mysterious end. But a
deadly night lies upon our eyes, poor sister; for how shall
we sustain our hard life, wandering over some distant land
or over the billows of the sea?

ISMENE

I do not know! May murderous Hades take me, so that I
share, poor creature, my aged father's death, for my future
life for me is not worth living!

CHORUS

O two best of daughters, you must bear bravely what the
god sends, and not burn in excess with passion! Your path
cannot be found fault with!

ANTIGONE

So one may regret the loss even of sorrows! For what was
never dear was dear, when I had him in my arms! O father,

1678 ἐν Canter: εἰ codd.

1682 φερόμενον Kunhardt: φερόμεναι t, coni. Hermann: φαινό-
μεναι fere cett.

1689–92 Ismenae tribuit Turnebus, Antigonae codd.

1694 τὸ θεοῦ καλῶς φέρειν Ll.-J. post Bergk et Wilamowitz: τὸ
φέρον ἐκ θεοῦ καλῶς φέρειν χρή codd.

1695 μηδ' ἔτ' Bellermann: μηδ' codd.   post ἄγαν add.
οὕτω codd., del. Burton

1697 suppl. Hartung

1698 μηδαμὰ . . . ἦν Brunck: μηδαμῇ δὴ τὸ φίλον codd.

1700 ὦ πάτερ, ὦ φίλος,
ὦ τὸν ἀεὶ κατὰ γᾶς σκότον εἱμένος·
οὐδ' ἐκεῖ ὢν ἀφίλητος ἐμοί ποτε
καὶ τᾷδε μὴ κυρήσῃς.

ΧΟΡΟΣ

ἔπραξεν —

ΑΝΤΙΓΟΝΗ
ἔπραξεν οἷον ἤθελεν.

ΧΟΡΟΣ

1705 τὸ ποῖον;

ΑΝΤΙΓΟΝΗ
ἇς ἔχρῃζε γᾶς ἐπὶ ξένας
ἔθανε· κοίταν δ' ἔχει
νέρθεν εὐσκίαστον αἰέν,
οὐδὲ πένθος ἔλιπ' ἄκλαυτον.
ἀνὰ γὰρ ὄμμα σε τόδ', ὦ πάτερ, ἐμὸν
1710 στένει δακρῦον, οὐδ' ἔχω
πῶς με χρὴ τὸ σὸν τάλαιναν
ἀφανίσαι τόσον ἄχος.
ὤμοι, γᾶς ἐπὶ
ξένας θανεῖν ἔχρῃζες, ἀλλ'
ἐρῆμος ἔθανες ὧδέ μοι.

1702 ἐκεῖ ὢν Jebb: γέρων codd.
1709 ἀνὰ Hermann: ἀεὶ vel αἰεὶ codd.
1713 ὤμοι Wecklein: ἰὼ μὴ fere codd.

O dear one, O you who are clothed in the eternal darkness
of the earth, not even there shall you be without my love
and hers!

CHORUS

He fared . . .

ANTIGONE

He fared just as he wished!

CHORUS

How?

ANTIGONE

He died in the foreign land as he desired; and he occupies
a bed shady for ever, nor did he fail to leave behind mourn-
ing with tears. For this eye of mine, father, laments for you
with weeping, nor do I know how I can make away with
such great grief, unhappy one! Alas, you wished to die in a
foreign land, but you died thus, far from me!

SOPHOCLES

ΙΣΜΗΝΗ

1715 ὦ τάλαινα, τίς ἄρα με πότμος
ἐπιμένει σέ τ᾽, ὦ φίλα,
πατρὸς ὧδ᾽ ἐρήμας;
< × – ∪ – × – ∪ –
– ∪ ∪ – ∪ – – >

ΧΟΡΟΣ

1720 ἀλλ᾽ ἐπεὶ ὀλβίως ἔλυ-
σεν τέλος, ὦ φίλαι, βίου,
λήγετε τοῦδ᾽ ἄχους· κακῶν
γὰρ δυσάλωτος οὐδείς.

ΑΝΤΙΓΟΝΗ

πάλιν, φίλα, συθῶμεν.

ΙΣΜΗΝΗ

ὡς τί ῥέξομεν;   στρ. β′

ΑΝΤΙΓΟΝΗ

1725 ἵμερος ἔχει μέ τις —

ΙΣΜΗΝΗ

<τίς οὖν;>

ΑΝΤΙΓΟΝΗ

τὰν χθόνιον ἑστίαν ἰδεῖν —

ΙΣΜΗΝΗ

τίνος;

ΑΝΤΙΓΟΝΗ

πατρός, τάλαιν᾽ ἐγώ.

ISMENE

Poor sister, what fate awaits me and you, my dear one, far as we are from our father?

Two lines of ISMENE are missing.

CHORUS

But since he resolved the end of life in happiness, my friends, leave off this grieving! For none is proof against misfortune.

ANTIGONE

My dear one, let us hasten back!

ISMENE

For what purpose?

ANTIGONE

A longing possesses me . . .

ISMENE

What longing?

ANTIGONE

To see the home beneath the earth . . .

ISMENE

Whose home?

ANTIGONE

Our father's, unhappy one that I am!

1715 post πότμος add. αὖθις ὧδ' ἔρημος ἄπορος (e v. 1735) codd., del. Reisig   lacunam hic statuit Lachmann

1717 post hunc v. lacunam statuit Masqueray

1721 ante τέλος add. τὸ codd., del. Bergk

1725 suppl. Gleditsch

ΙΣΜΗΝΗ

θέμις δὲ πῶς τάδ' ἐστὶ νῷν;

1730   οὐχ ὁρᾷς;

ΑΝΤΙΓΟΝΗ

τί τόδ' ἐπέπληξας;

ΙΣΜΗΝΗ

καὶ τόδ', ὡς —

ΑΝΤΙΓΟΝΗ

τί τόδε μάλ' αὖθις;

ΙΣΜΗΝΗ

ἄταφος ἔπιτνε δίχα τε παντός.

ΑΝΤΙΓΟΝΗ

ἄγε με, καὶ τότ' ἐπενάριξον.

<ΙΣΜΗΝΗ

— —

ΑΝΤΙΓΟΝΗ

— — ∪ — — >

ΙΣΜΗΝΗ

αἰαῖ, δυστάλαινα, πῇ δῆτ'

1735   αὖθις ὧδ' ἐρῆμος ἄπορος

αἰῶνα τλάμον' ἕξω;

ΧΟΡΟΣ

φίλαι, τρέσητε μηδέν.

ΑΝΤΙΓΟΝΗ

ἀλλὰ ποῖ φύγω;   ἀντ. β′

ISMENE

But how is that right for us? Do you not see . . .

ANTIGONE

Why do you rebuke me thus?

ISMENE

. . . this also, that . . .

ANTIGONE

Why do you do this again?

ISMENE

He descended with no burial, apart from all!

ANTIGONE

Take me there, and then kill me also!

One line, divided between the two sisters, is missing.

ISMENE

Alas, wretched am I! Where in the future, bereft and help-less, shall I maintain my miserable life?

CHORUS

My friends, fear nothing!

ANTIGONE

But where shall I take refuge?

1729 ἐστὶ νῷν Ll.-J.: ἐστί; μῶν codd.
1733 ἐπενάριξον Elmsley: ἐξεν- K: ἐνάριξον cett.   post hunc v. lacunam statuit Meineke

ΧΟΡΟΣ

καὶ πάρος ἀπεφύγετον —

ΑΝΤΙΓΟΝΗ
<τὸ τί;>

ΧΟΡΟΣ

1740   <τὰ> σφῷν τὸ μὴ πίτνειν κακῶς.

ΑΝΤΙΓΟΝΗ

φρονῶ —

ΧΟΡΟΣ
τί δῆθ᾽ ὅπερ νοεῖς;

ΑΝΤΙΓΟΝΗ

ὅπως μολούμεθ᾽ ἐς δόμους
οὐκ ἔχω.

ΧΟΡΟΣ
μηδέ γε μάτευε.

ΑΝΤΙΓΟΝΗ

μόγος ἔχει.

ΧΟΡΟΣ
καὶ πάρος ἐπεῖ<χε>.

ΑΝΤΙΓΟΝΗ

1745   τοτὲ μὲν ἄπορα, τοτὲ δ᾽ ὕπερθεν.

ΧΟΡΟΣ

μέγ᾽ ἄρα πέλαγος ἐλάχετόν τι.

1739 suppl. Bergk
1740 suppl. Hermann

594

CHORUS
Even before this you had escaped . . .

ANTIGONE
What?

CHORUS
. . . an ill turn in your fortunes.

ANTIGONE
I am minded . . .

CHORUS
What is in your mind?

ANTIGONE
I do not know how we shall return home.

CHORUS
Do not even try to!

ANTIGONE
Trouble holds us!

CHORUS
Even earlier it held you!

ANTIGONE
Then we were helpless, now things are worse!

CHORUS
So a great sea of trouble has been your lot!

1741 ὅπερ νοεῖς Graser: ὑπερνοεῖς codd.
1744 suppl. Wunder
1745 ἄπορα Wunder: πατέρα r: πέρα cett.

ΑΝΤΙΓΟΝΗ

ναὶ ναί.

ΧΟΡΟΣ

ξύμφημι καὐτός.

ΑΝΤΙΓΟΝΗ

φεῦ, φεῦ· ποῖ μόλωμεν, ὦ Ζεῦ;
ἐλπίδων γὰρ ἐς τί\<ν' ἔτι\> με
1750 δαίμων τανῦν γ' ἐλαύνει;

ΘΗΣΕΥΣ

παύετε θρῆνον, παῖδες· ἐν οἷς γὰρ
χάρις ἡ χθονία νὺξ ἀπόκειται,
πενθεῖν οὐ χρή· νέμεσις γάρ.

ΑΝΤΙΓΟΝΗ

ὦ τέκνον Αἰγέως, προσπίτνομέν σοι.

ΘΗΣΕΥΣ

1755 τίνος, ὦ παῖδες, χρείας ἀνύσαι;

ΑΝΤΙΓΟΝΗ

τύμβον θέλομεν
προσιδεῖν αὐταὶ πατρὸς ἡμετέρου.

ΘΗΣΕΥΣ

ἀλλ' οὐ θεμιτὸν κεῖσ' \<ἐστὶ\> μολεῖν.

ΑΝΤΙΓΟΝΗ

πῶς εἶπας, ἄναξ, κοίραν' Ἀθηνῶν;

1749 ἐς τίν' ἔτι Hermann: ἐς τί codd.
1751-53 Theseo tribuit Heath, choro codd.
1752 νὺξ ἀπόκειται Martin: ξυναπόκειται vel συν- codd.

ANTIGONE

Yes, yes!

CHORUS

I too say so!

ANTIGONE

Alas, alas! Where are we to go to, O Zeus? To what expectations is the god now driving me?

Enter THESEUS.

THESEUS

Cease your lamentation, girls! One should not mourn for those for whom the darkness below the earth is a treasure graciously bestowed; the gods would resent it!

ANTIGONE

Son of Aegeus, we supplicate you!

THESEUS

What is the request you wish me to grant?

ANTIGONE

We wish to see with our own eyes our father's tomb!

THESEUS

But it is not permitted that you should go there!

ANTIGONE

What do you mean, lord of Athens?

1758 suppl. Brunck

ΘΗΣΕΥΣ

1760 ὦ παῖδες, ἀπεῖπεν ἐμοὶ κεῖνος
μήτε πελάζειν ἐς τούσδε τόπους
μήτ᾽ ἐπιφωνεῖν μηδένα θνητῶν
θήκην ἱεράν, ἣν κεῖνος ἔχει.
καὶ ταῦτά μ᾽ ἔφη πράσσοντα κακῶν
1765 χώραν ἕξειν αἰὲν ἄλυπον.
ταῦτ᾽ οὖν ἔκλυεν δαίμων ἡμῶν
χὠ πάντ᾽ ἀίων Διὸς Ὅρκος.

ΑΝΤΙΓΟΝΗ

ἀλλ᾽ εἰ τάδ᾽ ἔχει κατὰ νοῦν κείνῳ,
ταῦτ᾽ ἂν ἀπαρκοῖ· Θήβας δ᾽ ἡμᾶς
1770 τὰς ὠγυγίους πέμψον, ἐάν πως
διακωλύσωμεν ἰόντα φόνον
τοῖσιν ὁμαίμοις.

ΘΗΣΕΥΣ

δράσω καὶ τάδε καὶ πάνθ᾽ ὁπόσ᾽ ἂν
μέλλω πράσσειν πρόσφορά θ᾽ ὑμῖν
1775 καὶ τῷ κατὰ γῆς, ὃς νέον ἔρρει,
πρὸς χάριν· οὐ δεῖ μ᾽ ἀποκάμνειν.

ΧΟΡΟΣ

ἀλλ᾽ ἀποπαύετε μηδ᾽ ἐπὶ πλείω
θρῆνον ἐγείρετε·
πάντως γὰρ ἔχει τάδε κῦρος.

[1764] κακῶν Hermann: καλῶς codd.
[1773] ὁπόσ᾽ Porson: ὅσ᾽ vel ὅσα codd.

THESEUS

Girls, that man instructed me never to go near to those regions and not to tell any among mortals of the sacred tomb that holds him. And he said that if I did this I would keep my country always free from pain. So the god heard me promise this, and the lord of oaths, the son of Zeus, who hears all words.

ANTIGONE

Well, if this accords with his wish, that is sufficient! But send us to ancient Thebes, in the hope that we may prevent the slaughter that is coming to our brothers!

THESEUS

I will do that, and anything in my power that will be helpful to you and agreeable to the one below the earth, who is lately departed; I must not relax my efforts!

CHORUS

Come, cease your lament and do not arouse it more! For in all ways these things stand fast.

1776 post οὐ add. γὰρ codd., del. Hermann
1777 μηδ᾽ Elmsley: μήτ᾽ codd.